Database
Developer's Guide
with Delphi™ 2

Ken Henderson

SAMS
PUBLISHING

201 West 103rd Street
Indianapolis, Indiana 46290

SAMS Developer's Guide

This book is dedicated to my wife, Teresa, who I adore and love unconditionally, and to my three children: Nicole, Ryan, and Amanda, whose little moments of growth inspire me.

Publisher	Richard K. Swadley
Acquisitions Manager	Greg Wiegand
Development Manager	Dean Miller
Managing Editor	Cindy Morrow
Marketing Manager	Gregg Bushyeager
Assistant Markering Manager	Kristina Perry

Acquisitions Editor
Chris Denny

Development Editor
Angelique Brittingham

Software Development Specialist
Cari Skaggs
Steve Straiger

Production Editor
James Grass

Copy Editors
Nancy Albright, Margaret Berson
David Bradford, Anne Owen
Kris Simmons, Tonya Simpson

Technical Reviewer
Danny Thorpe

Editorial Coordinator
Bill Whitmer

Technical Edit Coordinator
Lynette Quinn

Formatter
Frank Sinclair

Editorial Assistants
Carol Ackerman
Andi Richter
Rhonda Tinch-Mize

Cover Designer
Tim Amrhein

Book Designer
Alyssa Yesh

Copy Writer
Peter Fuller

Production Team Supervisor
Brad Chinn

Production
Mary Ann Abramson, Carol Bowers,
Mona Brown, Michael Brumitt,
Charlotte Clapp, Jason Hand,
Sonja Hart, Louisa Klucznik,
Ayanna Lacey, Clint Lahnen,
Steph Mineart, Julie Quinn,
Laura Robbins, Bobbi Satterfield,
Andrew Stone, Tina Trettin,
Susan Van Ness, Mark Walchle,
Colleen Williams

Indexer
Charlotte Clapp, Joy Dean Lee

Overview

Contents

18   ReportSmith   531

IV Advanced Topics

19   Business Rules Part I   575

Foreword

February 1996

Once upon a time, your choices for database application development tools for the Windows environment were pretty simple, and pretty bleak: you could build your app using a visual database forms interpreted scripting tool, or you could build the app using a low-level compiled programming language with a library of database access routines tacked on. The visual tools allowed you to throw together a prototype application fairly quickly, but their interpreted script languages lacked the power, performance, and reliability needed to graduate out of the prototype arena. Using compiler tools, you could realize the programming flexibility, runtime performance, and reliability that mission critical applications demand, but at the cost of tens or even hundreds of man-years of full-time software development. If you needed the data security, integrity, and centralized management services of a SQL database server, your application development costs and headaches just about doubled. It was a time of great frustration for database administrators (DBAs) and Information Services directors under pressure to produce custom database applications and enterprise information management systems—you could choose fast development, or fast and reliable execution, but not both. It's easy to measure this kind of industry frustration—just count the number of tried and discarded database development tools gathering dust on a DBA's top shelf.

In February 1995, Borland launched Delphi 1.0, a new product designed from the ground up to combine visual object-oriented program design tools, a high performance optimizing compiler, and a powerful client/server database component architecture. Delphi's object-oriented component architecture promotes code reuse between applications, reducing development time and effort. Delphi's Object Pascal language is clean, readable (maintainable), and powerful, with features such as structured exception handling to make the stability and reliability of Delphi applications second to none. The Borland Database Engine at the heart of Delphi's database architecture provides vendor-independent database support for a dizzying array of SQL servers and PC database file formats through native file drivers and ODBC drivers. In Delphi, Borland created a whole new category of database application development: rapid application development (RAD) *and* fast, reliable program execution.

Almost exactly one year later, Borland launched Delphi 2.0, a full-bore 32-bit development environment for producing database applications for Windows 95 and Windows NT. Delphi 2.0 raises the performance and RAD standards set by Delphi 1.0 by an order of magnitude: new compiler optimizations for two to three times faster program execution (20 to 50 times faster than interpreted tools), new and enhanced data aware components, code reuse enhancements through visual form inheritance, and a host of new database support features including cached updates, filters, schema caching, and multithreaded background query execution.

Combine Delphi's phenomenal market success with its strong support for SQL database servers and SQL queries against local "PC database" tables, and you wind up with a lot of SQL server DBAs wondering if Delphi could be their "silver bullet" application development tool—and many times more PC programmers wondering what SQL is. This book is invaluable to both kinds of programmers: it is both a "Delphi for DBAs" and a "SQL for Delphi programmers" handbook. The full spectrum of database application development issues is covered here: database design theory and practice, SQL syntax (ANSI standard and Sybase syntax), Delphi database components, SQL driver configuration and performance tuning, Delphi reporting tools, and even application deployment procedures. The level of specific detail in these pages on what each SQL driver or Delphi database component option does and the ramifications of each possible setting goes far beyond anything I've seen in any Delphi or SQL programming book.

Considering author Ken Henderson's background and tireless quest for the *right* tool to build SQL database applications, that level of detail comes as no surprise. Ken is one of those DBAs with a dangerously overloaded top shelf of dusty products that failed to meet his database programming needs. For Ken, high standards for tools and broad SQL expertise are simply survival skills: when you work with SQL tables containing 100 *million* rows, *everything* has a tangible effect on performance! A few hours of research and experimentation up front can mean the difference between query results in minutes versus query results in days.

Almost since the day he first got his hands on Delphi, Ken has been a constant source of information and perspective for the Delphi development team. Want to know how Delphi stacks up to another client/server product? Call Ken—he's probably already used it. Want to know how a particular Delphi feature performs when run against astronomically huge datasets? Call Ken—he's got databases so massive they have their own satellites.

Most of the time, though, Ken identifies issues and sends the info before we've even asked the question. On one such phone call about a year ago, I said "Gee, Ken, you could fill a book with tips like this!" And so he has, in the pages before you. Regardless of whether your expertise is in SQL or in Delphi, I can guarantee you'll learn quite a bit from this book. I certainly did.

Danny Thorpe

Danny Thorpe is a Delphi R&D engineer at Borland International.

Acknowledgments

Special thanks to my friend and mentor, Neil Coy, who first introduced me to Turbo Pascal several years ago; to Kim Kokkonen, for the friendship and example he has given me over the years; to all the wonderful people at Sams Publishing—particularly Chris Denny, Angelique Brittingham, and James Grass, for their patience and hard work; to my friend and colleague Danny Thorpe, for his countless helpful suggestions and just for listening to me; to my staff, who has had to deal with the tremendous demands this project has made on my time; and, finally, to my parents, who gave me the means of writing this book in the first place and who encourage me to press on.

About the Author

Ken Henderson is a database developer and DBA with more than 10 years experience. He is the author of several commercial software packages, including programmer productivity aids and software libraries. He is also a frequent speaker at industry trade shows. Currently, he is a consultant specializing in database administration and client/server architecture.

Henderson may be reached at `74763,2305@compuserve.com`.

Introduction

My goals for this book were threefold: first, provide a thorough treatment of the subject of database development with Delphi; second, provide a road map whereby database developers who use Delphi in their everyday work can find their way; and, third, provide a complete reference that can be used again and again, long after the book itself has been read. Only you, as the reader, can be the judge of whether I've accomplished these goals.

Who Should Read This Book

If you develop or intend to develop any type of database application using Delphi, this book is for you. You don't need to be an SQL expert to use this book—the book teaches you SQL. You also don't need to be a Delphi expert—the book teaches you Delphi from the perspective of database development. If you're an advanced user, the book provides insight into advanced topics like proper business rules deployment and concurrency control. If you're a beginner, the book covers entry-level topics like database design and the building blocks of Delphi database applications. The book provides all you need to get up to speed, including a tutorial that steps you through building a complete Delphi database application, then upsizing it to a client/server platform. If you fall somewhere between the beginner and advanced user levels, there's also plenty here for you, as well. The book traverses a number of subjects that users of all levels should find useful. If Delphi database development is your game, you've come to the right place.

Which Delphi?

Which Delphi you choose depends largely on your needs. Delphi 2.0 comes in three flavors: the Desktop version, the Developer version, and the high-end Client/Server suite. My personal recommendation is this: if you're serious about database development under Delphi, get the client/server edition. Client/server isn't the wave of the future; it's the wave of the present. The client/server version of Delphi provides more tools and better support for SQL server-based development than either of the other two versions. It's well worth its higher price.

Conventions

Throughout this book, I use a more-relaxed, less-formal writing style. I stress practicality in this book; rigidity and ostentation are expressly avoided. To that end, you'll notice that I interchange many terms that are functionally equivalent in database lingo. I use the terms *row* and *record* identically, for example. I also use *field* and *column* interchangeably. Sometimes I preceed the name of a Delphi component class name using the customary "T" prefix, and sometimes I don't. I might sometimes slip and pronounce SQL as "sequel" rather than "S-Q-L." I think adherence to these sorts of superficial customs has to be less important than the actual content of the text. In writing this book, I have tried to emulate the way people speak. When people get away from their Victorian pretensions and use language they're comfortable with, they usually communicate more effectively. And communicating effectively is what I'm trying to do here, even if I do occasionally begin a sentence with a conjunction.

Organization

The book is organized into four major parts, "Getting Started," "Tutorial," "Reference," and "Advanced Topics."

"Getting Started" gives you the basic tools you'll need throughout the rest of the book. An introduction to SQL is provided, a discussion on naming conventions is broached and insights into database and application design are offered.

The "Tutorial" section takes you through the complete process of developing a Delphi database application. You'll learn everything you need to know, from start to finish, to create a robust, full-featured database application using Delphi. The section concludes with upsizing the application to a client/server platform.

The "Reference" section covers a variety of topics that you may refer to individually. A comprehensive discussion of the Delphi database component class hierarchy is provided, with each component class being discussed separately and completely. ReportSmith and InterBase, two subjects you'll want to become familiar with for doing Delphi client/server development, are also covered in-depth.

"Advanced Topics" ventures into a number of topics that should prove useful as you delve deeper into database and client/server development. Proper business rules application, concurrency control, developing your own database components and trouble-shooting database connections are all covered exhaustively. This section also includes a discussion on application deployment. No stone is left unturned regarding advanced database development in Delphi.

Language Wars?

I think it would be disingenuous of me to feign no partiality to Delphi when I've just written a book on it. The fact is, I've waited years for Delphi. I tried tool after tool, looking for something that was sophisticated enough to handle *any* serious development task, yet intuitive enough for people who are, by trade, database analysts to use. When Delphi came into being and I discovered it, I wholeheartedly embraced it. Do I think there's a best language or a best tool? Of course I do! Just like I have favorite foods and clothes that I prefer over others, I have a favorite database development tool—and that tool is Delphi.

Conventions Used in This Book

This book uses the following conventions:

- Menu names are separated from menu options by a slash. For example, File/Open means "Select the File menu and choose the Open option."
- New terms appear in *italic*.
- All code appears in monospace, as do column and event names.
- Placeholders in code appear in *italic monospace*.
- When a line of code is too long to fit on only one line of this book, it is broken at a convenient place and continued to the next line. The continuation of the line is preceded by a code continuation character ➥. You should type a line of code that has this character as one long line without breaking it.

I

Getting Started

1

Delphi: The Silver Bullet?

Every two or three years or so, it seems that someone else has a new "silver bullet"—a single tool or technology that will help you develop bug-free software in record time. Back in the mid-eighties, CASE was the new buzzword. Toward the late 1980s, OOP was the panacea to cure all ills. Of late, it's been client/server. Who's right? Is anyone right?

The popular opinion on all this is that there is no silver bullet—no single development tool that can do it all. The thinking is that if a tool produces applications quickly, it probably generates inefficient executables. If it enables you to easily build forms using a visual paradigm, it probably gets in the way of doing low-level coding. A tool that's fluent in client/server probably doesn't "speak" Paradox at all. So the thinking goes.

I won't try to convince you that Delphi is the silver bullet the programming world's been waiting for. I will say, however, that it represents a colossal shift in the direction in which visual tools have been going since they first came on the scene. Delphi is the first Rapid Application Development (RAD) tool to meld quick application development with an optimizing compiler. To this it adds scaleable database technology, making for the most potent mix of programming technology ever before seen on the personal computer. It may not be the silver bullet, but it *is* awfully close.

For all its amenities, Delphi still won't produce bug-free software without proper design. It won't design applications for you or decide what your users need, either. It also won't think for you or solve world hunger. It's just a tool—it does what you *tell* it to.

The focus of this book is to help you learn to *tell* Delphi to do what you need—to wield Delphi's power to forge robust applications. Specifically, this book is aimed at helping you become proficient in database application development. By the time you're finished, you should know all you ever wanted to know about database and client/server applications development using Delphi.

The Nitty-Gritty

Let's talk about some specifics now. First of all: Why Delphi? Why would you want to use Delphi rather than some other tool like PowerBuilder or Visual Basic?

As I've said, Delphi successfully marries visual application development with an optimizing compiler. That's not true of other tools, including PowerBuilder and VB. The optimizing compiler in Delphi is no slouch, either. It's the latest in a long line of successful Pascal compilers from Borland. These compilers have earned a deserved reputation for producing executables that are low on resource usage and high on performance. Delphi's Object Pascal compiler is no exception.

An optimizing compiler is not enough, though. Developers these days want an application development *platform* that is comprehensive enough to meet their every need, yet nimble enough to enable them to solve most any programming problem. They want an object framework, but they want a tool that lets them code in assembly language, if need be. They'll normally need to generate .EXE files, but they want a tool that can produce .DLLs and device drivers, too, if necessary. They want quick database application development, but they want something that doesn't force them to carry around a database engine in applications that aren't database-related.

Delphi is all these things and more. It's as though Borland took all the best elements found in modern Windows development tools and wove them into a single product. Yes, Delphi provides an exhaustive component class library that alleviates much of the coding required in other tools. On the other hand, you can still write procedures in assembly language, if you'd like. You can drop components onto a form to build almost any type of application, but you can still interact directly with the Windows API, hooking messages and communicating with other processes at will. You can generate normal Windows EXEs with the press of a key, but you can build DLLs, device drivers, and console applications, too. And even though Delphi is expressly database-oriented, you can write any sort of Windows application you'd like with it—anything from an editor to a Windows shell to a screen saver—it's up to you. In fact, Delphi itself is written in Delphi!

Add to all this the two-way nature of the tools and the sophisticated debugger that's built into the Delphi development environment, and you have a software tool that's hard to beat. Delphi's integrated debugger is a lean first cousin of Borland's award-winning Turbo Debugger. And its two-way tools enable you to modify forms visually *or* textually and freely move objects between the two methods. Basically, they threw in everything *up to and including* the kitchen sink.

In summary, the reasons for choosing Delphi are manifold. Among them are the following:

- A comprehensive object framework
- A fast, native-code compiler
- An integrated debugger
- High-level database access
- Sophisticated two-way tools

In each of these areas, one of two things is usually the case. Either other tools are completely void of anything similar, or Delphi's technology is simply better.

No Limits

With all the talk about Delphi's impressive list of features, you might wonder if there's something missing. You might wonder if you will eventually run into a wall and find something that you just can't do in Delphi.

This is not likely. Unlike most other rapid application development tools, Delphi is fully extensible—you can extend it in so many different ways that you should rarely, if ever, encounter a task that Delphi is not up to. Whether it's database work or developing a Windows NT console application, Delphi can do it as no other program can.

Here's a brief summary of the options that make Delphi so extensible:

- Direct access to the Windows API
- Built-in assembler; supports inline code
- Can be used to create custom VCL and OCX components
- Can be used to create DLLs and other "secondary" Windows object types
- Fully object-oriented—you can inherit from component classes already included or build your own from scratch

In terms of object-orientation, I should point out that not all OOP solutions are created equal. Many tools feign object-orientation but are not OOP tools in the strictest sense of the term. Supporting an "object" data type does not an OOP tool make. Some tools provide a traditional OOP model; but it's too slow to use, so it goes unused. An OOP tool must pass four basic criteria in order to be truly object-oriented:

- **Inheritance**—New object types must be able to be synthesized from existing ones by inheriting their attributes and method procedures.
- **Polymorphism**—Object methods must be callable without respect for the actual object type in which the method resides. That is, the Show method, for example, performs radically different tasks when drawing a button control versus a grid control, but the call is the same. Also, provided they both descend from a common ancestor, calling the ancestor's Show method using an instance of either the grid or button control should properly display the correct control.
- **Encapsulation**—Data and program code must be locatable within single entities. That is, an object must be able to store both data elements (as a record structure does) and procedure elements (called methods). Procedural elements within an object must have automatic access to data elements within the object.
- **Primary methodology**—Here's the big one. The object-orientation of a tool must be the primary method of constructing program code, not an afterthought or add-on. Since it's the primary means of coding, the OOP technology present in the tool must be efficient enough to use productively, else the tool itself is suspect because its primary means of producing code cannot be used productively.

Delphi meets these criteria in the same way that C++ and other traditional OOP environments do. In fact, Borland's Pascal compiler was object-oriented before either Microsoft C or Borland C was. The OOP technology in Delphi is not an afterthought, but rather the basis for the entire environment. With the addition of visual development tools, Borland has removed much of the tediousness frequently associated with OOP development.

Scaleability

One of the first things that comes to mind with any database development tool is *scaleability*—the ability to work with data on different platforms. Sure, the tool works great with dBASE tables, but how is it with Sybase tables? Delphi answers these questions and more by providing some of the best scaling to be found in a RAD tool. Specifically, it does the following:

- Supports both local tables and those that reside on remote database servers
- Supports heterogeneous queries and access to multiple DBMS platforms from within a single application
- Allows applications to be easily moved from DBMS to DBMS by providing platform-independent database access through the Borland Database Engine
- Provides fast native drivers for the major client/server platforms
- Comes with complete ODBC support

The bottom line to all this is that Delphi is the consummate database developer's tool. Whether it's local or SQL Server–based tables, Delphi provides the tools you need to get the job done. Chances are, you'll get it done a lot quicker and with a lot less stress, too.

What's Ahead

Here's a brief rundown of what's ahead in the rest of the book. This should give you some assistance in deciding what parts of the book would be most useful to you.

Chapter 2, "Comparisons with Other Tools," helps you along in the journey from other tools to Delphi. If you're a PowerBuilder, Visual Basic, C, or xBase programmer, this chapter is for you.

Chapter 3, "Building Blocks," tours the building blocks used in creating Delphi applications. If you're new to Delphi, you'll want to be sure to visit this one.

Chapter 4, "Conventions," relates my thoughts regarding naming conventions. If you don't already have your own ideas about naming conventions, you might check this one out before beginning to build applications.

Chapter 5, "A No-Nonsense Approach to SQL," is a layman's guide to SQL. If you've never used SQL, or just need a refresher, have a look at this chapter—it'll give you the essentials without burying you under needless detail.

Chapter 6, "Database Design 101," explores relational database design theory and the ways in which it applies to Delphi database development. If you're unfamiliar with relational theory or want to sharpen your skills, be sure to read this chapter.

Chapter 7, "Application Design 101," extends the discussion of database design to cover database application design. Chapters 6 and 7 are a companion set and are good reading for anyone interested in developing database applications.

Chapter 8, "Your First Real Database Application," begins Part II, "Tutorial," of this book, which continues through Chapter 14, "Moving up to Client/Server." The Tutorial section takes you through the process of designing a full-featured database application, then upscaling it to an SQL server. If you're new to Delphi database development, this section is a must-have.

Chapter 15, "Database Component Reference Part I," begins Part III, "Reference," of the book. This chapter and Chapter 16, "Database Component Reference Part II," provide a complete reference for the Delphi database hierarchy. One of the goals of this book is to save you from having to shuffle back and forth through an armload of manuals. You can use these two chapters to learn the fundamentals of the Delphi database component hierarchy.

Chapter 17, "InterBase," covers the InterBase database server in depth. If you've purchased the Client/Server Suite edition of Delphi, you already have a version of InterBase at your disposal. This chapter takes you through all the nuances of using InterBase with your Delphi applications.

Chapter 18, "ReportSmith," covers the essentials of using Borland's ReportSmith, the report writer included with Delphi, in your applications. Designing various types of reports is discussed, as well as augmenting reports with DLL calls and user-defined SQL queries. Integration with Delphi is explored, and tips on using ReportSmith reports in your applications are given. If you use or think you might use ReportSmith in your applications, this chapter might be worth studying.

Chapter 19, "Business Rules Part I," begins the Advanced Topics section of the book. This chapter and Chapter 20, "Business Rules Part II," cover the correct implementation of business rules in Delphi applications. If you're interested in learning about business rules and why and how they should be implemented, check out these two chapters.

Chapter 21, "Concurrency Control," explores the subject of concurrency control in Delphi database applications. Although much of this is handled for you automatically by the Borland Database Engine, there are still several issues that you'll want to be aware of if you intend to develop and deploy large-scale database applications. This chapter explores Delphi's methods for dealing with concurrency control and the ways you can tweak it to your advantage.

Chapter 22, "Advanced SQL," covers advanced SQL programming. If Chapter 5 was just enough to whet your appetite, you'll want to consume this chapter, as well. Advanced topics like stored procedure creation, view construction, and the use of triggers are all covered in this chapter. Between this chapter and Chapter 5, you should be able to ingest all you ever wanted to know about SQL.

Chapter 23, "Optimizing Delphi Client/Server Applications," goes through a number of techniques for optimizing Delphi client/server applications. If you intend to deploy your applications on database servers, this chapter is for you. Optimizations with regard to performance are explored, as well as optimal SQL coding techniques and database design philosophies.

Chapter 24, "Delphi's Database Drivers Demystified," removes the cloud of mystery surrounding Delphi's database drivers. Many of the supported drivers have their own idiosyncrasies, and this chapter explores them. Techniques are provided for optimizing your applications to work well over a network, as well as tweaking the network to adequately support your applications. If you have problems getting your database connections to work properly, or if you simply want to learn how to tweak them to work optimally, this chapter should prove an invaluable resource.

Chapter 25, "The Borland Database Engine," covers the internals of the Borland Database Engine. You'll learn how to make direct BDE API calls and how to use them to supplement the facilities surfaced in Delphi's database components.

Chapter 26, "Building Your Own Database Components," shows you how to develop your own database components. You'll learn to inherit from existing components as well as to create your own from scratch. Several examples take you step-by-step through the process of creating useful database components for Delphi.

Chapter 27, "Deploying Your Applications," introduces you to all the issues surrounding the deployment of Delphi database applications. If you intend to distribute the applications you write to third parties, this chapter should be a source of much useful information.

Summary

There are a number of good reasons to choose Delphi over other development environments. Delphi offers these features:

- A sophisticated object framework
- A native-code compiler
- Integrated debugging
- Database access abstraction
- Comprehensive two-way tools

Beyond its native features, Delphi is also more extensible than other tools. Some of the things that make Delphi extensible are:

- Direct access to the Windows API
- Inline assembly language support
- Generation custom VCL and OCX components
- Creation of DLLs and other auxiliary Windows object types

■ Complete OOP implementation—you can inherit from included component classes or build new ones

Many environments that feign object-orientation are not true OOP tools. Real object-oriented tools have the following four characteristics:

■ **Inheritance**—New object types must be "synthesizeable" from existing objects by inheriting their attributes and method procedures.

■ **Polymorphism**—Object method procedures must be callable without regard to the actual type of the object in which the method resides.

■ **Encapsulation**—Data and program code must be contained within a single entity.

■ **Primary methodology**—the object-orientation of a tool must be the chief method of constructing program code, not an afterthought or add-on.

Many tools claim scaleability, but Delphi's scaleability provides the following features:

■ Supports both local and remote tables

■ Supports heterogeneous queries and multiple DBMS applications

■ Provides platform-independent database access

■ Comes with native drivers for the major client/server DBMSs

■ Provides complete ODBC support

In a word, Delphi is the consummate database developer's tool!

2

Comparisons With Other Tools

Because Delphi is fortunate enough to have been born late in the world of visual development, it benefits from the technology pioneered by a number of different tools. Borland has taken what it liked from a variety of approaches to application development and woven it into a single, comprehensive "super-tool." This is great for Delphi; it stands on the shoulders of those that have gone before it. It combines the best of a number of different visual development strategies.

The downside of this, though, is that it copies none of them. That is, you won't find a one-to-one relationship between the method of doing things in Delphi and that in any other tool you've ever used before. Delphi is a different animal. This means that you may find migrating your applications a bit of a challenge. You may initially find Delphi's way of doing things somewhat daunting. Rest easy, though—it isn't as bad as it might seem.

The purpose of this chapter is to assist you in moving to Delphi from other environments. I discuss major design concepts of the other tools, provide language cross-references between them and Delphi, and explore features they share with Delphi. I also point out differences in approaches to solving development problems. In general, I try to at least mention major issues that you should consider when migrating from the tools covered. I cover some areas in depth; I merely touch upon others.

Although this discussion could easily be the subject of its own book, this chapter applies the "80-20" rule—giving you the essentials for migrating, without going into exhaustive detail. Hopefully, you'll glean enough from the topics presented to migrate your applications successfully. The key is in understanding the differences between the Delphi "philosophy" and the philosophy ingrained in other tools. Once you understand this, the rest is easy.

Without further ado, let's begin our discussion of the issues involved in coming from other tools to Delphi. I'll start with C and C++.

C and C++

Because database access under C is largely dependent upon the framework used, this section focuses solely on the differences (and similarities) between the C and Object Pascal programming languages. Most C and C++ programmers who do database development have found a C-based database toolkit or framework that they use to build applications. Delphi is so tightly coupled with its own built-in database access tools that comparisons with these toolkits are difficult at best. The level of functionality and the issues involved with building applications using them vary from toolkit to toolkit. Most of them aren't as full-featured or as tightly linked with their host language environments as Delphi's database access is. This section, therefore, focuses exclusively on the language issues involved with coming from C to Delphi.

Historically, visual development tools are known for their large resource footprints and relatively poor performance. One of the promises made by the original proponents of client/server computing was that client computers could one day be down-sized because all the real work would be done by the server. This intent has been largely thwarted by the fact that most tools available for developing client/server applications, though increasingly easy to use, generate inefficient executables. Today, client machines are being revved up with enough horsepower to have been considered server machines just a few short years ago. This is no doubt due in part to the bloated executables that many client/server development tools are producing. It seems that no one really understands the art of building an efficient client/server development environment.

It isn't as though client/server application development is really optional these days, though. More and more, customers are demanding the increased stability and performance of dedicated database servers. They want the applications that talk to those servers to be Windows-based, too. Developers are left caught in the middle—a marketplace that demands Windows client/server applications and a dearth of good tools with which to build them.

The normal answer to this conundrum is the use of C or C++ as the host language for the application. If an application needs to be truly fast and efficient, tools such as PowerBuilder and Visual Basic just won't cut it. C compilers produce executables that are faster and more efficient than those produced by most of today's client/server development tools. The tradeoff, though, is that C compilers are also much more difficult to use. A complex application will often take several times longer to build in C than it would in a dedicated client/server environment. Originally intended as a machine-independent assembly language, C is not well suited to developing complex Windows-based client/server applications.

Given the choice of the two types of tools—those that are easy to use but produce inefficient executables, and those that generate efficient executables but are difficult to use—what's the developer to do? Enter Delphi. Unlike its predecessors, Delphi produces *efficient* applications *quickly.* You should not assume that coming from C or C++ to Delphi means that you're stepping off into the quagmire of slow executables and huge resource usage. If Delphi is anything, it is nimble. Based on the Turbo Pascal product line, Delphi furthers the speedy development metaphor to now include Windows development. And it does so without compromising the reputation for producing tight code that Turbo Pascal has enjoyed for years.

Common Misconceptions Regarding Object Pascal and C

Misunderstanding the directions for getting somewhere is the best way to get lost. Misconceptions regarding your journey to Delphi will run you aground, as well. In this section, I'll discuss some of the common misconceptions related to coming to Delphi from C.

> **NOTE**
>
> In this section, I use C and C++ interchangeably. The issues discussed apply equally to either of them. Many developers use the two together of necessity, so it seems reasonable to cover them both with one broad stroke.

Misconception 1

Delphi generates less efficient executables than C compilers do.

Delphi executables are native in every sense of the word, just like most C compilers. In contrast to tools like Visual Basic and PowerBuilder, Delphi applications require no runtime DLL, interpreter, or p-code engine. Delphi executables often rival those produced by C compilers in performance, too. Like most C compilers, Delphi makes use of several different optimization techniques to further streamline the executables it produces, including:

- Short-circuit Boolean evaluation
- Case statement jump table generation
- Constant string folding
- Redundant pointer load elimination (especially within `With` blocks)
- Near call optimizations
- Code segment merging
- Automatic jump sizing (in `asm` statements)
- Block-level smart-linking
- `While false` loops removed

Additional optimizations in 32 bits include register variables, loop induction variables, and common subexpression elimination.

Delphi's compiler is based on several generations of Borland's award-winning Turbo Pascal product line, so it's had plenty of time to learn the process of producing fast executables quickly.

Misconception 2

Delphi takes longer to generate executables than C compilers do.

Borland's Pascal compilers are legendary for their ability to compile programs at warp speed. Delphi will typically compile programs several times faster than a C compiler can. By Delphi's standards, C compilers are terribly slow. This is due to several factors. First, Delphi's compiler is a single-pass compiler. Unlike C, the Pascal language is designed to be translated to machine language in just one trip through the source code. Functions are declared before they are used, and there is no preprocessor to deal with. Second, Delphi's proprietary object module format includes enough information to make header files unnecessary. Delphi still supports include files, but header files, as they are normally used with C compilers, are obsolete. Borland's promotional materials for Delphi rate the compiler at 350,000 lines per minute. All marketing rhetoric aside, Delphi's compiler is quite probably the fastest Windows compiler on the planet.

The header file issue demonstrates a fundamental difference between the C and Object Pascal languages: C compilers assume they will have access to the entirety of a project's source code at compile-time. Header files are a way of tricking the C compiler into thinking it has the source code to all modules. Delphi's Object Pascal compiler does not need the source code to a unit when its compiled .DCU file is available. Enough information is contained in the DCU of each unit to allow it to be linked into an executable without referencing its source code. Delphi's compiled DCU modules are faster, leaner, and smarter than C++'s pre-compiled headers.

Misconception 3

Delphi's Object Pascal language is not as rich as C; many data types, programming constructs, and operators present in C are absent from Object Pascal.

You'll find that Object Pascal is up to the C/C++ challenge. It sports a language syntax that is as full-featured as C and easier to use in many ways. It is concise, but not restrictive; complete, but not overladen. The following sections summarize some of the similarities and differences between these two languages.

Data Types

Object Pascal supports a wide array of variable types, including some not found in C. Most notably, C doesn't have a separate string type, nor does it support sets. Table 2.1 cross-references C variable types with their corresponding Pascal data types. The table also includes a few Pascal data types that aren't present in C or C++. Those listed as N/A are not supported by the specified language. Notice that the two are pretty much even as far as basic data types are concerned.

Table 2.1. C and Object Pascal data type cross-reference.

C/C++ type	*Object Pascal type*
char	char
char *	pchar
char charvar[]	pchar
unsigned char	byte
signed char	shortint
N/A	boolean
int	integer
unsigned int	word
long	longint
unsigned long	cardinal
float	single
double	double
long double	extended

continues

Table 2.1. continued

C/C++ type	*Object Pascal type*
N/A	string
struct	record
enum	enumerated data type (no keyword)
N/A	set
void *	pointer

Regarding Pascal's `boolean` data type, C pundits would argue that C's equivalent mechanism is to use a zero int value as boolean `false` and a non-zero int as boolean `true`. It isn't quite that simple, though. In Pascal, the compiler knows the value can only be either true or false, so only the first bit of the byte that stores the `boolean` is examined to determine its value. Note that Object Pascal also defines the `ByteBool`, `WordBool`, and `LongBool` types for equating non-zero boolean values with True.

As I mentioned, C doesn't support a separate `string` data type. In C, strings are handled using arrays of characters. This means that you can't program long in C without having to deal directly with pointers. Object Pascal supports a separate `string` data type and automatically generates code to handle assignment and concatenation of string variables. That is, you do not need to use functions like C's `strcpy()` and `strcat()` to assign or concatenate Object Pascal strings. For example, in C you write:

```
char firstname[31]
.....
strcpy(firstname,name);
```

In Object Pascal, you use:

```
firstname : string;
.....
firstname:=name;
```

Furthermore, in C you use:

```
fullname=strcat(fullname,lastname);
```

Whereas in Object Pascal, you use:

```
fullname:=fullname+lastname;
```

In C, the first character of a string can be accessed like so:

```
firstname[0]='J';
```

Whereas in Object Pascal, it's

```
firstname[1]:='J';
```

Similarly to C strings, Object Pascal strings are null-terminated. However, unlike C strings, Object Pascal strings also contain a length integer. This means that an Object Pascal string need not be scanned for a null-terminator to determine its length. The length of the string is stored with it and is readily accessible. Because of this, accessing Object Pascal strings will normally be faster than accessing null-terminated ones. This also means Pascal strings can contain arbitrary binary data (including nulls) without loss of information and without requiring special encoding schemes.

Object Pascal strings have a theoretical limitation of 2 gigabytes. In actuality, this means that Object Pascal strings are limited only by available memory. Another nice feature of Delphi's strings is that the compiler automatically converts to and from C-style strings. As Table 2.1 indicates, the Object Pascal equivalent of the C char * type is the pchar type. Since the Windows API makes extensive use of the pchar type, it's helpful that Delphi provides native support for it. Even more useful, though, is the fact that Delphi handles converting between its string variables and pchar variables automatically—you can simply type-cast one to the other.

Set data types are also missing from C. In Pascal, sets are collections of bit flags used to store groups of related items. These items must all be of an ordinal type that allows no more than 256 possible values. Object Pascal provides a rich suite of operators and procedures for working with sets. The closest approximation of a set in C is a structure consisting of bit flags, though you must improvise operations on these pseudo-sets yourself.

Windows Data Types

Windows itself has a number of specialized data types (each with a base type in C) that Delphi also supports. Table 2.2 cross-references these types with their C and Object Pascal counterparts.

Table 2.2. C and Object Pascal Windows data type cross-reference.

C/C++ Windows type (WINDOWS.H)	*C/C++ base type*	*OP Windows type (WINTYPES.PAS)*	*OP base type*
BOOL	int	bool	wordbool
BYTE	unsigned char	byte	byte
UINT	unsigned int	word	word
WORD	unsigned int	word	word
LONG	long	longint	longint
LPSTR	char far *	PChar	PChar
WPARAM	unsigned int	word	word
LPARAM	long	longint	longint
LRESULT	long	longint	longint
HANDLE	unsigned int	thandle	word
HINSTANCE	unsigned int	thandle	word
HWND	unsigned int	hwnd	word

Coding Constructs

Delphi also supports a complete set of coding constructs comparable to that of C and C++. Though some of them are implemented differently, Delphi supports the full range of code building blocks needed to create complex applications.

Assignment

C uses the equal sign (=) to assign values to variables, whereas Pascal uses : = (colon equal). You use == (double equal) to test for equality in C, but the equal sign (=) is used in Pascal. Additionally, C assignments return a value, so they can be used in expressions. Fortunately, Object Pascal does not support this problematic syntax.

Code Blocks

In C, a compound statement or "code block" is delimited with braces. For example,

```
{
 clrscr();
 printf("A line in a compound statement\n");
}
```

Whereas in Object Pascal, you use

```
begin
 clrscr;
 writeln('A line in a compound statement');
 end;
```

while loop

In C, a while loop is coded

```
while (a+b==c) callsubroutine;
```

Whereas in Object Pascal, you write

```
while a+b=c do callsubroutine;
```

The principle differences between the two are that C requires parentheses around the conditional expression, and Pascal requires the use of the do keyword.

do while loop

In C, a do while loop takes this form:

```
do {
 callsubroutine;
 callanotherroutine;
}while (a+b==c);
```

Whereas in Object Pascal, you use

```
repeat
 callsubroutine;
 callanotherroutine;
until (a+b<>c);
```

Note the differences between the two blocks of code. They are due to fundamental differences in the way the two languages implement the do...while loop. First, the statements between the repeat and the until in the Object Pascal code execute *until* an expression is true, not *while* it is true. Second, the Object Pascal code does not require code block delimiters to execute multiple statements; C's do...while does.

for loops

In C, a for loop looks like

```
for (n=1;n<m;n++) callsubroutine;
```

In Object Pascal, it's

```
for n=1 to m do callsubroutine;
```

The for loop construct typifies the differences between C and Object Pascal as programming languages. Object Pascal's for loop construct is rather plain compared to its C counterpart. In C, the construct is completely open-ended and flexible. While this is powerful, it sometimes leads to coding constructs that bear little resemblance to for loops. Pascal's stricter requirements also make it easier for the compiler to optimize the loop control variable.

In C, when you want to iterate through a for loop in reverse, you simply change the third of the for construct's three expressions to use the decrement operator (--) rather than the increment operator (++). In Object Pascal, on the other hand, you change the to keyword to downto. One major difference between the two languages is that Object Pascal only enables you to increment through the loop one ordinal value per iteration—you can't cycle through the loop by more than one step at a time. C's open syntax, on the other hand, lets you do whatever you please. The ideal approach is probably somewhere between the two.

if Statements

In C, an if construct looks like this:

```
if (a+b==c) dosomething;
else dosomethingelse;
```

In Object Pascal, it looks like this:

```
if a+b=c then dosomething
else dosomethingelse;
```

There are three principle differences between the two implementations. First, C requires parentheses around the conditional expression, but Object Pascal does not. Second, Object Pascal requires the use of the keyword then—C does not. Third, C requires an if to be terminated with a semicolon, even if it precedes an else, but Object Pascal does not allow a semicolon before else.

case Statement

C's case construct is implemented as its switch statement and takes the form

```
switch(a) {
case 1: dosomething; break;
case 2: dosomethingelse; break;
case 3: doyetanotherthing; break;
case 4: doitagain; break;
case 5: ;
case 6: ;
case 7: doyetanotherthing; break;
case 8: doitagain; break;
case 9: doyetanotherthing; break;
default dotherightthing;
}
```

The Object Pascal case statement takes this form:

```
case a of
1: dosomething;
2: dosomethingelse;
3,5..7,9: doyetanotherthing;
4,8: doitagain;
else dotherightthing;
end;
```

Note the differences between the two. First, the C code requires the use of the break keyword in order for most of the case statements to work properly. Second, Object Pascal supports multiple case selector values on the left of the colon—C does not. Third, the C switch statement requires compound statement delimiters, whereas the Object Pascal code does not.

NOTE

Be aware that although Object Pascal supports multiple case selector values on the left of the colon, these values cannot overlap. Overlapping case selector values is a poor coding practice, anyway, and should be avoided. When you overlap selector values, you are essentially identifying two different actions to take place for the same value. In most languages, none but the first of the case selectors will actually be reached in the sequence of execution. This is a confusing, if not illegal, coding style.

Function and Procedure Declarations

In C, a function declaration takes the form

```
int max(int parm1, int parm2)
{
 if (parm1 > parm2) return(parm1);
 else return(parm2);
}
```

Whereas in Object Pascal, it looks like this:

```
function max(parm1, parm2 : integer ) : integer;
begin
 if parm1 > parm2 then result:=parm1
 else result:=parm2;
end;
```

Returning Results

Note that C uses the `return` function to return a result to the caller, whereas Object Pascal uses the predefined result variable to return it. All Object Pascal functions have a built-in `result` variable whose whole purpose is to return a value to the function's caller. Note that C's `return()` function exits immediately to the caller, whereas assigning Object Pascal's result variable does not immediately exit the function. To return immediately from a function or procedure in Object Pascal, use the `exit` procedure.

Functions Versus Procedures

Note Object Pascal's use of the function keyword. This is done to distinguish a function from a procedure. In Pascal, functions that do not return anything are known as procedures. That is, C's `void someroutine();` is identical to Object Pascal's `procedure someroutine;`.

Table 2.3 summarizes the similarities and differences between Object Pascal and C/C++ coding constructs.

Table 2.3. C and Object Pascal coding construct cross-reference.

Element	C/C++	Object Pascal
Code blocks	{...}	begin...end
While loop	while (1) statement;	while true do statement;
Do while loop	do statement while (1);	repeat statements; until false;
For loop	for (n=1;n<m;n++) statement;	for n:=1 to m do statement;
If-else	if (1) statement; else statement;	if true statement else statement;

continues

Table 2.3. continued

Element	C/C++	Object Pascal
Case	`switch(n) {case 1:code;break;}`	`case n of 1:code;end;`

Function	`int fname(int parm)`	`function`
		`fname(parm:integer) :`
		`integer;`

Procedure	`void fname(int parm)`	`procedure` `name(parm:integer);`

Operators

Object Pascal supports a rich suite of operators, as well. Table 2.4 cross-references some of the more notable operators supported by C and Object Pascal. Those listed as N/A are not supported by the specified language.

Table 2.4. C and Object Pascal operator cross-reference.

Operator	C/C++	Object Pascal
Pointer dereference	`*somepointer`	`somepointer^`
Assignment	`=`	`:=`
Increment	`++`	`Succ, Inc;`
Decrement	`--`	`Pred, Dec;`
Assignment-increment	`+=`	`Inc(x,y)`
Assignment-decrement	`-=`	`Dec(x,y)`
Equality	`==,>=,<=,!=`	`=,>=,<=,<>`
Bitwise operators	`¦,^,&,>>,<<`	`or, xor, and, shr, shl`
Logical operators	`¦¦,&&`	`or, and`
Sets	N/A	`in,+,-,*`
String concatenation	N/A	`+`

Note that Object Pascal's `Succ` and `Inc` routines are only approximations of the C `++` and `--` operators. First, though you can increment a number using `Inc`, you can't use `Inc` in an expression—it's a procedure. Second, though `Succ` can be used in an expression, it leaves the original value unchanged. These same caveats apply to the `Pred` and `Dec` routines, as well.

Misconception 4

It is more difficult to create "secondary" Windows executable code such as DLLs and device drivers in Delphi than it is in C-based tools.

Not only is Delphi capable of creating secondary Windows executables like DLLs, it is, in fact, better at it than most C tools. The entirety of the Windows API is readily accessible via Delphi's Windows unit. Also, special language extensions aid in the creation of Windows executables.

Creating DLLs

Delphi can easily create DLLs, device drivers, and other types of Windows executables. In fact, Delphi includes extensions to the Pascal language to allow for easy creation of DLLs. You don't need C's module definition file to build DLLs. For example, here's the code to create a simple DLL in Object Pascal:

```
library MaxLib;
function max(parm1, parm2 : integer ) : integer; export;
begin
 if parm1 > parm2 then result:=parm1
 else result:=parm2;
end;
exports
 max index 1;
 begin
 end.
```

Note the use of the special `library` keyword. This tells Delphi to generate a DLL rather than an EXE file. Also, note the two variations of the `export` keyword. The first tells the compiler to generate the special entry and exit code that functions exported from a DLL require. The second use (`exports`...) tells Delphi which functions in the DLL to actually export. This is necessary because Delphi's compiler is a single-pass compiler—it must know at the time it actually translates the `max` function into machine code that the function is to be exported. Further, by separating the function of generating the prologue-epilogue code from that of actually exporting routines, Object Pascal enables you to set up callback functions without actually having to export them from a DLL. The `export` keyword can even be used to flag routines as callbacks in EXE files. Note that, in contrast to C, none of this requires the use of a module definition (DEF) file or an import library.

Delphi can also be used to create device drivers and other types of Windows executables. The complete Windows API is surfaced in Delphi's `Windows` unit (the equivalent of C's `WINDOWS.H`), so you can interact directly with the API if need be. The section on Visual Basic presents a SendKeys function that's written entirely in Object Pascal—no area of Windows programming is out of Delphi's reach.

Additionally, because Delphi supports inline machine language and has a built-in assembler, there is virtually nothing you can do using C that you can't also do with Delphi. You can even create OCXs with Delphi that you can then use with packages like Visual Basic, though these can't be created in Visual Basic itself.

Not only is Delphi every bit as capable as C in this regard, it is, in fact, *more* capable because it includes Windows-specific language extensions that C itself does not have.

Misconception 5

Delphi can't handle large projects.

There is a misconception among veteran and novice developers alike that C is the tool of choice for the really large projects. I've had people who couldn't code their way out of a paper bag in C tell me this. This simply reflects a lack of knowledge. Not only is Delphi quite adept at handling large projects, but built-in PVCS support (and hooks for other version control systems), an integrated project manager, smart linking, and a comprehensive class library make Delphi a better choice than most, if not all, C/C++ tools.

Delphi's Maximum Project Size

With abbreviated unit names that all reside in the current directory, you're limited to about 600 very large units per project. In practice, this means there's no functional limit on the number of source code modules or forms that a Delphi project can have. Delphi can handle as large a project as any Windows C compiler.

Team Development Support

Furthermore, Delphi's team development support is simple but elegant. If you have a large project on which many programmers are working, Delphi's integrated PVCS support may come in handy. Delphi detects the presence of PVCS on your machine and takes special advantage of it if present. Part of the Delphi Open Tools interface is its version control system socket. Though the client/server edition of Delphi provides a sample module to talk to PVCS, other version control system manufacturers are providing interface modules to talk to their systems as well. Delphi's support for version control software is as good as, if not better than, other language tools that support team development.

Using DLLs Written in C in Delphi

Because Object Pascal and C are so comparable in terms of language features, interfacing with DLLs written in C does not have to be terribly difficult. The cross-reference tables listed in the previous sections should get you started. The main thing to keep in mind is that you'll need to translate the function headers and data types used in the C code to their Object Pascal equivalents. Think in terms of the size of the variable you're dealing with, not necessarily its language type.

Import Units

In Object Pascal, function header information is stored in the interface section of the unit in which the function lives. Prototypes for functions that live in DLLs are normally declared in an "import" unit, though they do not have to be. In an import unit, the body of a function that is imported from a DLL is replaced with a reference to the DLL using the `external` keyword. DLL-based functions can be referenced by name or by index. No checking is performed by the compiler, so the DLL need not even be present at compile-time.

No Import Library

Most C programmers use an import library to aid them in interfacing with DLLs, but Delphi programmers have no need to. The interface to a DLL is encapsulated entirely in the source code to the import unit. When a Delphi application references a function that resides in a DLL, the DLL is loaded and the function referenced, just as it would be if the calling application were written in C.

FAR PASCAL Not Needed

Although C programmers use the `FAR PASCAL` designation to interface DLL-based routines, Delphi programmers can safely omit it. This is because any routine declared in the interface section of a unit (in this case, the import unit) is automatically a `far` routine. (If the routine is not declared in the interface section of a unit, you'll need to flag it with `FAR; EXPORT;`) Also, Delphi uses the `PASCAL` calling convention by default, so you don't need to specify it, either. Note that Delphi also supports the `cdecl` and `stdcall` calling conventions.

C Macros

Macros as used in C are handled using a couple of different mechanisms in Delphi. Simple constant declarations can be replaced with equivalent Object Pascal constant declarations. For example, in C you would write

```
#define SUCCESS 1
```

This could be coded as follows in Pascal:

```
const SUCCESS=1;
```

However, more complex macros, such as those involving expressions, will require replacement by Object Pascal functions. The following example in C

```
#define addem(a,b) ((a+b))
```

would have to be replaced by an Object Pascal function such as

```
function addem(a,b: variant) : variant;
begin
 result:=a+b;
end;
```

DLL-based *Varargs* Routines

DLL-based functions that allow a variable number of parameters to be passed to them (such as Windows' own `wsprintf()` function) cannot be used directly by Object Pascal. There is a way around this, though, if you must use one of these unruly beasts.

First, you could code the call to the routine in assembly language (embedded within your Object Pascal source) using Delphi's built-in assembler, BASM. You would place this call in a "wrapper" function that your application would call instead of the varargs function. This function would in turn set up the stack and reverse the parameter order before calling the varargs routine.

Second, if you don't feel like resorting to assembly language, you could write a C-based DLL that acts as a messenger between the Delphi application and the DLL in question. This is especially easy to do if you do not actually take advantage of the function's variable parameters ability.

You set this up by creating a C-based DLL that surfaces its own version of the function you want to call but does not allow a variable number of parameters. It, in turn, makes the requisite call to the varargs function, acting as a kind of function "go-between," passing the parameters you specified to it and returning any function results from it. In your Object Pascal code, you import the go-between function rather than the varargs function.

Converting Function Prototypes

Following are a couple of examples showing the process of converting a function header written in C to Object Pascal. They demonstrate the syntactical differences between the two languages and the manner in which one variable type is translated to another. Let's take a simple example to begin with. A function header declared as

```
UINT FAR PASCAL _export GetWinmacroVersion();
```

would translate to the following line in the interface section of an Object Pascal unit:

```
function GetWinmacroVersion : Word;
```

It could take the following form in the implementation section:

```
function GetWinmacroVersion; external 'WINMACRO';
```

Now let's take a more complex example. In C, a function header declared as

```
pTMacroContext FAR PASCAL _export InstallHook( HWND, UINT, UINT, BOOLEAN,
➥BOOLEAN, BYTE, BYTE, BOOLEAN);
```

might look like this in Object Pascal:

```
function InstallHook(_CallingWindowHook : HWND; _MaxMacroNum, MaxMacroLen :
➥word; _FastPlayback, _SystemWide : boolean; _RecordMouse : TRecordMouse;
➥ _MouseBase : TMouseBase; _CancelChecking : boolean) : pTMacroContext;
```

Of course, the example code is presuming the definition of some custom data types (TRecordMouse, TMouseBase, and pTMacroContext), but you get the idea.

Conclusion

As you can see, Delphi's Object Pascal supports a rich language syntax rivaling that of C, or any other programming language, for that matter. Pascal's structure has made it a favorite in the classroom for years. Borland's enhancements have also made it a favorite in the developer community. When the dust from all the hype surrounding C++ has settled, it's apparent that Object Pascal is as capable any other language. It could also be argued that Object Pascal's tighter syntax and strong data typing make it better suited to the treacherous world of Windows development than C or C++.

One of the things I personally like best about Object Pascal is the conciseness of its runtime library compared with that of C. Object Pascal is not governed by any committee. Borland basically controls the language definition and has always sought to keep it and its runtime library small and succinct. There aren't 15 ways to perform a given function—there's normally just one. This is as it should be. More than anything else, this brevity means you won't spend hours wading through a runtime library reference manual searching for the explanation of some unknown function you've discovered in reading someone else's code, only to discover that it's just an obscure substitute for one you use all the time.

C suffers from the same malady as the UNIX operating system. Initially intended as a modular platform capable of extension, it has been expanded to the point of collapse. C as a programming language initially had a very clear purpose: to provide the power of assembly language in a processor-independent programming language. Though it began life as a very small package, every C guru since then has played tinker toys with it—building on whenever possible. This has continued to the point that C has become a monstrosity that compilers find unwieldy and developers find intimidating. Add to this the bureaucracy of management by committee, and you see why C is in the shape it's in. Fortunately, Object Pascal suffers from none of this.

PowerBuilder

This section on PowerBuilder is divided into two parts, "Conceptual Issues" and "Language Issues." The "Conceptual Issues" section covers general design differences and subtleties of approach within the two products. The section entitled "Language Issues" covers the nuts-and-bolts of moving from PowerBuilder to Delphi. Data-type cross-references, function cross-references, and control cross-references are provided.

Conceptual Issues

The most striking thing you encounter when coming from PowerBuilder to Delphi is *speed*—Delphi's got it, PowerBuilder doesn't. PowerBuilder's interpretive code execution is no match for that of a real compiler. Applications built with PowerBuilder are also saddled with the huge memory footprint of its runtime interpreter DLLs. This slows things down even more. And don't look for PowerBuilder's C code translator and compiler to dramatically improve things, either. A turtle with a rocket strapped to its back is still a turtle.

No Interpreter DLLs

Delphi, on the other hand, is a true native code compiled language; Delphi requires no runtime engine or DLL set. Executables built with Delphi are complete in and of themselves. You could even build a product like PowerBuilder *in* Delphi.

Database Access Requires DLLs

Still, I should point out that Delphi's database access is handled through the Borland Database Engine (BDE), which is composed of DLLs. Although it's technically true that Delphi applications do not require runtime DLLs, if your applications access databases using the default mechanism for doing so (the BDE), they will most certainly require support DLLs at runtime.

Nevertheless, this is a far cry from requiring runtime *interpreter* DLLs. Database support DLLs represent one of the few things in PowerBuilder that could be reasonably labeled "speedy." This is largely due to the fact that they aren't written in PowerBuilder itself, but in C. Likewise, Delphi's DLLs provide swift, application-independent access to databases—they don't function as any kind of runtime interpreter. Furthermore, though Delphi may require DLLs for database access, you can write applications all day long that aren't database applications and therefore require no support libraries. Communications programs, editors, low-level machine control software—you name it—are all doable in Delphi without DLLs.

Replacing the BDE

Because Delphi applications do not inherently require runtime DLLs, it's also possible to eliminate the database DLL dependency by replacing the BDE with some other database mechanism. Already vendors are scrambling to fill this niche. One of them, SuccessWare, Inc., offers a new version of their popular Rock-E-T database component set just for Delphi. Another, TurboPower Software, plans to soon release a set of Delphi VCL components to support their popular Btree Filer database. Other vendors have similar plans. All of these mean that there are alternatives to the DLLs that constitute the BDE. They all link directly into the executable and eliminate the need for database support DLLs. This just isn't possible with PowerBuilder.

Why the DLLs?

With all that said, it's really not surprising that Borland would package its database technology in the form of DLLs. After all, these DLLs provide database access to a number of Borland products, not just Delphi. These include Paradox for Windows, dBASE for Windows, Borland C++, and the former Borland product, Quattro Pro for Windows (although QPW uses an older version of the DLLs, the concept is the same). The idea is that once installed on the machine, all Borland products can then share the libraries. This goes for applications you build, too. Once the BDE is installed on a client's machine, there's no need to reinstall it with each new application you build using your spiffy new tool. This turns out to be a nice compromise between ultimate application independence and the modularity of inter-application code sharing.

DataWindows

A mainstay of PowerBuilder development is the use of *DataWindows*. Few PowerBuilder developers could live without them. Fortunately, Delphi provides a component that encompasses much of the functionality of the DataWindow. It's called the DBCtrlGrid component. On it, you can drop controls and arrange them any way you like. You can display as many rows in a DBCtrlGrid as will fit on the screen, scrolling through your DataSet at will. Unlike Delphi's DBGrid component, individual DataSet rows can take up multiple screen rows. Delphi and PowerBuilder have completely different object models, but DBCtrlGrid provides a close facsimile of the DataWindow construct without succumbing to its "one-size-fits-all" mentality.

Form Inheritance Versus Class Inheritance

Another popular PowerBuilder feature is that of DataWindow inheritance. You can set up a virtual class hierarchy that enables you to inherit the attributes of one DataWindow while building another.

Delphi provides this same ability in a much more elegant fashion. First and foremost, Delphi is an OOP environment. This means that when you inherit from one class to create another, you're creating a true OOP descendant class. You get all the benefits of a real OOP implementation, like polymorphism and encapsulation, when you create new Delphi objects through inheritance.

Second, Delphi supports visual form inheritance. You aren't making a static copy of a form when you inherit from it to create another. Changes to the ancestor are reflected in the descendant. Because Delphi's form classes are natively compiled, there's also no penalty for constructing elaborate form hierarchies. You can store the forms you build in the Object Repository and inherit from them to build other forms. The same is true for data modules— you can inherit from them as well. You get the best of both worlds: the ease of use of visual form inheritance and the speed of native code executables.

Automatic Syntax Checking

There is one PowerBuilder feature missing from Delphi that developers will appreciate. The annoying auto-syntax feature (you know, the one that prohibits exiting the code painter until the code is syntactically correct) is not present in Delphi. You can code all day long, introducing syntax errors to your heart's content. Delphi attempts to highlight Object Pascal syntax as you work in the code editor, but that's about it until you initiate a compile. If the compiler finds problems in your code, it lists them in the Messages window. Compiler errors, hints, and warnings are all listed in this window. You can jump to the code referenced by a given error, hint, or warning by double-clicking it in the Messages window.

The interesting thing to note, here, is that what PowerBuilder is actually doing when you exit the code painter is tokenizing your code. PowerBuilder generates pseudo code (p-code) from the PowerScript you write. This is then coupled with an executable file. This whole process takes about the same amount of time as a Delphi compilation to native code. The difference being that PowerBuilder's p-code must still be translated to native machine code at runtime by the interpreter DLLs.

Exception Handling

Truly robust application development tools provide some level of support for exception handling. An exception is defined as anything that happens other than what is expected. Delphi brings to Object Pascal the same facility that C++ programmers enjoy, that of class-level exception handling. Basically, Delphi classes are exception-aware—they handle most exceptions automatically. Exceptions are classes themselves and may be derived by the developer as well.

Essentially, Delphi provides a complete facility for managing the unexpected. Everything from an error connecting to a database server to a Windows Access Violation can be handled using Delphi's exception-handling mechanism.

PowerBuilder, by contrast, has exceedingly weak error-handling abilities. Most functions are capable of detecting errors, but the default behavior is nearly always to ignore the problem and continue. The global `SystemError` event provides a meager facility for detecting and handling errors, but PowerBuilder as a whole is barren of any real exception-handling ability.

Language Issues

Due to fundamental differences in the way PowerBuilder and Delphi work, it's difficult to draw exact comparisons between specific language elements. Nevertheless, this section attempts to draw similarities between the two environments where possible. The comparisons presented here aren't meant to be exhaustive—they're only meant to get you started.

Data Types

PowerBuilder data types are a mix of traditional Object Pascal data types and objects. Table 2.5 summarizes some of these.

Table 2.5. PowerBuilder and Object Pascal data type cross-reference.

PowerBuilder type	Object Pascal type or class	Kind
Blob	TBlobField	Class
Boolean	Boolean	Type

PowerBuilder type	Object Pascal type or class	Kind
Date, DateTime, Time	TDateTime	Type
Decimal	TFloatField	Class
Double	Double	Type
Integer	Integer	Type
Long	Longint	Type
Object	TObject, TComponent	Class
Real	Real	Type
String	PChar	Type
UnsignedInteger	Word	Type
Structure	Record	Type

Controls

Although drawing comparisons between their supported data types is somewhat challenging, comparing the visual controls supported by PowerBuilder and Delphi is a little easier. This is due to the fact that many of the controls they provide are actually a part of Windows itself. Table 2.6 lists several of these.

Table 2.6. PowerBuilder and Object Pascal component cross-reference.

PowerBuilder control	Delphi component	Delphi Palette page
Application	TApplication	N/A
CheckBox	TCheckBox	Standard
CommandButton	TButton	Standard
DataWindows	TDBCtrlGrid	Data controls
DropDownListBox	TComboBox	Standard
Group	TGroupBox	Standard
HScrollBar, VScrollBar	TScrollBar	Standard
ListBox	TListBox	Standard
MDI Client, Windows	TForm	N/A
Menus	TMainMenu	Standard
MultiLineEdit	TMemo	Standard

continues

Table 2.6. continued

PowerBuilder control	Delphi component	Delphi Palette page
Picture	TImage	Additional
PictureButton	TBitBtn	Additional
SingleLineEdit	TEdit	Standard
StaticText	TLabel	Standard

Many of these controls are merely wrappers around standard Windows controls, so they share much common ground. The table's third column lists the Delphi toolbar palette page where the component resides. Those listed as N/A do not reside on the component palette. For example, the TApplication class is created automatically by Delphi for every application—you do not install it yourself.

Functions

Cross-referencing functions in the two environments is a little more difficult. This stems from fundamental differences in the way the two environments work. Delphi's language, Object Pascal, was designed to be used as a general purpose programming language, whereas PowerBuilder's language, PowerScript, was designed for the sole purpose of supporting the PowerBuilder environment. These two different approaches yield vastly different function sets. Nevertheless, the tables in this section do their best to compare them.

Date/Time Functions

The main difference between date/time functions in PowerBuilder and Object Pascal is that Object Pascal's date/time data type, TDateTime, is capable of date arithmetic without the aid of supporting functions. Consequently, one doesn't use a host of functions to add dates, extract date segments, and so on. You perform the date calculations needed, then format the result to your liking using Delphi's general purpose date-formatting routine, FormatDateTime. Table 2.7 summarizes the similarities between PowerBuilder and Delphi in this area.

Table 2.7. PowerBuilder and Object Pascal date/time function cross-reference.

PowerBuilder function	Delphi function
Day	FormatDateTime
DayName	FormatDateTime
DayNumber	DayOfWeek

PowerBuilder function	Delphi function
DaysAfter	N/A
Hour	FormatDateTime
Minute	FormatDateTime
Month	FormatDateTime
Now	Time
RelativeDate	N/A
RelativeTime	N/A
Second	FormatDateTime
SecondsAfter	N/A
Today	Date
Year	FormatDateTime

Note the absence in Delphi of PowerBuilder's DaysAfter/SecondsAfter and RelativeDate/RelativeTime functions. These are unnecessary in Delphi because date and time variables can be added and subtracted from each other directly. Unlike PowerBuilder, there's no need for a set of functions to perform these operations.

Delphi's TDateTime data type is a floating-point type made of two parts: the day portion and the time portion. Days are stored as the whole number portion of the float and reflect the number of days since 12/30/1899. The time portion is the fractional part of the float and stores the time as a fractional part of the day.

Also note the repeated references to Delphi's FormatDateTime function. The FormatDateTime function is a general purpose data-formatting routine that formats TDateTime values and returns them as strings. You specify a formatting string and a TDateTime value in your call to FormatDateTime.

If you want to treat a value extracted by FormatDateTime as a numeric value, as you can do in PowerBuilder, you'll need to convert it to an integer using Delphi's StrToInt function. To return results comparable to PowerBuilder's Day function, for example, you would have to convert the value returned from FormatDateTime using StrToInt(FormatDateTime('d', Date)).

Numeric Functions

With few exceptions, numeric functions in Delphi and PowerBuilder are quite similar. The standard functions one would expect to find in any modern programming language are present in both tools. Table 2.8 illustrates this.

Table 2.8. PowerBuilder and Delphi numeric function cross-reference.

PowerBuilder function	Delphi function
Abs	Abs
Ceiling	Ceil
Cos	Cos
Exp	Exp
Int	Int
Log	Ln
Max	MaxValue
Min	MinValue
Mod	Mod
Pi	Pi
Rand	Random
Randomize	Randomize
Round	Round
Sin	Sin
Sqrt	Sqrt
Tan	Tan
Truncate	Trunc

Note that Delphi's Math unit defines a number of other mathematical functions missing from PowerBuilder. You'll find that Delphi's rich suite of math functions (available only in the Developer and Client/Server suite products) is a superset of that found in PowerBuilder. And, what functions aren't available right out of the box you can easily write in Delphi's Object Pascal.

String Functions

Both PowerBuilder and Delphi support the standard roster of string functions found in most development tools. Delphi's support is more complete because it also supports the speedy Object Pascal string type—a string type that is faster by design than either C or PowerBuilder strings. Table 2.9 summarizes the similarities between the string functions found in PowerBuilder and those found in Delphi.

Table 2.9. PowerBuilder and Object Pascal string function cross-reference.

PowerBuilder *function*	*Delphi* String *function*	*Delphi* PChar *function*
Asc	Ord	Ord
Char	Chr, #chr	Chr, #chr
Fill	FillChar	FillChar
Left	Copy	StrLCopy
Len	Length	StrLen
Lower	LowerCase	StrLower
LeftTrim	LTrim	StrFmt
Mid	Copy	StrLCopy
Pos	Pos	StrPos
Replace	N/A	N/A
Right	Copy	StrLCopy
RightTrim	RTrim	StrFmt
Space	FillChar	StrFmt
Trim	Trim	StrFmt
Upper	UpperCase	StrUpper

Note that Delphi doesn't include a function comparable to PowerBuilder's Replace function, though writing one would not be difficult. And, unlike PowerBuilder, there's no performance penalty associated with writing custom functions; in fact, most of Delphi is written in Delphi.

File Functions

Like most modern PC programming languages, both Delphi and PowerBuilder support a wide variety of file-management routines. Because of its background as a traditional programming language, though, Object Pascal's support is significantly more complete than PowerBuilder's. Table 2.10 compares the more important file-management functions of the two environments.

Table 2.10. PowerBuilder and Object Pascal file function cross-reference.

Function	*PowerBuilder* *syntax*	*Delphi* *syntax*
Check file existence	FileExists	FileExists
Close file	FileClose	FileClose

continues

Table 2.10. continued

Function	PowerBuilder syntax	Delphi syntax
Delete file	FileDelete	DeleteFile
Move within file	FileSeek	FileSeek
Open file	FileOpen	FileOpen
Read file	FileRead	FileRead
Rename file	N/A	RenameFile
Return file attributes	N/A	FileGetAttr
Return file date	N/A	FileGetDate
Return file size	FileLength	FileSize
Search for a file	N/A	FileSearch
Search using wildcards	N/A	FindFirst/FindNext
Set file attributes	N/A	FileSetAttr
Set file date	N/A	FileSetDate
Write file	FileWrite	FileWrite

Note the close similarity between the majority of the functions in the two products—they each follow a very logical syntactical path. Object Pascal excels in this area because it is a traditional programming language. I should also mention that the `FileListBox` and `DirectoryListBox` components (and other similar ones) provide a wealth of file services in and of themselves. For example, you don't need to write `FindFirst/FindNext` code to populate a `ListBox` component with a list of files; the `FileListBox` component does that for you.

Coding Constructs

The coding constructs supported by PowerBuilder are rather basic—you should have no trouble learning their counterparts in Object Pascal. First and foremost a script language, PowerScript is nothing to write home about as a programming language. It emulates BASIC in many ways. In the following sections are some of the more important PowerScript programming constructs, cross-referenced with their Object Pascal equivalents.

IF Statements

In PowerBuilder, the `IF` construct takes two forms: the single-line statement and the multi-line statement. The single-line statement takes the following form:

```
IF a=b THEN Doit(a) ELSE Doit(b)
```

The multi-line statement takes the form

```
IF a=b THEN
 Doit(a)
ELSEIF a=c THEN
 Doit(c)
ELSEIF a=q THEN
 HALT
ELSE
 Doit(d)
END IF
```

By contrast, the basic Object Pascal `if` construct looks like this:

```
if a=b then doit(a) else doit(b);
```

The equivalent of PowerScript's multi-line `if` construct as previously coded would be

```
if a=b then doit(a)
else if a=c then doit(c)
else if a=q then halt
else doit(d);
```

There is no explicit `else if` construct in Object Pascal—you simply follow an `else` with another `if` statement. Object Pascal also makes no distinction between single-line and multi-line `if` constructs. If you want to code a multi-line `if` construct, simply follow the `if` with a `begin..end` pair, denoting a statement block.

Note PowerScript's requirement of an `END IF` following the multi-line `IF`. This is reminiscent of BASIC. Note also that, like BASIC, a block of statements may be coded between the `IF` and `ELSE` statements without the need of any kind of code block delimiters. Finally, note that a PowerScript `IF` statement requires at least one action as its object. This is, again, the way that most versions of BASIC work.

CASE Statement

PowerBuilder's `CASE` statement takes the following form:

```
CHOOSE CASE a
CASE 1
  Doit(a)
CASE 2
 Doit(b)
CASE 3 TO 9
 Doit(c)
CASE ELSE
 Doit(d)
END CHOOSE
```

The same statement in Object Pascal would look like this:

```
Case a of
1 : Doit(a);
2 : Doit(b);
3..9 : Doit(c);
else Doit(d);
end;
```

Note the multiple case selectors supported by the ellipses (...) in the Object Pascal code. PowerScript supports this feature with the TO keyword. Also note that Object Pascal, like most natively compiled languages, does not support PowerScript's ability to use expressions as CASE selectors. That is, you can't use an expression in place of a case constant (to the left of the colon) in an Object Pascal case statement. This is because Delphi's compiler optimizes your code by turning the case statement into a "jump table." Each case constant represents an exact location in the table to which code execution will "jump" based on the value of the selector. Obviously, this precludes the use of expressions that the compiler cannot evaluate at compile-time. You can use expressions in Delphi case selectors, but they have to be *constant ordinal* expressions.

This scheme also prohibits case constant overlap—you can't represent the same value in the case constant list twice. For example, the following Object Pascal code is illegal:

```
case a of
1 : Doit(a);
2 : Doit(b);
2..9 : Doit(c);{<- illegal because it overlaps with the previous case constant}
else Doit(d);
end;
```

It works in PowerBuilder, however (in PowerScript terms, of course).

This is a dubious coding style and should be avoided. It sets up two different actions to occur for the same selector value. The 2 in the 2..9 case constant has no logical effect on the code because, even if it were allowed by the compiler, it would never be acted on by the program; execution would never reach it. PowerScript is able to support this syntax and that of having expressions as case selectors because it is interpreted, not compiled, and because it treats the CHOOSE CASE statement merely as a series of IF statements. That is, it performs no jump table optimization similar to Delphi.

WHILE LOOP, UNTIL LOOP, DO WHILE LOOP, DO UNTIL LOOP

PowerScript packs the functionality of all four of these loops into its DO...LOOP syntax. Consequently, it can take the following four forms:

```
DO WHILE c<d
  c=c+1
LOOP
DO UNTIL c=d
  c=c+1
LOOP
DO
  c=c+1
LOOP WHILE c<d
DO
  c=c+1
LOOP UNTIL c=d
```

The equivalent code in Object Pascal would be

```
while c<d do inc(c);

while c<>d do inc(c)
repeat
 inc(c)
until c>=d;

repeat
 inc(c);
until c=d;
```

Note that Object Pascal has no direct equivalents of PowerScript's DO UNTIL...LOOP or DO...LOOP WHILE constructs. This isn't as significant as it might seem, though—you just code the conditional expression on the while...do or repeat...until statements a bit differently.

FOR loop

In PowerBuilder, the classic FOR loop construct takes the form

```
FOR counter = 1 to 10
 x = x*5
NEXT
```

Whereas in Object Pascal, you would code the same loop like so:

```
for counter:=1 to 10 do x:=x*5;
```

Note the BASIC-like syntax employed by PowerScript. Note also the requirement of the NEXT keyword, even when only one line of code is contained within the loop. The syntax offered by Object Pascal is more concise than this, using the more advanced approach of delimiting multiple statements as code blocks, and never requiring a NEXT-type keyword.

Conclusion

Delphi and PowerBuilder share many common concepts because they serve similar purposes. Migrating from PowerBuilder to Delphi is not as difficult as it might at first seem. The key is to avoid trying to make Delphi work like PowerBuilder. It comes to the table with its own ways of doing things. Once you make the journey to Delphi, stay there. If you follow the "Delphi way," you'll be rapidly producing robust applications before you know it.

Visual Basic and Access

As with the section on PowerBuilder, this section is divided into two parts: conceptual issues and language issues. The "Conceptual Issues" section covers general design differences and approach subtleties within the Visual Basic and Delphi environments. The "Language Issues" section covers the nuts and bolts of moving from Visual Basic to Delphi. Coding construct cross-references, function cross-references, and control cross-references are provided for these two products.

Because the programming language in Microsoft Access is just another flavor of Visual Basic, many of the issues covered in this section apply equally well to either of them. Microsoft is rapidly moving all its applications that have need of a macro language to use a rendition of Visual Basic in that capacity. If you are using Word or Excel, for example, many of the concepts presented in this section may be familiar to you as well.

Conceptual Issues

Of the products covered here, Visual Basic is the most like Delphi—well, kind of. Their user interfaces are much the same, but the fundamental technology upon which each of them is based is radically different. Visual Basic is an interpreter-based product. Delphi, on the other hand, is a native compiler-based product. Furthermore, Visual Basic makes use of the BASIC programming language, but Delphi employs Object Pascal.

Many have touted Delphi as Borland's "VB Killer." When Delphi first shipped, a PC Week headline proclaimed, "New Contender Knocks Out Aging Champion." This might be a possibility if only Visual Basic could box at the same weight as Delphi. Rather than a "VB Killer," Delphi feels more like "VB: The Next Generation."

The User Interface

The most striking similarity between the two programs is the user interface. Both programs work by dropping objects onto a canvas. In Visual Basic, these are known as controls; in Delphi they're components. In both programs, you configure these controls visually using a property window. Delphi also sports a number of enhancements to the visual development metaphor made popular by Visual Basic.

Compiling Versus Tokenizing

One of the biggest differences between Visual Basic and Delphi is that Delphi generates native-code executables—it's a true compiler. Unlike Visual Basic, which generates semi-interpreted EXE files, Delphi's executables are composed of machine language, not pseudo-code that must be interpreted at runtime.

This means that there's no automatic tokenization of your code as you write it. Unlike Visual Basic, no compilation occurs in Delphi until you initiate a compile yourself. Delphi will highlight your Object Pascal syntax as you work, but it does not compile and link your code until you tell it to. You can do this just by running an application, because Delphi automatically compiles an application's changed files prior to executing it.

The only drawback to this is that errors in your code are not caught until the compiler is initiated. Unlike Visual Basic, Delphi doesn't check for errors in your code when you exit a line. This is normal for language products that aren't line-oriented. In contrast to both C and Pascal, the BASIC programming language is line-oriented, so it's relatively easy to catch errors as you type. On the other hand, free-form languages like C and Pascal could require a significant amount of time to determine whether a given statement is syntactically correct, because it will often depend on other statements, all of which may be stretched out over several lines. Consequently, you almost never see this feature in C and Pascal language products. This is really a non-issue, though, because Delphi's compiler is so incredibly fast. It compiles source code faster than some tools can even save a project to disk.

Control Arrays

Control arrays are normally used in Visual Basic for two purposes: to allow several controls to share event code and to support the creation of controls at runtime. Control arrays, as such, aren't supported by Delphi, but you can still do all the things normally done with Visual Basic's control arrays and much more.

To allow code to be shared by a number of controls:

1. Click the first control.
2. Shift-click the rest of them.
3. Establish the method they are all to call using the Events page in the Object Inspector. You can use an existing method handler or create a new one by double-clicking the event's combo box.

This method even allows controls of different types to share a common event, something not possible in Visual Basic. For example, you could set up a TEdit and its corresponding label to invoke the same code when either of them are clicked.

If you need to change a property setting for a group of components at runtime, a simple loop will do. Consider the following Object Pascal code fragment:

```
var
 Index : Word;
begin
 for Index:=0 to pred(ComponentCount) do
  If Components[Index] is TEdit then
   With TEdit(Components[Index]) do
    Text:='Key your entry here';
end;
```

The code fragment changes the caption of all the TEdits (TextBoxes in Visual Basic) on the form. It makes use of the Components property of the Form class. Components is an indexed property that returns pointers to the components on a form by index. Notice that the syntax for accessing an indexed property is very similar to that for accessing an array. As we walk through the components on the form, we test each one to see if it's a TEdit component, and, if it is, we set its Text property. Note that you could substitute any component type and any supported property in place of the TEdit component and Text property in the code fragment.

Runtime Type Information

The code shown in the preceding section makes use of an advanced feature in Delphi known as Run-Time Type Information (RTTI). This is the sort of feature you normally find in interpreted languages, not compiled ones. It's implemented by the is function in Delphi. Most compiled languages have no way of knowing a variable's type at runtime. A variable is normally just a collection of bytes that the program itself happens to know how to handle because the compiler generates different code to handle different types of variables. This example uses RTTI to determine which components on the form are of a particular type so that we can change a property specific to the component type. Obviously, this isn't as automatic as being able to assign all the controls at once, but it works well and runs at native code speed.

The second reason developers use Visual Basic control arrays is to create new controls at runtime. Visual Basic's mechanism for creating controls at runtime requires that you supply a template from which the new control is created. Delphi doesn't have this limitation—you can create new components to your heart's content without any kind of template. Consider the following Object Pascal code fragment:

```
var
 bt : TButton;
begin
 bt:=TButton.Create(Self);
 bt.Parent:=Self;
 bt.Name:='Button'+IntToStr(c);
 bt.Caption:=bt.Name;
 inc(c);
end;
```

Each time it's called, a new button is created. There's no need for a control array of any type, though the new control appears in the form's Components indexed property list. Also note that these new controls are automatically destroyed when the form is destroyed.

Variant Data

Unlike most natively compiled languages, Delphi's Object Pascal supports variant data types. You can define a variable as a variant and assign any simple data type to it that you want. Assignments to and from a variant are handled automatically by the compiler—you don't have to be cognizant of the type of data you're working with.

Note that Delphi's TField component defines a variant property named Value that you can use to generically access a field's underlying data. Regardless of the data type of the underlying field, Value will enable you to assign and retrieve values from it.

That said, let me make a recommendation: make judicious use of variants—don't go overboard with them. Although convenient, variant data types are a questionable coding practice for a couple of reasons. Since the type of data they hold at runtime can be changed simply by assigning a value of a different type to them, variant types leave the developer open to all sorts of human error. For example, consider the following two button-click handlers coded in Visual Basic:

```
Sub Command1_Click ()
 Customer = 0
 Cust.Text = Customer
End Sub

Sub Command2_Click ()
```

```
  Customer = "NONE"
  Cust.Text = Customer
End Sub
```

It's not obvious from the code what it is that the programmer is attempting to do with each assignment of the Customer variable. Does he actually intend to assign a numeric value at one time and a character string at another? Who knows? The fact is, because Customer is a variant data type, Visual Basic allows this to go unnoticed. Add to this the fact that variant is the default data type for Visual Basic variables, and you have a programming language that is an accident waiting to happen.

GLOBAL.BAS

Common functions in Visual Basic are organized into a single file, GLOBAL.BAS, which then makes the functions visible to the rest of the project. This is a bit cumbersome in actual practice and leads to huge GLOBAL.BAS files containing hordes of unrelated functions.

Object Pascal's approach, on the other hand, is more sensible and follows established conventions in other programming languages. Object Pascal introduces the concept of units—compiled code modules referenced by source code wanting to use routines contained within them. These modules can be organized logically so that they provide a particular type of function to source code that uses them. For example, unlike Visual Basic, you could create one unit containing special string-handling functions and another that contains special file-handling routines. These modules could be used by the entire application or just by the other modules that need the services they provide. This approach leads to easier code maintenance and more efficient memory utilization.

Another point to be made along these lines is the limitation in Visual Basic of every source code file having to be associated with a form except GLOBAL.BAS. Object Pascal doesn't have this limitation and allows files to be used in a project that aren't necessarily related to any particular form. This flexibility allows functions and procedures to be properly scoped without losing the services they provide.

SendKeys

One of the favorite mechanisms for controlling other programs from Visual Basic is through the use of the SendKeys function. SendKeys allows keypresses to be faked in the target application. The application then behaves as though the keys were actually being typed into it.

Despite the handiness of this facility, Delphi has no equivalent function. Control of other applications is supported by OLE Automation and DDE, but not by any kind of SendKeys implementation. The source code in Listing 2.1 includes both a SendKeys function and an AppActivate function that you can use in your own programs.

Custom Code: New functions—*SendKeys* and *AppActivate*

Listing 2.1 provides a unit named SndKey32 that enables you to send keys to other applications. It provides the equivalent of the Visual Basic SendKeys and AppActivate routines, and even supports Visual Basic's SendKeys syntax. AppActivate finds a window using a name you supply and makes it the current input focus. SendKeys takes a string of characters, translates them into keys, and sends them to the current input focus.

Listing 2.1. SndKey32.PAS.

```
unit sndkey32;

interface

Uses SysUtils, Windows, Messages;

Function SendKeys(SendKeysString : String) : Boolean;
Function AppActivate(WindowName : String) : boolean;

implementation

Function SendKeys(SendKeysString : String) : Boolean;
type
  WBytes = array[0..pred(SizeOf(Word))] of Byte;

  TSendKey = record
    Name : String;
    VKey : Byte;
  end;

const
  {Array of keys that SendKeys recognizes.

  If you add to this list, you must be sure to keep it sorted alphabetically
  by Name because a binary search routine is used to scan it.}

  MaxSendKeyRecs = 41;
  SendKeyRecs : array[1..MaxSendKeyRecs] of TSendKey =
  (
    (Name:'BKSP';          VKey:VK_BACK),
    (Name:'BS';            VKey:VK_BACK),
    (Name:'BACKSPACE';     VKey:VK_BACK),
    (Name:'BREAK';         VKey:VK_CANCEL),
    (Name:'CAPSLOCK';      VKey:VK_CAPITAL),
    (Name:'CLEAR';         VKey:VK_CLEAR),
    (Name:'DEL';           VKey:VK_DELETE),
    (Name:'DELETE';        VKey:VK_DELETE),
    (Name:'DOWN';          VKey:VK_DOWN),
    (Name:'END';           VKey:VK_END),
    (Name:'ENTER';         VKey:VK_RETURN),
    (Name:'ESC';           VKey:VK_ESCAPE),
    (Name:'ESCAPE';        VKey:VK_ESCAPE),
    (Name:'F1';            VKey:VK_F1),
    (Name:'F2';            VKey:VK_F2),
    (Name:'F3';            VKey:VK_F3),
    (Name:'F4';            VKey:VK_F4),
    (Name:'F5';            VKey:VK_F5),
```

```
   (Name:'F6';                    VKey:VK_F6),
   (Name:'F7';                    VKey:VK_F7),
   (Name:'F8';                    VKey:VK_F8),
   (Name:'F9';                    VKey:VK_F9),
   (Name:'F10';                   VKey:VK_F10),
   (Name:'F11';                   VKey:VK_F11),
   (Name:'F12';                   VKey:VK_F12),
   (Name:'F13';                   VKey:VK_F13),
   (Name:'F14';                   VKey:VK_F14),
   (Name:'F15';                   VKey:VK_F15),
   (Name:'F16';                   VKey:VK_F16),
   (Name:'HELP';                  VKey:VK_HELP),
   (Name:'HOME';                  VKey:VK_HOME),
   (Name:'INS';                   VKey:VK_INSERT),
   (Name:'LEFT';                  VKey:VK_LEFT),
   (Name:'NUMLOCK';               VKey:VK_NUMLOCK),
   (Name:'PGDN';                  VKey:VK_NEXT),
   (Name:'PGUP';                  VKey:VK_PRIOR),
   (Name:'PRTSC';                 VKey:VK_PRINT),
   (Name:'RIGHT';                 VKey:VK_RIGHT),
   (Name:'SCROLLLOCK';            VKey:VK_SCROLL),
   (Name:'TAB';                   VKey:VK_TAB),
   (Name:'UP';                    VKey:VK_UP)
   );

{Extra VK constants missing from Delphi's Windows API interface}
VK_NULL=0;
VK_SemiColon=186;
VK_Equal=187;
VK_Comma=188;
VK_Minus=189;
VK_Period=190;
VK_Slash=191;
VK_BackQuote=192;
VK_LeftBracket=219;
VK_BackSlash=220;
VK_RightBracket=221;
VK_Quote=222;
VK_Last=VK_Quote;

ExtendedVKeys : set of byte =
[VK_Up,
 VK_Down,
 VK_Left,
 VK_Right,
 VK_Home,
 VK_End,
 VK_Prior,   {PgUp}
 VK_Next,    {PgDn}
 VK_Insert,
 VK_Delete];

const
 INVALIDKEY = $FFFF {Unsigned -1};
 vkKeyScanShiftOn = $01;
 vkKeyScanCtrlOn = $02;
 vkKeyScanAltOn = $04;
 UnitName = 'SendKeys';
```

continues

Listing 2.1. continued

```
var
  UsingParens, ShiftDown, ControlDown, AltDown, FoundClose : Boolean;
  VKey,PosSpace : Byte;
  I, L, NumTimes, MKey : Word;
  KeyString : String[20];

procedure DisplayMessage(Message : String);
begin
  MessageBox(0,PChar(Message),UnitName,0);
end;

function BitSet(BitTable, BitMask : Byte) : Boolean;
{   inline($5A/$58/$20/$D0/$74/$02/$B0/$01);}
begin
  Result:=Boolean(BitTable and BitMask);
end;

procedure SetBit(var BitTable : Byte; BitMask : Byte);
{   inline($58/$5F/$07/$26/$08/$05);}
begin
  BitTable:=BitTable or Bitmask;
end;

Procedure SendKeyDown(VKey: Byte; NumTimes : Word; GenUpMsg : Boolean);
var
  Cnt : Word;
  ScanCode : Byte;
begin
  ScanCode:=Lo(MapVirtualKey(VKey,0));
  For Cnt:=1 to NumTimes do
    If (VKey in ExtendedVKeys)then begin
      keybd_event(VKey, ScanCode, KEYEVENTF_EXTENDEDKEY,0);
      If (GenUpMsg) then
        keybd_event(VKey, ScanCode, KEYEVENTF_EXTENDEDKEY or KEYEVENTF_KEYUP, 0)
    end else begin
      keybd_event(VKey, ScanCode, 0 ,0);
      If (GenUpMsg) then keybd_event(VKey, ScanCode, KEYEVENTF_KEYUP,0);
    end;
end;

Procedure SendKeyUp(VKey: Byte);
var
  ScanCode : Byte;
begin
  ScanCode:=Lo(MapVirtualKey(VKey,0));
  If (VKey in ExtendedVKeys)then
    keybd_event(VKey, ScanCode, KEYEVENTF_EXTENDEDKEY and KEYEVENTF_KEYUP, 0)
  else keybd_event(VKey, ScanCode, KEYEVENTF_KEYUP,0);
end;

Procedure SendKey(MKey: Word; NumTimes : Word; GenDownMsg : Boolean);
begin
  If (BitSet(Hi(MKey),vkKeyScanShiftOn)) then SendKeyDown(VK_SHIFT,1,False);
  If (BitSet(Hi(MKey),vkKeyScanCtrlOn)) then SendKeyDown(VK_CONTROL,1,False);
  If (BitSet(Hi(MKey),vkKeyScanAltOn)) then SendKeyDown(VK_MENU,1,False);
  SendKeyDown(Lo(MKey), NumTimes, GenDownMsg);
  If (BitSet(Hi(MKey),vkKeyScanShiftOn)) then SendKeyUp(VK_SHIFT);
  If (BitSet(Hi(MKey),vkKeyScanCtrlOn)) then SendKeyUp(VK_CONTROL);
```

```
    If (BitSet(Hi(MKey),vkKeyScanAltOn)) then SendKeyUp(VK_MENU);
  end;

  {Implements a simple binary search to locate special key name strings}

  Function StringToVKey(KeyString : String) : Word;
  var
    Found, Collided : Boolean;
    Index : Byte;
    Bottom, Top, Middle : Byte;
  begin
    Found:=false;
    Result:=INVALIDKEY;
    Bottom:=1;
    Top:=MaxSendKeyRecs;
    Found:=false;
    Collided:=false;
    Middle:=(Bottom+Top) div 2;
    Repeat
      Collided:=((Bottom=Middle) or (Top=Middle));
      If (KeyString=SendKeyRecs[Middle].Name) then begin
        Found:=True;
        Result:=SendKeyRecs[Middle].VKey;
      end else begin
        If (KeyString>SendKeyRecs[Middle].Name) then Bottom:=Middle
        else Top:=Middle;
        Middle:=(Succ(Bottom+Top)) div 2;
      end;
    Until (Found or Collided);
    If (Result=INVALIDKEY) then DisplayMessage('Invalid Key Name');
  end;

  procedure PopUpShiftKeys;
  begin
    If (not UsingParens) then begin
      If ShiftDown then SendKeyUp(VK_SHIFT);
      If ControlDown then SendKeyUp(VK_CONTROL);
      If AltDown then SendKeyUp(VK_MENU);
      ShiftDown:=false;
      ControlDown:=false;
      AltDown:=false;
    end;
  end;

begin
  Result:=false;
  UsingParens:=false;
  ShiftDown:=false;
  ControlDown:=false;
  AltDown:=false;
  I:=1;
  L:=Length(SendKeysString);
  If (L=0) then Exit;
  While (I<=L) do begin
    case SendKeysString[I] of
    '(' : begin
            UsingParens:=True;
            Inc(I);
```

continues

Listing 2.1. continued

```
        end;
')' : begin
        UsingParens:=False;
        PopUpShiftKeys;
        Inc(I);
      end;
'%' : begin
        AltDown:=True;
        SendKeyDown(VK_MENU,1,False);
        Inc(I);
      end;
'+' : begin
        ShiftDown:=True;
        SendKeyDown(VK_SHIFT,1,False);
        Inc(I);
      end;
'^' : begin
        ControlDown:=True;
        SendKeyDown(VK_CONTROL,1,False);
        Inc(I);
      end;
'{' : begin
        NumTimes:=1;
        If (SendKeysString[Succ(I)]='{') then begin
          MKey:=VK_LEFTBRACKET;
          SetBit(Wbytes(MKey)[1],vkKeyScanShiftOn);
          SendKey(MKey,1,True);
          PopUpShiftKeys;
          Inc(I,3);
          Continue;
        end;
        KeyString:='';
        FoundClose:=False;
        While (I<=L) do begin
          Inc(I);
          If (SendKeysString[I]='}') then begin
            FoundClose:=True;
            Inc(I);
            Break;
          end;
          KeyString:=KeyString+Upcase(SendKeysString[I]);
        end;
        If (Not FoundClose) then begin
            DisplayMessage('No Close');
            Exit;
        end;
        If (SendKeysString[I]='}') then begin
          MKey:=VK_RIGHTBRACKET;
          SetBit(Wbytes(MKey)[1],vkKeyScanShiftOn);
          SendKey(MKey,1,True);
          PopUpShiftKeys;
          Inc(I);
          Continue;
        end;
        PosSpace:=Pos(' ',KeyString);
        If (PosSpace<>0) then begin
            NumTimes:=StrToInt(Copy(KeyString,Succ(PosSpace),Length(KeyString)-
➥PosSpace));
```

```
                KeyString:=Copy(KeyString,1,Pred(PosSpace));
              end;
            If (Length(KeyString)=1) then MKey:=vkKeyScan(KeyString[1])
            else MKey:=StringToVKey(KeyString);
            If (MKey<>INVALIDKEY) then begin
              SendKey(MKey,NumTimes,True);
              PopUpShiftKeys;
              Continue;
            end;
          end;
      '~' : begin
              SendKeyDown(VK_RETURN,1,True);
              PopUpShiftKeys;
              Inc(I);
            end;
      else  begin
              MKey:=vkKeyScan(SendKeysString[I]);
              If (MKey<>-1) then begin
                SendKey(MKey,1,True);
                PopUpShiftKeys;
              end else DisplayMessage('Invalid KeyName');
              Inc(I);
            end;
      end;
    end;
  Result:=true;
  PopUpShiftKeys;
end;


{
Converts a string of characters and key names to a Winmacro-compatible
macro, then plays them back as a macro.  Supports the Visual Basic SendKeys
syntax, as documented in the description of the StringToMacro function (above).
}

{AppActivate

This is used to set the current input focus to a given window using its
name.  This could be used for a variety of tasks, but is especially useful
for ensuring a window is active before sending it input messages via either
a macro or the SendKeys function.

}

Function AppActivate(WindowName : String) : boolean;
var
  WindowHandle : HWND;
begin
  Result:=true;
  WindowHandle:=FindWindow(nil,PChar(WindowName));
  If (WindowHandle<>0) then begin
    SendMessage(WindowHandle, WM_SYSCOMMAND, SC_HOTKEY, WindowHandle);
    SendMessage(WindowHandle, WM_SYSCOMMAND, SC_RESTORE, WindowHandle);
  end else Result:=false;
end;
end.
```

Sending Keys

You call SendKeys using the following syntax:

```
SendKeys('+call me if you need anything--]+(kh)~');
```

The SendKeys routine takes the string you pass it and translates it into key sequences which it then pokes into the current input focus. Note that this parameter is an Object Pascal string, so it can theoretically be any size up to 2GB.

SendKeys Syntax

The following modifiers, keys, and key names are supported by the SendKeys function. Table 2.11 lists the supported modifier keys.

Table 2.11. Supported SendKeys modifier keys.

Symbol	Modifier
+	Shift
^	Control
%	Alt

Surround sequences of characters or key names with parentheses in order to modify them as a group. For example, +abc shifts only a, while +(abc) shifts all three characters.

In addition to modifier symbols, SendKeys also recognizes certain special characters. Table 2.12 lists these characters.

Table 2.12. SendKeys supported special characters.

Symbol	Function
~	Enter
(	Begin modifier group
)	End modifier group
{	Begin key name text
}	End key name text

Normal Characters Supported By *SendKeys*

Any character that can be typed is supported. Surround the modifier keys listed in Table 2.11 with braces in order to send as normal text.

In addition to modifier and special keys, SendKeys also recognizes many key names. Table 2.13 lists the key names that SendKeys recognizes (surround the SendKeys with braces, as in the following example).

Table 2.13. SendKeys supported key names.

Key name	Windows key code
BKSP, BS, BACKSPACE	VK_BACK
BREAK	VK_CANCEL
CAPSLOCK	VK_CAPITAL
CLEAR	VK_CLEAR
DEL	VK_DELETE
DELETE	VK_DELETE
DOWN	VK_DOWN
END	VK_END
ENTER	VK_RETURN
ESC	VK_ESCAPE
ESCAPE	VK_ESCAPE
F1	VK_F1
F2	VK_F2
F3	VK_F3
F4	VK_F4
F5	VK_F5
F6	VK_F6
F7	VK_F7
F8	VK_F8
F9	VK_F9
F10	VK_F10
F11	VK_F11
F12	VK_F12
F13	VK_F13
F14	VK_F14
F15	VK_F15
F16	VK_F16
HELP	VK_HELP

continues

Table 2.13. continued

Key name	Windows key code
HOME	VK_HOME
INS	VK_INSERT
LEFT	VK_LEFT
NUMLOCK	VK_NUMLOCK
PGDN	VK_NEXT
PGUP	VK_PRIOR
PRTSC	VK_PRINT
RIGHT	VK_RIGHT
SCROLLLOCK	VK_SCROLL
TAB	VK_TAB
UP	VK_UP

Follow the key name with a space and a number to send the specified key a given number of times (for example, {left 6}).

Here's another example using SendKeys:

```
If AppActivate('Test.txt - Notepad') then

  SendKeys('abc123{left}{left}{left}def{end}456{left 6}ghi{end}789');
```

These two functions provide all the functionality of the corresponding Visual Basic routines and have the advantage of being customizable. For example, you can add your own key names to SendKeys. If you want to use a key name that SendKeys doesn't include, or if you want to change a name to be more intuitive, you can make the necessary modifications to the SendKeys source. You can't do that with Visual Basic.

Component Inclusion Versus Component Use

A major architectural difference between Visual Basic and Delphi is that native Delphi components are built into an application's executable, rather than merely included with it. Visual Basic OCXs are really just DLLs in disguise. Each OCX used by an application brings with it the full overhead of a DLL under Windows. Because of this, Visual Basic developers make a habit of carefully paring down the controls associated with a project to just those that the project requires. Failing to do this wastes significant resources when developing an application of any size.

Contrast this with Delphi, whose components are all natively compiled and live in a single DLL at design time. This conserves memory while developing, but still keeps components immediately available for use by the developer. At runtime, these components reside in the application's executable—there's no need for a DLL or other component file.

Creating New Components

Visual Basic itself can't create OCX controls. This must be done using another tool, such as a C or Pascal compiler, capable of creating DLLs. If an OCX that a developer is using doesn't have some needed feature, a new component must be found—you can't extend OCX components using Visual Basic.

Delphi, on the other hand, allows full subclassing and extension of its native component format. In fact, because it supports OCX controls, you can also extend them, as well—even if you don't have source code to the OCX. The New Component option on Delphi's File menu is used to create new component classes. When selected, it presents a list of available components from which you may descend a new component class. Once a descendant and name for the new class is selected, Delphi generates the necessary source code and places you in it in the code editor. You can then easily add whatever functions you want, then install the new component onto the component palette. Once installed, the new component can be used like any other component.

Language Issues

Because they're both Windows-based visual development environments, Visual Basic and Delphi share a lot of common ground. Aside from providing similar interfaces, they also utilize a lot of the same application building blocks. These building blocks include visual and nonvisual controls, form properties, coding constructs, and so on. In this section, you'll get to meet some of the common language features of Visual Basic and Delphi.

Controls

There is a corresponding component in Delphi for each standard control in Visual Basic. Many of these components even have similar properties because they interface the same built-in Windows control. Table 2.14 summarizes the similarities between the Visual Basic and Delphi control sets.

Table 2.14. Visual Basic and Delphi control cross-reference.

VB control	*Delphi component*	*Delphi palette page*
CheckBox	TCheckBox	Standard
ComboBox	TComboBox	Standard
CommandButton	TButton	Standard
CommonDialog	TOpenDialog	Dialog
	TSaveDialog	Dialog
	TFontDialog	Dialog

continues

Table 2.14. continued

VB control	Delphi component	Delphi palette page
	TColorDialog	Dialog
	TPrintDialog	Dialog
	TPrinterSetupDialog	Dialog
	TFindDialog	Dialog
	TReplaceDialog	Dialog
DirListBox	TDirectoryListBox	System
DriveListBox	TDriveComboBox	System
FileListBox	TFileListBox	System
Frame	TGroupBox	Standard
Gauge	TGauge	Samples
Graph	TChart	VBX
Grid	TStringGrid	Additional
HScrollBar, VScrollBar	TScrollBar	Standard
Image	TImage	Additional
Label	TLabel	Standard
ListBox	TListBox	Standard
MaskEdBox	TMaskEdit	Additional
MMControl	TMediaPlayer	Additional
OleControl	TOleContainer	System
OptionButton	TRadioButton	Standard
Outline	TOutline	Additional
Shape	TShape	Additional
SpinButton	TSpinButton	Samples
SSCommand	TBitBtn	Additional
TextBox	TEdit, TMemo	Standard
Timer	TTimer	System

Note that Visual Basic defines a single component for the Windows multi-line text edit control, whereas Delphi defines two separate components for it. Note also Delphi's use of separate components for each of the Windows common dialog types, whereas Visual Basic combines them into just one control. Finally, note that Delphi provides a number of components absent from Visual Basic. If you have purchased any of these components separately for use with Visual Basic, you may be able to replace them with those supplied by Delphi.

Forms

Just as they present many of the same controls, Visual Basic and Delphi also share many of the same form features. This is largely due to the fact that they are both just surfacing the user interface inherent to all Windows applications. The following sections detail the similarities between form events, properties, and methods in Visual Basic and Delphi.

Form Properties

Table 2.15 cross-references the supported form properties of Visual Basic with those of Delphi.

Table 2.15. Visual Basic and Delphi form properties cross-reference.

Visual Basic form property	*Delphi form property*
ActiveControl	ActiveControl
ActiveForm	ActiveForm
BackColor	Color
BorderStyle	BorderStyle
Caption	Caption
Enabled	Enabled
FontBold, FontItalic, FontStrikThru, FontUnderline	Font.Style
FontName	Font.Name
FontSize	Font.Size
ForeColor	Font.Color
HDC	Canvas
Height	Height
HelpContextID	HelpContext
Hwnd	Handle
Icon	Icon
KeyPreview	KeyPreview
Left	Left
MDIChild	FormStyle
MousePointer	Cursor
Name	Name
Picture	Picture

continues

Table 2.15. continued

Visual Basic form property	Delphi form property
ScaleHeight	ClientHeight
ScaleWidth	ClientWidth
Tag	Tag
Top	Top
Visible	Visible
Width	Width
WindowState	WindowState

Form Methods

Because they both implement many of the same form properties, it's no surprise that Visual Basic and Delphi share a number of the same form methods as well. A form method is a procedure that is part of the form itself. Form methods often provide the means by which the form is caused to perform certain actions, such as printing or displaying itself. Table 2.16 compares the Visual Basic and Delphi form methods.

Table 2.16. Visual Basic and Delphi form method cross-reference.

Visual Basic form method	Delphi form method
Circle	Canvas.Ellipse, Canvas.Arc
Hide	Hide
Line	Canvas.LineTo
Move	SetBounds
PrintForm	Print
Print	Canvas.TextOut
Refresh	Refresh
SetFocus	SetFocus
Show	Show
TextHeight	Canvas.TextHeight
TextWidth	Canvas.TextWidth
Zorder	BringToFront, SendToBack

Form Events

Just as they share many common form methods, Delphi and Visual Basic also share many of the same form events. A form event is something that happens to the form, such as it being clicked with the mouse. Code is associated with the event that is executed when the event occurs. Table 2.17 summarizes the similarities and differences between Visual Basic and Delphi in this regard.

Table 2.17. Visual Basic and Delphi form event cross-reference.

Visual Basic *form event*	*Delphi* *form event*
Activate	OnActivate
Click	OnClick
DblClick	OnDblClick
Deactivate	OnDeactivate
DragDrop	OnDragDrop
GotFocus	OnGotFocus
KeyDown	OnKeyDown
KeyPress	OnKeyPress
KeyUp	OnKeyUp
Load	OnCreate
LostFocus	OnLostFocus
MouseDown	OnMouseDown
MouseMove	OnMouseMove
MouseUp	OnMouseUp
Paint	OnPaint
QueryUnload	OnQueryClose
Resize	OnResize
Unload	OnDestroy

Variable Scoping

Variable scoping rules control the visibility of a variable to the outside world. If a variable is said to be "out of scope" in a particular routine, this means that it cannot be accessed by that routine, though it may be accessible elsewhere in the program. Table 2.18 compares the Visual Basic and Delphi variable scoping levels.

Table 2.18. Visual Basic and Delphi variable scope cross-reference.

Visual Basic	Delphi
Global	Global
Local	Local
Module	Unit
N/A	Object Level
Static	Typed constant

String Functions

The wealth of string functions found in both Object Pascal and Visual Basic is consistent with what one would expect of a modern programming language. Note that Object Pascal's support is more complete because it supports both C-style null-terminated strings (PChar) and Object Pascal length-byte strings. It should be noted that Visual Basic strings are neither C-style strings nor Object Pascal-style strings. Functionally speaking, they are the equivalent of C-style strings because they can store data of up to 2GB in size. Despite this, they differ internally from the C-style string and should not be treated as such. (See Table 2.19.)

Table 2.19. Visual Basic and Delphi string function cross-reference.

Visual Basic string function	Delphi string function	Delphi PChar function
Format	Format	StrFmt
Instr	Pos	StrPos
Lcase	LowerCase	StrLower
Len	Length	StrLen
Mid	Copy	StrCopy
N/A	Delete	N/A
N/A	IntToHex	StrFmt
N/A	LoadStr	LoadString
N/A	N/A	StrRScan
Str	IntToStr, Str	IntToStr, Str
StrComp	CompareText	StrLComp
Ucase	UpperCase	StrUpper
Val	StrToInt, StrToFloat	N/A

Conclusion

Because of the similarities between Visual Basic and Delphi, moving from VB to Delphi shouldn't be terribly difficult. One of the more challenging aspects of leaving Visual Basic might be having to unlearn old habits. BASIC in general and Visual Basic in particular allow coding styles and programming conventions that are questionable, if not dangerous. Depending on one's coding style, it may be difficult to get away from them. Take heart, though—it's worth the effort. Work with Delphi for a while, and you'll never go back.

The xBase Dialects: dBASE, Clipper, FoxPro, and So Forth

You may be an xBase developer wanting to migrate completely to Delphi. Or, you may want to enhance existing systems with modules written in Delphi. You may want to move certain of your more resource-intensive applications to Delphi, leaving the rest in their original host environment. Whatever your needs, if you need help getting from xBase to Delphi, this section is for you.

This section covers the myriad of issues you may encounter when coming from the xBase dialects to Delphi. Some issues are specific to a given dialect; most are applicable to all xBase dialects. The topics presented here are not divided into coding and conceptual issues sections because the line between the two is extremely blurred in the xBase dialects.

Ragged Arrays

Ragged arrays (as made popular by Clipper) are supported in Delphi via variant arrays. Variant arrays are defined at runtime and can contain elements of any data type, including other variants. You use the VarArrayCreate function to construct variant arrays. For example, here's the construction of a variant array with 10 elements, all of type variant:

```
var
  MyVar : Variant;
begin
  MyVar:=VarArrayCreate([0,9],varVariant);
end;
```

Once the array is created, you can store any type of data you'd like in its elements. (See Table 2.20.)

Table 2.20. Lists key procedures and functions related to variant arrays.

Procedure/function	Purpose
VarArrayCreate	Creates a variant array
VarArrayOf	Creates a variant array on-the-fly using a list of elements
VarArrayRedim	Resizes a variant array
VarArrayDimCount	Returns the number of dimensions in a variant array
VarArrayLowBound	Returns the low bound of a variant array dimension
VarArrayHighBound	Returns the high bound of a variant array dimension
VarIsArray	Returns True when passed a variant array

Indexes

This section deals with accessing xBase indexes. I show you some techniques for creating indexes and accessing them at runtime. I also discuss the supported index file formats and the functions available to you when creating expression-based indexes.

Supported Index File Formats

Out of the box, the Borland Database Engine (BDE) supports the maintained index (MDX) format native to dBASE IV and the NTX format native to Clipper. This doesn't mean that you can't use other formats. Because the BDE supports ODBC access, you can make use of ODBC drivers that work with whatever format you like. Intersolv, for example, publishes an ODBC driver that works with the FoxPro index file format.

Another option is to completely replace the BDE. You can do that, too. SuccessWare, Inc., publishes a version of its popular Rock-E-T database library that can completely eliminate the need for the BDE in your applications. Rock-E-T also supports the FoxPro and Clipper proprietary index file formats.

Creating Indexes

A favorite (and often necessary) process that xBase programmers include in their applications is a routine to rebuild indexes. Creating runtime indexes in a Delphi application can be easily done through two methods. The easiest way is to use the AddIndex method of the Table component. It takes the following form:

```
procedure AddIndex(const Name,Fields:string; Options:TIndexOptions);
```

TIndexOptions is defined as follows:

```
TIndexOptions = set of (ixPrimary, ixUnique, ixDescending, ixCaseInsensitive,
➥ixExpression);
```

So, to create an index using this method, simply write:

```
Table1.DeleteIndex('CUSTOMER'); {Do this first if it already exists}
Table1.AddIndex('CUSTOMER', 'CUSTOMER;NAME', [ixUnique, ixCaseInsensitive]);
```

A second way to create an index at runtime is to use Delphi's Local SQL to build it using the CREATE INDEX statement. To do this, follow these steps:

1. Drop two Query components onto the form in your application where you'd like to locate your re-indexing code. The first of these will be used to delete your index, if it exists. The second will be used to create the index. Though these functions could be performed by a single Query component, there's really no reason to do it this way, and splitting their functions makes the programming *you* have to do simpler.

2. Set both Query components to point to the appropriate alias or directory where the index resides or will reside.

3. If there's any chance that the index will exist prior to your attempt to create it, key a SQL DROP INDEX statement into the SQL property of the first Query. It should look something like the following:

   ```
   DROP INDEX "CUSTOMER.DBF".CustNo
   ```

   where CUSTOMER.DBF is the name of the table on which the index was built, and CustNo is the name of the index tag itself. This is necessary because your attempt to create the index will fail if it already exists.

5. Key a SQL CREATE INDEX statement into the SQL property of the second Query. It should take the form

   ```
   CREATE INDEX CustNo on "CUSTOMER.DBF" (CustNumber)
   ```

   where CustNo is the name of the index to create, CUSTOMER.DBF is the name of the table on which the index will be created, and CustNumber is the name of the field on which the table will be indexed.

6. Drop a button onto the form, label it Reindex, and attach the following code to it:

   ```
   Query1.ExecSQL; {Include this line if you need to drop the index first}
   Query2.ExecSQL;
   ```

7. When you run the application, click the button. The index should be dropped, then re-created with the name and key you specified.

NOTE

Delphi supports only the dBASE IV style MDX "maintained" index file format. Non-maintained indexes are not supported.

> **NOTE**
>
> It's also possible to build indexes using direct calls to the Borland Database Engine API (IDAPI), but there's really no need to. The methods presented in this chapter should insulate you from having to call the BDE directly.

Expression Indexes

Using the `Table` component's `AddIndex` method, you can create expression-based indexes using the `ixExpression` option. For example, you could use the following syntax to create an expression-based index:

```
Table1.AddIndex('DATESHIP','DTOS(DateShip)',[ixExpression]);
```

Table 2.21 lists the functions that Delphi supports in conjunction with dBASE-style expression indexes.

Table 2.21. Functions supported in dBASE expression indexes.

ABS	ACOS	ALIAS	.AND.
ANSI	ASC	ASIN	AT
ATAN	ATN2	BITAND	BITLSHIFT
BITOR	BITRSHIFT	BITSET	BITXOR
CEILING	CENTER	CHR	COS
CTOD	DATABASE	DATE	DAY
DBF	DELETED	DIFFERENCE	DOW
DTOC	DTOR	DTOS	ELAPSED
EMPTY	EXP	FCOUNT	FIELD
FIXED	FLDCOUNT	FLOAT	FLOOR
FV	HTOI	ID	IIF
INT	ISALPHA	ISBLANK	ISLOWER
ISUPPER	ITOH	LEFT	LEN
LENNUM	LIKE	LOG	LOG10
LOWER	LTRIM	MAX	MEMLINES
MIN	MLINE	MOD	MONTH
.NOT.	OEM	.OR.	OS
PAYMENT	PI	PROPER	PV
RANDOM	RAT	RECNO	RECSIZE
REPLICATE	RIGHT	ROUND	RTOD

RTRIM	SECONDS	SIGN	SIN
SOUNDEX	SPACE	SQRT	STR
STUFF	SUBSTR	TAN	TIME
TRIM	UPPER	VAL	VERSION
YEAR			

Searching Expression Indexes

If you use an xBase-style expression index, be aware that the Table component's FindKey routine won't work. You'll have to use GotoKey or one of the Lookup methods instead. Assuming the use of the expression index previously created, the following code demonstrates this:

```
Table1.SetKey;
Table1.FieldByName('DATESHIP').AsString:='06/06/96';
If not Table1.GotoKey then MessageBox(0, 'Not found',
    'Error',MB_APPLMODAL);
```

Selecting an Index at Runtime

In the xBase dialects, you use SET INDEX or SET ORDER to change indexes at runtime. In Delphi applications, you set the Table component's IndexName property to do this. Set this to the name of the tag within the MDX file, not the name of the file itself. The BDE assumes the filename of a maintained index will be the same as the table on which it is built.

Code Blocks

Because code blocks as implemented in the xBase dialects require an interpreter or some such, they aren't supported directly in Delphi. There is, however, a workaround that provides this interpreter-based functionality to Delphi applications. It involves the use of Object Pascal's procedure and function variables in conjunction with its open array parameters. Basically, you can write a fairly generic AEval routine by using the following technique:

```
type
  prShowString = procedure(StringToShow: string);

const
  Suits : array[1..4] of string = ( 'Hearts', 'Clubs', 'Diamonds', 'Spades');

procedure ShowString(StringToShow: string);
begin
  StringToShow:=UpperCase(StringToShow);
  ShowMessage(StringToShow);
end;

procedure AEval(const AnArray: array of string; ShowProc: prShowString);
Var
  Index: Integer;
begin
```

```
  for Index := Low(AnArray) to High(AnArray) do
    ShowProc(AnArray[Index]);
end;

procedure DisplayEm;
begin
 AEval(Suits, ShowString);
end;
```

Note the way that the DisplayEm routine passes the ShowString parameter to the AEval routine as a procedural parameter. Inside AEval, it is then called like any other procedure, once for each element in the array. Notice the fact that the array is passed into AEval without the bounds information (for example, [1..4]) normally required with Pascal arrays. This is because the parameter is an open array—it could have any number of parameters. When the function receives the open array parameter, the Low and High functions are used to determine the number of elements in the array and loop through it accordingly.

Now let's consider a more complex example. In the following example, we not only call a function for each member of an array, we also set each member of the array using the function.

```
type
 fnAddSalesTax = function(Price : Single) : Single;
const
 Prices : array[1..5] of Single = (4.50, 2.10, 1.31, 3.89, 5.56);
function AddSalesTax(Price : Single) : Single;
const
 Rate = 0.07;
var
 Tax : Single;
begin
 Tax:=Price * Rate;
  Result:=Price+Tax;
end;
procedure AEval(var AnArray: array of Single; AddTaxFunc: fnAddSalesTax);
Var
 Index: Integer;
begin
 for Index := Low(AnArray) to High(AnArray) do
  AnArray[Index]:=AddTaxFunc(AnArray[Index]);
end;
procedure CalcEm;
begin
 AEval(Prices, AddSalesTax);
end;
```

Note the use of the var keyword in the open array declaration of the AEval function. This ensures that the array is passed by address, not value, so that it can be modified by the AEval routine.

Functions

When the concept of the User-Defined function was first introduced in Clipper, it was considered a major enhancement to the language. The other xBase dialects at the time did not allow the user to build his own functions to extend the language. Contrast this with Object Pascal, which has always supported user-defined functions and procedures—even from the very first version of Turbo Pascal.

Object Pascal functions have the following form:

```
function AddSalesTax(Price : Single) : Single;
const
 Rate = 0.07;
var
 Tax : Single;
begin
 Tax:=Price * Rate;
  Result:=Price+Tax;
end;
```

Note the use of the `result` variable to return the function's result. All Object Pascal functions have a predefined `result` variable whose whole purpose is to return the function's result. This is similar to the `return()` function in the xBase dialects, but more flexible because the value can be tested and further manipulated before the function actually returns to the caller. Assigning the `result` variable does not cause the flow of execution to return to the caller. Use the `exit` procedure if you want to return immediately to the caller of a function or procedure.

xBase and Delphi Function Cross-Reference

Table 2.22 is a cross-reference of key xBase and Delphi functions. The different dialects have different functions, so making an exhaustive comparison between those functions and the functions in Object Pascal would be difficult. Nevertheless, this should get you started.

Table 2.22. Delphi and xBase function cross-reference.

xBase function	*Delphi function*
AT()	Pos
CHAR()	Chr
COL()	WhereX
CTOD()	StrToDate
CURDIR()	GetDir
DATE()	Date
DISKSPACE()	DiskFree
DTOC()	DateToStr
EXP()	Exp
FCLOSE()	FileClose
FOPEN()	FileOpen
FREAD()	FileRead

continues

Table 2.22. continued

xBase function	Delphi function
FWRITE()	FileWrite
FCREATE()	FileCreate
FERASE()	DeleteFile
FILE()	FileExists
LEN()	Length
LOWER()	LowerCase
MEMOLINE()	TMemo.Lines[ ]
MEMOREAD()	TMemo.Lines.LoadFromFile
MEMOWRITE()	TMemo.Lines.SaveToFile
MLCOUNT()	TMemo.Lines.Count
MOD()	Mod
ROUND()	Round
ROW()	WhereY
STR()	IntToStr
SUBSTR()	Copy
TIME()	Time
UPPER()	UpperCase
VAL()	Val, StrToInt, StrToFloat

Custom Code: New Functions—xBase-like Object Pascal Functions

Because of the ease with which Object Pascal can be extended, it's a simple matter to construct Object Pascal functions that emulate those xBase routines not already present in the language. Listing 2.2 is an Object Pascal unit that does just that. It supplies many of the xBase functions that have no direct equivalents in Object Pascal.

Listing 2.2. The xBase unit provides a number of xBase functions not found in Object Pascal.

```
unit Xbase;
{Object Pascal routines that emulate popular xBase routines}
interface

Uses
 SysUtils,
 Windows;

function Pad(InString: String; Len: Integer): String;
function LPad(InString: String; Len: Integer): String;
```

```
function LeftString(InString: String; Len: Integer): String;
function RightString(InString: String; Len: Integer): String;
function Replicate(Ch: Char; Len: Integer): String;
function Space(Len: Integer): String;
function Empty(InString: string): boolean;
function CDOW(InDate : TDateTime) : String;
function CMonth(InDate : TDateTime) : String;
function Day(InDate : TDateTime) : Integer;
function IsAlpha(InString : String) : Boolean;
function IsDigit(InString : String) : Boolean;
function IsLower(InString : String) : Boolean;
function IsUpper(InString : String) : Boolean;
function RAt(SubString, InString : String) : Integer;
function Year(InDate : TDateTime) : Word;
function Seconds : Longint;

implementation

function Pad(InString: String; Len: Integer): String;
begin
 Result:=Format('%-*s',[Len, InString]);
end;

function LPad(InString: String; Len: Integer): String;
begin
 Result:=Format('%*s',[Len, InString]);
end;

function LeftString(InString: String; Len: Integer): String;
begin
 Result:=Copy(InString,1,Len);
end;

function RightString(InString: String; Len: Integer): String;
begin
 Result:=Copy(InString,Succ(Length(InString)-Len),Len);
end;

function Replicate(Ch: Char; Len: Integer): String;
begin
  SetLength(Result,Len);
  FillChar(Result[1],Len,Ch);
end;

function Space(Len: Integer): String;
begin
 Result := Replicate(' ', Len);
end;

function Empty(InString: string): boolean;
begin
 Result:=(Length(InString)=0) or (Trim(InString) = '');
end;

function CDOW(InDate : TDateTime) : String;
begin
 Result:=FormatDateTime('dddd',InDate);
end;
```

continues

Listing 2.2. continued

```pascal
function CMonth(InDate : TDateTime) : String;
begin
 Result:=FormatDateTime('mmmm',InDate);
end;

function Day(InDate : TDateTime) : Integer;
begin
 Result:=StrToInt(FormatDateTime('d',InDate));
end;

function IsAlpha(InString : String) : Boolean;
begin
 Result:=(UpCase(InString[1]) in ['A'..'Z']);
end;

function IsDigit(InString : String) : Boolean;
begin
 Result:=(InString[1] in ['0'..'9']);
end;

function IsLower(InString : String) : Boolean;
begin
 Result:=(InString[1] in ['a'..'z']);
end;

function IsUpper(InString : String) : Boolean;
begin
 Result:=(InString[1] in ['A'..'Z']);
end;

function RAt(SubString, InString : String) : Integer;
Var
 I : Integer;
 TempInString, TempSubString : String;
begin
 TempInString:='';
 TempSubString:='';
 {Reverse both strings for use with the Pos function}
 For I:=Length(InString) downto 1 do
  TempInString:=TempInString+InString[I];
 For I:=Length(SubString) downto 1 do
  TempSubString:=TempSubString+SubString[I];
 Result:=Pos(TempSubString,TempInString);
 If Result<>0 then Result:=Succ((Length(InString)-Result)-Pred(Length(InString)));
end;

function Year(InDate : TDateTime) : Word;
begin
 Result:=StrToInt(FormatDateTime('yyyy',InDate));
end;

function Seconds : Longint;
var
 HH, MM, SS, MS : Word;
begin
 DecodeTime(Time,HH,MM,SS,MS);
```

```
 Result:=(HH*3600)+(MM*60)+SS;
end;

end.
```

Optional Function Parameters

By design, Object Pascal requires that all parameters defined for a function or procedure be passed to it. Naturally, this precludes the construction of routines that take an indeterminate number of parameters. There is an exception to this, though. You can pass a varying number of items to a function by using Object Pascal's open arrays. Consider the following two essentially equivalent code fragments—one in Clipper, the other in Object Pascal:

```
* Clipper
LISTSONG("Feel Like Makin Love", "Shooting Star", "Anna")
LISTSONG( "Cut Loose", "Peace")
PROCEDURE LISTSONG(Song1,Song2,Song3)
DEFAULT Song3 to "NONE"
 ? Song1
 ? Song2
 ? Song3
RETURN

{Object Pascal}
procedure ListSong(Songs : array of string);
var
 I, NumSongs : Word;
begin
 NumSongs := High(Songs);
 For I:=Low(Songs) to NumSongs do
  ShowMessage(Songs[I]);
 If NumSongs < 2 then ShowMessage('NONE'); {Default the third parameter}
end;
ListSong(['Feel Like Makin Love', 'Shooting Star','Anna']);
ListSong(['Cut Loose', 'Peace']);
```

Note that the Object Pascal code is more flexible from the standpoint that it theoretically allows any number of parameters to be passed to it, whereas the Clipper code allows only three. On the other hand, the Clipper code is more flexible in that any type of variable could be passed to it. You could change the Object Pascal code to use a variant array instead of an open array to accomplish this same thing. Here's a code sample that does just that:

```
{Object Pascal}
procedure ListSong(Songs : variant);
```

```
var
 I, NumSongs : Word;
begin
 NumSongs := VarArrayHighBound(Songs);
 For I:=VarArrayLowBound(Songs) to NumSongs do
  ShowMessage(Songs[I]);
 If NumSongs < 2 then ShowMessage('NONE'); {Default the third parameter}
end;
ListSong(VarArrayOf(['Feel Like Makin Love', 'Shooting Star','Anna']));
ListSong(VarArrayOf(['Cut Loose', 'Peace']));
```

The next section discusses untyped parameters in Delphi functions.

Untyped Function Parameters

Like BASIC, the xBase languages support untyped function parameters. You can also pass untyped parameters to Object Pascal functions and procedures. You do this by using Object Pascal's variant data type. Variants can receive or be assigned to any data type. The compiler generates the appropriate code to ensure that they translate to and from the actual data types. For example, consider the following two equivalent pieces of code. Again, one of them is coded in Clipper, the other in Object Pascal.

```
* Clipper
DEBUGMSG("ENTERED FOR LOOP")
DEBUGMSG(4)
PROCEDURE DEBUGMSG(P1)
MSG="NONE"
DO CASE
 CASE VALTYPE(P1) = "C"
   MSG=P1
 CASE VALTYPE(P1) = "N"
   MSG=LTRIM(STR(P1))
ENDCASE
? "DEBUG MESSAGE= "+MSG
RETURN

{Object Pascal}
Procedure DebugMsg(p1 : variant);
Var
 Msg : String;
begin
 Msg:='NONE';
 case VarType(p1) of
  varString : Msg:=p1;
  varInteger : Msg:=p1;
 end;
 ShowMessage('DEBUG MESSAGE='+Msg);
end;
DebugMsg(['ENTERED FOR LOOP']);
DebugMsg([4]);
```

Note that the Object Pascal code is actually more flexible than the corresponding Clipper code because it does not have to convert P1 based its underlying data type, as the Clipper code does. The compiler generates all code necessary to convert variants to and from actual data types.

VarType

Note the use of the VarType function to determine the p1 parameter's data type. VarType has the following possible return values as shown in Table 2.23.

Table 2.23. VarType return values.

Identifier	Value
varEmpty	$0000
varNull	$0001
varSmallint	$0002
varInteger	$0003
varSingle	$0004
varDouble	$0005
varCurrency	$0006
varDate	$0007
varOleStr	$0008
varDispatch	$0009
varError	$000A
varBoolean	$000B
varVariant	$000C
varUnknown	$000D
varByte	$0011
varString	$0100
varTypeMask	$0FFF
varArray	$2000
varByRef	$4000

Indexed Record Location

Delphi's equivalent of the xBase SEEK command is LookUp. LookUp is a method of the DataSet components and accepts as its parameters the same kind of variant array that was mentioned in the previous section. The following example performs an indexed record seek on the database table associated with Table1.

```
Table1.Lookup('Name',VarArrayOf(['DOE, JOHN']),[foCaseInsensitive]);
```

Non-Indexed Record Location

Delphi's equivalent of the xBase LOCATE command is its own LookUp or Locate method. The LookUp and Locate functions work regardless of whether there's an index on a given table, so they're similar to xBase's LOCATE command in that regard.

Filters

Non-indexed filtering, analogous to the xBase SET FILTER TO construct is supported by Delphi's Locate Filters. You set up local filtering by entering an expression into the Filter property of a DataSet, then toggling the DataSet's Filtered property to True. You can also use the DataSet's OnFilterRecord event to filter rows. See Chapter 15, "Database Component Reference Part I," for more information on local filters.

Traversing a Table

Because Delphi is so visually oriented, iterating programmatically through a database is a lot less necessary in Delphi applications than it is in the xBase environments. Nevertheless, there are occasions where this is needed, so I'll take you through a comparison between doing this in xBase and doing it in Object Pascal.

To bump a record at a time through a table, xBase code like the following is used:

```
USE C:\DATA\DELPHI\WORKORD\INVENT INDEX INVENT
SET ORDER TO INVNUM
GO TOP
DO WHILE .NOT. EOF()
 SKIP
ENDDO
USE
```

In Delphi, the process is even simpler:

```
With Table1 do begin
  Open; {Assumes component has been setup properly}
  While not Eof do Next;
 tClose;
end;
```

The code is simpler in Delphi because, even though you're navigating the data manually, you still set up as much of the task as possible visually using the Delphi Form Designer. This includes the directory location and physical filename of the table, the index tag, and so on. You could also avoid having to explicitly open the table at runtime by opening it at design-time.

Writing Text Files

In the xBase dialects, writing to a text file involves a bit of needless hoop-jumping. The following code illustrates this:

```
SET ALTE TO "MWATERS.TXT"
SET ALTE ON
SET CONS OFF
? "GOOD MORNING LITTLE SCHOOL GIRL"
SET CONS ON
SET ALTE OFF
SET ALTE TO
```

In Delphi, the same thing can be accomplished in a number of better ways. For one thing, nearly all the controls that support multiple lines of text or items of some sort include a SaveToFile method for writing the contents of the component to disk. For example, the TMemo component supports this; therefore, using it you'd write

```
Memo1.Lines.SaveToFile('MWATERS.TXT');
```

to accomplish the same thing as the xBase code, provided, of course, that the TMemo's Lines property contained the appropriate text.

Using Object Pascal's basic file-management routines would more closely follow the approach taken in the xBase code. Here's an example of that approach:

```
const
 Song : String = 'GOOD MORNING LITTLE SCHOOL GIRL';

var
  F: TextFile;
begin
  AssignFile(F, 'mwaters.txt');
  Rewrite(F);
  try
    writeln(F, Song);
  finally
    CloseFile(F);
  end;
end;
```

Note the Pascal example's use of exception-handling code. The line that follows the finally keyword is executed regardless of whether there's an error writing to the file. This makes the Pascal code more bullet-proof (and more readable) than the corresponding xBase code.

Conclusion

Despite the radical differences in their approach to solving database development problems, moving from xBase to Delphi is fairly straightforward. More than anything else, things suddenly get much easier with Delphi than they ever were in the xBase world.

A challenge facing xBase developers who want to move to Delphi is giving up the convenience of interpreter-specific things like code blocks and moving up to the more structured, but slightly less convenient, equivalents in Delphi. Going from a relatively unstructured language to one that enforces a degree of uniformity can be difficult. But the end result makes it all worthwhile. With Delphi, you get to "have your cake and eat it, too." You get to keep the file structures and database formats you've been used to, and you get to see once-sluggish applications invigorated with the speed of optimized machine code.

What's Ahead

In the next chapter, you'll explore the building blocks that make up Delphi applications. You'll learn about programs and libraries, components and units, and the pieces that make up each of them. This will give you some very fundamental insights into the way that applications are constructed in Delphi.

Summary

In this chapter, you learned many of the caveats, pitfalls, and general issues regarding the journey to Delphi from other tools. Specifically, you explored the process of moving from C/C++, PowerBuilder, Visual Basic, and the xBase dialects. If you are moving from one of these to Delphi, the information contained in this chapter should prove invaluable to you.

3

Building Blocks

Although *Database Developer's Guide with Delphi 2* isn't intended as a beginner's book, I thought it appropriate to touch briefly on the building blocks of a Delphi application. You might be coming from a database environment that differs greatly from Delphi; if so, a brief discussion of Delphi basics could be beneficial. If you're familiar with Delphi concepts and have already begun developing applications, you might want to skip this chapter and go straight to Chapter 4, "Conventions."

In this chapter, you learn the pieces that make up the Delphi puzzle. You are introduced to Delphi projects and libraries. You get acquainted with Object Pascal units, forms, data modules, and include files. Last, but not least, you meet the cornerstone of Delphi application development—the component.

What Are Projects?

Depending on the software you're using, the term *project* can have a number of different meanings. Usually, a project is the top-level container for all the objects in an application. Its purpose is to relate the files that make up an application to one another—to establish dependency relationships between them. A single project usually acts as the repository for all the objects in an application. Of course, this isn't always the case. Sometimes an application is composed of multiple projects. Sometimes a project covers more than just a single application. In most development tools, though, a project produces a single executable file.

Delphi Projects

In Delphi, a project is a master list of all the files that make up a single application. Delphi projects are unusual in that, aside from filling the traditional role of projects, they are also source code. That is, a Delphi project is Object Pascal source code that you can view and modify if necessary.

> **NOTE**
>
> Although it is possible to modify a Delphi project file manually, you shouldn't need to do so. Because Delphi might change parts of the file, it's a good idea to avoid making your own modifications to it. A change you make could confuse Delphi, or Delphi might overwrite an alteration that you've made to the file.

Because Delphi projects are stored as source code and reside in the operating system as files, project names are limited only by Pascal's identifier restrictions. Project and unit names must begin with a letter and may include letters, digits, and underscores. No spaces or periods are permitted. Listing 3.1 is a small Delphi project file.

Listing 3.1. The RentalMan project file.

```
program RENTMAN;

uses
  Forms,
  anyform in 'ANYFORM.pas' {fmAnyForm},
  RSYSMAN0 in 'RSYSMAN0.pas' {fmRSYSMAN0},
  rentdata in 'RENTDATA.pas' {dmRentalMan},
  dbform in 'DBFORM.pas' {fmDatabaseForm},
  editform in 'EDITFORM.pas' {fmEditForm},
  REMPENT0 in 'REMPENT0.PAS' {fmREMPENT0},
  RWKTENT0 in 'RWKTENT0.PAS' {fmRWKTENT0},
  cgrdform in 'CGRDFORM.pas' {fmControlGridForm},
  RTENCGD0 in 'RTENCGD0.PAS' {fmRTENCGD0},
  RPROCGD0 in 'RPROCGD0.PAS' {fmRPROCGD0},
  mstrform in 'MSTRFORM.pas' {fmMasterDetailForm},
  gridform in 'GRIDFORM.pas' {fmGridForm},
  RWORGRD0 in 'RWORGRD0.PAS' {fmRWORGRD0},
  RWORMDE0 in 'RWORMDE0.PAS' {fmRWORMDE0},
  RCALGRD0 in 'RCALGRD0.PAS' {fmRCALGRD0},
  RCALEDT0 in 'RCALEDT0.PAS' {fmRCALEDT0},
  reputili in 'reputili.pas',
  anyreprt in 'ANYREPRT.pas' {frAnyReport},
  RPROLST0 in 'RPROLST0.PAS' {frRPROLST0},
  About in '\PROGRAM FILES\BORLAND\DELPHI 2.0\OBJREPOS\ABOUT.pas' {AboutBox},
  RABTBOX0 in 'RABTBOX0.pas' {fmRABTBOX0};

{$R *.RES}

begin
  Application.Title := 'RentalMan Maintenance System';
  Application.HelpFile := 'rentman.hlp';
  Application.CreateForm(TfmRSYSMAN0, fmRSYSMAN0);
  Application.CreateForm(TdmRentalMan, dmRentalMan);
  Application.CreateForm(TfmREMPENT0, fmREMPENT0);
  Application.CreateForm(TfmRWKTENT0, fmRWKTENT0);
  Application.CreateForm(TfmRTENCGD0, fmRTENCGD0);
  Application.CreateForm(TfmRPROCGD0, fmRPROCGD0);
  Application.CreateForm(TfmRWORGRD0, fmRWORGRD0);
  Application.CreateForm(TfmRWORMDE0, fmRWORMDE0);
  Application.CreateForm(TfmRCALGRD0, fmRCALGRD0);
  Application.CreateForm(TfmRCALEDT0, fmRCALEDT0);
  Application.CreateForm(TfrRPROLST0, frRPROLST0);
  Application.CreateForm(TfmRABTBOX0, fmRABTBOX0);
  Application.Run;
end.
```

The *program* Keyword

In Listing 3.1, note the use of the program keyword. It tells the compiler that this file is to become its own executable. In a dynamic link library or unit, the program keyword would be replaced by library or unit, respectively.

The *Uses* Statement

The Uses statement lists the Object Pascal units that Delphi links to build the executable. *Units* are the molecules of Delphi applications. Any unit whose source code is more recent than its compiled code is automatically recompiled when you compile or run the project file. Some environments refer to this as a "make."

The Forms unit in Listing 3.1 is part of Delphi's own Visual Component Library and defines the characteristics of Delphi forms. The other units listed correspond to the forms that have been added to the project. Each line lists the name of the unit, the operating system file in which it resides, and the name of the form that the unit contains. The name of a form is the name assigned to its Name property in the Delphi Object Inspector. With the advent of long filename support in Delphi, the name of the unit and the name of the file in which it resides are identical, minus, of course, the file's extension. During compilation, if the Delphi compiler can't find a unit using its long name, it will attempt to find it using its truncated, or short, name.

The *$R* Directive

The $R compiler directive instructs the compiler to include the specified Windows resource with the project. The asterisk tells the compiler the resource file has the same base name as the project. Delphi creates a resource file corresponding to every module in a project, including the project file itself. If these resource files are not present when the application is linked, Delphi issues a File not found *xxx*.RES message.

Application.CreateForm

The Application.CreateForm statements load the project's forms into memory. Usually, every form in a project is listed here. Using the Options/Project menu selection in the Delphi Integrated Development Environment (IDE), you can control whether a form is created automatically for you. Each form is stored in its form instance variable (in this case Form1 and fmInventory, respectively), which is defined in the interface section of the form's unit. Because the project file uses the units that define the form instance variables, it can "see" these variables and pass each of them to the Application.CreateForm routine. Application.CreateForm then loads the specified form into memory and returns a pointer to it in the instance variable.

The order in which the Application.CreateForm statements are listed is significant in that it determines the order in which the forms are created. The first form created by Application.CreateForm is the application's main form. If you want to change the order of form creation, use the Options/Project menu selection; don't edit your project source code file.

Application.Run

`Application.Run` starts the ball rolling as far as your application is concerned. It enters the loop that runs your application.

Delphi Libraries

Delphi provides a convenient mechanism for building Windows dynamic link libraries (DLLs). Unlike most other Windows programming languages, Delphi actually includes special syntax for building DLLs. You use two keywords to implement Delphi's DLL support, `library` and `export`. The `library` keyword takes the place of the `program` keyword in the previous example. It tells Delphi to build a DLL rather than an EXE file. The `export` keyword has two uses. First, it flags individual routines in the DLL as exportable—meaning that special prologue-epilogue code is generated for them by Delphi's compiler, as Windows requires. Second, in its plural form, it causes the DLL to actually export the functions so that other executables can call them. Listing 3.2 is the source code to a small library.

Listing 3.2. The StrUtil library.

```
library StrUtil;
Uses
  SysUtils;
function Pad(InString: String; Len: Integer): String; export;
begin
 Result:=Format('%-*s',[Len, InString]);
end;
function LPad(InString: String; Len: Integer): String; export;
begin
 Result:=Format('%*s',[Len, InString]);
end;
exports
  Pad index 1,
  LPad index 2;
begin
end.
```

Libraries are very similar in form to programs. Note the use of the `library` keyword in place of `Program` at the top of Listing 3.2. Notice how both functions are flagged with the `export` keyword. Failing to set them up this way causes the `exports` directive at the end of the library source to fail. The `exports` statement tells Delphi to export the `Pad` and `LPad` routines from the DLL so that other executables can call them.

Delphi Units

Along with forms, units are the molecular building blocks of Delphi applications. Units house the forms that make up your application's visual appearance. Furthermore, they store supplemental code that you write to support the functions your application provides.

Each form you add to your project comes with its own unit source. This unit source contains a class definition that is a reflection of the visual representation of the form. For each component you add to the form, Delphi's form designer modifies the class definition to reflect the new component. Each time you add an event handler to the form, the event handler code is stored in the unit file. Nearly all the coding you do in Delphi is done in unit files. Listing 3.3 is the source to a simple unit file.

Listing 3.3. The source to a Delphi unit.

```
unit RTENCGD0;

interface

uses
    Windows, Messages, SysUtils, Classes, Graphics, Controls, Forms, Dialogs,
    CGRDFORM, Buttons, DBCtrls, StdCtrls, ExtCtrls, Mask, DBNavSch, DBCGrids;

type
    TfmRTENCGD0 = class(TfmControlGridForm)
      teTenantNo: TDBText;
      deName: TDBEdit;
      deEmployer: TDBEdit;
      deEmpAddress: TDBEdit;
      deEmpCity: TDBEdit;
      deEmpState: TDBEdit;
      deEmpZip: TDBEdit;
      deHomePhone: TDBEdit;
      deWorkPhone: TDBEdit;
      deICEPhone: TDBEdit;
      deLeaseBeginDate: TDBEdit;
      deLeaseEndDate: TDBEdit;
      deMovedInDate: TDBEdit;
      deMovedOutDate: TDBEdit;
      deRentDueDay: TDBEdit;
      dePetDeposit: TDBEdit;
      deComments: TDBEdit;
      Label1: TLabel;
      dkLawnService: TDBCheckBox;
      Label2: TLabel;
      Label3: TLabel;
      Label4: TLabel;
      Label5: TLabel;
      Label6: TLabel;
      Label7: TLabel;
      Label8: TLabel;
      Label9: TLabel;
      Label10: TLabel;
      laName: TLabel;
```

```
    Label12: TLabel;
    Label13: TLabel;
    Label14: TLabel;
    Label15: TLabel;
    Label16: TLabel;
    Label17: TLabel;
  private
    { Private declarations }
  public
    { Public declarations }
  end;

var
  fmRTENCGD0: TfmRTENCGD0;
  DefaultPetDeposit : Integer;

implementation

uses rentdata;

{$R *.DFM}

initialization
  DefaultPetDeposit:=150;
end.
```

The *interface* Section

Note the division of the unit into the interface, implementation, and initialization sections. The interface section contains the header information for the unit. This includes the function and procedure declarations and the variable, constant, and type definitions you want to be visible to the outside world. For you C programmers out there, this is the equivalent of C's .H file. Unlike in C, you don't need to store this section in a separate source code file so that other modules can include it. A compiled unit stores its interface information in its header. When another module references this unit in its Uses statement, Delphi looks at the header of the compiled unit, *not* its source code, to determine the interface it presents.

This approach enables you to distribute Delphi units as object code only—without the need of a header file of any kind. Furthermore, it does away with the redundancy of recompiling a header file each time a module that includes it is compiled. (Precompiled header files address this issue to an extent, but not all C compilers support them.) This approach is better than that taken by most C compilers and represents the next logical step beyond C's header file approach.

The *implementation* Section

The implementation section contains the unit's actual programming code. Items you place here are visible only to the unit itself unless you also list them in the interface section. The typical organization of a unit places a function's declaration in the interface section and its code in the implementation section.

The Form Instance Variable

Note the form instance variable in the var section of the unit's interface:

```
var
    fmRTENCGD0: TfmRTENCGD0;
```

This defines a variable named `fmRTENCGD0` as type `TfmRTENCGD0`. `TfmRTENCGD0` is a third-generation descendant of the `TForm` class created for you by Delphi's visual form designer. `fmRTENCGD0` is the variable that the project file initializes when it calls `Application.CreateForm`. Because this variable is defined in the `interface` section of the unit, other modules that reference the unit in their `Uses` clauses, including the project file, can see the variable and modify it if necessary.

The *initialization* Section

When you need to set up code that executes when a unit is first loaded, put it in the unit's `initialization` section. Anything placed here is executed when the application loads. The order in which a given unit's `initialization` code executes is determined by the unit's position in the project source file's `Uses` statement. In Listing 3.3, the `initialization` section consists of the lines between the word `initialization` and the end of the unit:

```
initialization
    DefaultPetDeposit:=150;
end.
```

When the application is first loaded, the `DefaultPetDeposit` variable is initialized to 150. The application can then reference the variable without having to be concerned with first initializing it.

Delphi Forms

Delphi forms provide your application's on-screen appearance. Most of the design work you do in Delphi's visual form designer is stored in a form file. When you set a property or move a component, you are modifying settings that are stored in the module's form file.

Because Delphi's tools are true two-way tools, it's possible to edit a form as text, save it, and then see the changes you made reflected visually. Listing 3.4 is the text version of a small form.

Listing 3.4. The text representation of a simple form.

```
inherited fmDatabaseForm: TfmDatabaseForm
    Left = 75
    Top = 124
    Width = 554
    Caption = 'fmDatabaseForm'
    PixelsPerInch = 96
    TextHeight = 13
```

```
inherited paTop: TPanel
  Width = 546
end
inherited paMiddle: TPanel
  Width = 546
end
inherited paBottom: TPanel
  Width = 546
  object paRight: TPanel
    Left = 385
    Top = 1
    Width = 160
    Height = 37
    Align = alRight
    BevelOuter = bvNone
    TabOrder = 0
    object bbOK: TBitBtn
      Left = 4
      Top = 8
      Width = 75
      Height = 25
      TabOrder = 0
      Kind = bkOK
    end
    object bbCancel: TBitBtn
      Left = 82
      Top = 8
      Width = 75
      Height = 25
      TabOrder = 1
      Kind = bkCancel
    end
  end
  object bbPrintForm: TBitBtn
    Left = 280
    Top = 8
    Width = 75
    Height = 25
    Caption = 'Print Form'
    TabOrder = 1
    OnClick = bbPrintFormClick
    Glyph.Data = {
      76010000424D7601000000000000760000002800000020000000100000000100
      0400000000000000010000130B0000130B00000000000000000000000000000000
      8000008000000080800080000000800080008080000007F7F7F00BFBFBF000000
      FF0000FF000000FFFF00FF000000FF00FF00FFFF0000FFFFFF00300000000000
      00033FFFFFFFFFFFFFFF088888888888888077777777777777F0888888888888
      8880777777777777777F0000000000000000FFFFFFFFFFFFFFFF0F8F8F8F8F8F
      8F80777777777777777F08F8F8F8F8F8F8F9F07777777777777777F0F8F8F8F8F8F8F
      8F80777777777777777F7F0000000000000000007777777777777777F3330FFFFFFFF
      03333337F3FFFF3F7F333330F0000F0F03333337F77773737F333330FFFFFFFF
      03333337F3FF3FFF7F333330F00F000003333337F773777773333330FFFF0FF0
      33333337F3FF7F3733333330F08F0F0333333337F7737F7333333330FFFF0033
      33333337FFFF77333333333300000033333333337777773333333}
    NumGlyphs = 2
  end
  object DBNavigator1: TDBNavSearch
    Left = 8
```

continues

Listing 3.4. continued

```
      Top = 8
      Width = 253
      Height = 25
      TabOrder = 2
    end
  end
end.
```

Data Modules

Delphi supports a special type of form known as a *data module*. You create a data module by selecting New Data Module from Delphi's File menu. Data modules enable you to group non-visual controls—usually database components—on to a central form. You can then reference these data modules from other forms in the application in order to access their database components. You can also add data modules to Delphi's Object Repository and inherit, copy, or use them, like other Repository members. Note that you can't drop visual controls on to a data module—only non-visual controls are allowed.

Include Files

Like most language tools, Delphi's compiler supports include files. *Include files* enable you to establish common sections of code that you want to share among a number of modules. Because Delphi recompiles include files each time it encounters them in source code, you'll want to restrict their use and utilize units instead whenever possible.

A common use of an include file is to list compiler directives common to several units and to cause those units to be automatically recompiled when you alter the contents of the include file. The following segment is an example of such a file from the WinMacro Windows Macro Engine source:

```
{$A+,B-,F-,G+,I-,K+,N-,P+,Q-,R-,S+,T-,V+,W-,X+}
{$IFNDEF DEBUG}
{$D-,L-,Y-}
{$ELSE}
{$D+,L+,Y+}
{$ENDIF}
```

> **NOTE**
>
> You can find the complete WinMacro source code on the CD-ROM included with this book.

The primary purpose of the code is to enable you to easily toggle compiler options related to debugging. Note the {$IFNDEF DEBUG} line. It simply states that if you haven't defined a custom compiler directive named DEBUG, the three options related to debugging, $D, $L, and $Y, should be switched off. Conversely, if you have defined DEBUG, the three options are switched on. If all the modules in an application include this file, you can easily toggle whether they are compiled with debugging-related switches turned on just by defining or undefining the DEBUG switch. This is simpler than having to toggle all three options from the Delphi Options/Project dialog box.

Once the file is defined, you include it in your source code files by using the $I compiler directive, like so:

```
{$I WINMACRO.INC}
```

Delphi Components

Components are the atomic building blocks of Delphi applications. They combine to build forms, just as atoms combine to make molecules.

Behind the visual representation you see in Delphi's form designer, components are composed of Object Pascal source code. Listing 3.5 lists the source code to a simple component.

Listing 3.5. Custom code for a new component—TArrayTable.

```
{
ArrayTable Delphi Component

Provides an array-like interface to a table.

Use the syntax:

Records[RecNum].Fields[FieldNum].AsType

to access individual field values.

Written by Ken Henderson.

Copyright (c) 1995 by Ken Henderson.
}
unit Arraytab;

interface

uses
  SysUtils, Windows, Messages, Classes, Graphics, Controls,
  Forms, Dialogs, DB, DBTables;
```

continues

Listing 3.5. continued

```
type
  TArrayTable = class(TTable)
  private
    { Private declarations }
    function GetRecord(RecNum : Longint) : TDataSet;
  protected
    { Protected declarations }
  public
    { Public declarations }
    property Records[RecNum : Longint] : TDataSet read GetRecord;
  published
    { Published declarations }
  end;

procedure Register;

implementation

function TArrayTable.GetRecord(RecNum : Longint) : TDataSet;
begin
  First;
  MoveBy(RecNum);
  Result:=Self;
end;

procedure Register;
begin
  RegisterComponents('Data Access', [TArrayTable]);
end;

end.
```

This component subclasses Delphi's Table component and adds a single public property to it, Records. Records enables you to treat the table as one large array. For example, the following syntax returns the third field from the fifth record in the table as a string (both the new Records property and TTable's own Fields property are zero-based):

```
Table1.Records[4].Fields[2].AsString;
```

As you can see, this added functionality came at a very small price. The process was even simpler with Delphi's New/Component option on the File menu. Using the New/Component option, you specify the ancestor class (in this case, TTable), the name of the new class, and the page on which it is to reside. Delphi then generates the necessary source code for you.

> **NOTE**
>
> Something that might not be obvious from looking at TArrayTable's source code is that using the Records property physically moves the record pointer. Because of the nature of Delphi's database controls, there's no way around this. Setting a bookmark from within the component wouldn't be of any use because TTable's Fields property always points to the current record. In code that uses this component, you might want to use a bookmark to save your position in the table so that you can return to it after the reference to the Records property.

Note the Register procedure at the end of Listing 3.5. A Delphi component is added to the toolbar palette via the RegisterComponents procedure. Its first parameter denotes the toolbar palette page on which the new component is to reside. The second parameter lists the component to register. Separate multiple components' names with commas (within the brackets).

What's Ahead

In the next chapter, I introduce some standard conventions for naming application objects. The subject of naming conventions is no one's favorite; it's about as interesting as a book on dental flossing. Nevertheless, establishing sound guidelines on the naming of the objects you just learned about can save you headaches down the road.

Summary

In this chapter, you learned about the following concepts:

- A project is the collection of files that make up a Delphi application.
- A library is a Windows dynamic link library (DLL) and exports routines for other modules to use.
- In conjunction with forms, units are the molecular building blocks with which Delphi applications are built.
- Forms constitute the visual representation of a Delphi application.
- An include file is used to share a common snippet of code among several modules.
- Components are the atomic building blocks with which forms and, hence, units are made.

4

Conventions

Of the many things you can do to make life easier for yourself when you develop software, few are as beneficial as adhering to standard naming conventions and following consistent coding practices. I felt this important enough to talk about before we actually build any applications because I see it as very fundamental to solid application development.

In this chapter, I give you my thoughts on the conventions you should follow when naming Delphi application elements. These include both server and client constructs, and I talk about each of them separately.

Note that the following suggestions are just that: suggestions. Use whatever works for you. Being consistent is more important than following any particular convention.

Object Pascal Program Elements

We begin with Delphi program elements. Delphi program elements include components, forms, data modules, units, variables, constants, and so on. In short, anything other than database server constructs are considered Delphi program elements in this discussion. Database server constructs include tables, indexes, views, triggers, stored procedures, rules, defaults, and so forth. You learn Delphi program elements first.

> **NOTE**
>
> Because of the diverse nature of today's networking environments, I recommend that you stay away from Windows 95/NT long filenames when naming elements. While it's true that Delphi itself will handle filenames longer than eight characters just fine, you may have to interact with a networking operating system (NOS) or host computer that does not. This is fairly likely given that the focus of this book is on database application development and your databases will often reside on other computers.
>
> I know that it's tempting to utilize this handy advance in PC OS technology, but I recommend you avoid doing so for the immediate future when naming files you create with Delphi. Someday, most networks and host computers will support long filenames, as well, and there will no longer be any reason to avoid using them.

Directories

I start with directories because I believe them to be very important. The physical location of your files is at least as important as what they contain. In my case, I keep all data of any type in a first-level subdirectory called DATA on my hard disk. This enables me to back up all the data on my machine just by backing up DATA and its subdirectories.

Under DATA, I place a subdirectory for each application I use—one for WordPerfect for Windows, one for Delphi, one for Quattro Pro for Windows, and so on. This helps me find a file that's produced by a particular application. This strays from the document-centric philosophy all the vendors seem to be pushing; nevertheless, it helps me.

> **NOTE**
>
> Keep in mind that Windows 95 defines a directory that's analogous to my DATA directory called My Documents. You may want to store your files in subdirectories under My Documents instead. Also note that Windows 95 introduces the concept of the folder—basically the same thing as a directory—and you can create these folders using the Windows 95 Explorer.

Under each program's subdirectory, I place a subdirectory for each of my projects. For example, the RentalMan project developed in the Tutorial section of this book resides in C:\DATA\DELPHI\RENTMAN. I don't use extensions on my directories. I do use sensible names—names that would make sense to me if, instead of residing on a computer, these directories were files in a file cabinet—because that's what they emulate. All the files for a particular project reside in directories of this type. If a project spans multiple programs, I create an identically named subdirectory under each program's subdirectory. You might have your own way of doing things, but as I've said, this works for me.

Project Names

My project names are something sensible that can be squeezed into the 8.3 filenaming convention. As I've said, I avoid the use of Windows 95/NT long filenames in my Delphi projects. Because I never change the extensions of Delphi project files, I'm limited to just eight characters. These always have the same name as the directory in which they reside. This way, if I move the file elsewhere temporarily or give it to a colleague, I can easily determine where it came from.

Filenames

I strive to name my files sensibly and "expandably." By expandably, I mean that I regularly designate one to two digits at the end of the filename as sequence digits. These digits enable me to have multiple versions of a file without resorting to renaming the file. That is, this chapter of the book lives in a file named DBD0400. As I make modifications to the file, it becomes DBD0401, DBD0402, and so on. This way I know what the most recent version is without looking at a time stamp. Furthermore, I can easily move all the files at once or zip them or whatever, using file masks.

I also prefix my filenames with at least one character identifying the project in which they reside. This gives all the files in a particular project a similar look and makes them easier to manage. For example, the Rental Maintenance Management System that you'll build in the Tutorial section of this book uses R as the first character of all of its files.

I usually follow my prefix with three to six characters describing the *general* use of the file. If the file has no purpose more specific than its general use, I use all six characters for the portion of the filename up to the sequence number. If it has both a general and a specific use, I use three characters for the general use and three for the specific use. For example, the Rental Maintenance Management System contains a file whose purpose is to provide an edit dialog box for the CALLS table. This file is named RCALEDT0, for Rental maintenance management system, CALl EDiT dialog box. You can use a variety of combinations to achieve the desired end. Some people even break the six characters I mentioned into verbs and nouns—the verb describing the action that is to occur and the noun specifying the object of the action.

Another facet of filenaming that people often overlook is naming a file something that you can easily pronounce. Some folks go nuts with filenames and make each character in a filename signify something different. Don't do this. These types of mainframe-style names are hard to remember and harder to talk about. You'll often find yourself conversing with a team member about a particular file. Naming the file something that you can say easily helps with this. For example, in conversing about the aforementioned file, I might say, "Hey, Joe, you remember that M-Call-Edit file we worked on six months ago?" To which he'd reply, "Why, of course I do, Ken, thanks to those brilliant naming conventions you invented!"

Unit Names

As with filenames, a unit name can be virtually as long as you want it to be, though unit names are only significant through 63 characters. As I've said, I would avoid creating filenames that exceed eight characters in length. Whatever name you give to a unit is used by Delphi to create its corresponding .PAS file in the operating system, so using a unit name that's longer than eight characters will create a corresponding file in Windows that is also longer than eight characters.

Component Names

Because there's no one-to-one relationship between components and filenames, I think you should name components as descriptively as you can stand. Name them in a manner that is as spoken-language-like as possible and makes sense to you. Temper your zeal in this with what you are willing to type over and over. I also recommend the use of mixed case with component names. Because you can't have spaces in a component name, mixing the case of the words contained therein helps provide a break between them. Finally, as you'll see in the next section, I recommend prefixing all Pascal *types* (include component definitions, which are class types) with a capital T. This is a convention used by Borland throughout Delphi's Visual Component Library (VCL). For example, the array table component presented in Chapter 3,

"Building Blocks," is named TArrayTable. The T signifies an Object Pascal–class type, and the next two words describe the component's function.

When setting the Name property of Delphi's built-in components, I use a two-character lower-case mnemonic at the front of the name to signify the type of component. For example, a Memo component begins with me and an Edit control with ed. The remainder of the name consists of something descriptive, like edCustomerName, or meComments. Table 4.1 summarizes my recommendations for abbreviating Delphi component names. Note that I've included the Form and Data Module classes in this list because you'll want to name them sensibly, as well.

All the dialog components in the list are abbreviated with a single character followed by an underscore (_). This should make them stand out in your code. Note also that, as a rule, all the database controls corresponding to standard components (for instance, DBEdit corresponds to the Edit control) are abbreviated using the letter d followed by the first character of the standard component's abbreviation (for example, Edit is abbreviated ed, while DBEdit is abbreviated de). I've done this to make them easier to remember.

Table 4.1. Delphi components and suggested abbreviations

Component	Abbreviation
AutoObject	ao
BatchMove	bm
Bevel	be
BiGauge	bg
BiPict	bp
BiSwitch	bs
BitBtn	bb
Button	bu
Calendar	ca
ChartFX	ch
CheckBox	ck
ColorDialog	c_
ColorGrid	cg
ComboBox	cb
Database	db
DataModule, DBMemo	dm
DataSource	ds
DBCheckBox	dk

continues

Table 4.1. continued

Component	Abbreviation
DBComboBox	dc
DBEdit	de
DBGrid	gr
DBImage	di
DBListBox	dl
DBLookupComboBox, DBLookupCombo	lc
DBLookupListBox, DBLookupList	ll
DBNavigator	na
DBRadioGroup	dg
DBText	te
DdeClientConv	cc
DdeClientItem	ci
DdeServerConv	sc
DdeServerItem	si
DirectoryListBox	dy
DirectoryOutline	do
DrawGrid	dr
DriveComboBox	rc
Edit	ed
FileListBox	fl
FilterComboBox	fc
FindDialog	n_
FontDialog	f_
Form	fm
Gauge	ga
GraphicsServer	gs
GroupBox	gb
Header	he
HeaderControl	hc
HotKey	hk
IBEventAlerter	ie

Component	Abbreviation
Image	im
ImageList	il
Label	la
ListBox	lb
ListView	lv
MainMenu	mm
MaskEdit	md
MediaPlayer	mp
Memo	me
Notebook	nb
OleContainer	ol
OpenDialog	od
Outline	ou
PageControl	pc
PaintBox	pb
Panel	pa
PopupMenu	pu
PrintDialog	p_
PrinterSetupDialog	i_
ProgressBar	pr
QRBand	qb
QRDBCalc	qc
QRDBText	qt
QRDetailLink	qd
QRGroup	qg
QRLabel	ql
QRMemo	qm
QRPreview	qp
QRShape	qh
QRSysData	qs
Query	qu
QuickReport	qr

continues

Table 4.1. continued

Component	Abbreviation
RadioButton	rb
RadioGroup	rg
ReplaceDialog	r_
Report ·	rp
RichEdit	re
SaveDialog	s_
ScrollBar	sa
ScrollBox	sx
Session	se
SpeedButton	sb
SpinButton	su
SpinEdit	sd
StatusBar	st
StoredProc	sp
StringGrid	sg
TabbedNotebook	tn
TabControl	tc
Table	ta
TabSet	ts
Thread	th
Timer	ti
TrackBar	tb
TreeView	tv
UpdateSQL	us
UpDown	ud
VCFirstImpression	vf
VCFormulaOne	vo
VCSpeller	vs

Note that I've used the same abbreviation for a few of the controls in the list. The DBLookupComboBox and DBLookupCombo controls, for example, share a single abbreviation moniker. This is due to the fact that DBLookupCombo, a Delphi 1.0 component, has been replaced by

DBLookupComboBox, a Delphi 2.0 component. DBLookupCombo has been kept around for compatibility only. As a rule, you won't use both of them in the same application. I've also used the same abbreviation for the DataModule form class and the DBMemo component due to the fact that these two entities are so different that you could never mistake one for the other when looking at program code. The context of the code itself will tell you which one you're looking at.

Type Names

Type names follow much the same conventions as component names. Begin all type definitions with a capital T, and use descriptive words for the rest of the declaration. Limit your names to what you are willing to type repetitively. Use mixed case to make the words in your names more readable. Finally, because all class definitions are types as well, follow these conventions with them, too. The following is a sample type definition:

```
TRecordMouse = (rmAll, rmNone, rmClicksAndDrags);
```

Constant Names

When you're typing constants, I recommend the use of all uppercase characters, just as is normally done with #define's in C. This distinguishes *constants,* which can't change, from *variables*, which can, in your code. For example, the following is a constant declaration from the source to the LiveQuery component mentioned in Chapter 26, "Building Your Own Database Components":

```
DEFAULTCREATEVIEWSQL = 'CREATE VIEW %s AS ';
```

Variable Names

I use mixed case and complete words for my variable names. Variable names should be descriptive but not so long as to be a pain to type. The following are some examples of good variable names, again from the TLiveQuery source:

```
TemporaryDB : TDatabase;
WorkSQL : TStrings;
```

Procedure and Function Names

Procedures and function names should follow fairly closely those of variables. The one exception is that you should make an attempt to distinguish functions that take no parameters from variable names. That is, the following line is ambiguous in that it isn't clear from looking at the code whether SalesTax is a function or a variable name:

```
x:=SalesTax;
```

To disambiguate these two, add the `Get` prefix to functions of this type. In fact, it's a good idea to prefix *most* functions with `Get`, although there are situations in which it doesn't make sense to do so. For example, `FileOpen` is a function; prefixing it with `Get` is nonsensical.

A convention followed by Borland in the VCL source code is the use of `Set…` for procedures that set a property value and `Get…` for those that return the value of a property.

Object Pascal Coding Styles

Another area in which it pays to standardize is coding styles. You usually find about as many coding styles as people, but if you can at least adhere to a consistent style yourself, you'll find your own code easier to read and maintain. I discuss my thoughts on `If…else` constructs, `begin…end` blocks, and comment delimiters. As with object names, it is more important to be consistent than to follow any particular convention, including mine.

If…else Constructs

One of the things I like to do in my `If…else` constructs is to delimit the conditional expression with parentheses even though they're not required by default. The reason I do this is twofold. First, I find this style easier to read than those without parentheses. Second, and more importantly, I can add a second conditional expression without changing the first. Unlike C, Pascal doesn't require parentheses around a single conditional expression, so the following syntax is completely legal:

```
If x=1 then y:=z;
```

However, two or more expressions in a single `If` statement require parentheses around each expression:

```
If (x=1) or (x*2=4) then y:=z;
```

If you code an `If` statement with a single expression as in the first example, adding the second expression requires the placement of parentheses around both the second expression and the first. Add to this the fact that there's no penalty for having parentheses around a single conditional expression, and there's really no reason not to have them.

Begin…end Pairs

Another convention I follow not only with `If…else` statements but also with other block-oriented constructs is to put the `begin` of a `begin…end` block on the same line as the construct itself. In the case of the `If` statement, this means that the `begin` is on the same line as the `If`. Because Pascal is a free-form language, you can actually put the `begin` anywhere you want—on the same line as the `If`, on the next line, or down five lines; it makes no difference because the code generated by the compiler is the same. The following is an example of my convention:

```
If (x=1) then begin
  y:=z;
  closefile;
end;
```

Opinions vary widely on this; some people code `If` statements in the following way:

```
If x=1 then
  begin
    y:=z;
    closefile;
  end;
```

I dislike this approach because it takes an extra line of screen space. You especially want to avoid this in light of the small default size of Delphi's code window. Furthermore, the appropriate amount of indentation needed by the `begin` statement is not immediately clear; should it be indented the same as the `If` because it's not actual code but a delimiter? Or, should it be indented to the right of the `If` because the code it contains is dependent upon the `If`? What about the code *between* the `begin...end` delimiters? How should it be indented in relation to the `begin` or the `If`? In my style, the `begin` is on the same line as the `If`, so the indentation issue disappears. Furthermore, the `end` acts as a terminator for the `If`, which is its actual function anyway. Finally, the code between the two is indented to the right of the `If`, not the `begin`, showing its dependency on the `If`, which, I think, is as it should be.

Another approach taken by some developers is to capitalize the `begin...end` pair. I don't care for this because anything capitalized in a section of code seems to jump off the screen and yell at you. This seems inappropriate for mere delimiters that don't even translate to machine code when the program is compiled. Capitals should be reserved for identifiers that need to get your attention (such as constants), not `begin...end` pairs that are liable to be all over a screenful of Object Pascal code.

Comments

Object Pascal supports three different comment styles: `(*..*)`, `{...}`, and `//`. For normal commenting—comments that document or explain a section of code—I use `{...}`. For temporarily commenting out a section of code so that I can see how the program functions without it, I use `(*..*)`. This makes it easy to find sections I've temporarily commented out so that I can uncomment or remove them, as the need arises. For single-line comments or to disable a single line of code, I use `//`.

If you need to nest comments or use one of the delimiters in the text of a comment, you might have to depart from your normal way of doing things. For example, in detailing the syntax of a `SendKeys` function in its source code, I needed to use the brace delimiters { and } within the comment itself because they are part of the `SendKeys` syntax. This precluded the use of the braces as comment delimiters because the compiler would have been confused by the ones in the comment's text. Fortunately, I could use the (*..*) pair to delimit the comment.

Database Server Constructs

Over the years, I've learned to name my SQL server constructs consistently to maintain my sanity. Large databases are like large programs; the more sensibly you've named things, the easier you get around. If you name your objects consistently, they become server-based guideposts—they help you find your way in the database.

Not only does using consistent naming conventions aid you in administrating your databases, it also makes queries easier to construct and easier to read. The whole idea of SQL is to provide a query language that is structured, yet spoken-language-like and easy to follow. If you name your objects sensibly and consistently, you ensure that your SQL is as easy to ingest as possible.

As with Object Pascal program objects, the suggestions provided here are just one way of doing things. It's more important to do what works for you and do it *consistently* than to follow my conventions to the letter.

Databases

Databases, as covered here, are collections of tables, not the tables themselves. I always name databases in all lowercase. This is significant because most database servers are case sensitive by default. I prefix the first part of the name with up to three characters identifying the system to which the database belongs. I also usually distinguish master databases from transactional databases using up to four characters after the prefix. A *master* database is one that contains tables that rarely change and in which you look up names and descriptive information. *Transactional* databases contain transactional data, which can change daily, that is either keyed by users or collected from equipment. Sometimes these types of databases are created as separate entities, sometimes they're combined into a single database. You can take advantage of their being separate by naming them accordingly.

I sometimes include a sequence number as the last digit or two of the name. This allows for multiple versions of the same database but is rarely used in actual practice. Using these conventions, I might, for example, name an accounting master database `actmast0`. `act` identifies this database as belonging to the accounting system, `mast` signifies that this is a master database, and `0` signifies that this is the first in a possible series of like databases.

Notice the eight-character limitation employed. This is done so that an SQL script used to build this database that possibly resides on a Novell file server can have the same name as the database it creates. Although the script might initially reside on your local hard drive (and therefore could use Win32's long filenames), it's a good idea to voluntarily keep filenames short so the filename never has to change, regardless of where it resides.

Tables

I always create table names in all uppercase. This makes them stand out in large stored procedures and in server object listings. Tables are the most important object in the database, so this is fitting.

As for the table names themselves, I aim for a single- or double-word description that can be kept to eight characters or less. I use no sequence numbers; I keep the names as simple as possible. The idea here is to make SQL queries simple to write. The more complicated the table name is, the more difficult it is to read and remember. Single-word identifiers are best. For example, INVOICES, ORDERS, and CUSTOMER are all good table names.

Again, notice the adherence to the eight-character limitation. This allows the SQL script files that create these objects to be named after them, regardless of the operating system.

Indexes

Most dialects of SQL do not permit direct access to table indexes from within queries, so naming them is largely a non-issue. I name mine after the table on which they're built, appending their individual index numbers to the end of the name. For example, I would name the first index for the CUSTOMER name CUSTOMER01, the second CUSTOMER02, and so forth. These numbers correspond to the index number assigned by Sybase SQL Server, my main platform, and make it easier to write time-critical queries that force the use of a particular index.

Views

You should name views in the same way you name tables. Views and tables play the same role in SQL queries, so this makes sense. Some people distinguish views by tacking a lowercase v or vw to the front or back of the name, but this isn't a must.

Stored Procedures

I name stored procedures in all lowercase. The use of lowercase is just a method of always acknowledging the case that you must use when you refer to the procedure because most servers are case sensitive.

Some people append sp to the front or back of a stored procedure name, but this isn't really necessary. You hardly ever use a stored procedure in the same context that you would another object, such as a table. That is, you rarely see SELECT * FROM *storedprocname*, and you never see EXEC *tablename*. If you make a habit of selecting from stored procedures as though they were tables (supported on the InterBase platform, for example), you might want to tack sp on to your stored procedure names; otherwise, I wouldn't bother.

As far as actual names, I usually adopt a name for stored procedures that is similar to what I use for Object Pascal units. I use a single character to identify the application to which the procedure belongs. I then follow this with a three- to six-character section identifying the procedure's *general* and *specific* functions. Finally, I include a digit or two as a sequence number, so that I can easily manage multiple versions of the same procedure.

For example, in following the example given in the filenaming conventions discussed previously, I would choose the name RCALLST0 for a procedure that lists the CALLS table in the Rental Maintenance Management System. The R identifies the system that the procedure belongs to, CAL signifies that the procedure works with the CALLS table, LST means that the procedure will list its table, and 0 indicates that this is the first of a possible series of similar procedures.

Note the adherence to the eight-character name limitation. This allows the SQL script files that create these objects to be named after them, regardless of the operating system.

> **NOTE**
>
> Both Sybase and Oracle support naming multiple stored procedures using a single base name. In Oracle, you "overload" to designate the actual procedure you want to use. In Sybase, you follow the name of a procedure with a semicolon and the sequence number of its member procedure that you want to use. I recommend you avoid using both of these facilities. They're generally unwieldy and not worth the confusion they introduce.

Rules

If your server supports rules, you should name them descriptively and use with mixed case. You should also name them according to the type of data they allow in a column, not what they don't allow. That is, a rule that prevents the entry of zero into a field could be named NonZero. A rule that forces an entry of M or F into the Sex field could be named MaleFemale. SQL queries rarely refer to rules, so their names are, to a large degree, insignificant. Rules are the types of database objects that won't likely have their own SQL CREATE scripts, so there's no reason to keep their names to eight characters.

Defaults

If your server supports column default objects, you should name them for the field to which they correspond, if they correspond to just one, and for the default value they supply, using mixed-case letters. That is, a default that is bound to the Sex field and defaults to F should be named SexFemale. SQL queries rarely refer to defaults directly, so their names are relatively unimportant. Domains are the types of objects that are not likely to have their own SQL CREATE scripts, so there's no reason to limit their names to just eight characters.

Domains

I like to name domains after the column they will define, followed by the word TYPE. For example, a domain that will be used to define the CustomerNo column would be named CustomerNoTYPE. This signifies that the domain defines the CustomerNo column and, within a CREATE TABLE statement, distinguishes the domain from built-in data types. A domain is the type of database object that is not likely to have its own SQL CREATE script, so there's no reason to keep its name to eight characters.

Constraints and Exceptions

I name constraints and exceptions using a message-type approach that identifies what the problem is when a constraint is violated or an exception is raised. The idea behind this approach is to notify the user of the problem using the name of the object alone since some tools do not reliably relay server-based messages (particularly messages associated with constraints). For example, a foreign key constraint that ensures that a valid customer number is entered might be called InvalidCustomerNo. This way, if the constraint is violated and the front-end tool at least relays the name of the constraint from the server, the user will have an idea of what the problem is. I take the same approach with exceptions, though hopefully the text of the exception itself, not its name, will be displayed by the front-end tool. Exceptions and constraints are another of those types of objects that are not likely to have their own SQL CREATE script, so there's no reason to keep their names to eight characters.

Generators

As with domains, I name generators after the column they will service. I also append GEN to the end of generator names. For example, a generator that services the CustomerNo column would be named CustomerNoGEN. Generators are the type of objects that are not likely to have their own SQL CREATE script. There's therefore no reason to keep their names to just eight characters.

Cursors

Because of their transient nature, I often name cursors using a single letter. I also like to distinguish those that allow updates from those that don't. I do this by tacking the word UPDATE on to the end of the identifier.

There is another school of thought that says that a cursor should be named after its associated table. For example, a cursor declared on the TENANT table that allows updates and deletions might be named TENANTUPDATE.

As with all these conventions, you can use what works best for you. Personally, I find the first method to be easier to deal with.

Triggers

Triggers should be named for their associated tables, followed by a verb or verbs indicating the trigger's catalyst(s). A trigger can be activated by an INSERT, UPDATE, or DELETE, so this verb will be some combination of the words Insert, Update, and Delete. For example, a trigger that executes when a row is inserted or updated in the TENANT table would be named TENANTInsertUpdate. One that executes when a record is deleted from the WORDERS table would be named WORDERSDelete. Triggers are the types of database objects that won't likely have their own SQL CREATE scripts, so there's no reason to keep their names to only eight characters.

Columns

Columns are the most popular object in SQL queries, so naming them descriptively is important. Column names should be mixed-case and spoken-language-like. Don't be afraid to be a little wordy with these names; those who have to maintain your SQL in years to come will thank you for it. The names should consist of enough identifiers to make the column's role in the database obvious. Columns that represent the same entity in a database, such as CustomerNo, should be named identically in all tables. If you abbreviate an element such as Number or Address, abbreviate it consistently in all column names. For example, don't abbreviate Number in the customer number field as CustomerNum, then abbreviate it in the order number column as OrderNo. Abbreviate it consistently everywhere it's used. Examples of good column names include OrderNo, ShippingAddress, SampleWeight, and AverageWellDepth.

What's Ahead

In the next chapter, you learn the phases of application design and development. I take you through each phase individually and discuss it in terms of the project you'll undertake in the Tutorial section of this book.

Summary

Naming your program and database server objects can sometimes be tedious, but the effort is well worth it. Not only will your code be easier to read for those who follow you, but it will also be easier for *you* to read six months after you write it. The same is true for maintaining a consistent coding style. Although you might differ in style from others who look at your work, if you are consistent, they will eventually catch on. Using good naming conventions and following a consistent coding style takes your mind off trying to remember what something is or where it resides on disk and enables you to focus instead on the more important aspects of application development.

In this chapter, you learned my recommendations for naming Object Pascal and database server elements. Additionally, I shared with you my thoughts on Object Pascal coding conventions. Here's a brief summary of what you learned:

- You should place projects in a sensible directory structure; where you put something is at least as important as what you put there.

- You should name project files descriptively so that you can easily determine what the project's executable is supposed to do. You should name the project filename and directory identically.

- At least for now, you should avoid using Windows 95/NT long filenames. Filenames should conform to the 8.3 filenaming convention standard, regardless of their host operating system. I've suggested the format of the MCALEDT0 example, but you can use whatever works for you. Files should also be named such that their names lend themselves to conversation.

- Although units can have very long names, they should be named the same as their corresponding filenames, that is, they should follow the 8.3 naming standard. Good filenames alleviate the need for long unit names.

- Component class names, as with all Pascal type names, should begin with a T, be mixed case, and describe the component's function.

- You should name constants in uppercase.

- You should name variables in mixed case and as language-like as possible.

- I personally prefer to surround all Pascal conditional expressions with parentheses, even though it is not always necessary. This makes coding additional conditional expressions easier.

- I also prefer to place the begin of a begin...end pair on the same line as the statement to which it is related.

- Object Pascal supports three distinct comment styles. The // style is for single line comments. The {...} and (*..*) sets are for multiline comments. You should use one set for true comments and the other for commenting code.

- The goal of naming database objects is to turn the database into a large road map that shows how to navigate itself. In short, this boils down to making it easier to write and maintain SQL queries.

- Database names should be all lowercase, descriptive of the system to which they belong, and kept to eight characters in length.

- Table and view names should be all uppercase, as descriptive as possible, and kept to eight characters in length.

- Stored procedure names should follow the same rules as file and unit names in the Object Pascal section.

- You should name rules and defaults descriptively, but their names are largely unimportant because SQL queries rarely refer to them.

- Domains should be named after the column they will be used to define, followed by the word TYPE.

- Generators should be named after the column they will service, followed by the word GEN.

- A trigger should be named after its associated table, followed by a verb or verbs indicating its catalyst(s).

- Exceptions and constraints should be named using a message-type approach that identifies the problem with a constraint violation or exception using the name of the object alone.

- Cursors should be named using single alphabetic letters.

- Columns are the most popular entity in SQL queries, so you should name them descriptively. You should use mixed case and whole words in your column names.

5

A No-Nonsense
Approach to SQL

My goal in this chapter is to remove the mystery surrounding SQL. To people unfamiliar with it, learning SQL can be a daunting prospect, despite the fact that it's a relatively simple query language. I think this is largely due to the way that SQL is usually presented in books and training materials. Often, every syntax element of every command is presented in one session, along with a good dose of relational database theory, and the reader is left to sort through it all to figure out what's important and what's not.

This chapter expressly avoids such an approach. Instead, I take you step by step through the process of creating database objects, adding data to them, and querying the database, in one sitting. It's a pragmatic approach. The chapter attempts to cut to the chase and "give you the goods" as quickly as possible. The idea is to be concise, yet thorough—to cover all the basics of SQL, without getting into non-essential topics.

I've organized this tour into two sections. You should be able to work through the first section, "Quick Start," in a single session. The second section ties up a few loose ends by addressing entry-level SQL topics omitted from the "Quick Start" section. Advanced SQL is covered in Chapter 22, "Advanced SQL."

> **NOTE**
>
> I don't assume any prior knowledge of SQL. If you already have a basic working knowledge of SQL, you may want to skip this chapter and go straight to Chapter 6, "Database Design 101."

> **NOTE**
>
> I do assume that you have an SQL database server of some type and a means of sending SQL commands to it. This chapter uses the Local InterBase server that's included with Delphi Client/Server, though you can use any server that is reasonably compliant with the ANSI '92 SQL specification.

Quick Start

As they say, practice makes perfect. The quickest way to learn to swim in the SQL ocean is to simply jump in, so without further ado, let's get started.

Choosing an SQL Editor

One of the first things you need to do is to select an SQL editor. An SQL editor is a tool you use for entering and executing SQL commands. All of the examples in this chapter are done using the Windows Interactive SQL (WISQL) utility that comes with the Local InterBase Server.

I recommend you use it to begin with. If you're a Sybase SQL Server user, you might want to use the included ISQL utility. Otherwise, you might use some third-party utility like Datura's Desktop DBA or Embarcadero's DB Artisan. The tool you use needs to be able to send SQL commands to your server and display any results they return.

Command Terminators

Executing commands in most SQL dialects requires a command terminator of some type. A command terminator tells the SQL editor to process the text just entered as a single SQL command. InterBase and Oracle, for example, use the semi-colon (;) as a command terminator. In some editors, the command terminator is also the firing mechanism that sends the SQL to the server for processing. Sybase's line-oriented ISQL editor uses the go keyword this way. With many SQL editors, including InterBase's own WISQL, the terminator is optional. With others, including Sybase's ISQL utility, it's required. See your SQL editor documentation for more information.

> **NOTE**
>
> When you compile stored procedures and other constructs on the InterBase platform that include embedded SQL statements, use of a command terminator is not optional, no matter what editor you're using. That is, some SQL commands, including the CREATE PROCEDURE statement, are themselves composed of other SQL statements that you do not want to run when you execute CREATE PROCEDURE in your SQL editor. You want them to run when you execute the procedure itself, not the SQL statement that creates it. To pull this off, you must use the SET TERMINATOR command to temporarily change the editor's default command terminator during the creation of the procedure. This subject is covered in detail in Chapter 22.

A Word About SQL Vendors and Dialects

In this chapter, I make a regular point of comparing the two distinct families of SQL syntax to each other. Those two families are the Sybase family and the ANSI family. Sybase SQL Server, and its licensed cousin, Microsoft SQL Server, both use an SQL syntax that varies widely from the ANSI standard, in many respects. InterBase, Oracle, and most other DBMSs adhere pretty much to the ANSI SQL standard, with each vendor adding its own enhancements to the basic ANSI syntax. The examples in this chapter use InterBase's syntax, so many of them would require modification to work on SQL Server. Also, be aware that when I mention the Sybase syntax used to do something, the syntax would probably work for Microsoft SQL Server, as well. Likewise, when I list InterBase syntax, it's probably a safe assumption that the syntax would work for any ANSI SQL-compliant vendor, including Oracle.

Creating a Database

You may already have a database in which you can create some temporary tables for the purpose of working through the examples in this chapter. If you don't, creating one is easy enough. In SQL, you create databases using the SQL CREATE DATABASE command. The exact syntax varies from vendor to vendor, but here's the InterBase syntax:

```
CREATE DATABASE 'C:\DATA\IB\ORDENT'
LENGTH=100 USER username PASSWORD password ;
```

You could key this syntax into the InterBase ISQL utility to create your database, or, you could select a menu option in InterBase's WISQL utility to create it. Using WISQL, you use the Create Database option from the File menu to create a database. Here are the steps for doing that:

1. Start the Windows Interactive SQL tool (WISQL) (it should be in your Delphi program folder).

2. Select the Create Database option from WISQL's File menu.

3. Type C:\DATA\IB\ORDENT into the Database field of the Create Database dialog, replacing C:\DATA\IB with a valid path. Of course, you may want to create a special directory in advance in which to store your database objects.

4. Type a valid user name and password into the appropriate entry boxes. The default user should be SYSDBA; you may want to use it for the time being.

5. Type Length=100 into the Database Options field on the form. Specifying a length of 100 tells InterBase to create a database that's 100 pages long. The default size of an InterBase page is 1KB, so 100 pages=100KB.

6. Click the OK button. InterBase should create the database and connect you to it. In the future, you'll use the Connect to Database option from the File menu to connect to the database without creating it first.

Creating Tables

Once a database has been established, you're ready to get started building database objects. Begin by creating three tables. Tables are created using the SQL CREATE TABLE statement. Enter the following syntax into your SQL editor and execute it:

```
CREATE TABLE CUSTOMER
(
CustomerNumber          int
LastName                char(30)
FirstName               char(30)
StreetAddress           char(30)
City                    char(20)
State                   char(2)
Zip                     char(10)
)
```

This builds the CUSTOMER table. Next, build the ORDERS table using similar syntax:

```
CREATE TABLE ORDERS
(
OrderNumber                 int
OrderDate                   date
CustomerNumber              int
ItemNumber                  int
Amount                      float
)
```

Now that the ORDERS table is built, only one remains. Create the ITEMS table using the following syntax:

```
CREATE TABLE ITEMS
(
ItemNumber                  int
Description                 char(30)
Price                       float
)
```

> **NOTE**
>
> Using the NULL/NOT NULL designation is optional on most servers. Note, however, that they default the designation differently. InterBase, for example, complies with the ANSI SQL standard and defaults columns to NULL if you do not indicate a preference. SQL Server defaults to NOT NULL if neither is specified. In practice, it's a good idea to always specify one or the other.

Inserting Data

The SQL INSERT statement is used to add data to a table a row at a time. Use the following syntax to add data to each of the three tables. First, add three rows to the CUSTOMER table by executing the following syntax in your SQL editor:

```
INSERT INTO CUSTOMER
VALUES(1,'Doe','John','123 Sunnylane','Anywhere','OK','73115')

INSERT INTO CUSTOMER
VALUES(2,'Doe','Jane','123 Sunnylane','Anywhere','OK','73115')

INSERT INTO CUSTOMER
VALUES(3,'Citizen','John','57 Riverside','Reo','AR','65803')
```

Now, add four to the ORDERS table using this syntax:

```
INSERT INTO ORDERS
VALUES(101,'07/07/95',1,1001,123.45)

INSERT INTO ORDERS
VALUES(102,'07/08/95',2,1002,678.90)
```

```
INSERT INTO ORDERS
VALUES(103,'07/09/95',3,1003,86753.09)

INSERT INTO ORDERS
VALUES(104,'07/10/95',1,1002,678.90)
```

Finally, add three rows to the ITEMS table with this syntax:

```
INSERT INTO ITEMS
VALUES(1001,'WIDGET A',123.45)

INSERT INTO ITEMS
VALUES(1002,'WIDGET B',678.90)

INSERT INTO ITEMS
VALUES(1003,'WIDGET C',86753.09)
```

Note that none of the INSERT statements specify a list of fields, only a list of values. This is because the INSERT command defaults to inserting a value for all the columns in a table in the order in which they appear in the table. You could have specified a field list for each insert using the following syntax:

```
INSERT INTO ITEMS (ItemNumber, Price)
VALUES(1001,123.45)
```

Note also that you don't have to follow the order the fields appear in the table when you specify a field list, *but the list of values must match the order you specify*. Here's an example of that syntax:

```
INSERT INTO ITEMS (Price, ItemNumber)
VALUES(123.45, 1001)
```

The *SELECT* Command

You can quickly check the contents of each table using the SQL SELECT command. Issue a SELECT * FROM *tablename*, replacing *tablename* with the name of the table you want to check (for example, CUSTOMER, ORDERS, or ITEMS). At this point, the CUSTOMER and ITEMS tables should have three rows each, and the ORDERS table should have four.

Figure 5.1 shows the CUSTOMER table as it appears when SELECT * is issued in the WISQL utility.

Figure 5.2 shows the ORDERS table as it appears when SELECT * is issued in the WISQL utility.

Figure 5.3 shows the ITEMS table as it appears when SELECT * is issued in the WISQL utility.

FIGURE 5.1.

The ISQL output for
CUSTOMERS.

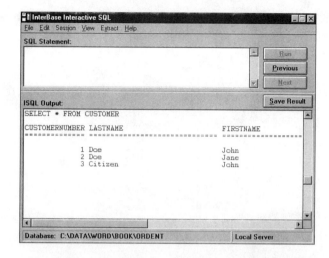

FIGURE 5.2.

The ISQL output for
ORDERS.

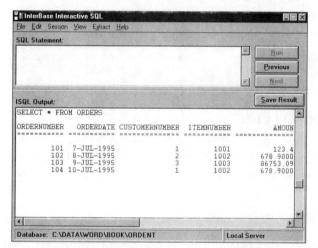

NOTE

Note that the implementation of the FROM clause varies from platform to platform. It's required on some platforms and optional on others. For example, InterBase SELECT statements require a FROM clause, even if you don't select any table columns. Sybase SQL Server, by contrast, only requires you to include a FROM clause if you are selecting columns from a table. SELECT statements that do not involve table columns do not require a FROM clause in SQL Server SELECT statements. For example, if you select a Sybase system function, like getdate(), you don't need a FROM clause.

FIGURE 5.3.

The ISQL output for ITEMS.

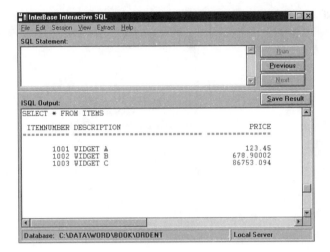

The SELECT * syntax causes all the columns in the table to be returned. You could change it to use a comma-delimited field list, instead, like so:

```
SELECT CustomerNumber, LastName, State FROM CUSTOMER
```

This syntax qualifies what fields you'd like to see. Figure 5.4 lists the output from this query.

Expression Columns

A column in the SELECT statement's column list can consist of more than just a column in a table. It can also consist of expressions containing absolute values and functions. Some SQL dialects support functions that return useful data without even referencing a column. For example, here's the SQL syntax to return the current date and time on a Sybase server:

```
SELECT getdate()
```

Here's InterBase SQL syntax to return the last name of each customer in the customer table in uppercase (see Figure 5.5):

```
SELECT UPPER(LastName), FirstName
FROM CUSTOMER
```

Aggregate Columns

Aggregate columns are actually functions that perform some calculation on a set of data. Examples of aggregates are the COUNT, SUM, AVG, MIN, and MAX functions. Here are some examples of their use.

```
SELECT COUNT(*) FROM CUSTOMER
```

FIGURE 5.4.

A SELECT that uses a field list.

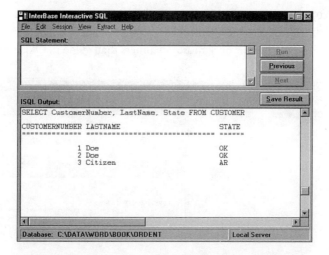

FIGURE 5.5.

Using the UPPER function in a SELECT statement.

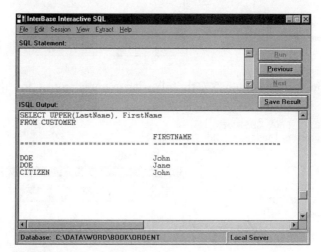

The preceding statement tells you how many customers are on file.

```
SELECT MAX(Amount) FROM ORDERS
```

The preceding statement reports the dollar amount of the largest order on file, whereas the following statement returns the total dollar amount of all orders on file:

```
SELECT SUM(Amount) FROM ORDERS
```

The *WHERE* Clause

The SQL WHERE clause is used to qualify the data returned by a SELECT statement. Here are some examples:

```
SELECT * FROM CUSTOMER
WHERE State='OK'
```

This example returns only those customers that reside in Oklahoma (see Figure 5.6).

FIGURE 5.6.

Using a WHERE clause in a SELECT statement.

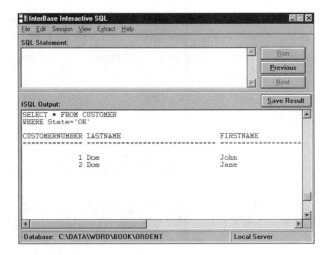

As illustrated by Figure 5.7, the following example returns only those customers whose street address contains the word "Sunny."

```
SELECT * FROM CUSTOMER
WHERE StreetAddress LIKE '%Sunny%'
```

FIGURE 5.7.

Using a WHERE clause with LIKE in a SELECT statement.

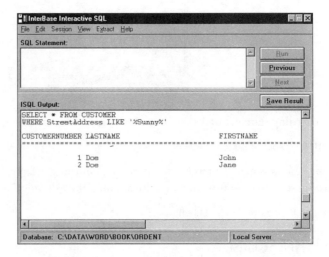

The following example returns only the orders exceeding $500, as Figure 5.8 illustrates.

```
SELECT * FROM ORDERS
WHERE Amount > 500
```

FIGURE 5.8.

Orders exceeding $500.

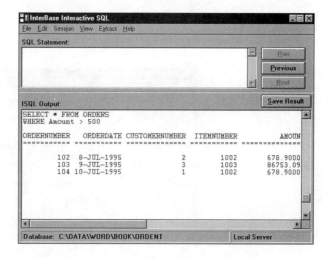

The following example returns only those orders occurring between July 8 and July 9, 1995, inclusively. (See Figure 5.9.)

```
SELECT * FROM ORDERS
WHERE OrderDate BETWEEN '07/08/95' AND '07/09/95'
```

FIGURE 5.9.

Using the WHERE clause with BETWEEN.

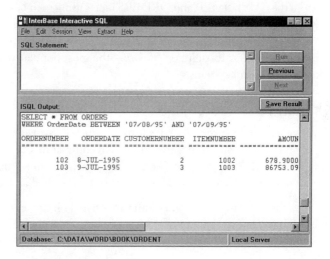

Joins

The WHERE clause is also used in joining one table with another to create a combined result set. Joining one table with another using the WHERE clause consists of two changes to the basic SELECT statement syntax: you specify additional tables in the SELECT statement's FROM clause, and you link related fields in the tables using equality conditions in the WHERE clause. (See Figure 5.10.) Here's an example:

```
SELECT CUSTOMER.CustomerNumber, ORDERS.Amount
FROM CUSTOMER, ORDERS
WHERE CUSTOMER.CustomerNumber=ORDERS.CustomerNumber
```

FIGURE 5.10.

The CUSTOMER table joined with the ORDERS table.

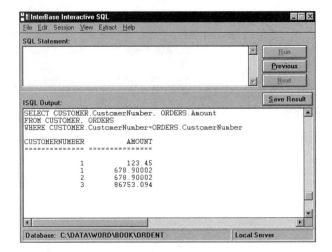

Notice the inclusion of the ORDERS table in the FROM clause. Also notice the use of the equal sign to join the CUSTOMER and ORDERS tables using their CustomerNumber fields. The table on the left of the equal sign is said to be the outer table, and the one on the right is the inner table. They're also commonly referred to as the left and right tables, respectively, indicating their positions in a left-to-right, or *left join*—the most popular type of join used in relational database management systems.

Inner Joins Versus Outer Joins

The type of left join just mentioned is formally known as an *inner* join. An inner join returns rows only if the join condition is met. This is in contrast to an outer join, which returns rows regardless of whether the join condition is met. When the join condition is not met for a given row in an outer join, fields from the inner table are returned as NULL.

The syntax for constructing an outer join varies based on the server and the ANSI SQL level it supports. There are two versions of the basic outer join syntax. The Sybase SQL Server syntax looks like this:

```
SELECT CUSTOMER.CustomerNumber, ORDERS.Amount
FROM CUSTOMER, ORDERS
WHERE CUSTOMER.CustomerNumber*=ORDERS.CustomerNumber
```

Note the use of the asterisk to the left of the equal sign. This signifies a left outer join on the Sybase platform. Outer joins can also be right outer joins, but left outer joins are by far more popular. The Sybase syntax for a right outer join is similar to that of the left outer join, with the asterisk located on the right of the equal sign rather than on the left, like so:

```
SELECT CUSTOMER.CustomerNumber, ORDERS.Amount
FROM CUSTOMER, ORDERS
WHERE CUSTOMER.CustomerNumber=*ORDERS.CustomerNumber
```

Right outer joins are most useful in finding orphans—keys that exist in the table on the right, but not in the one on the left.

ANSI Join Syntax

The ANSI syntax for a left outer join looks like this (see Figure 5.11):

```
SELECT CUSTOMER.CustomerNumber, ORDERS.Amount
FROM CUSTOMER LEFT OUTER JOIN ORDERS
ON CUSTOMER.CustomerNumber=ORDERS.CustomerNumber
```

FIGURE 5.11.

The CUSTOMER and ORDERS tables joined using an ANSI-SQL outer join.

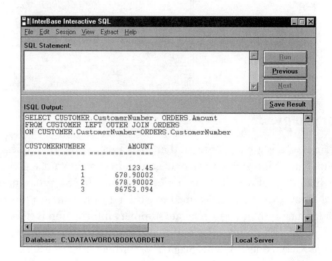

For right outer joins or left inner joins, you simply replace LEFT with RIGHT, or OUTER with IN-NER, respectively.

> **NOTE**
>
> InterBase doesn't support the Sybase convention of constructing *outer* joins in the WHERE clause—it supports the ANSI syntax only. By contrast, it *does* support the construction of *inner* joins using the WHERE clause.

Subqueries

A subquery is a SELECT statement within the WHERE statement of a query that's used to qualify the data returned by the query. (See Figure 5.12.) You generally use a subquery to return a list of items that you then test a column in the calling query against. Here's an example:

```
SELECT * FROM CUSTOMER
WHERE CustomerNumber IN (SELECT CustomerNumber FROM ORDERS)
```

FIGURE 5.12.

A subquery within the
WHERE clause of another
query.

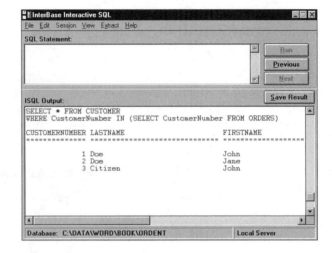

GROUP BY

Because SQL is a set-oriented rather than a record-oriented query language, statements that group data are integral to the language and, in concert with aggregate functions, are the means by which the real work of data retrieval is done. dBASE programmers find this approach unusual because they are accustomed to working with data on a record-by-record basis. Looping through a table in order to generate summary information is the way things are normally done in PC database products, but not in SQL. A single SQL statement can do what 10 or even 50 lines of Xbase code can. This magic is performed using the SELECT statement's GROUP BY clause in conjunction with SQL's aggregate functions. Here's an example of the use of GROUP BY:

```
SELECT CUSTOMER.CustomerNumber, sum(ORDERS.Amount) TotalOrders
FROM CUSTOMER, ORDERS
WHERE CUSTOMER.CustomerNumber=ORDERS.CustomerNumber
GROUP BY CUSTOMER.CustomerNumber
```

This query returns a list of all customers along with the total amount of each customer's orders. (See Figure 5.13.)

How do you know which fields to include in the GROUP BY clause? The rule of thumb is to include all the fields from the SELECT statement's column list that are not aggregate functions or absolute values. Take the following SELECT statement as an example:

```
SELECT CUSTOMER.CustomerNumber, CUSTOMER.LastName, CUSTOMER.State,
➥sum(ORDERS.Amount) TotalOrders
FROM CUSTOMER, ORDERS
WHERE CUSTOMER.CustomerNumber=ORDERS.CustomerNumber
```

If you'd written that statement, you'd need the following GROUP BY clause:

```
GROUP BY CUSTOMER.CustomerNumber, CUSTOMER.LastName, CUSTOMER.State
```

FIGURE 5.13.

A query that uses the
GROUP BY clause.

Some servers, including InterBase, enforce this rule—they won't attempt to execute queries that break it. Others, including Sybase SQL Server, will attempt to execute the query, though the results returned will probably be other than what you'd expect. For example, consider the following query:

```
SELECT CUSTOMER.LastName, COUNT(*) NumberWithName
FROM CUSTOMER
```

It might appear that this query would list all the last names found in the customer table, giving a count for the number of occurrences for each, but that's not the case. InterBase won't even execute this query—it's missing its GROUP BY clause. Sybase will execute it, rendering a count of *all* the records in the table for *each* row returned. This means that the count returned refers to all the records in the table, not just those with a particular last name. A dead giveaway that a query is flawed in this way is when its aggregate function results are identical in each result row. A query suffering from this malady will run forever against large sets of data. In this example, NumberWithName would list the *total* number of rows in the table, in *each* returned result row. Properly written, the preceding query looks like this:

```
SELECT CUSTOMER.LastName, COUNT(*) NumberWithName
FROM CUSTOMER
GROUP BY CUSTOMER.LastName
```

This query lists the number of customers with each last name from the CUSTOMER table, as illustrated in Figure 5.14.

HAVING

The HAVING clause is used to limit the rows returned by a GROUP BY clause. Its relationship to the GROUP BY clause is similar to the relationship between the WHERE clause and the SELECT itself. It works like a WHERE clause on the rows in the result set rather than on the rows in the query's tables. (See Figure 5.15.)

FIGURE 5.14.

The results as they should appear when the query is constructed properly.

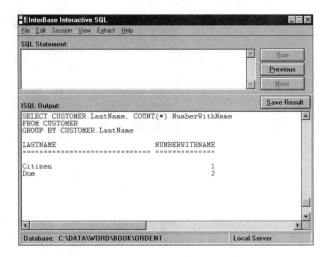

There is almost always a better way of qualifying a query than by using a HAVING clause. In general, HAVING is less efficient than the WHERE clause because it qualifies the result set *after* it has been organized into groups; WHERE does so *beforehand.* Here's an example of the use of the HAVING clause:

```
SELECT CUSTOMER.LastName, COUNT(*) NumberWithName
FROM CUSTOMER
GROUP BY CUSTOMER.LastName
HAVING CUSTOMER.LastName<>'Citizen'
```

Properly written, this query should place its selection criteria in its WHERE clause, not its HAVING clause, like so:

```
SELECT CUSTOMER.LastName, COUNT(*) NumberWithName
FROM CUSTOMER
WHERE CUSTOMER.LastName<>'Citizen'
GROUP BY CUSTOMER.LastName
```

Some servers (such as Sybase SQL Server) recognize HAVING clause misuse and correct it when they optimize a query for execution. Others don't detect it, so you'll have to be careful, especially when querying extremely large tables, since using a HAVING clause in place of WHERE criteria usually inhibits table-index use.

ORDER BY

You use the ORDER BY clause to order the rows in the result set. (See Figure 5.16.) Here's an example:

```
SELECT * FROM CUSTOMER
ORDER BY State
```

Here's another example:

```
SELECT FirstName, LastName
FROM CUSTOMER
ORDER BY LastName
```

FIGURE 5.15.

Using the HAVING *clause to limit the rows returned by a* GROUP BY *clause.*

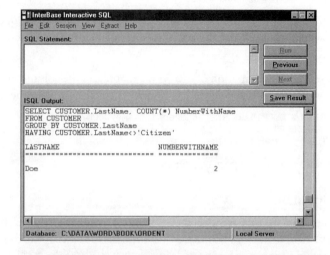

FIGURE 5.16.

Using the ORDER BY *clause.*

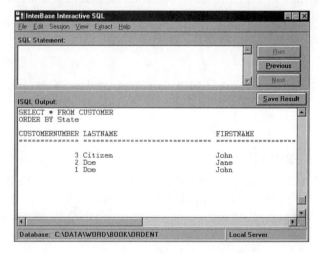

Column Aliases

You may have noticed that I use logical column names for aggregate functions like COUNT() and SUM(). Labels such as these are known as *column aliases* and serve to make the query and its result set more readable. In ANSI SQL, you place a column alias immediately to the right of its corresponding column in the SELECT statement's field list. For example, in the preceding query, the column alias of the COUNT() aggregate is the NumberWithName label. You can use column aliases for any item in a result set, not just aggregate functions. For example, the following example substitutes the column alias LName for the LastName column in the result set:

```
SELECT CUSTOMER.LastName LName, COUNT(*) NumberWithName
FROM CUSTOMER
GROUP BY CUSTOMER.LastName
```

Note, however, that you cannot use aliases in other parts of the query, like the WHERE or GROUP BY clauses. You must use the actual column name or value in those parts of the SELECT statement.

Sybase supports a variation of this syntax that places the column alias to the left of the column, separating it from the column name with an equal sign, as in the following:

```
SELECT CUSTOMER.LastName, NumberWithName=COUNT(*)
FROM CUSTOMER
GROUP BY CUSTOMER.LastName
```

InterBase doesn't support this syntax.

Table Aliases

Rather than always having to specify the full name of a table each time you reference it in a SELECT command, you can define a shorthand moniker for it to use instead. You do this by specifying a *table alias* for the table in the FROM clause of the SELECT statement. Place the alias to the right of the actual table name, as illustrated here:

```
SELECT C.LastName, COUNT(*) NumberWithName
FROM CUSTOMER C
GROUP BY C.LastName
```

Notice that the alias can be used in the field list of the SELECT list, before it is even syntactically defined. This is possible because references to database objects in a query are resolved before the query is executed.

The Finish Line

This concludes the Quick Start part of the SQL tour. You should now be able to create a database, create tables, and populate those tables with data. You should also be familiar with the basic mechanics for querying those tables using the SQL SELECT command.

A Few Additional Comments

The following section ties up a few loose ends and covers other entry-level SQL topics not covered in the "Quick Start" section of this chapter. Chapter 22 continues the discussion on SQL in greater depth.

The *CONNECT* Command

In most SQL dialects, you use the CONNECT command to change the "database context"—to connect to and use a specific database. Both InterBase and Oracle use this syntax. Use the DISCONNECT command to reverse a CONNECT command.

With Sybase SQL Server, the USE command changes the database context. Unlike CONNECT, USE provides access to only one database at a time. There is also no equivalent to DISCONNECT in Sybase's SQL dialect.

The *UPDATE* Command

Without a doubt, you'll eventually want to change the data you've loaded into a table. You use the SQL UPDATE command to do this. It works much like the dBASE REPLACE ALL command. Here's the syntax:

```
UPDATE CUSTOMER
SET Zip='90210' WHERE City='Beverly Hills'
```

Though the WHERE clause in the preceding query might cause it to only change a single row, depending on the data, you can update all the rows in the table by omitting the WHERE clause:

```
UPDATE CUSTOMER
SET State='CA'
```

You can also update a column using columns in its host table, including the column itself, as in:

```
UPDATE ORDERS
SET Amount=Amount+(Amount*.07)
```

In Sybase's SQL dialect, you can also update the values in one table with those from another. Here's an example:

```
UPDATE ORDERS
SET Amount=Price
FROM ORDERS, ITEMS
WHERE ORDERS.ItemNumber=ITEMS.ItemNumber
```

The *DELETE* Command

You use the DELETE command to delete rows from tables. To delete all the rows in a table, use this syntax:

```
DELETE FROM CUSTOMER
```

Some servers provide a quicker, table-oriented command for deleting all the rows in a table, like the dBASE ZAP command. The Sybase syntax is:

```
TRUNCATE TABLE CUSTOMER
```

The DELETE command can also include a WHERE clause to limit the rows deleted. Here's an example:

```
DELETE FROM CUSTOMER
WHERE LastName<>'Doe'
```

COMMIT and *ROLLBACK*

A group of changes to a database is formally known as a transaction. The SQL COMMIT command makes these transactions permanent. Think of it as a database save command. ROLLBACK, on the other hand, throws away the changes a transaction might make to the database—it functions like a database undo command. Both of these commands affect only the changes made since the last COMMIT—you cannot roll back changes you've just committed.

On some platforms, including Sybase SQL Server, you must expressly start a transaction in order to explicitly commit it or roll it back. InterBase's WISQL utility begins a transaction automatically (by issuing the equivalent of the InterBase SET TRANSACTION command) when it first loads. When you exit the utility, it asks whether you'd like to commit your work. You can commit or roll back your work at any time using the Commit Work and Rollback Work options on WISQL's File menu.

Summary

In this chapter, you've been introduced to the *lingua franca* of relational databases, SQL. Though its syntax has been extended in many different directions by DBMS vendors, SQL is basically a very simple language, as you've discovered.

The next chapter discusses the basics of database design. The skills you've acquired in this chapter should prove especially useful in designing databases and database applications.

6

Database Design 101

This chapter and the one that follows cover database application design from a pragmatist's point of view. They introduce various concepts of database theory and application design and show you how to apply those concepts in your work. These chapters are intended for those with limited database application development experience. If you're already familiar with basic relational database and application design, you might want to skip straight to Chapter 8, "Your First Real Database Application."

The formal processes for building a database application are as follows:

1. Define the purpose and goals of the application.
2. Design the database foundation and application processes needed to meet those goals.
3. Develop the design into an application by creating the requisite database and program objects.
4. Test the application for compliance with the established goals.
5. Install the application for production use.

This chapter focuses on the parts of the list that apply to database design. The next chapter focuses on those that relate to application design. I've organized the chapters this way only to make the material easier to digest—the two subjects are so dependent on each other that it would be futile to try to completely separate them.

My approach to database application design differs from that of most people. Rather than bore you with a long discourse on database theory, I'd rather be more pragmatic—more practical. I don't care to discuss the fine details of Dr. E. F. Codd's historic paper or the mathematics behind database normalization. There are plenty of books out there that do that already. I also won't talk about the different types of database management systems; I'll assume that you are working with a relational database of some type. You won't see any mention of CASE tools for database or application design, either. CASE tools are great, but unfortunately, not everyone has them or knows how to use them. Moreover, I view CASE tools as "luxury" or "convenience" items. Like remote controls and microwave ovens, they're nice to have and are certainly time-savers, but they're largely unneeded and tend to make us a bit lazy. Consequently, I'll stick with what comes in the Delphi box.

Now that you've heard what won't be covered, I bet you're wondering what will be. I'll concentrate on concepts that you can quickly put into practice. I'll focus more on the practical aspects of database application design than on its theoretical aspects.

A common pitfall of database and application design is concentrating too much on theory and not enough on implementation. This kind of imbalance leads to poorly implemented databases and database applications. An application's implementation is what the user sees, so it's important to place adequate emphasis on it. You'd never buy a house whose floor fell through the minute you walked in—no matter how promising the blueprint looked. The same is true with applications that look great on paper but deficient on-screen. A good developer strives to build applications that work well in theory *and* in practice.

Something else you'll notice about this chapter and the one that follows is that I won't discuss *database* design as though it were a separate subject from database *application* design. Why? Because I believe the two are inseparably linked. I've never designed a database that was not intended to be accessed in some way by a front-end application. Remember: the database is just a means to an end—it's your way of providing the service the client has requested. The database application is the conduit between the user and the database. It, too, is just a tool for servicing your client. Both the database and its dependent applications must work together to provide solutions your clients will find acceptable.

In this chapter, I'll give you tips, tricks, and shortcuts that I use in my work when designing database applications. I'll hang these thoughts on a solid theoretical framework—I'm not throwing database theory out the window here. On the contrary, I'm employing it in its intended use—to produce robust database applications.

Defining the Purpose of the Application

The first step in designing any application—database or otherwise—is to define the purpose of the application. An application's statement of purpose should consist of a single sentence describing the subject, the verb, and the verb's object. The subject is always the application, such as "This system..." or "The RENTALMAN System..." The verb describes what the application is supposed to do, for example, "The system will manage...", or "The RENTALMAN System will track..." The object denotes the recipient of the application's actions, for example, "The system will manage summer camp registration," or "The RENTALMAN System will track rental property maintenance."

The statement of purpose needs to be as simple and concise as you can make it. Don't waste time with flowery language or needless information. For example, avoid "for the organization" and "for the client" at the end of the statement because these are normally implicit.

Once you've developed a statement of purpose for the application, show it to the potential users of the new application and see if they agree. Don't be surprised if they don't understand your brevity, but try to get them to sanction your statement as accurate and complete. Assure them that the specific goals of the application are to be addressed separately.

Defining the Goals of the Application

Once the statement of purpose is in place, it's time to determine the specific goals of the application. What, specifically, is the application going to do? You should probably keep this to no more than three or four major tasks, if possible. It's a great idea to develop these items using an outline. These goals should further define the application's statement of purpose, not go beyond it. Follow the same three-part format you used with the statement of purpose, for example:

The RENTALMAN System will track maintenance on rental properties:

- Record incoming calls from tenants
- Generate work orders and track progress
- Provide historical information on individual properties

Make sure you cover all the major functions of the application, but don't overdo it with needless details. Also be sure that the tasks you list don't overlap—don't list a task that's covered by another task already on the list.

Designing the Database Foundation and Application Processes

This stage is where the database itself is designed. Most people separate the database part of this step from the application design process, but I think that's a mistake. As I've said, a database is a means to an end—it's the means by which you satisfy your client's requirement to store and retrieve data. A database and the application that runs atop it are inexorably linked. By extension, their designs are also intertwined. That's why I cover database design and database application design in the same discussion.

Data Modeling

The first thing you must do in building a database is to determine what tables are needed and what these tables need to contain. *Data modeling* is the formal term for the process in which you do this. There are several recognized approaches to data modeling, each with its own merits. The first is *application-centric* modeling, and the second is *kind-centric* modeling.

- Application-centric modeling seeks to fully satisfy the data needs of an application with a single database. In application-centric modeling, each application has it own, essentially private, set of tables. The tables do not relate to the outside world—the application and database are essentially a world unto themselves.
- Kind-centric modeling organizes tables into databases according to the kinds of data they represent. For example, the company's product list table might live in its sales database, whereas the inventory of parts used to build those products resides in its manufacturing database. A report that showed the amount of profit on each product would have to reference both tables, though they reside in completely different databases.

Generally speaking, kind-centric modeling is the preferred approach. It better leverages a company's investment in its existing database resources. It also cuts down on redundant database tasks, effectively normalizing the organization's data bank.

On the other hand, application-centric modeling has advantages of its own. For one thing, with this approach, the access by a user to the database objects used by an application can be coordinated through a single database. Applications that use hundreds of tables spread across dozens of databases can present a real challenge as far as user security and database administration is concerned.

Furthermore, copying an application's dependent objects from server to server (for example, from a development server to a production server or from a production server to a backup server) is complicated by magnitudes when those objects reside in many different databases. Taking a snapshot of the data for the purposes of backing it up is also difficult because most DBMS's do not support cross-database snapshots. Sybase, for example, supports single database snapshots: once a backup is begun on a given database, all data written to the backup device will be consistent as of a single point in time. This isn't the case with multiple databases. After restoring the sales and manufacturing databases from a backup, you may find that they do not match—that products exist in the sales database that manufacturing knows nothing about.

With respect to Delphi itself, storing database objects in multiple databases requires multiple BDE (Borland Database Engine) aliases to access those objects, and hence multiple connections to what is probably a single database server. Without some hoop-jumping, you'll have to log into that same database server multiple times—once for each database you are accessing.

Finally, as far as commercial applications go, it's rare that you'll be able to utilize databases or tables that your clients already have. You need a canned solution—something that can be installed and used right out of the box without regard to other applications. Usually, an application-centric approach works best for this type of development.

Personally, I use a combination of the two approaches. I begin any database application design by figuring out what it is the application needs to do, then I determine what tables are needed to enable it to do this. Next, I check the other databases at my disposal to see if any of them have the entities I need. If they do, I make use of them in one of two ways. I either use multiple aliases and bear the full burden of accessing multiple databases, or I create an SQL VIEW in the application's primary database for each external table referenced. I use this VIEW, rather than its base table, in the application. The application's primary database is a kind-centric database that is either created in conjunction with the project or one that already exists. Using this method eliminates the insistence by the BDE on a separate login for each database because all objects appear to it to exist in one database. At the same time, it preserves the "kind-centricity" of the databases—a VIEW doesn't copy its base table; it merely references it through an SQL query. I find this approach to be a good compromise between the two methodologies.

NOTE

Keep in mind that not all servers support references by objects in one database to those in another. InterBase, for example, doesn't support these types of external references. This means than an InterBase VIEW in one database cannot reference tables in a another database. By contrast, many platforms, among them Sybase SQL Server and Oracle, do support these types of external object references. If you intend to take the approach of creating a data modeling hybrid, as I have, you'll want to ensure that your server supports external references before doing so.

Database Terms

Before proceeding, I think it would be a good idea to talk about the basic building blocks of relational databases. As I've said, I don't intend to enter into a prolonged discussion of database theory. On the other hand, a working knowledge of basic concepts is essential to proper database design.

For all the talk these days about *databases*, many people seem to be confused as to what exactly a database is. Thanks to PC-based DBMS's, many people are under the impression that a database and a physical file are the same thing. Some people think a Quattro Pro worksheet is a database. Others have been lead to believe that a WordPerfect merge file is. DBASE's .DBF extension (*DataBase File*) doesn't help either. There seems to be a lot of confusion over what is essentially a simple concept.

A good way to think of a database is as a file cabinet. Each folder represents a *table* and each sheet in each folder represents a *record*. As discussed in the previous section on data modeling, a database is usually the collection of all the data of a particular kind. Several related types of data usually exist within each kind. These types of data are known as *record types* or *entity classes* and are embodied in tables. In its most basic form, then, a database is simply a collection of tables.

> **NOTE**
>
> When talking about databases, it's important to keep physical organization separate from logical organization. The fact that a database is physically composed of either a single file or numerous files has nothing to do with its logical layout. Some database formats, for example dBASE and Paradox, use numerous tables to store their elements. Some, namely Access, use just one. This difference has nothing to do with their use or functionality as databases.

Next on the list is the key element in database construction, the *table*. Think of a table as a two-dimensional surface divided into rows and columns. As in a spreadsheet, the *rows* represent the *records* in the table, and the *columns* represent the *fields*. You can equate each table to a folder in our metaphorical database filing cabinet.

A *record* corresponds to a real-world data object. It might be an invoice, a withdrawal from a savings account, or a listing in the phone book. Records are the "meat-and-potatoes" of the database. Database purists prefer the use of *row* rather than record. This book uses the two terms interchangeably. In their simplest form, databases and tables are really just mechanisms for organizing records. In our analogy, a record is a sheet within a folder in our database file cabinet. If the folder were titled "INVOICES," we would expect each element therein to be an invoice of some type. According to our analogy, then, each invoice would be the equivalent of a record in the INVOICES table.

The records in a database are known as *entities*—instances of a particular record type or entity class. Tables house all the entities of a particular entity class. Just as a folder in a filing cabinet ideally contains all the items of a given type (for example, the entirety of a company's invoices), so does a table in a database contain all the records of a given type. These records make up the real data of the database. Many end-users tend to look at data from a record-centric point of view.

A *field* is an element within a record. Analogous to a column in a spreadsheet, a field represents a characteristic of the object represented by a record. Database purists prefer the use of column rather than field. This book uses the two terms interchangeably. An example of a field would be the address field in a customer table. In and of itself, the address is meaningless. In the context of its entity class, though, it describes a customer's address.

An *attribute* is the intersection between a row and a column in a table. That is, the value of a given field within a particular record is known as an attribute. Just as rows of a particular type of data are known as entity classes, a column of a particular type is known as an *attribute class*.

An *entity identifier* is a field or set of fields that distinguish a record from the others in the table. It uniquely identifies each record in a table. An example of an entity identifier would be the invoice number field in an invoice table. The invoice number in each record of the invoice table is unique to that one record. If you save the value of the invoice number field and go elsewhere in the table, you can always return to the original record using only the invoice number as the key.

A *primary key* is the field or fields in a table that are used as its entity identifier. As an identifier, the value of a table's primary key is always unique to each record. The fields that make up a primary key are also normally used to build an index on the table for fast access to its rows.

A *foreign key* is a field or fields in a table that, while not used as its identifier, is often used in joins with other tables. For example, using the invoice table example, the customer number field in an invoice table might be set up as a foreign key. The customer number field does not uniquely identify individual invoice records—you might have several invoices for a single customer. However, the customer table might be joined with the invoice table to produce a listing of sales by customer. This would most likely be done using the customer number field in each table. The customer number field would probably be the primary key of the customer table and a foreign key of the invoice table.

A *join* is the logical relation of one table to another using a common key. The tables involved are commonly referred to as the left and right side of the join, referring to the SQL syntax for constructing joins. A join normally returns a result set with elements from both tables. The SQL syntax for constructing a join has the following form:

```
SELECT TENANT.TenantNo, TENANT.Name, PROPERTY.Address
FROM TENANT, PROPERTY
WHERE TENANT.TenantNo=PROPERTY.TenantNo
```

Joins come in two basic flavors: inner joins and outer joins. An inner join returns no rows from either table if the join condition is not met. An outer join returns rows from the table on the left regardless of whether the join condition is met. If the condition is not met, fields in the result set that reside in the table on the right are returned as NULL. The SQL syntax example in the preceding paragraph demonstrates an inner join. Following is the same query expressed as an outer join:

```
SELECT TENANT.TenantNo, TENANT.Name, PROPERTY.Address
FROM TENANT LEFT OUTER JOIN PROPERTY ON TENANT.TenantNo=PROPERTY.TenantNo
```

Notice the use of the LEFT OUTER JOIN syntax in the second query. This causes the query to return the rows in the table on the left regardless of whether a match is found in the table on the right using the tables' TenantNo fields.

Refine Your Goals into Operational Processes

To continue designing your application, further divide the goals you outlined in the previous step into operational processes. Make the list as exhaustive and detailed as you can. Continue to refine the list until you have processes that appear to operate on single database objects, for example:

The RENTALMAN System will track maintenance on rental properties, including:

- Record incoming calls from tenants
- Log calls from tenants as they are received
- Assign calls received to a new or existing work order

Determine the Database Objects Needed to Service Your Processes

Once this is done, you're ready to begin developing database objects to service the processes you've outlined. Looking closely at the processes you've defined, determine what database tables will be needed to service them. For example, in the processes listed in the preceding example, it's evident that the following tables will be needed:

- A table in which to store tenant calls
- A tenant table
- A property table
- An employee table

■ A work order table

■ A resources table for tracking the resources used in completing a work order

Check Existing Databases for These Objects

In the interest of avoiding an application-centric database design, check the other databases at your disposal to see if these objects already exist. You may need the assistance of your Database Administrator (DBA) to determine this. For example, you may find that, with the exception of the work order and resources tables, all of the tables mentioned earlier exist elsewhere in a rental management database of some type. If they do, you'll want to use them rather than create your own. Of course, you'll need to ensure that they contain all the fields you need. Adding additional fields to these tables may be necessary, and the sooner you know this, the better.

Begin the Database Framework

Now it's time to translate your work so far into database objects and program processes. Once you decide on a formal list of tables and their relations to one another, it's time to build your preliminary database framework. I call it preliminary because it will probably change. Before you're done, it may change many times—this is to be expected. In the early stages of database application development, the database design must be sufficiently malleable so as to be able to handle your growing understanding of what the application needs to do. Later, it must be a sturdy framework capable of supporting the application you build on top of it. Tweaking the database design in the early stages of the project is much easier than doing so after the application is built. Don't be afraid to change things that you find deficient about your initial design. Nothing is carved in stone at this point.

Construct a Field Repository

When designing tables for the database, think about the items the table needs to store. Using the list of tables you developed earlier, build a list of all the informational elements the application needs to track. Consolidate these items into a single master list of all the fields that will exist in the database. List each field only once, and determine the optimal data type and size for each. Think of your master list as a field repository—you use the fields in it to build your tables. Some tools refer to this master list as a data dictionary or reference table. In Delphi, you implement this type of field repository using *attribute sets* in the Database Explorer. You can equate the fields in the repository to field *templates*—they define how a given database attribute will look in all the tables in which it appears.

Think Efficiency

Think about efficiency, too. Ask yourself, "What's the smallest data type I can use for this field and still store its largest possible value?" If the field will never need to store a value greater than 255, store it as a byte or tinyint value. Use integers instead of floating-point values, when possible. Use variable character types instead of fixed-character types when the length of a character field may vary considerably from record to record.

User Data Types

If your target platform supports them, now is a good time to think about user-defined data types. A user-defined data type is just a shorthand way of referring to a data type the server already supports. InterBase calls them "domains." They provide an easy and consistent method of defining similar table columns. For example, suppose that you have several fields in your field repository that represent names of some type, say, CustomerName, VendorName, and EmployeeName. Let's say you want all three fields to be variable-length character fields of 40 bytes each. Rather than define all three fields as VARCHAR(40), you could instead define a user data type called, say, NameTYPE, that is itself defined as a variable character data type of 40 bytes in length. You would then use NameTYPE, rather than VARCHAR(40), as the data type for the three fields. This is a safer and more readable way of defining similar fields.

Describe Your Data

I've also found it helpful to write a one-line description for each field in the field repository. Describe the data contained in the field and the allowable values it may have, if applicable. This helps ensure that you actually understand the role each field will play in the database. Optionally, you could include the description for each field in a table as a comment in the table's SQL CREATE statement. Describing fields this way helps eliminate redundancy and helps clarify your understanding of the data. In multi-programmer projects, it also helps others understand your thinking when you constructed a given table.

Use the Field Repository to Build Table Definitions

Next, use these attributes to reassemble your tables. Copy the refined field definitions from the field repository to the table structures you previously outlined. You should see your database design slowly beginning to take shape.

Code Your Definitions in SQL

Something I've found helpful at this stage is to go ahead and code the table structures in SQL. That is, write an SQL CREATE statement for each of the tables. This forces you to formalize the definition of each table. It also causes you to make decisions regarding the actual SQL data types you'll use. You'll have to decide which fields can and cannot be left empty, and define them as either NULL or NOT NULL, accordingly. Despite the fact that your server probably defines a default for the NULL/NOT NULL designation, specify it anyway—it makes for better clarity. Doing this also begins the real work of creating the tables because you can later use these CREATE statements to build them (using tools like Database Desktop, building a table using SQL is optional, but writing the CREATE statements is still good practice). For example, you might write the following CREATE statement for the TENANT table:

```
CREATE TABLE TENANT
(
 TenantNo       smallint      NOT NULL,
 Name           varchar(30)   NOT NULL,
 Employer       varchar(30)
 EmpAddress     varchar(30)
 EmpCity        varchar(30)
 EmpState       char(2)
 EmpZip         char(10)
 HomePhone      char(10)
 WorkPhone      char(10)
 ICEPhone       char(10)
 LeaseBegin     datetime      NOT NULL,
 LeaseDuration  tinyint       NOT NULL,
 MovedIn        datetime      NOT NULL,
 MovedOut       datetime      NOT NULL,
 RentDueDay     tinyint       NOT NULL,
 PetDeposit     money
 LawnService    bit           NOT NULL
)
```

Organize the Tables by Type

Divide the tables into base and transactional tables. Base tables contain items that are unique by definition. An example of a base table would be one that lists state capitals. Because there is only one capital per state, the capitals table is a base table. Base tables are often used to translate codes, numbers or abbreviations into something more meaningful. For example, a table that lists the properties owned by the rental company would be considered a base table.

A transactional table receives data collected from equipment or keyed by users. It changes frequently and is the most volatile part of the database.

Master/Detail Tables

One of the attributes of relational databases is that they do not allow duplication of data *within* an individual table. Consequently, data is instead duplicated *among* tables. This happens because the primary key of one table must be duplicated as the primary or foreign key of another in order to establish a relationship between them. These relationships come in two basic flavors: one-to-one relationships and one-to-many relationships. One-to-one relationships are fairly rare. Usually data contained in a second table that is accessed through a one-to-one relationship can instead be included in the first table. One-to-many relationships, by contrast, are ubiquitous—they form the basis for most PC database applications. (Note that many-to-one relationships are really just one-to-many relationships reversed.) Tables involved in one-to-many relationships are commonly referred to as master/detail tables.

Within the transactional table group, determine which tables depend on others to provide meaningful information. These tables are called *detail* tables; the tables on which they depend are called *master* tables. Detail tables depend on other tables to be truly useful—they normally store line-item data. They are also known as "child" or "slave" tables.

Sometimes a table plays a dual role—it acts as the detail for one table and the master for another. Whatever the case, master/detail tables are usually linked by a combination of primary and foreign keys. In addition to the key fields by which it is linked to the master table, a detail table usually stores a line or sequence number of some type. This is what distinguishes detail records participating in a one-to-many relationship with a master table from one another. A good example of a master/detail relationship is a pair of tables that store invoice information. Normally, one table functions as the master table and stores the header information for each invoice. The second table acts as the detail table and stores the line items for each invoice.

Visually Relate the Tables

Next, I've found it's helpful to visually diagram the relationships between tables. *Entity relation* diagrams show the way that entities (records) in one table relate to entities in another. These don't need to be anything elaborate or use complex symbols. The purpose of an ER diagram is to visually relate tables, and you can do that without using special symbols. Although there is a formal design specification for ER diagrams, simply drawing boxes on a sheet of paper and connecting them with lines may work for you. Or, you may want to take a more formal approach. Whatever you do, be sure you understand the ways in which your tables are related before you proceed. Figure 6.1 illustrates an ER diagram that follows the more formal style. Figure 6.2 illustrates one that follows a less formal one.

FIGURE 6.1.

An entity relation diagram for the TENANT and PROPERTY tables that follows the formal ER diagram style.

FIGURE 6.2.

An entity relation diagram for the TENANT and PROPERTY tables that follows a less formal ER diagram style.

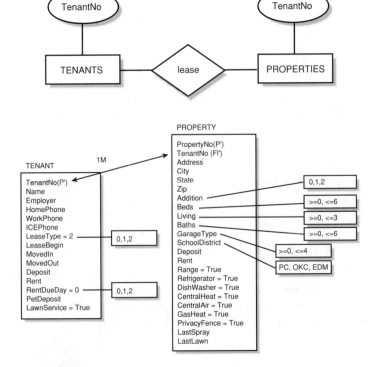

Another helpful thing that I've found is to create schematics of the entire database design. That is, I create a single diagram that shows the rough relationships between the tables in the database. This bird's-eye view of the database helps you better understand what data the database contains and how the tables in the database relate to one another. Figure 6.3 illustrates such a diagram.

FIGURE 6.3.

A database schematic shows the relationships between the tables in a database.

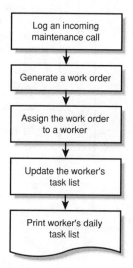

Data Flow Diagrams

Something else that I've found useful is to build data flow diagrams for the processes that make up the application. Data flow diagrams are a carryover from the 1950's when computers first began to be used in business. They are task-oriented rather than data-oriented. Using special symbols, they depict the steps that make up a process and the tables and devices it uses. Figure 6.4 illustrates a typical data flow diagram.

FIGURE 6.4.
A typical data flow diagram.

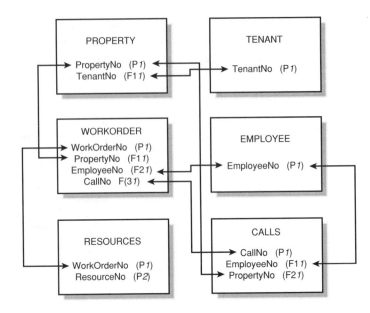

Normalize the Database

The process of transforming data into the relational form discussed in Dr. E. F. Codd's famous 1970 paper, "A Relational Model of Data for Large Share Data Banks," is called *normalization*. Simply put, normalization is the elimination of redundant data from each table in a database. The purpose of normalization is twofold: to eliminate unnecessary copies of data, and to provide for maximum flexibility in both table structures and front-end applications as future changes are made to the database.

You'll want to normalize the tables in your database before you get very far into the design of the application. Sometimes the process of normalization yields additional tables that you did not include in your original design. Knowing about these as early as possible will help prevent wasted development effort.

Normalization is formally divided into five *forms* or stages, *first normal form* through *fifth normal form*. These obscure terms really just refer to the five sets of relational criteria that a table either does or does not meet. Each successive stage builds on the previous one. Though there are technically five forms, in practice you'll probably use just the first three. The last two are generally regarded as too specialized to be applicable to commonplace database design.

First Normal Form

In order for a table to be considered normalized to first normal form, each of its fields must be completely *atomic*, and it must contain no *repeating groups*. A field is atomic when it contains only one element of data. For example, an `Address` field that contains not only a street address but also a city, state, and zip code is not atomic. Columns designed this way must be split into multiple fields in order to be fully compliant with first normal form.

A repeating group is a field that is repeated within a record definition for the sole purpose of storing multiple values for the attribute. For example, we could have taken the approach in designing our TENANT table of storing the property the tenant was renting within the TENANT table rather than separately in the PROPERTY table. This fails to allow for the possibility that a single tenant, for example a restaurant chain, might rent more than one property. To address this exclusively within the TENANT table, we would have to decide on the maximum number of properties a tenant might rent, then add the requisite supporting fields to the table. These repetitive fields would be repeating groups.

Some database tools provide direct support for repeating groups, and, as such, are inherently non-relational. Obviously, they can't be relational tools if they violate first normal form. An example of such a tool is Advanced Revelation. Its multi-valued fields are actually repeating groups. Using them, which is a popular practice in AREV applications, violates first normal form. Another example is the COBOL programming language. COBOL was invented before the relational database and therefore carries with it baggage from the pre-relational days of databases. In particular, COBOL's `groupname occurs several times` syntax is a direct violation of first normal form. This isn't surprising, though, because COBOL was originally designed to work with network databases rather than relational ones.

What all this boils down to is that repeating groups are a very poor database design practice. First, using the TENANT table example, every tenant record includes the repeating property fields whether they are used or not. Second, repeating groups present a challenge when it comes to processing the data they represent. In particular, properly formatting them on printed reports can be difficult. Not only do you have to deal with series of records, but you also have to deal with series of fields, turning a one-dimensional task into a two-dimensional one. Third, if the maximum number of properties that a tenant may rent needs to be increased, the structure of the TENANT table must be changed, along with any applications that access it.

Second Normal Form

In order for a table to be normalized in second normal form, each of its non-key fields must be fully dependent upon the table's primary key and on each field in the primary key when the primary key is composed of multiple fields. This means that each non-key field must be uniquely identified by the primary key and its component fields.

Let's take the example of an invoice table again. If the table's primary key consists of the `LocationNo` and `InvoiceNo` fields, storing the name of the Location in each record would violate second normal form. This is because the `LocationName` field wouldn't be uniquely identified by the entirety of the primary key. It would depend only on the `LocationNo` field—the `InvoiceNo` field would have no effect on it. Instead, the `LocationName` field should be retrieved from the LOCATION table through a join whenever it's needed, not permanently stored in the INVOICE table.

Third Normal Form

In order for a table to be normalized in third normal form, each of its non-key fields must be fully dependent upon the table's primary key and independent of each other. So, along with meeting the qualifications of second normal form, each non-key field in a table must be independent of the other non-key fields.

Let's return to our INVOICE table example. Let's say that the primary key of the table is again both LocationNo and InvoiceNo. One of the non-key fields in the table would probably be the CustomerNo field. If, along with the CustomerNo field, the CustomerName field was also stored in the INVOICE table, the table would fail the criteria for third normal form because the CustomerNo and CustomerName fields would be dependent on one another. If the CustomerNo field was changed, certainly the CustomerName field would need to change with it, and vice versa. The CustomerName field should instead be left in the CUSTOMER table and accessed through a join when needed.

Fourth Normal Form

Fourth normal form prohibits independent entities from being stored in the same table when many-to-many relationships exist between them. Returning to the INVOICE table example, let's assume that only one item can be listed on each invoice, and that the INVOICE table includes a Vendor column and an Item column. The Vendor column refers to the seller of the item on the invoice, "Vendor X," for example. The Item column contains the company's code for a given type of product that it buys regularly, say, copy machine paper. There may be many records in the INVOICE table that refer to Vendor X—after all, Vendor X sells lots of things, not just copy machine paper. Likewise, there may be numerous records in the table that list copy machine paper—after all, the company buys it from a number of vendors, not just Vendor X. The columns then, Vendor and Item, are said to have a many-to-many relationship between them. For every Item in the INVOICE table, there may be numerous vendors, and for every Vendor in the INVOICE table there may be numerous items. Fourth normal form requires that you store these entities in separate tables and that you create a relation table for maintaining links with tables having many-to-many relations with other tables.

Of course, since the two columns have a many-to-many relationship between them, they aren't really independent in the first place, so they already violate third normal form. This is the reason fourth normal form is generally considered too esoteric to be of practical use in actual applications. The parts of it that matter are already covered by third normal form.

Fifth Normal Form

Fifth normal form requires that you be able to reconstruct your original data from the normalized tables into which it was translated. This means that if you start with tables that aren't normalized, you should be able to cut and paste your way back to them once they've been normalized. The main thing this accomplishes is help ensure that you don't lose any data in the process of normalization. For example, if you start with the INVOICE table, previously mentioned, that includes both a CustomerNo and a CustomerName column, normalizing the database should cause you to create a separate CUSTOMER table and move the CustomerName column to it. You would, of course, copy the CustomerNo column to the table as well. If you made the mistake of simply removing the CustomerName column from the INVOICE table, you wouldn't be able to reconstruct your original un-normalized table since CustomerName would no longer exist in your new design. Your design, then, would violate fifth normal form.

In practice, the concept of retaining all the elements in a database during normalization is so intuitive that it's a given. Of course you don't blindly throw away data elements. No one does. Nevertheless, fifth normal form exists to help you ensure that this is the case.

Normalize, But Don't Overdo It

Once you begin normalizing your data, it's important not to get too carried away. Overdoing it when normalizing can have a devastating effect on performance. For example, in a normalizing frenzy, you might be tempted to set up a separate table for the employer information currently stored in the TENANT table. After all, `Employer` and `EmpAddress` are clearly dependent upon one another in violation of third normal form. But what real benefit would you realize in doing this? None at all, actually. The fact is, each employer and its related information is only of interest to us in the context of the tenant with which it's associated. You have no need to list, for example, all tenants working for a given employer. Nor would you ever want to change all employer-related information *en masse*. Because of this, setting up a separate table for tenant employers would be a waste of time.

There are also times when *limited de-normalization* is the only way to get the performance you need. This is especially possible when working with large amounts of data. For example, suppose that you've built an application that processes hundreds of thousands of credit card receipts each day. Among other things, each receipt lists the card number, the amount of the transaction, and the card's expiration date. At the end of each day's work, your system needs to be able to print a report of all the credit cards used, the net amount of the day's transactions for each card, and the expiration date of each card. Because you can easily join to the base credit card table to retrieve the expiration date of each card, you wisely normalize the credit card transaction table by not storing the expiration date from the receipts in it.

Even though the expiration date is read from each credit card when it is used and sent to you as part of the receipt record, you elect not to use the one in the transaction itself, preferring instead to use the one from the credit card base table. This is a better relational design, but unfortunately that extra join you must do to retrieve the expiration date makes the report run twice as long. It runs so long, in fact, that your client finds the application's performance unacceptable.

Speaking only in terms of database design, the answer to this, of course, is to store and use the expiration date as it is received in each transaction. Although this introduces redundancy into the database, it is *controlled redundancy*, which is done by design for a specific purpose. This is an acceptable deviation from strict relational database theory.

The rule to follow when introducing controlled redundancy into a database design is to *first* fully normalize the database, *then* introduce redundancy only where absolutely necessary.

Database Rules

Now that the tables are completely normalized, the next step is to define the database-level rules for each table. These rules further define the relationships between the tables and the characteristics of each field.

Keys

Key fields identify the access methods that you intend to use to get at a table's rows. Keys you select in this stage will translate later into indexes. Pick all the keys you need, but don't select fields as keys unnecessarily. Unneeded indexes waste disk space and slow down your DBMS. Also, don't bother selecting the first field or fields of a composite key as a separate key. For example, if Location and InvoiceNo form the primary key for the INVOICE table, there's no need to also flag Location as a separate key. Nearly all DBMS's support partial key searches, so creating an index over the Location column, for example, would waste disk space and DBMS resources.

> **NOTE**
>
> Note that partial key searches only work left-to-right, not right-to-left. So, given the preceding example, if you wanted to search the INVOICE table using only the InvoiceNo column, you'd need a separate index on the InvoiceNo column.

> **NOTE**
>
> Also keep in mind that, unlike dBASE and Paradox tables, SQL tables do not have a natural row order. Even when a table is indexed, you can't count on rows being returned in a particular order without specifying that order in your queries. Of course, in practice, rows usually follow the order of a table's clustered index, if the server supports clustered indexes and one has been created. Remember, though, that SQL itself does not assume any natural table order and expressly forbids any such assumptions in queries. One of the major principles of SQL is that elements that affect the result set returned by a query should be defined by the query, not by the presence or absence of trivialities like indexes. Look at indexes as a way to improve your database performance, don't look at them as a means of ordering data.

Primary Keys

Review the tables in your database and specify a primary key for each. In my diagrams, I label each field of a primary key with a capital *P*, followed by a superscripted number signifying its order in the composite key, if applicable. See Figure 6.2 for an illustration of this.

Keep in mind that the primary key can be a composite key—it can be made of more than one field. The primary key you select should be inherently unique and should be the most popular access path you plan to take into the table's data. That is, think about the way in which a table's data will be used. How will it most often be queried? What field(s) in this table might another table reference in a constraint? (See the section later in this chapter on Constraints for more information). For example, using the TENANT table described earlier, it's obvious that tenant records are uniquely identified by the TenantNo field. This field will, no doubt, be used to govern constraints established in other tables. It's therefore the logical choice as TENANT's primary key.

Note that the column or columns you identify as a table's primary key will be used to construct a primary key constraint, as outlined later. Creating a primary key constraint not only forces values to be unique within a column, it also creates a unique index over the column.

Secondary Keys

Use secondary keys to establish secondary access paths into a table. These are less popular but essential paths into the data. Don't get too carried away—later the key selections you've made here will be translated into indexes, and needless indexes waste disk space and slow down your DBMS. Creating a new index from scratch takes less time than incrementally maintaining the index for many SQL servers. This is exactly the opposite of performance issues usually observed in PC databases. SQLApps often create secondary indexes only when needed, and destroy them afterwards.

Flag fields as secondary keys that you think might participate in a join, especially as the right side of an outer join. Also establish fields as secondary keys that you think users will frequently use to search the table. In my diagrams, I use an uppercase "S" followed by a number signifying the secondary key's order among the other secondary keys. I superscript a second number to designate the field's order in a composite key, if applicable.

TIP

Remember that there's no reason to flag the first field or fields of a composite key as a separate key. Nearly all database platforms support partial left-to-right key searches, so you'll still get index-type access when you query a table using the first field(s) of a multi-part key.

Constraints

There are three basic types of constraints: primary key constraints, foreign key constraints, and check constraints (some platforms refer to column defaults as constraints, as well; column default are discussed later in the section entitled "Defaults"). Primary key constraints ensure that values are unique within a table. Foreign key constraints ensure that values in one table exist in another. Check constraints guarantee that a column's values meet a given set of criteria.

Primary Key Constraints

Primary key constraints ensure that the data contained in a given column is unique across a table. Creating a primary key constraint also creates a unique index over the column in question. If you attempt to insert a duplicate value into a column that has a primary key constraint attached to it, your INSERT operation will fail.

Foreign Key Constraints

Next up are foreign key constraints. Foreign key constraints are *foreign* in that they are not the table's primary key, but instead exist as the primary key of a different, or foreign, table. Establishing a foreign key constraint does two things: first, it creates an index on the relevant column in the host table, and, second, it creates a bi-directional integrity constraint between the host table and the foreign table.

Using the PROPERTY table as described, an obvious foreign key would be the TenantNo field. This is because you would naturally only want values in PROPERTY's TenantNo column that also exist in the TENANT table.

Foreign key constraints are bi-directional in nature. That is, not only does the constraint restrict the values a field may have, but once a value is stored in the field, it prevents the deletion or modification of the corresponding value in the second table. For example, using the TENANT and PROPERTY tables mentioned previously, the TenantNo field in the PROPERTY table must allow only tenant numbers that exist in the TENANT table. Likewise, once a given tenant number is stored in the PROPERTY table, the corresponding record in the TENANT table must not be deleted. Doing so would orphan the TenantNo stored in the PROPERTY table and would prevent using it to determine the current inhabitants of the property. In my diagrams, I use an uppercase "F" followed by a number signifying the foreign key's order among the other foreign keys. I superscript a second number to designate the field's order in a multi-field (composite) foreign key, if applicable. See Figure 6.2 for an illustration of this.

Check Constraints

Check constraints ensure that a value matches a given criteria or is a member of a specific set of values before it is allowed into a field. A check constraint's governing criteria is fixed—it's something you come up with at design time. For example, using the PROPERTY table from the preceding example, you might want to restrict the allowable values for the GarageType field to 0-4 because you know that all of the properties either have no garage (type 0) or have a one-, two-, three-, or four-car garage, respectively. In my diagrams, a field with a check constraint attached to it is identified with a line connecting it to a rectangle containing the governing criteria, as seen in Figure 6.2.

> **NOTE**
>
> Though you can define column defaults and check constraints using Delphi's Database Explorer, I recommend you only do this as a last resort. You should only implement a data integrity or business rule on the client-side of a database application when you aren't able to build the rule into the database itself. You should place as much of your business rules implementation as possible on your server or in your local DBMS in order to ensure that they are respected by as many tools and applications as possible.

Defaults

The next class of database rules to establish are the default values for the fields in each table. Review each table and determine which, if any, of the fields should have a default value assigned to them. Normally, you set up defaults for fields that you may want to omit explicitly setting at runtime. For example, using the PROPERTY table, you might default the Range field to True because the rental company normally provides an electric range in all its properties. In my diagrams, I signify a field's default value using an equal sign and the value to the right of the field definition, as illustrated in Figure 6.2.

> **NOTE**
>
> Though you can change a field's default value once it's been created when using local tables, you can't do so on many database server platforms, including InterBase. If you want to define a default value for a server-based column, chances are that you'll need to establish it when you create the table.

Create the Database Objects

Once the inter-table dependencies, rules, keys, and so on have all been defined, your database design is basically complete. You are now ready to implement this design by creating the corresponding database objects. This entails creating a database in which to store your database objects, if necessary, then creating the tables, indexes, constraints, rules, defaults, etc., necessary to actualize your design.

It's important to realize the correlation between database design elements and physical database objects. Often there is a one-to-one correspondence. Table 6.1 summarizes these relationships.

Table 6.1. Correlation of database design elements and database objects.

Design element	Database object
Database	Database
Table	Table
Primary key	Primary key constraint, unique index
Secondary key	Secondary index
Foreign key	Foreign key constraint, secondary index
Check constraint	Check constraint or trigger
Default	Default constraint or trigger

NOTE

The examples in the following sections show you how to use SQL to create your database objects. You could actually use any tool you like so long as it's able to create the database objects you need. I use SQL in the following sections because it enables you to look under the hood, so to speak, and see the fine details of what's involved with creating your database objects. SQL is also fairly pervasive; most database tools speak some dialect of SQL.

Creating the Database

You may need to create a database before you can even get started implementing your database design. This may consist of a directory or folder on a disk drive for local DBMS's or an actual server-based database object for remote ones. Obviously, if you merely need to create a subdirectory, you'll use operating system commands to do so. If you need to create a database on a remote database server, you can usually use SQL to create it. The exact syntax and supported extensions of the SQL CREATE DATABASE command vary from platform to platform, but the following InterBase syntax should get you started:

```
CREATE DATABASE "C:\DATA\DELPHI\RENTMAN\RENTAL.GDB"
USER "SYSDBA" PASSWORD "masterkey"
LENGTH=100;
```

NOTE

Note that you can't use the CREATE DATABASE command from within InterBase's WISQL utility, you'll have to use the ISQL utility instead. WISQL prepares all queries before executing them and you can't prepare a CREATE DATABASE statement. WISQL has a separate menu item for creating a new database: File/Create Database.

Note the use of the C:\DATA\DELPHI\RENTMAN\RENTAL.GDB device. The database could theoretically consist of any number of device files, possibly spread across several different disk drives. This points out a major difference between client/server DBMSs and local DBMSs. Normally, local DBMSs, such as dBASE and Paradox, do not support spanning a single database object over multiple disk drives unless the underlying operating system can make the multiple drives appear as a single volume. High-end client/server systems do not suffer from this limitation.

Tables

If you wish, you can use the SQL you developed earlier as a starting point for creating your tables. You can also use a tool like Database Desktop to create them. If you're working with a client/server back-end, you may already have a tool of choice for doing these sorts of things.

Even though the establishment of keys and constraints is normally done at the same time a table is created, I've separated them here so that you can easily see the different functions performed by each task.

> **NOTE**
>
> The dBASE file format does not directly support many advanced database features like required fields and unique indexes. Consequently, as far as local DBMS's are concerned, the examples that follow will often apply only to Paradox. Paradox tables are my preferred file format when designing non-client/server database applications.
>
> When building client/server applications that are to run on a stand-alone machine, I utilize the Local InterBase Server (LIBS). It delivers full ANSI SQL support on stand-alone PCs and allows applications to be easily scaled up to utilize a separate database server when the time comes. The following examples should also work with LIBS.

Required Fields

One thing that you will probably establish at table creation time is which fields are required fields. Though it is certainly possible to implement required fields in your front-end only, I don't recommend this. If you flag a field as being required at the database level, you ensure that it's required regardless of the front-end.

In SQL, required fields are defined using the NOT NULL syntax. On some platforms NOT NULL is the default, but it's a good practice to specify it anyway. Fields that aren't required get the NULL designation. On most platforms, this designation is specified at the time the table is created and cannot be changed afterward.

NOTE

Delphi's Local SQL doesn't support the NULL/NOT NULL designation. Note that this limitation is only present in Delphi's Local SQL—the SQL dialect you use to query Paradox and dBASE tables. Borland's Local InterBase Server (LIBS) supports a full implementation of ANSI SQL syntax, including the use of NOT NULL to identify required fields.

When dealing with local tables, you can use Database Desktop to select which fields are required. Click the 1. Required Field checkbox in Database Desktop's Create Table dialog to flag a field as required.

TIP

The fact that Local SQL doesn't support the NULL syntax doesn't preclude you from using it anyway, provided your back-end supports it. Because the Borland Database Engine passes SQL statements for remote tables straight to the server, the SQL syntax you can use is limited only by what's supported on the back-end.

The following is a sample Local SQL CREATE TABLE command for the PROPERTY table that was mentioned previously:

```
CREATE TABLE "PROPERTY.DB"
(
PropertyNo      smallint,
TenantNo        smallint,
Address         varchar(30),
City            varchar(30),
State           char(2),
Zip             char(10),
Addition        varchar(20),
Beds            smallint ,
Living          smallint,
Baths           smallint,
GarageType      smallint,
SchoolDistrict  smallint,
Deposit         money,
Rent            money,
Range           boolean,
Refigerator     boolean,
DishWasher      boolean ,
CentralHeat     boolean,
CentralAir      boolean,
GasHeat         boolean,
PrivacyFence    boolean ,
LastSpray       date,
LastLawn        date
)
```

Now, here's that same SQL script customized for the InterBase platform:

```
CREATE TABLE PROPERTY
(
PropertyNo        INTEGER                   NOT NULL,
TenantNo          INTEGER,
Address           VARCHAR(30)               NOT NULL,
City              VARCHAR(20)               NOT NULL,
State             VARCHAR(2)                NOT NULL,
Zip               VARCHAR(10)               NOT NULL,
Addition          VARCHAR(15)               NOT NULL,
Beds              SMALLINT                  NOT NULL,
Living            SMALLINT                  NOT NULL,
Baths             SMALLINT                  NOT NULL,
GarageType        SMALLINT                  NOT NULL,
SchoolDistrict    VARCHAR(15)               NOT NULL,
Deposit           DOUBLE PRECISION          NOT NULL,
Rent              DOUBLE PRECISION          NOT NULL,
Range             VARCHAR(1)                NOT NULL,
Refrigerator      VARCHAR(1)                NOT NULL,
DishWasher        VARCHAR(1)                NOT NULL,
CentralHeat       VARCHAR(1)                NOT NULL,
CentralAir        VARCHAR(1)                NOT NULL,
GasHeat           VARCHAR(1)                NOT NULL,
PrivacyFence      VARCHAR(1)                NOT NULL,
LastSprayDate     DATE,
LastLawnDate      DATE,
PRIMARY KEY (PropertyNo)
);
```

And here it is tailored for the Sybase platform:

```
CREATE TABLE PROPERTY
(
PropertyNo        smallint         NOT NULL,
TenantNo          smallint         NOT NULL,
Address           varchar(30)      NOT NULL,
City              varchar(30)      NOT NULL,
State             char(2)          NOT NULL,
Zip               char(10)         NOT NULL,
Addition          varchar(20)      NOT NULL,
Beds              tinyint          NOT NULL,
Living            tinyint          NOT NULL,
Baths             tinyint          NOT NULL,
GarageType        tinyint          NOT NULL,
SchoolDistrict    tinyint          NOT NULL,
Deposit           smallmoney       NOT NULL,
Rent              smallmoney       NOT NULL,
Range             bit              NOT NULL,
Refigerator       bit              NOT NULL,
DishWasher        bit              NOT NULL,
CentralHeat       bit              NOT NULL,
CentralAir        bit              NOT NULL,
GasHeat           bit              NOT NULL,
PrivacyFence      bit              NOT NULL,
LastSpray         smalldatetime
LastLawn          smalldatetime
)
```

Note the use of the NULL/NOT NULL designation to flag fields as either optional, or required, respectively.

NOTE

InterBase, like all ANSI SQL '92 compliant servers, defaults to allowing null values in columns. If you attempt to redundantly flag a column with NULL in a CREATE TABLE statement, your create operation will fail. You should therefore simply leave the designation off of columns that are to allow null values. Sybase, by contrast, defaults to the NOT NULL designation (though you can change this via a server configuration switch), but you can still flag fields with NOT NULL in your CREATE TABLE statements without error. As I've said, if your server allows it, I recommend you always spell out the NULL/NOT NULL designation when you create tables.

Primary Keys

Once you've created the table and established which fields are required, you're ready to specify the table's primary key. In SQL, you do this with the PRIMARY KEY constraint. Although you could have specified it when you originally created the table, I've separated the two tasks so that you can easily distinguish them from one another. To designate its primary key once a table has been created, you use the SQL ALTER TABLE command. Its syntax is as follows:

```
ALTER TABLE PROPERTY
ADD PRIMARY KEY (PropertyNo)
```

Specifying a primary key constraint also creates a unique index over the specified columns. In terms of indexing, creating the primary constraint executes Data Definition Language (DDL) statements similar to the following:

```
CREATE UNIQUE INDEX RDB$PRIMARY1 ON PROPERTY (PropertyNo)
```

Secondary Keys

Once your primary keys are created, you're ready to establish your secondary keys. As mentioned, secondary keys establish secondary access paths into a table. These are less traveled but important paths into the data. An example of a secondary key for the PROPERTY table would be the Address column. It's likely that a user of the table would want to look up a piece of property using its street address rather than its property number. By creating a secondary index on Address, you help speed this access. You use the CREATE INDEX command to create secondary indexes. Here's an example:

```
CREATE INDEX PROPERTY02 ON PROPERTY (Address)
```

Foreign Keys

Once you've defined your primary and secondary keys, the next step is to define your foreign key constraints. As mentioned, foreign keys are fields in a table that reference primary keys in other tables. In the preceding example, the TenantNo field in the PROPERTY table is a foreign key. Though it does not uniquely identify the records in the PROPERTY table, and, hence, is not the table's primary key, it is the primary key of the TENANT table. To apply a foreign key constraint to the TenantNo field in the PROPERTY table, the following syntax is used:

```
ALTER TABLE PROPERTY
ADD CONSTRAINT INVALID_TenantNo FOREIGN KEY (TENANTNO)
REFERENCES TENANT(TENANTNO)
```

Defining a foreign key constraint creates a secondary index over the column(s) in question. In terms of indexing, creating the preceding foreign key constraint executes a DDL statement similar to the following:

```
CREATE INDEX RDB$FOREIGN4 ON PROPERTY (TenantNo)
```

Constraints

A check constraint is one that references a fixed set of values. As mentioned before, a prime example of the use of such a constraint is the GarageType field in the PROPERTY table. You know that all the properties owned by the rental company have one- to four-car garages, or no garage at all, so you can safely limit the values in the GarageType field to 0-4. You could code a constraint to do this using the following SQL syntax:

```
ALTER TABLE PROPERTY
ADD CONSTRAINT INVALID_GARAGETYPE CHECK (GarageType>=0 and GarageType<=4)
```

Defaults

Next on the list is the establishment of default values for the fields in each table. Don't be surprised if you're unable to supply a large number of fields with default values—there will be many where this simply isn't possible. Sometimes, though, it's helpful to establish default field values in advance—especially in data-entry intensive applications. In applications of this type, your users will be especially appreciative of any keystrokes you can save them by defaulting field values where possible.

Resist the temptation to build default field values into your front-end application. The proper place for such mechanisms is in the database itself. This is fundamental to proper database design. It is most appropriately a database, not an application, task. Placing defaults on the database itself ensures that, regardless of the front-end, columns receive appropriate values when a row is added to a table.

Delphi automatically detects column default values and reflects them when you add records to a DataSet. The SQL required to add a defaulted column to an existing table takes the form:

```
ALTER TABLE TENANT
ADD RentDueDay SMALLINT
DEFAULT 15
```

Triggers

A trigger is a typically small compiled SQL program that executes when a given event occurs on a table. The three events most commonly associated with triggers are row inserts, deletions, and updates. On some platforms, you're also able to specify whether a trigger executes before or after an event, as well.

If your database design includes a master/detail relationship between two or more tables, you may need to make use of a trigger to keep them synchronized. This is especially true if your DBMS platform does not support cascading deletes. A cascading delete replicates a record deletion in a master table through its dependent tables. That is, deleting a row in the master table causes a "ripple effect" through its related detail tables, deleting all related rows in those detail tables.

Though SQL's constraint mechanism covers most referential integrity bases, cascading deletes is one it may not cover, depending on your platform. If you need to create a trigger to handle cascading deletes, the basic syntax is as follows:

```
CREATE TRIGGER Delete_Detail FOR WORDERS
  BEFORE DELETE
    POSITION 0
  AS BEGIN
    DELETE FROM WODETAIL
    WHERE WODETAIL.WorkOrderNo=Old.WorkOrderNo;
  END
```

Notice the use of the logical "Old" table. This is the mechanism whereby you refer to the values in the row about to be deleted in the associated table. Be aware of the danger of modifying a primary key field in an insertion trigger: the row changes location after BDE posts it, so BDE is unaware the row has moved.

> **NOTE**
>
> The Sybase equivalent of the logical "Old" table in the preceding example is named "deleted." You can use it to refer to columns in a row that's about to be deleted. You can also use the logical "inserted" table to refer to values about to be added to the table.

Craft the Rest of the Database

Repeat this process for every table in your database design. Each table will present its own challenges and nuances, but soon you will have a database foundation on which you can build a robust database application.

What's Ahead

In the next chapter, you'll see how the five formal processes for building database applications apply to designing the applications themselves. You'll take the concepts inherent in the five formal processes and learn to use them in the design and construction of database applications. Such things as form creation, application motifs, user-interface considerations, and testing your applications will be discussed in Chapter 7, "Application Design 101."

Summary

In this chapter, you were introduced to the five formal processes for building database applications. You learned to apply the parts of these processes that relate to databases to designing your database foundation and its relevant objects. The chapter concluded with showing you how to translate your design into actual database objects. Here's a list of the subjects broached in this chapter:

- Defining the purpose and goals of your application
- Designing the requisite database foundation and application processes
- Data modeling
- Database terms
- Refining your goals into operational processes
- Determining the database objects needed to service your processes
- Constructing a field repository from which to build table definitions
- Coding your definitions in SQL
- Organizing your tables by type
- Visually relating your tables
- Setting up data flow diagrams
- Normalizing your database
- Database rules, keys, constraints, and defaults
- Creating your database objects
- Creating the database itself
- Constructing tables
- Flagging required fields
- Setting up primary, secondary, and foreign keys
- Creating defaults and triggers

7

Application Design 101

The previous chapter listed the five processes or stages of database application development. To reiterate, the five steps are:

1. Define the purpose and goals of the application.
2. Design the database foundation and application processes needed to meet those goals.
3. Develop the design into an application by creating the requisite database and program objects.
4. Test the application for compliance with the established goals.
5. Install the application for production use.

Chapter 6, "Database Design 101," focused on the elements of the five processes that relate to database design. This chapter focuses on their relation to application design. Because database design and application design are so closely related, it's difficult to determine where one ends and the other begins. I tend to think of database application design in terms of a grid with two columns—one for database design and one for application design—whose rows consist of the five formal processes. Use whatever analogy works best for you. The key thing is to understand that database design and application design are inseparably linked.

Let's now pick up where we left off in Chapter 6 and continue with the five formal processes for designing database applications.

> **NOTE**
>
> At this point, you should already have constructed your database, as outlined in Chapter 6. Your tables, rules, constraints, indexes, triggers, and defaults should all be in place before proceeding.

Designing the Database Foundation and Application Processes

Now that the database foundation has been laid, it's time to move on to building the application processes needed to meet your application's goals. The database acts as a platform on which the rest of the application is built. It's important to finalize it as much as possible before getting too far into the application-building phase. Changes made to the database after the application is built can result in significant portions of the application having to be redesigned or rewritten.

A Word About Software Development

Before we get down to the business of designing applications, I'd like to give you my thoughts on software development as a whole. This is just an aside, but I think it's very important that you keep what you're doing in perspective as you design applications.

There's no "right way" to develop applications. No single system covers all application software development. Like the master chef who sometimes works from his head and sometimes from a recipe, you'll want to decide for yourself when to go "by the book" and when to "wing it." The object, here, is to find an approach that works best for you and that works for most of the development you do—then stick with it.

Software development is considered by most people to be a science. Some view it as an artistic science, but a science nonetheless. After all, you earn a BS, *not* a BA, in Computer *Science*, not Computer *Art*. There's no class on artistic software development, no course named "Software Craftsmanship 101." I nevertheless view software development as more of an art or a craft than a science. The distinction between art and craft being that a craft is utilitarian in purpose—things produced by means of a craft have a use beyond that of artistic appreciation.

Like carpentry, pottery, and other crafts, software development must abide by certain physical laws in order to produce desirable results. After all, even the potter knows to use good clay when making his pots or risk having them fall apart. The carpenter uses a level to ensure the straightness of his work and a square to ensure the accuracy of its angles. But that's where it ends. The potter can make whatever he wants and still call it pottery. The carpenter can build whatever fancies him, innovating to his heart's content, and the fruit of his labor will still be carpentry. And the process the craftsman uses to craft his work, whether it be with his bare hands, with a hammer and saw, or with tools of his own making, is largely irrelevant. The emphasis is on the object, not the means of creating it. Thus, there's no "right way" to make pottery. There's no fixed set of steps that carpenters always follow when building things. So it is with software development.

The world of software development today reminds me of the furniture industry of the mid-nineteenth century. For time immemorial, furniture had been constructed one piece at a time, in a shop full of highly skilled craftsmen. Each craftsman built the pieces of furniture he worked on from start to finish. Each piece was hand-tooled and built with such precision that the craftsman proudly inscribed his name on it. It was his personal guarantee that the piece was as good as he could make it.

Then came the Industrial Revolution. Suddenly, craftsmanship was out and glue and staples were in. High quality was out and low price was in. A streamlined, cost-cutting process was developed for constructing furniture quickly. The process became manufacturing, rather than creating—the builders were assembly-line workers, not craftsmen.

A natural outgrowth of this departure from craftsmanship was the use of machines to build furniture. In conjunction with the assembly-line mentality that preceded it, mechanized furniture manufacturing all but eliminated the need for humans to build furniture. The upshot of all this was that the quality of the furniture being produced went down dramatically. Because machines necessarily operate using a prescribed, fixed set of steps in doing what they do, innovation suffered as well. No longer did the individual craftsman guarantee his work—there were no craftsmen. The skills of those humans involved with furniture manufacturing were dumbed down to that of mere worker bees, with little or no thought for individuality, creativity, or making a quality product.

This sort of assembly-line mentality is pervasive through most of American industry, not just the furniture business. It has brought with it both blessings and curses. True, most goods can be produced more cheaply now than ever before. But at what cost? Are we really getting the *same* goods cheaper, or are we getting *cheaper* goods cheaper? And has the extinction of the skilled craftsman actually made quality goods more, not less, expensive?

What does all this have to do with database application development? Simple. Remember, it all began with reducing what was essentially a craft to mere manual labor that *anyone*, skilled or not, could do. Machines were left to do the real work. With this degradation came the inevitable consequence of lower quality goods and the virtual elimination of innovation. Software development could certainly suffer the same fate. The school of thought that says there is a "right way" and a "wrong way" to develop applications denies the software craftsman the freedom to leave his own mark on his creation. It stymies creativity and leaves scant room for innovation. This is why I contend there's no "right way" to build software. Just as there's no "right way" to make pottery or do carpentry, there's no fixed set of steps that will produce a good application every time.

So, bear this in mind when you sit down to write database applications. I've purposely avoided arranging this chapter and the preceding one as some sort of series of concrete steps that one always follows to the letter when developing database applications. The suggestions I've given you are just that: suggestions. Use the ones you find useful; omit those you do not.

Decide the Type of Application

The first step in designing the processes that make up an application is to decide exactly what type of application you're building. Applications can be organized into two distinct types: transaction processing systems and decision support systems. Generally speaking, decision support systems are utilized by management to achieve a bird's-eye view of some portion of a company's data. Transaction processing systems, on the other hand, are responsible for the entry and manipulation of this data. Decision support applications need only access data in a read-only fashion. Transaction processing systems need to be able to both read *and* write data. Because of this fundamental difference between the two types of applications, you need to decide what type of application you plan to build before getting started.

Chart the Application's Operational Processes

Using the list of operational processes you developed in Chapter 6, chart the flow of each separate application process graphically. You can use formal flow-charting symbols or just handwritten statements of what is to happen procedurally in the application—whatever works for you. Figures 7.1 and 7.2 illustrate a couple of different approaches to flow charting. The level of detail you need to go to here depends on a number of factors. First, you may be able to mentally envision the processes that make up the application without needing to lay them out visually. Second, the application may be simple enough so as not to need any complex flow charting. Third, time constraints may be such that you don't have the luxury of spending as much time planning as you might like. Whatever the case, be sure that you fully understand each operational process in your application before proceeding.

FIGURE 7.1.

A simple approach to process flow charting.

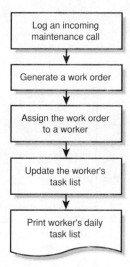

Visually Link Related Processes

Once you've charted the operational processes that make up the application, visually link any related processes. For example, if a battery of reports is to be printed each month following a closing process, show the link between the two processes.

Once you've visually linked related processes, construct a chart that overviews the application, a system flow chart, if you will. Although a given piece of data may not go through all the operational processes that make up your application, build a schematic that illustrates the processes that make up the application anyway. This will give you a better overall understanding of the scope of the application.

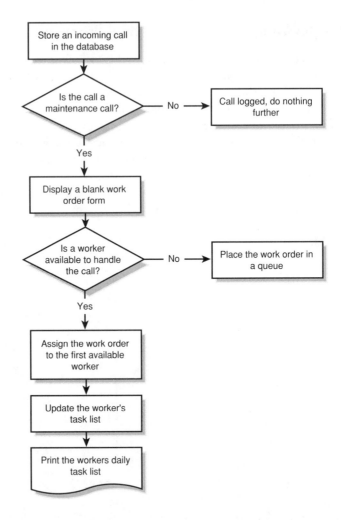

FIGURE 7.2.

A more formal approach to process flow charting.

Label Operational Elements by Type

Next, you should go through the elements that make up your operational processes and label each one according to the type it represents. Decide which nodes will have corresponding forms or reports and which will have non-interactive support code. Each node should have one of these associated with it. Within those elements that have associated forms, decide what type of forms they will have. Will the form be a decision support form, a transaction support form, or a data-entry form? Label the elements that make up your operational processes accordingly. I usually go ahead and label each node with the name I intend to use for the corresponding form, report, or source code unit. Figure 7.3 illustrates this labeling technique.

FIGURE 7.3.

The nodes within application processes labeled by type.

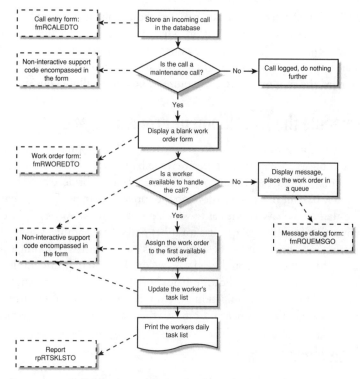

Design Form and Report Hierarchies

Once you've roughly determined what forms and reports are needed by your application, design a separate hierarchy for your forms and reports to take advantage of Delphi's visual form inheritance support. That is, organize your forms and reports into general classes that build upon one another. For example, you should define a top-level form for your application from which all others will descend. If you later need to change an attribute of all the forms in your application, chances are you'll be able to make the change in just one place. The same is true for the report form hierarchy. Since you'll probably end up designing most of your reports using Delphi's QuickReport components, it makes sense to design a report form hierarchy, as well.

Identify and Acquire Third-Party Support Code

Once you've gone through this process, attempt to determine which, if any, support libraries and third-party code you might need. One popular library that I make use of in my Delphi applications is the Orpheus Visual Component Library from TurboPower Software. Another is Asynch Professional, from the same vendor. In a large shop, you may need to speak with another team leader or resource manager about utilizing support libraries that have been developed internally by the organization. The time when you decide which processes will have associated forms and which will have associated non-interactive code is a good time to determine what support libraries you might need. Far better to do this now than to delay until you actually need the support library to acquire it, possibly stalling your project until it arrives.

Schedule the Development Process

The next thing you need to do is schedule the development of the forms and support code your application requires. There are three basic factors that affect this scheduling. First, your client may require that certain parts of the application be developed before others. For example, you may be commissioned to develop the application in pieces, deploying each piece separately. The client may have an idea as to which pieces he'd like to see first. Second, some parts of the application may be prerequisites for other parts. For example, you may need to develop a suite of string-handling routines before you can proceed with developing a routine that parses a text file. If this is the case, you'll need to develop these prerequisite modules first. Third, developing some parts of the application before others may aid you in your development effort. For example, building an application's main form prior to its other forms will assist you in building these other forms since you can test them at runtime from the main form's menu.

Time Lines

The process of scheduling a project along a time line is indeed a black art. It's a complex process that varies from individual to individual. It's further complicated by the prospect of team development efforts. I'm not as interested in the amount of time needed to complete your application as I am in the order of events. I'll leave the time estimates to you (after all, that's what they pay *you* for!).

Build the Application

Next up is the actual development of the application according to the schedule you've constructed. The craft of developing source code in a structured manner is outside the scope of this book. Keep in mind that the emphasis on *source code* design has been lessened a great deal by the emergence of visual tools like Delphi. The emphasis has instead shifted to *form* design, which is covered in the next section.

Form Design

The approach you take to form design depends heavily on the type of application you're building and on the type of forms you're building for that application. This is why it's important to decide the application and form types in advance, as mentioned previously.

The following comments are some general guidelines on form design. Again, many of these are subjective—use only the ones you find helpful. They're divided into four sections: guidelines that apply to all forms, those that apply to decision support forms, those that apply to transaction processing forms, and those that apply to data-entry forms.

■ Decide on a *motif.* An important decision you'll want to make early on regarding your application's visual appearance is that of an application *motif.* The motif you select governs the visual appearance of the forms that make up the application. Three popular motifs are already in widespread use in the world of Windows applications. They are: Corel PerfectOffice, Lotus SmartSuite, and Microsoft Office. If you choose the Corel PerfectOffice motif, your application and the forms in it will resemble Quattro Pro and WordPerfect. If you choose SmartSuite, your application will resemble Lotus 1-2-3 and WordPro. If you choose Microsoft Office, you'll imitate Word and Excel. Figures 7.4, 7.5, and 7.6 show an example of each of the interfaces.

FIGURE 7.4.

The Novell PerfectOffice interface.

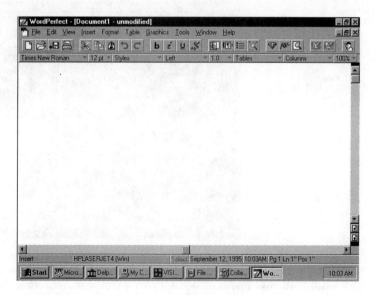

FIGURE 7.5.

The Microsoft Office interface.

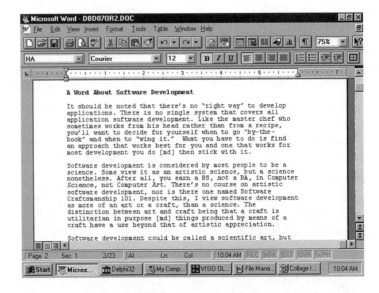

FIGURE 7.6.

The Lotus SmartSuite interface.

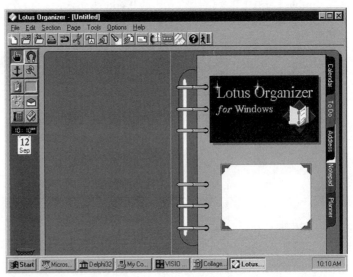

The obvious reason for adhering to an already-established user-interface motif is that your users will enjoy instant familiarity with your application and find it easier to get up to speed. Additionally, mimicking a major vendor's visual interface gives your application a seemingly more professional appearance.

■ Don't add unneeded features. Inundating your client with useless information wastes his time and yours. Pretend you're the user of the application, then determine what features would and would not be useful to you. Too often, language features or nifty interface elements determine what functions make it into an application. The user's needs should instead determine what it is that the application does.

■ Construct a separate hierarchy for your forms and reports in order to take advantage of Delphi's visual form inheritance support. Create a top-level form for your application from which all others will descend. If you later need to change some facet of all the forms in your application, chances are you'll be able to change just the top form. This is also true for the report form hierarchy. Since you'll probably create most of your reports using Delphi's QuickReport components, you'll want to create a report form hierarchy, as well.

■ Be consistent, both internally and externally. *Internal consistency* involves being consistent from form to form. Utilizing a form hierarchy should help you with this. *External consistency* means being consistent with other applications. This is why I suggest you choose a motif early on. The fonts, background colors, size of display elements, toolbar placement, and so on, should match other mainstream Windows applications.

■ Build SDI, not MDI, forms. There was a time when MDI (Multiple Document Interface) forms were preferred over SDI (Single Document Interface) forms. Alas, the pendulum has again swung the other direction and now Microsoft recommends that applications adhere to the SDI convention. This is just a general guideline, and there's certainly something to be said for MDI applications. However it appears, at least for now, that the trend is toward the SDI interface.

■ Don't display more than one type of information on a single form. For example, don't display both invoices and payment vouchers on the same screen—keep the form as straightforward as possible. Usually, a form should not encompass more than one type of source document at a time.

■ Make use of Windows' common dialog boxes. It's silly to build your own open and save dialogs when Windows already provides them. Delphi envelopes the standard Windows dialogs in easy-to-use components that you can simply drop onto a form. Use these where possible to save yourself time and to conserve system resource usage. You can find Delphi's dialog components on the Dialogs page in the component palette.

■ Use a neutral background color (such as clBtnFace which defaults to gray) for your forms. This affords a more professional look, is easier on the eyes, and displays properly on more types of video cards and monitors than louder colors.

■ Use SpeedButton groups to show the mode an application is currently in. You can set up a SpeedButton group by setting the GroupIndex property of a set of SpeedButtons to a non-zero number. You'll also want to set the group's AllowAllUp property to False. SpeedButtons defined this way stay down when clicked until another button in the group is clicked, much like the buttons on old push-button car radios. If your application can only have one of several modes at a time, this is an effective means of both allowing the mode to be easily changed and displaying the application's current mode simultaneously. Note that you can set an individual SpeedButton's Down property to True to cause it to appear in the down position.

■ Present large mouse targets. Large buttons and easily located radio button groups make applications easier to navigate than a form that's chock-full of microscopic controls.

■ Include a menu option for each button on a form and include menu items for commands not on forms. For those that prefer the use of the keyboard over the mouse, this can be a big time-saver. Also, by providing keyboard shortcuts for the options in your applications, you provide support for voice recognition programs that pull off their magic using keyboard macros.

■ Include menu accelerators for commonly used menu commands. If you want to add an accelerator key to a form without associating it with a menu item, first create a dummy menu item with the desired accelerator key and attach the code you want to execute to the item's OnClick event. Next, make the menu item invisible (at runtime) by setting its Visible property to False in the Object Inspector. When your application runs, the accelerator key will still be active, even though the menu item is hidden.

■ Establish label accelerators for key fields on a form. To do this, first establish a label accelerator key using a Label control's Caption property (use the & character to denote the accelerator key). Next, set the FocusControl property of the Label control to the component that is to receive the input focus when the Label's accelerator is pressed.

■ The location and function of navigation devices should be the same from form to form and between applications. If you locate a DBNavigator control at the bottom of one form and the top of the next, you aren't being consistent within the application and could conceivably confuse your users. It's far better to locate controls that perform the same or similar functions in the same place on each form.

■ Use a consistent font for button captions. It's important to keep user-interface elements as unobtrusive as possible. If a user has to stop and squint to try to read a label on a button, you've failed in this task. It's preferable to have some buttons that are larger than they really need to be than to try to economize every inch of screen space.

■ In my opinion, sans serif fonts are easier to read than fonts with serifs. Use sans serif fonts like Arial rather than those with serifs, like Times New Roman, when possible.

■ Use fly-over hints. Fly-over hints are the little pop-up labels that display when the mouse pointer pauses over some significant screen element. These are great for letting a user know what a given control does (especially a toolbar button) without clicking it.

■ Include on-line help in your applications. Professional Windows applications include a complete on-line help database that includes links between related topics. You should also set up your forms to support context-sensitive help. You do this with the `HelpContext` property of the form and the controls on it. When help is then requested while a given control on a form has focus, the Windows help facility will automatically jump to the relevant topic in your help database. See Chapter 13, "Finishing Touches," to learn more about developing Windows help files.

■ Build an About Box form and include your application's name, its current version number, and the name of your company (if applicable). You might also consider providing a technical support phone number, a copyright notice, if applicable, and information on Windows resource usage. The product name, version number and copyright notice should be linked into your application using a Windows VERSIONINFO resource. See Chapter 13 for more information about including version resources.

■ Include a toolbar in your applications. This is done in all three of the application design motifs discussed earlier and is the convention in modern Windows applications. Delphi includes a special `TSpeedButton` component just for this purpose.

■ Include a status bar in your applications. You can use the built-in Windows 95 StatusBar component for this. You can find the StatusBar component on the Win95 page in the component palette.

■ Establish a default field (by setting its `TabOrder` to `0`) on forms that include input fields.

■ Use the page and tab controls to condense large numbers of controls into a relatively small screen space. This is now the preferred approach in Windows 95 and has been a standard convention in Borland products for years.

■ Associate a distinctive icon with your application. This is not a form issue but a user-interface issue nonetheless. The application icon you establish is the one that appears in the Windows Explorer and in the Alt+Tab "cool switch" list, so it's important that your users are able to distinguish it from other applications. Set the icon associated with a Delphi application using the Project/Options/Application menu selection in the Delphi IDE.

■ Target your forms for the lowest screen resolution in use by your users. This is probably VGA resolution, so you can safely target VGA's 640×480 resolution in your forms. The best way to do this is to switch the resolution on your own video adapter to VGA. Forms you develop at resolutions too high for VGA to display properly will be clipped to fit it—something you obviously want to avoid.

■ Do not rely on on-line help to explain the basic use of your application. In most cases, its use should be obvious without having to dig though a manual or read the on-line help.

■ Prototype the forms you create as soon as possible for your clients so that you can be sure they share your vision for the application's visual interface. I've found that Delphi itself is ideal for this—in many cases, I've designed forms with the client right at my side.

Decision Support Forms

Decision support forms are typically used by people who, while possibly not the most computer-literate people in an organization, typically wield more influence than other types of users. They need *decision* support applications because they have some role in the decision-making process. There is a truism about such users: the level of computer skill they have acquired is inversely proportional to the level of management at which they reside. Thus, the challenge with decision support forms is to keep them simple, yet informative. The following suggestions will help you to do that.

■ Occupy most of the display area. Typically, managers like to see things as simplified and spread out as possible. You may also find that the managers at your organization rarely run more than one application at a time under Windows, so maximizing your application's form windows is a permissible thing to do.

■ Keep it simple; avoid cluttering a form with a large amount of detail or tabular data. Generally, managers want just the facts, and they want them as palatable and simple as possible. Don't bother with large amounts of transactional data—the manager probably isn't interested in it.

■ Use graphs where possible to visually display the relevance of data to other data. Depending on the manager, graphs can be a very powerful way of summarizing complex data sets. If the manager is comfortable with abandoning raw figures in favor of graphical ones, graphs can give your application a very polished and professional appearance with a minimum of effort. You should still, however, provide a means of "drilling down" to the underlying raw data, lest the manager attempt to glean exact figures from your charts.

■ Remove list components and other data-entry niceties if the application reads, but does not write, data. If the decision support application is to be used merely to report on and view data, data-entry support devices (such as DBListBox or DBLookupComboBox controls) can and should be removed to conserve system resources. You can replace these list components with DBText or even TLabel controls to display description-type fields without resorting to a full-blown combo-box or list box component.

- Control access to the data from the database or network server—avoid application-based security. Management-level users tend to dislike messages telling them that they lack access rights for a particular application function, so avoid these where possible.

- Do not include functions in the application that the management personnel who use the application cannot access. Avoid grayed-out menu items and disabled buttons as this could tend to confuse them. If an option is not available to a given user of a decision support application, set its `Visible` property to `False` and make it invisible (or remove it altogether), rather than merely disabling it.

Interactive Forms

Second only to decision support forms, interactive forms are the form type most often found in applications. They provide the means whereby data is normally entered, edited, and deleted. The typical user of an interactive form is someone who is more computer-literate than those at the manager level in an organization. These persons might be administrative assistants, computer operators, or other clerical personnel. An interactive form, then, needs to be as straightforward as possible and as conducive to effective data navigation and manipulation as possible.

- Consider augmenting or replacing Delphi's `DBNavigator` buttons with standard buttons. Though powerful and easy to use, the `DBNavigator` control lacks certain basic features like a search facility and the ability to assign accelerator keys or labels to its built-in buttons.

- Group controls for ease of use. Arrange controls in such a way as to make their selection intuitive and logical. Place related controls in close proximity to one another. Align related radio group items. Place related buttons next to each other. This will help your users become familiar with your forms more quickly and will help avoid user errors.

- Use accelerator keys for command buttons and entry fields. Accelerator keys are a must, especially for the keyboard-inclined. Arrange accelerator keys logically, not positionally, giving buttons preference over labels. That is, if you have a field at the top of the screen whose label happens to begin with the letter *A* and you also have a button at the bottom of the screen that's labeled *Add*, set the accelerator key of the button, not the field, to Alt+A. It's probably less likely that the user will want to jump to the field at the top of the screen than that he'll want to trigger the button using a shortcut key.

- Establish a logical tab order. Set up a tab order that enables the user to jump logically from field to field and from button to button on the form in a left-to-right, top-to-bottom fashion.

■ Use the Kind property of Delphi's TBitBtn control to establish both an OK button and a Cancel button where appropriate. Setting a button up as an OK button automatically sets its Default property to True, making it the form's default button. This means that the user can press Enter to end the editing of the current record and can press Esc to abort it.

■ Consider using a right-click pop-up menu in place of or in addition to command buttons. Some users prefer the use of the right-click pop-up menu made popular by Borland. If your users fit this category, setting up such a menu in your Delphi applications is very easy to do.

Data-Entry Forms

Data-entry forms are normally used for "heads-down" data entry. These forms are used primarily for getting data into a database. The emphasis here is on speed rather than on screen aesthetics or other application niceties like fly-over hints and drop-down list boxes. Data-entry forms are usually quite terse and include only the most essential elements. Typically, a user of this type of form is a data-entry operator who will be looking mainly at source documents, not the screen, during the entry of the data. Special emphasis is placed on the keyboard in data-entry forms because mouse use requires visual interaction.

Here's a list of tips that should help you build better data-entry forms:

■ Use a bold, monospace font for text boxes. Evenly spaced fonts are easier to read at a glance, although they take up more screen space. When speed is the issue—as it probably would be in data-entry forms—use monospace fonts. Boldfacing the text areas in these boxes also makes them easier to read.

■ Remove unneeded buttons and fields. Remove those controls on the form that aren't needed for quick data entry. For example, if you know that your user will never need to look up an account number, remove the account lookup button — it just takes screen space. Considered convenience features in normal transaction processing forms, these kinds of elements get in the way of rapid data entry.

■ Relate DataSet components underlying data-aware controls on a form using Delphi's master/detail facility. Don't make the user click a button or do anything else to see the detail related to a given master displayed. Relate the tables using the appropriate property selections so that they are automatically synchronized on screen.

■ Use accelerators that are easy to hit. Don't require athletic jumps to get to your accelerator keys. Assign accelerator keys based on use, not position on the screen. If two controls would naturally have the same intuitive hot key, give it to the control that is likely to be used most, not the one that's positionally first on the form. Assign some other accelerator to the lesser-used control. For those keys that the user hits often, make the keys as simple as possible.

- Set the default button to an Add button, not an OK button, where appropriate. Unlike normal transaction processing forms, make the default button an Add button—one that adds new records—in forms where adding records is the form's primary use. This will make things go much faster when a user has to add several records in succession.

- Keep forms as small as possible. Unlike other types of forms, this form should be as small as possible because this allows it to be repositioned and reduces eyestrain. Users of this type of form will typically be looking at source documents of some type, not the screen, so open the form as a normal, not a maximized or minimized, window.

Another thing you may want to consider is remapping the Enter key to function like the Tab key. You may find that your users prefer using the Enter key as if it were the Tab key, especially in entry forms. In the world of DOS applications, Enter normally moves the cursor from field to field on the screen, as the Tab key does in Windows. Keep in mind that you are deviating from an established standard in Windows applications if you decide to do this in your applications.

The method for doing this in Delphi is very simple. The steps are as follows:

- Set the form's KeyPreview property to True; it defaults to False.
- Attach code to the form's OnKeyDown event similar to that shown in Listing 7.1.

Listing 7.1. A routine for translating Enter to Tab in Delphi applications.

```
procedure TForm1.FormKeyUp(Sender: TObject; var Key: Word;
  Shift: TShiftState);
begin
  if ((Key=VK_RETURN) and (Shift=[])) then
    Key:=VK_TAB;
end;
```

Note that, because of the KeyPreview setting, the form, rather than the current control, gets the key as it's pressed. It then checks the key to see if it's the Enter key, and, if so, determines whether the shift keys (Alt, Ctrl, or Shift) are being pressed. If the Enter key alone was pressed, the code translates the key received by the event to the Tab key using the VK_TAB constant.

Report Design

Report writing is covered in more detail in Chapter 12, "Reports." Still, here are some suggestions regarding report design that you may find helpful:

- Use Delphi's QuickReport components to design your reports when possible. They're easier to set up and use than external report writers if, for no other reason, they are built into your application. You don't have to shell to a report runtime of any type to run a QuickReport-based report.

■ For those reports too complex for the QuickReport components, use a graphical report writer to build your reports, if possible. Popular report writers include ReportSmith, R&R SQL Report Writer for Windows, and Crystal Reports (see Chapter 18, "ReportSmith," for more information). Using a graphical report writer has many benefits. First, reports are created and modified visually. This is easier, faster, and less error-prone than creating reports using Object Pascal source code. Second, mechanisms like control breaks, headers, footers, and summarization are built into all decent report writers—you don't have to write any code to use them. Third, you can choose to allow your users to modify the reports you design or base new reports on them without their having to modify application source code.

■ Use stored procedures, if your platform supports them, to do as much of the report's work as possible. This keeps the majority of the action on the database server, which is where it should be in properly designed client/server applications. It also makes testing the data retrieval portion of your report easier because you can do it outside of the report writer. Furthermore, it separates the data retrieval function from the data display function, so you can more easily switch report writers or retrieve a report's data directly into a Delphi application.

■ If you use stored procedures to drive your reports, set them up to call a procedure that updates a report log table on your server when the procedure begins and ends. This will give you useful information on the overall performance of your reports, and it has the added benefit of letting you know what reports users are running the most and when they are running them. The following code is a sample Transact-SQL (Sybase's dialect) for creating such a procedure.

```
CREATE PROCEDURE reportlog @StartEnd char(6),@ReportName char(30) as
insert into REPORTLOG
select @StartEnd, getdate(), suser_name(), @ReportName
```

Once this procedure is in place, you would use the following SQL syntax to call it:

```
/*
Log the start of the report procedure
*/
exec reportlog 'STARTED','MAINTENANCE REPORT BY WORK TYPE'
/*
Do the work of the procedure
*/
...
/*
Log the end of the report procedure
*/
exec reportlog 'ENDED','MAINTENANCE REPORT BY WORK TYPE'
.
```

■ Include the report's internal name, the current date and time, and the user name of the user running the report (if available) in the page heading of your reports. Including the date and time helps distinguish multiple versions of the same report from each other and gives an idea of the age of the report if it is viewed at some later date. Including the report's internal name helps you track down the "source" to the report should you need to work on it in the future. Having the user name in the report header can give you a user contact to discuss the problem further with. Figure 7.7 shows a properly designed report page heading.

FIGURE 7.7.

A properly designed report.

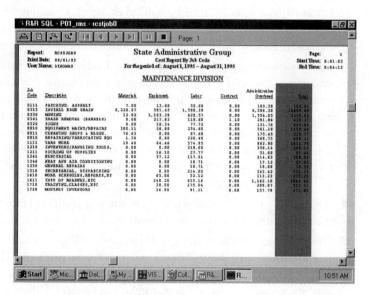

■ Include any criteria used to qualify the data displayed on a report in its page header. If the user supplied dates or other criteria in your front-end application, put them in the report's page header. This is imperative because data may be missing from the report due to the criteria specified in the front-end. This could in turn confuse the user. This is particularly likely when there is a significant amount of time between the running of the report and a subsequent review of it. Figure 7.7 illustrates the inclusion of a report's criteria in its heading.

■ Use proportional fonts for headers and nonproportional ones for data. Proportional fonts give your reports a more polished look and take full advantage of the high-end printers most everyone uses these days. Furthermore, they distinguish reports generated by a modern PC-based system from those generated on older, less capable legacy systems. Unfortunately, proportional fonts have the disadvantage of making it difficult to align columnar data. That is, because the numeral *1* may be narrower than, say, the numeral *5* when printed, proportional fonts are less than ideal for columnar data that must be aligned. Fixed-pitch fonts should be used instead. Typically, I use a proportional font like Arial or Times New Roman in the heading of a report and a nonproportional font like Courier New in the body of the report. See Figure 7.7 to see the proper use of proportional and nonproportional fonts.

■ When you need an underline in a report, use the font underline attribute. In many report writers, you can embed graphical elements, including lines and boxes, in the reports you build. Underlines drawn this way waste printer memory and slow down the report because the line is a graphic, not a text or font element.

Another common practice dating back to the days of chain printers is the use of the underscore character (_) to underline text. Lines drawn this way waste valuable vertical space on the report because they are actually located on the line beneath the one they are attempting to underline. Getting the length of lines drawn this way to correspond with the columnar data above them is also difficult when proportional fonts are used. Use the underline attribute of whatever font you're using rather than either of these methods when you need to underline items in a report. Figure 7.7 shows the proper use of underlines in reports.

■ Right-justify numbers that represent numeric quantities. Left-justify numbers that are used as identifiers (such as stock numbers, invoice numbers, and so forth).

■ Use advanced print formatting features, like shading and bold font attributes, to make report elements stand out. There's really no reason not to use the available features of today's printers to give your reports a more polished look. Printers of just a few years ago lacked many of the advanced formatting features that are standard on today's printers. Keep in mind, though, that your client's printer needs to support the features you intend to use. When converting from legacy systems, I've found that making judicious use of advanced printing features makes users especially happy. It seems to actualize the promises they've been made regarding how much better the technology they're being sold is than what they've been using. See Figure 7.7 for the use of advanced print formatting techniques to give a report a polished appearance.

■ Prototype the reports you create as soon as possible for your clients so that you can both be sure that there is a mutual understanding of what each report is supposed to look like and do. As with Delphi, you may even be able to use your report writer itself to construct prototypes of reports with the user at your side. This helps avoid confusion and redoing work later on.

Testing the Application for Compliance with the Established Goals

The subject of application testing and quality assurance is a book unto itself. Although covering it in-depth is outside the scope of this book, here are a few suggestions regarding testing the application you've just developed:

■ Establish a formal procedure for reporting and responding to anomalies that are discovered in your application. A common practice is to develop a form or, even better, a small application to be used for this purpose. Include such essential information as a number for each report, the steps needed to reproduce it, the type of report (bug, suggestion, or information request) and the response of the developer(s) to the report.

■ Set up a mechanism for easily distributing bug-fixes and updates to your clients as the need arises. One way I've done this is to build a small application that runs in the user's Windows Startup folder and checks the time stamp of the executable on the local hard disk against the one on a network or dial-up server. If the local copy is older, I replace it with the remote version.

■ Include and display a version number in all your applications. Increment the minor version number whenever you send out a new release, even a bug-fix. As mentioned previously, you should use a Windows VERSIONINFO resource (covered in Chapter 13) to do this.

■ Ask yourself whether the application fulfills the basic purpose you defined for the application. For example, you might ask yourself, "Does the application effectively track rental property maintenance?"

■ Compare the features that ended up being included in the application with the goals you originally established for it. Be sure that you didn't overlook anything or incorrectly implement a major goal of the application. It may be that the goals need to be revised to reflect changes made to the application's intended use by the client.

■ If possible, set up a machine that is identical to those the application will run on and install and test the application using it. Be especially careful to reproduce the processor chip, available memory and disk resources, and the video adapter in use at your client sites. Attempt also to duplicate the desktop and network operating systems in use. If your user is a Windows NT user, test your app under NT. If the user is a Windows 95 user, make sure you test it under Windows 95. It's also a good idea to run the applications that your clients use alongside your application to be sure that they're compatible.

■ Check your database constraints to be sure that they do what they're supposed to. Try to insert invalid data through your application into the database to ensure that it's rejected. Try to get passed both the lower and the upper boundaries of constraints that are range-oriented. Attempt to delete rows with dependent keys. See if the database will allow you to add duplicate values for columns that are not supposed to allow them. Try to omit fields that you know are required.

■ Conduct concurrency testing. If the application is to be used by more than one person, have a number of testers try it out simultaneously. Have the testers attempt to update the same row concurrently and have one user attempt to delete a row another is editing. Test your database's locking facilities to make sure that updates by multiple users aren't lost and occur in a timely fashion.

■ If the application is database server- or network-based, verify that the access rights you've defined operate as they're supposed to. Ensure that password retry lock-outs work as expected. Make sure that users have the rights they need to get to the parts of the application you intend for them to use. Attempt to violate the access rights for each level you've defined. Attempt to delete or update rows using logins that should not have the access privileges to do so—this will help ensure that your access restrictions work as expected.

■ Have coworkers and people not affiliated with the project test the application before clients see it.

■ If the application is to go into wide distribution, establish a small beta test group of key users to test the application before it is actually released.

■ Conduct usability testing with users of different skill levels. Your application may work correctly, but it may be too difficult to use. Allowing users of different skill sets to try the application out will help you determine this.

■ Remember that the user has the final word on whether the application meets his or her needs.

Installing the Application for Production Use

Application deployment is covered in detail in Chapter 27, "Deploying Your Applications." However, here are a few ideas to get you started:

■ As mentioned previously, set up a test machine that emulates the target user environment and install your application there before installing it anywhere else.

■ Seek to impact the user's machine as little as possible. Avoid modifying any more configuration parameters than absolutely necessary.

■ Size up your client's site to determine whether additional hardware or software needs to be installed before your application can be. For example, if you intend to communicate with a client/server DBMS over TCP/IP, you'll need TCP/IP protocol support on your client's machines. You may need to contact your network administrator for assistance with this.

■ Create an installation program using Delphi's InstallShield Express tool to handle installing your application and its supporting files on to client machines. Chapter 27 discusses InstallShield in depth.

What's Ahead

The next chapter begins the Tutorial section, wherein I take you through the creation of an actual client/server database application. The design process is covered first, followed by the development of the application using local tables. The section ends with upsizing the completed application to a full-blown client/server system.

Summary

Hopefully, you have gleaned enough from this and the preceding chapter to begin developing real database applications. Using the basic tools given here, you should have all you need to be well on your way. Regarding database design, remember that emphasis must be placed on the practical, not just the theoretical. Sometimes the rules must be bent in order to meet the client's needs. Regarding application design, remember that there's no "right way" to develop, no fixed set of steps that produces a good application every time. Software development is a craft, not an exact science.

As with any highly skilled craft, there are certain guidelines you should follow when developing applications. You must be careful, though, not to let the "assembly-line" mentality restrict your ability to create and innovate. Innovation is one area in which software development seems to be fading fast. Find the method of development that works best for you, then use it to effectively solve your client's problems.

II

Tutorial

8

Your First Real Database Application

This chapter begins the Part II, "Tutorial," portion of this book. Here you'll begin to build a moderately complex database application using Delphi. This application will be known as the Rental Maintenance Management System, RENTALMAN for short. You'll be introduced to the most important aspects of developing robust database applications under Windows. As in the rest of the book, I stress the pragmatic—what actually works—in the concepts presented here. This is especially true of the Tutorial section of the book, whose whole purpose is to lead you by the hand through the labyrinth that is Windows database application development.

As pointed out in Chapter 6, "Database Design 101," the five formal processes for building a database application are as follows:

1. Define the purpose and goals of the application.
2. Design the database foundation and application processes needed to meet those goals.
3. Develop the design into an application by creating the requisite database and program objects.
4. Test the application for compliance with the established goals.
5. Install the application for production use.

This chapter covers the first of the five steps and parts of the second and third steps. You'll do much of the work in this chapter without ever setting foot in Delphi. Properly designing *any* type of complex application requires thorough planning before any actual development begins.

Defining the Purpose of the Application

The first thing you need to do is define what it is the application is to do. You do this by defining its statement of purpose. This statement of purpose should consist of a sentence that includes a subject, a verb, and the verb's object. The subject is always the application, for instance, "The RENTALMAN System…." The verb describes what the application is supposed to do, such as "The RENTALMAN System will track…." The object denotes the recipient of the application's actions, for example, "The RENTALMAN System will track rental property maintenance."

The statement of purpose needs to be as concise as possible. Don't bother with flowery language or trivial details. Avoid clauses like "for the organization" and "for the client" at the end of the statement since these are implicit.

The application that is detailed in this chapter and those that follow has a very simple purpose: managing the maintenance work performed on rental property. So, simply put, the purpose of the sample application can be stated as:

"The RENTALMAN System will track maintenance on rental properties."

Defining the Goals of the Application

Once you've formulated a statement of purpose, you're ready to define specific goals for the application. You'll need to determine what exactly it is that the application is supposed to do. Keep the goals you come up with to no more than three or four major tasks, if possible. I've found it's helpful to develop these tasks using an outline. The goals you come up with should further define the application's statement of purpose, not exceed it. Follow the same three-part format you used with the statement of purpose. For example:

"The RENTALMAN System will track maintenance on rental properties."

- ■ Record incoming calls from tenants
- ■ Track progress on maintenance work
- ■ Provide historical maintenance information

Make sure you cover all the major functions of the application, but don't overdo it with needless details—remember: these are major goals of the application, not specific form or report features. Also, be sure that the goals you define don't overlap—don't list a task that's covered by a task already on the list.

Once you've defined the goals of the application, it's time to design the database and program objects necessary to accomplish them.

Designing the Database Foundation and Application Processes

Let's begin by designing the database objects necessary to service the RENTALMAN application. You begin the process of database design by modeling the database objects necessary to meet your application's goals. For the purpose of this tutorial, I'll assume that you don't have other databases or database objects that you want to utilize when building this application. You'll build a single database to house all the objects used by this application. In that sense, then, the approach to data modeling taken here will be *application*-centric, rather than *kind*-centric. Chapter 6 outlines the relative strengths and weaknesses of each approach.

The next step in building your database foundation is to refine your application goals into operational processes. The idea here is to translate the goals of the application into the actual processes needed to accomplish those goals. From this, you'll extrapolate the database objects that the processes require in order to function.

The operational processes for the RENTALMAN application might be as follows:

The RENTALMAN System will track maintenance on rental properties:

■ Record incoming calls from tenants:

    ■ Log calls from tenants as they are received

    ■ Assign calls received to a new or existing work order

■ Track progress on maintenance work:

    ■ List open work orders

    ■ Generate a task schedule for each employee

■ Provide historical maintenance information:

    ■ List the maintenance history for a particular piece of property

    ■ List the properties on which a particular type of work has been performed

Once you've determined the individual operational processes for your application—what it is, specifically, that the application is to do—you're ready to deduce what tables and other database objects are needed to support these processes.

Determine the Database Objects Needed to Service Your Processes

Looking closely at the processes you've defined, determine what database tables will be needed to service them. For example, in the processes previously listed, it's evident that the following tables will be needed:

■ A table in which to store tenant calls

■ A tenant table

■ A property table

■ An employee table

■ A work order table

■ A work order detail table

■ A work type table for classifying the types of maintenance performed

The logic we use to arrive at this list is as follows:

■ The first major goal of the application is to record incoming calls from tenants. Obviously, in order to store these calls in a database, we need a CALLS table of some type. Furthermore, in the interest of a fully normalized database, we want a TENANT table, as well. After all, we wouldn't want to have to record the same information repeatedly each time a given tenant called in. Lastly, we need a PROPERTY table if we're to associate tenant calls with rental properties. Omitting this would force us to redundantly store property-specific information for each call made on a property. In the interest of building a normalized database, we avoid this. (Database normalization is discussed in Chapter 6.)

■ The second major goal of the application is to track the progress of maintenance work as it is being performed. When a tenant calls, you want to be able to tell him when you'll get to his property. Furthermore, you want to effectively manage the maintenance work itself, ensuring that calls are being addressed in a timely fashion and that an employee doesn't spend an inordinate amount of time on a single call. Obviously, if you're to track maintenance work as it's being performed, you need a work order table of some type. Because a given work order might need to list several smaller work items, a related detail table is needed, as well.

■ Finally, because it's desirable to know the properties at which a given type of work has been performed (such as annual air conditioning maintenance), a classification of the work performed is necessary. In relational DBMS terms, the best way to implement this is to store a code in each work order detail line that identifies the type of work being performed. A master or lookup table would then be created so that these codes could be translated into meaningful descriptions, hence the inclusion of the "work type" table.

Checking Existing Databases

In a situation where you're not creating the first database objects at a client location, the next step would be to check existing databases to see if any of the objects your design calls for already exist. For the purposes of this application, though, we'll assume that no such objects exist and that you need to create a new database from scratch in which they will all reside.

Construct a Field Repository

Once you've determined what tables you need, the next step is to decide what columns those tables need to contain. Using the list of tables you developed earlier, build a list of the informational elements that each table needs to contain. Tables 8.1 through 8.7 are preliminary listings for each of the tables we've defined so far.

Table 8.1. Column list for the TENANT table.

Table	Column
TENANT	TenantNo
	Name
	Employer
	EmpAddress
	EmpCity
	EmpState

continues

Table 8.1. continued

Table	Column
	EmpZip
	HomePhone
	WorkPhone
	ICEPhone
	LeaseBeginDate
	LeaseEndDate
	MovedInDate
	MovedOutDate
	RentDueDay
	PetDeposit
	LawnService
	Comments

Table 8.2. Column list for the PROPERTY table.

Table	Column
PROPERTY	PropertyNo
	TenantNo
	Address
	City
	State
	Zip
	Addition
	BedRooms
	LivingAreas
	BathRooms
	GarageType
	SchoolDistrict
	Deposit
	Rent

Table	Column
	Range
	Refigerator
	DishWasher
	CentralHeat
	CentralAir
	GasHeat
	PrivacyFence
	LastSprayDate
	LastLawnDate
	Comments

Table 8.3. Column list for the CALLS table.

Table	Column
CALLS	CallNo
	CallDateTime
	PropertyNo
	Description
	Priority
	WorkOrderNo
	Comments

Table 8.4. Column list for the WORDERS table.

Table	Column
WORDERS	WorkOrderNo
	PropertyNo
	EmployeeNo
	StartDate
	EndDate
	Comments

Table 8.5. Column list for the WDETAIL table.

Table	*Column*
WDETAIL	WorkOrderNo
	LineNo
	WorkTypeCode

Table 8.6. Column list for the EMPLOYEE table.

Table	*Column*
EMPLOYEE	EmployeeNo
	Name

Table 8.7. Column list for the WORKTYPE table.

Table	*Column*
WORKTYPE	WorkTypeCode
	Description
	TaskDuration

Notice that I kept each table name to eight characters or less. This is in keeping with the naming conventions spelled out in Chapter 4, "Conventions." Also note the use of mixed case in naming each table's columns. Again, the reasons for this are detailed in Chapter 4.

I should point out here that this application is being designed with a very narrow purpose in mind—to track maintenance on rental properties. If it were to be used as a full-blown rental property management system, some of the table structures might change a bit. The design I've presented provides most of the features of the full-blown design while keeping it simple enough to cover in the limited space we have for doing so.

Once you've defined items that make up each table, the next step in creating your field repository is to consolidate these items into a single master list of all the fields that will exist in the database. List each field only once, and determine the optimal data type and size for each. Think of your master list as a field or domain repository—you use the entries in it to build your tables. Some tools refer to this master list as a data dictionary or reference table. Delphi uses the term *Attribute Set* to refer to this type of information. You can equate these attributes to field *templates*—they define how a given database attribute will look in all the tables in which it appears.

First, we'll create a consolidated list of all the columns listed in the table definitions already defined. (See Table 8.8.)

Table 8.8. A preliminary field repository for the RENTALMAN System.

Column	Column	Column
Addition	EmpState	PetDeposit
Address	EmpZip	Priority
Baths	EndDate	PrivacyFence
Beds	GarageType	PropertyNo
CallDateTime	GasHeat	Range
CallNo	HomePhone	Refigerator
CentralAir	ICEPhone	Rent
CentralHeat	LastLawnDate	RentDueDay
City	LastSprayDate	SchoolDistrict
Comments	LawnService	StartDate
Deposit	LeaseBeginDate	State
Description	LeaseEndDate	TaskDuration
DishWasher	LineNo	TenantNo
EmpAddress	Living	WorkOrderNo
EmpCity	MovedInDate	WorkPhone
EmployeeNo	MovedOutDate	WorkTypeCode
Employer	Name	Zip

Now take the composite list of columns and assign attributes to each one. For the moment, just concern yourself with the data type of each field. If you already know the DBMS platform on which your database will reside, go ahead and use its supported data types at this stage. Because the RENTALMAN System is being designed to run on the Paradox platform, I'll use data types that are native to the Paradox environment.

Table 8.9 is a partially completed field repository for the RENTALMAN System.

Table 8.9. A partially completed field repository for the RENTALMAN System.

Column	Type
Addition	Alpha
Address	Alpha

continues

Table 8.9. continued

Column	Type
BathRooms	Short
BedRooms	Short
CallDate	Date
CallTime	Time
CallNo	AutoIncrement
CentralAir	Logical
CentralHeat	Logical
City	Alpha
Comments	Alpha
Deposit	Money
Description	Alpha
DishWasher	Logical
EmpAddress	Alpha
EmpCity	Alpha
EmployeeNo	AutoIncrement
Employer	Alpha
EmpState	Alpha
EmpZip	Alpha
EndDate	Date
GarageType	Short
GasHeat	Logical
HomePhone	Alpha
ICEPhone	Alpha
LastLawnDate	Date
LastSprayDate	Date
LawnService	Logical
LeaseBeginDate	Date
LeaseEndDate	Date
LineNo	Short
LivingAreas	Short
MovedInDate	Date
MovedOutDate	Date

Column	Type
Name	Alpha
PetDeposit	Money
Priority	Alpha
PrivacyFence	Logical
PropertyNo	AutoIncrement
Range	Logical
Refigerator	Logical
Rent	Money
RentDueDay	Short
SchoolDistrict	Alpha
StartDate	Date
State	Alpha
TaskDuration	Number
TenantNo	AutoIncrement
WorkOrderNo	AutoIncrement
WorkPhone	Alpha
WorkTypeCode	Short
Zip	Alpha

The next step in constructing the field repository is to determine the optimal size for each field. The rule of thumb is to set a column to the *smallest* possible size that allows it to store the *largest* value it will ever need to store. For some types of fields—date or Boolean fields, for example—the required storage space for a column may be fixed, so specifying a column size is a non-issue. Exact column sizing becomes more important as the number of rows in your database increases—a few bytes of waste per row can add up quickly when there are several million rows in a table. For small- to medium-sized databases, though, character fields are usually the only field type you'll need to worry about sizing.

Table 8.10 is a revised field repository with the sizes for each column specified.

Table 8.10. A partially completed field repository for the RENTALMAN System.

Column	Type	Size
Addition	Alpha	10
Address	Alpha	30

continues

Table 8.10. continued

Column	Type	Size
BathRooms	Short	
BedRooms	Short	
CallDate	Date	
CallTime	Time	
CallNo	AutoIncrement	
CentralAir	Logical	
CentralHeat	Logical	
City	Alpha	20
Comments	Alpha	100
Deposit	Money	
Description	Alpha	30
DishWasher	Logical	
EmpAddress	Alpha	30
EmpCity	Alpha	20
EmployeeNo	AutoIncrement	
Employer	Alpha	30
EmpState	Alpha	2
EmpZip	Alpha	10
EndDate	Date	
GarageType	Short	
GasHeat	Logical	
HomePhone	Alpha	10
ICEPhone	Alpha	10
LastLawnDate	Date	
LastSprayDate	Date	
LawnService	Logical	
LeaseBeginDate	Date	
LeaseEndDate	Date	
LineNo	Short	
LivingAreas	Short	
MovedInDate	Date	
MovedOutDate	Date	

Column	Type	Size
Name	Alpha	
PetDeposit	Money	
Priority	Alpha	
PrivacyFence	Logical	
PropertyNo	AutoIncrement	
Range	Logical	
Refigerator	Logical	
Rent	Money	
RentDueDay	Short	
SchoolDistrict	Alpha	10
StartDate	Date	
State	Alpha	2
TaskDuration	Number	
TenantNo	AutoIncrement	
WorkOrderNo	AutoIncrement	
WorkPhone	Alpha	10
WorkTypeCode	Short	
Zip	Alpha	10

NOTE

Note that a column's size specification refers to the number of bytes required to store the field, not the number of digits it allows. This distinction is particularly important for numeric fields, where the difference this makes can be dramatic. A numeric field that is *sized* at one byte can store values as high as 255, whereas a numeric field that is limited to numbers of a single *digit in length* cannot represent values greater than 9. It's important to remember that field *sizes* and field *lengths* are two different things.

User Data Types

If your target platform supports user-defined data types, now is a good time to think about them. A user-defined data type is just a shorthand way of referring to a data type the server already supports. InterBase calls them "domains." User data types provide an easy and consistent method of defining similar table columns. Careful inspection of the preceding column definitions reveals several potential user data types. Table 8.11 includes the most obvious ones.

Table 8.11. Potential user-defined data types.

User-defined data type	Affected columns	Type	Base Req	Allowable values	Default
RoomCountType	BathRooms, BedRooms, LivingAreas, GarageType	Short	Y	0–4	
AddressType	Address, EmpAddress	Alpha(30)	Y		
CityType	City, EmpCity	Alpha(20)	Y		OKC
CommentsType	Comments (all tables)	Alpha(100)	N		
DescriptionType	Description (all tables)	Alpha(30)			
NameType	Name, Employer	Alpha(30)	Y		
PhoneType	HomePhone, WorkPhone, ICEPhone	Alpha(10)	Y		
StateType	State, EmpState	Alpha(2)	Y		OK
ZipCodeType	ZipCode, EmpZipCode	Alpha(10)	Y		

User-defined data types provide a safer and more readable way of defining fields with similar attributes. The fact that Paradox doesn't support user-defined data types shouldn't stop you from using them while designing your tables. If nothing else, they act as a kind of database shorthand and help avoid inconsistencies in table definitions. Regardless of whether you're able to utilize user data types when you actually build your tables, you'll find it's still helpful to use them when designing your field repository. There's certainly no harm in using them in the design stage, if not in the actual building of the tables.

Notice that the preceding user data type definitions include columns indicating whether fields based on them are required, what their allowable values are, and what default value to supply them with, if any. The next step in fleshing out your field repository is to add this same information for the fields that won't be defined using these user data types. You do this by inspecting the remaining fields in the repository for any fixed validation rules or defaults that could be applied to them. What you're looking for are the types of rules that transcend the table boundary—the kinds of rules that apply to columns regardless of the table in which they reside. Some fields will be required fields, some won't. Some will have a fixed set of allowable values, some will reference other tables, and some will allow any value. Some columns will have a default value, and some won't. A given column may be required in one table but not in another. For example, the `TenantNo` column is required in the TENANT table, but not in the PROPERTY table, because a rental property may be vacant. You'll have to look at each column in the repository to see if a global validation rule or default can be applied to it.

It's helpful at this stage to get as much of this type of work out of the way as possible. It will save you time when you begin to create the tables themselves. Here's a completed field repository that lists validation and default settings that apply to columns globally across the database. You'll define table-specific field validations and defaults when you reconstruct your tables using the definitions in your field repository. (See Table 8.12.)

Table 8.12. A completed field repository for the RENTALMAN System.

Column	Type	Size	Req	Allowable values	Default
Addition	Alpha	10	Y		ROCKKNOLL
Address	AddressType		Y		
BathRooms	RoomCountType				
BedRooms	RoomCountType				
CallDateTime	Timestamp		Y		Current date and time
CallNo	AutoIncrement		Y		
CentralAir	Logical		Y		T
CentralHeat	Logical		Y		T
City	CityType				
Comments	CommentsType				
Deposit	Money		Y		Rent
Description	DescriptionType				
DishWasher	Logical		Y		T
EmpAddress	AddressType		Y		
EmpCity	CityType				
EmployeeNo	AutoIncrement		Y		
Employer	NameType				
EmpState	StateType				
EmpZip	ZipCodeType		Y		
EndDate	Date		N		

continues

Table 8.12. continued

Column	Type	Size	Req	Allowable values	Default
GarageType	RoomCountType				
GasHeat	Logical		Y		T
HomePhone	PhoneType				
ICEPhone	PhoneType				
LastLawnDate	Date		N		
LastSprayDate	Date		N		
LawnService	Logical		Y		T
LeaseBeginDate	Date		Y		
LeaseEndDate	Date		Y		
LineNo	Short		Y		
LivingAreas	RoomCountType				
MovedInDate	Date		Y		
MovedOutDate	Date		N		
Name	NameType				
PetDeposit	Money		Y		$0
Priority	Alpha		Y	L,M,H	'M'
PrivacyFence	Logical		Y		T
PropertyNo	AutoIncrement		Y		
Range	Logical		Y		T
Refigerator	Logical		Y		T
Rent	Money		Y		$650
RentDueDay	Short		Y	1,15	1
SchoolDistrict	Alpha	15	N		PUTNAM CITY
StartDate	Date		Y		
State	StateType				
TaskDuration	Number		Y		
TenantNo	AutoIncrement		Y		
WorkOrderNo	AutoIncrement		Y		
WorkPhone	PhoneType				
WorkTypeCode	Short		Y		
Zip	ZipCodeType				

Notice that I've left the elements defined by user data types blank in the listing here. This helps ensure that the corresponding field attributes are consistent from table to table because they are defined solely by the user data type.

Note also that we've omitted a few attribute details from the repository (such as edit and display mask specifications for each column). We'll address these minor details when we implement the RENTALMAN database design using the Database Desktop.

I should also point out that there are a few database attributes specified here that you won't be able to define when building the RENTALMAN System's Paradox database objects. For example, in the PROPERTY table design, the Deposit column defaults to the value of the Rent column because a property's security deposit is usually equal to a month's rent. For situations like this one, you'll set the column's default value from within the corresponding Delphi application.

Use the Field Repository to Build Table Definitions

Next, decompose your field repository into its composite tables. Copy the refined field definitions from the field repository to the table structures you previously outlined. You should see the RENTALMAN database design slowly beginning to take shape. Tables 8.13 through 8.19 include a revised definition for each of the tables in the RENTALMAN System.

Table 8.13. The finalized table design for the TENANT table.

Column	Type	Size	Req	Allowable values	Default
TenantNo	AutoIncrement		Y		
Name	NameType		Y		
Employer	NameType				
EmpAddress	AddressType				
EmpCity	CityType				
EmpState	StateType				
EmpZip	ZipCodeType				
HomePhone	PhoneType				
WorkPhone	PhoneType				
ICEPhone	PhoneType				
LeaseBeginDate	Date		Y		
LeaseEndDate	Date		Y		
MovedInDate	Date		Y		

continues

Table 8.13. continued

Column	Type	Size	Req	Allowable values	Default
MovedOutDate	Date		N		
RentDueDay	Short		Y	1,15	1
PetDeposit	Money		Y		$0
LawnService	Logical		Y		T
Comments	CommentsType				

Table 8.14. The finalized table design for the PROPERTY table.

Column	Type	Size	Req	Allowable values	Default
PropertyNo	AutoIncrement		Y		
TenantNo	AutoIncrement		N		
Address	AddressType				
City	CityType				
State	StateType				
Zip	ZipCodeType				
Addition	Alpha	15	Y		ROCKKNOLL
BedRooms	RoomCountType				
LivingAreas	RoomCountType				
BathRooms	RoomCountType				
GarageType	RoomCountType				
SchoolDistrict	Alpha	15	N		PUTNAM CITY
Deposit	Money		Y		Rent
Rent	Money		Y		$650
Range	Logical		Y		T
Refigerator	Logical		Y		T
DishWasher	Logical		Y		T
CentralHeat	Logical		Y		T
CentralAir	Logical		Y		T

Column	Type	Size	Req	Allowable values	Default
GasHeat	Logical		Y		T
PrivacyFence	Logical		Y		T
LastSprayDate	Date		N		
LastLawnDate	Date		N		
Comments	CommentsType				

Table 8.15. The finalized table design for the CALLS table.

Column	Type	Size	Req	Allowable values	Default
CallNo	AutoIncrement		Y		
CallDateTime	Timestamp		Y		Current date and time
PropertyNo	Long				
Description	DescriptionType				
Priority	Alpha		Y	L,M,H	L
WorkOrderNo	Long		N		
Comments	CommentsType				

Table 8.16. The finalized table design for the WORDERS table.

Column	Type	Size	Req	Allowable values	Default
WorkOrderNo	AutoIncrement		Y		
PropertyNo	Long		Y		
EmployeeNo	Long		Y		
StartDate	Date		Y		
EndDate	Date		N		
Comments	CommentsType				

Table 8.17. The finalized table design for the WDETAIL table.

Column	Type	Size	Req	Allowable values	Default
WorkOrderNo	Long		Y		
LineNo	AutoIncrement		Y		
WorkTypeCode	Short		Y		
Comments	CommentsType				

Table 8.18. The finalized table design for the EMPLOYEE table.

Column	Type	Size	Req	Allowable values	Default
EmployeeNo	AutoIncrement		Y		
Name	NameType				

Table 8.19. The finalized table design for the WORKTYPE table.

Column	Type	Size	Req	Allowable values	Default
WorkTypeCode	Short		Y		
Description	DescriptionType		Y		
TaskDuration	Number		Y		

Organize the Tables by Type

The next step in designing the RENTALMAN database is to segregate the list of tables defined so far into base and transactional tables. Base tables contain items that are by definition unique. Transactional tables receive data collected from equipment or keyed by users. An example of a base table would be the PROPERTY table. Because each record in the PROPERTY table represents a unique item—a piece of rental property—it's a base table. Base tables are often used to translate codes, numbers, or abbreviations into something more meaningful. They're usually static and change little over time. Transactional tables, by contrast, change often and are the most volatile part of a database. The CALLS table is a transactional table because it will be used to store tenant calls as they are received each day. It will probably grow larger over time, whereas the PROPERTY table won't increase in size unless additional properties are purchased by the rental company. Table 8.20 shows the way I'd break down the tables.

Table 8.20. The tables of the RENTALMAN System organized by type.

Base tables	Transactional tables
TENANT	CALLS
PROPERTY	WORDERS
WORKTYPE	WODETAIL
EMPLOYEE	

Master/Detail Tables

The next step in developing the database design is to further refine the preceding list into master and detail tables. Within the transactional table group, determine which tables depend on others to provide meaningful information. These tables are called *detail* tables; the tables on which they depend are called *master* tables. Detail tables depend on other tables to be truly useful—they normally store line-item data. They are also known as "child" or "slave" tables.

In the preceding list, the WODETAIL table serves as a line item table to the WORDERS table. This is due to the fact that it's of very limited use without the WORDERS table. WORDERS contains much of the essential information about the work to be done. Without it, we don't even know the piece of property on which the work is to be done or which employee is to do it. In that sense, then, WODETAIL is dependent upon WORDERS, making WORDERS a master table and WODETAIL its detail, or slave, table.

Visually Relate the Tables

The next step in designing the RENTALMAN database is to visually diagram the relationships between its tables. *Entity relation* diagrams show the way that entities (records) in one table relate to those in another. These don't need to be anything elaborate or use fancy symbols. The purpose of an ER diagram is to visually relate tables, and you can do that without using special symbols. Though there is a formal design specification for ER diagrams, simply drawing boxes on a sheet of paper and connecting them with lines may work for you. Or, you may wish to take a more formal approach. Figures 8.1 through 8.7 demonstrate how to visually relate tables to one another. The first five use the formal ER diagram style; the rest use a less formal one.

FIGURE 8.1.

An entity relation diagram for the EMPLOYEE and WORDERS tables that follows the formal ER diagram style.

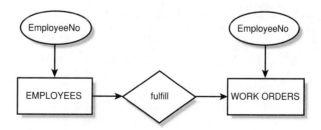

FIGURE 8.2.

An entity relation diagram for the TENANT and PROPERTY tables that follows the formal ER diagram style.

FIGURE 8.3.

An entity relation diagram for the CALLS and WORDERS tables that follows the formal ER diagram style.

FIGURE 8.4.

An entity relation diagram for the WORDERS and WODETAIL tables that follows the formal ER diagram style.

FIGURE 8.5.

An entity relation diagram for the WORDERS and CALLS tables that follows the formal ER diagram style.

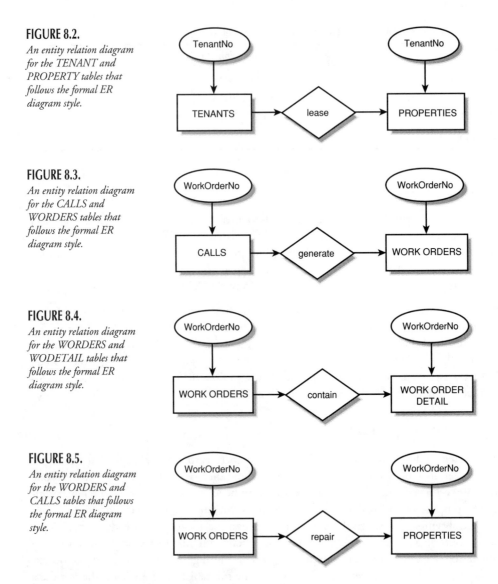

Figures 8.6 and 8.7 follow a less formal, but more informative, style.

FIGURE 8.6.

An entity relation diagram for the TENANT and PROPERTY tables that follows a less formal ER diagram style.

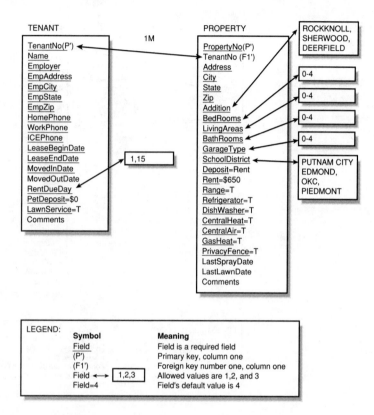

I'd strongly suggest that you complete an informal ER diagram, like the two shown in Figures 8.6 and 8.7, for each of the tables and entity relationships in the RENTALMAN database before proceeding. This will make the steps that follow much simpler.

Database Schematics

Another helpful thing that I've found is to create a schematic of the entirety of an application's database design. That is, I create a single diagram that shows the rough relationships between the tables in the database. This bird's-eye view of the database helps you better understand what data the database contains and how the tables in the database relate to one another. Figure 8.8 shows a database schematic for the RENTALMAN System.

FIGURE 8.7.

An entity relation diagram for the CALLS and PROPERTY tables that follows a less formal ER diagram style.

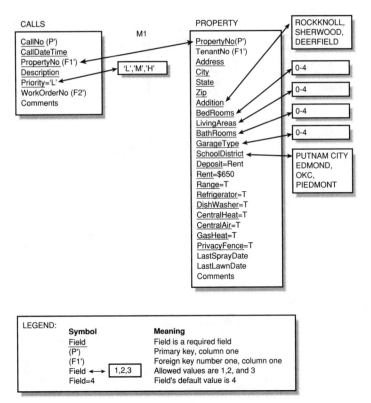

Normalize the Database

Although the RENTALMAN database is already third-normal form compliant in terms of normalization, there are a few elements of its design that merit further discussion. Going through these can be helpful in understanding the normalization process. (Database normalization is discussed in detail in Chapter 6.)

First, notice that the TENANT table does not contain a PropertyNo attribute. This may seem strange given that tenants certainly lease properties, as the ER diagram in Figure 8.8 illustrates. The connection between the PROPERTY and TENANT tables is established through the TenantNo column of the PROPERTY table. Why? Because a single tenant—say a business of some type—may rent several different properties. If the link between the two tables was established through a PropertyNo column in the TENANT table, a single tenant could rent just one property. By placing the link in the PROPERTY table, a given tenant may lease any number of properties, but a single property can be home to just one tenant. This is an equitable solution and keeps the design as flexible as possible while remaining practical as well.

FIGURE 8.8.

A database schematic shows the relationships between the tables in a database.

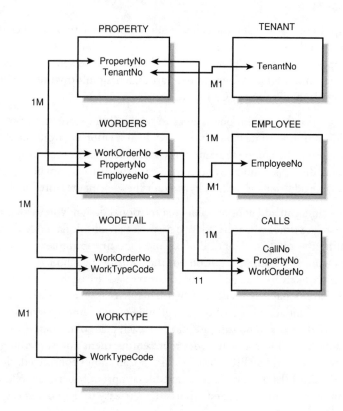

Another oddity of this design is the inclusion of the employer information in the TENANT table. The entirety of the information relevant to a tenant's employer is stored within each tenant record. This is in clear violation of third-normal form because the employer-related fields are obviously dependent upon one another. Why would you want to do this? The answer is simple. The fact is that the user will never want to query the database by employer. The employer information serves no purpose except to allow tenants to be contacted at their place of employment should the need arise. Outside the context of a tenant record, the employer information is useless. The rental company doesn't care how many tenants work for a given employer. It therefore makes more sense to store the employer information within each tenant record than to have the user maintain an EMPLOYER base table and link the tables relationally. This allows the employer information to be stored and retrieved without the baggage of a second database table.

Another seeming curiosity of the design is the absence of a TenantNo column in the CALLS table. After all, tenants place the calls, right? The reason for this, again, is that, first, several properties may be rented by a single tenant. Second, the focus of the maintenance work isn't on the tenant; it's on the property in need of repairs. When a tenant calls in, the Delphi form responsible for logging the call will allow a property to be selected. Once this is supplied, the name of the property's current tenant will be displayed on screen. This keeps the focus on the property in need of repair while still allowing the person taking the call to verify the relevant tenant information. When the need arises, tenant information can be extracted using the property information in the CALLS table.

A question might also be raised as to why I didn't store the list of school districts and home additions in separate tables and access them relationally from the PROPERTY table. After all, by storing the complete name for a school district in each property record, the design both wastes disk space and prevents the name of the district from being easily changed. Ditto for the housing addition, as well. Why weren't these elements stored in separate tables?

Any time you add another table to a relational design, you further complicate it to an extent. There are times when the relative merits of an additional table do not justify further complicating the database design. Both of these are fine examples of such a situation. First, neither the name of a housing addition nor the name of the school districts referenced by the application are likely to change. Second, the projected size of this database is small- to medium-sized. The additional disk space used by the name of, say, a school district rather than a short code representing it will probably be negligible overall. And by storing the complete names of the school district and housing addition for each piece of property with it in the database, we alleviate the need to translate codes representing them into something meaningful in forms and reports that display PROPERTY data. So, all things considered, the storage of these elements in the PROPERTY table is an acceptable compromise between following strict relational theory and constructing forms and reports that are easy to design and easy to use.

Understanding these issues should help you better grasp the overall philosophy employed in database design.

Completing the Design

To finish off the RENTALMAN database design and proceed with actually creating it, you'll need to establish the primary and foreign keys for each table, the constraints between tables, if any, and any default values not already specified. You'll find that much of this work is already done. In fact, if you created the ER diagrams as previously instructed, you should already have these definitions set up. If not, you'll want to establish them before proceeding.

Keys

Key fields identify the access methods that you intend to use to get at a table's rows. Keys you select in this stage will be used later to build indexes. Pick all the keys you need, but don't select fields as keys needlessly. Keys you select become indexes in the database and unnecessary indexes waste disk space and slow down your DBMS.

Primary Keys

Review the tables in the RENTALMAN database and specify a primary key for each. In my diagrams, I label each field of a primary key with a capital "P", followed by a superscripted number signifying its order in the composite key, if applicable. See Figure 8.6, shown previously, for an illustration of this.

The primary key you select for each table should be inherently unique and should be the most popular access path you plan to take into the table's data. That is, think about the way in which a table's data will be used. How will it most often be queried? What field(s) in this table might another table reference in a constraint? (See the following section on Constraints for more information.) For example, using the TENANT table, it's obvious that the most popular access path into the table's data is through the TenantNo field. This field will, no doubt, be used to govern constraints established in other tables. It's therefore the logical choice as the table's primary key. Table 8.21 shows my primary key selections for the RENTALMAN database.

Table 8.21. Primary keys for the RENTALMAN database.

Table	Primary key
TENANT	TenantNo
PROPERTY	PropertyNo
CALLS	CallNo
WORDERS	WorkOrderNo
WODETAIL	WorkOrderNo, LineNo
EMPLOYEE	EmployeeNo
WORKTYPE	WorkTypeCode

Foreign Keys

Next up are foreign keys. Foreign keys are *foreign* in that they are not the table's primary key, but instead probably exist as the primary key for a different, or foreign, table. Use foreign keys to establish secondary access paths into a table. These are less popular, but essential, data access paths.

Using the PROPERTY table, an obvious foreign key would be the TenantNo field. This is because a listing of all current tenants would logically include the property or properties they've rented. TenantNo wouldn't be the right choice as the primary key for this table because it's not likely to be the most popular access path into the table, nor is it guaranteed to be unique. TenantNo works much better as a foreign key.

Flag fields as foreign keys that you think might participate in a join, especially as the right side of an outer join. Also establish fields as foreign keys that you think users will frequently use to search the table. In my diagrams, I use an uppercase "F" followed by a number signifying the foreign key's order among the other foreign keys. I superscript a second number to designate the field's order in a multi-field (composite) foreign key, if applicable. See Figure 8.6 for an illustration of this.

Table 8.22 shows my foreign key selections for the RENTALMAN database.

Table 8.22. Foreign keys for the RENTALMAN database.

Table	*Foreign keys*
PROPERTY	TenantNo
CALLS	PropertyNo; WorkOrderNo
WORDERS	PropertyNo; EmployeeNo
WODETAIL	WorkTypeCode

Constraints

Next come the database rules—these are formally known as constraints. Constraints restrict the type of data a given column can contain. Constraints usually ensure that a value matches a given criteria or is a member of a specific set of values before it is allowed into a field. The set of allowable values might be fixed; that is, it might be a set of values you come up with at design time. For example, using the PROPERTY table, you might want to restrict the allowable values for the GarageType field to 0-4 because you know that all of the properties either have no garage (type 0) or have a one-, two-, three-, or four-car garage, respectively. A field with a fixed set of allowable values is identified with a line connecting it to a rectangle containing the set of allowed values, as seen in Figure 8.6.

The set of allowable values may also depend entirely upon another table. In this case, you'll usually establish the constraint by using a foreign key definition. Some DBMS platforms enable you to specify constraints that exceed the meager abilities of a foreign key constraint.

A constraint that depends upon another table is usually bi-directional. That is, not only does the constraint restrict the values a field may have, but once a value is stored in the field, it prevents the deletion of the corresponding record in the second table. For example, using the TENANT and PROPERTY tables mentioned previously, the TenantNo field in the PROPERTY table allows only tenant numbers that exist in the TENANT table. Likewise, once a given tenant number is stored in the PROPERTY table, the corresponding record in the TENANT table must not be deleted. Doing so would orphan the TenantNo stored in the PROPERTY table and would prevent using it to determine the current inhabitants of the property.

If you've created the ER diagrams (the less formal style) as instructed earlier, you should already see the constraints for the RENTALMAN database depicted visually in your diagrams. Between fixed constraints and foreign key definitions, the constraints needed by the RENTALMAN database should already be in place. Tables 8.13 though 8.19 depict the fixed constraints for the tables in the RENTALMAN database.

Defaults

The next class of database rules to establish are the default values for the fields in each table. Review each table and determine which, if any, of the fields should have a default value assigned to them. Normally, you set up defaults for fields that you may want to omit explicitly setting at runtime. For example, using the PROPERTY table, we might default the Range field to True because the rental company normally provides an electric range and self-cleaning oven in all its properties. In my diagrams, I signify a field's default value using an equal sign and the value to the right of the field definition, as illustrated in Figure 8.6. Tables 8.10 though 8.17 depict the column defaults for the tables in the RENTALMAN database.

Develop the Design into an Application

The next section will concern itself with the first portion of the third major step in database application development—that of actually creating the database objects. We'll use Borland's Database Desktop to create these objects, though you could also use Paradox for Windows, if you wanted. If you're already a Paradox user, you may find that you're more comfortable with it than with Database Desktop. Database Desktop is actually just a stripped-down version of Paradox. This means that anything Database Desktop can do, Paradox can do as well. Furthermore, there are features in Paradox that are missing from the Database Desktop.

Create the Database Objects

Now it's time to create the database objects. Your design is complete, and it's time to give it life by creating the database objects it defines.

You'll use the Database Desktop to build these objects. You'll begin by keying in the column lists that were designed previously and conclude by constructing each table's requisite indexes and referential integrity constraints.

Create a Directory

Because the RENTALMAN System will initially be Paradox-based, your database tables will reside on a local hard disk rather than on a SQL server. Because of this, it's a good idea to create a separate directory on your hard disk in which to store these tables.

Mine is: C:\DATA\DELPHI\RENTMAN. You'll want to create this directory before proceeding. This directory will perform the same function as a database on a SQL server—it will house the database objects you create for your application.

Fire Up Database Explorer

Start Delphi and select Explore from the Database menu. Database Explorer has a variety of uses—you'll use it here to create a Borland Database Engine alias. You'll need a BDE alias before you can get started creating database objects.

Click on the Database tab, if it isn't already selected, then click the Databases entry in the treeview below it. Next, right-click the Database entry and select New on the ensuing menu.

You're then prompted to select a database driver for your new BDE alias. Because this database will be Paradox-based, select Standard and click OK.

Next, you're prompted for the name of the new database alias. Type RENTMAN and press Enter. Next, click the Path entry in the right-hand pane and type the name of the directory in which you intend to store your Paradox tables for the RENTALMAN System (such as C:\DATA\DELPHI\RENTMAN), then press Enter.

Next, click the Apply button in Database Explorer's toolbar. It's the blue arrow that curves to the right. This saves your new alias definition to the IDAPI.CFG file.

Figure 8.9 illustrates what the screen should look like when you're done.

FIGURE 8.9.

The Database Explorer as it should look once your new alias is defined.

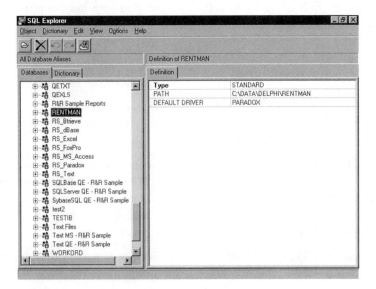

Now that you've created a new BDE alias, it's time to create the tables themselves. We'll use the Database Desktop for this, so start up the Database Desktop now.

To begin with, click DBD's File menu and select Working Directory. Next, click the Aliases dropdown and select the RENTMAN alias from the list, then click OK. This will cause the tables you create to be placed into the disk directory that you specified when you defined the alias.

Now click the File menu again and select Table from the New submenu. Select either Paradox for Windows 5.0 or Paradox for Windows 7.0 in the ensuing dialog, then click OK to select it. You're now presented with the Create table dialog box. (See Figure 8.10.)

FIGURE 8.10.

The Database Desktop Create table dialog box.

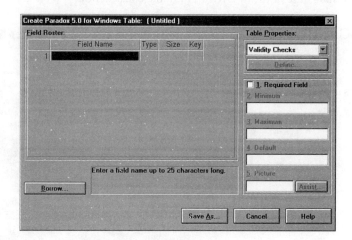

The WORKTYPE Table

Using the finalized table definitions from earlier in this chapter, we'll define each table in our database design. Let's start with the WORKTYPE table. Table 8.23 lists its finalized definition.

Table 8.23. The finalized table design for the WORKTYPE table.

Column	Type	Size	Req	Allowable values	Default
WorkTypeCode	Short		Y		
Description	DescriptionType		Y		
TaskDuration	Number		Y		

> **NOTE**
>
> Because of the inter-relationships between tables, you'll want to create less dependent tables first. In other words, if tables A and B reference table C through a foreign key constraint, it makes sense to build table C first so that it will be available when you build tables A and B.

Begin by defining the field names, types, and lengths for each field. Go ahead and mark the primary key for the table, the WorkTypeCode column, as the table's key. Figure 8.11 illustrates this first stage of the WORKTYPE table construction.

FIGURE 8.11.

The first stage of the WORKTYPE table construction.

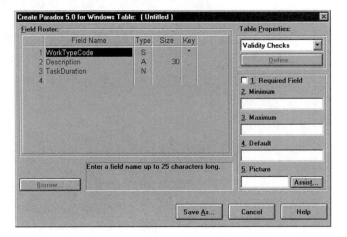

Now, go back through the field list and click the dialog's 1. Required checkbox for each column that's listed as a required field in the preceding table layout. All three fields are required, so you'll need to click the checkbox for each of them.

> **NOTE**
>
> Note that you can press Alt+1 (because the 1 is underlined) in order to check/uncheck the 1. Required checkbox. You may find that this is faster than clicking it repeatedly with a mouse.

This completes the definition of the WORKTYPE table. By specifying the WorkTypeCode field as the table's primary key, you cause Database Desktop to create a unique index over the WORKTYPE table whose key is the WorkTypeCode field. Click the Save As button to save your definition. Type WORKTYPE as the name of the new table and click OK in the Save As dialog to create the table. Because you specified the RENTMAN alias earlier, the table will be created in the directory pointed to by the alias. Note that you don't need to specify an extension—Database Desktop supplies one based on the type of local table you're working with: DB for Paradox tables and DBF for dBase tables. Your new table will be created as WORKTYPE.DB in the operating system.

The TENANT Table

We'll next create one of the system's larger tables—the TENANT table. Table 8.24 shows its finalized table design.

Table 8.24. The finalized table design of the TENANT table.

Column	Type	Size	Req	Allowable values	Default
TenantNo	AutoIncrement		Y		
Name	NameType		Y		
Employer	NameType				
EmpAddress	AddressType				
EmpCity	CityType				
EmpState	StateType				
EmpZip	ZipCodeType				
HomePhone	PhoneType				
WorkPhone	PhoneType				
ICEPhone	PhoneType				
LeaseBeginDate	Date		Y		
LeaseEndDate	Date		Y		
MovedInDate	Date		Y		
MovedOutDate	Date		N		
RentDueDay	Short		Y	1,15	
PetDeposit	Money		Y		$0
LawnService	Logical		Y		T
Comments	CommentsType				

Select File/New/Table again, and choose Paradox for Windows 5.0 or 7.0 as the table type. Then, using the previous design, enter the column information for the TENANT table just as you did for the WORKTYPE table. Remember to check the 1. Required box for those fields that are required fields. TenantNo is the table's primary key. Figure 8.12 illustrates the completion of this entry.

FIGURE 8.12.

The completed column definition of the TENANT table.

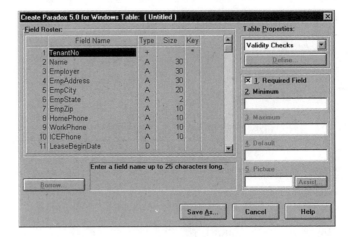

Now you're ready to assign defaults and other constraints to the columns. Click on the RentDueDay column in the list. Enter 1 as the column's default value in the 4. Default entry box. Enter {1,15} in the columns Picture entry box. This limits the values the field can store to 1 and 15 only.

Next, click the PetDeposit column and set its default to 0. Finally, click the LawnService column and set its default to True.

Because we know we'll want to search the tenant list by name, let's create a secondary index over the table that uses the Name column as its key. Click the Table Properties dropdown and select Secondary Indexes from the list. Next, click the Define button. The Define Secondary Index dialog is presented. The left side of the dialog lists the fields in the TENANT table. Double-click the Name field. (See Figure 8.13.)

FIGURE 8.13.

The Define Secondary Index dialog box.

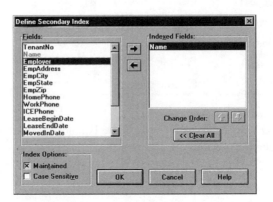

Click OK to save your index definition. You'll then be prompted for an index name. Type TENANT02_Name. This tells us that this index is the second one over the TENANT table (the primary key is the first index) and that its key is the Name column.

There are no other indexes or referential integrity constraints over the TENANT table, so you're finished with it once you create the TENANT02_Name secondary index. Figure 8.14 shows the completed TENANT table definition. Click the Save As button to save the table definition as before.

FIGURE 8.14.

The completed TENANT table definition.

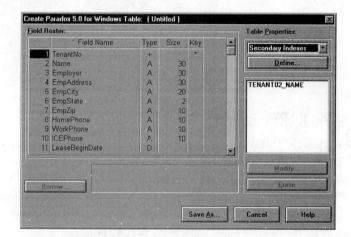

The EMPLOYEE Table

Next, create the EMPLOYEE table using the same techniques that you used to create the other tables. Table 8.25 lists its finalized definition.

Table 8.25. The finalized table design of the EMPLOYEE table.

Column	Type	Size	Req	Allowable values	Default
EmployeeNo	AutoIncrement		Y		
Name	NameType				

Be sure to flag the table's columns using the 1. Required checkbox and be sure to label the EmployeeNo column as the table's primary key. Figure 8.15 shows the completed EMPLOYEE table layout.

FIGURE 8.15.

The completed EM-PLOYEE table definition.

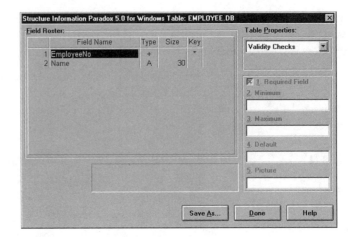

The PROPERTY Table

Next up is the PROPERTY table. It's a little more interesting than the tables you've built so far because it contains a wider variety of column types and external references. Bring up the Create table dialog in Database Desktop and key in the column definitions listed as shown in Table 8.26.

Table 8.26. The finalized table design of the PROPERTY table.

Column	Type	Size	Req	Allowable values	Default
PropertyNo	AutoIncrement		Y		
TenantNo	AutoIncrement		N		
Address	AddressType				
City	CityType				
State	StateType				
Zip	ZipCodeType				
Addition	Alpha	30	Y		ROCKKNOLL
BedRooms	RoomCountType				
LivingAreas	RoomCountType				
BathRooms	RoomCountType				
GarageType	RoomCountType				
SchoolDistrict	Alpha	15	N		PUTNAM CITY
Deposit	Money		Y		Rent

Column	Type	Size	Req	Allowable values	Default
Rent	Money		Y		$650
Range	Logical		Y		T
Refigerator	Logical		Y		T
DishWasher	Logical		Y		T
CentralHeat	Logical		Y		T
CentralAir	Logical		Y		T
GasHeat	Logical		Y		T
PrivacyFence	Logical		Y		T
LastSprayDate	Date		N		
LastLawnDate	Date		N		
Comments	CommentsType				

Don't forget to flag the required fields appropriately and remember to set up the default value for each field that has one. Figure 8.16 shows this first stage of the PROPERTY table's construction.

FIGURE 8.16.

The first stage of the PROPERTY table's construction.

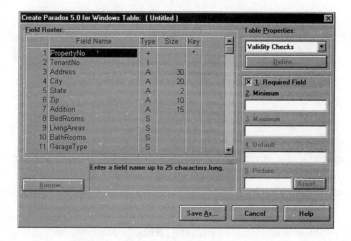

The next step in defining the PROPERTY table is to define the referential integrity constraints that control the data it may store. Click the Table Properties dropdown list box and select Referential Integrity from it. You'll then see Database Desktop's Referential Integrity dialog. In the Fields list on the left, double-click the TenantNo field. In the Table list on the right, double-click the TENANT table. This establishes the relationship between the TenantNo columns of both tables. Essentially, this defines the TenantNo column as a foreign key in the PROPERTY table that references the TENANT table. Any TenantNo that's stored in the PROPERTY table must first exist in the TENANT table. Likewise, any TenantNo that's in use in the PROPERTY table cannot be deleted from the TENANT table. Figure 8.17 shows what the dialog should look like once you're done. Click OK to save your constraint. When prompted for a referential integrity name, type TENANTTenantNo. This tells us at a glance that the column referenced by the constraint is the TenantNo column in the TENANT table.

FIGURE 8.17.

The Referential Integrity dialog box.

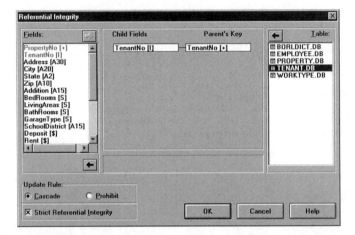

NOTE

Note that Database Desktop creates a secondary index over any column you set up with a referential integrity constraint. So, not only did the previous step create the RI constraint you specified, it also created a secondary index (named TenantNo, after its base column) over the PROPERTY table.

The final order of business with the PROPERTY table is the creation of a secondary index over the Address column. It's a pretty safe bet that users will want to access properties based on where they're located. Click the Table Properties dropdown list and select Secondary Indexes, then click the Define button.

As before, you're presented with the Define Secondary Index dialog. Double-click the Address field, then click OK. Type PROPERTY03_Address for the index name and click OK. The 03 in the name signifies that this is the third index over the table (the primary key index is the first index, and the automatically-created secondary index is the second one). You've now defined a secondary access path into the data that will speed access to it.

Figure 8.18 shows what the completed PROPERTY table definition should look like.

FIGURE 8.18.

The completed PROP-ERTY table.

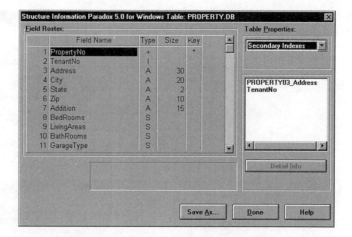

The WORDERS Table

Using the finalized definition in Table 8.27, create the WORDERS table using the Database Desktop. Be sure to flag the appropriate fields as required fields.

Table 8.27. The finalized table design for the WORDERS table.

Column	Type	Size	Req	Allowable values	Default
WorkOrderNo	AutoIncrement		Y		
PropertyNo	Long		Y		
EmployeeNo	Long		Y		
StartDate	Date		Y		
EndDate	Date		N		
Comments	CommentsType				

Once you've defined the columns, create referential integrity constraints on the PropertyNo and EmployeeNo columns that reference the PROPERTY and EMPLOYEE tables, respectively. Name them PROPERTYPropertyNo and EMPLOYEEEmployeeNo, respectively.

Next, define a secondary index over StartDate column named WORDERS04_StartDate. Figure 8.19 shows what the Create table dialog should look like when you're done.

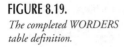

FIGURE 8.19.
The completed WORDERS table definition.

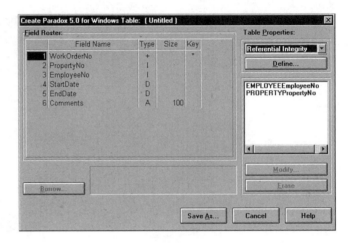

Click the Save As button and name the table WORDERS. You've now completed the WORDERS table definition.

The WODETAIL Table

You're now ready to proceed with the WODETAIL table. WODETAIL is the line item detail table for the WORDERS table. WORDERS is the master, and WODETAIL is the detail or slave table. Table 8.28 is the finalized definition.

Table 8.28. The finalized table design for the WDETAIL table.

Column	Type	Size	Req	Allowable values	Default
WorkOrderNo	Long		Y		
LineNo	Short		Y		
WorkTypeCode	Short		Y		
Comments	CommentsType				

Create the WODETAIL table using the Database Desktop just as you have the other tables. Figure 8.20 shows the completed column definitions for the WODETAIL table.

Once you've created the WODETAIL table to match the column specifications shown previously, create two referential integrity constraints. The first one refers to the WorkOrderNo column of the WORDERS table. The second refers to the WorkTypeCode column of the WORKTYPE table.

FIGURE 8.20.

The first stage of the WODETAIL table definition.

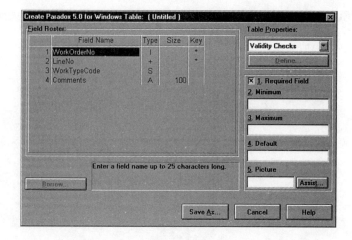

The CALLS Table

Now you're ready to create the last table in the RENTALMAN database, the CALLS table. Table 8.29 shows its finalized table definition.

Table 8.29. The finalized table design for the CALLS table.

Column	Type	Size	Req	Allowable values	Default
CallNo	AutoIncrement		Y		
CallDateTime	Timestamp		Y		Current date and time
PropertyNo	Long				
Description	DescriptionType				
Priority	Alpha	1	Y	L,M,H	L
WorkOrderNo	Long		N		
Comments	CommentsType				

Create it according to the previous specifications. Don't forget the Allowable Values and Default settings. Specify a picture mask of {L, M, H} in order to restrict values for the Priority field to "L", "M", or "H". The completed field list is shown in Figure 8.21.

FIGURE 8.21.

The completed field list for the CALLS table.

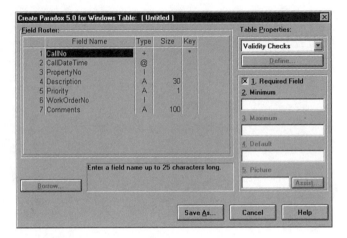

Once you've set up the columns for the CALLS table, define two referential integrity constraints. Set up the first one to reference the PropertyNo column in the PROPERTY table. The second one needs to reference the WorkOrderNo column in the WORDERS table. Also, create a Secondary Index on the CallDateTime column. This will speed up the generation of the reports that sort the table by date and time. Figure 8.22 shows the completed CALLS table definition.

FIGURE 8.22.

The completed CALLS table definition.

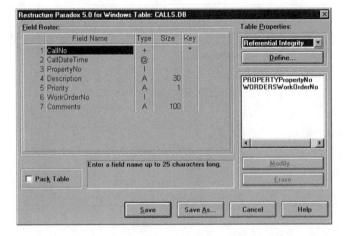

What's Ahead

Once you've completed the construction of the CALLS table, you're done with the creation of the Paradox database object necessary to service the RENTALMAN System. In the next chapter, we'll begin creating the requisite Delphi program objects needed to accomplish the application's goals. The foundation you've constructed in this chapter will serve as a sturdy yet flexible platform on which to build a full-featured Delphi database application in the chapters to come.

Summary

In this chapter, you designed and then implemented the RENTALMAN System's database. You defined the purpose and goals of the application, then designed and created the database objects necessary to meet those goals. In doing so, you garnered the following skills:

■ Determining the database objects that your application requires

■ Constructing a field repository

■ Using the field repository to build table definitions

■ Organizing your tables by type

■ Visually relating your tables

■ Creating database schematics

■ Normalizing your database

■ Creating keys, constraints, and defaults

■ Turning your design into actual database objects

9

First Steps

Now that your database objects have been created, you're ready to proceed with designing and developing the RENTALMAN application. The process of designing database applications is detailed in Chapter 7, "Application Design 101." You might want to review it before proceeding.

Let's begin by reiterating the five steps involved in database application development. We'll then pick up where we left off in Chapter 8, "Your First Real Database Application." These steps are:

1. Define the purpose and goals of the application.
2. Design the database foundation and application processes needed to meet those goals.
3. Develop the design into an application by creating the requisite database and program objects.
4. Test the application for compliance with the established goals.
5. Install the application for production use.

In Chapter 8, you completed the entirety of the first step and the first halves of steps two and three. In this chapter, you'll begin work completing the second and third steps by developing application objects to correspond to the database objects you created in Chapter 8.

Designing RENTALMAN's Database Foundation and Application Processes

Now that the database foundation has been laid, it's time to move on to building the processes needed to meet the application goals of the RENTALMAN System. The database acts as a platform on which the rest of the application is built. It's important to finalize it before getting too far into the application-building stage. Changes made to the database after the application is built can result in significant application pieces having to be redesigned or rebuilt.

Decide the Type of Application You're Building

According to Chapter 7, the first step in building any application is to decide what type of database application you're building. There are basically two choices: transaction processing systems and decision support systems. Generally speaking, decision support systems are utilized by management to achieve a bird's-eye view of some portion of a company's data. Transaction processing systems, on the other hand, are responsible for the entry and manipulation of this data. While decision support applications need only access data in a read-only fashion, transaction processing systems need to be able to both read *and* write data. This fundamental difference between the two types of applications is the reason you need to decide what type of application you plan to build before getting started.

The RENTALMAN System is definitely a transaction processing application. Users will need to be able to add, change, and delete data, so the system falls outside the realm of decision support applications. On the other hand, some of the information rendered by the application will probably be used in the decision-making process, so, as with many applications, this one is a bit of a hybrid. For our purposes, though, we'll design it as a transaction processing application.

Chart the Application's Operational Processes

Using the list of operational processes you developed in Chapter 8, chart the flow of each separate application process graphically. It's helpful at this stage to revisit the list of application goals for the system. To reiterate, these are:

The RENTALMAN System will track maintenance on rental properties:

- Record incoming calls from tenants:
    - Log calls from tenants as they are received
    - Assign calls received to a new or existing work order
- Track progress on maintenance work:
    - List open work orders
    - Generate a task schedule for each employee
- Provide historical maintenance information:
    - List the maintenance history for a particular piece of property
    - List the properties on which a particular type of work has been performed

In Chapter 8, we extracted the tables the system will need from the goals listed previously. These are:

> A table in which to store tenant calls
> A tenant table
> A property table
> An employee table
> A work order table
> A work order detail table
> A work type table for classifying the types of maintenance performed

When you chart the operational flow of the system, you can rely on formal flow-charting symbols or just use handwritten statements of what each process does—whatever works for you. Figure 9.1 illustrates a simple system flow chart for the RENTALMAN System.

Because the RENTALMAN System is a rather simple one from a design standpoint, a single-process flow chart can pretty much cover the entire system. With a more complex system, you might have several disparate-process flow charts. You could then link these into a system flow chart so that you better understand the overall boundaries of the system.

FIGURE 9.1.

A simple system flow chart for the RENTALMAN System.

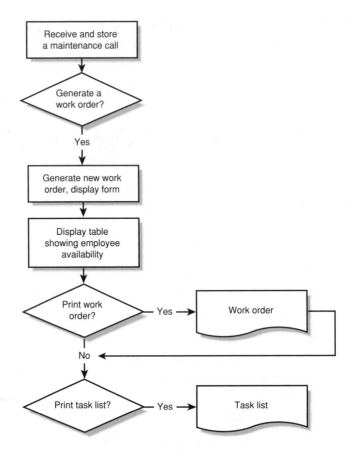

Label Operational Elements by Type

The next step is to go through the elements that make up the system's operational processes and label each one according to the type it represents. Here we'll decide which nodes will have corresponding forms or reports and which will have non-interactive support code. Each node should have one of these three associated with it. Using the flow chart in Figure 9.1, let's label each node according to the element it represents. At this stage, I usually go ahead and label each node with the name I intend to use for the corresponding form, report, or source code unit, as well. Figure 9.2 illustrates a more complete system flow chart for the RENTALMAN System.

FIGURE 9.2.

The nodes within the RENTALMAN system flow chart labeled by type.

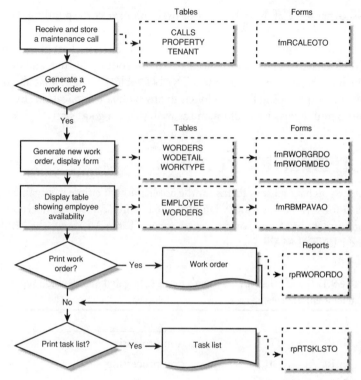

By studying the flow chart, we can come up with most of the forms and reports that the application will require. The list so far is (notice that the form names I've selected here follow the naming conventions outlined in Chapter 4, "Conventions"):

- fmRSYSMAN0—The system's main menu
- fmRCALEDT0—The call entry/edit form
- fmRCALGRD0—The call list grid
- fmRWORMDE0—The work order master/detail form
- fmRWORGRD0—The work order list grid
- fmREMPENT0—The employee quick entry form
- fmREMPGRD0—The employee list/edit grid
- fmRWKTGRD0—The work type list/edit grid
- fmRWKTENT0—The work type quick entry form
- fmRPROCGD0—The PROPERTY table control grid
- fmRTENCGD0—The TENANT table control grid
- rpRWORORD0—The work order print report
- rpRTSKLST0—The employee task list report

Note that some of the entries in this list don't have corresponding symbols in the flow chart in Figure 9.2. This is because many of these are implicit—you don't need a flow chart symbol to tell you that you'll need them. For example, if the flow chart points out the need for a PROPERTY table, you'll obviously need a form for adding, editing, and deleting PROPERTY table entries. The same is true for the TENANT table. Also note that a main system form (the first one in the preceding list) is implicit in any database application. Even though there are other forms and reports we could name as well, this is a good start.

Organize the Forms

Once you have a list of forms for the application, it's time to organize them. Decide what type each form is. Forms usually fall into one of three categories: decision support forms, transaction processing forms, or data-entry forms. Table 9.1 shows the breakdown of the forms for the RENTALMAN System.

Table 9.1. The RENTALMAN System's forms segregated into decision support, transaction processing, and data-entry forms.

Form	Type
fmRCALEDT0	Transaction processing
fmRCALGRD0	Transaction processing
fmRWORMDE0	Transaction processing
fmRWORGRD0	Transaction processing
fmREMPENT0	Data-entry
fmREMPGRD0	Transaction processing
fmRWKTGRD0	Transaction processing
fmRWKTENT0	Data-entry
fmRPROCGD0	Transaction processing
fmRTENCGD0	Transaction processing

As you can see, most of the forms are transaction processing forms. Only two are quick data-entry forms, fmREMPENT0 and fmRWKTENT0, and none are pure decision support forms. Note that I left off the application's main form, fmRSYSMAN0, and the reports frRWORORD0 and frRTSKLST0. This process of form segregation doesn't really apply to them. A system's main form doesn't need classification, and reports are, by design, decision support elements.

Design a Form Hierarchy

Now that you've segregated the forms into their respective types, it's time to design a form hierarchy. Because Delphi supports visual form inheritance, making use of a form hierarchy can save you lots of time designing forms. You can design an ancestor form that all similar forms inherit from. Then, when you need to make a change to a given type of form (say, the quick data-entry forms in your application), you can simply change the ancestor form and your modification will ripple through to its descendants.

Classes of Delphi Forms

The first step in designing a form hierarchy is to classify your forms by function. Delphi database forms can be divided into four general functional classes. These are:

- Entry/edit—Simple forms that represent a single record from a single table
- Grid—Forms that show several rows from a single table in a manner similar to a spreadsheet (each row occupies a single screen row)
- Control grid—Forms that show several rows from a single table (each row can occupy multiple screen rows)
- Master/detail—Forms that show a row or rows from two or more related tables

Now let's take the list of forms we've developed thus far and organize them into one of the four classes as shown. Table 9.2 shows the breakdown.

Table 9.2. The RENTALMAN System's forms organized into form classes.

Form	Class
fmRCALEDT0	Edit/entry
fmRCALGRD0	Grid
fmRWORMDE0	Master/detail
fmRWORGRD0	Grid
fmREMPENT0	Edit/entry
fmREMPGRD0	Grid
fmRWKTGRD0	Grid
fmRWKTENT0	Edit/entry
fmRPROCGD0	Control grid
fmRTENCGD0	Control grid

Given this breakdown, it's obvious that the RENTALMAN System has representatives from all four functional groups. It therefore makes sense to include ancestor forms for all four groups in the form hierarchy. Figure 9.3 illustrates a simple form hierarchy.

FIGURE 9.3.

A form hierarchy for the RENTALMAN System.

```
                        ┌──────────────┐
                        │   AnyForm    │
                        └──────┬───────┘
                               │
                               ▼
                        ┌──────────────┐
                        │ DatabaseForm │
                        └──────┬───────┘
                    ┌──────────┴──────────┐
                    ▼                     ▼
            ┌──────────────┐      ┌─────────────────┐
            │   EditForm   │      │ MasterDetailForm│
            └──────┬───────┘      └─────────────────┘
          ┌────────┴────────┐
          ▼                 ▼
   ┌──────────────┐   ┌──────────────┐
   │   GridForm   │   │  ControlGrid │
   └──────────────┘   └──────────────┘
```

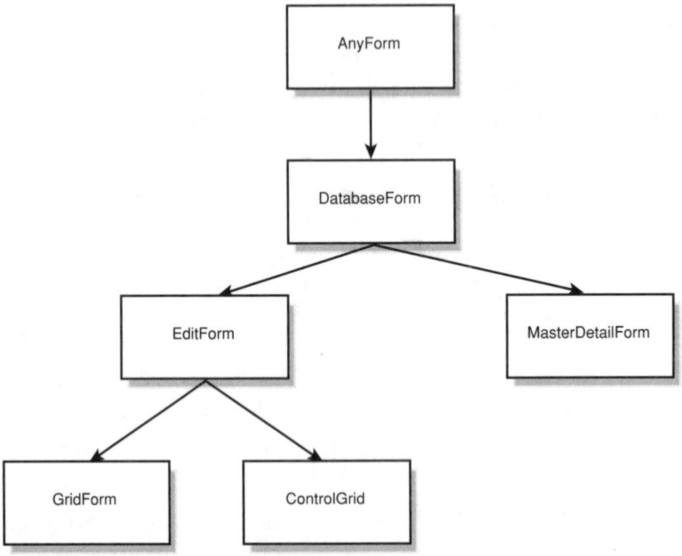

You'll create each of these ancestor forms first, then save them to Delphi's Object Repository so that you can inherit from them when you build new forms.

Note the inclusion of the form class AnyForm at the top of the hierarchy. You can use this form to ensure that all the forms in the RENTALMAN application—even non-database forms—have a consistent look and feel. When you create a new form for the RENTALMAN System, be sure to inherit from the AnyForm class.

Schedule the Development Process

Even though the next step (as listed in Chapter 7) is to schedule the development process, formulate a time line, and so forth, I'll skip that for the time being. In your own projects this is a good next step, but it's not applicable in a tutorial setting such as this one.

Build the Application

At long last, you're finally ready to begin actually building the application. You'll take the design we've developed thus far and put it into action. As I've said before, there's no *right* way to build an application. You may want to deviate from some of the design or development decisions made here and in the following chapters. Feel free to do so—few of them are key to the application working properly—most are a matter of preference. What I'm attempting to do in this and the ensuing chapters is introduce you to a wide variety of real database application development issues. You may find alternate paths through these issues that work better for you.

Start a New Project

Fire up Delphi and select File|New Application. Delphi presents you with a new project and a blank form.

Construct a Data Module

The next step in building the application is to create a data module form. A data module is a special type of form designed for holding non-visual controls like database access controls. The data modules presented in this book are database-oriented. That is, they store all the tables in a given database. In this case, the data module in the RENTALMAN application will include a `Table` and `DataSource` component for every table in the RENTALMAN system. I recommend that you create a data module for every database that you might want to access with Delphi applications. You don't have to put all the tables in a given database in a single data module. I recommend you do so when possible, however, because this enables you to save the data module to the Delphi Object Repository where you and others can reuse it when building applications. This helps ensure consistency across your applications and enables you to make changes to Delphi's access to a given database from a single place—the Object Repository.

So, select File|New Data Module. You'll be presented with a small form onto which you can then drop non-visual components. Click the `Name` property in the Object Inspector and change it to dmRentMan.

You may want to resize the form so that it's quite a bit larger before proceeding. Next, click the Data Access page on Delphi's component palette, and drop a `Database` component onto the form. Change its `AliasName` property in the Object Inspector to point to the RENTMAN alias you created in Chapter 8. Next, change its `DatabaseName` and `Name` properties to dbRENTMAN. Once you've done this, drop seven `Table` components and seven `DataSource` components onto the data module form.

> **TIP**
>
> You can quickly drop several copies of the same component by pressing Shift before you click the component in the palette. Then, each time you click on a form in Delphi's visual designer, you get another copy of the component. To end this repetitive drop mode, click the pointer arrow in the component palette.

Next, set the `DatabaseName` property of all seven `Table` components to point to the dbRENTMAN application-specific alias you previously created.

> **TIP**
>
> You can quickly select several components at once by dragging a selection rectangle over them. You do this by positioning the mouse pointer to the left and above the leftmost component, holding down button one, then dragging the rectangle that subsequently appears so that it encompasses the controls that you want to select. When you release button one, the controls within the rectangle will be selected.

Next, change the Name and TableName properties of the Table components to match the list in Table 9.3.

Table 9.3. Component and table names for the RENTALMAN System.

Name	*TableName*
taTENANT	TENANT
taPROPERTY	PROPERTY
taCALLS	CALLS
taWORDERS	WORDERS
taWODETAIL	WODETAIL
taEMPLOYEE	EMPLOYEE
taWORKTYPE	WORKTYPE

Once you've done this, reselect all seven tables and set their Active properties to True. This has the effect of opening all seven tables and will cause them to be automatically opened by any application that uses the data module. Figure 9.4 shows what the form should look like so far.

Now that the table components have been set up, it's time to set up the DataSource components. Change the DataSet and Name properties of the DataSource components to match the following list:

DataSet	*Name*
taTENANT	dsTENANT
taPROPERTY	dsPROPERTY
taCALLS	dsCALLS
taWORDERS	dsWORDERS
taWODETAIL	dsWODETAIL
taEMPLOYEE	dsEMPLOYEE
taWORKTYPE	dsWORKTYPE

Figure 9.5 shows the completed data module.

FIGURE 9.4.

The RENTALMAN System's data module.

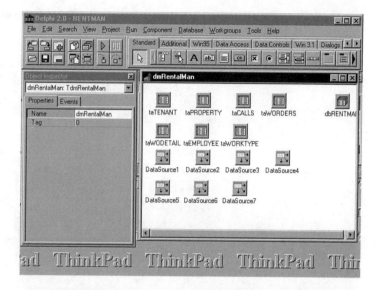

FIGURE 9.5.

The completed RENTALMAN System data module.

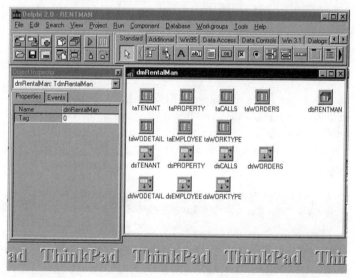

Now that the data module is completed, let's save it to the Object Repository. Right-click on the data module itself and select Add to Repository. Type dmRentalMan for the Title and Data module form for the RENTMAN database for the Description. Select Data Modules in the Page dropdown list box, then click OK. You'll then be asked whether you want to save the file first. Click Yes and enter \data\delphi\rentdata for the filename, substituting whatever directory you want for \data\delphi. Figure 9.6 shows the Add To Repository dialog box.

FIGURE 9.6.

Adding the dmRentalMan data module to the Object Repository.

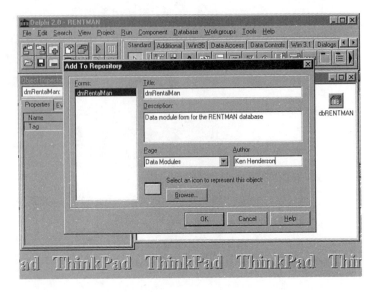

Now that you've added the dmRentalMan data module to the Object Repository, you'll be able to use it whenever an application needs access to the RENTMAN database.

Create the Form Hierarchy

The next step in developing the RENTALMAN application is to create the form hierarchy that was designed earlier. You'll also be able to reuse this form hierarchy in other systems you build with Delphi. To reiterate, the hierarchy defines six forms: a top level form, a database form, an edit form, a grid form, a control grid form, and a master/detail form. Let's begin by creating the top level form.

> **NOTE**
>
> The form dimensions in this chapter and throughout the rest of the book take a lowest-common-denominator approach to screen size—they assume VGA resolution. If you're operating at a higher resolution, some of the component size specifications—particularly the width and height properties—may need to be changed to match your resolution. Failing to scale these dimensions proportionately to your video resolution could make some of the forms appear askew.

AnyForm

Double-click the system menu of the data module form to close it, then click the New Form button (or select New/Form from the File menu). You should see a form named Form2 appear in Delphi's visual form designer. You'll customize this form and save it as the AnyForm form class (from the form preceding hierarchy) in the Object Repository.

Change the form's Name property to fmAnyForm, then change its Position property to poScreenCenter. Once you've done this, drop three Panel controls onto the form, arranging them vertically. Name them paTop, paMiddle, and paBottom, respectively. Set the Align property of the paTop panel to alTop, and delete the value in its Caption property. Set its Height property to 117. Set the Align property of the paBottom panel to alBottom and delete its caption, as well. Set its Height to 39. Set the Align property of the paMiddle panel to alClient and set its Height property to 117. Delete its Caption property as well.

In case you're wondering, we're designing this first form with three panels because the forms in this system will generally follow a three-panel design. Some won't need three panels, but most will. We're also defaulting the Position property of the form to ensure that each form in the system displays consistently. Figure 9.7 shows what the new form should look like.

FIGURE 9.7.

The completed AnyForm *class.*

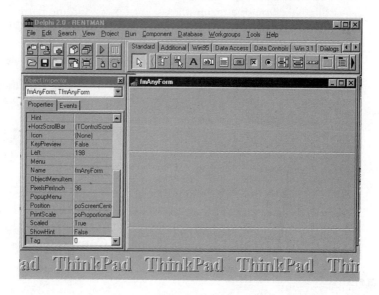

Now that the form's complete, you'll want to save it to the Object Repository. Right-click the form and select Add to Repository. Enter fmAnyForm for its Title and Top-level generic form class for its Description. Select Forms from the Page dropdown, then click OK. Figure 9.8 illustrates the completed dialog box.

Save the form as *data**delphi*\anyform, once again replacing *data**delphi* with the directory of your choice.

FIGURE 9.8.

Adding the AnyForm *form class to the Object Repository.*

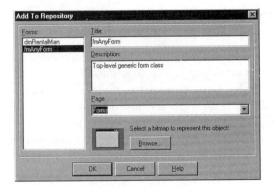

DatabaseForm

Now that the base form has been created, you can proceed with creating the DatabaseForm class. Select File/New from the menu, then select Forms. On the Forms page, click the AnyForm icon, then click Inherit on the right side of the dialog box. Click OK to create the new form. You should see a form named fmAnyForm2 appear in the Delphi visual form designer. You'll notice that it has inherited all the visual attributes of the original AnyForm class.

Change the form's Name property to fmDatabaseForm. Next, click the paBottom panel to select it, and then drop a DBNavigator component onto its left side. Follow this by reselecting the paBottom panel, then dropping a fourth Panel component onto its right end. Set the new Panel component's Name property to paRight, set its Align property to alRight, and set its BevelOuter property to bvNone. Delete its caption, and drag its left border to the right end of the DBNavigator control.

Next, drop two BitBtn's side by side onto the new panel. Place the leftmost button as close as possible to the left edge of its host panel. Resize the panel so that it is just large enough to contain the two buttons. Set the Kind property of the leftmost BitBtn to bkOK, the rightmost to bkCancel. Name the OK button bbOK and the Cancel button bbCancel.

Once you've finished with this, you've completed the DatabaseForm class. Figure 9.9 shows the completed form.

By way of explanation, I had you drop a fourth panel onto the paBottom panel in order to ensure that the form's OK and Cancel buttons will always be in its lower-right corner, no matter how the form is sized. Because the fourth panel is docked at the right side of the dialog box and the buttons "live" on it, they'll remain docked, too.

You're now ready to save the form to the Object Repository. Right-click the form and select Add to Repository. Enter fmDatabaseForm for the Title and Generic database form class for the Description. Select Forms in the Page dropdown list box, then click OK. Save the file as \data\delphi\dbform.

FIGURE 9.9.

The completed
DatabaseForm class.

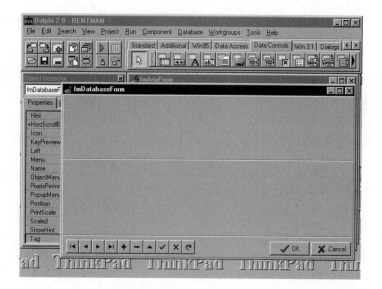

EditForm

Now that you've completed the DatabaseForm class, you're ready to proceed with the EditForm class. The purpose of the EditForm class is to provide a base for forms that edit a single table a row at a time. This form descends from the DatabaseForm class you just created, so click File/ New, then select DatabaseForm from the Forms page. Click the Inherit radio button, then click OK. You should see a form named fmDatabaseForm2 in the Delphi visual form designer. Change the form's caption to "EditForm," and its Name to fmEditForm.

Next, click on the paMiddle Panel component and set its Visible property to False. Once you've done this, set the Height property of the paTop panel to 233. This will have the effect of removing the paMiddle Panel component from the form, which is what we want. You might be wondering why I didn't just have you delete the paMiddle component. The reason for this is that Delphi won't let you delete a component in a descendant form that was introduced in one of its ancestors. Because AnyForm introduced paMiddle, we can't delete it in EditForm.

Once you've done this, you're finished with the EditForm class. Figure 9.10 shows the completed form.

Save it to the Object Repository with fmEditForm as its Title and Generic database edit form class as its Description. Store it on the Forms page. My suggested filename is *data**delphi*\editform.

FIGURE 9.10.

The completed EditForm *class.*

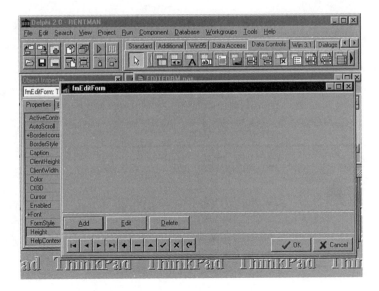

GridForm

The next class in the hierarchy is the GridForm class. It's a descendent of the EditForm class, so click File/New and select EditForm from the Forms page of the ensuing dialog box. Click Inherit, then click OK. You should see a form named fmEditForm2 in the Delphi form designer. Change the form's Name to fmGridForm and its caption to "GridForm."

The only change you'll make to this form is to drop a DBGrid component onto it. Select the paTop Panel component, then click the DBGrid component on the Data Controls palette page. Drop it onto paTop and set its Align property to alClient so that it takes up all the empty space on the panel component. Once you've done this, you're finished. Figure 9.11 shows what the form should look like.

Save the form to the Object Repository with fmGridForm as its Title and Generic database grid form class as its Description. Store it on the Forms page. My suggested filename is *data**delphi*\gridform.

FIGURE 9.11.

The completed GridForm *class.*

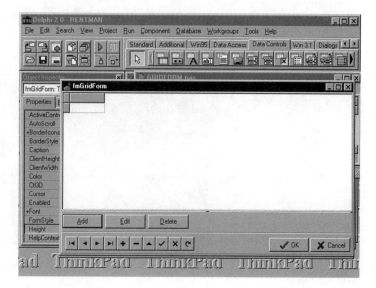

ControlGridForm

The next form class to define is the ControlGridForm. It, too, descends from EditForm, so click File/New and select EditForm from the Forms page of the New Items dialog box. Click Inherit and click OK. You should see a form named fmEditForm2 displayed in the visual form designer. Change the form's Name to fmControlGridForm.

The only difference between this form and the GridForm is that you'll drop a DBCtrlGrid rather than a DBGrid onto the paTop panel. Select the paTop Panel component, then drop a DBCtrlGrid component (located on the Data Controls palette page) onto it. Unfortunately, DBCtrlGrid doesn't have an Align property, so you'll have to size it manually so that it takes up the empty space on the panel. Figure 9.12 shows what the new form should look like.

Once you've done this, you're ready to save the form to the Object Repository. Save the form to the Object Repository with fmControlGridForm as its Title and Generic database control grid form class as its Description. Store it on the Forms page. My suggested filename is *data**delphi*\\cgrdform.

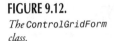

FIGURE 9.12.
The `ControlGridForm`
class.

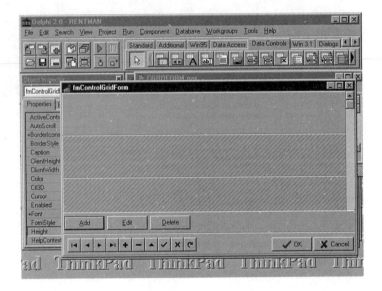

MasterDetailForm

The next and final form class in the hierarchy is the `MasterDetailForm`. It descends from `DatabaseForm`, so click File/New and select `DatabaseForm` from the Forms page of the New Items dialog box. Click Inherit and click OK. You should see a form named `fmDatabaseForm2` displayed in the visual form designer. Change the form's `Name` to `fmMasterDetailForm`.

The one change you'll make to this form is to add a `DBGrid` to the `paMiddle Panel` component. Click the `paMiddle` component to select it, then drop a `DBGrid` component (from the Data Controls page of the component palette) onto it. Set the `DBGrid`'s `Align` property to `alClient` so that it occupies all the available space on the `paMiddle` panel. Figure 9.13 shows the new form.

Once you've done this, you're ready to save the form to the Object Repository. Save the form to the Object Repository with `fmMasterDetailForm` as its Title and `Generic database master/ detail form class` as its Description. As with the other forms in the hierarchy, store it on the Forms page. My suggested filename is *data**delphi*\mstrform.

Now that you've created the base form classes and defined a working form hierarchy, you're ready to begin creating real forms. Nearly all the forms you create in the RENTALMAN System will descend from one of the form classes you just defined.

FIGURE 9.13.

The MasterDetailForm class.

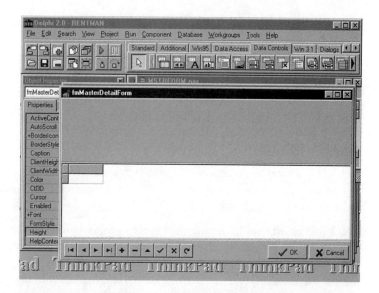

You can save the data module form and the form hierarchy form classes you just defined as a single Delphi project so that you can later easily load them as a set and work on them together. You'll find this to be especially handy in light of the fact that you can't open one of the repository forms in the visual designer without its ancestor forms loaded in advance. You'll have to load them as a set.

To save these forms as a stand-alone project, just save your current project, naming it something like "formrepo" for "form repository project." I recommend that you store it in the same directory that the forms themselves reside in. If you're prompted to name the original new form that was presented when you first created the project, you can use its default name, "unit1," because it's inconsequential as far the repository is concerned. In fact, you may want to remove it from the project before saving it.

The Main Form

The next step in building the RENTALMAN application is to build the application's main form. You begin this project by starting a new project, so click File/New and select Application.

Next, click File/New again and select Forms. Then click the fmAnyForm class and select Inherit. Finish by clicking OK to create the new form. You should then see a form named fmAnyForm2 in the visual designer. Change its Name to fmRSysMan0 and its caption to "Rental Maintenance Management System." Set its WindowState to wsMaximized. This will cause the RENTALMAN application to take up the entire screen when it begins.

Now select both the paTop and paBottom panels and set their Height properties to 30 pixels. The top panel will house application speed buttons; the bottom panel will be our application status bar.

Next, drop a MainMenu component anywhere on the form and set its Name to mmRentMan. This will be the application's main menu. Now, double-click the MainMenu component to start Delphi's menu designer tool.

Add a File menu item by setting the Caption property of the default menu item to "&File." The ampersand defines *F* as the menu item's hot key. Next, set up the File menu's first item to have a caption of "&Log a call" and a shortcut key of F2. You'll add each of the menu items for the File menu in the same manner. Table 9.4 summarizes the contents of the File menu.

Table 9.4. Items for RENTALMAN's File menu.

Caption	Shortcut
&Log a call	F2
&Print setup	None
E&xit	None

Next, add a Tables menu (set its caption to "&Tables") at the same level as the File menu (the root level) and add the items in Table 9.5 to it.

Table 9.5. Items for RENTALMAN's Tables menu.

Caption	Shortcut
&Calls	F3
&Property	F4
&Tenants	F5
&Work Orders	F6
&Employees	F7
W&ork Types	F8

The next menu to add is the Reports menu. It lives at the root level with the File and Tables menus (set its caption to "&Reports"). Add the items in Table 9.6 to it.

Table 9.6. Items for RENTALMAN's Reports menu.

Caption	Shortcut
&Work Order	F9
&Task List	F10

Finally, finish up the menu system by adding a Help menu at the same level as the other menus. Add it by setting the caption of the empty item on the right of the Reports menu to "&Help." Add a Contents item to the Help menu, setting its caption to "&Contents." Complete the Help menu by adding an About item with a caption of "&About."

Figure 9.14 shows the completed MainMenu.

FIGURE 9.14.
The completed RENTALMAN MainMenu *component.*

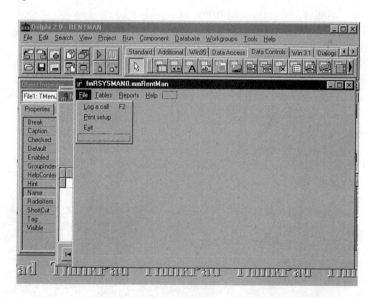

You've now finished the RENTALMAN System's main menu, so close the Delphi menu designer.

SpeedButtons

Now you'll set up speed buttons to access the system's more popular functions. Click the paTop panel to select it, then drop five SpeedButton components onto it, side by side. Select them all and right-click to bring up the menu. Click Align... and select Space equally in the Horizontal pane of the dialog box and Tops in the Vertical pane, then click OK.

Name the SpeedButton components sbLogCall, sbProperty, sbTenants, sbWorkOrders, and sbPrintSetup, respectively. You can set their glyphs to whatever you want—Delphi comes with several that you may find useful. They're located in the …images\buttons subdirectory under your Delphi program directory. Table 9.7 shows my suggestions for the five buttons.

Table 9.7. Suggested SpeedButton glyph settings.

Button	Glyph
sbLogCall	Phonerng.bmp
sbProperty	Property.bmp
sbTenants	Picture.bmp
sbWorkOrders	Tools.bmp
sbPrintSetup	Printer.bmp

Once you've added these buttons, we'll add a Help SpeedButton to the right of the paTop panel. First, click the paTop component to select it. Next, drop a Panel component onto the right end of the paTop panel. Clear its caption and set its BevelOuter property to bvNone. Set its Align property to alRight and set its Name property to paRight. Size it to be a little larger than a SpeedButton component. Now, drop a SpeedButton component onto the paRight component. Set its Name to sbHelp and set its glyph to Help.bmp in the previously mentioned directory. Because the panel is docked on the right of the form, the Help button will always remain there, as well. Figure 9.15 shows the form with the SpeedButton components in place.

FIGURE 9.15.
The RENTALMAN System's speed bar.

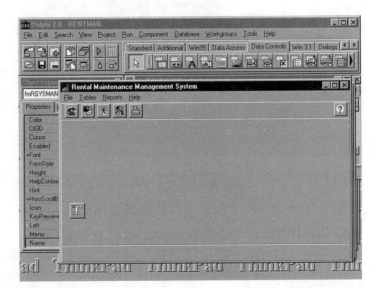

The Status Bar

Now that you've completed the speed bar, the only thing that remains to do on the system's main form is the construction of its status bar. Select the paBottom panel, then drop a StatusBar component (located on the Win95 component palette page) on to it. Name the StatusBar stRentalMan and set its Align property to alClient. Next, double-click its Panels property and add three panels to the list. Set the Text property of the first one to Status, the second one to User and the third one to Version. Set the Width of the Status panel to 275 and the Width of the User and Version panels to 150, then click OK.

Figure 9.16 shows the completed form.

FIGURE 9.16.

The RENTALMAN System's main form.

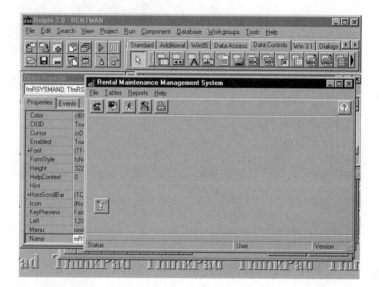

Test the Main Form

Now let's fire up the application to see what the main form looks like at runtime. Before you do anything, though, save the project so you won't lose your work if there's a problem. You'll want to remove Unit1 from the project (you don't need it at this point) by clicking the Remove from Project button or selecting Remove from Project from the Project menu. Be sure it's Unit1, not Unit2, that you remove. This will have the added effect of making fmRSYSMAN0 the application's main form in the Delphi project manager, which is what you want.

You can save your project and all its related files by either clicking the Save Project button or selecting Save All from the File menu. For the time being, I'd suggest you store the project in the same directory as the RENTMAN alias, C:\DATA\DELPHI\RENTMAN, by default. Save the Unit2 file as RSYSMAN0. Name the project itself RENTMAN.

Once you've saved the project, click the Run button or press F9 to run the application and test out the main form. Figure 9.17 shows what the main form should look like at runtime.

FIGURE 9.17.
*The first run of the
RENTALMAN application.*

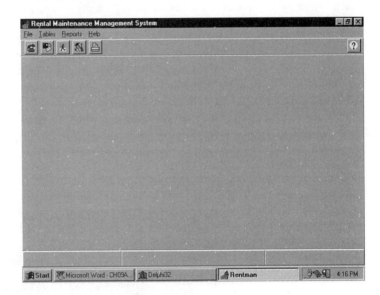

FIGURE 9.17.
*The first run of the
RENTALMAN application.*

What's Ahead

You've just completed the first stage of the development of the RENTALMAN application. In the remaining chapters of the Tutorial section, you'll construct the rest of the forms and other objects necessary to bring the RENTALMAN System to life.

Summary

In this chapter, you completed the design phase of the RENTALMAN application development project. You designed and created a form hierarchy for the project from which all its forms will descend, and you created a data module to service the data needs of the application. You also built the application's main form, fmRSYSMAN0, and placed speed buttons and a status bar on it.

Here's a brief rundown of the subjects covered in this chapter:

- ■ Designing RENTALMAN's database foundation and application processes
- ■ Identifying the type of application you're building
- ■ Charting the application's operational processes
- ■ Labeling operational elements by type
- ■ Organizing your forms
- ■ Designing and building a form hierarchy
- ■ Constructing a data module

■ Creating the `AnyForm`, `DatabaseForm`, `EditForm`, `GridForm`, `ControlGridForm`, and `MasterDetailForm` generic form classes

■ Building RENTALMAN's main form

■ Setting up speed buttons on a form

■ Adding a status bar to a form

10

First Forms

Now that you've completed the system's main form, you're ready to move on to the rest of the application. The first thing you need to do before constructing additional forms is to add a data module form to your application. This form will supply the RENTALMAN application with the database access that it needs.

Building a Data Module

If the RENTALMAN application is running, close it now. Next, select File/New from the Delphi main menu. On the Data Modules page, click the dmRentalMan selection and choose Use (not Inherit). This will add the Data Module you created earlier to the project. Rather than creating a new form, this adds the existing form to the RENTMAN project. Figure 10.1 illustrates the process of adding the form.

FIGURE 10.1.

*Adding the dmRentalMan
Data Module to the project.*

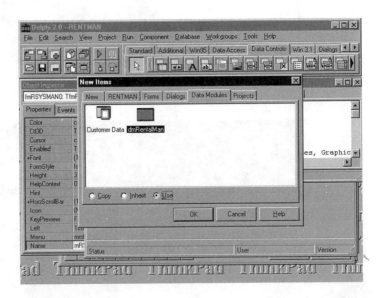

You may be wondering why you shouldn't inherit from the dmRentalMan Data Module in the Object Repository and create one of your own. After all, this would enable you to make changes to the module without affecting other projects. The reason for this is simple. Whenever you inherit from a form in the Object Repository, Delphi adds it and all of its ancestor forms to the project. This in and of itself isn't a problem. What is a problem, though, is that dmRentalMan defines an application-specific database alias that its tables then use. Application-specific alias names must be unique across a project. If you attempt to inherit from a form that defines one of these, you automatically break this rule because the same alias name would then be defined in two different forms—the form that originally defined it and its newly created descendant. This generates an error condition, and Delphi will refuse to create the second form because of it. Hence, the selection of Use rather than Inherit.

If you weren't using an application-specific alias, this wouldn't be a problem, but, as I've said previously, I recommend that you make use of a central Database component in your applications, and this requires the application-specific alias.

The one drawback to this approach is that changes you make to the objects on the Data Module form while building your application will cascade through to other applications that also make use of it. In some situations, this would be undesirable. However, in this situation, it's a reasonable assumption that any business rules you design on the application side for the RENTALMAN System would also be applicable to other projects. That is, you'd want them in place in *any* application that references the RENTMAN database, not just the RENTALMAN application itself.

Customize the Data Module

The first thing you'll do in building the RENTALMAN application is customize the Data Module form, dmRentalMan, to include column-specific information from the field repository you constructed in Chapter 8, "Your First Real Database Application." You'll add things like display properties, edit restrictions, and so forth to many of the fields in the tables referenced by the Data Module. Later, when you build forms that use these tables, your settings will be reflected in data-aware controls that you link with the tables.

Customizing the TENANT Table

Begin this customization by right-clicking the taTENANT column on the dmRentalMan Data Module form. In the ensuing dialog box, right-click again and select Add fields. You should then see all the fields in the TENANT table added to the list and the first one, taTENANTTenantNo, selected in the Delphi Object Inspector. (See Figure 10.2.)

We'll now add an edit mask for the Name, Employer, and EmpState fields. An edit mask restricts or modifies the data that is keyed into a field. Click on the Name field in the list, then double-click its EditMask property in the Object Inspector. In the Input Mask Editor dialog box, type the > character into the form's Input Mask entry box. This will cause all characters typed into the TENANT table's Name field to be uppercased. (See Figure 10.3.)

FIGURE 10.2.

Adding fields by using the Fields Editor.

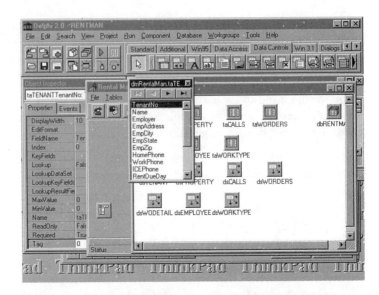

FIGURE 10.3.

Specifying an edit mask for the Name column.

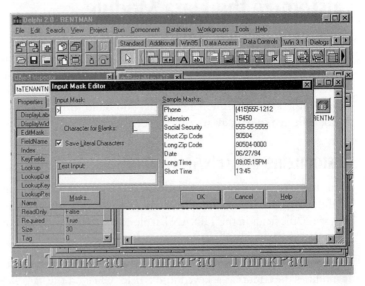

Next, click OK to save your mask and repeat the process for the `Employer` and `EmpState` columns.

Next up is the `EmpZip` column. Because it's a ZIP code field, we'll apply one of Delphi's built-in masks to it. Select it in the field list, then double-click `EditMask` in the Object Inspector. Notice that the Sample Masks list has two ZIP-code–oriented masks: Short Zip Code and Long Zip Code. Select Long Zip Code, then click OK. This will format ZIP codes entered into the field so that they match the standard U.S. business ZIP code format.

Next up are the HomePhone, WorkPhone, and ICEPhone columns. Select all three fields in the field list, then double-click the EditMask property in the Object Inspector. Notice that the first entry in the Sample Masks list is the Phone mask. Select it, then click OK. This will apply the mask to all three fields.

TIP

You can quickly select consecutive fields in the Delphi Fields Editor by positioning on the first field that you want to select, then pressing Shift-Down to select each successive field. You can select non-consecutive fields by pressing Shift+F8 while positioned on the first one, then moving to each additional field that you want to select and pressing the spacebar.

Now select the LeaseBeginDate, LeaseEndDate, MovedInDate, and MovedOutDate columns, and apply Delphi's built-in Date mask to them. Once you've done this, you're done with the TENANT table and ready to move on to the PROPERTY table.

Customizing the PROPERTY Table

Begin customizing the taPROPERTY component by invoking the Fields Editor and adding the table's fields to the component, as you did with the taTENANT component. Next select the BedRooms field from the list of fields, and click on the MinValue property in the Object Inspector. Notice that the minimum and maximum value restrictions you established in Database Desktop aren't reflected in Delphi's Object Inspector. Unfortunately, neither Delphi's own Table components nor the Database Explorer correctly import or use these settings. The main purpose of setting them, then, is to protect the data itself.

Even though neither Database Explorer nor Delphi itself reflect these field attributes, they must still respect them. In fact, any application that accesses the tables in the RENTMAN database, including Paradox itself, will have to respect the constraints you put in place on its tables. So, even though the MinValue and MaxValue properties aren't set in Delphi's Object Inspector, attempting to store a value outside the range you established when you built the table will fail. Your application will display an appropriate message if this occurs, and your user will then know what the problem is. Hopefully, a future version of Delphi will correctly import and use these settings.

Now select the LastLawnDate and LastSprayDate fields in the field list, then double-click the EditMask property in the Object Inspector. Select the Date mask from the Sample Masks list and click OK. Once you've done this, you're finished with the taPROPERTY component.

Customizing the CALLS Table

Next up is the CALLS table. Right-click the taCALLS component and add its fields in the Fields Editor. Next, click its CallDateTime field and double-click the EditMask property in the Object Inspector. Key the following mask into Input Mask field: !99/99/00 90:00;1;_, then click OK. (See Figure 10.4.)

FIGURE 10.4.

Setting the EditMask for the CallDateTime field.

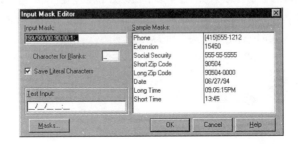

For now, this is all we'll do to the CALLS table. Let's move on to the WORDERS table.

Customizing the WORDERS Table

As you've done with the other tables, add the fields for the WORDERS table to the taWORDERS component. Once you've done this, select the StartDate and EndDate fields in the Fields Editor, then double-click the EditMask property in the Object Inspector. Select the built-in Date edit mask and click OK. This change is the only one you will make for the moment to the taWORDERS table. You're now ready for the EMPLOYEE table.

Customizing the EMPLOYEE Table

Add the fields from EMPLOYEE.DB to the taEMPLOYEE table component then select the Name field in the Object Inspector. Double-click its EditMask property and set it to the > character, as you did when customizing the TENANT table. Figure 10.5 demonstrates this change.

FIGURE 10.5.

Setting the EditMask property for the EMPLOYEE table's Name column.

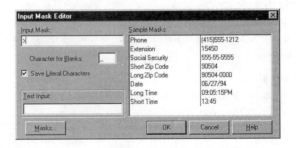

Customizing the WODETAIL and WORKTYPE Tables

Although we won't make any changes at this point to the taWODETAIL or taWORKTYPE table components, go ahead and add each table's respective fields to its corresponding table component. I recommend that you always create field components for the tables you access within your Delphi applications. Accessing a database field through its own component is the fastest way to get at it directly, should you need to. If you need to get at the current value of a field (such as to search another table, display on a form, and so forth), you'll need to access the field directly.

The EMPLOYEE Quick Entry/Edit Form

The next step we'll take in building the RENTMAN application is to create the EMPLOYEE table's quick entry form, fmREMPENT0. There are a couple of ways to go about this. I'll first take you through the easy way—using the Database Form Expert—and then through the "hard" way, building the form manually in Delphi's visual form designer. The Database Form Expert won't make use of our form hierarchy. Therefore, it isn't a permanent solution for creating simple forms for the RENTALMAN System. We'll explore it anyway so that you can get a feel for the potential of Delphi form experts. In Chapter 26, "Building Your Own Database Components," I'll show you how to create your own form expert.

Creating the Form Using the Database Form Expert

Start the Database Form Expert by choosing File/New from the Delphi menu, then selecting Database Form on the Forms page of the New Items dialog box. The purpose of a form expert is to build a form by asking you questions about what it should look like. It begins these questions by asking what type of form to create (simple or master/detail) and whether to use Table or Query components on the form. For now, just take the defaults and click the Next button. (See Figure 10.6.)

The expert then asks what table you'd like to make use of on the form. Begin by selecting the dbRENTMAN alias in the Drive or Alias name dropdown list box. Once you select dbRENTMAN, the list of tables changes to reflect the tables in the RENTMAN database. Double-click the EMPLOYEE table near the top of the list. (See Figure 10.7.)

Next, you're presented with a list of fields from the EMPLOYEE table. You can select them one at a time with the > button, or all at once using the >> button. Click the >> button, then click Next to proceed. (See Figure 10.8.)

FIGURE 10.6.

*The opening screen of the
Database Form Expert.*

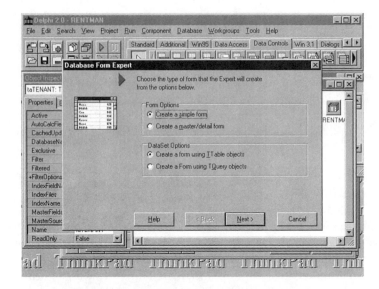

FIGURE 10.7.

*Selecting a table in the
Database Form Expert.*

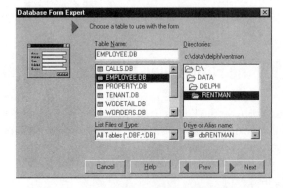

FIGURE 10.8.

*Selecting fields in the
Database Form Expert.*

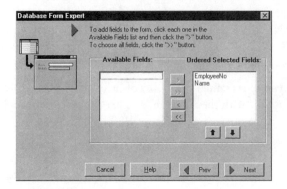

The next form presented by the expert asks you to select an orientation for the fields on the new form. You have three choices, Horizontal, Vertical, and Grid. Take the default, Horizontal, by clicking the Next button.

The next and final form presented by the Database Form Expert asks whether you want to generate the form as your application's main form. A checkbox at the top of the form enables you to select whether to "Generate a main form." Although this defaults to checked (or True), uncheck it. Your application already has a main form, fmRSYSMAN0, so you don't need to create this form as one. Finish up by clicking the Create button to generate the new form. Figure 10.9 shows the new form.

FIGURE 10.9.

The EMPLOYEE entry/ edit form as created by the Database Form Expert.

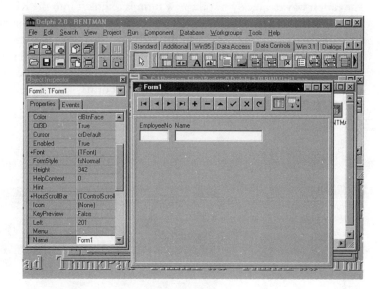

Note that the form includes its own Table and DataSource components. The forms you create will use the Table and DataSource components on the application's Data Module form, dmRentalMan. You can change this form to use them as well by following these steps:

■ Delete both the Table and the DataSource components from the form.

■ Select the Use Unit option from Delphi's File menu, then double-click the rentalman unit in the listing of available units. (See Figure 10.10.)

FIGURE 10.10.

Linking units together with the File/Use Unit option.

- Select the DBNavigator component on the form along with the two DBEdit components.
- Change the DataSource property of all three components to the dmRentalMan.dsEMPLOYEE DataSource. (It should be in the drop-down list for the DataSource property.)

Now, when you test the form, you'll actually be working with the RENTALMAN System's own Table and DataSource components.

Testing the New Form

The easiest way to quickly test the new form is to link it into the RENTALMAN application. To do this, select the fmRSYSMAN0 form, then select Use Unit from the File menu, and choose the Unit1 unit from the list. Next, double-click the form's MainMenu component. Select the Tables menu, and double-click the Employee menu item. This will place you in Delphi's code editor so that you can attach program code that executes when the menu item is clicked. Because your new form still has its default name, Form1, key the following single line of code into the code editor:

```
Form1.Show;
```

See Figure 10.11.

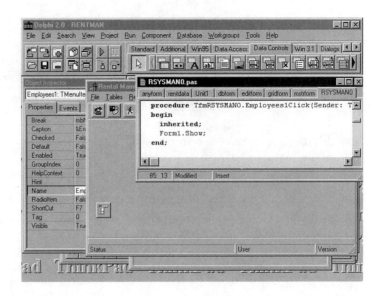

This will cause your new form to be displayed when either the Employees item on the Tables menu is clicked or its accelerator key (F7) is pressed.

Now let's run the application to try out the new form. Press F9 or click the Run button to execute the RENTALMAN application.

Once the application starts, press F7 to display the new form. Figure 10.12 shows what the new form should look like at runtime.

FIGURE 10.12.

The new form as it appears at runtime.

Once the form is displayed, you can add records, delete, or edit them—the form is fully functional. Click the + button on the DBNavigator to add a record, or click the - to delete it. Once you've viewed the new form, close both it and the RENTALMAN application and return to Delphi.

Removing the New Form from the Project

Because the new form doesn't use the form hierarchy that you built, remove it from the project by clicking the - button on the Delphi button bar or by selecting the Remove from project option on Delphi's Project menu. When the list of units in the project is then displayed, select the Unit1 unit for removal. When asked whether to save the unit, answer No.

Building the New Form Using Delphi's Visual Designer

Now that you've seen the "easy" way to build a database form in Delphi, I'll take you through the hard way. "Hard" is certainly a relative term, here, though—neither way is exceptionally difficult.

Begin by selecting File/New from Delphi's menu. Select the Forms page, then select fmEditForm from the list of forms. Click the Inherit radio button, then click OK. You should see a new form named fmEditForm1 loaded into the visual form designer. Change its Name property to fmREMPENT0 and its caption to "EMPLOYEE Quick Entry/Edit Form."

Once you've done this, drop two label components onto the left side of the form and align them vertically, one right above the other. Set the caption of the top label to "&EmployeeNo" and the caption of the bottom one to "&Name." Follow this with two DBEdits on the right side of the form, also aligned vertically and aligned horizontally with the two labels. Name the top DBEdit deEmployeeNo and the bottom one deName. Size the deName component so that it's at least twice as wide as the deEmployeeNo component. It'll surface the Name field from the EM-PLOYEE table, so it needs to be plenty large. Figure 10.13 shows the new form so far.

FIGURE 10.13.

The fmREMPENT0 form with its labels and DBEdits in place.

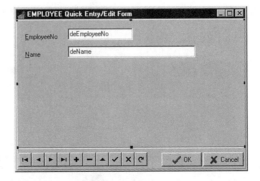

TIP

You can quickly drop data controls and labels on to a form by dragging TField components from a DataSet's fields list. Here's how:

- Bring up the dmRentalMan data module in the visual form designer and position it so that you can see the target form.
- Right-click the dmRentalMan DataSet whose fields you want to use and select Fields editor from the pop-up menu.
- Drag a field from the Fields editor to your target form. You should see both a data control and a corresponding label created on the target form.
- Note that you can specify which control to create for a given field by defining the TControlClass property of a Delphi's Attribute Set (in the Database Explorer), then applying that Attribute Set to the field.

Linking with the Data Module Form

Next, you'll link this form with the application's Data Module so that you can reference its database object. Select Use Unit from the File menu and select the rentdata unit from the list. Now select the form's DBNavigator and DBEdit controls. Set their DataSource property to point to the dmRentalMan.dsEMPLOYEE DataSource component. Now, unselect all three controls, and set the DataField property of each of the two DBEdits to point to its respective field in the EM-PLOYEE table. deEmployeeNo references the EmployeeNo column, and deName references the Name column. After you do this, set the FocusControl property of the top label to point to the deEmployeeNo control and the FocusControl property of the bottom one to point to the deName control.

Once you've completed these steps, the EMPLOYEE Quick Entry/Edit Form is essentially done. Save it before you proceed as REMPENT0.PAS.

Testing the New Form

Once you've saved your new form, you're ready to test it. To test it, you'll want to attach it to the menu system of your application's main form. Select the fmRSYSMAN0 form in the visual form designer and double-click its mmRentMan menu component. Select the Tables menu and double-click the Employee option. Change the Form1.Show line you entered earlier to fmREMPENT0.Show. This will cause the new form to be displayed when the Employee menu item is selected. Now close the menu designer and click Use Unit on the File menu. Double-click the REMPENT0 unit in the list. This will cause the system's main form, RSYSMAN0, to use the unit that defines the fmREMPENT0 form so that your call to its Show method will compile and work properly. Now save your project, then run the application. Figure 10.14 shows the completed form as it should appear at runtime.

FIGURE 10.14.

The completed fmREMPENT0 form.

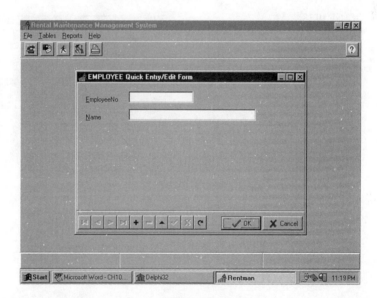

The WORKTYPE Quick Entry/Edit Form

Now that you've successfully created the EMPLOYEE form, you're ready to move on to the Work Type Quick Entry/Edit Form. Rather than lead you by the hand, I'm going to let you complete this form without me. Here are some general guidelines that should be of use to you:

■ The new form's Name is fmRWKTENT0, and its caption is "Work Type Quick Entry/Edit Form."

- It descends from fmEditForm, just like the EMPLOYEE form.
- Be sure to define accelerator keys for the labels you drop (using the "&" character in their captions) and be sure to set their FocusControl properties to point to their corresponding DBEdit controls.
- Remember to name the form's components in accordance with the naming conventions spelled out in Chapter 4, "Conventions."
- The form's data-aware controls should reference the dmRentalMan.dsWORKTYPE DataSource component.
- Remember that you'll need to do a File/Use Unit of the rentalman unit in order to "see" its database objects.
- Remember to connect the DBEdit components to their corresponding fields in the WORKTYPE table using the DataField property.

Figure 10.15 shows what the completed form should look like.

FIGURE 10.15.

The completed fmRWKTENT0 form.

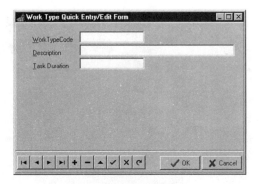

Once you've completed the form, link it into the application's main menu using the same steps you took to link the EMPLOYEE form.

What's Ahead

In the next chapter, we'll customize the two forms you just created a little further, then create several more. We'll make some changes to the quick entry forms that make them quicker to navigate and use. And we'll use visual form inheritance to save lots of time making these changes.

Summary

In this chapter you constructed a data module and two of the data entry forms needed by the RentalMan System. Creating these forms entailed accomplishing a number of smaller tasks.

Specifically, you:

- Created a new data module
- Customized DataSet components on the data module
- Created a quick entry/edit form for the EMPLOYEE table
- Created a new form using the Database Form Expert
- Removed the new form from the RentalMan project
- Constructed new forms using Delphi's visual form designer
- Established a link between new forms you created and a data module form
- Created a quick entry/edit form for the WORKTYPE table

Hopefully, you'll find that these smaller tasks have equipped you with the skills needed to take on RentalMan's more complex forms. We'll tackle them next.

11

Forms, Forms, and More Forms

In this chapter, you'll build the remainder of the data-entry forms for the RENTALMAN System. These forms will allow editing of the TENANT, PROPERTY, CALLS, and WORDERS tables. Building the wide variety of forms needed by the RENTALMAN System will give you a thorough introduction to constructing Delphi forms for use in database applications.

The TENANT and PROPERTY forms that you'll build are unusual in that they make use of the DBCtrlGrid component, Delphi's answer to the PowerBuilder DataWindow. A DBCtrlGrid enables you to display multiple records from the same table in a grid-like fashion. The distinction between a standard DBGrid and a DBCtrlGrid is that each table row can take up multiple screen rows in a DBCtrlGrid—that's not true with DBGrid. In DBGrid controls, each table row occupies exactly one row in the grid. You'll use the grid control for the CALLS and WORDERS forms, and the DBCtrlGrid for the TENANT and PROPERTY forms.

The TENANT Form

The TENANT form is a descendant of the fmControlGridForm class, so select File/New from Delphi's menu, then click on the Forms page in the New Items dialog box. Select fmControlGridForm, click on Inherit, then click on OK. You should see a form named fmControlGridForm1 in the visual designer.

Change the form's Name property to fmRTENCGD0 and its caption to "Tenant Edit Form." Next, select Use Unit from the File menu and select rentdata from the list. This will make the RENTALMAN System's Data Module form, dmRentalMan, available to your new form.

> **NOTE**
>
> You may want to unlock the form's controls before proceeding. This will make visually manipulating its controls easier. To do this, select the Lock Controls option on the Edit menu to remove the check beside it. The controls need to be unlocked only if you locked them previously on this form or on one of its ancestors—they're not locked by default.

The first thing you need to do with this form is resize it. Set its Height property to 400 and its Width property to 565. This will enable you to place the numerous fields of the TENANT table more easily.

Removing Inherited Components

Note that all three of the buttons you added to fmEditForm are present on this form. Because this form isn't designed to be a quick-entry form, you don't really need them. Nevertheless, you can't delete them because Delphi doesn't let you delete controls in a form that were introduced in one of its ancestors. There are, however, ways to remove them for all practical purposes and reclaim the space they take up on the form.

Click on the paMiddle panel and set its Enabled and Visible properties to False. Because it's a container for the three buttons you added earlier, this also disables them as well, which is what we're actually after here. Disabling the panel isn't worth much to us in and of itself except that this also disables its dependent components. Follow this by setting the Height property of the paTop component to 333. paMiddle and its buttons should then disappear from the form.

You might be wondering why it was necessary to disable the button controls. After all, what would it hurt to have their accelerator keys available even if they themselves aren't visible? Whether the controls are visible or not, their accelerator keys are still active until you disable them. This means that pressing a button's accelerator key would have the same effect as clicking the button. Basically, the button wouldn't be removed at all, it would merely be invisible. It's really just a matter of taste, but I personally don't like to set up "hidden" or unlabeled hot keys. If a given key does something special, it should be obvious from looking at the screen, in my opinion. If you don't agree, feel free to leave them enabled.

Configuring the *DBCtrlGrid*

Next, click on the DBCtrlGrid component and change its Width property to 552 and its Height property to 334. Notice that Delphi changes the 334 to 333. This is because your DBCtrlGrid is set up to handle three table rows by default, so there are three panes within the control. Because these three panes must be sized evenly, the total height of the control must be evenly divisible by three. The number 333 is evenly divisible by three, but 334 isn't. Finish configuring the DBCtrlGrid component by setting its DataSource property to dmRentalMan.dsTENANT.

There are 18 fields in the TENANT table. Sixteen of these are editable text fields, one is a read-only text field, and one is a Boolean field. Drop one DBText control, 16 DBEdit controls, and one DBCheckBox control onto the first of the DBCtrlGrid's three panels. Don't drop anything on the panels covered with gray diagonal lines. These panels are off-limits. Arrange the DBText control so that it is in the top left of the panel. This component will display the TenantNo column from the table. Position one of the DBEdit controls so that it is the last of the controls in the pane and on a line by itself—it will service the Comments column in the TENANT table.

> **TIP**
>
> To drop a given control repeatedly without having to return to the component palette after each drop:
> ■ Press and hold the Shift key.
> ■ Click the component in the palette (you can then release the Shift key).

■ Click the form once for each copy of the component you want to drop.

■ Click the pointer icon in the component palette to end repetitive drop mode.

Once you've dropped these components onto the form, set the Height property of each one to 19.

TIP

To change the properties of more than one component at a time:

■ Click the first component.

■ Press and hold the Shift key.

■ Click the remaining components.

■ Press F11 to jump to the Object Inspector. Only the properties common to all selected controls show up in the list. If you change one of the property values, you change it for all selected components.

■ You can also right-click any of the selected components to display a menu of actions that apply to all selected controls.

Table 11.1 shows the Name, Label, and DataField for each of the components on the DBCtrlGrid.

Table 11.1. DBCtrlGrid components and their attributes.

Name	*Label*	*Component*	*DataField*
teTenantNo	TenantNo	DBText	TenantNo
deName	Name	DBEdit	Name
deEmpAddress	Employer Address	DBEdit	EmpAddress
deEmpCity	City	DBEdit	EmpCity
deEmpState	State	DBEdit	EmpState
deEmpZip	Zip	DBEdit	EmpZip
deHomePhone	Phone/Home	DBEdit	HomePhone
deWorkPhone	Work	DBEdit	WorkPhone
deICEPhone	Emergency	DBEdit	ICEPhone
deLeaseBegin	LeaseBegin	DBEdit	LeaseBegin

Name	Label	Component	DataField
deLeaseEnd	LeaseEnd	DBEdit	LeaseEnd
deMovedIn	MovedIn	DBEdit	MovedIn
deMovedOut	MovedOut	DBEdit	MovedOut
deRentDueDay	RentDueDay	DBEdit	RentDueDay
dePetDeposit	PetDeposit	DBEdit	PetDeposit
dkLawnService	LawnService	DBCheckBox	LawnService
deComments	Comments	DBEdit	Comments

Note that the labels of all but the dkLawnService component will have to be dropped onto the DBCtrlGrid separately as Label components.

Figure 11.1 shows all the components in place.

FIGURE 11.1.

The DBCtrlGrid and its components.

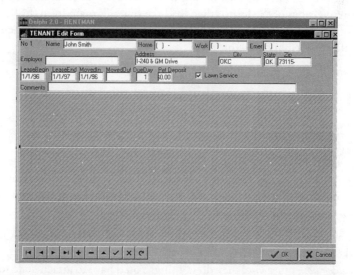

When not linked to an open DataSet, a DBEdit control always displays its component name in the edit box portion of the control. That is, unlike the standard Edit component, there is no way to clear the contents of an unlinked or closed DBEdit at design time. The component, however, will clear at runtime. This is in contrast to the Edit component, which can be cleared at design time by deleting the contents of its Text property.

Setting the Tab Order

Once you have the components in place, make sure their TabOrder properties are set correctly. You can view/change the TabOrder settings for all the controls at once using Delphi's Tab Order editor. Invoke the editor by selecting Tab Order from Delphi's Edit menu, then use the arrows to move a given component up or down in the list.

The only thing that remains to be done on the form is to set the DataSource property of the DBNavigator component. Set it to the same DataSource as the DBCtrlGrid, dmRentalMan. dsTENANT. Once you've done this, the form is ready to be wired into fmRSYSMAN0 for testing.

Linking the Form into the Application

To test the new form, you'll need to hook it into the menu system of your application's main menu. Save your form now as RTENCGD0.PAS (R is for the RENTALMAN System, TEN signifies the TENANT table, and CGD stands for dbControlGrid; 0 provides support for multiple versions of the form), then load the system's main form, fmRSYSMAN0, into the visual form designer and double-click the Tenants option on its Tables menu. Key the following code into the Delphi code editor:

```
fmRTENCGD0.ShowModal;
```

Then press F12 to return to the form designer.

ShowModal

If you're even a little familiar with Windows programming, you may be wondering why I have you displaying the form in a modal fashion. In other words, why didn't I just use the Show method rather than ShowModal? After all, ShowModal prevents you from switching to another form in the application until you close the modal form.

The reason for this is simple. Because the form's exit buttons, bbOK and bbCancel, both set the form's ModalResult property, they cause the form to exit properly *if the form is a modal dialog box*; otherwise, they do nothing. You'd have to attach code to both buttons in order to get them to close a non-modal dialog box, and it's easier for the time being to skip this. For now, we'll just display the form modally.

Testing the TENANT Form

Next, select Use Unit from the File menu and select RTENCGD0 from the list. This links the unit that encompasses the fmRTENCGD0 form with RENTALMAN's main form so that you can display it from the main form's menu system. Now, save your project and run it.

CAUTION

It's a good idea to save your work before running an application. This ensures that you do not lose your work if the application has a problem. This can be done for you automatically if you click the Autosave options/Editor files checkbox on the Tools/Options/Preferences menu. You can also save your project by clicking Delphi's Save Project SpeedBar button or by selecting Save All from the File menu.

TIP

Nearly anything you can do in Delphi with the mouse can also be done with the keyboard. Table 11.2 lists some keys that you may find useful. Note that some of these keys are only active if you are using Delphi's default keyboard layout.

Table 11.2. Some common keyboard shortcuts.

Key	*Function*
F11	Jump to the Object Inspector
F12	Jump to the code editor or form designer; toggle between them
Ctrl+Enter	Same as mouse double-click in the Object Inspector
Alt+Down	Drop down a list in the Object Inspector
Tab, Arrows	Move between properties or controls
Ctrl+Arrows	Move the current component in the form designer
Shift+Arrows	Size the current component in the form designer
Shift+F12	Select a form
Alt+0	Select a window
F9	Run the application
F1	Help for the current component in the form designer
F5	Toggle debugger breakpoint at the current line in the code editor
Ctrl+Tab	Jump to the next file tab in the code editor
Ctrl+Shift+Tab	Jump to the previous file tab in the code editor

Once inside the RENTALMAN application, press F5 to display the new form. Figure 11.2 shows what the new form should look like.

FIGURE 11.2.

The TENANT form as it appears at runtime.

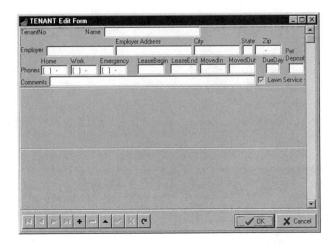

Adding Test Data

Now click the DBNavigator's row insert button (the + button) and add a row to the table. Repeat this until you have four new rows in the table.

Enhancing the Form

Careful inspection of the form once it's populated with data reveals that the phone fields aren't wide enough. However, there's no place to expand them. You'll have to rearrange the form to really get it right.

Maximizing the Form

In situations like this, it makes more sense to maximize the form than to spend hours economizing every inch of screen space. Though there are times when you'll want to avoid large forms (such as when you're building quick entry forms), doing so is usually not a problem. Maximize the TENANT form, then set its WindowState property to wsMaximized. As mentioned in Chapter 8, if your screen resolution exceeds that of your users, keep in mind that your forms may be clipped down to fit the lower resolution when displayed on your users' machines.

Rearranging the Form

Once you've maximized the form, you're in a better position to rearrange it. Move the phone fields up to the first line of the form, beside the deName field. You'll have to make some adjustments to some of the other components on the form, but you should find that you now have plenty of room to expand the phone fields. Another option here would be to shrink the font that they're using, but I don't recommend this. If at all possible, keep the fonts you use consistent within each form and between forms. Table 11.3 lists each component and the properties that are relevant to its positioning in the DBCtrlGrid.

Table 11.3. The components of the DBCtrlGrid and their placement.

Name	Left	Top	Width
teTenantNo	20	3	29
deName	87	1	147
deEmployer	51	33	147
deEmpAddress	230	33	143
deEmpCity	395	33	87
deEmpState	486	33	24
deEmpZip	513	33	70
deHomePhone	268	2	77
deWorkPhone	377	2	77
deICEPhone	484	2	77
deLeaseBeginDate	2	64	50
deLeaseEndDate	63	64	50
deMovedInDate	118	64	50
deMovedOutDate	172	64	50
deRentDueDay	232	64	26
dePetDeposit	275	64	29
deComments	56	84	497
dkLawnService	350	61	87

Resetting the Tab Order

One consequence of moving the phone DBEdits up next to the deName field is that the form's tab order now needs to be adjusted. Select Tab Order from the Delphi Edit menu and reorder the tab stops so that the phone fields immediately follow the deName component. Figure 11.3 illustrates the Edit Tab Order dialog box.

FIGURE 11.3.

Setting the tab order for the components on the TENANT form.

Aligning Components

Be sure to use the Align and Size options on Delphi's right-click menu to quickly and accurately align the controls on your form. You can easily align controls horizontally and vertically and size them to match one another using the pop-up menu in the form designer.

TIP

Always click the control that is to be stationary first when aligning a number of controls at once. This is because the form designer expects the "reference" component to have been selected first and aligns the other controls with it.

Expanding the *DBCtrlGrid*

One thing you may notice now that the form is maximized is that you now have quite a bit more vertical room on the form. In fact, you have so much more room that you can add a fourth row to the DBCtrlGrid. Click the DBCtrlGrid and change its RowCount property to 4 in the Object Inspector. You should now see the surface of the DBCtrlGrid divided into four panes. Figure 11.4 illustrates the revised version of the TENANT form.

FIGURE 11.4.

The new, improved TENANT form.

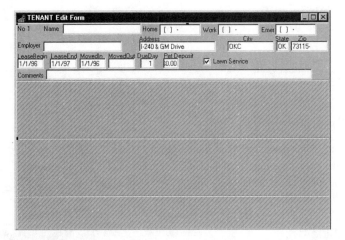

Setting Up the SpeedButton

Now that you've hooked the TENANT form into RENTALMAN's menu system, it's time to activate its corresponding SpeedButton as well. If the application is still running, close it. Load RENTALMAN's main form, fmRSYSMAN0, into the form designer and click on the

SpeedButton component you set up for the TENANT form, sbTenants. Press F11 to switch to the Delphi Object Inspector, then click the Events page. Click the dropdown list for the OnClick event and select Tenants1Click from the list. Tenants1Click is the name of the event that Delphi created when you double-clicked the Tenants option on the Tables menu in your main form's menu system. If you'll recall, you keyed in the following code for the Tenants1Click event:

```
fmRTENCGD0.ShowModal;
```

By setting the stTenants' OnClick to Tenants1Click, you cause the menu item and the SpeedButton to function identically. (See Figure 11.5.)

FIGURE 11.5.

Linking the Tenants SpeedButton and menu item.

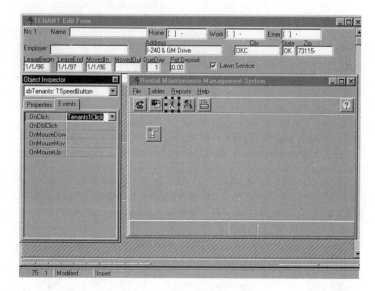

Now that you've linked it with the Tenants menu item, when you click the stTenants SpeedButton, you'll see the TENANT form just as if you had clicked the menu option. You can also associate fly-over hints with your SpeedButtons so that their functions are obvious. We'll cover these in Chapter 13, "Finishing Touches."

Testing the Revised Form

Now that you've completed the changes to the TENANT form, let's run it again and see what it looks like at runtime. Figure 11.6 shows the TENANT form populated with data at runtime.

Once you've completed the enhancements, you're finished with the TENANT form for the time being. Close the application and return to Delphi. Let's move on now to the PROPERTY form.

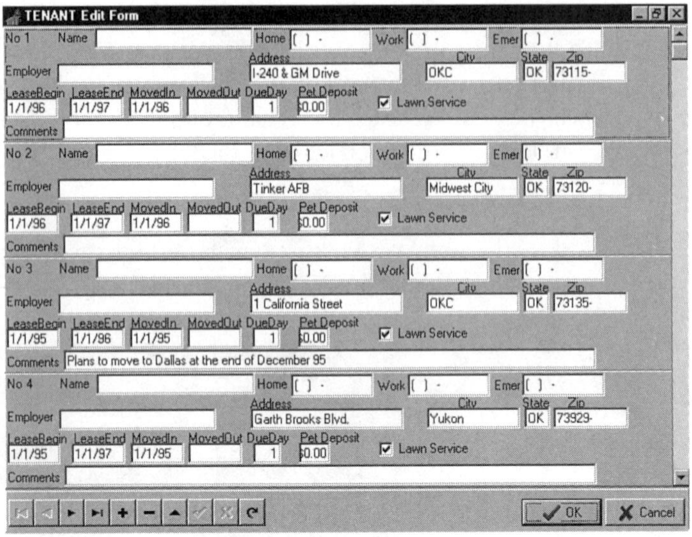

FIGURE 11.6.

*The new, improved
TENANT form at
runtime.*

FIGURE 11.6.

The new, improved TENANT form at runtime.

The PROPERTY Form

Click File/New from Delphi's menu and select the Forms page in the New Items dialog. Click the fmControlGridForm icon again, click Inherit, then click OK. You should see a new descendant form of the `fmControlGridForm` class in the form designer. You'll turn this form into one that edits the PROPERTY table.

Begin your customization of the form by renaming it to fmRPROCGD0 and setting its caption to Property Edit Form. Set its `WindowState` to `wsMaximized` and maximize the form. Go ahead and save the form now to the C:\DATA\DELPHI\RENTMAN directory and name it RPROCGD0.PAS.

Configuring the *DBCtrlGrid*

There are 24 columns in the PROPERTY table; seven of them are Boolean columns, and the rest are either text or numeric columns. Additionally, you'll add a special lookup column to translate the table's `TenantNo` column into something more meaningful—the tenant's name. Drop 15 `DBEdits`, seven `DBCheckBoxes`, one `LookupComboBox`, and one `DBText` component onto the top pane of the `DBCtrlGrid`. The `DBText` component will display the `PropertyNo` column. The `LookupComboBox` control will display the `Name` field from the TENANT table. It will also allow the PROPERTY table's `TenantNo` column to be set using the list of tenant names from the TENANT table. The control is two-way in that sense: it both displays data from the TENANT table based on the PROPERTY table's `TenantNo` column and also sets the `TenantNo` column using values from the TENANT table.

The 15 DBEdit controls will cover the PROPERTY table's textual columns, and the DBCheckBoxes will cover its Boolean fields. Be careful not to drop components onto anything but the topmost pane on the DBCtrlGrid—the other panes are off-limits.

Position the DBText component so that it's the top leftmost component on the DBCtrlGrid. Position the other components as shown in Figure 11.7.

FIGURE 11.7.

The first version of the PROPERTY form.

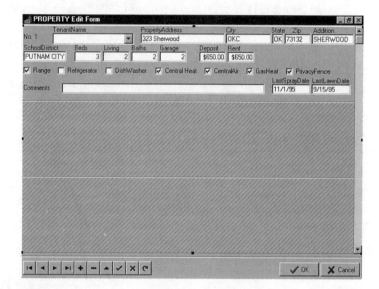

Linking the Components with the PROPERTY Table

There are four steps you must follow in order to link these components with the fields in the PROPERTY table. These steps are:

- You need to link the dmRentalMan Data Module with your new form. Select Use Unit from the File menu and select rentdata from the list of units.

- Next, set the DataSource property of the DBCtrlGrid component to the dmRentalMan.dsPROPERTY DataSource. While you're at it, set the DataSource property of the form's DBNavigator component to dmRentalMan.dsPROPERTY as well.

- Once you've set the DataSource property, create a Lookup field for the PROPERTY table that retrieves the Name column in the TENANT table using PROPERTY's TenantNo column. To do this, do the following:

  - Load the dmRentalMan Data Module into the visual designer.
  - Right-click the PROPERTY table and select Fields Editor.

■ Right-click the field list and select New field.

■ Type `TenantName` for the new field's Name, select String for its Type, and specify 30 for its Size.

■ Click the Lookup radio button, then set the Key Fields entry (in the Lookup definition section of the dialog) to TenantNo.

■ Select taTENANT as the lookup field's Dataset, then set its `Lookup Keys` property to TenantNo.

■ Set the Result Field entry to the Name field in the TENANT table, then click OK.

■ Click on each component in the `DBCtrlGrid` and set its `DataField` property to the appropriate PROPERTY table field, as specified in Table 11.4.

Table 11.4. The `DBCtrlGrid`'s components and their attributes.

Name	*Label*	*Component*	*DataField*
tePropertyNo	No.	DBText	PropertyNo
dcTenantName	TenantName	LookupComboBox	TenantName
deAddress	PropertyAddress	DBEdit	Address
deCity	City	DBEdit	City
deState	State	DBEdit	State
deZip	Zip	DBEdit	Zip
deAddition	Addition	DBEdit	Addition
deSchoolDistrict	SchoolDistrict	DBEdit	SchoolDistrict
deBedRooms	Beds	DBEdit	BedRooms
deLivingAreas	Living	DBEdit	LivingAreas
deBathRooms	Baths	DBEdit	BathRooms
deGarageType	Garage	DBEdit	GarageType
deDeposit	Deposit	DBEdit	Deposit
deRent	Rent	DBEdit	Rent
dkRange	Range	DBCheckBox	Range
dkRefrigerator	Refrigerator	DBCheckBox	Refrigerator
dkDishWasher	DishWasher	DBCheckBox	DishWasher
dkCentralHeat	CentralHeat	DBCheckBox	CentralHeat
dkCentralAir	CentralAir	DBCheckBox	CentralAir

Name	Label	Component	DataField
dkGasHeat	GasHeat	DBCheckBox	GasHeat
dkPrivacyFence	PrivacyFence	DBCheckBox	PrivacyFence
deComments	Comments	DBEdit	Comments
deLastSprayDate	LastSprayDate	DBEdit	LastSprayDate
deLastLawnDate	LastLawnDate	DBEdit	LastLawnDate

Lookup Fields

The TenantName field doesn't actually exist in the PROPERTY table but is instead a lookup field. A lookup field is a special type of column that is used to retrieve data located in a second table. In this case, the TenantNo column in the PROPERTY table is used to look up the Name column in the TENANT table.

By using lookup fields, you can easily reference values in other tables without any coding. The DBGrid, DBCtrlGrid, DataListBox, and LookupComboBox are all "lookup-field–aware" controls and will automatically update these fields as needed. In fact, DBGrid and DBCtrlGrid provide a dropdown list for fields that they determine are lookup fields. This means that not only does the control display the correct field from the lookup table, but it also lets you set the lookup's corresponding column in the current table using the dropdown list. Note that other types of components (for instance, DBEdit) *don't* automatically update lookup fields—you'll have to do it manually if you intend to use these controls with lookup fields.

Live Data at Design Time

After the components are linked with their corresponding database fields, you should see the first row of data in the DBCtrlGrid while still designing the form. This is because the PROPERTY table is already opened (we opened all the tables on dmRentalMan when we designed it), and Delphi displays live data when you attach a data-aware control to an open DataSet at design time.

Resetting the Tab Order

You may find that you need to re-establish the form's tab order once you've placed the components on the DBCtrlGrid and aligned them. To do this, select Tab Order from the Edit menu and use the arrow buttons to move components up and down in the tab order list. The components' tab order should match their physical layout on the form so that tabbing from one component to another does what the user expects.

Label Accelerators

Note that we aren't assigning any label accelerator keys to the labels on any of the forms in this chapter. This is because there are simply too many labels for this to be practical, and it's highly unlikely that a user would make much use of them anyway.

Table 11.5 lists the components on the DBCtrlGrid and their relevant display properties.

Table 11.5. The components of the DBCtrlGrid and their placement.

Name	Left	Top	Width
tePropertyNo	22	14	30
dcTenantName	56	14	152
deAddress	220	14	158
deCity	380	14	85
deState	467	14	21
deZip	489	14	50
deAddition	541	14	79
deBedRooms	97	47	50
deLivingAreas	150	47	50
deBathRooms	203	47	50
deGarageType	256	47	50
deSchoolDistrict	2	47	80
deDeposit	330	47	50
deRent	383	47	50
dkRefrigerator	66	74	79
dkDishWasher	155	74	80
dkCentralHeat	248	74	80
dkCentralAir	340	74	67
dkGasHeat	418	74	64
dkPrivacyFence	493	74	87
dkRange	2	74	53
deLastLawnDate	542	105	73
deLastSprayDate	467	105	73
deComments	74	105	379

Testing the PROPERTY Form

Once you've set up all the components and their properties, you're ready to test the PROPERTY form. Let's begin by wiring it into the application's main form, fmRSYSMAN0.

Linking the PROPERTY Form into the Application

Load the fmRSYSMAN0 form into the visual designer, then select Use Unit from the File menu. Double-click the RPROCGD0 unit in the list. This links the PROPERTY form with the main form so that you can display the PROPERTY form from within the main form's menu system.

Next, select the Tables menu on the main form and double-click the Property item. This should place you in the Delphi code editor. Once you're there, key in the follow source code:

```
fmRPROCGD0.ShowModal;
```

Remember that this causes the form to be displayed modally. That is, you can't do anything else in the application until you exit the form. We do this so that the OK and Cancel buttons that are already on the form will work correctly out of the box.

When you double-clicked the Property option in the Tables menu, Delphi created a class method (a procedure or subroutine) in its code editor named `Property1Click`. When called, `Property1Click` executes the single line of previously listed code that you keyed in. At present, the only time `Property1Click` is called is when the Property item is clicked with the mouse. Let's now link this same procedure to the stProperty SpeedButton.

Setting Up the SpeedButton

If you're still in the code editor, press F12 to return to the visual form designer, then click the stProperty SpeedButton component near the top of the form. Now press F11 to go to the Object Inspector and click the Events page. Click the dropdown list next to the `OnClick` event and select Property1Click from the list. This will cause the SpeedButton to behave identically to the menu option when clicked. This is more efficient than simply calling the `Property1Click` routine from an `stPropertyClick` routine because it alleviates the need for a separate procedure to service the `Click` event of the `SpeedButton` component.

Now save your work and run the application. Once the RENTALMAN System is on the screen, press F4 to invoke the Property dialog box. Figure 11.8 shows what the form should look like at runtime.

Note that you'll want to add some test data to the PROPERTY table to really give it a thorough testing. Figure 11.8 shows three rows of test data that I keyed in myself.

FIGURE 11.8.
The PROPERTY form as it appears at runtime.

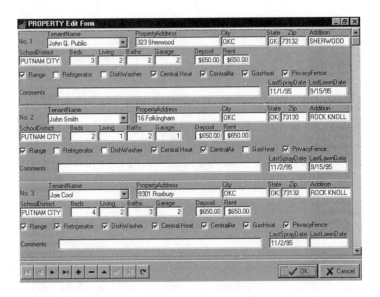

There are certainly other things you could do to both forms, but I think you've done enough that the process of building database forms should be second nature to you, particularly those that utilize the DBCtrlGrid component. In the next section, we'll cover the WORDERS and CALLS forms. They each require two forms and utilize the DBGrid component extensively.

The WORDERS Form

WORDERS is unique among the other forms in that it uses a master/detail metaphor to display data from the WORDERS and WODETAIL tables. These two tables are linked at the database level through referential integrity constraints. You'll link them visually on the WORDERS form by establishing a relationship between their Table components on the dmRentalMan Data Module.

If the RENTALMAN application is running now, close it. Next, select File/New from the Delphi menu. When the New Items dialog box is presented, select the fmGridForm generic form class and inherit from it. You should see a new form named fmGridForm1 loaded into Delphi's visual form designer.

This form will be the first thing that a user sees when the Work Orders option is selected from RENTALMAN's main menu. From this screen, a user will decide whether to insert, edit, or delete rows from the WORDERS table. If either insert or edit is selected, a second form, fmRWORMDE0, will be displayed that presents a master/detail visual metaphor for editing the WORDERS and WODETAIL tables simultaneously.

The Grid Form

The grid form gives a bird's-eye view of the WORDERS table. It enables the user to quickly peruse the work orders on file, something that should prove to be useful. On the other hand, the master/detail form allows the editing of a single WORDERS row along with its corresponding detail rows from WODETAIL. This form will also be unusual in that its database controls will not all reference the same DataSource. The controls on the top of the form will reference the WORDERS table, and the DBNavigator and DBGrid components on the bottom of the form will reference the WODETAIL table.

Note that we could drop a second DBNavigator onto the master/detail form and associate it with the WORDERS table—eliminating the need for the grid form. However, then you could not quickly browse the entirety of the WORDERS table. Rows would have to be negotiated sequentially, something the user would find undesirable with a transaction-oriented table like WORDERS. Also, the presence of two DBNavigators on a single form could tend to be confusing. It seems better to avoid it altogether.

Change the form's name to fmRWORGRD0 and its caption to "Work Order Selection Form." Once you've done this, save it as RWORGRD0.PAS.

There isn't much to do to this form to get it up and running. You'll begin by creating two lookup fields to retrieve descriptive information from other tables, and you'll finish by setting the DataSource property of the form's database components.

Creating the Lookup Fields

Bring up the dmRentalMan Data Module in the visual designer now and right-click the WORDERS table. Select Fields Editor, then right-click the list of fields. Select New field, then type PropertyAddress as the new field's name. Select String for its Type, and specify a Size of 30. Click Lookup, then set the Key Fields entry to PropertyNo. Set the DataSet entry to taPROPERTY, then set the Lookup Keys entry to PropertyNo, as well. Finish up by setting the Result Field to Address, then click OK to exit the dialog box. This will cause the Address field to be retrieved from the PROPERTY table and stored in the Work Order table's PropertyAddress lookup field. You should see your new field added to the bottom of the field list.

Now right-click the field list a second time and select New field again. This time you'll define a lookup field to retrieve the Name field from the EMPLOYEE table. This will enable you to display the name of the EMPLOYEE to whom a work order has been assigned. Name this field EmployeeName, set its Type to String, and set its Size to 30.

You'll now set the relevant properties in the Object Inspector, just as you did with the PropertyAddress field. Click Lookup, then set the Key Fields entry to EmployeeNo. Set the DataSet entry to taEMPLOYEE, then set the Lookup, Keys entry to EmployeeNo, as well.

Finish up by setting the Result Field to Name, then click OK to exit the dialog box. This will cause the Name field to be retrieved from the EMPLOYEE table using the EmployeeNo column in both tables and stored in WORDERS' EmployeeName lookup field.

Establishing a Master/Detail Relationship

While you're in the dmRentalMan Data Module, establish the master/detail relationship between the WORDERS and WODETAIL tables. This way, you can set up a master/detail form where the two tables are visually synchronized. Click the WODETAIL table, then press F11 to switch to the Object Inspector. Set the table's MasterSource property to point to the dsWORDERS DataSource. Next, click the ellipsis to the right of the MasterFields property to bring up Delphi's Field Link Designer.

The Field Link Designer

You'll use the Field Link Designer to visually establish a relationship between the WORDERS and WODETAIL tables. The left pane lists the columns in the WODETAIL table; those in the right are from the WORDERS table. Click the WorkOrderNo column in both lists, then click Add. (See Figure 11.9.)

FIGURE 11.9.

The Delphi Field Link Designer.

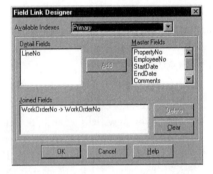

Clicking the WorkOrderNo column in both lists creates a link between the two tables using their WorkOrderNo column. The detail or slave table will appear as though it only contains rows whose WorkOrderNo column matches that of the current record in the master table. This will facilitate the two tables being visually linked on the master/detail form that you'll build momentarily. Note that you could have just typed WorkOrderNo into the MasterFields and IndexFieldNames properties—you're not required to use the Field Link Designer.

Using a Query to Increment a Field

Once you've defined the relationship between the WORDERS and the WODETAIL tables, you'll need to set up a Query component to supply the LineNo column in the WODETAILS table.

Drop a `Query` component onto the form and change its name to quWODETAILLineNo. Set its Database to dbRENTMAN and its DataSource to dsWORDERS. Double-click its `SQL` property, then key in the following query:

```
select max(LineNo) LineNo from WODETAIL
where WorkOrderNo = :WorkOrderNo
```

This query uses the `WorkOrderNo` column from the WORDERS table (because you specified dsWORDERS as the `Query`'s DataSource) to determine the next detail line number when adding rows to the WODETAIL table.

Once you've keyed in your query, click OK to exit the SQL editor. Next, right-click the `Query` component and select Fields editor. Right-click the fields list and select Add fields, then click OK to add the one field returned by the query. You can then close the Fields editor. Once you've done this, double-click the `Query`'s `Params` property and set the parameter's type to `Integer`, then click OK to save your change.

The *OnNewRecord* Event

Now that the `Query` component is set up, you need to add the appropriate code to taWODETAIL's `OnNewRecord` event to utilize it. Click the taWODETAIL `Table` component, then click the Events page in the Object Inspector. Scroll down to the `OnNewRecord` event and double-click it. Key the following code into the Delphi code editor:

```
taWODETAILWorkOrderNo.AsInteger:=taWORDERSWorkOrderNo.AsInteger;
 with quWODETAILLineNo do begin
  ParamByName('WorkOrderNo').AsInteger:=taWODETAILWorkOrderNo.AsInteger;
  Open;
  taWODETAILLineNo.AsInteger:=quWODETAILLineNoLineNo.AsInteger+1;
  Close;
 end;
```

The first line of code assigns the `WorkOrderNo` field in the current record of the WORDERS table to the `WorkOrderNo` field in the new record in WODETAIL. Notice the use of `ParamByName` to reference the parameter you defined earlier when you coded your SQL. The `Query` component is then opened (which executes its SQL) to retrieve the highest line number in WODETAIL for the current WorkOrderNo. This number is then incremented and assigned to the new record. This ensures that detail line numbers are sequential for each work order detail line that you add.

> **CAUTION**
>
> This method of determining a sequential numeric value for a table column is given only as an example of how to use `Query` components when adding rows to a table. Depending on the DBMS platform, this technique might not work correctly if rows are being added to a table by more than one user at a time.

> **NOTE**
>
> One thing you could do to enhance the performance of the application would be to prepare the quWODETAILLineNo `Query` when the dmRentalMan form is created. You could do this by placing a call to quWODETAILLineNo.Prepare in the Data Module's `OnCreate` event handler. The `Query` component's `Prepare` method sends a query to the database engine for parsing and optimization. The idea is that once the query has been prepared, all that needs to be sent to the server are the query's parameters. If the parameters change, only their new values need to be sent back to the server, not the entire query. This means that using `Prepare` is only advantageous with parameterized queries—queries, like this one, that receive parameters from outside the `Query` component. Although it's not required, using `Prepare` is a good idea because it could potentially make your queries run faster.

You might be wondering why we didn't just define `LineNo` as an auto-increment field. If we had, we wouldn't have to use a `Query` component to increment the number each time, it might seem. The problem with this, though, is that we don't actually want a sequential number here. What we want is a number that is sequential *within each work order*, not one that's sequential across the WODETAIL table. Thus, an auto-increment field wouldn't have done the trick for us—we need a more flexible method, and a `Query` component fits the bill perfectly.

Assigning a Column Default at Runtime

While you're on the dmRentalMan form, let's assign an `OnNewRecord` event for the WORDERS table, as well. Though you didn't define a default for the `StartDate` column in the RENTMAN database design, defaulting it to today's date would save having to key it, should a work order be keyed the same day it is to be started, which is likely. Click the taWORDERS component, then double-click the `OnNewRecord` event in the Object Inspector. Key the following code into the code editor:

```
taWORDERSStartDate.AsFloat:=Date;
```

This will assign the current date to the `StartDate` column. There are times when a database attribute, like a column default, must be implemented through program code. This is an example of such a situation. Of course, your preference should always be to define these attributes at the database level, if at all possible. If you can't define a column default through a default constraint, you might try a trigger (if your DBMS platform supports triggers). If you can't implement the default using either a default constraint or a trigger—which is the situation here—you may have to resort to program code. The disadvantage to defining the default with your Object Pascal program code is that other applications that update the table (for example, Paradox) won't be aware of or respect the default you implemented in your code. That's why it's always better to define database attributes in the database.

Assigning the *DataSource* Property

Once you've completed the work on dmRentalMan, you're ready to assign the DataSource properties for the Work Order form's DBNavigator and DBGrid components. Bring up the WORDERS form in the visual form designer, then click Use Unit on the File menu. Double-click the rentdata unit—this will link your new form with the dmRentalMan Data Module. Next, select both the DBGrid and the DBNavigator components, then switch to the Object Inspector and change their DataSource properties to dmRentalMan.dsWORDERS. This will set your form up to edit the WORDERS table in the RENTMAN database.

Configuring the Columns Displayed by *DBGrid*

Only one thing remains to do on the WORDERS grid form before you can test it. You need to edit the columns displayed by the DBGrid component to be more logical. Some of the columns in the WODETAIL table don't need to be displayed; they're already displayed elsewhere on the screen. Also, you don't need to display both a lookup's key field and its result field; all you really want is the result field. Furthermore, you don't want these result fields at the end of the column list where they're less visible, you want them as prominently displayed as possible.

Click on the DBGrid component, and double-click its Columns property in the Object Inspector. Next, click the Add All Fields button in the Columns Editor. Once all the fields are added, note that the two lookup fields you defined are at the bottom of the list. This isn't what you want. Click on the PropertyAddress lookup field and drag it up in the list so that it's just below the PropertyNo column. Drag the EmployeeName column up in the list so that it's just below the EmployeeNo column. Next, click on the PropertyNo column in the list, then click the Delete button to delete it. Do the same thing for the EmployeeNo column. This will remove these two columns from the DBGrid, but leave them intact in the table. Figure 11.10 illustrates the DBGrid Columns Editor dialog box. Once you've removed these columns, you're finished editing columns, so click OK.

FIGURE 11.10.

You use the DBGrid Columns Editor dialog box to configure the columns displayed by a DBGrid *component.*

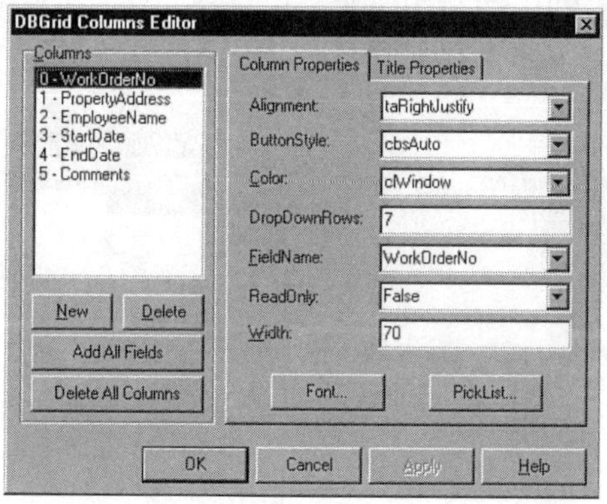

> **NOTE**
>
> Note that you were able to avoid setting up special column headings (using the Title Properties page of the Columns Editor) for the fields displayed by the DBGrid due to the sensible field-naming conventions we've used. That is, thanks to readable field names and the use of mixed case to differentiate the words in each field name, there's little reason to configure separate column headings for each column. This saves you both time and headaches.

Linking the Grid Form into the Application

You're now ready to hook the WORDERS grid form into the application. Bring up RENTALMAN's main form, fmRSYSMAN0, and double-click the Work Orders option on its Tables menu. This should place you in Delphi's code editor. Code a call to fmRWORGRD0's ShowModal method, as you've done with all the other forms. In case you need a refresher, here's the line of code you need:

```
fmRWORGRD0.ShowModal;
```

As mentioned, this enables the form's OK and Cancel buttons to work correctly out of the box. While you're at it, configure the corresponding SpeedButton, as well. Press F12 to return to the form designer, then click the sbWorkOrders SpeedButton component. Click the Events page in the Object Inspector, then click the dropdown list next to the OnClick event and select WorkOrders1Click from the list. This causes the SpeedButton and the Work Orders menu item to function identically.

Testing the Form

You're now ready to test your new form. Save your project, then press F9 to compile and run the application. Once inside the RENTALMAN application, press F6 to bring up the WORDERS grid form. Figure 11.11 shows the form at runtime.

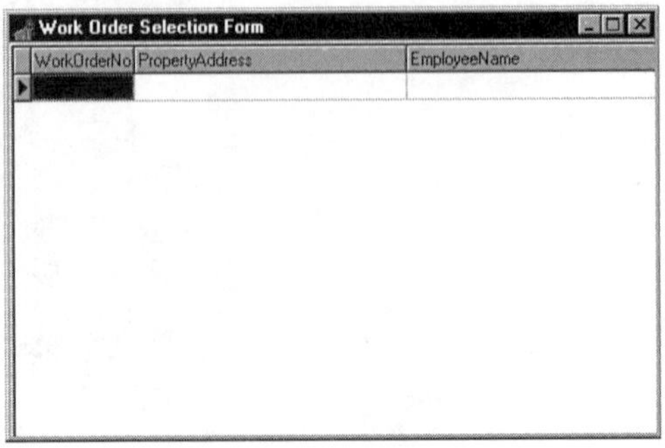

FIGURE 11.11.

The WORDERS grid form as it appears at runtime.

Enhancing the Form

There's one flaw in the form design that is immediately obvious. Although the form is set up to allow selection of work orders, it actually provides a very small window into the WORDERS table. If a form is going to enable you to easily select from a number of rows, it should display as many rows as possible. Furthermore, it should display as many columns as possible so that you can easily distinguish records from one another. If you attempt to maximize the form at runtime, you see that the paMiddle component takes up an inordinate amount of screen real estate and that the grid doesn't display any more rows than it did before. What you'll have to do is maximize the form in the visual form designer and adjust the sizes of the affected panels.

If the application is still running, exit it and return to Delphi. Now, select the form component itself in the visual designer (you may have to use the dropdown list in the Object Inspector because the form itself may be difficult to click on) and change its WindowState property to wsMaximized in the Object Inspector. Now return to the visual designer and maximize the form. Next, select the paTop component and set its Height to 385 in the Object Inspector. As I mentioned in the introduction to the Tutorial section, if you're using a resolution that's higher than that supported by the VGA standard, this height setting may not work for you—385 is the number for VGA. If you're using some other resolution, just be sure that your form looks like the one in Figure 11.12.

FIGURE 11.12.

The revised WORDERS grid form.

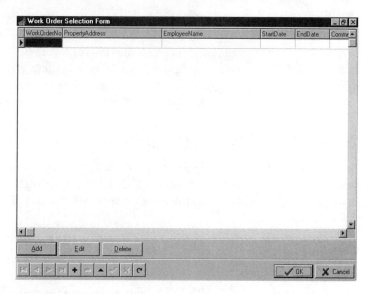

Making a *DBGrid* Read-Only

There's one more issue to address before you're completely done with the form. This form is supposed to function only as a row selector for the WORDERS table—it's not supposed to allow editing of the table itself. One of the reasons for this is that a form that edits the

WORDERS table will also need to allow the WODETAIL table to be edited because they're intrinsically linked. Another form, the fmRWORMDE0 dialog box, will allow editing of both tables simultaneously. The grid form need only allow row selection.

Given all that, you'll need to do a couple of things to implement it. First, you'll need to set the DBGrid's ReadOnly property to True in the Object Inspector. This prevents any editing of the data using the grid control. Data is displayed, but can't be changed.

Overriding *DBNavigator*

Once you've made the grid read-only, double-click the form's DBNavigator component. This should place you in the Delphi code editor. Once you're there, key in the following code:

```
With DBNavigator1 do
  case Button of
  nbInsert : begin
        DataSource.DataSet.Insert;
        fmRWORMDE0.ShowModal;
      end;
  nbEdit  : begin
        DataSource.DataSet.Edit;
        fmRWORMDE0.ShowModal;
      end;
  end;
```

This overrides the behavior of the nbInsert and nbEdit buttons. It first either inserts a new row or configures the DataSet to edit the current one, then calls the WORDERS master/detail form, fmRWORMDE0. This takes the responsibility of editing the WORDERS table from the grid form and gives it to the master/detail form instead. Note that this code won't compile until you've created the fmRWORMDE0 form. You'll create that form next.

The WORDERS Master/Detail Form

Select File/New from the Delphi menu and click the Forms page in the New Items dialog box. Click the fmMasterDetailForm icon, click Inherit, then click OK. Change the form's Name to fmRWORMDE0 and its caption to Work Order Edit Form. Save the form as RWORMDE0.PAS.

Lookup Fields

Prior to doing anything on the new form, let's define a lookup field for the taWODETAIL DataSet to retrieve the WORKTYPE table's Description field. To do this, bring up the dmRentalMan Data Module in the visual designer and right-click its taWODETAIL DataSet. Select Fields editor, then right-click again and select New field. Key WorkTypeDescription in the Name box, select String as the data Type, and specify 30 for the field's Size. Click the Lookup radio button, then set the Key Fields entry to WorkTypeCode. Set the DataSet entry to taWORKTYPE, then set the Lookup Keys entry to WorkTypeCode, as well. Finish up by setting the Result field to Description, then click OK to exit the dialog box. This will enable you to set the WorkTypeCode column in the WODETAIL table using the work-type descriptions stored in the WORKTYPE table. It will also translate WorkTypeCode values already in the WODETAIL table into their corresponding Description values on the form. Now that you've defined the new field, close the Fields editor and reload the new form in the visual form designer.

Setting the *DataSource* Property

Before you drop any components onto the form, let's set the DataSource property of the DBGrid and DBNavigator controls. Click Use Unit on the File menu and select rentdata from the list. This gives you access to the database controls on the dmRentalMan Data Module form. Next, select both the DBGrid and the DBNavigator components and change their DataSource properties to dmRentalMan.dsWODETAIL. The top of the form will display the current row in the WORDERS table, and the lower half will display its corresponding rows in the WODETAIL table.

Posting Detail Rows in Master/Detail Forms

Because of the form's two-table nature, you'll need to code a special routine to post a pending master record prior to adding detail records. This is because the referential integrity constraints that we put in place in the WODETAIL table insist that WorkOrderNo values stored in WODETAIL must first exist in WORDERS. Obviously, if a new record has been added, but not yet posted, to the WORDERS table, it does not yet exist as far as the referential integrity constraints are concerned. This results in an attempted post of a new detail row failing until its master record has been posted.

To handle this, deselect the DBGrid component, then double-click the DBNavigator component. This should place you in the DBNavigator1Click method in the Delphi code editor. Key in the following Object Pascal code:

```
with dmRentalMan.taWORDERS do
  if (State in [dsEdit, dsInsert]) and
    (Modified) then begin
    Post;
    Edit;
  end;
with DBNavigator1.DataSource.DataSet do
  case Button of
  nbEdit : Edit;
  nbInsert : Insert;
  end;
```

What this code does is check the state of the WORDERS table, and, if it's being edited or a new row is being added, posts any pending changes. It then immediately places the table back in edit mode so that you can still make changes to it. Because taWORDERS and taWODETAIL are linked in a master/detail relationship, this post has the effect of putting the taWODETAIL component back in browse mode, so the preceding case statement determines what button was clicked and reissues the edit or insert command.

> **NOTE**
>
> Technically speaking, it isn't necessary to check the State of the taWORDERS DataSet. It will always be in either edit or insert mode—that's the whole purpose of the work order master/detail form. However, it's still a good practice to check the mode of a DataSet before issuing a Post. A call to the Post method will generate an exception if the DataSet isn't in edit or insert mode.

Configuring the Columns Displayed by *DBGrid*

Once you've set up the DBNavigator, you're ready to configure the columns for the DBGrid component. Select the DBGrid component, then double-click its Columns property in the Object Inspector. Click Add All Fields, then remove the WorkOrderNo and WorkTypeCode columns from the list. You don't need to display the WorkOrderNo in the grid—it will already be on the top of the form, and you won't need the WorkTypeCode because you're provided a lookup field to display/edit it. Next, move the WorkTypeDescription up in the list, just below the LineNo column. Finish up by setting the Read-Only property to True for the LineNo column, then click OK to save your changes.

Dropping Components onto the Form

The WORDERS table has six columns—one of them is a read-only column, two are lookup columns from other tables, and the last three are simple text and date fields. Drop one DBText component, two LookupComboBox components, and three DBEdit components onto the paTop panel.

> **NOTE**
>
> As it relates to selecting a visual component to use with a particular field type, there's no distinction between numeric, date, and string table columns—you use the same components for all three data types. That is, a DBEdit might reference a string column, it might reference a date column, or it might reference a numeric column. You don't use one type of component for character data and another for numeric—there's no distinction between them at the component level.

Once you've dropped all the components, set their DataSource properties to dmRentalMan.dsWORDERS. Table 11.6 lists the components you need to drop and their key properties.

Table 11.6. The work order header components and their attributes.

Name	Label	Component	DataField
teWorkOrderNo	No.	DBText	WorkOrderNo
dcPropertyAddress	PropertyAddress	LookupComboBox	PropertyAddress
dcEmployeeName	EmployeeName	LookupComboBox	EmployeeName
deStartDate	StartDate	DBEdit	StartDate
deEndDate	EndDate	DBEdit	EndDate
deComments	Comments	DBEdit	Comments

Note that the labels for each component will have to be dropped onto the panel separately as Label components. Table 11.7 lists each component and its corresponding positional property settings. You can use this information to help you set up the form as Figure 11.13 depicts.

Table 11.7. The components of the paTop panel and their placement.

Name	Left	Top	Width
teWorkOrderNo	25	12	36
dcPropertyAddress	88	12	145
dcEmployeeName	248	12	145
deStartDate	8	51	76
deEndDate	96	51	76
deComments	8	86	401

FIGURE 11.13.

The WORDERS master/ detail form.

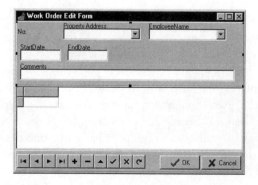

Testing the WORDERS Master/Detail Form

To test the fmRWORMDE0 form, you'll need to link it into the RENTALMAN application. Rather than attach it to the main menu, you'll attach it to the WORDERS grid form, fmRWORGRD0.

Linking the Master/Detail Form with the Grid Form

Load the WORDERS grid form that you designed previously into the visual form designer. Select Use Unit from the File menu and double-click your master/detail unit's name, RWORMDE0. This will allow the code you supplied earlier for the DBNavigator control to compile and work properly. While you're at it, let's set up the DBGrid control so that when it's double-clicked, the form behaves as if you'd clicked the Edit button. Click on the DBGrid component, then click the Events page in the Object Inspector. Click the dropdown list next to the OnDblClick event, and select btEditClick from the list. This will make double-clicking the grid do the same thing as clicking the Edit button.

Now, save your project and run the application. Figure 11.14 shows what the new form should look like at runtime.

FIGURE 11.14.

The WORDERS master/detail form at runtime.

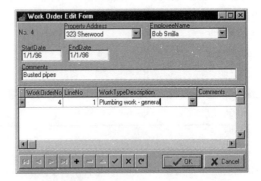

Enhancing the Form

After displaying the form at runtime, it's evident that there's an important enhancement you could make. Even though the property address is displayed at the top of the work order, what isn't displayed is the name and phone number of the person living there. Furthermore, if the rental property management company had two properties in adjacent cities with a similar street address, the worker might get confused and go to the wrong property. It would certainly be handy to list the name and phone number of the current tenant on the work order, as well as the city, state, ZIP code, and housing addition of the rental property.

Using a Query to Display Support Information

Like a lot of good ideas, this one's a little tricky to implement. In order to derive a TENANT row using the WORDERS table, you'll have to take the PropertyNo column from the WORDERS table and look up the corresponding PROPERTY record. Once you have the PROPERTY row, you can take its TenantNo column and look up the corresponding TENANT row. In database terms, this is known as a multilevel join. It is necessary because the database is normalized.

There are a couple of ways to go about constructing the multilevel join. First, you could simply issue calls to each table's FindKey method and manually look up any information you wanted. Second, you could issue an SQL query to perform the multilevel join and return the information you're looking for. We'll use the second approach.

The quTenantInfo Query

Begin by bringing the dmRentalMan Data Module back up in the visual designer. Drop a Query component onto the form. Change its name to quTenantInfo and its Database to dbRENTMAN. Double-click its SQL property and enter the following query:

```
select Name, HomePhone, City, State, Zip, Addition
from PROPERTY p,
TENANT t
where p.PropertyNo=:PropertyNo
and p.TenantNo=t.TenantNo
```

Once you've keyed in this query, click OK to save it.

Next, right-click the quTenantInfo Query component and select Fields editor. Right-click again from the Fields editor and select Add fields. Click OK to add the six fields returned by the query. Once you've done this, double-click the query's Params property and set the parameter's type to Integer, then click OK to save your change.

Now that the Query component is fully defined, the next step is to add a DataSource component to the form so that you can reference the Query with data-aware controls. Drop a DataSource component onto the Data Module and change its Name to dsTenantInfo. Set its DataSet property to point to your new Query component, quTenantInfo.

Linking the Query with the Form

Now that this is done, you're ready to wire the query into the WORDERS master/detail form so that it can retrieve the information you're after. Following this, you'll drop some components onto the form to display the information returned by the query.

Preparing the Query

Bring the WORDERS master/detail form back up in the form designer and select the form component itself (you may have to select it using the dropdown list in the Object Inspector because it's obscured by other controls). Click the Events page in the Object Inspector, then double-click the OnCreate event. Once you're in the Delphi code editor, key in the following line:

```
dmRentalMan.quTenantInfo.Prepare;
```

As mentioned previously, preparing a query that receives external parameters (a *parameterized query*, in Delphi lingo) can help it run faster. Calling Prepare sends the query to the database engine for parsing and optimization before you actually run it. Though calling Prepare isn't required, if you don't call it prior to opening a parameterized query, Delphi will call it for you. In fact, Delphi will call it each and every time you open the query. It makes sense, then, to go ahead and call it when the form that will use it is created.

Rearranging the Form

Now that the Query is all set up, move the deStartDate and deEndDate components (and their labels) to the right of the form to make room for the tenant information. Once you've moved them, drop six DBText components and six labels onto the form in their place. Name the components using the naming conventions outlined in Chapter 4, "Conventions," and used throughout this chapter. Set the DataSource property of all six DBText controls to dmRentalMan.dsTenantInfo. Set the DataField property of each control to its corresponding field in quTenantInfo's result set. You can use the dropdown list next to the DataField property to select from the list of available fields.

Triggering Query Execution

Now that the components are in place, the only thing remaining is deciding what event will trigger the execution of the query. There are two good candidates. The first event that should cause the query to execute is the display of the form itself. If a user edits a work order, you'll need to execute the query the moment the form comes up in order to display the relevant information. The second catalyst should be the selection of an item in the dcPropertyAddress LookupComboBox. That is, when a user clicks an item in the dcPropertyAddress box, you'll want to execute the query in case the selected property has changed. If the property that the work is to be performed on has changed, obviously the tenant information is also likely to change.

To attach the execution of the query to the display of the form, select the form component (you may have to use the dropdown list in the Object Inspector because the form is covered by other components), then click the Events page in the Object Inspector. Scroll down to the OnShow event and double-click it. This should place you in the Delphi code editor. Once you're there, key in the following code:

```
with dmRentalMan.quTenantInfo do begin
  If Active then Close;
    ParamByName('PropertyNo').AsInteger:=dmRentalMan.taWORDERSPropertyNo.AsInteger;
  Open;
 end;
```

The code closes the `Query` component if it's open, then reopens it. Because your new components are linked to the `dsTenantInfo` DataSource, this will have the effect of updating them.

Now that you've written a handler for the `OnShow` event that executes the query, you can make use of it for the `OnClick` event of the `dcPropertyAddress` component. Press F12 to return to the form designer, then click the `dcPropertyAddress` LookupComboBox. Select the Events page in the Object Inspector, then click the dropdown list next to the `OnClick` event, and select FormShow from the list. This will cause the query to execute both when the form is initially displayed and any time that the `dcPropertyAddress` component is clicked.

Figure 11.15 shows how the revised form should look.

FIGURE 11.15.

The revised WORDERS master/detail form.

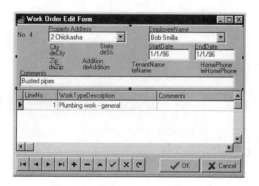

Testing the Form

Save your work now and run the application to see how well we did. Figure 11.16 shows the form as it should now appear at runtime.

FIGURE 11.16.

The revised fmRWORMDE0 form as it should appear at runtime.

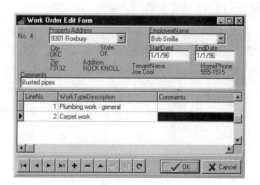

Resizing a Form with Panels

Note that, due to the optimal use of `Panel` components on the form, you can maximize or resize the form, and it will retain the same general proportions. Maximize the form now to see this. Figure 11.17 shows the form as it appears when maximized.

FIGURE 11.17.

The WORDERS master/ detail form can be maximized or resized without being distorted.

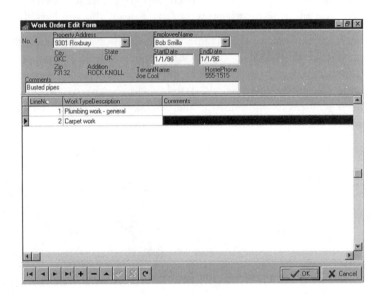

Further Enhancements

There's one more enhancement you can make to the form that would make it even more usable. Because each `WorkTypeCode` has a `TaskDuration` associated with it in the WORKTYPE table, it would make sense for the application to calculate how long the work order's tasks should take and adjust the work order's `EndDate` accordingly. The best way to do this is by using an SQL query.

Building a Query with the Query Builder

NOTE

Delphi's Visual Query Builder is not included with all versions of the product. If your version does not include it, skip to the section entitled "Testing the Enhancements."

Exit the RENTALMAN application and return to Delphi. Next, bring up the dmRentalMan Data Module in the form designer and drop a Query component onto it. Change the query's name to quWorkDuration and set its Database to dbRENTMAN. Next, right-click the Query component and select Query Builder from the menu. A dialog box asks you for the database to use. Double-click the dbRENTMAN database. The next dialog box prompts for the tables you'd like to use. Double-click the WODETAIL table first, then double-click the WORKTYPE table. Click Close to proceed. The next display you see shows the two tables side-by-side, as illustrated in Figure 11.18.

FIGURE 11.18.

The main screen of Delphi's Query Builder.

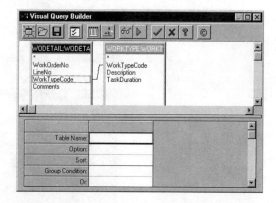

Drag the WorkTypeCode column in the WODETAIL table over to the WorkTypeCode column in the WORKTYPE table. You should then see a line connecting the two. This establishes a join between the two tables on the WorkTypeCode column.

Now you're ready to define what you'd like to retrieve from the tables based on the join. Double-click the WorkOrderNo column in the WODETAIL table to add it to the Query. You should see it at the bottom of the Query Builder's main form. Scroll down to its Criteria field and type = :WorkOrderNo to qualify the data it returns. Next, click the a+b icon in the Query Builder's button bar—you should see the Expression dialog box. You'll use this form to define the expression that totals the work duration for a given work order. Type WorkDuration in the Expression Name box. Next, select WORKTYPE from the Tables dropdown. Once you've selected the WORKTYPE table, double-click the sum() function in the Functions list, then double-click the TaskDuration field in the Columns list. Next, click the Save button, then click Close to return to the Query Builder's main form. (See Figure 11.19.)

Once back in the Query Builder's main form, click the Play button to test your query. You should see a result window like the one in Figure 11.20.

FIGURE 11.19.

The Expression dialog box of Delphi's Query Builder facility.

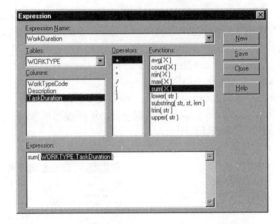

FIGURE 11.20.

The Query Builder's result window.

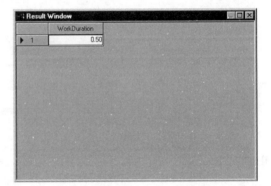

Close the result window, then click the View SQL icon in the Query Builder's button bar (it's the Glasses icon). The SQL that's generated by the Query Builder should look something like the following:

```
SELECT ( sum( WORKTYPE.TaskDuration ) ) as WorkDuration ,
 WODETAIL."WorkOrderNo"
FROM "WODETAIL.DB" WODETAIL , "WORKTYPE.DB" WORKTYPE
WHERE ( WODETAIL.WorkTypeCode = WORKTYPE.WorkTypeCode )
 AND
 (
 ( WODETAIL."WorkOrderNo" = :WorkOrderNo )
 )
```

A simplified version of the query would look like this:

```
SELECT SUM(WORKTYPE.TaskDuration) WorkDuration
FROM WODETAIL, WORKTYPE
where WODETAIL.WorkTypeCode = WORKTYPE.WorkTypeCode
and WorkOrderNo = :WorkOrderNo
```

This query will total the amount of work represented in the detail portion of the work order. At runtime, you'll supply the WorkOrderNo parameter so that the query sums up only the rows that correspond to the current work order.

Close the SQL Statement window, then close the Query Builder facility. Your new query will be saved automatically to the SQL property of the quWorkDuration component.

Using the Query in the Form

Next, right-click the new Query component and select Fields editor. Right-click the Fields editor and select Add fields. Select WorkDuration from the list and click OK, then close the Fields editor. This will enable you to easily refer by name to the column that's returned by the query.

Once you've defined a field component for the query, double-click the Query's Params property and set the parameter's type to Integer, then click OK to save your change.

The *AfterPost* Event

Now that the Query component is complete, you're ready to link it into the WODETAIL table. Click the taWODETAIL component, then click the Events page in the Object Inspector. Double-click the AfterPost event and key in the following code:

```
with quWorkDuration do begin
  if Active then Close;
  ParamByName('WorkOrderNo').AsInteger:=taWODETAILWorkOrderNo.AsInteger;
  Open;
  taWORDERSEndDate.AsFloat:=taWORDERSStartDate.AsFloat+
   quWorkDurationWorkDuration.AsFloat;
end;
```

Date Arithmetic in Delphi

As you can see, this bit of code executes the query, then adds its result to the StartDate column in the WORDERS table. This approach is based on two basic premises. The first is that Delphi stores date/time values as floating-point numbers. The integer part of the number is the number of days since 12/30/1899. The floating-point portion of the number is the time of day, expressed as a fractional part of the day. This enables you to add days to a date simply by adding whole numbers to it. The second premise is that the WORDERS table will be pointed to the correct record because you are currently editing it. In other words, you scroll the WORDERS table to a given row when you select a work order with your grid form. This row remains the current row in the WORDERS table until you move the cursor again. The bottom line to this is that you don't have to scan the WORDERS table to find the correct row to update—you're already there.

The *AfterDelete* Event

Note that the Post event isn't the only event that should cause a recalculation of the WorkDuration. You'll also want to do it after a delete in the WODETAIL table, so select the AfterDelete event in the Object Inspector, click the dropdown list next to it and select taWODETAILAfterPost from the list. This will make both events behave identically.

Testing the Enhancements

Now let's run the application to test it. As you add or delete line items on a work order, you should see its EndDate adjusted accordingly. Note that the work order form is automatically updated as you change the EndDate column on the dmRentalMan Data Module form—you don't have to do anything special to see the update. Also note that, even though you're adjusting the EndDate column by adding and deleting work order detail lines, this doesn't preclude you from overriding the calculated EndDate and supplying your own. You can still key in your own EndDate just as you could before installing the quWorkDuration component.

One Last Bell

There's one final enhancement that would make the work order master/detail form still more useful. Because employees will regularly be assigned to work orders, it wouldn't make much sense to let an employee be assigned to a new work order who's already working on another— a worker can't be in two places at one time. So, it would be sensible to filter the list of employees that the user can select on the work order form to include only those who are actually available. Workers that are unavailable shouldn't be on the list.

Filters

The best way to do this through a local filter on the EMPLOYEE table. By *local*, I mean that the filter will be enforced by the application, not the DBMS. All the records in the EMPLOYEE table will come to the application, as they must, but only those that list available employees will be visible from within the work order edit form.

Building a Query for Use Within a Filter

If the RENTALMAN application is still running, close it and return to Delphi. Load the dmRentalMan Data Module form into the visual designer. Next, drop a Query component onto the form, change its name to quEMPLOYEEAVAILABLE, and set its Database to dbRENTMAN. Double-click its SQL property, then key in the following query:

```
select max(EndDate) EndDate
from WORDERS
where EmployeeNo = :EmployeeNo
and WorkOrderNo <> :WorkOrderNo
```

This query returns the last date a given employee will be busy completing a work order. It retrieves this information by returning the latest EndDate value from the WORDERS table for the employee.

Once you've keyed in your query, click OK to exit the SQL editor. Next, right-click the Query component and select Fields editor. Right-click the fields list and select Add fields, then click OK to add the one field returned by the query. You can then close the Fields editor. Once you've done this, double-click the Query's Params property and set the parameter's type to Integer, then click OK to save your change.

Now that the query is set up, you're ready to wire it into the EMPLOYEE table. Click the taEMPLOYEE component, then double-click the OnFilterRecord event in the Object Inspector. Key in the following code:

```
if Screen.ActiveForm.Name = 'fmRWORMDE0' then begin
  with quEmployeeAvailable do begin
   If Active then Close;
   ParamByName('EmployeeNo').AsInteger:=taEMPLOYEEEmployeeNo.AsInteger;
   ParamByName('WorkOrderNo').AsInteger:=taWORDERSWorkOrderNo.AsInteger;
   Open;
   Accept:=(Trunc(quEmployeeAvailableEndDate.AsFloat)<=Date);
  end;
 end else Accept:=True;
```

Notice that this routine uses the Name property of the ActiveForm to determine whether the work order master/detail form is the current one. If it's not the current form, no filtering is performed. As you'll see in a moment, this is just an extra precaution to ensure that the EMPLOYEE table is filtered only when appropriate.

I should point out here that it would be slightly more efficient to simply use the form class itself, rather than its Name property, to identify the current form. In other words, you could have written the preceding opening if statement as

```
if Screen.ActiveForm = fmRWORMDE0 then ...
```

This, however, would have required that the dmRentalMan unit, rentdata, use the unit containing fmRWORMDE0. Because RWORMDE0 already uses the rentdata unit itself, this would create a circular unit reference, something you want to avoid when possible.

The *Filtered* Property

Once you've keyed in the preceding code, load the master/detail form back into the form designer and double-click its OnShow event in the Object Inspector. Add the following line of code to the OnShow event handler:

```
dmRentalMan.taEMPLOYEE.Filtered:=True;
```

Then return to the Object Inspector and double-click the OnClose event. Key in the following line of code for that event:

```
dmRentalMan.taEMPLOYEE.Filtered:=False;
```

This ensures that the EMPLOYEE table is filtered only when the fmRWORMDE0 form is on the screen.

Testing Once More

Now run the application and test your work. When you select from the dropdown list of employees on the work order form, you should see only those employees that aren't currently involved in other projects (it's assumed that an employee who is scheduled to complete a work order on a given day will be available for more work that same day). Now, close the application and return to Delphi.

Disabling the Filter

Despite the fact that it's generally a bad idea to double-schedule an employee, there are situations where the rental management company might want to do it anyway. An example would be when the employee finishes a job early and is ready for another. Without the ability to override your filter, the employee couldn't be scheduled to work on another project without first editing the last one he worked on. With this in mind, let's devise a way for the user to disable the filtering mechanism when needed.

Begin by moving the dkEmployeeName component as far left as you can without over-running the dkPropertyAddress component. Next, drop a CheckBox component to the immediate right of the dkEmployeeName component and delete its caption. Name it ckFilterAvailable. Size the component so that it's just wide enough to display the checkbox—you'll provide its caption separately. Double-click its Checked property to check the box. Now, drop a Label component to the right of the checkbox. Size it so that it's about 35 pixels high and about 50 pixels wide. Set its AutoSize property to False, and its WordWrap property to True, then set its caption to "Only show available workers?." Now, click the checkbox, then switch to the Events page in the Object Inspector and double-click its OnClick event. Key the following code into the Object Inspector:

```
dmRentalMan.taEMPLOYEE.Filtered:=ckFilterAvailable.Checked;
```

This will cause the clicking of the checkbox to toggle taEMPLOYEE's Filtered property. Now click the Label component you dropped to the right of the checkbox. Switch to the Object Inspector, click the dropdown list next to the OnClick event and select the ckFilterAvailableClick event. This will cause a click of the label to have the same effect as clicking the checkbox. Under normal circumstances, you wouldn't have to bother setting this up—clicking a checkbox's caption normally toggles the checkbox. The difference here is that, because the CheckBox component's built-in caption doesn't support word wrap, you had to drop a label onto the form rather than use the one provided by the component. Because your caption label is actually a separate component, it must be linked to the checkbox manually.

Another solution would be to eliminate a caption altogether and simply use a fly-over hint to label the checkbox. When the user then rested the mouse over the checkbox, its description would display in the form of a fly-over hint. Creating fly-over hints is discussed in Chapter 13, "Finishing Touches."

The final thing you need to do to finish this form is change the form's OnShow event to assign taEMPLOYEE's Filtered property based on the status of the checkbox's Checked property. You can no longer assume that it's safe to always set Filtered to True—the user may have toggled it to False on the work order master/detail form. So, click the fmRWORMDE0 form (you may need to select it in the Object Inspector), then double-click its OnShow event. Change this line:

```
dmRentalMan.taEMPLOYEE.Filtered:=True;
```

to the following:

```
dmRentalMan.taEMPLOYEE.Filtered:=ckFilterAvailable.Checked;
```

This will cause the form to take into account the status of the checkbox when it assigns the taEMPLOYEE component's Filtered property.

This completes the work order master/detail form, fmRWORMDE0. You're now ready to move on to the CALLS form.

The CALLS Form

Like the WORDERS table, the CALLS table will be serviced by two different forms. The first of these will be a grid form and the second will be an edit form. The grid form will be used for selecting records, and the edit form will be used for editing records.

The Grid Form

Select File/New from the Delphi menu and Inherit from fmGridForm to create a new form. Change the form's Name to fmRCALGRD0 and its caption to "Call Selection Form." Save the form as RCALGRD0.PAS.

Accessing the Data Module

You'll next need to link the new form with RENTALMAN's Data Module in order to make use of the CALLS Table and DataSource objects. Select Use Unit from the File menu, then double-click rentdata from the list. Next, select the DBGrid and DBNavigator components, and set their DataSource property to dmRentalMan.dsCALLS. This will link both controls to the CALLS table in the database.

Lookup Fields

You're now ready to define a lookup field for the taCALLS component that will translate the PropertyNo column into its corresponding Address. Switch to the dmRentalMan Data Module and right-click the taCALLS component. Right-click the field list and select New field. Name the new field PropertyAddress, set its Type to String, and its Size to 30. Click Lookup, then OK, to save your definition. In the Object Inspector, set the field's LookupDataSet to taPROPERTY, its LookupDetailField and LookupMasterField to PropertyNo, and its LookupResultField to Address, then close the Fields editor.

Defining a Column Default at Runtime

Next on the agenda is the definition of a default for the CallDateTime field in the CALLS table. Click the Events page in the Object Inspector, then scroll to the OnNewRecord event and double-click it. Key in the following line of code to execute when a new row is added to the CALLS table:

```
taCALLSCallDateTime.AsFloat:=Now;
```

This code uses Delphi's Now function to set the CallDateTime field to the current date and time.

Configuring the Columns Displayed by *DBGrid*

Switch back to the fmRCALGRD0 form and click the DBGrid component. Double-click its Columns property and click Add All Fields. Next, remove the PropertyNo column and drag the PropertyAddress column up in the list prior to the Description field. Set the CallNo field to Read-Only, then click OK to exit.

Turning a *DBGrid* into a Row Selector

Now set the DBGrid's Read-Only property to True. Remember, this form is to be used to select rows only. Now click the Events page in the Object Inspector, and click the dropdown next to the OnDblClick event. Select the btEditClick event. This will make double-clicking the grid have the same effect as clicking the Edit button.

Maximizing the Form

Set the form's WindowState to wsMaximized, then maximize it. Resize the paTop component so that the paMiddle component is automatically sized to about 39 pixels high.

Overriding *DBNavigator*

Now double-click the DBNavigator component and supply the following code:

```
With DBNavigator1 do
  case Button of
  nbInsert : begin
         DataSource.DataSet.Insert;
         fmRCALEDT0.ShowModal;
       end;
  nbEdit   : begin
         DataSource.DataSet.Edit;
         fmRCALEDT0.ShowModal;
       end;
  end;
```

This will override the default behavior or the DBGrid control and cause it to invoke the fmRCALEDT0 form when the Edit or Insert button is clicked.

Linking the Form into the Application

Now load the application's main form, fmRSYSMAN0, and double-click the Calls option on its Tables menu. Key in a call to the ShowModal method of the new form. While you're at it, set up the corresponding SpeedButton as well. Click the sbCalls SpeedButton component, then click the dropdown next to the OnClick event in the Object Inspector. Select Calls1Click and save your project. This will cause the SpeedButton and menu item to function identically.

Figure 11.21 shows the completed CALLS grid form.

FIGURE 11.21.

The completed CALLS grid form.

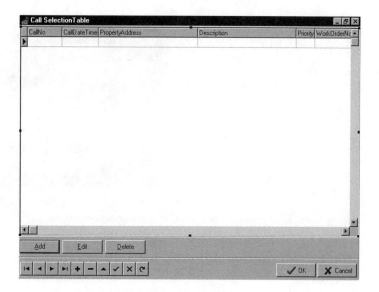

The Edit Form

Now that the grid form is complete, you're ready to move on to the edit form. Create a new descendant of the fmEditForm in the form designer. Name it fmRCALEDT0 and set its caption to "Call Edit Form."

Preventing a Form from being Resized

Set the forms BorderStyle property to bsDialog and its BorderIcons property to biSystemMenu. Next, select Use Unit from the File menu and double-click the rentdata unit. Save the form as RCALEDT0.PAS.

Populating the Form with Components

Drop three DBEdit controls, one LookupComboBox, one DBComboBox, and seven DBText controls onto the paTop panel of the new form. Drop corresponding Label components for each of the controls. Set the DataSource of the DBNavigator control, the topmost DBText control, and all the other editable controls to dmRentalMan.dsCALLS. These components will interact with the CALLS table. Set the DataSource of the remaining DBText controls to dmRentalMan.dsTenantInfo. These components will display the tenant and address information returned by the quTenantInfo Query component you built earlier. One of the advantages of placing the quTenantInfo component on the dmRentalMan form is that you can use it from any form that uses the Data Module, including this one.

Arrange the components so that the DBText component you attached to the dsCALLS DataSource is in the upper left of the panel and so that the form generally matches Figure 11.22.

FIGURE 11.22.

The preliminary CALLS edit form.

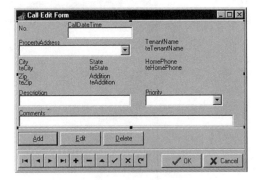

Set the DataField property of each component according to Table 11.8.

Table 11.8. The components of the paTop panel and their key properties.

Name	*Label*	*Component*	*DataField*
teCallNo	No.	DBText	CallNo
deCallDateTime	CallDateTime	DBEdit	CallDateTime
dcPropertyAddress	PropertyAddress	LookupComboBox	PropertyAddress
deDescription	Description	DBText	Description
dcPriority	Priority	DBComboBox	Priority
deComments	Comments	DBEdit	Comments
teCity	City	DBText	City
teState	State	DBText	State
teZip	Zip	DBText	Zip
teAddition	Addition	DBText	Addition
teTenantName	TenantName	DBText	TenantName
teHomePhone	HomePhone	DBText	HomePhone

Triggering Query Execution

Now that the components are in place, the only thing left is deciding what event will trigger the execution of the quTenantInfo query. There are two good candidates. The first event that should cause the query to execute is the display of the form itself. If a user edits or enters a call record, you'll need to execute the query the moment the form comes up in order to display the relevant information. The second catalyst should be the selection of an item in the dcPropertyAddress LookupComboBox. That is, when a user clicks an item in the dcPropertyAddress box, you'll want to execute the query in case the selected property has changed. If the property involved in that call has changed, obviously the tenant and address information is also likely to change.

To attach the execution of the query to the display of the form, select the form component (you may have to use the dropdown list in the Object Inspector because the form is covered by other components), then click the Events page in the Object Inspector. Scroll down to the OnShow event and double-click it. This should place you in the Delphi code editor. Once you're there, key in the following code:

```
with dmRentalMan.quTenantInfo do begin
  If Active then Close;
      ParamByName('PropertyNo').AsInteger:=dmRentalMan.taCALLSPropertyNo.AsInteger;
  Open;
 end;
```

The code closes the Query component if it's open, then reopens it. This will have the effect of updating the components that you attached to the dsTenantInfo DataSource.

Now that you've written a handler for the OnShow event that executes the query, you can make use of it for the OnClick event of the dcPropertyAddress component. Press F12 to return to the form designer, then click the dcPropertyAddress LookupComboBox. Select the Events page in the Object Inspector, then click the dropdown list next to the OnClick event and select FormShow from the list. This will cause the query to execute both when the form is initially displayed and any time that the dcPropertyAddress component is clicked.

Linking the CALLS Form with the WORDERS Master/Detail Form

The last step to be performed for this form is to link it with the work order master/detail form. This form will allow work orders to be generated and edited from within it without returning to RENTALMAN's main menu. Select Use Unit from the File menu and double-click the RWORMDE0 unit. Next, click the paMiddle panel, then drop a Button control just to the right of the Delete button. Change the Button's Name to btGenerateWorkOrder and its caption to "&Generate Work Order." Size it so that it's able to display the entire caption.

Now, double-click the new button and key the following code into the Delphi code editor:

```
With dmRentalMan do begin
  If (taCALLSWorkOrderNo.AsInteger=0) then begin
   taWORDERS.Insert;
```

```
    taCALLSWorkOrderNo.AsInteger:=taWORDERSWorkOrderNo.AsInteger;
    taWORDERSPropertyNo.AsInteger:=taCALLSPropertyNo.AsInteger;
  end else begin
   If not taWORDERS.FindKey([taCALLSWorkOrderNo.AsInteger]) then
    raise EDatabaseError.Create('Work Order has been deleted');
  end;
end;
fmRWORMDE0.ShowModal;
```

FindKey

This code does several important things. First, it distinguishes between a generation of a new work order and an edit of an existing one by looking at the WorkOrderNo column of the CALLS table. Second, if the action to be taken is an edit, the routine uses the FindKey method of the taWORDERS component to scroll the DataSet to the correct work order record. Lastly, notice that the code checks the result of the FindKey to ensure that it's successful, and, if not, raises an exception. Although this should never be possible because of the referential integrity constraint between the CALLS and WORDERS tables, if it were to occur, an error message would be displayed and the work order form would be skipped. Control would then return to the CALLS form. This is exactly what you'd want in that situation.

Dynamically Setting a Button's Caption

The only thing that remains to be done is to dynamically set the caption of the btGenerateWorkOrder button based on whether clicking it will produce a new work order or edit an existing one. The best place to do this is in the form's OnShow event. Select the form, then double-click its OnShow event in the Object Inspector. Once you're in the Delphi code editor, add this code to the bottom of the procedure already in place:

```
If (dmRentalMan.taCALLSWorkOrderNo.AsInteger=0) then
   btGenerateWorkOrder.Caption:='&Generate Work Order'
else
   btGenerateWorkOrder.Caption:='Edit &Work Order';
```

> **NOTE**
>
> Note that whatever code is added to the OnShow event handler will also get executed when the dcPropertyAddress component is clicked, due to your having set its OnClick event to point to the FormShow method. That's fine in this case, but it's something you'll want to be aware of as you customize the form.

Testing the CALLS Edit Form

Save your project and run the application. Figure 11.23 shows what the CALLS edit form should look like at runtime.

FIGURE 11.23.
The completed CALLS form at runtime.

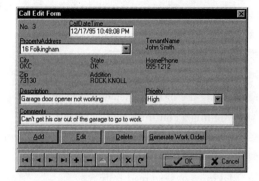

What's Ahead

Now that you've completed the lion's share of the forms in the RENTALMAN System, you're ready to move on to building reports. In the next chapter, you'll create RENTALMAN's end-user reports and link them into the application.

Summary

In this chapter, you created four forms: the TENANT form, the PROPERTY form, the WORDERS form, and the CALLS form. You learned the nuts and bolts of real form construction. Each of these forms has its own nuances and peculiarities; by having dealt with them, you garnered valuable skills that will help you in your own applications.

Here's a list of the form construction issues you addressed with each form in this chapter:

- The TENANT form
    - Removing inherited components
    - Configuring `DBCtrlGrid`
    - Setting the tab order
    - Linking the form into the application
    - Using modal forms
    - Aligning components
    - Setting up the speedbutton
- The PROPERTY form
    - Linking the components with the PROPERTY table
    - Setting up lookup fields
    - Viewing live data at design time
    - Establishing label accelerators

- The WORDERS form
  - Establishing a master/detail relationship
  - Using the field link designer
  - Using a `Query` to increment a field
  - Making use of the `OnNewRecord` event
  - Assigning a column default at runtime
  - Assigning the `DataSource` property at runtime
  - Configuring the columns displayed by `DBGrid`
  - Making a `DBGrid` read-only
  - Overriding `DBNavigator`
- The WORDERS master/detail form
  - Posting detail rows in master/detail forms
  - Linking the master/detail form with the grid form
  - Using a `Query` to display support information
  - Preparing a `Query`
  - Triggering `Query` execution
  - Resizing a form with panels
  - Building a `Query` with the Query Builder
  - Using the `AfterPost` event
  - Performing date arithmetic in Delphi
  - Using the `AfterDelete` Event
  - Implementing local filters
  - Building a `Query` for use within a filter
  - Purpose of the `Filtered` property
  - Disabling a filter
  - The CALLS grid form
  - Accessing the Data Module
  - Turning a `DBGrid` into a row selector
- The CALLS edit form
  - Linking the CALLS form with the WORDERS master/detail form
  - Using `FindKey` to lookup records
  - Dynamically setting a button's caption

12

Reports

In this chapter you'll build the reports needed by the RENTALMAN System. You'll design five reports and link them into the RENTALMAN application. Specifically, these reports include the following:

- A form report to print work orders
- A columnar report to list the PROPERTY table
- Mailing labels for the TENANT table
- A cross-tab Maintenance By Work Type report
- A columnar task list report

Methods of Building Delphi Reports

There are basically four methods you can use to build reports for Delphi applications. You can simply print a Delphi form, you can construct a report using Delphi's QuickReport components, you can build a report in an external report writer like ReportSmith, or you can write Object Pascal program code that produces a report. You'll use each one of these methods in this chapter.

Types of Reports

Business reports can be classified into four primary report types: forms, labels, columnar reports, and cross-tab reports. A form report prints just one record per page (or one master record and its corresponding detail records). A good example of this type of report is an invoice form report. It prints just one invoice per page.

A columnar report is a report in the traditional sense. It lists data in a series of parallel columns. There are normally several rows per page. A columnar report may include groupings that arrange and summarize its rows, using a column or columns from the source data. A typical example of a columnar report is one that provides a listing of a company's customers.

A mailing-labels report is just that: a report that prints labels for the purpose of mass mailings and the like. You can specify the type of label to print and the number of labels to print across each page. Normally, these labels are printed on special printer paper that comes with adhesive mailing labels attached to it. A good example of a mailing-label report is one that prints CUSTOMER table records for use in billing accounts-receivable customers.

Cross-tab reports cross tabulate data in the same way that a spreadsheet does. That is, in contrast to a columnar report, a cross-tab report not only lists data in columns, but can also arrange data so that row and column values intersect, in a manner similar to a spreadsheet. A good example of a cross-tab report is one that lists sales by state and by quarter. The left-most column of the report would list each state, and each row would list the sales by quarter for that state. If you wanted to find the second-quarter sales for a given state, you'd find the intersection between the second-quarter column and the appropriate state row.

You'll build all four types in this chapter. The Work Order print you design will be a form report. You'll create this report by simply printing the fmRWOREDT0 form itself. You'll learn to print simple reports of this type using only Delphi forms and standard components.

You'll list the PROPERTY table in a columnar report that you'll build using Delphi's QuickReport components. You'll find that most reports can be built using these components.

You'll construct a mailing-label report to list out the TENANT table using ReportSmith. You'll select both the number of labels to print and the criteria by which to select records when you build this report.

You'll next build a cross-tab report that summarizes the maintenance work on each property by the type of work performed. This one will also be built using ReportSmith.

You'll finish up by building a task-list report using only Object Pascal code. This will acquaint you with the old-fashioned way of building reports. You'll use simple looping constructs and terminal-output statements to format and print the report.

The Work Order Form Report

Let's begin with the Work Order form report. You build this report by printing your Delphi work order master/detail form.

Begin by loading the RENTALMAN System's main form, fmRSYSMAN0, into the Delphi visual form designer and dropping a `PrinterSetupDialog` component onto the form. In keeping with the naming conventions set forth in Chapter 4, "Conventions," name the component `i_RENTALMAN`. Now, double-click the Print setup option on RENTALMAN's File menu and type the following code:

```
i_RENTALMAN.Execute;
```

Next, return to the visual designer and link the sbPrintSetup SpeedButton with the Print setup menu item's OnClick handler; it should be named Printsetup1Click. This will cause your Print Setup dialog box to display when the menu item or SpeedButton is clicked. Figure 12.1 shows what it looks like at runtime.

Among other things, the Print Setup dialog box enables the user to change the printer to send output to. All good Windows programs that send output to a printer include a printer-setup dialog box.

FIGURE 12.1.
*The Print Setup dialog
box, at runtime.*

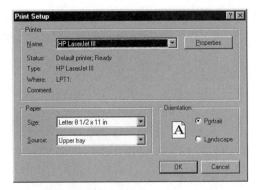

Setting Up the Work Order Report Menu Item

Next, link the Work Order option on the Reports menu with the Work Orders option on the Tables menu. Because your master/detail form will do its own printing, all you want to do when a user selects the Work Order option on the Reports menu is display the work-order selection form, fmRWORGRD0. This form is displayed when the Tables/Work Orders menu option is clicked, so it's appropriate to link the two menu items.

The Print Button

Now, load the fmRWORMDE0 form into the visual designer and widen it so that there's room for a Print button to the left of its OK button. A width of about 500 pixels should be about right.

Next, select the paBottom Panel component and drop a BitBtn component onto it. Change the button's Name to bbPrint, its Caption to &Print, and its Glyph to Images\Buttons\ print.bmp (Images should be a subdirectory under your main Delphi directory). After you've done this, double-click the button—this should place you in the button's OnClick event handler in Delphi's code editor. Type in the code shown in Listing 12.1.

Listing 12.1. Printing the fmRWORMDE0 form.

```
Tag := Longint(WindowState);
WindowState:=wsMaximized;
for I:=0 to ComponentCount-1 do
  If (Components[I] is TButton) or
     (Components[I] is TDBNavigator) or
     (Components[I] is TSpeedButton) then
       With Components[I] as TControl do begin
         Tag:=Longint(Visible);
         Visible:=False;
       end;
Print;
for I:=0 to ComponentCount-1 do
  If (Components[I] is TButton) or
```

```
      (Components[I] is TDBNavigator) or
      (Components[I] is TSpeedButton) then
        With Components[I] as TControl do
          Visible:=Boolean(Tag);
WindowState:=TWindowState(Tag);
```

Be sure to define I as an integer value in the procedure's header. For example:

```
var
  I : Integer;
```

will do just fine.

The purpose of this code is three-fold. Its first objective is to hide components that you wouldn't want on a form report prior to printing the form. For example, you wouldn't want buttons on the printed version of the form—they serve no purpose. The second objective is to print the form itself using its Print method. This will send a copy of the form as it appears on-screen to the printer. The final objective involves restoring the hidden components to their original status.

There are several important aspects of the code that I should point out. First, notice the extensive use of the Tag property. Tag is a long integer property that is included in every Delphi component and has no predefined purpose—you can do whatever you'd like with it. This code uses Tag at two different levels: it uses the Form component's Tag property to store/retrieve WindowState, and it uses each component's Tag property to store/retrieve its Visible property. Although you could certainly get by without saving and restoring either of these, you'd be making assumptions about the form that may not be valid. You don't know whether WindowState will always be initially set to wsNormal. You might decide the form looks better maximized. You also don't know that all the form's components will always be initially visible. Under certain circumstances, you might decide to hide some of the components on the form. If you make the assumption that all components are initially visible, printing the form and returning all components to a visible state would then reveal these hidden components. The code listed previously is a much more robust solution.

Another important aspect of the code is the use of the Components property. Components is an indexed property of controls that can contain other components, like TForm. The previous code uses it to look at each component on the form, determines whether it should be on the printed form, then sets its Visible property accordingly. You can use the Components property to quickly set properties for a group of controls at runtime.

The third major aspect of the preceding code is the use of runtime type information (RTTI). The is and with...as constructs use RTTI to perform their magic. Even though Delphi's compiler produces native machine code, you can still determine the specific data type of a class at runtime. This is normally not the case with native-code compilers. Runtime type information has historically been the exclusive province of interpretive products such as Visual Basic.

Native-code products don't usually have the ability to check the data type of a particular element because machine language itself contains no such information. Variables are reduced to offsets and sizes when source code is translated to object code. Delphi's RTTI capability gives you the best of both worlds: native code compilation *and* useful data-type information at runtime. This ability enables you to generically examine the components on the form and set them appropriately.

The fourth thing I should point out is the use of typecasting to set each component's `Visible` property. Not all components have a `Visible` property (none of the nonvisual components do, for example), so it's not possible to simply say:

```
with Components[I] do begin
  Tag:=Longint(Visible);
  Visible:=False;
end;
```

Because the base component class does not have a `Visible` property, the preceding code fragment will not set the `Visible` property of `Components[I]` at all. Instead, the assignment of the property will fall out to the next scoping level, which is that of the form class itself because you're within a method of the form. The end result, then, would be that you'd set *the form's* `Visible` property, something you definitely don't want to do.

The Object Browser

What you must do in order for this to work properly is find the ancestor class that defines the `Visible` property. The first common ancestor of Delphi's visual controls that defines the `Visible` property is the `TControl` component class. How do I know this? By examining the Delphi class hierarchy. There are two ways to examine this hierarchy. The first, and easiest, is to use the Object Browser. Once you've compiled your project at least once, the Browser option becomes available on Delphi's View menu. Click the View/Browser menu option to bring up the Object Browser. You can then scroll the class hierarchy in the left pane until you see the class or classes in which you're interested. You can also search for an element of the hierarchy by name. For example, if you scroll the list until you see the `TButton` component, you'll notice that it's an immediate descendent of `TButtonControl` and a second-level descendent (grandchild) of `TWinControl`. `TWinControl`, in turn, is an immediate descendent of `TControl`. If you scroll the right pane, you'll find `TControl`'s `Visible` property.

The other way to investigate the heritage of a particular class is to study the VCL source code. There is much that you can learn from exploring the VCL source. It's not as easy as simply popping up the Object Browser, but you get a lot more information than the Browser can provide. You start with the unit that defines the class in which you're interested and work backward from there. You may have to use a text-search utility (such as grep) to locate the unit that defines a particular class, but Borland has named the units fairly well, so this isn't as bad as it sounds. You can look at the type definition for each class to determine its ancestor. This information is contained in the first line of each class definition. For example, the first line of the TButton class definition is:

```
TButton = class(TButtonControl)
```

This tells us that TButton is a descendent of TButtonControl. Furthermore, the first line of TButtonControl's definition is:

```
TButtonControl = class(TWinControl)
```

This tell us that TButtonControl descends from TWinControl. Both TButton and TButtonControl are defined in the Stdctrls unit. Careful inspection of both of them reveals that neither defines the Visible property, so you'll have to keep going. The TWinControl class is defined in the Controls unit. It's first line looks like this:

```
TWinControl = class(TControl)
```

and a check of its class definition reveals that it doesn't define a Visible property, either. If you check it's ancestor, TControl, you'll find that it does define the Visible property. That's why we can use the TControl class to typecast any visual component on the form to set its Visible property.

> **NOTE**
>
> Note that the typecasts performed by the form print code are known as *checked typecasts*—they're checked for validity at runtime. If you typecast a class instance using a class type that is not the instance's class type and not the class type of any of its ancestors, an exception will be raised.
>
> The unchecked form of typecasting, by contrast, is implemented through the following syntax:
>
> ```
> With TControl(Components[i]) do
> ```
>
> With unchecked typecasts, if you miscast a class instance, your application will most likely generate an access violation and go down in flames. Checked class typecasts are just as functional and much safer; use them whenever possible.

Another interesting aspect of the form-printing code is that the list of controls being checked doesn't include the TBitBtn class. Why not? After all, there are certainly TBitBtn's present that you wouldn't want to print. You just dropped one, the bbPrint button, onto the form. How does the following code

```
If (Components[I] is TButton) or
(Components[I] is TDBNavigator) or
(Components[I] is TSpeedButton) then
```

account for the TBitBtn component class? Once again, the answer lies in the class hierarchy. You must remember that the RTTI is operator returns true when you test a particular class instance using its own class type *or that of any of its ancestors.* That last clause is the important part. Because TBitBtn is *a descendent* of TButton, testing for TButton covers TBitBtn as well. Unfortunately, TSpeedButton doesn't descend from TButton, as one might think, so it must be checked separately.

A Shorter Path?

You might argue that, rather than looping through all the components on the form, it would make more sense to simply hide the handful of components on the form that shouldn't be printed. Likewise, you could maximize the form at design time, alleviating the need to do so at runtime. For example, you could code a small routine like so:

```
DBNavigator1.Visible:=False;
bbOK.Visible:=False;
bbCancel.Visible:=False;
bbPrint.Visible:=False;
```

This code is certainly shorter than the preceding procedure, but the problems with this approach are many. First, adding even one additional button to this form would require updating the preceding code. That's not true of the earlier approach. Second, adding any nonprinting controls (such as buttons) to any of this form's *ancestors* would cause the same problem. Third, the preceding coding style doesn't allow for the possibility that a given control might be invisible to begin with. That is, you were to take into consideration that a control (based on various factors) might be hidden to begin with, the preceding code would have to have a line of code for each control to store off its Visible status prior to setting it, then a line for each control to reset its Visible status following the print. You'd soon have as many lines as are in the first, and far more flexible, approach. Finally, maximizing the form may be desirable from a printing standpoint, but it may not be from a design standpoint. For whatever reason, you might not want it to take up the whole screen. If not, you shouldn't be forced to maximize it at design time just to get it to print correctly.

The bbPrint button's OnClick code, as was originally designed, can be used in any Delphi application and with any form. It's a solution that you can make use of in your own applications. You could even copy the Print button and its OnClick code to the fmAnyForm class in the form hierarchy you designed and effectively add a print capability to all the forms in the RENTALMAN System.

Printing Multiple Rows

You can easily switch a form from printing just the current row in a table to printing multiple rows from the table. For example, to print all the work orders on file, you could write:

```
With taWORDERS do begin
```

```
First;
While not(EOF) do begin
fmRWORMDE0.bbPrintClick(Self);
Next;
end;
end;
```

Print Forms

Keep in mind that you can design forms whose whole purpose is to be printed. For example, you could inherit from the work-order master/detail form and create a form just for printing work orders. On this form, you could do various things to make the form print more legibly, including using color combinations that print well (some popular screen combinations, like black text on gray, should be avoided) and making use of borders and other things that enhance the appearance of printed reports. On this form, you could set the Visible property of those components that shouldn't be printed to False at design time—there'd be no need to do it at runtime. Although we won't do it in this chapter, you may find this preferable to printing forms originally designed for display only.

> **NOTE**
>
> Note that building reports through printed forms is the least efficient way to get printed output. Since the form image is sent to the printer as a large bitmap, your printer will need lots of memory in order to print it. Some printers won't be able to print it at all. Printing a form this way will also take longer than printing the equivalent report via almost any other means. Also, since printing a form is essentially printing its screen image, the quality of print you receive will depend on the relatively lower resolution of your video card versus the relatively high resolution of a printer.

Alternative Methods of Creating Form Reports

Form reports can also be designed using either Delphi's QuickReport components or from within ReportSmith. You may find designing complex form reports using one of these alternative methods easier than merely printing Delphi screen forms. For simple form reports like this one that would typically be for internal use only, TForm's Print method is adequate. However, for more complex reports, a more flexible method may be required. As you'll see throughout the rest of the chapter, designing reports using these alternative methods is quite easy.

Testing the Form Report

You're ready now to test the new report. Save your project and run the application. Click the Reports/Work Order option (or press F9) and you should see the Work Order Selection form.

Select a work order, then click edit. Next, click your Print button and you should see the form maximize, hide its button controls, print, then return to normal display. Now exit the application and return to Delphi.

> **NOTE**
>
> Note that you can use TForm's PrintScale property to control the manner in which a form is rendered by its Print method. The default setting, poProportional, causes the form to print very similarly to the way it displays. The same number of pixels per inch in use when a form is displayed are used when it's printed. poPrintToFit causes the form to print using the same screen proportions, but sized so that it just fits the printed page. poNone turns off any special scaling or sizing. This may result in a printed form differing significantly from its on-screen counterpart, because the resolution of today's displays can't match that of most printers.

Property-List Columnar Report

You'll build the next report using Delphi's QuickReport components. You'll see through this exercise that building reports using the QuickReport components is only slightly more difficult than building them using standard screen components. You'll also find that these components are up to the task of producing most types of reports. You will probably also discover that the QuickReport components offer the fastest route to professional business reports in Delphi applications.

Some Groundwork First

One of the nicest things about Delphi is that you'd be hard-pressed to find a programming task that it isn't able to handle. Unlike other tools, you will have to go to great pains to ever "hit the wall" in Delphi. Dynamic Link Libraries (DLLs) are no exception. Not only is Delphi just as capable as the leading C++ products at producing DLLs, it is, in fact, easier to use than most of them in this regard.

REPUTILS.DLL

Before you begin developing reports, you'll need to construct a simple DLL to house utility functions that the reports in this chapter will use. DLLs are popular mechanisms for extending Windows applications, including report writers, because their functions can be defined and loaded at runtime (that is, dynamically). Although it's unnecessary to encompass functions that the QuickReport components will use within DLLs, doing so will make the functions also available to reports designed in ReportSmith. By placing the functions in their own DLL, you make them available to nearly any Windows application, including all the leading report writers.

To construct a DLL in Delphi, select New from the File menu and double-click the DLL option in the ensuing dialog. You should see a DLL "skeleton" loaded into the Delphi code editor. For now, you'll add just one function to the DLL for use by other executables. You'll construct a function that calls the Win32 GetUserName API function to retrieve the current user's name from the system. You'll use this in the headings of reports you create. Change the DLL skeleton that Delphi has provided to match Listing 12.2.

Listing 12.2. The REPUTILS Dynamic Link Library.

```
library Reputils;

{ Important note about DLL memory management: ShareMem must be the
the first unit in your interface section's USES clause if your DLL
exports any procedures or functions that pass string parameters or
function results. This applies to all strings passed to and from
your DLL—even those that are nested in records and classes. ShareMem
is the interface unit to the DELPHIMM.DLL, which must be deployed
along with your DLL. To avoid using DELPHIMM.DLL, pass string
information using PChar or ShortString parameters. }


uses
  SysUtils,
  Classes,
  Windows;

function GetWindowsUserName(UserName : PChar) : PChar; stdcall; export;
var
  Name : Array[0..30] of Char;
  NameLen : Integer;
begin
  NameLen := sizeof(Name);
  If GetUserName(Name, NameLen) then StrCopy(UserName,Name)
  else StrCopy(UserName,'UNKNOWN');
  Result := UserName;
end;

exports
  GetWindowsUserName;
end.
```

Note that the best way to change the name of the DLL is to save it as the name you wish to use; there's no need to edit the library line itself. For now, save the DLL's .DPR file to the same directory in which you're storing the RENTALMAN project.

There are a couple of changes the preceding code makes to the default DLL skeleton that I should point out. First, notice the addition of the Windows unit to the DLL's uses list. This is done to provide access to the GetUserName API function. The Windows unit interfaces Win32 API functions so that they may be called like normal Delphi functions.

The next thing I should point out is the use of the PChar data type for both the parameter and the return value of the GetWindowsUserName function. Although Delphi's other string types are more flexible and easier to use than the PChar type, PChar is more compatible with a larger number of Windows applications and development tools. This is a valid concern when writing something that could potentially be used by a number of different applications; you should use data types that are as language-independent as possible. Because PChars are identical to the C/C++ *char type, they're fairly ubiquitous. Making use of them in DLLs you build with Delphi will make your DLLs more accessible by a greater number of applications.

Finally, notice the use of the exports keyword in the DLL source code. This syntax makes the listed functions and procedures available to other executables, alleviating the need for the module definition file that is required by many C/C++ products when building DLLs.

If you haven't already done so, save your project and compile it. You should now have a ready-to-use DLL in the same directory as the RENTALMAN project.

After you've constructed the DLL, you're ready to create an interface unit for it. Although not required to use the DLL, an interface unit enables you to call functions that reside in DLLs as though they were built-in Delphi functions. The Windows unit, mentioned previously, is an example of an interface unit. Delphi provides it to interface the DLLs (and other executables) that make up the Win32 API.

Reload the RENTALMAN project, then select the New option from Delphi's File menu and double-click the Unit selection. Change the unit skeleton provided by Delphi to look like the following:

```
unit REPUTILSi;
interface
function GetWindowsUserName(UserName : PChar) : PChar;
implementation
function GetWindowsUserName(UserName : PChar) : PChar; external 'REPUTILS';
end.
```

Remember that the easiest way to change the name of the unit is to save it using the name you prefer—there's no need to edit the preceding unit line. Save the unit before proceeding.

Now that you've created an interface unit for your DLL, you're ready to proceed with building the reports using Delphi's QuickReport components. You'll make use of REPUTILS.DLL in these reports.

A Report Hierarchy

Just as you created a form class hierarchy before designing the principle forms that make up the RENTALMAN System, you could also design a form hierarchy on which to base the reports that the system needs. Reload the formrepo.dpr project that you created in Chapter 9, "First Steps," and select New from the File menu. Click the Forms page and inherit from the fmAnyForm class to create a new form. Name this new form frAnyReport and save it as ANYREPRT.PAS. This form will be the report form hierarchy's equivalent to the fmAnyForm class in the standard form hierarchy.

You'll drop several components onto this new form in setting up your default report-form class. All reports that you design using Delphi's QuickReport components will then inherit from this class and be consistent with each other. This will give all your reports a standard look and feel—something your users will no doubt appreciate.

Utilizing a report-form hierarchy is similar to using templates in other report-writing tools. Delphi's form inheritance, however, is actually superior to report-writer templates because changes to report-form ancestor classes cascade through to descendent forms. Changing some detail on all the reports in an application is as easy as making the change to an ancestor form that they share.

Figure 12.2 illustrates the basic layout that we'll use for the reports in the RENTALMAN System.

FIGURE 12.2.

The basic report layout for the RENTALMAN System.

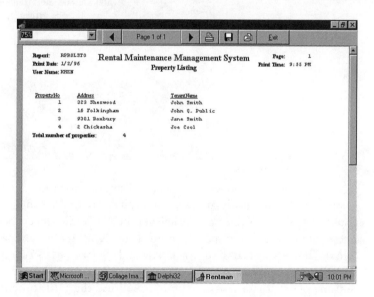

Drop a QuickReport component onto the top panel of the new form and name it qrAnyReport. Set its TitleBeforeHeader property to True so that any title band you add to your reports will print before the page heading of the first page. Next, drop four qrBand components onto the paMiddle component. Set the BandType property of the first band to rbPageHeader, the second to rbColumnHeader, the third to rbDetail, and the fourth to rbSummary. Table 12.1 summarizes the components on frAnyReport and their settings so far.

Table 12.1. frAnyReport's preliminary components and their settings.

Name	Property	Value
qrAnyReport	TitleBeforeHeader	True
qbPageHeader	BandType	rbPageHeader
qbColumnHeader	BandType	rbColumnHeader
qbDetail	BandType	rbDetail
qbSummary	BandType	rbSummary

Next, drop eight qrLabel components and four qrSysData components onto the qbPageHeader band. Arrange the components as shown in Figure 12.3.

FIGURE 12.3.

The frAnyReport form as it initially appears.

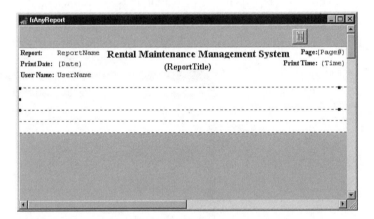

As a rule, qrLabel components are used to display information that doesn't change when the report is run—data that is somewhat static. The qrSysData components, on the other hand, display data that is derived at runtime and may indeed change when the report is executed. These components return special system elements like the current page number or the system date and time. Note that the qlReportName and qlUserName label components are exceptions to this rule. Neither of these components represent static values; they're both determined at runtime. The qlUserName component will use the DLL function you defined earlier, GetWindowsUserName, to display the name of the user printing the report. The qlReportName component will use some simple string manipulation (and the fact that you're using the naming conventions specified in Chapter 4) to return a name for the report. You'll set each of these up using its OnPrint event. Table 12.2 lists the key settings of these new components.

Table 12.2. Key settings of the new components on frAnyReport.

Name	Property	Value
qlReportName	Caption	ReportName
qsPrintDate	Data	qrsDate
qlUserName	Caption	UserName
qlReportTitle	Data	qrsReportTitle
qsPage	Data	qrsPageNumber
qsPrintTime	Data	qrsTime

In order to make use of the GetWindowsUserName function, you'll need to reference its interface unit. You'll recall that you built the REPUTILI interface unit earlier for the express purpose of making the functions in the REPUTILS.DLL easier to access. Click the Add to project button on the Delphi toolbar and select the Reputili.pas file from the list. Next, find the implementation section of the frAnyReport unit and add the code lines

```
Uses
REPUTILI;
```

to it. This will enable you to use the GetWindowsUserName function as though it were a built-in Delphi function (see Figure 12.4).

FIGURE 12.4.

Adding Reputili.pas unit to the implementation section of frAnyReport.

Now that the function contained in the DLL is accessible by frAnyReport, you can use its GetWindowsUserName function to supply the qlUserName component with data. Click the qlUserName component, then double-click its OnPrint event in the Object Inspector. You use the OnPrint event of the QuickReport components to override their default print behavior. In this case, you'll override the printing of qlUserName's caption and instead print the user name returned by the GetWindowsUserName function.

Key the following code into the Delphi code editor:

```
Value:=GetWindowsUserName(Temp);
```

Note that the procedure supplies a variable, Value, that you assign to override the default print behavior of the component. Here, you assign the GetWindowsUserName function to Value. Note that, even though GetWindowsUserName returns a PChar data type, Delphi's compiler takes care of converting the PChar to a String value so that it can be assigned to Value. Add the definition of the Temp variable to the method procedure's header, like so:

```
var
Temp : Array[0..30] of char;
```

The entire procedure looks like this:

```
procedure TfrAnyReport.qlUserNamePrint(sender: TObject; var Value: string);
var
  Temp : Array[0..30] of Char;
begin
inherited;
  Value:=GetWindowsUserName(Temp);
end;
```

Notice that Value is passed as a var parameter. This means that the variable is passed by address and that you can change its value from within the procedure. Notice also that the procedure uses a static character array in place of the PChar variable that GetWindowsuserName requires. Delphi converts these automatically and allows the two to be used interchangeably.

Next, click the qlReportName component, double-click its OnPrint event in the Object Inspector, then key the following line of code:

```
Value:=Copy(Name,3,8);
```

This code uses the Object Pascal substring function, Copy, to extract an eight-character segment of the form's Name property beginning with its third character. Why do we begin with the third character? Remember the naming conventions from Chapter 4? Forms are named using the convention fmXXXXXXXX, where fm signifies that the object is a form. Because the remaining eight characters specify the name of the form, or, in our case, the name of the report, it's safe to derive the report name by dropping the first two characters and returning the remainder of the form's Name property. The Copy function is used to extract these characters and return them in the Value parameter, which is then printed.

After you've finished with the OnPrint events for the qlUserName and qlReportName components, you're done with frAnyReport, so save it. You can ensure that your new form is syntactically correct by selecting the Syntax Check option from Delphi's Project menu. After you're sure everything is correct, save your new form to Delphi's Object Repository so that you may base new reports on it. (See Figure 12.5.)

FIGURE 12.5.

*The Add to Repository
dialog box.*

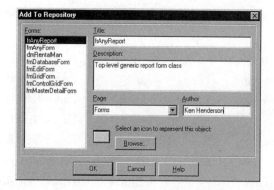

Now that frAnyReport is created, the next step you could take would be to define a complete report-form hierarchy. We'll skip that for now; you can fill out the rest of the hierarchy later, if you'd like. With the report-form hierarchy, the most important form class is the top-level form, frAnyReport. The minimal benefits of constructing a complete report-form hierarchy aren't enough to justify the space in this book necessary to detail it.

Creating the PROPERTY List Report

Reopen the RENTALMAN project and create a new report form by inheriting from the frAnyReport form class in the Object Repository. Name this form frRPROLST0 and save it as RPROLST0.PAS.

Next, give the new form access to the dmRentalMan data module by selecting the Use unit option on the File menu (dmRentalMan's unit name is rentdata). After you've done this, set the DataSource property of the qrAnyReport component to the PROPERTY table's DataSource, dmRentalMan.dsPROPERTY. Set qrAnyReport's ReportTitle property to Property Listing.

Now that you've established a link between the new report form and the PROPERTY table, you're ready to set up the components needed to list the table's rows. The report will include the PropertyNo, Address, City, State, Zip, Addition, and TenantName column from each row in the dsPROPERTY DataSource. You'll recall that TenantName is a lookup column that actually comes from the TENANT table, not the PROPERTY table.

Drop eight qrLabel components onto the qbColumnHeader band and space them out horizontally so that they can be used as headings for the columns in the detail band. Situate the two right-most qrLabels vertically so that one is above the other. These labels will be used to display the text Current Tenant on two separate lines. Now, change each component's Caption property to match the column it will represent from the table. After you've done this, select all seven of the lower qrLabel components and change their Font property to Times New Roman 10 pts. and check the Underline attribute checkbox. Table 12.3 lists the key properties of the qrLabel components and their values.

Table 12.3. Key properties of the label components and their settings.

Name	Top	Caption	Font
qlCurrent	1	Current	Times New Roman 10 pts.
qlPropertyNo	17	No.	Times New Roman 10 pts. (underlined)
qlAddress	17	Address	Times New Roman 10 pts. (underlined)
qlCity	17	City	Times New Roman 10 pts. (underlined)
qlState	17	State	Times New Roman 10 pts. (underlined)
qlZip	17	Zip	Times New Roman 10 pts. (underlined)
qlAddition	17	Addition	Times New Roman 10 pts. (underlined)
qlTenant	17	Tenant	Times New Roman 10 pts. (underlined)

Now drop corresponding qrDBText components onto the qbDetail band. You'll need to drop seven of them, positioning each under one of your column headings. Set the Font property of all seven components to Courier New, 10 pts. Set the DataSource of each to dmRentalMan .dsPROPERTY. Point each DataField property to the appropriate column in the dsPROPERTY DataSource.

Table 12.4 shows the Name, DataField, and Font of each component on the detail band.

Table 12.4. Detail-band components and their attributes.

Name	DataField	Font
qtPropertyNo	PropertyNo	Courier New 10 pts.
qtAddress	Address	Courier New 10 pts.
qtCity	City	Courier New 10 pts.
qtState	State	Courier New 10 pts.
qtZip	Zip	Courier New 10 pts.
qtAddition	Addition	Courier New 10 pts.
qtTenantName	TenantName	Courier New 10 pts.

Figure 12.6 shows the form so far.

FIGURE 12.6.

The RPROLST0 as it looks after its column heading and detail bands have been set up.

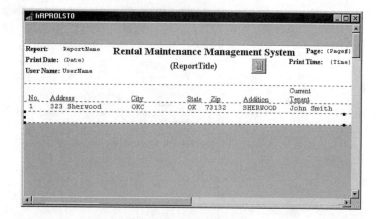

Now that the detail columns and their headings are in place, you're ready to add one last touch to the report. Drop a qrLabel and a qrDBCalc component onto the qbSummary band. Position the qrLabel at the far left of the band and the qrDBCalc to its immediate right. Set the Caption of the qrLabel to Total number of properties: and its Font to Times New Roman, 10 pts., Bold. Set the DataSource property of the qrDBCalc to the dmRentalMan.dsPROPERTY DataSource and double-click its DataField property to set it to the first column in dsPROPERTY. Set its Operation property to qrcCount and its Font to Courier New, 10 pts. This will cause a count of the total number of properties to be printed on the last page of the report.

Linking the Report into the Application

In order to test and use the report, you'll need to link it into the RENTALMAN application. To do this, you'll need to do two things:

■ Use the report form's unit in the application's main unit, RSYSMAN0

■ Add a menu item and support code for the new report to the application's main menu

Begin these steps by reselecting the fmRSYSMAN0 form in the form designer. Click Use unit on the File menu and double-click RPROLST0 in the list. This will enable you to reference the report form contained in the RPROLST0 unit.

Next, double-click the form's MainMenu component and click the blank menu option on the Reports menu. Set its Caption to &Property List and its ShortCut to F11. Now, double-click the item and type the following code into the code editor:

```
frRPROLST0.QuickReport1.Preview;
```

This line of code causes the new report to be displayed on-screen where it may be printed, saved, or canceled.

After you've completed these steps, you're ready to test the new report. Save the project and run the application. Figure 12.7 shows the report at runtime.

FIGURE 12.7.

*The Property Listing report
as it appears at runtime.*

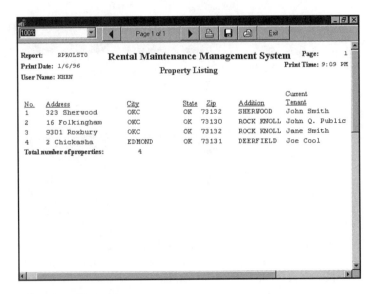

Enhancing the Base Report Class

It's a good idea to print the criteria that govern a report on the report itself. Usually, this information is printed on a title page or in the report's page heading. Although the Property List report isn't controlled by any external criteria, you can still add a component to frAnyReport to allow reports to print their governing criteria when applicable. In the case of the Property List report, you'll simply disable this component.

Exit the application and load the frAnyReport base form class into the visual designer. Drop a qrLabel component just below the qsReportTitle component. Name it qlCriteria and set its Caption to Report Criteria. Set its Font to Courier New, 10 pts. and change its Align property to taCenter. Widen it so that it spans the breadth of the page heading and set its AutoSize property to False. Figure 12.8 shows the new component.

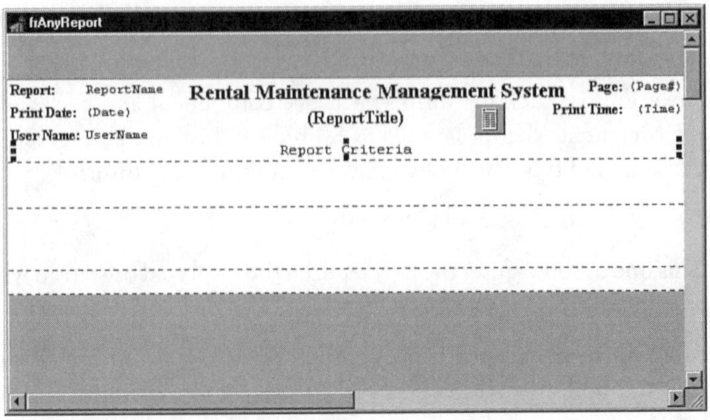

FIGURE 12.8.

*The qlCriteria
component is used to print
a report's controlling
criteria on the report itself.*

Save the form, then reload the frRPROLST0 form into the form designer. You should see the new component on your report form; it's a descendant of frAnyReport. (See Figure 12.9.)

FIGURE 12.9.

Changes you make to frAnyReport are reflected in its descendant forms, such as frRPROLST0.

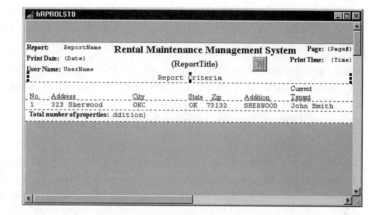

Click the qlCriteria component in your report form and press F11 to switch to the Object Inspector. Delete the component's Caption property and save the form. When you run the Property List report, the qlCriteria component will be invisible.

Building Reports in ReportSmith

You'll find that Delphi's QuickReport components are adequate for most of your reporting needs. Some types of reports, however, are more easily done using a report writer. Complex financial reports or ones that involve a large number of columns are often easier to construct using a report writer. These tools come in a variety of flavors, the three most popular being ReportSmith, R&R Report Writer, and Crystal Reports. The leading report writers are all very similar—you should use the one that works best for you.

One advantage of building reports using a report writer is that they can be modified by your users or used by them as a basis for new reports. This means, of course, that your users will have to purchase the report writer you used to build the reports; most vendors only enable you to include a runtime version with your software. They'll also have to be trained in the use of your chosen tool. As easy as they are, report writers still require a certain amount of competency in order to be used.

Because tampering with your reports could cause you support headaches, you may wish to prevent your users from doing it. It's far more preferable to allow users to create reports *based on* your reports than to allow them to modify the reports themselves.

In this chapter, you'll use Borland's ReportSmith to build report writer-based reports. ReportSmith is widely respected as a first-rate database report writer. You can purchase it separately or with Delphi. Because both are Borland products, you'll find that ReportSmith integrates better with Delphi than does any other stand-alone report writer. The latest version of ReportSmith is a full, 32-bit product that can share database connections with Delphi applications.

You'll begin writing ReportSmith reports by redeveloping the Property Listing report that you originally designed using Delphi's QuickReport components. Doing this will enable you to accurately compare the relative strengths and weaknesses of these two methods of report creation. You'll follow this with a mailing-label report (something report writers are particularly useful for) that lists the TENANT table.

Load the dmRentalMan data-module form into the visual form designer. Because of the way in which Delphi and ReportSmith communicate, you'll probably prefer to drop your Report components onto the data-module form of applications you design. Although this isn't a necessity, doing so allows Delphi and ReportSmith to share a single database connection. When sharing a database connection between Delphi and ReportSmith, only the DataSets that reside on the same form as a Report component can be selected from within the report writer.

Drop a Report component (located on the Data Access component palette page) onto the dmRentalMan form and name it reRPROLST0. Set its `ReportName` to `rprolst0` and its `ReportDirectory` to `C:\DATA\DELPHI\RENTAMAN`. Right-click the component and select Edit Report from the menu. You should see ReportSmith started.

Next, click Columnar Report in the Create a New Report dialog box. You'll see the Tables dialog. Click its Add Table button. When the Select Table dialog is presented, select Delphi as the table Type and click the Server Connect button. The Tables list should then display all the DataSet components in your Delphi application that share a form with a Report component. In this case, the DataSets on dmRentalMan should be displayed. (See Figure 12.10.)

FIGURE 12.10.

ReportSmith's Select Table dialog box.

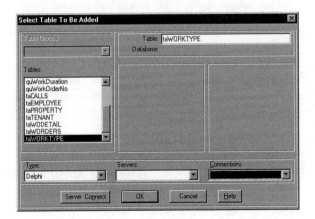

Double-click the taPROPERTY table, which should return you to the Tables dialog. Click the Done button to return to ReportSmith's main edit screen. You should then see the columns from the PROPERTY table arranged in a sample report layout that you can modify. Figure 12.11 shows the first rendition of the property list report.

FIGURE 12.11.

ReportSmith's main screen shows a default report layout for the PROPERTY table.

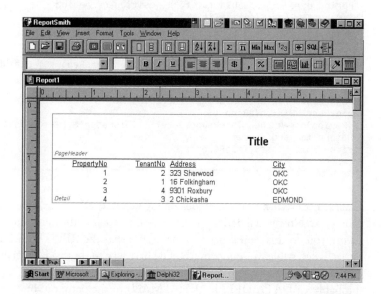

You'll make several changes to this report in order to get it presentable. After you've made the appropriate changes, this report will serve as a model for other reports. You'll standardize the page header and establish the appropriate fonts for the detail section of the report. Because most reports have at least a page header and a detail section, this will save you time when you create new reports.

Derived Fields

Before you begin dropping elements onto the page header, you'll need to set up a couple of calculated fields. ReportSmith refers to calculated fields as *derived fields*. You'll need to define two derived fields: one to return the report's name as a formatted string, the other to return the current Windows user name. You'll use the REPUTILS Dynamic Link Library (DLL) that you created earlier to return the current user name.

Click the Derived Fields option on ReportSmith's Tools menu. In the Derived Field Name field of the ensuing dialog box, type ReportName and click the Add button. In the next box, type GetReportName in the Macro Name field and click the New button. Next, type the text in Listing 12.3 into the Macro Formula field of the Edit Macro dialog box.

Listing 12.3. Adding the macro formula.

```
' A function to return the name of the current report without a path or extension.
' NOTE: this function depends on the report name being originally in 8.3 format.
Sub GetReportName()
  SlashPos=0      'Variable to store position of backslash
  PeriodPos=0     'Variable to store position of period
ThisReport$=Right$(ActiveTitle(),12)
' Loop removing all directories from the name
SlashPos=InStr(ThisReport$,"\")
Do While SlashPos<>0
ThisReport$=Mid$(ThisReport$,SlashPos+1,Len(ThisReport$)-SlashPos)
SlashPos=InStr(ThisReport$,"\")
Loop
' Now remove the extension, if there is one
PeriodPos=InStr(ThisReport$,".")
If PeriodPos<>0 then ThisReport$=Left$(ThisReport$,PeriodPos-1)
' Return the end result
DerivedField UCase$(ThisReport$)
End Sub
```

Click OK to return to the previous dialog box and OK again to return to the Derived Fields dialog box. Now you'll define a derived field to retrieve the current user name from Windows. Before you do this, you'll need to make sure that the REPUTILS.DLL file that you created earlier is accessible to ReportSmith. The best way to do this is to make sure it's in a directory on the system PATH. You can do this by adding the RENTALMAN project's home directory (probably C:\DATA\DELPHI\RENTMAN) to the path, or you can copy REPUTILS.DLL to a directory that is already on the PATH, such as C:\WINDOWS.

After you've done this, you're ready to create the UserName derived field. Key UserName into the Derived Field Name box of the Derived Fields dialog box, then click the Add button. In the Choose a Macro dialog box, type GetUserName into the Macro Name box, then click the New button. Next, type the following macro code into the Macro Formula box of the Edit Macro dialog box:

```
Declare Sub GetWindowsUserName Lib "REPUTILS" (ByVal usrnam as String)
Sub GetUserName()
UName$=string$(30," ")
GetWindowsUserName(ByVal UName$)
DerivedField UName$
End Sub
```

This function calls the GetWindowsUserName function in your REPUTILS DLL. Notice that the Declare Sub code is situated outside the main body of the function and that it imports the DLL function by name. You can import DLL functions and procedures by ordinal index, as well. Although not as flexible, this method of importing DLL-based functions is faster than referencing them by name.

Note that the call to `GetWindowsUserName` treats the function as though it were a procedure. You can safely ignore the return value of this function. `GetWindowsUserName` copies its return value to the parameter that you pass into it, so you need not store its return value in a separate variable. This is also true within Delphi itself—you don't have to make use of a function's return value. You can call the function as though it were a procedure—although as a rule, I recommend you avoid this and use a procedure instead of a function when a routine does not need to return a value.

Click OK in the Edit Macro dialog and again in the Choose a Macro dialog box. Click Done in the Derived Fields dialog box to return to ReportSmith's main screen.

Begin by deleting all the columns on the report except the `PropertyNo`, `Address`, `City`, `State`, `Zip`, and `Addition` columns. You can delete a column simply by clicking on it and pressing the Delete key. You can select a number of contiguous columns at once by dragging a rectangle around them (which selects them) and pressing the Delete key. Notice that when you delete a column, its column heading vanishes with it. This is because ReportSmith is in column-edit mode. You can toggle between column and field-edit mode by clicking the appropriate button on ReportSmith's toolbar.

Before proceeding, set the `PropertyNo` column's heading to `No`. Set the font of the column headings to Times New Roman, 10 pts. and enable the underline attribute. Change the font of the columns themselves to Courier New, 10 pts. Resize the columns so that they all fit on the screen at once; there's no reason for them to spread out horizontally, and moving them to a single screen will make designing the report easier. Figure 12.12 shows what the report should look like thus far.

Now click the Title field in the page-heading section of the report and change it to Property Listing. Set its font to Times New Roman, 14 pts., Bold. Next, drop a text field onto the page-heading section, just above the Property Listing field. Set its text to `Rental Maintenance Management System` and its font to Times New Roman, 14 pts., Bold. Center the two fields horizontally on the page. (See Figure 12.13.)

FIGURE 12.12.

*An early version of the
ReportSmith version of the
Property List report.*

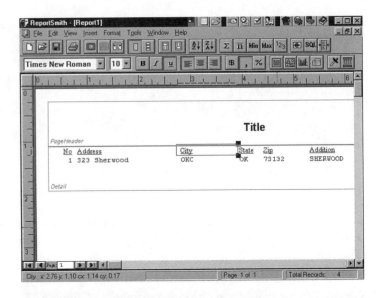

FIGURE 12.13.

*The PageHeader section of
the new report as it should
initially appear.*

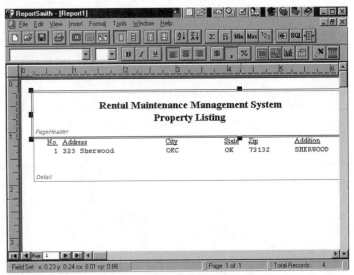

You're now ready to set up the remainder of the page heading fields, including the UserName and ReportName derived fields you built earlier. Begin by dropping a text field onto the upper-left corner of the page heading and setting its text to Report:. Set its font to Times New Roman, 10 pts., Bold.

Next, drop the `ReportName` field to the right of this label. To drop the `ReportName` field, select ReportSmith's Insert/Field menu option, then select Derived Fields in the Insert Field dialog's drop-down list. Unclick the Include field name checkbox, then drag ReportName from the list to the page header section. Change its font to Courier New, 10 pts.

Once you've placed the `ReportName` derived field, you're ready to drop the PrintDate system field. You'll position it just below the `ReportName` field on the left side of the page heading section. Drop a text field onto the left side of the page heading whose text is set to `Print date:`. Set its font to Times New Roman, 10 pts., Bold.

Next, click Field on ReportSmith's Insert menu again, then select System Fields in the Insert Field dialog. Drag Print Date just to the right of its corresponding label. As with the `ReportName` field, set its font to Courier New, 10 pts. Figure 12.14 illustrates the proper placement of the `ReportName` and `Print Date` fields.

FIGURE 12.14.

The proper placement of the `ReportName` *and* `Print Date` *fields on the new report.*

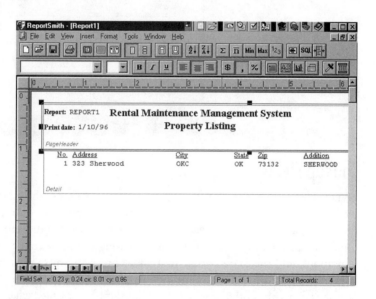

Now that you've placed the `ReportName` and `Print Date` fields, you're ready to insert the `UserName` field. Drop a text field onto the left of the page-heading section, beneath the `Print Date` field. Set its text to `User name:` and its font to Times New Roman, 10 pts., Bold. Follow this by dragging the `UserName` derived field (be sure to omit the field name) to its immediate right. Format the `UserName` field to use the Courier New, 10 pts. font.

After the left side of the page heading is taken care of, you're ready to move on to the right side. There are only two fields to go on the right side of the page-heading section: the `Page Number` field and the `Print Time` field. They are both system fields.

Drop the Page Number field and the Print Time field onto the right side of the page header, include text labels for both of them, and format each of them to match the fields on the left of the section. After you've completed the construction of the page header, save your new report as RPROLST0. Figure 12.15 illustrates the completed page heading of the new report.

FIGURE 12.15.

The completed page header for the new Property Listing report.

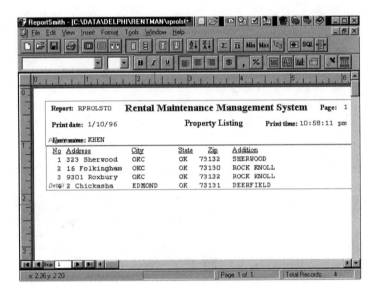

Lookup Fields

You may have noticed that the lookup fields that are a part of the taPROPERTY DataSet were not included in the fields that ReportSmith imported from Delphi. An example of such a field is the TenantName field in the taPROPERTY DataSet; it provided the name of the tenant currently occupying a given property. Unfortunately, sharing a database connection with Delphi has some limitations, and this is one of them. To make matters worse, you can't perform the lookup yourself from within ReportSmith by linking the tables in question together. The ability to link one table with another from within ReportSmith is disabled when ReportSmith and Delphi share a database connection.

To remedy this, you have two options. First, you could set up a query component in Delphi that performs the join for you and returns the composite rows. ReportSmith could then use this DataSet, rather than the taPROPERTY component, for its data source. Second, you could change the report so that it does not attempt to share a database connection with Delphi.

ReportSmith can talk directly to the Borland Database Engine, just as Delphi can. You can simply replace the table connection that references Delphi with one that works directly with the BDE. This is probably the best of the two methods for handling situations where your data needs are more sophisticated than the DataSets currently defined in your Delphi application can provide.

To change a report that you originally designed to share a connection with Delphi so that it communicates directly with the BDE, select the Tables option from ReportSmith's Tools menu. Next, click the Replace table button and change the connection Type, in the ensuing dialog box, to the BDE alias you want to use (RENTMAN, in this case), then double-click the name of the table you want in the Files list. (See Figure 12.16.)

FIGURE 12.16.

Changing a report from sharing a database connection with Delphi to communicating directly with the BDE.

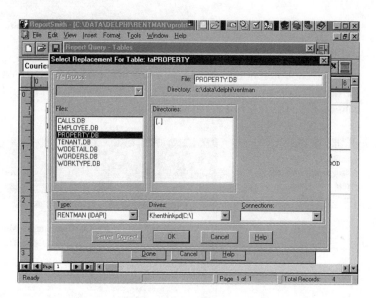

After you're back in the Table dialog, click the Done button to activate your change. ReportSmith will then change the report's data source without affecting the report itself. The fields that you've placed on the report remain intact.

Now that the report is talking directly with the BDE, you can construct the link with the TENANT table that's needed to retrieve tenant names. To do this, bring up the Tables dialog again and click the Add table button, then double-click the TENANT table in the list. Next, click the Add new link button in the Tables dialog. In the Create New Table Link dialog, notice that ReportSmith has already set up a link between the two tables based on the TenantNo column. (See Figure 12.17.)

FIGURE 12.17.

The Create New Table Link dialog box.

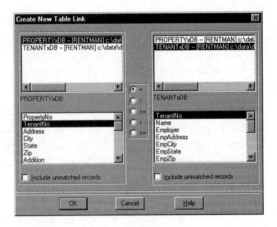

Click OK to save your new link, then click Done in the Tables dialog to return to ReportSmith's main screen. You'll notice that all the fields in the TENANT table have now been placed to the right of those from the PROPERTY table. Remove all the TENANT fields except the Name column from the report. Figure 12.18 shows the revised report.

FIGURE 12.18.

The revised Property Listing report links the PROPERTY and TENANT tables.

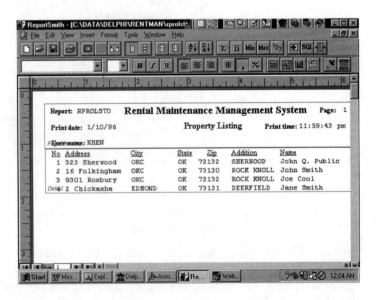

With this change, you now have the basic equivalent of the RPROLST0 report you built earlier using Delphi's QuickReport components. To finish up, you need to add a text field to the page heading of the report as a placeholder for the report's criteria, and you also need to add a summary field to the bottom of the report that counts the total number of properties.

Drop a text field onto the report's page header and center it below the Property Listing field. Set its text to Report criteria and its font to Courier New, 10 pts.

Next, select the `PropertyNo` column and click the Count button on ReportSmith's toolbar (it's the one with the 123 label). After you've done this, click the Header/Footer option on the Insert menu. Leave Entire Report_Group selected and click the Footer checkbox in the Header/Footer dialog box, then click OK. (See Figure 12.19.)

FIGURE 12.19.

Insert headers and footers using the Header/Footer dialog box.

After you've done this, ReportSmith inserts a footer section just below the report's detail section. You can now insert fields in this section that will print on the last page of the report. Drop a text field onto the left side of this new section and set its text to `Total number of prop-erties:`. Set its font to Times New Roman, 10 pts., Bold. Next, click Field on ReportSmith's Insert menu and select Summary Fields in the Insert Field dialog box. Uncheck the Include field name checkbox and drag the PropertyNo-Count field to the right of the text field you just dropped in the summary section. Set its font to Courier New, 10 pts. Finish up by saving your completed report. Figure 12.20 shows what it should now look like.

FIGURE 12.20.

The Property Listing report as it appears in ReportSmith.

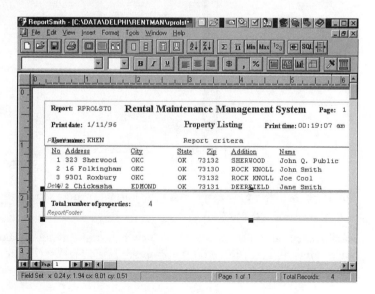

Now that you've fully defined the report, you can use it as the basis for other reports. There are basically two ways to go about this. You can save the report as a formatting *style* that you may then apply to other reports, or you can save the report in its entirety, then load and modify it when building a new report. Personally, I prefer the second method, although I'd have to admit that it's sort of a "whittle and spit" approach to report-form inheritance. We'll try both methods and you'll see why I prefer the second one.

Click the Report Style option on the ReportSmith Format menu. Next, click the New button and type AnyReport into the ensuing dialog box, then click OK. Click the Done button to return to ReportSmith. This saves the formatting information of the current report as a report style, naming it AnyReport.

To see the effects of the new style, click the New report button on the ReportSmith toolbar. Click OK to create a Columnar report, then add the TENANT table to the report and return to ReportSmith's main screen. Figure 12.21 shows the initial appearance of the report.

FIGURE 12.21.

The Tenant Listing report before the AnyReport style has been applied to it.

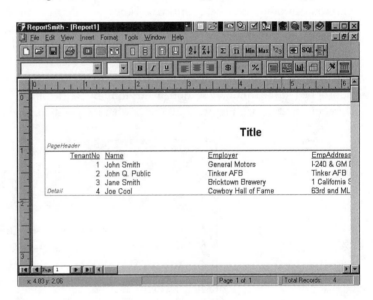

Now click the Report Style option on the Format menu a second time, select the AnyReport style, and click the Apply button.

You'll see several subtle changes to the new report, including the alteration of the detail and header fonts to match those on the Property Listing report. Figure 12.22 shows the altered report.

FIGURE 12.22.

The Tenant Listing report after the AnyReport style has been applied to it.

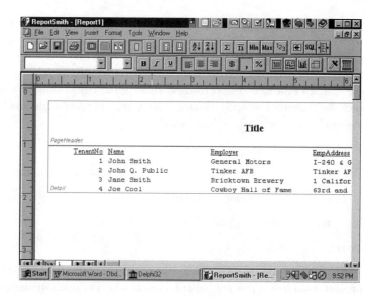

Unfortunately, the actual fields from the other report aren't brought in by the style—you must add those yourself. And this points out the principle advantage to the second approach I mentioned previously. When you load a copy of a report and modify it to create a new report, you automatically get all the fields in the original report, including those in its page header. You could call this a "poor man's" report-form inheritance—you simulate Delphi's form inheritance within ReportSmith by using existing reports as the basis for new reports.

Although you probably won't want the detail columns from the first report, they're easy enough to delete. Moreover, you *will* want the page heading fields and their attributes—and they'll all be present along with the report macros that you created to return values for some of the fields in the heading. This saves you time in creating new reports and provides virtually the same benefits as using report styles.

To store the Property Listing report as a template that you can then use to build other reports, simply save the report using a generic name like AnyReprt (I've omitted the *o* to keep the name to eight characters). After the report is saved using this generic name, you can build new reports by simply loading and modifying it. The possibility that you might want to do this is the reason that I had you add the Report criteria text field previously. This report doesn't actually have any governing criteria, but reports you base on it might (thus the criteria field). For this report, you can simply remove the field.

Testing the Report

Now that the report is complete, you're ready to test it. Although you previously built a Property List report using Delphi's QuickReport components, it's still a good idea to test the one you've developed in ReportSmith to ensure that you understand what you've done in ReportSmith thus far.

To test the report, save the report (its name should be RPROLST0.RPT), close ReportSmith, and return to Delphi. You should be placed in the dmRentalMan data module. Change the Preview property of the Report component, reRPROLST0, to True so that you can preview the report before printing it. Next, load the fmRSYSMAN0 form into the form designer and add the rentdata unit to its Uses clause by clicking the Use Unit option on the File menu. Next, click the Property List option on the main form's Reports menu and comment out the line of code in its click event. That line should be:

```
frRPROLST0.QuickReport1.Preview;
```

You can comment it out by placing a double slash at the beginning of the line, like so:

```
// frRPROLST0.QuickReport1.Preview;
```

Next, type the following line:

```
dmRentalMan.reRPROLST0.Run;
```

This will cause the report to be displayed on the screen (due to the setting of the Preview property) when the Property List option is clicked. The user can then perform a variety of functions, including both printing the report and saving it to disk. The save-to-disk function enables you to save the report's output in a number of formats, including the Excel, Lotus 1-2-3 and Quattro Pro spreadsheet formats as well as several text formats.

To see the new report in action, save your project and run it. Once inside RENTALMAN, click the Property List option on the Reports menu to run the report. Figure 12.23 shows the report at it appears in ReportSmith's runtime view.

FIGURE 12.23.

The Property List report as it appears in ReportSmith's runtime viewer.

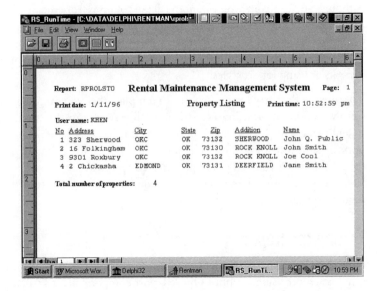

Close the runtime viewer and return to the application, then close the application and return to Delphi. Restore the code associated with the Property List click event to its previous state by uncommenting the original line of code and removing the call to the Report component's Run method. Because the QuickReport version of the report is more tightly integrated with Delphi, we'll use it rather than the one just designed in ReportSmith.

Mailing Labels

The next report you build in ReportSmith will be one that prints mailing labels using data from the TENANT table. Change the name of the reRPROLST0 Report component on dmRentalMan to reRTENLBL0 and set its ReportName property to rtenlbl0. Next, right-click the component and select Edit Report. You should then be placed in ReportSmith. Select Label Report from the list of report types and add the TENANT table (using the RENTMAN BDE alias, as before) to the report.

You'll be immediately placed into ReportSmith's Insert Field dialog box. From there, you can drag the fields from the TENANT table onto the label report. Drag the Name field from the list onto the upper corner of the label Report, then click the dialog's Done button.

Next, add the PROPERTY table to the report using the Table option on the Tools menu. Add a link between the TENANT and PROPERTY tables using the Add new link button on the Tables dialog box. The default link that ReportSmith builds is correct; you need to link the two tables using the TenantNo column.

After you've linked the tables, bring up the Insert Field dialog and drag the Address, City, State, and Zip fields onto the label report. (See Figure 12.24.)

FIGURE 12.24.
The initial Tenant Mail Labels report.

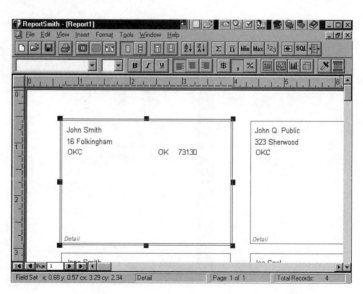

You'll notice in Figure 12.24 that the `City` and `State` fields are not formatted very well. This is due to the fact that the `City` field is being padded to its maximum length, regardless of the actual data that it contains. This padding produces a noticeable gap on the label report between the `City` and `State` fields that causes the report to look odd.

The solution to this problem is found by creating a derived field that combines the three fields, `City`, `State`, and `Zip` into a single, properly formatted field that can be used instead of the fields themselves on the report.

Create a new derived field named `CityStateZip`. Set the field up so that it's defined by a macro named `GetCityStateZip`. Type this code into the macro:

```
DerivedField Trim$(Field("City"))+", "+ Trim$(Field("State"))+ " "+
➡Trim$(Field("Zip"))
```

This one-line macro procedure takes the `City`, `State`, and `Zip` fields and combines them into a single string. In so doing, it removes unnecessary spaces from the beginning and ending of each field. This means that the fields go from being formatted like

CITY   STATE   ZIP

to instead being formatted like

CITY, STATE ZIP

which is the way that mailing labels should be formatted.

Save your macro and newly defined derived field and drag the new field onto the label report. Delete the `City`, `State`, and `Zip` fields from the report. Position the `CityStateZip` derived field so that it occupies the portion of the label formerly occupied by the three fields. (See Figure 12.25.)

FIGURE 12.25.

The Tenant Labels report with its City, State, *and* Zip *fields reformatted.*

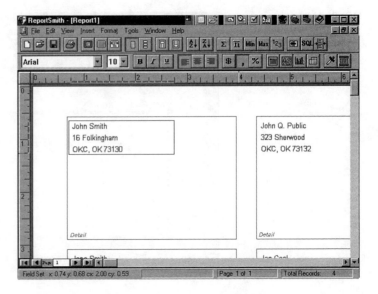

Selecting a Label Type

The final thing you need to do is select the type of labels that you wish to use. ReportSmith comes with built-in support for Avery labels and also supports user-defined labels. To specify the type of label that you'd like to use, select Page Setup from ReportSmith's File menu and click the Labels radio button. A common type of address label is the Avery 5160 Address label. Select it now from the Label type and dimensions drop-down list, then click OK. Figure 12.26 shows the effects of the change.

FIGURE 12.26.

The Tenant mailing label report uses Avery 5160 address labels.

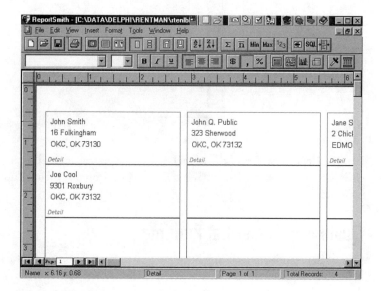

Running the New Report

Save the report, now, as RTENLBL0 and return to Delphi. Next, load RENTALMAN's main form, fmRSYSMAN0, and add a new option to its Reports menu. Add an option named `Tenant Mailing &Labels` to the menu and type the following code into its click event:

```
dmRentalMan.reRTENLBL0.Run;
```

This will cause the labels to be initially displayed on-screen (because the `Preview` property is set to `True`). Save your project, then run the application. Click the new option on the Reports menu to make sure that it works correctly. Figure 12.27 shows what the new report should look like.

FIGURE 12.27.

The Tenant Mailing Labels report as it appears at runtime.

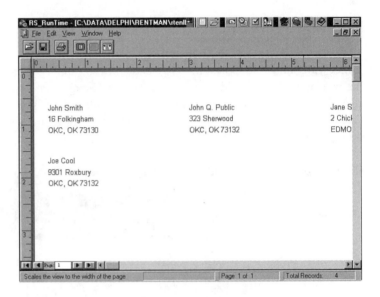

Exit the ReportSmith and the RENTALMAN application and return to Delphi. Next, right-click the Report component and select Edit Report from the menu. You should see ReportSmith reloaded.

Qualifying a Report at Runtime

One of the realities of building business reports that people will actually use is that users want to be able to qualify the data that will appear on reports they run. They rarely want entire tables dumped. This is a real-world need, and ReportSmith has an elegant solution for it.

Report Variables

ReportSmith defines a special type of field known as a report variable. You set up these special fields so that they are requested at runtime and used to control the data being printed on the report. You can also optionally print them in the report's header. ReportSmith allows these to be toggle selections, simple text entry, and list- and table-based entries. You can display one field from a table and specify another, or you can build your own list of values and use them instead. The prompt and dialog-box title you specify will be displayed at runtime when the user is prompted to supply values for the report variables you've defined.

Select Tools/Report Variables and define a new report variable called SelectedTenantName. Set the new field's data type to String, its dialog title to Tenant Name and its Prompt to Enter a tenant name for which to print labels. Set its property to Type-in and its Maximum property to 30, then click New. Click Done to exit the dialog. Figure 12.28 shows the completed dialog box.

FIGURE 12.28.

Report variables prompt for report criteria at runtime.

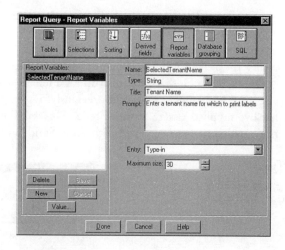

In order to limit the data returned by the report using this new variable, you must modify the row Selections utilized by the report's query. To do this, click Selections on the Tools menu. Next, click the button next to the Include records in the report... line in the upper-left corner of the dialog box and select Add selection criteria from the pop-up menu. Click the TENANTxDB.TenantNo element in the criteria and change it to TENANTxDB.Name. Change is equal to to is patterned like and change the text element to report variable. Because you have only one report variable, ReportSmith automatically selects it and places it in your selection criteria. Click Done to apply your criteria. Figure 12.29 shows the completed Selections criteria.

FIGURE 12.29.

The Report Query Selections dialog box.

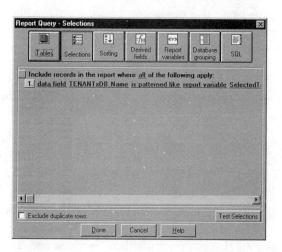

When you're prompted to supply the report variable you just defined, type in % (without the quotes) because % is the SQL wildcard character and will therefore allow all the rows to be returned while testing the report.

Testing the Report

Save your report and return to Delphi. Run the application again and notice what happens when you click the Tenant Mailing Labels option on the Reports menu. You see a dialog box prior to the report running that prompts you for a tenant name to print. You can supply an entire name, or just a pattern, as we did previously. Figure 12.30 illustrates the dialog box. Notice that I've supplied %Smith as the criteria. This will limit the labels printed to the two customers whose last names end with Smith: John Smith and Jane Smith.

FIGURE 12.30.

Prompting for parameters for the Tenant Mailing Label report.

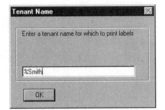

You've now completed the mailing labels report. Your next report will be a crosstab report. This one will be a bit more complex than the labels report you just designed. It will involve several tables and summarize the data from them in a spreadsheet-like format.

Crosstab Reports

The crosstab report you're about to create will summarize the amount of maintenance done at each property by the type of work performed. Each row of the report will list a rental property, with columns indicating the amount of time spent on each type of work on that property. Using the report, one could easily determine whether a given type of work—say, annual air-conditioner maintenance—had been performed at a property and how much time was spent doing it. Furthermore, the total maintenance on each property could be easily determined by simply looking at the row total for each property. Finally, the total time spent on a given type of work could be deduced by looking at the report's column totals.

If the report is still on the screen, close it and exit the application. Next, drop a new Report component onto the dmRentalMan data module and name it reRMANWKT0. Set its ReportName property to RMANWKT0. Change its Preview property to True so that the report will initially display on the screen when you run it.

Next, right-click the component and select Edit Report. You should see ReportSmith started. Click the Cancel button in the Create a New Report dialog and open the AnyReport generic report template that you created earlier. Go ahead and resave the AnyReport template using the name RMANWKT0 (click Save As on the File menu) to ensure that you don't accidentally modify your template.

Now, bring up the Report Query - Tables editor on the Tools menu and remove both tables from the report. Notice that the links between the two tables also disappear. After you've done this, add the WODETAIL, WORDERS, PROPERTY and WORKTYPE tables to the report. Establish a link between the WODETAIL and WORDERS tables using `WorkOrderNo` as the key. Establish another link between the WORDERS and PROPERTY table using `PropertyNo` as the key. Finally, establish a link between the WODETAIL table and the WORKTYPE table using `WorkTypeCode` as the key field. After you've built these table links, click the Done button to exit the Tables dialog box.

Once back in the main ReportSmith screen, change the report's title line from `Property Listing` to `Maintenance by Work Type`. Next, delete all the columns that ReportSmith has automatically inserted into the detail area. After the columns are gone, select the Detail section itself and delete it. You can't insert crosstabs into the Detail section of a report; they must be inserted into a header or footer section.

Now that you've removed the Detail section of the report, resize the Page footer section so that it occupies as much of the screen area as possible. Delete the text label and the total field that you inserted into the page footer of the original AnyReport template.

Next, select Crosstab from the Insert menu to create a crosstab object that you may then insert into the footer. Once inside the Crosstab Report dialog, drag the `Address` column from the PROPERTY table to the Rows list, drag the WORKTYPE table's `Description` field to the Columns list and its `TaskDuration` column to the Values list. After you've done this, click the crosstab's Options button (the left-most Options button, not the ones under each of the lists) and uncheck the Fix Cell Size and Labels options. Set the crosstab's Null Value String to N/A and click OK. After its options are set, click OK to finish defining the crosstab.

You'll next notice ReportSmith pause briefly while it generates the crosstab. After it's finished, the mouse pointer changes to a crosstab bitmap, and you can click anywhere in the report to insert it. Click the Page footer section to insert the crosstab. Figure 12.31 shows what it should look like.

Because of the large number of columns that could potentially be contained within the crosstab, you'll want to change the paper size and orientation of the report. Click the Page Setup option on the File menu, and change the report's orientation to landscape and its paper size to legal paper. This allows as many columns as possible to fit on the report. Keep in mind that you'll need to move the fields in the report's page header because you've changed the width of the printed page.

You've now completed the report, so you're ready to wire it into the application. Save the report and return to Delphi. Load the fmRMANSYS0 form into the visual designer and double-click its `MainMenu` component. Insert a new menu item just before the Tenant Mailing Labels item and set its Caption to `&Maintenance by Work Type`. Double-click it and type in a call to the new `Report` component's `Run` method:

```
dmRentalMan.reRMANWKT0.Run;
```

FIGURE 12.31.

This crosstab cross-references rental properties with the maintenance on them.

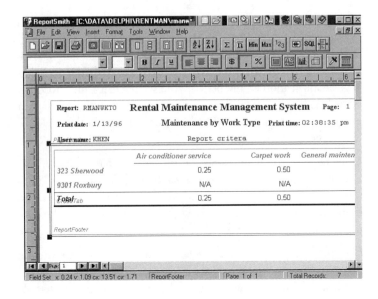

This will cause the report to be displayed in preview mode when you select the new menu item. Now save your project and run the application. Select the new menu item, and you'll see the report shown in Figure 12.32.

FIGURE 12.32.

The Maintenance by Work Type report as it appears at runtime (here, it's zoomed to 50 percent of its actual size).

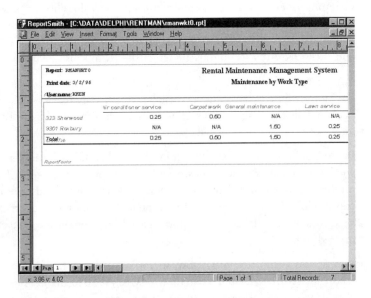

You've now completed your first sophisticated ReportSmith report. As you can see, complex reports can often be built with little or no coding.

The Task-List Report

You'll build the last report in this chapter using nothing but Object Pascal code. This will be a good exercise, if for no other reason than to cause a greater appreciation for the complexity of report-development tools such as ReportSmith and Delphi's QuickReport components. After you've done things the hard way, you can't help but be thankful for the many tools that Delphi provides to make report writing a breeze!

Drop a new Query component onto the dmRentalMan data module. Name it quTaskList and set its SQL as follows:

```
SELECT E.Name, P.Address, P.City, P.Addition, T.Description, T.TaskDuration
FROM EMPLOYEE E,
WORDERS W,
PROPERTY P,
WODETAIL D,
WORKTYPE T
WHERE E.EmployeeNo=W.EmployeeNo
and W.WorkOrderNo=D.WorkOrderNo
and W.PropertyNo=P.PropertyNo
and D.WorkTypeCode=T.WorkTypeCode
and W.StartDate <= :ListDate
and W.EndDate >= :ListDate
ORDER BY E.Name, P.Address, P.City, P.Addition, T.Description
```

This query will join the EMPLOYEE, WORDERS, PROPERTY, WODETAIL, and WORKTYPE tables to produce a comprehensive employee task list for a given date. Notice that the query defines a single parameter, :ListDate, that must be supplied in order for it to work properly. Bring up the property editor for the Query component's Params property and set ListDate's type to Date. Next, right click the Query component and add all of its fields as field components.

Now you're ready to set up the actual Object Pascal code that will produce the report. Load the application's main form, fmRSYSMAN0, into the form designer and click the Task List option on the Reports menu. Change its OnClick event handler to look like that shown in Listing 12.4.

Listing 12.4. The TaskList1Click event handler.

```
procedure TfmRSYSMAN0.TaskList1Click(Sender: TObject);
var
  LastName : String;
  CurrentLine : Byte;

  procedure PrintColumnHeadings;
  begin
      Writeln(PrintFile,'      '+Pad('Address',30), Pad('City',20),
➡Pad('Addition',20), Pad('Work',30), Pad('Time (Days)',15));
  end;
```

continues

Listing 12.4. continued

```
begin
  inherited;
  try
  Cursor:=crHourGlass;
  With dmRentalMan, quTaskList do begin
    ParamByName('ListDate').AsDate:=Date;
    Open;
    try
    BeginReport(poPortrait,Caption);
    try
    While not eof do begin
      CurrentLine:=9;
      PrintHeader('RTSKLST0',Caption,'Employee Task List',
➥ParamByName('ListDate').AsString);
      PrintColumnHeadings;
      While (not eof) and (CurrentLine<>PageLength) do begin
        Writeln(PrintFile);
        Writeln(PrintFile,'EMPLOYEE:  '+quTaskListName.AsString);
        Inc(CurrentLine,2);
        Repeat
          LastName:=quTaskListName.AsString;
          Writeln(PrintFile,'    '+ Pad(quTaskListAddress.AsString,30),
➥Pad(quTaskListCity.AsString,20),
          Pad(quTaskListAddition.AsString,20),
➥Pad(quTaskListDescription.AsString,30), Pad(quTaskListTaskDuration.AsString,15));
          Next;
          Inc(CurrentLine);
          Until (eof) or (CurrentLine=PageLength) or (quTaskListName.AsString <>
➥LastName);
      end;
    end;
    finally
      EndReport;
    end;
    finally
      quTaskList.Close;
    end;
  end;
  finally
  Cursor:=crDefault;
  end;
end;
```

This code is dependent on several other support functions and procedures. Type the code shown in Listing 12.5 into the RSYSMAN0 unit, just prior to the TaskList1Click method procedure.

Listing 12.5. Utility functions for the Task List report.

```
function Pad(InStr : String; TotalLen : Integer) : String;
begin
  Result:=InStr;
  While (Length(Result)<TotalLen) do Result:=Result+' ';
end;
```

```
function LPad(InStr : String; TotalLen : Integer) : String;
begin
  Result:=InStr;
  While (Length(Result)<TotalLen) do Result:=' '+Result;
end;

function Center(InStr : String; TotalLen : Integer) : String;
var
  NumSpace : Integer;
  Temp : String;
begin
  NumSpace := (TotalLen-Length(InStr)) div 2;
  Temp:='';
  While Length(Temp)<NumSpace do Temp:=Temp+' ';
  Result:=Temp+InStr+Temp;
  While Length(Result)<TotalLen do Result:=Result+' ';
end;

procedure PrintHeader(ReportName,SystemTitle,ReportTitle,Criteria : String);
begin
  If (Printer.PageNumber <> 1) then Write(PrintFile,^L);
  Writeln(PrintFile,Pad('Report: '+ReportName,25),
          Center(SystemTitle,LineLength-45),
          LPad('Page: '+IntToStr(Printer.PageNumber),25));
  Writeln(PrintFile);
  Writeln(PrintFile,Pad('Print date: '+DateToStr(Date),25),
          Center(ReportTitle,LineLength-45),
          LPad('Print time: '+TimeToStr(Time),25));
Writeln(PrintFile);
  Writeln(PrintFile,Pad('User name: '+UserName,25),
          Center('For: '+Criteria,LineLength-45));
  Writeln(PrintFile);
end;

procedure BeginReport(Orientation : TPrinterOrientation; Title :String);
var
  Temp : Array[0..30] of Char;
begin
  Printer.Orientation:=Orientation;
  Printer.Title:=Title;
  AssignPrn(PrintFile);
  Rewrite(PrintFile);
  With Printer.Canvas.Font do begin
    Name:='Courier New';
    Height:=10;
    Style:=[];
  end;
  LineLength:=(Printer.PageWidth div Printer.Canvas.TextWidth('X'))-5;
  PageLength:=(Printer.PageHeight div Printer.Canvas.TextHeight('X'))-2;
  UserName:=GetWindowsUserName(Temp);
end;

procedure EndReport;
begin
  CloseFile(PrintFile);
end;
```

The preceding functions and procedures rely on a handful of variables that are global to the RSYSMAN0 unit. Insert a var declaration section just prior to the {$R *.DFM} line in RSYSMAN0 like so:

```
var
  PrintFile : Text;
  LineLength : Integer;
  PageLength : Integer;
  UserName : String;
```

Finally, this new code requires the services of two external units, the Delphi Printers unit and the Reputili unit that you created earlier. The Printer unit provides an interface to much of the basic Windows printing interface. Reputili interfaces the functions contained in the REPUTILS.DLL, including GetWindowsUserName. Add both units to the Uses clause of the RSYSMAN0 unit.

Inside *TaskList1Click*

There are several points about the TaskList1Click procedure that merit discussion. First, notice the use of Object Pascal's standard Writeln procedure to send output to the printer. This is facilitated by the AssignPrn procedure. AssignPrn associates a text file with the default Windows print device. By opening and writing to this text file, you send printer output to Windows.

There are a couple of schools of thought regarding the proper way to print text in Windows applications. The first maintains that you should use the BeginDoc procedure to start a print job and the TextOut procedure to send output to the printer. This method has many advantages, including complete control over the appearance of the text and the ability to position the text exactly where you want it. The downside to this approach, though, is that it's somewhat complicated to set up and use. If you need that kind of control, I suggest you use a full-blown report writer; they usually provide a full range of facilities for controlling printer output.

The second school of thought regarding printing text under Windows espouses the approach taken here. The idea is to keep things as simple as possible; the task of printing sophisticated reports is left to report writers. By using standard output routines to send the printer output, you avail yourself of all the facilities those routines provide without needlessly complicating the process of getting your report to the printer. This simplistic approach keeps the code size small and easy to follow.

BeginReport

Let's reexamine each of the component pieces of the preceding code. Let's look first at the BeginReport routine. To reiterate, its text is as follows:

```
procedure BeginReport(Orientation : TPrinterOrientation; Title :String);
var
```

```
   Temp : Array[0..30] of Char;
begin
  Printer.Orientation:=Orientation;
  Printer.Title:=Title;
  AssignPrn(PrintFile);
  Rewrite(PrintFile);
  With Printer.Canvas.Font do begin
    Name:='Courier New';
    Height:=10;
    Style:=[];
  end;
  LineLength:=(Printer.PageWidth div Printer.Canvas.TextWidth('X'))-5;
  PageLength:=(Printer.PageHeight div Printer.Canvas.TextHeight('X'))-2;
  UserName:=GetWindowsUserName(Temp);
end;
```

Notice how the orientation of the report is passed into the routine as a variable of type TPrinterOrientation. TPrinterOrientation is defined by the Printers unit and has the possible values of poPortrait and poLandscape. Because page orientation is usually dependent upon the routine calling it, the routine expects it to be supplied when you initiate a print job.

The With Printer.Canvas.Font section sets the font that the report will use. For simplicity's sake, the entire report will be printed in a single font. Moreover, that single font will be a non-proportional TrueType font, Courier New. Unless you have a lot of time on your hands or feel you need an extra source of frustration in your life, I recommend you stay away from proportional fonts when "rolling your own" report-printing mechanism.

Notice the way in which LineLength and PageLength are calculated. The line

```
LineLength:=(Printer.PageWidth div Printer.Canvas.TextWidth('X'))-5;
```

divides the number of pixels on the printed page (taking into account the current paper size and page orientation) by the width of a single X in the current font. This is another good reason for using a non-proportional font. Because all characters are sized identically in non-proportional fonts, you can make calculations such as this one by using the TextWidth method function. Using a proportional font, however, invalidates this calculation; the process of determining the maximum number of characters per line gets much more complex. Note that the calculation subtracts 5 from the quotient to allow for left and right margins.

The GetWindowsUserName routine that you built earlier is called when the report job is initiated. Its result is stored in the UserName global variable for display in the report's page header. The BeginReport routine defines a scratch variable, the Temp character array, to pass to the GetWindowsUserName function.

The Title parameter that is passed into the routine is used to set the print job name used in the Windows print spooler and on network banner pages. If your network print configuration prints a banner page before each print job, you can use TPrinter's Title property to set the text it prints.

The `Pad`, `LPad`, and `Center` functions all perform a similar function. One of the challenges of formatting print output is getting columns containing variable length data sized appropriately. Another major challenge is in getting column headings and the data they represent to be sized evenly. If the heading over a column is longer than its data, the column must be sized to match the heading; if the data is wider, the column heading must be padded. These three functions pad the elements on the report so that they are easier to align. Along with using non-proportional fonts, consistently padding similar elements is the most important aspect of getting reports to print correctly.

PrintHeader

I've written the `PrinterHeader` routine in such a way that it should be modular enough to use in your own programs. Although I don't recommend that you print reports using only programming code, if you run into a situation where you must, you can use much of the code presented in this chapter, including the `PrinterHeader` routine. It takes as its parameters the `ReportName`, `SystemTitle`, `ReportTitle` and report criteria for display in the report's page heading. This flexibility should enable you to use it with virtually any type of report.

The line

```
If (Printer.PageNumber <> 1) then Write(PrintFile,^L);
```

sends a Ctrl+L character to the printer each time the `PrintHeader` routine is called, with the exception of the first time. Sending a Ctrl+L to almost any type of printer causes it to eject a page. You don't want to eject a sheet the first time the routine is called, or you waste a sheet of paper each time the report is printed.

You might be wondering why I didn't just call `TPrinter`'s `NewPage` routine. The reason for this is that you can't reliably mix the two approaches to printing under Windows mentioned previously. Calling `NewPage` while using standard file I/O to send printer output can result in page breaks occurring in curious places. The printer output and the page breaks get out of synch because you are using two different methods for initiating them.

Despite the fact that `NewPage` isn't used, `TPrinter`'s `PageNumber` property is still accurate and usable by the code. Even though the code presented here never calls `TPrinter`'s `NewPage` method, the fact that a page is ejected on the printer is still detected and reflected in the `PageNumber` property.

Note the use of the built-in `Date` and `Time` functions. In production code, you might want to store both of these when a print job is initiated and print the stored versions on the report itself. By printing the function results directly, you leave yourself open to the possibility that each page will print a different time on it—the current system time is re-retrieved with each call to the `Time` function. Furthermore, if a print job crosses the midnight boundary, you might have a similar problem with the date printed on each page. I've left the calls to the functions themselves in place for simplicity's sake.

Note the use of calculations based on the LineLength variable in the calls to the Center function for the system title, the report title, and the report criteria fields. This is done to allow the orientation of the printed page to be changed without invalidating the code used to print the page header. If the page orientation is switched to poPortrait, the page header will change dynamically along with it.

More on *TaskList1Click*

The line

```
ParamByName('ListDate').AsDate:=Date;
```

supplies the current system date to the quTaskList query as its ListDate parameter. This enables the Task List report to print the task assignments for the current day. After the parameter is assigned, quTaskList's Open method is called to initiate the query and return a result set.

Notice the use of try..finally blocks to insulate the code from exceptions. On inspecting the code, you'll find that there are three separate try..finally blocks. The first one ensures that the query is closed at the end of the routine, in the event there's a problem within the procedure. The second ensures that the text file the routine uses to send print output to Windows is closed when the routine terminates, regardless of whether the routine terminates normally or because of an error. The third one ensures that the cursor pointer is reset to its normal state when the print job ends.

The Repeat...Until (quTaskListName.AsString<>LastName) section handles the report's grouping. The idea within the report is to print a separate task list for each employee. Through the use of an ORDER BY statement in the SQL that drives the report, and due to the logic contained in the Repeat...Until loop, the report is able to do just that—each employee's task list is printed separately, one after the other.

One last thing I might mention about the report code. Notice that the mouse pointer is changed to an hour glass prior to the report beginning and restored afterward. It's important to let your users know that something's happening while the report runs. As with any task, the more feedback you can provide the user, the better. Another idea you might consider is the use of a progress graph. You could update the graph as you step through the quTaskList query result set. Little elements such as this give your applications a more polished look and make them more palatable for the user.

Previewing the Report

Another nice feature that you could implement is the ability to preview the report before printing it. This can easily be done by using Assign rather than AssignPrn to output your report. What you'll then get when previewing a report is a text file that contains the output that would have gone to the printer had you printed the report instead. You can then use the LoadFromFile method of the TMemo component to display this file in a scrollable window. If you then want to send the previewed report to the printer, you can simply use AssignPrn to initiate a print job, then write the TMemo's Lines property to the printer.

Save your project, then press F9 to compile and run the application. After RENTALMAN is loaded, pressing F10 prints the employee Task List report.

What's Ahead

In Chapter 13, "Finishing Touches," you'll complete the RENTALMAN application by applying a few finishing touches to it. Chapter 13 takes you through polishing your app to look and work more professionally. You'll learn how to set up a background bitmap, an application icon, Windows help, a status bar, and lots of other niceties. You'll then be left with a Delphi database application that is full-featured and robust.

Summary

You've now constructed reports in just about every way that they can be under Delphi. You learned to construct reports by printing forms, by using the QuickReport components, via ReportSmith and through Object Pascal code. Generally, you'll find that Delphi's QuickReport components are the easiest way to go, but you may also come to rely heavily on report-writer-based reports, as well. Whatever your needs, you should find yourself now sufficiently equipped to deal with the printing needs of the database applications you build with Delphi.

13

Finishing Touches

Now that you've finished designing your database and your application and have developed the requisite objects to implement that design, you're ready to spruce up the app a bit. RENTALMAN still lacks a few finishing touches—some things that will no doubt make it more professional in appearance and more usable.

The process whereby you go through an app after you've written it, looking for potential improvements is known as a *post-developmental review.* This phase of the development process is often slighted in terms of the importance placed upon it. Make no mistake about it, post-developmental review is a key phase in the application development cycle. It's important in that it lets you step back from the application and evaluate it as a user. It's also important in that it brings to light usability problems and other anomalies that your users may find objectionable, before they actually see the app. Programmers are some of the most demanding users of all; chances are, if your application can survive a review by software developers—including yourself—it's probably fairly robust.

This phase of the development process also enables you to incorporate changes that users have requested. You may have demonstrated the application to your users during the development process and discovered that a user needed some little nuance or other facility in the application that you hadn't thought of. The post-development review process is the place to address such things.

This phase of application development is also important in that it gives you a chance to polish your work. After some of the more mundane phases of the application's development have been completed, you can do a few things that are more fun, and, at the same time, enhance the application. This enables you to take even more pride in your work—and, I think you'll find, it makes the software-development process even more enjoyable.

The enhancements you'll make in this chapter to the RENTALMAN System include:

- Adding an application logo
- Changing the application's title and icon
- Adding Windows help (including context-sensitive help)
- Adding fly-over hints
- Activating the status bar
- Adding an About box
- Adding a form Print button (and other system-wide enhancements)
- Changing the forms to use `DBNavSearch`
- Adding a ReportSmith menu item
- Adding report front-end dialog boxes

After these changes are complete, you'll finish up by comparing the completed application with the original design and goals that were developed in earlier chapters. You'll test the application for compliance with those goals and for stability and usability in general.

Adding an Application Bitmap

There isn't much to adding a bitmap to an application. Some developers prefer to set up separate splash forms whose whole purpose is to display the bitmap. In the case of RENTALMAN, you simply add it to the application's main form, fmRSYSMAN0.

Before you can place it onto the form, though, you'll need to procure the bitmap. You can use one of the many canned ones that ship with Delphi, Windows, or some other package. Alternately, you can create your own using Delphi's Image Editor tool. You can access the Image Editor tool from Delphi's Tools menu or from your Delphi program folder. Figure 13.1 shows some of the author's world-famous line art created using the Image Editor tool.

FIGURE 13.1.

You can use Delphi's Image Editor tool to create spectacular bitmaps like this one.

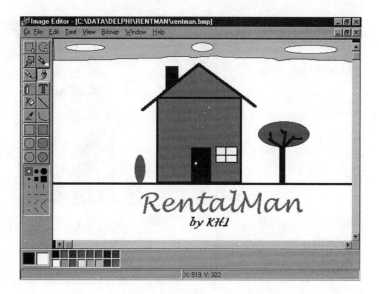

Reload the RENTALMAN project, if you've not already done so, and select the fmRSYSMAN0 form in the visual designer. Click the paMiddle Panel component, then drop an Image component onto it. Name the component imSplash and set its Alignment property to alClient. Next, double-click its Picture property and click the Load button in the ensuing dialog. From the Load picture dialog, select a bitmap and click Open. After you return to the Picture editor dialog, click OK.

For bitmaps that display on forms that might be resized, like this one, you'll want to ensure that the bitmap is large enough to accommodate the form's maximum size. If you're placing the bitmap on a Panel component, as we are here, you can simply maximize the form, then view the panel's Height and Width properties in the Object Inspector. Make your bitmap match the dimensions of the panel. In this case, this means that the bitmap needs to be 638 pixels wide and 380 high.

Alternatively, you can use a smaller bitmap and stretch it to fit its host area. I don't recommend this, though. Usually, this will have the effect of distorting a bitmap to the point of making it look silly. To cause a bitmap to stretch to fit its area, set its Stretch property to True.

Note that setting the Image component's Stretch property to True *does* have the benefit of allowing the bitmap to be shrunk to fit the form when it's reduced in size. You may find this preferable to cropping the bitmap. The important thing is to ensure that the bitmap looks correct when the form is displayed at its maximum size. In the case of fmRSYSMAN0, the form's maximum size is also its default size.

After you've placed the bitmap correctly, save the project, and run it. Figure 13.2 shows what the application looks like at runtime with its new bitmap.

FIGURE 13.2.

Adding a bitmap to the RENTALMAN application helps polish its appearance.

Specifying the Application's Title and Icon

After you've set up RENTALMAN's splash bitmap, you're ready to assign its application title and icon. By default, Delphi assigns the same canned icon image to every new application you build. If you only develop a handful of applications, this might be acceptable; over time, however, it can become a problem. An application's icon should give a quick, bird's-eye view of what it is the application does. It should also distinguish the application from other applications. In this section, you'll set up an application icon that does just that.

Once again, the first thing you need to do is come up with an image to use. Windows itself comes with a number of icons, as does Delphi. You can also use the Image Editor tool to build your own. Figure 13.3 illustrates more of the author's contribution to the art world.

FIGURE 13.3.

You can use Delphi's Image Editor tools to build icons for your applications.

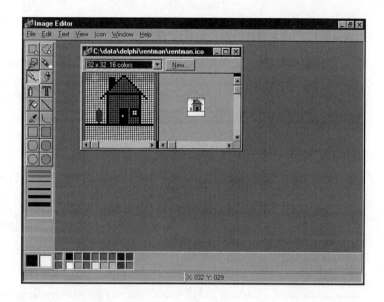

After you've got an icon, you're ready to link it into the application. To do this, select the Options item on the Project menu, then click the Application tab. Once on the Application page, type `RentaMan Maintenance System` into the Title box, then click the Load Icon button and specify your new icon. (See Figure 13.4.)

FIGURE 13.4.

You use the ProjectOptions/ Application menu option to associate an icon with your applications.

The title you specified will be used on the Windows task bar to identify your application. The icon you included will be used in a variety of places. Basically, it'll be referenced every time Windows needs an icon to represent your application. This icon will also carry through to your users' machines when you run an InstallShield-based set-up program to install your software.

Adding Windows Help

The subject of adding Windows help to applications has filled many a book. It's a complex topic and a world unto itself. Nevertheless, I think at least a cursory review of what's involved with creating Windows help for your applications is in order. All professional Windows applications include help systems.

Help-File Creation Utilities

Before we get started, I should mention that there are a number of good utilities to assist you in creating Windows help files. Among these, two stand out as the leaders of the pack: ForeHelp and RoboHelp. I'd encourage you to invest in one of these if you intend to get serious about Windows help-file generation. They will save you hours of painstaking work.

Help File Basics

In order to build Windows help files, it's necessary to understand what the components of a Windows help files are. You have three basic files that are a part of every help file: the help-project file (.HPJ), the help-contents file (.CNT), and the rich-text file (.RTF) containing the help text itself. The help-project file and the help-contents file are both text files. The help-text file is a rich-text-format file that can be created with a number of word processors including Microsoft Word. You merge these three files (and possibly others, as well) into your help file by compiling them with the Windows help compiler.

> **NOTE**
>
> The WordPad accessory that accompanies Windows can also read and write rich-text-format files, but it does not support all the formatting capabilities that you'll need to build Window help files. It doesn't support either footnotes or hidden text, so it's not usable as a Windows help-text editor.

Each of the tree files contains special instructions that control the make-up and behavior of the generated help file. Prior to Windows 95, you used to have to edit the help project and contents files manually if you did not have a third-party utility for doing so. Beginning with Windows 95, though, Microsoft has produced a much nicer editing facility and compiler for working with help files. The utility is called Microsoft Help Workshop, and it's included with Delphi.

Before you create the help project or contents file, though, you'll need to compose the help text itself. This file consists of free-form text with a handful of special characters and other text-formatting attributes that define the help topics themselves and the relationships between them.

You organize the text by topic, placing each topic on a separate page. Within each topic, you use custom footnote characters to denote a topic's title, its topic number, its browser sequence, and its index entries. You use special text attributes to denote hotspots—links from one topic to another. Table 13.1 summarizes these special characters and attributes.

Table 13.1. You use several different special characters and attributes to set up Windows help topics.

Symbol/Attribute	*Meaning*
#	Defines the topic ID that is used elsewhere to refer to this topic
$	Defines the topic title
K	Defines an index entry or set of entries
+	Defines this topic's order in its browser sequence
A	Defines an A-link keyword
!	Defines a macro to execute
*	Defines a build tag for conditional exclusion of Selected topics
>	Defines the window type to use
@	Indicates a comment in the topic
Double-underline	Indicates a *hotspot*—a jump to another topic
Hidden text	Identifies the topic ID to jump to

Only the first one, the topic ID symbol (also known as the *context string*) is actually required—the rest are optional. In practice, you use the first four—#, $, K, and +—more than the others.

Building the Help Text File

Now that you know what these symbols mean, let's put them to use. Start a new file in your Windows word processor. This word processor will have to support the RTF format, custom footnotes, double-underlines, and hidden text. The one most often used is Microsoft Word, but you can use any that meets the preceding qualifications.

Let's key three sample topics for the RENTALMAN System, plus a contents topic. You'll set up links between these topics and define index entries for each of them.

To begin with, key the following text for the Log a call menu item:

```
Log a call

Select this option to enter a maintenance call. You'll be asked to specify the
property that the call concerns.
```

Entering a Context String

Position the I-beam cursor just prior to the word `Log` and insert a # custom footnote (press Alt+I, in Microsoft Word 7.0). This will denote the topic's ID or context string. Key `LogCall` for the footnote's text. Other topics that establish links to this topic will use its context string to set up the link. You also use the topic ID in the Help Workshop—you'll map it to actual help-context numbers that your application can use.

Entering a Topic Title

Next, reposition the I-beam just before the word Log and insert a $ custom footnote. This will establish the topic's title. Key `Log a call` for the footnote's text. Windows allows topics to be looked up using their titles, so it's a good idea to establish titles for your help topics. The title you specify for a topic is displayed in the WinHelp History list, the Search dialog box, and the Bookmark menu. Usually, the title you specify will match the text on the topic's first line.

You should format the first line of the topic as you would any other type of title—whether it be a screen title, a paragraph title, or something similar. Use a larger point size and bold the title text to help it stand out.

Entering Topic Keywords

Now that you have a context string and a title for the topic, let's define some keywords for it as well. Insert a K custom footnote just prior to the word `Log` and set its text to `Log a call; Calls, logging; Calls, entering; Calls, adding`. These entries will appear in the help file's index, and they will help your users more easily locate topics of interest.

Insert a page break following your topic definition. All topic definitions end with a page break (press Ctrl+Enter in Microsoft Word). Figure 13.5 illustrates the completed topic. Notice that the spaces that Word places after its footnotes have been removed. I've done this because I've seen extraneous spaces confuse the help compiler. They serve no real purpose, so I recommend that you omit them from your help topics as well.

Now that the LogCall topic is defined, you're ready to define one for the Property topic on the Tables menu and the Work orders topic on the Reports menu. Let's begin with the Property topic.

Key the following help text for the Property menu item:

```
Property

Select this option to enter or update property records. If you are needing
➥ to log a maintenance call, see the Log calls help topic.
```

Insert footnotes for the topic's context string, title, and key words. Use the same sort of keywords you used for the LogCall topic. Don't forget to format the topic's first line appropriately. It needs to be consistent with the LogCall topic's first line.

FIGURE 13.5.

The completed LogCall topic.

Linking Two Topics via a Hotspot

After the topic is set up, you're ready to link it with the LogCall topic. Position the mouse to the immediate right (no space) of the Log calls string in the preceding text. Type LogCall, then select Log Call with the mouse and hide its text by setting its Hidden attribute to True (use the Format/Font menu item in Word 7.0). Next, select the Log calls string and set its double-underline attribute to True (again with Format/Font in Word 7.0). This will transform the Log calls string in the preceding text into a hotspot, causing the familiar green underline to appear under it. When the user clicks it, the LogCall topic will be displayed, as would be expected.

> **NOTE**
>
> Although hotspots are usually identifiable via their green underline attributes, this isn't always the case. A developer can turn off both the special coloring and the underline attribute. To see all the hotspots on a given help screen, press and hold Ctrl+Tab. All the hotspots should be displayed in reverse video when you do this.

Insert a page break following your topic definition. All topic definitions end with a page break. Figure 13.6 illustrates the completed topic.

FIGURE 13.6.

The completed Calls topic.

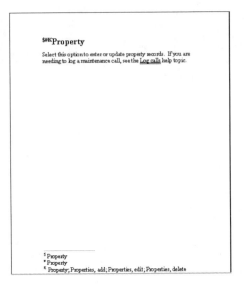

The last of the three topics is the Work Orders topic on the Reports menu. Key the following text for it (minus the quotes):

```
Work Order Print

This option allows you to select and print a work order. A work order lists
➡ the work to be done on a rental property due to a call from a
➡ tenant. See the Property and Log Call topics for more information.
```

Set this topic up using the three basic footnotes as you've done with the other two topics. After you've done that, you're ready to establish some links between the topics.

Begin by unlinking the Property topic; the hotspots you specify on this topic won't jump to other help topics. On the contrary, they'll display linked topics in pop-up windows. The only difference between setting up a hotspot to jump to another topic and setting one up to display the topic in a pop-up window is that you use a single underline, rather than a double underline, to underscore the hotspot.

Position the I-beam to the immediate right (no space) of the word Property. Key in the word Property a second time, then select it with the mouse and hide it as you did in the preceding example. Select the original Property and underline it (Ctrl+U in Microsoft Word).

Once you've done this, move to the immediate right of the Log Call string in the preceding text. Type LogCall, then highlight it and set its Hidden attribute to True. Finish up by selecting Log Call with the mouse and underlining it. Figure 13.7 illustrates the finished topic.

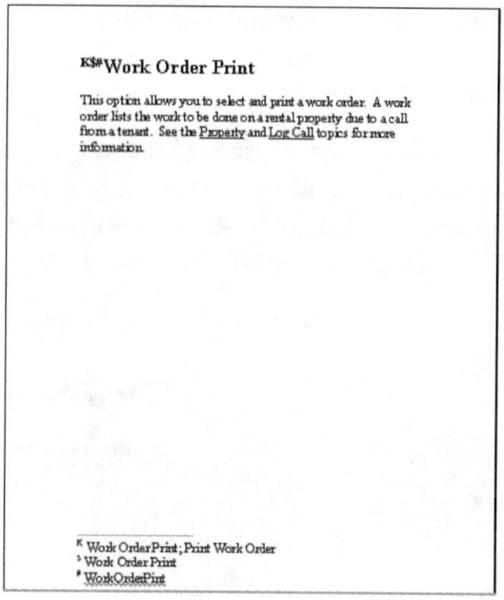

FIGURE 13.7.

The finished Work Order Print help topic.

K$#**Work Order Print**

This option allows you to select and print a work order. A work
order lists the work to be done on a rental property due to a call
from a tenant. See the Property and Log Call topics for more
information.

K Work Order Print; Print Work Order
$ Work Order Print
# WorkOrderPrint

After you've completed the Work Order Print topic, you're ready to move on to the Contents topic.

The Contents Topic

Even though you'll later define a separate contents file, you still need a Contents topic in your help file. This topic will consist of nothing but links to other topics. It will consist of a whole page of hotspots that jump to other pages in the help file.

The Contents topic is assumed by the help compiler to be the first topic in your help-text file, so move to the top of the file and insert a page break before the LogCall topic. Type the following text for the Contents topic:

```
RentalMan Maintenance System Contents

Log a call

Add or update property

Print work orders
```

After you've done this, set up the three basic footnotes for the topic, using the word Contents as their key.

When you have the footnotes completed, you're ready to move on to setting up the links with the other topics. These should be full-blown hotspots that actually jump to the other topics.

Position the I-beam to the immediate right of the `Log a call` string in the preceding text and type `LogCall`. Select `LogCall` and hide it, as you did in the previous example. Next, select `Log a call` and double-underline it.

Next, position to the immediate right of the `Add or update property` string in the preceding text and type `Property`. Follow this by selecting `Property` and hiding it. Finish up by selecting `Add or update property` and double-underlining it. Repeat this process for `Print work orders`, substituting WorkOrderPrint for the hotspot's key.

Figure 13.8 illustrates the completed Contents topic.

FIGURE 13.8.

The completed Contents dialog box.

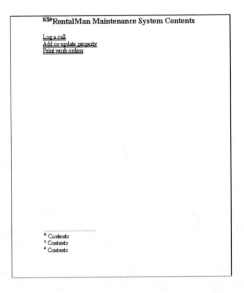

There's one last thing you should do before moving on to the help project and help contents file. You need to set up a browse sequence so that you can move sequentially through the topics in your help file. Inside WinHelp, this is done via the Browse buttons, which you'll enable in the Help Workshop program. Although you can define as many browse sequences as you want per help file, we'll keep things simple and define a single one for the entire file.

Position the I-beam to the immediate left of your Contents topic and insert a + custom footnote. Type `auto` for the footnote's text. Repeat this process for each of the remaining three topics. The `auto` specification tells the help compiler to number your topics sequentially for browsing. Although you can also specify a fixed sequence number for each topic, using `auto` is the most flexible way to do things because it enables you to insert additional topics without having to rearrange the browse sequence.

After you've finished setting up your browse sequence, you're done with the help-text file. Save it (make sure you save it in Rich Text Format, *not* in your word processor's native format) to your RENTMAN directory as rentman.rtf. You're now ready to move on to the help-project file and help-contents file.

Creating Your Help-Contents File

Prior to Windows 95, you had to create your help-contents file using a text editor if you did not have a third-party utility to assist you. You'd take this text file and another text file, your help-project file, and merge the two of them with your RTF file using Microsoft's DOS-based help compiler.

In conjunction with the release of Windows 95, Microsoft has released a graphical editor for these two text files called the Microsoft Help Workshop. You can also use Help Workshop to compile and test your help files. Delphi includes this utility; you should find it in your \Program Files\Borland\Delphi 2.0\Help\Tools directory. Its executable is HCW.EXE. Locate the file on your system and start it.

Help Author

The first thing you'll need to do is turn on the Help Author option on the File menu. Turning on Help Author affords several benefits. First, it causes additional information about your help system to be displayed while you're designing it, such as the topic numbers of your help topics as you navigate through them. Second, it enables you to move back and forth through your help file (regardless of whether you have enabled the Browse buttons) using Ctrl+Shift+Left Arrow and Ctrl+Shift+Right Arrow. You can also move to the beginning and end of your help file using Ctrl+Shift+Home and Ctrl+Shift+End.

Next, click the New option on the File menu and double-click Help Contents. Figure 13.9 shows this screen.

FIGURE 13.9.

The contents-definition dialog of the Microsoft Help Workshop.

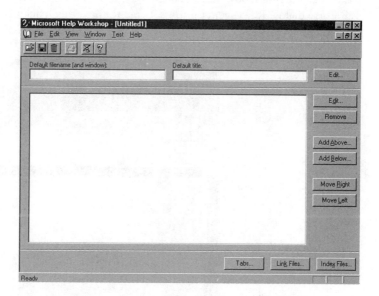

Key `.\rentman.hlp` into the Default filename (and window) entry box. Type `RentalMan Main-tenance System` in the Default title box. Next, click the Add Above button and key `RentalMan Maintenance System Contents` into the Title box of the ensuing dialog, and `Contents` into its Topic ID entry box. Click OK to save your new entry. (See Figure 13.10.)

FIGURE 13.10.

Key the first topic using a descriptive title and its context string from your .RTF file.

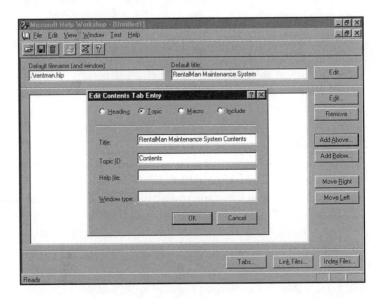

Next, click the Add Below button and key `Log a call` into the Title box of the Edit Contents Tab Entry dialog. Key `LogCall` into its Topic ID box, then click OK. Repeat the process for the remaining two topics in your help file. Figure 13.11 shows the completed list.

FIGURE 13.11.

The completed contents-file definition.

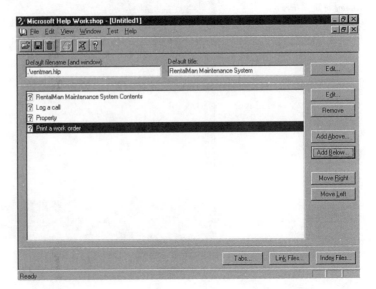

After you've added your last topic to the list, you're ready to save your contents file. Save it to your RENTMAN directory as rentman.cnt. Listing 13.1 shows what the file looks like in textual form.

Listing 13.1. The help-context file as generated by Help Workshop.

```
:Base .\rentman.hlp
:Title RentalMan Maintenance System
1 RentalMan Maintenance System Contents=Contents
1 Log a call=LogCall
1 Property=Property
1 Print a work order=WorkOrderPrint
```

Creating Your Help-Project File

Now that your help-contents file is created, you're ready to move on to the help-project file. Once again, the help-project file is actually a text file that Help Workshop manages for you. After you've set it up correctly, you can also use Help Workshop to compile your project.

> **NOTE**
>
> Even though both the contents file and the project file are text files that you could edit with an external editor, you shouldn't do this because Help Workshop manages these files for you. Editing them yourself could confuse it. Help Workshop itself warns against doing this, so I suggest you avoid it.

Select New from the File menu and double-click Help Project. The first thing Help Workshop does is prompt you for a filename for the project. Change to your RENTMAN directory and type in rentman for the project's name, then click the Save button. Help Workshop will append the magical HPJ extension to the file for you.

Figure 13.12 shows the project's initial appearance.

Adding Your .RTF and .CNT Files to the Project

Click the Options button and specify "Contents" as the Default topic and "Rental Maintenance System" as the Help title, then click the Compression tab and specify Maximum. Next, click the Files tab and specify your rentman.rtf file in the Rich Text Format (.RTF) files entry, and your contents file, rentman.cnt, in the Contents file box. After you've done this, save your Options settings by clicking OK to exit the dialog.

FIGURE 13.12.

RENTMAN.HPJ as it initially appears in Help Workshop.

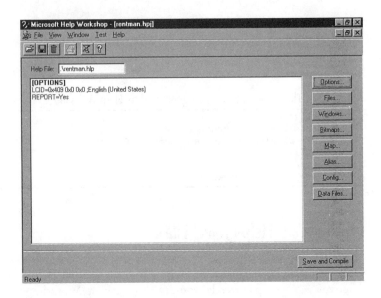

Adding Browse Buttons to the Project

Next, click the Windows button, then click Add in the ensuing dialog and type main in the Add New Window Type dialog. Click OK to save your new window type. Once you're back in the Window Properties dialog, click the Buttons tab and place a check mark in the Browse Buttons checkbox. This will enable WinHelp's Browse buttons so that you can navigate your help file using the browse sequence you defined earlier. If you now click the Macros tab of the same dialog, you'll see that Help Workshop has added the BrowseButtons() macro to your help project's global-macros list. This is what actually enables the buttons. Click OK to save your changes.

Mapping Context Strings to Help-Context Numbers

After returning to the Help Workshop main screen, click the Map button. Next, click Add, then key Contents into the Topic ID box and 0 (no quotes) into the Mapped numeric-value box. This will cause elements in the RENTALMAN application for which no help has been set up to display the help contents when the user requests context-sensitive help. Click OK to save your mapping.

Next, click Add again and, this time, add the LogCall topic ID with a numeric value of 100. It's a good idea to space out your help topics so that you can add new ones in between them if the need arises. Add the Property topic ID with a numeric value of 200 and the WorkOrderPrint ID with a value of 300. These numbers are the ones you'll use inside the RENTALMAN application to link program elements with the help system. You'll key these numbers into the HelpContext property of the appropriate components. When you get the mappings keyed in, click OK to save them. Figure 13.13 illustrates the completed mappings.

FIGURE 13.13.

The completed topic-ID mappings.

After you've defined your topic ID mappings, you're ready to save the help project and compile it. Click the Save and Compile button in the lower-left corner of the screen. Figure 13.14 shows the results of the compile.

FIGURE 13.14.

The compiler log shows the results of a help-project compilation.

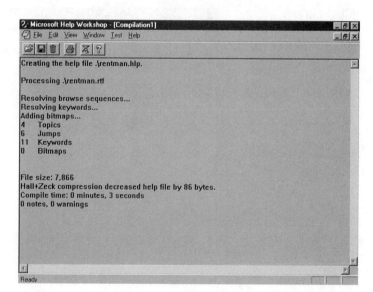

As you can see, the help file we've defined compiled smoothly and is now ready to be tested.

Testing Your Help File

You can easily test your help file without ever leaving Help Workshop. Select the Run WinHelp option on the File menu (or click the question mark on Help Workshop's toolbar). You should see the View Help File dialog. Select Contents in the Mapped Topic IDs drop-down list, then click OK. This drop-down list enables you to simulate an application program passing a help context ID to WinHelp. You could select any of the other available mappings to test them, as well. (See Figure 13.15.)

FIGURE 13.15.

The View Help File dialog box enables you to test your help file without leaving Help Workshop.

Click the View Help button to open your newly-created help file. You should see the Contents topic from your new file. (See Figure 13.16.)

FIGURE 13.16.

The Contents page from your new help file.

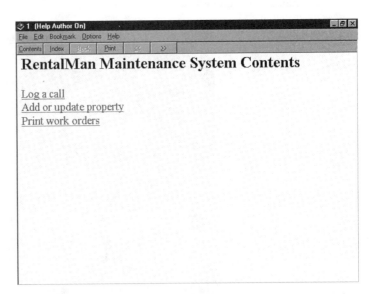

Click the Log a call topic on the Contents page. Figure 13.17 shows what you should see.

Now, click the Back button and return to the Contents page, then click the Property topic. Figure 13.18 shows what it should look like.

Return to the Contents page and click the Print a work-order topic. It should be displayed as shown in Figure 13.19.

FIGURE 13.17.

The LogCall topic as it appears at runtime.

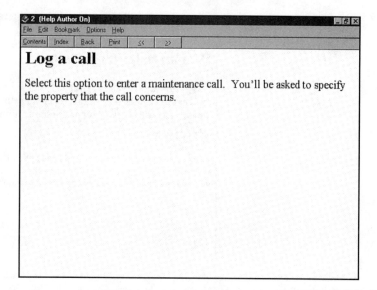

FIGURE 13.18.

The Property topic as it appears in your new help file.

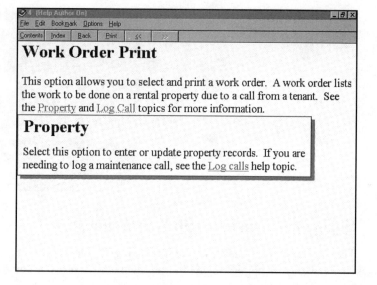

Finally, click the Contents button to see the runtime appearance of the contents file you created earlier. (See Figure 13.20.)

FIGURE 13.19.
*The WorkOrderPrint topic
as it appears at runtime.*

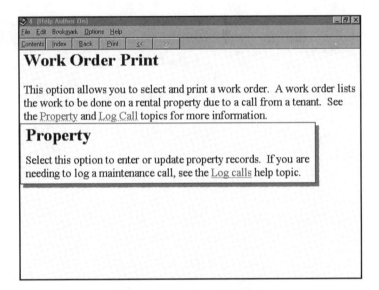

FIGURE 13.20.
*RENTMAN.CNT as it
appears at runtime.*

Linking the Help File with Your Application

The final, and most crucial, step in integrating Windows help into your application is to link the file with your application and set up the help-context IDs correctly.

Now exit Help Workshop and return to Delphi. Go ahead and turn off the Help Author feature before you exit Help Workshop. After you're back in Delphi, select the Application tab on the Project/Options menu item. You'll notice that the Help file entry is blank. Key `rentman.hlp` into the entry box and click OK.

Next, reload the fmRSYSMAN0 form into the visual form designer and double-click its `MainMenu` component to start the menu designer. After you're in the menu designer, click the Log a call option on the File menu and press F11 to jump to the Object Inspector. In the Object Inspector, change the menu item's `HelpContext` property to `100`, to reflect the mapping you gave it in

Help Workshop. Repeat the process for the Property and WorkOrderPrint topics, assigning them `HelpContexts` of `200` and `300`, respectively.

Now, finish up by setting up the Contents option on the Help menu. Double-click the `MainMenu` component, then double-click the Contents option on the Help menu. Key the following code into Delphi's code editor:

```
Application.HelpContext(0);
```

`HelpContext` is a method of the built-in Application object that calls WinHelp with a given topic ID. In this case, you're passing it `0`, which will invoke the Contents topic.

Next, click the Help button on RENTALMAN's speedbar, then press F11 to jump to the Object Inspector. Switch to the Events page and set its `OnClick` event to point to `Contents1Click`, the click event of the Contents menu option. Now, it does the same thing as the Contents option. Save your project and run it. You should be able to click the Contents option or the Help button on the speedbar to see the Contents topic in your new help file. Likewise, you can use the arrow keys to position over the Log a call, Property, or Work Order print-menu items and press F1 to see their respective help topics. (See Figure 13.21.)

FIGURE 13.21.

Pressing F1 while positioned on a menu item brings up help for the item in the help system.

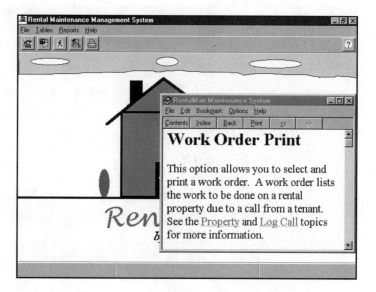

Adding Context-Sensitive Help

Although the concept has been around for years in a number of different packages, Windows 95 has brought the idea of context-sensitive help to the forefront with its new question-mark, window-frame icon. To add this type of help to your Delphi applications, you need to do two things. First, you need to enable the `biHelp BorderIcons` option. Second, you need to create the appropriate topics in your help file.

Because you've already got a handful of help topics in place in your help file, we'll just utilize them to illustrate setting up context-sensitive help in Delphi applications.

Because you won't be developing any new help topics to support context-sensitive help, all you need to do to enable it is set the `biHelp` border icon setting to `True` in the `BorderIcons` property on one of your forms, then set the `HelpContext` property on the form to reference an existing topic in the help file. Let's use the PROPERTY table's control grid form, fmRPROCGD0. Load it into the visual designer and toggle the `biHelp` option of its `BorderIcons` property to `True`. You'll need to also disable the biMinimize and biMaximize icons in order for the question mark icon to appear in the title bar. Next, click the `DBCtrlGrid` on the form and set its `HelpContext` to the value to which you mapped the `Property` help topic, `200`. This will enable you to bring up context-sensitive help for any control on the grid; components whose `HelpContext` is set to `0` inherit the `HelpContent` of their Parent. After you've configured the `HelpContext`, run the application. When the application starts, load the PROPERTY table's control-grid form, then click the question-mark icon and select one of the grid's components. You should see the Property help topic displayed in a pop-up window as illustrated in Figure 13.22.

FIGURE 13.22.

Your help topics become pop-up Windows when they're used with context-sensitive help.

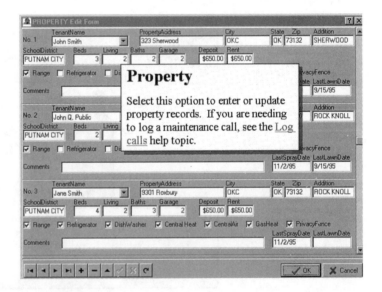

Adding Fly-Over Hints

Now that you've completed your help set-up, you're ready to move on to fly-over hints. There are only two things that you need to do to enable fly-over hints on a form. First, you need to set the form's `ShowHints` property to `True`; it's `False` by default. Second, you need to define hints for the components on the form.

Close the RENTALMAN application if it's currently running and return to Delphi. Next, load the system's main form, fmRSYSMAN0, into the form designer and toggle its ShowHint property to True. Next, set the Hint property of the speedbuttons on the form to something sensible. For example, the sbLogCall button should have a Hint that reads something like this: Click here to log a new maintenance call.

After you've set up a few hints, run the application. When you rest the mouse pointer over a component that has an associated hint, you'll see the hint pop up over the component.

Note that you can override the way that hints are displayed by default. For example, you could redirect your application's pop-up hints to its status line. To do this, you write a special procedure that is to handle your hints, then you assign it to the built-in Application object's OnShowHint event. This procedure has to follow the form:

```
procedure(var HintStr: string; var CanShow: Boolean; var HintInfo: THintInfo) of
➥object;
```

Here's a sample procedure that redirects the form's hints to its status line:

```
procedure TfmRSYSMAN0.RMShowHintProc(var HintStr: string; var CanShow: Boolean; var
➥HintInfo: THintInfo);
begin
  stRentalMan.Panels.Items[0].Text:=HintStr;
  CanShow:=False;
end;
```

You initially define this procedure in the public section of the TfmRSYSMAN0 class, like so:

```
public
    { Public declarations }
    procedure RMShowHintProc(var HintStr: string; var CanShow: Boolean; var
➥HintInfo: THintInfo);
```

Then you assign it in the FormCreate event of the TfmRSYSMAN0 class:

```
procedure TfmRSYSMAN0.FormCreate(Sender: TObject);
begin
  inherited;
  Application.OnShowHint:=RMShowHintProc;
end;
```

I don't recommend you do this—there are other problems presented by redirecting fly-over hints that you'll have to address if you intend for this to be truly functional. For one thing, you'll have to come up with a way to remove a hint from your status bar when it's no longer valid (for instance, if the user has moved off the item). If you leave the default mechanism in place, this is handled for you.

Activating the Status Bar

The next task on the list of user-interface improvements for the RENTALMAN application is the activation of the status bar. You'll recall that you added the status bar to the fmRSYSMAN0 form when you first designed it, but it hasn't been used since.

There are three elements that the status bar is set up to display: a status message indicating what's going on in the application, the name of the current user and the current version of the software. These are three elements that you'll find are handy to have displayed prominently on the screen. If a user calls with a problem, he can easily tell you which version of the software he's using just by looking at the bottom-right corner of the screen. And if you visit a client having a problem with your software, you can look at the application's status bar to determine which username he's logged into the system with, in case that's germane.

The first of the three elements is a no-brainer. All you do to display status messages on the status bar is update the bar before and after significant program events. For example, let's update the click-event code for the Log a call item on the File menu. Here's what the code looks like now:

```
procedure TfmRSYSMAN0.Logacall1Click(Sender: TObject);
begin
  inherited;
  dmRentalMan.taCALLS.Insert;
  fmRCALEDT0.ShowModal;
end;
```

All you need to do to enable a status message to display when this item is selected is surround the code with updates to the status message area of the stRentalMan component. Earlier, we designated this as the leftmost of the component's three areas, so the code would look like this:

```
procedure TfmRSYSMAN0.Logacall1Click(Sender: TObject);
begin
  inherited;
  try
    stRentalMan.Panels.Items[0].Text:='Add a maintenance call';
    dmRentalMan.taCALLS.Insert;
    fmRCALEDT0.ShowModal;
  finally
    stRentalMan.Panels.Items[0].Text:='';
  end;
end;
```

Adding the current username is equally simple. Because you've already made use of the GetWindowsUserName DLL function in your reports, you can easily make use of it here, as well. Select the fmRSYSMAN0 form component itself (not one of its components) and double-click its OnCreate event. After you're in the Delphi code editor, key the following code:

```
GetWindowsUserName(UserName);
stRentalMan.Panels.Items[1].Text:='User: '+String(UserName);
```

Add the following lines to the OnCreate's header:

```
var
  UserName : Array[0..30] of Char;
```

This routine will call the GetWindowsUserName function in the REPUTILS.DLL that you created earlier each time the form is shown. The username returned by the function will then be displayed on the status bar.

The third, and final, element that needs to be displayed on the status bar is the program's version number. When establishing version information for a Windows application, there are two ways to go about things: the easy way and the right way. The easy way consists of hard coding a version string constant, like so:

```
Const
  VersionStr : String[10] = '1.5';
```

You can also build a function that returns your current version, like so:

```
function VersionStr : String;
begin
  Result:='1.5';
end;
```

There are a number of convenient methods for doing this the easy way.

The right way, on the other hand, is not so effortless. The right way to define the version information for a Delphi application is to define a Windows VERSIONINFO resource.

The VERSIONINFO Resource Type

Why is this the right way? Because other tools can use the version information that you embed in your applications. For example, InstallShield automatically detects the presence of a Windows VERSIONINFO resource in your executables and constructs its Windows Registry keys accordingly. Likewise, a number of third-party utilities can examine Windows executables and report their version information. This is good for you—you can inspect your applications with industry-standard tools. It's good for your users; they can easily determine the current versions of the key applications they use.

Because Delphi has no native support for the VERSIONINFO resource type, you'll have to create the resource as a text file and compile it with the BRCC32 resource compiler provided with Delphi. You'll then link the resulting .RES file into your executable using the $R compiler directive.

VERSIONINFO resources are rather odd little beasts—bent on flexibility, they're a bit unwieldy. Here's the version resource from Delphi:

```
1 VERSIONINFO
FILEVERSION 1, 0, 0, 0
PRODUCTVERSION 1, 0, 0, 0
FILEOS VOS_DOS_WINDOWS32
FILETYPE VFT_APP
{
 BLOCK "StringFileInfo"
 {
  BLOCK "040904E4"
  {
   VALUE "CompanyName", "Borland International\000\000"
   VALUE "FileDescription", "Delphi32 Development Environment\000"
   VALUE "FileVersion", "2.00\000"
```

```
    VALUE "InternalName", "DELPHI32\000"
    VALUE "LegalCopyright", "Copyright \251 Borland International 1996\000\000"
    VALUE "OriginalFilename", "DELPHI32.EXE\000"
    VALUE "ProductName", "Delphi\000"
    VALUE "ProductVersion", "2.00\000"
  }

}

BLOCK "VarFileInfo"
{
 VALUE "Translation", 1033, 1252
}

}
```

The FILEVERSION and PRODUCTVERSION identifiers consist of two long integers, spread over four 16-bit integers. You can see that Delphi's internal-file version and product version both show it to be version 2.0.

The only other curious number is in the preceding BLOCK "040904E4" statement. You may be wondering what the significance of 040904E4 is. This number is a concatenation of the numbers that represent the language and character set in use. Windows defines tables that translate the two halves of this hexadecimal number string to signify the U.S. English language and the Windows Multilingual character set.

All the background information aside, how do you create your own version resource? It's simple. You can use a resource editor like Borland's Resource Workshop, or you can build your own as a text file and compile it with the resource compiler included with Delphi, BRCC32. Click the New option on Delphi's File menu and double-click Text in the ensuing dialog. Next, key the following resource information into the text file:

```
VERSIONINFO_1 VERSIONINFO
FILEVERSION 1, 0, 0, 0
PRODUCTVERSION 1, 0, 0, 0
FILEOS VOS_DOS_WINDOWS32
FILETYPE VFT_APP
{
 BLOCK "StringFileInfo"
 {
  BLOCK "040904E4"
  {
   VALUE "CompanyName", "Your Company\000\000"
   VALUE "FileDescription", "RentalMan Maintenance Management System\000"
   VALUE "FileVersion", "1.00\000\000"
   VALUE "InternalName", "RentalMan\000"
   VALUE "LegalCopyright", "Copyright © Your Company 1996\000\000"
   VALUE "OriginalFilename", "RENTMAN.EXE\000"
   VALUE "ProductName", "RentalMan Maintenance Management System\000"
   VALUE "ProductVersion", "1.00\000"  }

 }

 BLOCK "VarFileInfo"
```

```
  {
   VALUE "Translation", 0x409, 1252
  }

}
```

Replace *Your Company* with something more inventive, then save the file as RMANVER.TXT in the RENTMAN directory you created earlier (thanks to a quirk in Windows 95, you'll have to initially save the file with a .TXT extension). Next, shell to DOS and change to your RENTMAN directory. Rename your RMANVER.TXT file to RMANVER.RC, then compile it with the Borland Resource Compiler, like so:

```
"\program files\borland\delphi 2.0\bin\brcc32" RMANVER.RC
```

This will produce a file named RMANVER.RES, which you can then link to the RENTALMAN executable.

Return to Delphi and insert a blank line after the {$R *.DFM} line in RSYSMAN0.PAS. Next, type in the following line:

```
{$R RMANVAR.RES}
```

This will cause your VERSIONINFO resource to be included in the RENTALMAN executable when you compile it.

Now let's add code to the application to extract this information from itself and display it on the status line. Locate fmRSYSMAN0's OnCreate event in the Object Inspector and double-click it. You should see the code you added earlier to display the user name on the status bar. Listing 13.2 shows the lines you need to add to what you see in the code editor:

Listing 13.2. Code to extract the current application's version information.

```
VersionSize:=GetFileVersionInfoSize(PChar(Application.ExeName),Dummy);
  If (VersionSize<>0) then begin
    SetLength(VersionBuffer,VersionSize);
    SetLength(Version,VersionSize);
    If (GetFileVersionInfo(PChar(Application.ExeName), Dummy, VersionSize,
➡PChar(VersionBuffer))) and
      (VerQueryValue(PChar(VersionBuffer),'\StringFileInfo\040904E4\ProductVersion',Pointer
➡(Version), VersionSize))
then
      stRentalMan.Panels.Items[2].Text:='Version: '+Version;
  end;
```

Be sure to add the following lines to the FormCreate method's header so that it will compile successfully:

```
var
  VersionBuffer, Version : String;
  VersionSize : Integer;
  Dummy : Integer;
```

The code in Listing 13.2 uses three Windows API calls—`GetFileVersionInfoSize`, `GetFileVersionInfo`, and `VerQueryValue`—to return the application's version information. After this information is retrieved, it's displayed on the status bar.

Compile the application and run it. Figure 13.23 shows the effects of the changes to the RENTALMAN status bar.

FIGURE 13.23.

The status bar shows the application status, the current user name, and the application version.

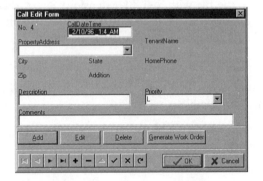

To illustrate how external programs utilize the VERSIONINFO resource in your applications, close down your app and start the Windows Explorer. Locate your RENTMAN directory using the Explorer, then right-click RENTMAN.EXE and select Properties from the pop-up menu. As you can see, besides the General tab present for all files, you have an additional one named Version. Click it and you should see the version information you specified in the VERSIONINFO resource. (See Figure 13.24.)

FIGURE 13.24.

The Windows Explorer recognizes and displays VERSIONINFO resources that are embedded into applications.

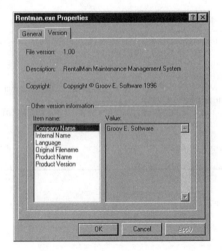

The ability to make use of the VERSIONINFO resource the way you just did is yet another example of Delphi's ability to access even the most minute of details in the Windows API. Whatever it is you need to do, you can probably find a way to do it with Delphi.

Adding an About Box

The next task on our wish list is to add an About box to the application. All good Windows apps have About boxes. An About box provides the user with critical information such as the program's author, its current version, technical-support numbers, and so on. Sometimes rogue developers even embed hidden messages or bitmaps in their About boxes. The About box in Delphi 1.0, for example, has a hidden picture of Anders Hejlsberg, Delphi's principle architect.

Return to Delphi and create a new form by inheriting from the About Box form in the Object Repository. Name the form fmRABTBOX0 and set its Caption to About RENTALMAN. Stretch it to be about 410 pixels wide, then stretch its panel component so that it remains proportional to the form. Lastly, double-click the form and change its FormCreate event handler to look like the code in Listing 13.3.

Listing 13.3. Your About box's FormCreate event handler assigns values to its crucial components.

```
procedure TfmRABTBOX0.FormCreate(Sender: TObject);
var
  VersionBuffer, VersionNoText, ProductNameText, LegalCopyrightText,
  CompanyText : String;
  VersionSize : Integer;
  Dummy : Integer;
begin
  inherited;
  VersionSize:=GetFileVersionInfoSize(PChar(Application.ExeName),Dummy);
  If (VersionSize<>0) then begin
    SetLength(VersionBuffer,VersionSize);
    SetLength(VersionNoText,VersionSize);
    SetLength(ProductNameText,VersionSize);
    SetLength(LegalCopyrightText,VersionSize);
    SetLength(CompanyText,VersionSize);
    If (GetFileVersionInfo(PChar(Application.ExeName), Dummy, VersionSize,
➡PChar(VersionBuffer))) and
      (VerQueryValue(PChar(VersionBuffer),'\StringFileInfo\040904E4\ProductVersion',Pointer
➡(VersionNoText), VersionSize)) and
      (VerQueryValue(PChar(VersionBuffer),'\StringFileInfo\040904E4\ProductName',Pointer
➡(ProductNameText), VersionSize)) and
      (VerQueryValue(PChar(VersionBuffer),'\StringFileInfo\040904E4\LegalCopyright',Pointer
➡(LegalCopyrightText), VersionSize)) and
      (VerQueryValue(PChar(VersionBuffer),'\StringFileInfo\040904E4\CompanyName',Pointer
➡(CompanyText), VersionSize)) then begin
        Version.Caption:=VersionNoText;
        ProductName.Caption:=ProductNameText;
        Copyright.Caption:=LegalCopyrightText;
        Comments.Caption:=CompanyText;
    end;
  end;
end;
```

Similar to the preceding code that displayed RENTALMAN's version on its status bar, this code uses the VERSIONINFO resource you defined earlier to retrieve application-specific information. This information is then displayed in RENTALMAN's About box.

To link your new About box with RENTALMAN's main form, assign the following code to the About option on fmRSYSMAN0's Help menu.

```
fmRABTBOX0.ShowModal;
```

After you've done this, select Use Unit from Delphi's File menu and add the RABTBOX0 unit to the main form's Uses statement. Next, run your application and click the About option. Figure 13.25 shows the new About box.

FIGURE 13.25.

Your new About box uses the VERSIONINFO resource you included earlier.

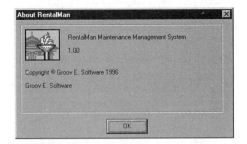

Adding a Form-Print Button

The next item on the wish list is a global form-print button. Were it not for Delphi's visual form inheritance, adding this would not be a trivial chore. But because of visual inheritance, this is a fifteen-minute task. Return to Delphi and load the DatabaseForm generic form class into the form designer. Drop a BitBtn component about one centimeter to the right of its DBNavigator component. Name the component bbPrintForm and set its Caption to Print Form. Set the button's Glyph property to the Print.bmp bitmapped file in the Images\Buttons subdirectory under your Delphi directory, then double-click the button and key the following single line of code:

```
Print;
```

Next, load the fmRWORMDE0 form into the visual designer. You'll notice that it now has two print buttons—one labeled Print, the other labeled Print Form. It doesn't need both of them, so you'll need to disable one. The one labeled Print Form is the new kid on the block that you introduced onto this form by adding it to his ancestor, DatabaseForm. Click the Print Form button on fmRWORMDE0 and set its Visible flag to False. Though you can't delete inherited components, you can make them invisible.

Finally, run the RENTALMAN application. All your forms now have the ability to print themselves. (See Figure 13.26.)

FIGURE 13.26.

Adding a Print button to all of your forms is a simple process when they all descend from a common ancestor.

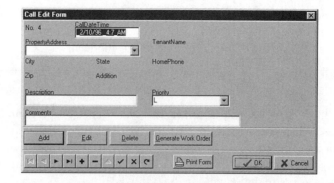

Replacing *DBNavigator* with *DBNavSearch*

The next item in the list of enhancements we discussed earlier is the replacement of the DBNavigator component with the DBNavSearch component. DBNavSearch is a DBNavigator-like component that adds a search button to the suite of buttons already present in DBNavigator. By clicking its magnifiying-glass button, you can search on any column or columns in a table. The component is profiled in Chapter 26, "Building Your Own Database Components" (you can find its complete source there). You can also find the component on the CD-ROM that accompanies this book. Install the component on Delphi's component pallete, then load the DatabaseForm back into Delphi's visual form designer.

Next, click the DBNavigator component on the DatabaseForm and note its name. Its name is the default name Delphi gives to a new DBNavigator when you first drop it onto a form, DBNavigator1. This information will be important when we replace it with the DBNavSearch component.

Now delete the DBNavigator component from the form and replace it with a DBNavSearch component. Change the DBNavSearch's Name to the name of the original DBNavigator component, DBNavigator1. Although this could be a bit confusing, it will save you work elsewhere in the application. Also, other than the addition of the search button, DBNavigator and DBNavSearch are identical in every respect.

You also may want to stretch the component to be a bit wider because it takes up no more space than the DBNavigator control does by default, yet includes an additional button.

Because you've deleted and redropped the DBNavigator1 component, links between it and its supporting code have been broken. You'll have to load forms that have attached special code to DBNavigator1 and reassociate that special code with your new navigator control. For example, load the fmRWORGRD0 form into the visual designer. You should see your DBNavSearch component in place at the bottom of the form. Click DBNavSearch, then switch to the Events page in the Object Inspector. Notice that there's no OnClick event defined for the navigator. Now double-click the OnClick. Surprisingly, you're placed into an existing OnClick event in the code editor. This happened because you had the foresight to name your new component the same as the original DBNavigator. Now that you've double-clicked the event, you've automatically reassociated it with the navigator component.

You'll need to repeat this process for each form in which code had been attached to the DBNavigator control. This includes fmRWORGRD0's detail form, fmRWORMDE0.

You'll also have to reset DBNavSearch's DataSource property on some of your descendent forms. When you deleted the DBNavigator component, this information was lost. Click the DBNavSearch component on the fmRWORGRD0 form and set its DataSource to dmRentalMan.dsWORDERS. Click the DBNavSearch on the fmRWORMDE0 form and set its DataSource to dmRentalMan.dsWODETAIL.

After you've relinked your forms with your new component, save the application and run it. After the application has started, hit F3 to bring up the CALLS table. You should see the DBNavSearch component at the bottom of the form. Click its search button (the magnifying glass) and key in some search criteria. (See Figure 13.27.)

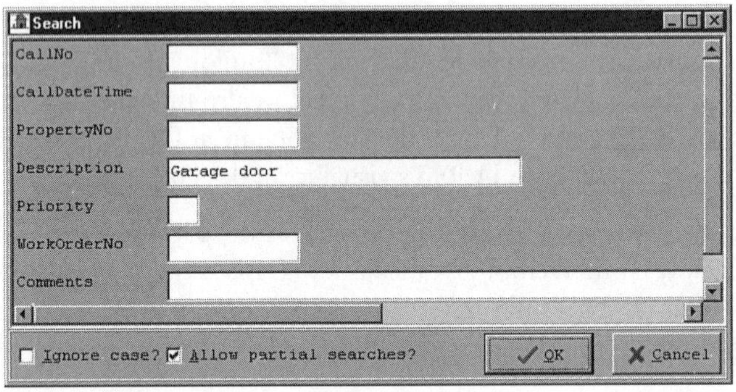

FIGURE 13.27.

By replacing the DBNavigator component with your DBNavSearch control, you've added a search ability to your database forms.

Adding a ReportSmith Menu Item

One of the things that people have come to expect in professional applications is the ability to create their own reports. Delphi doesn't provide any direct means of enabling the user to do this, but this doesn't prevent you from providing a link to the report writer of the user's choice.

You can't distribute the ReportSmith that's included with Delphi with your applications—you're licensed to include only the ReportSmith runtime engine. However, provided the user purchases his own copy of ReportSmith, you can easily link it into your Delphi applications so that he can develop custom reports without ever leaving your application.

To do this, there are two steps you'll need to take. First, you'll need to locate the ReportSmith main executable, RPTSMITH.EXE. Second, you'll shell to the executable to run ReportSmith.

Begin by reloading fmRSYSMAN0 into the visual-form designer and double-clicking its MainMenu component. Next, add a new item to the bottom of the Reports menu and set its Caption to "Run &ReportSmith." Double-click the item and change its OnClick event to look like Listing 13.4.

Listing 13.4. The OnClick event of the new Run ReportSmith menu option.

```
procedure TfmRSYSMAN0.RunReportSmith1Click(Sender: TObject);
var
  Key, Value, ReportSmithPath: string;
begin
  inherited;
  Key := LoadStr(SRptKey);
  Value := LoadStr(SRptDesignTimeValue);
  with TRegistry.Create do
  try
    RootKey := HKEY_LOCAL_MACHINE;
    OpenKey(Key, True);
    ReportSmithPath := ReadString(Value);
  finally
    Free;
  end;
  If (ShellExecute(Handle, nil, 'RPTSMITH.EXE', nil, PChar(ReportSmithPath),
➥SW_SHOWNORMAL) <= 32) then
    ShowMessage('Error starting ReportSmith');
end;
```

Add the DBConsts, Registry, and ShellAPI units to your Uses clause so that this code will compile.

The code in Listing 13.4 isn't terribly complex. First it locates the ReportSmith home directory in the Windows Registry. Second, it calls ShellExecute with the necessary parameters to invoke ReportSmith.

Note the use of the TRegistry component. TRegistry is a nonvisual component that you must instantiate at runtime if you intend to use it. Notice how the code never stores the return value of the TRegistry Create constructor—it simply uses it in a With statement that eventually frees the memory allocated by the constructor.

You'll also notice the use of a try...finally block to ensure that the memory allocated by TRegistry's Create constructor is released when the procedure ends—even if it ends due to an exception having been raised.

Notice that the code makes two calls to Delphi's string resource loader, LoadStr. Rather than hard-code the locations and names of ReportSmith Registry entries, the code uses the identifiers that Delphi itself uses. That is, because you're able to invoke ReportSmith from within the Delphi programming environment, obviously Delphi itself must have some means of determining the parameters necessary to start ReportSmith. By studying the Report VCL unit, you can see how this is done.

Essentially, Delphi defines two string resources that it uses to access ReportSmith. These are the `SRptKey` and the `SRptDesignTimeValue` strings. When you call `LoadStr`, you pass it an integer value that refers to the index of the string you want in Delphi's strings table. The `SRptKey` and `SRptDesignTimeValue` integer constants are defined in the DBConsts unit.

In Delphi's string table, `SRptKey` is set to `\\software\\borland\\ReportSmith\\3.00`, by default. This identifies the ReportSmith Registry key. `SRptDesignTimeValue` is set to "SQL Directory," by default, and denotes the Registry value under the ReportSmith key that identifies the home directory of the ReportSmith executable, RPTSMITH.EXE. Although you could code these yourself, it's preferable (and easier) just to use the ones provided by Borland. Note that the double slashes are for the RC compiler (string table resource); you would not need double slashes in Delphi code.

After the code locates the ReportSmith executable, it runs it using the `ShellExecute` Windows API call. The `ShellExecute` function is located in the ShellAPI unit—that's why you had to add ShellAPI to your Uses clause. It requires four parameters and takes the form:

```
function ShellExecute(hWnd: HWND; Operation, FileName, Parameters,
  Directory: PChar; ShowCmd: Integer): HINST; stdcall;
```

HWND is the caller's window handle—you can just pass it the current form's `Handle` property. `Operation` signifies what it is you want to do with the file; there are two options: Open and Print, the default being Open. `FileName` indicates the file that's to be spawned—RPTSMITH.EXE, in our case. `Parameters` stores any command-line options that you'd like to pass to `FileName`. `Directory` indicates the working directory to use when `FileName` is executed, and `ShowCmd` indicates the type of window to run the spawned process in; as a rule, `SW_SHOWNORMAL` should be used.

`ShellExecute` returns a handle to the spawned process with a value greater than 32 if the process starts correctly. If it doesn't, one of the error codes, as shown in Table 13.2, is returned.

Table 13.2. `ShellExecute` error codes.

Error code	*Cause*
0	Insufficient memory or resources
ERROR_FILE_NOT_FOUND	File to execute wasn't found
ERROR_PATH_NOT_FOUND	Working directory wasn't found
ERROR_BAD_FORMAT	Executable file is corrupted
SE_ERR_ACCESSDENIED	(Windows 95) access denied by Windows
SE_ERR_ASSOCINCOMPLETE	Filename association is incomplete

Error code	Cause
SE_ERR_DDEBUSY	Unable to perform DDE command due to DDE in progress
SE_ERR_DDEFAIL	DDE command failed
SE_ERR_DDETIMEOUT	DDE conversation timed out
SE_ERR_DLLNOTFOUND	(Windows 95) specified DLL wasn't found
SE_ERR_FNF	(Windows 95) specified file wasn't found
SE_ERR_NOASSOC	No application has been associated with the file
SE_ERR_OOM	(Windows 95) out of memory
SE_ERR_PNF	(Windows 95) specified path wasn't found
SE_ERR_SHARE	Share violation occurred

Adding Report-Confirmation Dialogs

The next item on the agenda is to set up confirmation dialogs for reports in RENTALMAN. Currently, when a report is selected from the menu or its hot key is pressed, the report runs without any type of confirmation. If the user accidentally presses the accelerator key that corresponds to a report-menu item, the report is immediately executed, possibly tying up the machine for a significant amount of time.

While doing things this way made it a little easier to code RENTALMAN's reports, professional applications don't behave this way. Any action that could conceivably take a long time to carry out or be potentially destructive should be confirmed.

Adding a confirmation dialog to your code is really quite simple. Load the fmRSYSMAN0 form into the visual-form designer and click the Task List item on its Reports menu. You should be placed into the code editor inside the item's OnClick event-handling procedure. Find the beginning of the procedure and key the following If statement:

```
If (MessageDlg('Print the Task List report?', mtConfirmation, mbYesNoCancel, 0)<>
➥mrYes) then
  Exit;
```

This line of code simply calls the built-in MessageDlg function and prompts for whether the report should be run. The first parameter to MessageDlg provides the prompt that's displayed in the dialog. The second parameter specifies the type of dialog to display—in this case, a confirmation-style dialog. The third parameter specifies the buttons to include in the dialog—here we've opted to include Yes, No, and Cancel buttons. The final parameter indicates a help-context ID. We'll leave this at zero, for now. You could set it to a help-topic ID if you wished.

Now, save your application and run it. Figure 13.28 illustrates the prompt at runtime.

FIGURE 13.28.

You can use the `MessageDlg` *function to confirm lengthy or destructive actions before carrying them out.*

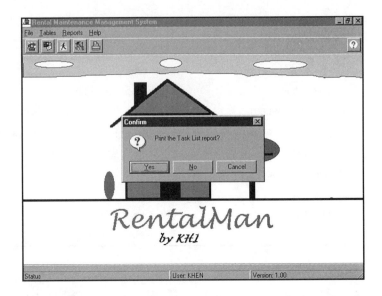

You can use this same technique to control the printing of any of RENTALMAN's reports. Simply place this line of code on the first line of the OnClick event handler for any of the report-menu items and change its prompt to match the report.

With this last enhancement, you've completed the items on the wish list that we formulated earlier in the chapter. The changes you've made have removed many of RENTALMAN's rough edges and will help it to be more intuitive and of a higher caliber as an appliction.

Testing the Application for Compliance with Your Original Goals

You may recall that the Tutorial section (of which this chapter is a member) began by listing the five steps necessary to build an application. To reiterate:

1. Define the purpose and goals of the application.

2. Design the database foundation and application processes needed to meet those goals.

3. Develop the design into an application by creating the requisite database and program objects.

4. Test the application for compliance with the established goals.

5. Install the application for production use.

You've finished the first three of these. You're now ready to complete the fourth step—you're ready to review the application you've just built to ensure that it meets the original goals that were set out for it.

The first order of business in evaluating the app's compliance with the established goals is to revisit exactly what those goals were. Here's the list we came up with in Chapter 8, "Your First Real Database Application":

The RENTALMAN System will track maintenance on rental properties:

- Record incoming calls from tenants
  - Log calls from tenants as they are received
  - Assign calls received to a new or existing work order
- Track progress on maintenance work
  - List open work orders
  - Generate a task schedule for each employee
- Provide historical maintenance information
  - List the maintenance history for a particular piece of property
  - List the properties on which a particular type of work has been performed

You should review each of these items individually to see whether the application you've just built meets them. I think you'll find that, in every case, the RENTALMAN application meets or exceeds the goals that were originally established for it.

This review process is important because it enables you to step back from the application and evaluate, as objectively as possible, whether the application does what it's supposed to. Forget all the bells and whistles—does it perform the function your client has asked for?

Remember that the client has the final say on whether your application meets his or her needs. It's important not to take rejection of your application by a client personally. People often don't know what they want until they see *what they don't want.* This is standard fare in the software-development business, and you shouldn't be discouraged by it.

Deploying your Application

The only step that remains of the original five listed is the deployment of the RENTALMAN application. That discussion is outside the scope of this chapter, but you can refer to Chapter 27, "Deploying Your Applications," for more on application deployment.

What's Ahead

In the next chapter, the final chapter in Part II, "Tutorial," you'll take the application you just finished and upsize it to a full-blown client/server implementation. Specifically, you'll change it from using Paradox tables to utilizing an InterBase database. Issues such as re-creating your database objects on the new platform, migrating your business rules, optimizing for database server use, and so forth, will be covered in depth.

Summary

Well, you've finally done it! You've just completed your first professional database application using Delphi. Hopefully you've garnered enough skills from this exercise to keep this from being your last such endeavor. The important thing is to dive in and enjoy yourself while you learn Delphi's way of doing things. I think you'll find that Delphi simplifies the process of application development so much that you can concentrate more on *what* it is your application is supposed to do—rather than on *how* to do it—and have a little fun along the way.

14

Moving Up to Client/Server

This is the final chapter in Part II, "Tutorial." In Chapter 8, "Your First Real Database Application," through Chapter 13, "Finishing Touches," you designed, developed, tested, and enhanced the RENTALMAN application. As designed, the RENTALMAN application works strictly with local tables. In this chapter we'll explore the process of scaling it upward to a client/server DBMS—specifically InterBase.

Starting the Server

If you've purchased the client/server version of Delphi, you already have a version of Borland's InterBase known as the *LIBS*—Local InterBase Server. If you're a Windows NT user, you'll use the Windows NT version of InterBase, instead. Chances are, one of the two is already running since, by default, Delphi's installation program sets InterBase up to run when you start Windows. It does this by updating the Windows Registry. The exact Registry key is `HKEY_LOCAL_MACHINE\SOFTWARE\Microsoft\Windows\CurrentVersion\Run`. You can update this value by right-clicking the InterBase server icon on your taskbar or by using the InterBase Configuration utility in your Delphi program folder.

Although you may not be an InterBase user, this chapter should still prove useful. The examples herein are written from the perspective of going from Paradox to InterBase, but there's no reason you couldn't target a different client/server platform. Many of the concepts presented here apply equally well to any client/server DBMS.

Whatever platform you're using, be sure your server is running and that you're able to connect to it before proceeding. See Chapter 24, "Delphi's Database Drivers Demystified," if you have trouble connecting to your server.

Getting the Data onto the Server

The first order of business when moving up to client/server is to get the data from your local tables onto the server. This can be done in a number of ways—I'll give you four of them.

First, and foremost, is Delphi's own Data Migration Expert. You can use it to copy your table definitions and their data to any target platform that Delphi supports. Data Migration Expert even enables you to modifying the *mappings* (the translation of field information on one platform to another) between the two platforms.

Another way to get the data onto the server is using the Database Desktop. You can use DBD's Copy option to copy a table's data (including its metadata) from one platform to another. You can also use its Borrow option while creating a new table on your target to import the structure of a local table—effectively importing the table's structure. If you do this, you'll still need to use DBD's Add facility to get the data across, since Borrow does not copy data.

Still another way to copy data from one platform to another is through the use of Delphi's `BatchMove` component. `BatchMove` copies data between two DataSets in the most expeditious manner possible. You could easily construct a simple application for moving local data to a SQL server.

Finally, you could simply connect to your server and execute the necessary SQL statement to create your tables. Although definitely the most time consuming, this is the preferred approach of many client/server old-timers—people who were client/server experts before the rash of GUI tools appeared.

If for no other reason than it's the tool Borland intended for this type of task, I'll take you through using the Data Migration Expert to port your data. You'll find that it's up to the task and simplifies the process of moving data from local tables to remote ones.

Before you can copy tables onto your server, though, you'll need to establish a database in which the tables will reside. This can be an existing InterBase database, or you can create a new one. I'll assume, for the purposes of this chapter, that you need to create one from scratch. After you've created the database, you'll need to create a BDE alias so that you can reference the database from inside of Delphi. I'll show you how to accomplish both tasks.

Creating a Database

Start up the InterBase Windows ISQL utility in your Delphi program folder. You'll use this table to create your database and to manipulate your database objects after they're on the server.

Select Create Database from WISQL's File menu. You'll next see the Create Database dialog. Specify `C:\DATA\DELPHI\RENTMAN\RENTMAN.GDB` for your Database, `SYSDBA` as your User Name and `masterkey` (or whatever SYSDBA's password is; `masterkey` is the default) as your Password, then click OK. This should create the database and connect you to it. (See Figure 14.1.)

FIGURE 14.1.

WISQL's Create Database dialog box.

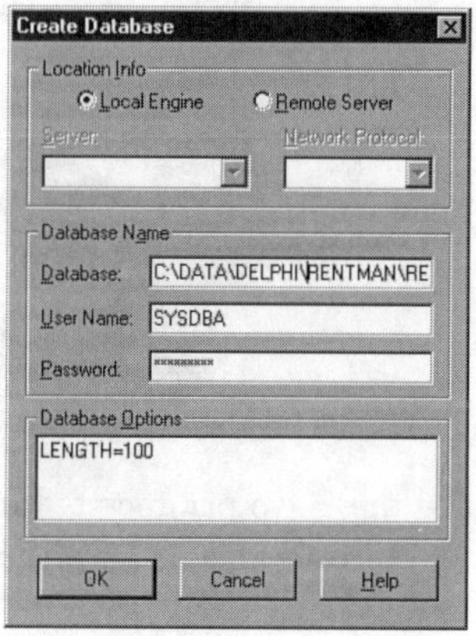

After the database is created, you're ready to proceed with defining your BDE alias.

Defining a BDE Alias

Exit WISQL for now and start up the BDE Configuration program. You'll find it in your Delphi program folder, as well. Click the Aliases page, then click New Alias. Key IB_RENTMAN for the new alias name and select INTRBASE as its type, then click OK. (See Figure 14.2.)

FIGURE 14.2.

The Add New Alias dialog in the BDE Configuration program.

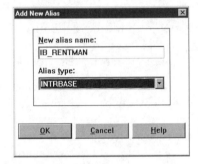

After the new alias is added, you'll need to specify a couple of configuration parameters. Click the SERVER NAME entry in the Parameters list and type C:\DATA\DELPHI\RENTMAN\RENTMAN.GDB. Next, click the USER NAME entry and key SYSDBA. (See Figure 14.3.)

FIGURE 14.3.

The BDE Configuration program's Alias definition screen.

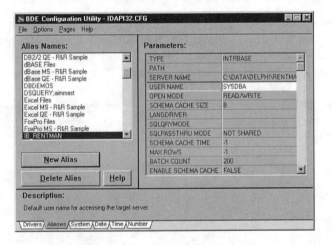

After you've specified these two parameters, you can save your work and exit the BDE Configuration program. You're now ready to use the Data Migration Expert to copy your data onto the server.

Using the Data Migration Expert

Start the Data Migration Expert—it's also in your Delphi program folder. (Note: DME is not included in all versions of Delphi.) The first screen you're presented with requests the source you want to copy from. You can specify either a source directory or a source alias. For our purposes, a source alias will do just fine, so find the RENTMAN alias in the list and double-click it. (See Figure 14.4.)

FIGURE 14.4.

The opening screen of the Data Migration Expert.

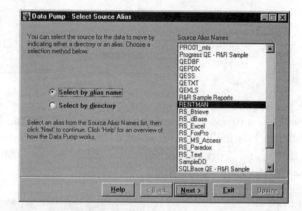

The next screen prompts for a target alias to copy the data to. Find IB_RENTMAN in the list and double-click it. (See Figure 14.5.)

FIGURE 14.5.

DME's Select Target Alias screen.

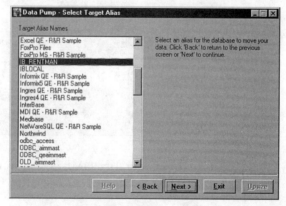

When you double-click an alias corresponding to a platform that requires passwords, you'll be prompted to enter one before proceeding. Enter your SYSDBA password (default is masterkey) into the login box that's presented by the Data Migration Expert.

You're next presented with the Select Tables to Move dialog. Click the double arrow (>>) button to select all the tables, then click Next. (See Figure 14.6.)

FIGURE 14.6.

The Select Tables to Move dialog box.

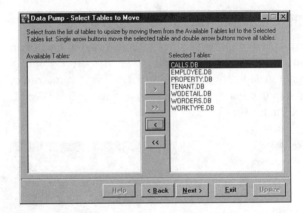

Next, you're given the opportunity to inspect and/or modify the manner in which your source data will be translated for insertion onto the target platform. If an item has a status of either Modified or Has Problem, click it, then click the Modify Mapping Information for Selected Item button and correct any problems DME has encountered. After you're finished, click the Upsize button. (See Figure 14.7.)

FIGURE 14.7.

The Inspect or Modify dialog of the Data Migration Expert.

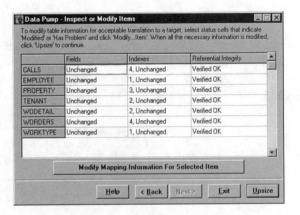

After you've successfully copied your data, DME presents you with a report that you may save to disk if you wish. Click Done to exit the Data Migration Expert utility.

Testing Your Copied Data

At this point, you can begin to test the data you've copied across to your server. Because you used a TDatabase component when you developed the RENTALMAN application, the change you need to make inside of Delphi in order to access your new platform is simple.

Load RENTALMAN's data module form, dmRentalMan, into the visual form designer and click its Database component, dbRentalMan. Next, double-click dbRentalMan's Connected property to close it, then change its AliasName property from RENTMAN to IB_RENTMAN, the name of your new alias. Next, select all seven of your Table components and set their Active properties to True in the Object Inspector. They were closed when you closed their database, dbRentalMan. Opening them should have the effect of reopening the dbRentalMan Database. Congratulations! You've just upscaled to your first client/server database application!

Not Quite That Simple

What? Got some errors when you tried to reopen your tables? Like they say, anything that sounds too good to be true probably *is* too good to be true. Rarely will you be able to simply change an AliasName property and convert a local, table-based application to a client/server based app. This is due to a number of factors. First, different platforms support different types of data. Despite your best efforts, and despite the near-psychic abilities of the BDE, your target platform may not even support the full range of standard SQL data types (that's the case here). Furthermore, even when two platforms support a given data type, they may do it differently. Both Paradox and InterBase support auto-incrementing fields, but they do so using completely different methods. So, it's up to you, the developer, to know both platforms well enough to make the necessary adjustments. You may have to adjust your application to match your server's capabilities. You may have to change a data type you thought you wanted to use to some other type because of deficiencies on your target. You may need to rewrite part of your application to more closely fit the way the target server works.

Beyond the issue of data types, different platforms also handle concurrency control differently. You may have to change some coding techniques that worked fine with Paradox tables but that cause too many locks under InterBase. You may find that a given practice is fine with local tables, but quite dangerous when talking to remote ones. You also may have to review your transaction-control methods. Techniques that work on one platform may cause you headaches on another. In short, you've got to completely retest your application to be sure that the design you came up with earlier is as bulletproof as you think it is. All DBMS platforms are not created equal—if they were, there'd be no reason for there to be so many of them.

The problems with this particular port are two-fold. First, InterBase does not have direct translations for two of the data types you used when you built the Paradox tables that make up the RENTALMAN database. It doesn't support Paradox's Logical type, and its DATE type contains both date and time information, not just date information, which your application is not expecting. The Delphi message LeaseBeginDate is not of the expected type indicates that Delphi was expecting a date-only type, but instead got InterBase's date/time type. This is due to a mismatch between the type of TField in use and its corresponding field in the table.

Fortunately, the solution to this problem is simple. All you need to do is bring up the Fields Editor for each of the DataSets (Tables and Queries, in this case) that contain either a date field or a logical field. Delete the date and logical fields from the field list (select them, then press Delete), then right-click and add them again. Delphi will take care of switching them to the correct TField types.

The second problem is related to the application itself. Even though the Data Migration Expert automatically switched the logical fields it encountered in your Paradox data to varchars, your application doesn't know this. If you run your application and bring up one of the two forms (fmRPROCGD0 or fmRTENCGD0) that use DBCheckBox components to service these Boolean fields, you'll find that they no longer work properly. This is due to the fact that the ValueChecked and ValueUnchecked properties of the DBCheckBoxes are still set up for true logical fields. Their values are True and False, respectively. What can you do about this? Simply select all the DBCheckBox controls on each form and switch their ValueChecked and ValueUnchecked properties to T and F, respectively. Once you've done this, the forms should work as expected.

Other Problems

One problem that isn't quite so obvious is the fact that InterBase doesn't support auto-increment fields in the same way that Paradox does. In Paradox, such fields have their own special data type. In InterBase, you must first create what's known as a Generator to create a new number to assign; second, you must set the field to the generated number from within a trigger. I'll show how to do both of these.

Start WISQL again, and connect to the InterBase database you just built. You connect to databases using the Connect to Database option on the File menu. After you've successfully connected, key the following syntax to create an InterBase generator:

```
CREATE GENERATOR CallNoGEN
```

Click the Run button to execute your SQL. Next, key the following syntax to create a trigger on the CALLS table that uses the CallNoGEN trigger to assign a default value for the CallNo column:

```
CREATE TRIGGER Generate_CallNo FOR CALLS
  BEFORE INSERT
  POSITION 0
  AS BEGIN
  NEW.CallNo - GEN_ID(CallNoGEN, 1);
END
```

There's an additional complication when adding a generator/trigger combo to a table that already has data in it: you must be careful to set the generator so that it does not create duplicate values for a unique index key. That is, because a unique index already exists on the CallNo column in the CALLS table, you'll have to be careful to set the generator so that the next value it returns does not conflict with those already in the table. This is easily done, though—you just use the SET GENERATOR command. Let's assume that the CallNo column in the last row of the CALLS table has a value of 3. To compensate for this, you just run the command:

```
SET GENERATOR CallNoGEN to 3
```

in WISQL. Of course, an alternative would be to delete the existing rows from the CALLS table. To do this, just key the following syntax into WISQL:

```
DELETE FROM CALLS
```

and click Run.

You'll need to add a generator/trigger combo to every table in the RENTALMAN database except the WODETAIL table. The SQL to set these up (run each command separately) is shown in Listing 14.1.

Listing 14.1. The SQL needed to create your generators and their associated triggers.

```
CREATE GENERATOR PropertyNoGEN

CREATE GENERATOR TenantNoGEN

CREATE GENERATOR WorkOrderNoGEN

CREATE GENERATOR WorkTypeCodeGEN

CREATE GENERATOR EmployeeNoGEN

CREATE TRIGGER Generate_PropertyNo FOR PROPERTY
  BEFORE INSERT
  POSITION 0
  AS BEGIN
    NEW.PropertyNo = GEN_ID(PropertyNoGEN, 1);
  END

CREATE TRIGGER Generate_TenantNo FOR TENANT
  BEFORE INSERT
    POSITION 0
  AS BEGIN
    NEW.TenantNo = GEN_ID(TenantNoGEN, 1);
  END

CREATE TRIGGER Generate_WorkOrderNo FOR WORDERS
  BEFORE INSERT
    POSITION 0
  AS BEGIN
    NEW.WorkOrderNo = GEN_ID(WorkOrderNoGEN, 1);
  END

CREATE TRIGGER Generate_EmployeeNo FOR EMPLOYEE
  BEFORE INSERT
    POSITION 0
  AS BEGIN
    NEW.EmployeeNo = GEN_ID(EmployeeNoGEN, 1);
  END
```

continues

Listing 14.1. continued

```
CREATE TRIGGER Generate_WorkTypeCode FOR WORKTYPE
  BEFORE INSERT
    POSITION 0
  AS BEGIN
    NEW.WorkTypeCode = GEN_ID(WorkTypeCodeGEN, 1);
  END
```

Unfortunately, this isn't the end of the story. Even though the database is properly set up to automatically increment your fields, your Delphi application knows nothing of this. Consequently, it won't display auto-incremented values provided by the generator, nor will it enable you to post rows to tables where the field being auto-incremented is also required—which is the case with all of the tables listed previously. In short, you're out of luck without doing some additional work.

The problem here is that Delphi doesn't directly support auto-incrementing fields in InterBase tables. Yes, the generators and triggers that you defined earlier will generate sequential numbers for their fields, as you'd expect. However, Delphi doesn't recognize the fact that these fields are auto-increment data types. And, because auto-incrementing fields aren't directly supported for InterBase tables, you can't use the Database Explorer to force the use of the TAutoIncField type inside your applications.

About the only thing you can do to aid in making use of auto-incrementing fields is to flag them as not being required. To do this, bring up the Fields Editor and toggle the auto-incrementing field's Required property to False in the Object Inspector.

Planning for Upsizing

Despite these minor data-type glitches, the basic process of moving RENTALMAN from Paradox tables to the InterBase platform has been fairly straightforward and painless. Because you had enough foresight to use a rich database format like Paradox for your local tables, there's pretty much a one-to-one correspondence between the table-level facilities in your local tables and those available on your InterBase server. Because of this, the Data Migration Expert was able to copy across your validity checks, defaults, and referential integrity constraints, in addition to your base-table definitions and their corresponding data, without a problem. Because you used sensible table and field names when you built your Paradox tables, the Data Migration Expert was able to copy them without a hitch, as well. In short, it pays to plan ahead. If you think you might be upsizing a local DBMS-based application to a server platform in the foreseeable future, use a least-common-denominator approach. That is, use just the features that are supported by both platforms. When you move from one to the other, things will go much smoother.

Business Rules

Depending on your source and target platforms, there's some chance that you may need to reconstruct your business rules. For example, if you're moving from dBASE to Sybase, you won't have any table-based referential integrity constraints or business-rule definitions because dBASE itself does not support them. If you're using a bland database format like dBASE, you've probably constructed your business rules inside your Delphi app, which isn't a good idea. (See Chapter 19, "Business Rules Part I," and Chapter 20, "Business Rules Part II," for more on proper business rule implementation.) When you move your application to a server-based architecture, you should move to server-based business rules, as well.

You have several weapons at your disposal in implementing business rules and referential integrity constraints on your InterBase server. In the following sections, I'll show you how to use primary- and foreign-key constraints, check constraints, defaults, and triggers to enforce your business rules at the server level. Remember that constructing your business rules on the server is almost always preferable to constructing them elsewhere because the server is the focal point of all database activity; applications cannot escape complying with the business rules you establish on the server.

Primary- and Foreign-Key Constraints

A primary-key constraint enables you to define a table's primary key, which in SQL terms, means that it must also be unique. Many tools require a unique key in order to edit or delete rows from a table; it is their only way of locating the row to change using a SQL UPDATE statement. Some platforms do not enforce the uniqueness of primary keys; nevertheless, it's bad form to have duplicate primary keys and you should avoid it.

To add a primary key constraint after your tables have been created, use the following syntax:

```
ALTER TABLE CALLS
ADD PRIMARY KEY (CallNo)
```

This syntax simply establishes that the CallNo column must be unique within the CALLS table. It also causes a unique-key index to be created, speeding access to the table. A primary-key index is also required for the object of a foreign-key reference. In short, you should always define a primary-key index on every table you build.

A foreign-key constraint ensures that a value in a given column on one table also exists in another. For example, one of the columns in the CALLS table is the WorkOrderNo column. Obviously, this column should always contain a valid WorkOrderNo—one that exists in the WORDERS table—if it contains a value at all. The way you ensure this is through a foreign-key constraint. Here's the syntax to set up a foreign-key constraint:

```
ALTER TABLE CALLS
ADD CONSTRAINT INVALID_WorkOrderNo
FOREIGN KEY (WorkOrderNo)
REFERENCES WORDERS
```

If you wanted to add one on the PropertyNo column, it would look like this:

```
ALTER TABLE CALLS
ADD CONSTRAINT INVALID_PropertyNo
FOREIGN KEY (PropertyNo)
REFERENCES PROPERTY
```

Notice the "negative" naming conventions of both constraints. This approach at least allows for the possibility that the user will understand what the problem is when he sees a constraint-violation exception.

> **NOTE**
>
> In order to report constraint violations to your Delphi apps, you can also define InterBase exceptions—messages to be displayed when a given exception, such as a constraint violation, occurs. See Chapter 17, "InterBase," for more information.

Check Constraints

Check constraints ensure that a value going into a given column passes a specified set of criteria. For example, the Data Migration Expert created a check constraint in your PROPERTY table that forces values in the GarageType column to be between 0 and 4. To add that same constraint manually, you'd use the following syntax:

```
ALTER TABLE PROPERTY
ADD CONSTRAINT INVALID_GarageType
CHECK (GarageType >=0 and GarageType<=4)
```

Defaults

Defaults do just what they sound like: they supply default values for columns. When you insert a row into a table without specifying a value for a column for which a default has been specified, the default is inserted into the new record. If you needed to add a column to a table and specify a default value for it, you'd use the following syntax:

```
ALTER TABLE TENANT
ADD RentDueDay SMALLINT
DEFAULT 15
```

Triggers

A trigger is a SQL procedure that executes when a given action occurs in a table. You created triggers previously to service the auto-increment fields in your database. You can also use them to perform other database functions, such as cascading deletes. Here's one that deletes the rows in the WODETAIL table that correspond to a WORDERS row being deleted:

```
CREATE TRIGGER Delete_Detail FOR WORDERS
  BEFORE DELETE
    POSITION 0
  AS BEGIN
    DELETE FROM WODETAIL
    WHERE WODETAIL.WorkOrderNo=Old.WorkOrderNo;
  END
```

This is a popular mechanism in local and server-based applications alike.

Sample SQL Script

This completes the discussion of reconstructing your business-rules logic on the server. Listing 14.2 provides a sample SQL script to help you through the process of moving business rules and referential integrity logic to your InterBase server.

Listing 14.2. A sample SQL script for the InterBase version of the RENTALMAN database.

```
/* Extract Database c:\data\delphi\rentman\rentman.gdb */

CONNECT "C:\DATA\delphi\rentman\rentman.gdb" USER "SYSDBA" PASSWORD "masterkey";


/* Table: CALLS, Owner: SYSDBA */
CREATE TABLE CALLS (CALLNO INTEGER NOT NULL,
        CALLDATETIME DATE NOT NULL,
        PROPERTYNO INTEGER NOT NULL,
        DESCRIPTION VARCHAR(30) NOT NULL,
        PRIORITY VARCHAR(1) NOT NULL,
        WORKORDERNO INTEGER,
        COMMENTS VARCHAR(100),
PRIMARY KEY (CALLNO));


/* Table: EMPLOYEE, Owner: SYSDBA */
CREATE TABLE EMPLOYEE (EMPLOYEENO INTEGER NOT NULL,
        NAME VARCHAR(30) NOT NULL,
PRIMARY KEY (EMPLOYEENO));


/* Table: PROPERTY, Owner: SYSDBA */
CREATE TABLE PROPERTY (PROPERTYNO INTEGER NOT NULL,
        TENANTNO INTEGER,
        ADDRESS VARCHAR(30) NOT NULL,
        CITY VARCHAR(20) NOT NULL,
        STATE VARCHAR(2) NOT NULL,
        ZIP VARCHAR(10) NOT NULL,
        ADDITION VARCHAR(15) NOT NULL,
        BEDROOMS SMALLINT NOT NULL,
        LIVINGAREAS SMALLINT NOT NULL,
```

continues

Listing 14.2. continued

```
              BATHROOMS SMALLINT NOT NULL,
              GARAGETYPE SMALLINT NOT NULL,
              SCHOOLDISTRICT VARCHAR(15) NOT NULL,
              DEPOSIT DOUBLE PRECISION NOT NULL,
              RENT DOUBLE PRECISION NOT NULL,
              RANGE VARCHAR(1) NOT NULL,
              REFRIGERATOR VARCHAR(1) NOT NULL,
              DISHWASHER VARCHAR(1) NOT NULL,
              CENTRALHEAT VARCHAR(1) NOT NULL,
              CENTRALAIR VARCHAR(1) NOT NULL,
              GASHEAT VARCHAR(1) NOT NULL,
              PRIVACYFENCE VARCHAR(1) NOT NULL,
              LASTSPRAYDATE DATE,
              LASTLAWNDATE DATE,
              COMMENTS VARCHAR(100),
PRIMARY KEY (PROPERTYNO));


/* Table: TENANT, Owner: SYSDBA */
CREATE TABLE TENANT (TENANTNO INTEGER NOT NULL,
              NAME VARCHAR(30) NOT NULL,
              EMPLOYER VARCHAR(30) NOT NULL,
              EMPADDRESS VARCHAR(30) NOT NULL,
              EMPCITY VARCHAR(30) NOT NULL,
              EMPSTATE VARCHAR(2) NOT NULL,
              EMPZIP VARCHAR(10) NOT NULL,
              HOMEPHONE VARCHAR(10) NOT NULL,
              WORKPHONE VARCHAR(10) NOT NULL,
              ICEPHONE VARCHAR(10) NOT NULL,
              LEASEBEGINDATE DATE NOT NULL,
              LEASEENDDATE DATE NOT NULL,
              MOVEDINDATE DATE NOT NULL,
              MOVEDOUTDATE DATE,
              RENTDUEDAY SMALLINT NOT NULL,
              PETDEPOSIT DOUBLE PRECISION NOT NULL,
              LAWNSERVICE VARCHAR(1) NOT NULL,
              COMMENTS VARCHAR(100),
PRIMARY KEY (TENANTNO));


/* Table: WODETAIL, Owner: SYSDBA */
CREATE TABLE WODETAIL (WORKORDERNO INTEGER NOT NULL,
              LINENO INTEGER NOT NULL,
              WORKTYPECODE SMALLINT NOT NULL,
              COMMENTS VARCHAR(100),
PRIMARY KEY (WORKORDERNO, LINENO));


/* Table: WORDERS, Owner: SYSDBA */
CREATE TABLE WORDERS (WORKORDERNO INTEGER NOT NULL,
              PROPERTYNO INTEGER NOT NULL,
              EMPLOYEENO INTEGER NOT NULL,
              STARTDATE DATE NOT NULL,
              ENDDATE DATE,
              COMMENTS VARCHAR(100),
PRIMARY KEY (WORKORDERNO));
```

```
/* Table: WORKTYPE, Owner: SYSDBA */
CREATE TABLE WORKTYPE (WORKTYPECODE SMALLINT NOT NULL,
        DESCRIPTION VARCHAR(30) NOT NULL,
        TASKDURATION DOUBLE PRECISION NOT NULL,
PRIMARY KEY (WORKTYPECODE));


/*  Index definitions for all user tables */
CREATE INDEX CALLS_CALLS04_CALLDATETIME ON CALLS(CALLDATETIME);

CREATE UNIQUE INDEX CALLS_INDEX1 ON CALLS(CALLNO);

CREATE INDEX CALLS_PROPERTYNO ON CALLS(PROPERTYNO);

CREATE INDEX CALLS_WORKORDERNO ON CALLS(WORKORDERNO);

CREATE UNIQUE INDEX EMPLOYEE_INDEX1 ON EMPLOYEE(EMPLOYEENO);

CREATE UNIQUE INDEX PROPERTY_INDEX1 ON PROPERTY(PROPERTYNO);

CREATE INDEX PROPERTY_PROPERTY03_ADDRESS ON PROPERTY(ADDRESS);

CREATE INDEX PROPERTY_TENANTNO ON PROPERTY(TENANTNO);

CREATE UNIQUE INDEX TENANT_INDEX1 ON TENANT(TENANTNO);

CREATE INDEX TENANT_TENANT02_NAME ON TENANT(NAME);

CREATE UNIQUE INDEX WODETAIL_INDEX1 ON WODETAIL(WORKORDERNO, LINENO);

CREATE INDEX WODETAIL_WORKTYPECODE ON WODETAIL(WORKTYPECODE);

CREATE INDEX WORDERS_EMPLOYEENO ON WORDERS(EMPLOYEENO);

CREATE UNIQUE INDEX WORDERS_INDEX1 ON WORDERS(WORKORDERNO);

CREATE INDEX WORDERS_PROPERTYNO ON WORDERS(PROPERTYNO);

CREATE INDEX WORDERS_WORDERS04_STARTDATE ON WORDERS(STARTDATE);

CREATE UNIQUE INDEX WORKTYPE_INDEX1 ON WORKTYPE(WORKTYPECODE);

ALTER TABLE CALLS ADD CONSTRAINT INVALID_PROPERTYNO
FOREIGN KEY (PROPERTYNO) REFERENCES PROPERTY(PROPERTYNO);

ALTER TABLE PROPERTY ADD CONSTRAINT INVALID_TenantNo
FOREIGN KEY (TENANTNO) REFERENCES TENANT(TENANTNO);

ALTER TABLE WODETAIL ADD CONSTRAINT INVALID_WorkOrderNo
FOREIGN KEY (WORKORDERNO) REFERENCES WORDERS(WORKORDERNO);

ALTER TABLE WODETAIL ADD CONSTRAINT INVALID_WorkTypeCode
FOREIGN KEY (WORKTYPECODE) REFERENCES WORKTYPE(WORKTYPECODE);

ALTER TABLE WORDERS ADD CONSTRAINT INVALID_PropertyNo
FOREIGN KEY (PROPERTYNO) REFERENCES PROPERTY(PROPERTYNO);
```

continues

Listing 14.2. continued

```
ALTER TABLE WORDERS ADD CONSTRAINT INVALID_EmployeeNo
FOREIGN KEY (EMPLOYEENO) REFERENCES EMPLOYEE(EMPLOYEENO);

ALTER TABLE CALLS ADD CONSTRAINT INVALID_WorkOrderNo
FOREIGN KEY (WORKORDERNO) REFERENCES WORDERS(WORKORDERNO);

CREATE GENERATOR CALLNOGEN;

CREATE GENERATOR PROPERTYNOGEN;

CREATE GENERATOR TENANTNOGEN;

CREATE GENERATOR WORKORDERNOGEN;

CREATE GENERATOR WORKTYPECODEGEN;

CREATE GENERATOR EMPLOYEENOGEN;

ALTER TABLE PROPERTY ADD
        CONSTRAINT INVALID_GARAGETYPE
        CHECK (GarageType>=1 and GarageType<=4)
;

ALTER TABLE PROPERTY ADD
        CONSTRAINT INVALID_LIVINGAREAS
        CHECK (LivingAreas>=0 and LivingAreas<=4)
;

ALTER TABLE PROPERTY ADD
        CONSTRAINT INVALID_BATHROOMS
        CHECK (BathRooms>=0 and BathRooms<=4)
;

ALTER TABLE PROPERTY ADD
        CONSTRAINT INVALID_BEDROOMS
        CHECK (BedRooms>=0 and BedRooms<=4)
;

ALTER TABLE CALLS ADD
        CONSTRAINT INVALID_PRIORITY
        CHECK (Priority in ('L','M','H'))
;

ALTER TABLE TENANT ADD
        CONSTRAINT INVALID_RENTDUEDAY
        CHECK (RentDueDay=1 or RentDueDay=15)
;

SET TERM ^ ;

/* Triggers only will work for SQL triggers */
CREATE TRIGGER GENERATE_CALLNO FOR CALLS
ACTIVE BEFORE INSERT POSITION 0
AS BEGIN
    NEW.CallNo = GEN_ID(CallNoGEN, 1);
  END
  ^
```

```
CREATE TRIGGER GENERATE_TENANTNO FOR TENANT
ACTIVE BEFORE INSERT POSITION 0
AS BEGIN
   NEW.TenantNo = GEN_ID(TenantNoGEN, 1);
  END
 ^

CREATE TRIGGER GENERATE_WORKORDERNO FOR WORDERS
ACTIVE BEFORE INSERT POSITION 0
AS BEGIN
   NEW.WorkOrderNo = GEN_ID(WorkOrderNoGEN, 1);
  END
 ^

CREATE TRIGGER GENERATE_EMPLOYEENO FOR EMPLOYEE
ACTIVE BEFORE INSERT POSITION 0
AS BEGIN
   NEW.EmployeeNo = GEN_ID(EmployeeNoGEN, 1);
  END
 ^

CREATE TRIGGER GENERATE_WORKTYPECODE FOR WORKTYPE
ACTIVE BEFORE INSERT POSITION 0
AS BEGIN
   NEW.WorkTypeCode = GEN_ID(WorkTypeCodeGEN, 1);
  END
 ^

CREATE TRIGGER DELETE_DETAIL FOR WORDERS
ACTIVE BEFORE DELETE POSITION 0
AS BEGIN
   DELETE FROM WODETAIL
   WHERE WODETAIL.WorkOrderNo=Old.WorkOrderNo;
  END
 ^
COMMIT WORK ^
SET TERM ; ^

/* Grant permissions for this database */
```

Concurrency Control and the Client/Server Model

Unlike local databases, you don't usually access SQL server data in a record-by-record fashion; many servers don't even lock individual rows. Instead, some larger object, usually a page or a segment, is locked to prevent changes one user makes from interfering with those of another. If enough of these locks occur on a single table, the server upgrades the lock to a table-wide lock, preventing other users from making changes to the table. The situation is quite different than it is with local tables.

You must be cognizant of the differences in concurrency control between local tables and server-based ones. You should do what you can to minimize lock contention. In particular, you'll want to avoid row-by-row processing at all costs. For example, here's some code to traverse the TENANT table, switching the LawnService column to False in the process:

```
With taTENANT do
  While not EOF do begin
    If taTENANTPetDeposit.AsFloat<>0 then
      taTENANTLawnService.AsBoolean:=False;
    Next;
  end;
```

Although this would be standard fare on local tables, it creates problems on database servers. It's also inefficient. Why? First, it creates a lock on the TENANT table every time it sets the LawnService field. This both blocks out other users momentarily and is a relatively slow way of doing things. Second, if enough rows are locked, it's possible that the server will upgrade the page or row locks on the server to a full-blown table lock, putting all other user changes on hold until the lock is released. Needless to say, this isn't the way you want to do things.

On the contrary, you want to use SQL to handle this. Either a stored procedure or a plain query will do, but the point is to avoid processing rows individually. Let the server do that— it's best at it. For example, the following SQL query will accomplish the same thing as the previously shown looping code:

```
UPDATE TENANT
SET LawnService="F"
WHERE PetDeposit<>0
```

It accomplishes the task in one pass and releases the lock(s) as soon as possible.

Transactions and Database Servers

Though Delphi supports transactions for local tables, you'll probably find that transactions play a much bigger role on client/server systems than they do with local DBMSs. It's to be expected that as your applications migrate to client/server platforms, they will have a larger number of users and, hence, will need to place more emphasis on concurrency control.

You may recall that a transaction is a group of database changes treated as a single batch. Either all the changes are applied to the database, or none of them are. As you move to client/server, such concerns as sizing the transaction log properly, being careful not to overrun it, committing and rolling back transactions, and so on, require much more attention than they did with local tables.

Delphi enables you to perform server-based transaction control via the TDatabase component. To begin a transaction, call TDatabase's StartTransaction method. To save the transaction to the database, call the Commit method. To cancel it, call Rollback. Calling these methods in a client/server environment is the same as issuing the equivalent SQL on the server. For example, calling TDatabase's StartTransaction method to start a transaction on an InterBase server is the same thing as issuing InterBase's SET TRANSACTION SQL command.

Transaction Isolation Levels

Another important area of transaction management is the use of transaction isolation levels to avoid lost data and lock conflicts. A transaction isolation level (TIL) affects your transaction's ability to see changes made by other transactions concurrent with it, and their ability to see changes made by your transaction.

You make use of transaction isolation levels via the TransIsolation property of the TDatabase component. TransIsolation can have one of three values: tiDirtyRead, tiReadCommitted, and tiRepeatableRead. tiDirtyRead returns any row changes that have been made—by this transaction or by others—even those that have not yet been committed. tiReadCommitted returns only row changes that have been committed. tiRepeatableRead returns rows as they originally appeared when the transaction was initiated. Rows appear unchanged for the duration of the transaction, even if another transaction commits row changes to the underlying tables while the transaction is in progress.

The possibility for lock conflicts between two transactions accessing the same database objects is governed by each transaction's isolation level. As a rule, the tiRepeatableRead and tiReadCommitted TILs reduce the possibility of lock conflicts the most. For example, say that you have two transactions, Tran1 and Tran2. If Tran1 is a tiReadCommitted transaction with read/write access, and Tran2 is a tiRepeatableRead transaction with read/write access, the two transactions only conflict when attempting to modify the same row. This reduces lock contention on the server and also provides a degree of security against lost updates. tiReadCommitted is the default transaction isolation level and should be adequate for most of your needs.

> **NOTE**
>
> Not all server platforms support all three transaction isolation levels. If your server does not support a particular isolation level, the BDE will choose the next most restrictive one that it does support. See Chapter 21, "Concurrency Control," for more information.

> **TIP**
>
> Most database servers enable you to monitor the locks they maintain on database objects. For example, you can use the sp_lock stored procedure to view locks on the Sybase and Microsoft platforms. You can monitor locks on the InterBase platform using the Lock Manager Statistics option in the InterBase Server Manager program. Monitoring a server's locking habits can help you tweak your apps so that they minimize lock contention and cooperate with each other as much as possible.

UpdateMode

You can use the UpdateMode property of the Table and Query components to control the type of SQL that's generated when you update a record. This enables you to balance performance when updating tables with protection against lost updates. UpdateMode has three possible values: upWhereAll, upWhereChanged, and upWhereKeyOnly. The setting you give this property determines the type of SQL WHERE clause that's used to locate a row for update.

When you make a change to a table or live query result set, a SQL UPDATE statement is generated to perform the modification on the server. If UpdateMode is set to upWhereAll, the WHERE clause of this UPDATE statement lists every column in the table or query. If UpdateMode is set to upWhereChanged, only the key fields and fields that you've changed are used. If UpdateMode is set to upWhereKeyOnly, the key fields alone are listed in the WHERE clause.

The default is upWhereAll, but you may find it too restrictive. In most cases, upWhereChanged is just as safe and can be considerably quicker than upWhereAll, depending on the number of columns in your table. As a rule, you probably shouldn't use upWhereKeyOnly without first speaking with your Database Administrator. If you need ultra-quick updates on a table to which you have exclusive access, upWhereKeyOnly can be handy to have. However, in multi-user environments, upWhereKeyOnly can have catastrophic side-effects that include the loss of updates by other users. Again, I recommend you use it only after consulting with your DBA.

You can see the effects of UpdateMode firsthand via Delphi's SQL Monitor tool. SQL Monitor enables you to "look under the hood" of the BDE and see the raw interaction between your app and the database. Among other things, you can see the SQL that your app sends to the server.

To see how this works, select the SQL Monitor tool from Delphi's Database menu and place a checkmark next to the Always on Top setting on its Options menu. Next, run your application and press F4 to display the fmRPROCGD0 form. Once the form is onscreen, change a value in one of its table rows and click the Post button on the DBNavSearch component at the bottom of the form. Now, scroll the top pane of the SQL Monitor window until you see an SQL UPDATE statement, then click it. This is the SQL code that your app sent to the server to carry out your table modification. Notice that the UPDATE lists all the fields in the table. (See Figure 14.8.)

Now, close the SQL Monitor and exit your application. Bring up the dmRentalMan Data Module in the form designer and change the UpdateMode property of the taPROPERTY component to upWhereChanged. Once you've switched UpdateMode, restart the SQL Monitor tool, then run your application. Make a second change to the PROPERTY table, then scroll the top pane in the SQL Monitor tool so that you can see the UPDATE statement that was generated. Click the UPDATE statement to see it fully displayed in SQL Monitor's lower pane. The number of columns listed in the UPDATE statement's WHERE clause should have dropped substantially. (See Figure 14.9.)

FIGURE 14.8.

Using upWhereAll *includes all the columns in a table.*

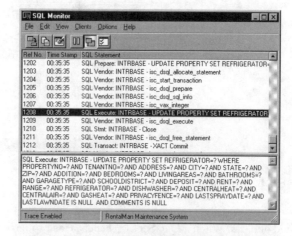

FIGURE 14.9.

Using upWhereChanged *safely reduces the number of columns used.*

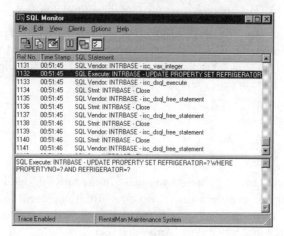

Now, close both your app and the SQL Monitor tool and change taPROPERTY's UpdateMode to upWhereKeyOnly. Next, save your work, then restart SQL Monitor and your application. Make another change to the PROPERTY table, then view your UPDATE statement in SQL monitor. As you can see, upWhereKeyOnly reduces the columns used to their lowest possible number. However, as mentioned previously, this is at the expense of safety. Figure 14.10 shows what you should see.

FIGURE 14.10.

*Using upWhereKeyOnly
reduces the number of
columns substantially.*

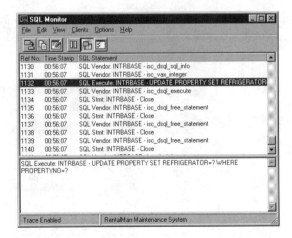

Cached Updates

One way of potentially minimizing lock contention on your database server is through the use of cached updates. When a DataSet's CachedUpdates property is set to True, changes you make to the DataSet are *cached*—stored locally—until you save them with ApplyUpdates.

Let's experiment with CachedUpdates to see how it works in practice. Load the dmRentalMan data module into Delphi's visual designer. Click the taTENANT table and set its CachedUpdates property to True. Next, load the fmRSYSMAN0 form and click the Tenant option on its Tables menu. Just after the line that reads:

```
fmRTENCGD0.ShowModal;
```

type

```
dmRentalMan.taTENANT.ApplyUpdates;
```

This will cause the changes you make in the fmRTENCGD0 form to be stored locally until you return from the form. After you return, they're sent to the server. Obviously, if you can reduce the number of updates you make against the server and its objects, you can reduce the potential for lock conflicts with other users.

Changing Queries to Stored Procedures and Views

Another popular practice when upsizing local database applications is to replace dynamic SQL queries with stored procedures and views. By changing a query to a stored procedure call, you cause the application to call SQL that's already been compiled—it should execute faster. Also, you trim down the SQL statement that must be sent from the client to the server. Instead of sending a potentially large body of text across the network, you send a tiny call to a stored procedure. In terms of efficiency, stored procedures are hard to beat.

Views enable you to convert simple queries into stored procedures that can be queried like tables. On the InterBase platform, you can define stored procedures that themselves can similarly be queries to tables and views, so the line between stored procedures and views is gray indeed. There are several queries within the RENTALMAN application that would make good stored procedures. For example, the SQL in the quWorkDuration Query component could be translated to this stored procedure:

```
SET TERM ^;
CREATE PROCEDURE GetWorkDuration (WONum INTEGER)
AS
BEGIN
  SELECT sum(WORKTYPE.TaskDuration)  as WorkDuration
  FROM WODETAIL, WORKTYPE
  WHERE WODETAIL.WorkTypeCode = WORKTYPE.WorkTypeCode
  AND   WODETAIL.WorkOrderNo=:WONum;
END ^
SET TERM ;^
```

After the stored procedure was defined, you'd simply replace the Query component with a StoredProc component and modify your program code accordingly. The net result is that you'd have a query that would no doubt run faster and be easier to access from different applications.

A good use of views in the RENTALMAN application would be to replace the many table-lookup field combinations with straight views. That is, instead of having a WODETAIL table defining a field that looks up information in the WORKTYPE table, you could replace it with a view that performs the join on the server. The view would appear to your application like any other table, but it would already include the Description and TaskDuration fields from the WORKTYPE table, so there'd be no need to access them via lookup fields. This is another example of the different mindset that must be taken when working with database servers rather than local DBMSs such as Paradox and dBASE.

TIP

The TLiveQuery component that's profiled in Chapter 26, "Building Your Own Database Components," enables you to easily create server-based views in a manner similar to setting up a TQuery component. As mentioned previously, using views can speed up your application and help eliminate lookup fields. See Chapter 26 for more information.

User Rights and Permissions

When you move from using local tables to using a database server, the dynamics of user rights and permissions change significantly. With multi-user Paradox applications, for example, you normally grant rights at the network or server level. Users are granted permissions on operating system files which correspond roughly with database tables. Some local table formats enable you to store all the tables in a database in a single physical file, but your users must still have adequate rights to the file. The permissions granted to users are usually limited allowing read or read/write access to a given file. For instance, most local platforms don't enable you to permit a user to write new rows to a table but prevent him from deleting existing rows from the table. The controls at your disposal are very simplistic indeed.

That all changes when developing applications for client/server platforms. Access to individual database tables, views, and procedures must be granted by a Database Administrator-type, who also creates user logins, groups, and so on. A full treatment of the subject of database administration is outside the scope of this book, but I should briefly touch on a few issues before proceeding.

Granting Rights with *GRANT*

GRANT is the SQL command used to grant user permissions. REVOKE is the command used to remove them. Both GRANT and REVOKE require three parameters: the permissions you're granting or revoking, the database object on which you're granting or revoking them, and the user whose rights you're changing. For example, you could use the following SQL command to grant permissions on the WORKTYPE table:

```
GRANT ALL ON WORKTYPE TO PUBLIC
```

This grants all rights (SELECT, INSERT, UPDATE, DELETE, and EXECUTE) to all users on the WORKTYPE table. Similarly, you could revoke those rights using:

```
REVOKE ALL ON WORKTYPE FROM PUBLIC
```

> **TIP**
>
> When first moving from local tables to a client/server platform, it can save time to grant and revoke user rights en masse. You can build ISQL scripts that utilize GRANT ALL ON *tablename* TO PUBLIC to grant user permissions to all your users at once. You can always go back after the fact and refine these access rights as needed.

You can issue more restrictive rights by replacing ALL with a list of permissions, like so:

```
GRANT SELECT, INSERT, UPDATE ON EMPLOYEE TO PUBLIC
```

You can also revoke those same permissions using a statement like this:

```
REVOKE SELECT, INSERT, UPDATE ON EMPLOYEE FROM PUBLIC
```

Note that you can replace PUBLIC with a list of users for whom to grant or revoke rights. Before you can do that, though, you'll need to create user logins. Unlike most client/server platforms,

InterBase doesn't support user groups (other than the predefined PUBLIC group, of course), and, unlike the Sybase and Microsoft platforms, server logins and database users are not separate from one another. Adding a user login gives the user the ability to connect to any database.

You can create user logins using the InterBase Server Manager. To do this, start the Server Manager from your Delphi program folder. Next, connect to a database by selecting the Database Connect option on the File menu.

Once you've connected to your database, select the User Security option on the Task menu. The User Security option enables you to add user logins. You should then see the InterBase Security dialog. Click the Add User button to add a user login. Key in a user name and password of your choice. Note that, try as you may, you can't enter a user name in lowercase letters—they're forced to uppercase. Despite this, the password you key in is case-sensitive. Not only can you use lowercase characters, but they're distinguished by the server from their uppercase counterparts. Figure 14.11 illustrates the User Configuration dialog.

FIGURE 14.11.

The User Configuration Dialog enables you to configure new users.

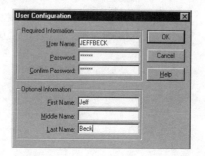

Once you've finished adding your user information, click OK to add the login to the server. You can now connect to any InterBase database using that new user name and password, though the user will have to be granted permissions for specific objects in order to access them. As mentioned previously, you grant these rights using the GRANT command. For example, to grant your new user rights to the TENANT table, you might enter the command:

```
GRANT ALL ON TENANT TO JEFFBECK
```

You could repeat this command for each table, view, and stored procedure in the database.

Note that you can extend the ability to grant user permissions to another user via the WITH GRANT OPTION clause of the GRANT command. Here's an example:

```
GRANT EXECUTE ON PROCEDURE LISTPROP TO JEFFBECK WITH GRANT OPTION
```

This command gives the user the ability to execute the stored procedure himself and to grant other users access rights to it using the GRANT command.

What's Ahead

Chapter 15, "Database Component Reference Part I" kicks off the Part III, "Reference," section of this book. This chapter covers Delphi's Data Access controls in depth, supplementing and enhancing the Delphi documentation when possible. If you're interested in the internals of Delphi's Data Access components, this chapter is for you.

Summary

The issues involved with upsizing to a client/server DBMS platform can be quite complex. We've just covered a few of them here. Suffice it to say, it's rarely as simple as changing an alias. On the other hand, Delphi's inherent scalability and the robustness of the BDE make the process much simpler than it would otherwise be. Couple this with advanced tools such as the Data Migration Expert, and you have all you need to move up to client/server when the need arises.

III

Reference

15

Database Component Reference Part I

The purpose of this chapter and the one that follows is to coalesce and augment the database class information available in the documentation that accompanies Delphi. The idea is to give you "one-stop shopping" as far as developing database applications with Delphi is concerned. As you begin to build complex database applications with Delphi, you will undoubtedly need to access specific class information regarding the database components. Using this chapter and the one that follows, you can find what you need right here.

The approach I've taken here is to divide the database-related components into two groups—those that provide database access to an application and those that utilize this access. In doing so, I've emulated the approach taken with Delphi's own toolbar—database controls are divided there into Data Access controls and, simply, Data Controls. These Data Controls are data-aware controls that require the Data Access controls in order to do anything useful. I cover Data Access controls in this chapter and Data Controls in Chapter 16, "Database Component Reference Part II."

I've intentionally omitted components that act only as support classes in the Delphi database class hierarchy. If a class is not actually a component—that is, if it's merely an ancestor of a component—I don't include it. This includes both the TDataSet and TDBDataSet component classes, for example. They're class ancestors of the TTable, TQuery, and TStoredProc components. My emphasis here is on components that you can work with using Delphi's visual tools. Although the ancestor class hierarchy is important, most of the properties, events, and methods that you'll need to be concerned with have been, by design, surfaced in Delphi's components.

Each component narrative consists of three sections:

■ A description of the component, its unit and class ancestor, and tables listing its key properties, methods, and events

■ A key elements section

■ A tasks section

The key properties, methods, and events tables are by no means exhaustive—see the Delphi documentation, or, better yet, the VCL source code, for complete lists of these. The idea is to give you a complete class reference without venturing into every nook and cranny of the VCL.

Hopefully, this chapter and the one that follows will prove a handy reference for you. Without further ado, let's begin with the TSession component.

TSession

Unit: DB   Class ancestor: TComponent

Because Delphi automatically creates a TSession component for you each time your application runs, you don't need to create one yourself. This built-in TSession can be referenced using Delphi's global Session variable.

Normally, you won't need more than one TSession per application. The only exception to this is when you're building multi-threaded database applications. When constructing multi-threaded database apps, you may need to use TSession components to open extra connections into your server in order to keep database access in one thread from interfering with that in another. You can drop as many TSession components as you need onto a form or data module, then utilize them in your Database and DataSet components. In a multi-threaded database application, you would typically set up one TSession per thread. Note that Delphi defines another global variable, Sessions, for tracking multiple Session components in a single application. Sessions is of type TSessionList and contains an entry for each Session component in the application.

Table 15.1 lists the key properties, Table 15.2 lists the key methods, and Table 15.3 lists the key events for TSession.

Table 15.1. TSession key properties.

Property	Description
DatabaseCount	Returns a count of the number of active TDatabases
Databases	Returns the array of active TDatabases
Handle	Provides access to the BDE handle—used for direct BDE calls
KeepConnections	Determines whether inactive connections are retained
NetFileDir	Specifies the location of PDOXUSRS.NET
PrivateDir	Specifies the location of temporary files
SessionName	Specifies the session name to publish to other components

Table 15.2. TSession key methods.

Method	Function
AddPassword	Adds a password to the current session (for Paradox connections)
CloseDatabase	Explicitly closes a TDatabase component
DropConnections	Drops all inactive TDatabase connections
FindDatabase	Locates a TDatabase by name
GetAliasNames	Returns the available BDE aliases
GetAliasParams	Returns the parameters for a given alias
GetDatabaseNames	Lists all available aliases, including local ones
GetDriverNames	Lists the available BDE drivers

continues

Table 15.2. continued

Method	Function
GetDriverParams	Returns the parameters for a given driver
GetPassword	Prompts for a password, returns True if successful
GetTableNames	Lists all tables in a given database
GetStoredProcNames	Lists all stored procedures in a given database
OpenDatabase	Explicitly opens a TDatabase
RemoveAllPasswords	Removes all Paradox-related passwords
RemovePassword	Removes a given Paradox-related password

Table 15.3. TSession key events.

Event	Catalyst
OnPassword	Occurs when the BDE needs a Paradox table password
OnStartup	Occurs when the session becomes active

Key Elements

TSession is the central control facility for an application's database connections. Use the DatabaseCount property to determine the number of active TDatabases and the Databases property to access them by index.

Similar to the Database component's DatabaseName property, the Session component's SessionName property enables you to specify a name to publish to other components. In a multi-threaded application, you would set this property to a name of your choice, then set the SessionName property of an associated Database and DataSet component (a Table, Query, or StoredProc) to match. By setting the SessionName of a Database, and, say, a Query component, to match the one used in a TSession, you specify which database connection the Query is to use. By extension, if you then interact with the Query from within a process thread, you've effectively specified which database connection the thread is to utilize. On some servers, this is a must because database access in one thread interferes with that of another.

The KeepConnections property determines whether inactive database connections are retained for temporary TDatabase components. Use DropConnections to drop all inactive database connections. Keep in mind that if all the current connections to a database server are inactive and you drop them, you'll have to log back into the server the next time you need to access it. There is, however, a way to set `KeepConnections` to `False` and still avoid being prompted for a user name and password each time the BDE reconnects to your back-end. This is covered in the discussion of the `Database` component later in this chapter.

The location of the BDE network control directory is stored in the `NetFileDir` property. Note that this is only used for Paradox tables. The directory path in which temporary files are located is stored in the `PrivateDir` property.

Tasks

Use the `TSession` component when you need to get at the internals of the BDE. You can access information such as alias lists, alias parameters, and driver settings. You can also make direct BDE API calls using `TSession`'s `Handle` property.

You can use the predefined `Session` instance variable to call `TSession` methods. The following are examples of `TSession` method calls:

```
Session.GetAliasNames(ListBox1.Items);
```

This method call replaces the contents of `ListBox1.Items` with the list of currently defined BDE aliases.

```
Session.GetDatabaseNames(ListBox1.Items);
```

This method call replaces the contents of `ListBox1.Items` with the list of all BDE and application-specific aliases.

```
Session.KeepConnections:=False;
```

This tells your application to drop inactive temporary database connections. Note that this affects only temporary database connections—those constructed by the BDE itself—not those you've explicitly created. Databases that have their own `TDatabase` component will use its `KeepConnections` property instead.

The main advantage of dropping inactive database connections is the conservation of network bandwidth. On local area networks (LANs), this may be barely perceptible. However, over wide area networks or dial-up connections, the difference this makes can be dramatic. Note that releasing unused database connections also frees up connections on the server and local PC resources, though this rarely justifies having to log back into the server repeatedly.

As mentioned previously, you can set up the `OnLogin` event of a `TDatabase` component such that the user is not actually required to log into the server each time the `TDatabase` reconnects, so dropping inactive connections is perhaps not as bad as it sounds. (See "Tasks" under `TDatabase`, for instructions on how to do this.)

TDatabase

Unit: DB   Class ancestor: TComponent

Although the explicit use of a TDatabase component is not required for database access, it does provide access to certain aspects of database connections that you cannot get to without one. Typically, you'll only have one TDatabase per application. Delphi instantiates a temporary TDatabase component internally if you do not include one in an application.

Table 15.4 lists the key properties, Table 15.5 lists the key methods, and Table 15.6 lists the key event for TDatabase.

Table 15.4. TDatabase key properties.

Property	Description
AliasName	Refers to the BDE alias used
Connected	Reflects whether the TDatabase is open
DatabaseName	Defines an application-specific database alias
DriverName	Specifies a driver type to use
KeepConnection	Toggles retention of inactive database connections
LoginPrompt	Toggles whether the user is prompted to log on

Table 15.5. TDatabase key methods.

Method	Function
Open	Explicitly opens a database connection
Close	Explicitly closes a database connection

Table 15.6. TDatabase key event.

Event	Catalyst
OnLogin	Occurs when a SQL TDatabase is opened and LoginPrompt is True

Key Elements

Use the DatabaseName property to define an application-specific, or local, BDE alias. Once you've specified a name here (it can be the same as the component's Name property, if you like), you'll see it "published" in the dropdown DatabaseName property list of DataSet components like TTable and TQuery. You can then select it from those lists to link the associated DataSet component with your TDatabase.

AliasName specifies the BDE alias that you want this TDatabase to use. It refers to an alias you've already defined using the BDE Configuration utility and uses it to get default settings. Note that this property and the DriverName property are mutually exclusive. Setting one automatically clears the other.

If you elect not to set an AliasName, use the DriverName property to identify a BDE driver that you want to use instead. This can include the STANDARD driver for local tables (dBASE and Paradox), or the INTERBASE, SYBASE, ORACLE, or MSSQL drivers for SQL database servers. As mentioned previously, the DriverName property and the AliasName property are mutually exclusive.

Toggling the Connected property opens and closes the database connection. You can set it to True in the Delphi Object Inspector to open a database connection while you're designing. If you open a DataSet that refers to your TDatabase, the TDatabase will automatically be opened. If you close a TDatabase that has associated DataSets, you'll close them as well.

> **NOTE**
>
> Note that if you define an application-specific alias, the form or data module that contains the associated TDatabase must be currently loaded in order for you to open DataSets that reference it.

To avoid logging in each time the database is opened, set the KeepConnection property to True.

If the LoginPrompt property is set to True, the user will be prompted for login information when connecting to the database server. You can override this using the OnLogin event (detailed in the following section, "Tasks").

Set the TransIsolation property to specify the transaction isolation level (TIL) to establish on the database server. The TIL you select affects your ability to see transactions originated by other users and their ability to see transactions you initiate.

Tasks

Your application must include a Database component to do any of the following:

- ■ Establish a permanent database connection
- ■ Establish local application-specific database aliases
- ■ Change server login parameters
- ■ Manipulate server-based transaction control mechanisms

Establishing Database Connections

Delphi applications connect to SQL-based database servers using the SQL Links drivers for the Borland Database Engine. These drivers provide access to the InterBase, Sybase, Oracle, and Microsoft DBMSs.

Typically, you'll use the Database Explorer or the BDE Configuration utility to construct database "aliases" through which your application will connect to these back-end servers. A BDE alias is no more than a named parameter list—a set of connection information that the BDE uses to connect you to your database. Once you've set up an alias, it appears in the DatabaseName property list of DataSet components like TTable and TQuery.

You can override the defaults provided by a BDE alias by editing TDatabase's Params property. The settings you make in Params override the parameters that are passed to the database engine.

Retaining Database Connections

Set the KeepConnection property of a TDatabase component to True to cause database connections to be retained even when no DataSets are open. This is necessary if you want to avoid having to log in the next time a connection is needed.

> **NOTE**
>
> Don't confuse TDatabase's KeepConnections property with the TSession's property of the same name. TSession's property only affects temporary TDatabase components, not those you create. Setting TSession's KeepConnections property will have no effect on whether your explicit TDatabase connections are retained.

Change Server Login Parameters

You can use TDatabase's OnLogin event handler to keep the default password dialog box from displaying when a connection is initiated. OnLogin gets passed two parameters, a TDatabase component that points to the database the user is trying to log on to, and a TStrings object for storing the required login parameters. Here's the header definition for a typical OnLogin event procedure:

```
procedure TForm1.Database1Login(Database: TDatabase; LoginParams: TStrings);
```

From inside the OnLogin procedure, you can use the TStrings' indexed Values property to access individual parameters, like so:

```
LoginParams.Values['SERVER NAME'] := 'BLUSERVER';
LoginParams.Values['USER NAME'] := 'muddy';
LoginParams.Values['PASSWORD'] := 'waters';
```

To prevent the default login dialog box from displaying, you'll have to at least set the PASSWORD parameter. You can gather the parameters you need from a dialog box of your own, you can retrieve them from another Database component, or you can hard-code them—it doesn't matter. If they leave your OnLogin procedure with values, Delphi will attempt to use them to establish a connection.

Application-Controlled Transaction Processing

Normally, Delphi handles transaction-related issues for you automatically by starting and committing transactions when your application attempts to make changes to a database. If this level of control isn't sufficient, you can guide transaction processing yourself using the TransIsolation property and the StartTransaction, Commit, and Rollback methods.

The TransIsolation property controls the transaction isolation level (TIL) on the database server. The TIL on the server controls the accessibility of transactions concurrent with yours to changes you've made and your transaction's ability to see changes they've made.

TransIsolation has three possible values, tiDirtyRead, tiReadCommitted, and tiRepeatableRead. It defaults to tiReadCommited. The three possible values of TransIsolation have the following significance:

- ■ tiDirtyRead—Uncommitted changes by other transactions are visible
- ■ tiReadCommitted—Only committed changes by other transactions are visible
- ■ tiRepeatableRead—Changes by other transactions to previously read data are not visible, which means that every time a transaction reads a given record, it always gets the *exact same* record

The StartTransaction method marks the beginning of a group of database changes that you want to be treated as a unit. They will either all be applied to the database or none of them will be.

Commit makes permanent the database changes that have occurred since the transaction was started. Think of it as a database save command.

Rollback discards the database changes that have been made since the transaction began. Think of it as a database undo command.

> **NOTE**
>
> You can also control transaction processing on your server using Passthrough SQL. To do this, you issue SQL commands that change the transaction processing on your server. Be aware that doing this with SQLPASSTHRUMODE set to SHARED AUTOCOMMIT or SHARED NOAUTOCOMMIT could cause your new TIL setting to affect other transactions initiated by your application.

See Chapter 21, "Concurrency Control," for more information on transactions.

TTable

Unit: DBTables   Class ancestor: TDBDataSet

TTable is a direct descendent of the DBDataSet class and an indirect descendant of the DataSet class. You access database tables using the TTable component. When you open a TTable, you establish a connection between your application and the table. You add, change, and delete rows in database tables using the TTable component.

Table 15.7 lists the key properties, Table 15.8 lists the key methods, and Table 15.9 lists the key events for TTable.

Table 15.7. TTable key properties.

Property	Description
Active	Toggles whether the DataSet is open
AutoCalcFields	Determines how calculated fields are calculated
BOF	Reflects whether the DataSet is at its beginning
CachedUpdates	Toggles whether updates are cached
Database	Identifies the TDatabase in use by the DataSet

Property	Description
DatabaseName	Names the alias used to connect to the database
EOF	Reflects whether the DataSet is at its end
Exclusive	Toggles whether other users can access the DataSet
FieldCount	Returns the number of fields in the DataSet
FieldDefs	Lists important information about fields in the DataSet
Fields	(Indexed) returns a specific field from the DataSet
Filter	Specifies an expression to filter records by
Filtered	Toggles whether the filtering specified by Filter or OnFilterRecord is active
FilterOptions	Controls the behavior of filters
IndexDefs	Lists important information about the DataSet's indexes
IndexFieldCount	Returns the number of fields in the current index key
IndexFieldNames	Specifies a set of fields as an index key
IndexName	Specifies the name of the index to use
IndexFields	(Indexed) returns a specific index field from the DataSet
KeyExclusive	Reverses the effect of the range and search functions
KeyFieldCount	Specifies the number of key fields to use in a search
MasterFields	Specifies the master fields in a master/detail relation
MasterSource	Specifies the master DataSource of a master/detail relation
Modified	Reflects whether the current record has been changed since the last Post or Cancel
ReadOnly	Determines whether the DataSet can be changed
RecordCount	Returns the number of rows in the DataSet
SessionName	Specifies the TSession component to use to connect to the database
State	Returns the state of the DataSet (for example, dsEdit or dsBrowse)
TableName	Specifies the physical name of the associated table
TableType	Specifies the type of (local) table
UpdateMode	Determines the type of SQL used to perform data changes
UpdateObject	Specifies the UpdateSQL component to use in conjunction with cached updates

Table 15.8. `TTable` key methods.

Method	Function
AddIndex	Creates a new index
Append	Appends a blank row to the DataSet
AppendRecord	Appends a row to the DataSet using specified values
ApplyRange	Activates range established by the `Set`/`EditRange` methods
ApplyUpdates	Saves cached updates to the database
BatchMove	Copies a batch of rows between DataSets
Cancel	Discards pending modifications to the current row
CancelRange	Cancels the effects of the `Set`/`EditRange` methods
CancelUpdates	Discards pending cached updates
ClearFields	Sets the current row's fields to their default values
Close	Closes the DataSet
CreateTable	Creates a new table
Delete	Deletes the current record
DeleteIndex	Deletes a secondary index
DeleteTable	Deletes the associated physical database table
Edit	Puts the DataSet in edit mode
EditKey	Allows search key values to be modified
EditRangeEnd	Allows editing of the upper key limit of a range
EditRangeStart	Allows editing of the lower key limit of a range
EmptyTable	Deletes all the rows in the DataSet
EnableControls	Enables associated data-aware controls
FetchAll	Reads all pending rows from the database
FieldByName	Returns a `TField` using its database field name
FindFirst	Finds a record using filter conditions you specify
FindNext	Finds the next record that meets the filter criteria
FindKey	Performs an exact search on the DataSet
FindNearest	Performs an inexact search on the DataSet
GetFieldNames	Returns a list of the fields in the DataSet
GetIndexNames	Returns a list of the DataSet's indexes
GotoKey	Performs an exact `SetKey`-based search on the DataSet
GotoNearest	Performs an inexact `SetKey`-based search on the DataSet

Method	Function
Insert	Inserts a blank row and allows it to be edited
InsertRecord	Inserts a row using supplied column values
Locate	Finds a record in a DataSet
LockTable	Locks a local table
Lookup	Finds a record in a DataSet and returns values from it
MoveBy	Moves the DataSet cursor by a given number of rows
Open	Opens the DataSet
Post	Saves pending modifications to the current row
RenameTable	Renames a local table
RevertRecord	Discards cached updates to the current row
SetKey	Puts the DataSet in a key-based search mode
SetRange	Puts the database in a range-based search mode
SetRangeEnd	Sets the upper limit of a range
SetRangeStart	Sets the lower limit of a range
UnlockTable	Unlocks a local table

Table 15.9. TTable key events.

Event	Catalyst
AfterCancel	Occurs following a Cancel
AfterClose	Occurs following the close of the DataSet
AfterDelete	Occurs following a Delete
AfterEdit	Occurs following an Edit
AfterInsert	Occurs following an Insert or Append
AfterOpen	Occurs after a DataSet is opened
AfterPost	Occurs following a Post
BeforeCancel	Occurs prior to a Cancel
BeforeClose	Occurs before the close of the DataSet
BeforeDelete	Occurs prior to a Delete
BeforeEdit	Occurs prior to an Edit
BeforeInsert	Occurs prior to an Insert or Append

continues

Table 15.9. continued

Event	Catalyst
BeforeOpen	Occurs before a DataSet is opened
BeforePost	Occurs prior to a Post
OnCalcFields	Occurs when calculated fields need values
OnDeleteError	Occurs when there is a problem deleting a record
OnEditError	Occurs when there is a problem editing a record
OnFilterRecord	Occurs when filtering is active and the DataSet needs a row
OnNewRecord	Occurs when a new record is added to the DataSet
OnPostError	Occurs when there is a problem posting a record
OnUpdateError	Occurs when there is a problem while applying cached updates
OnUpdateRecord	Occurs for each row saved by a call to ApplyUpdates

Key Elements

Use the DatabaseName property to specify the database you want to access. It points to either a local application-specific alias or one that you've defined using the Database Explorer or the BDE Configuration utility.

The TableName property points to the physical database table. On some platforms it may also include and the name of the table's home database and/or the table's owner.

Set the IndexName or IndexFields property to make use of a secondary index with the table. To establish a master-detail relationship with another table, set the MasterSource property to reference a DataSet that shares a common key with this one. Once MasterSource is set, specify the key fields in the master DataSource using the MasterFields property. These keys must correspond with those of the current index, as specified by IndexName or IndexFields. Note that you can double-click MasterFields to invoke Delphi's Field Link Designer, which enables you to establish master-detail relationships visually.

See Chapter 11, "Forms, Forms, and More Forms," to learn more about master-detail relationships.

Setting the Active property to True is identical to calling the DataSet's Open method—it opens the DataSet. Likewise, setting Active to False is the same as calling the DataSet's Close method—it closes the DataSet.

You can check the current status of a DataSet with the State property. It will have one of the following values:

■ `dsInactive`—The DataSet is closed.

■ `dsBrowse`—The DataSet is in `Browse` mode. The DataSet can be navigated, but changes can't be made to the data until the `State` is switched to `dsEdit`.

■ `dsEdit`—The DataSet is in `EUdit` mode and allows changes to the data.

■ `dsInsert`—The DataSet is in `Insert` mode.

■ `dsSetKey`—The DataSet is in `SetKey` mode because `SetKey` has just been called. When values are assigned to columns while in this mode, they are interpreted as search values. A subsequent `GotoKey` will search for a record using these values.

■ `dsCalcFields`—The `OnCalcFields` event handler is being called.

Tasks

The `First` method moves to the top of the DataSet, the `Last` method moves to the bottom. The `Prior` and `Next` methods move to the previous and next rows, respectively. Use the `MoveBy` method to move a number of rows forward or backward from the current row.

The `SetKey`, `FindKey`, `GotoKey`, `FindNearest`, and `GotoNearest` methods can be used to search the DataSet for a given set of field values.

Use the `BOF` property to determine whether the DataSet cursor is at its beginning. Use the `EOF` property to determine whether the cursor has reached the DataSet's end. These two properties can be useful in looping through the rows in a DataSet. For example, here's a simple routine that loops through a table's rows, displaying a field from each as it goes:

```
With taTENANT do begin
  First;
  While not EOF do begin
    ShowMessage('Name is: '+taTENANTName.Value);
    Next;
  end;
end;
```

CAUTION

Be careful that you don't make bad assumptions about the `BOF` and `EOF` properties. You can't assume that `BOF` will be `True` just because you're on the first row of a table. Nor can you assume that `EOF` will be `True` when you're on the last row of a table. Typically, an additional `Prior` or `Next` is required to set `BOF` or `EOF` to `True`. For example, the sequence `First`, `Next`, `Prior` won't reset `BOF` to `True`, but `First`, `Next`, `Prior`, `Prior` will. Note that `BOF` is `True` immediately after opening a table or calling the First method, and `EOF` is `True` immediately after calling the `Last` method.

The Append and Insert methods are used to add blank rows to a DataSet. Append adds a record to the end of the DataSet, whereas Insert adds it at the current cursor position. Append and Insert both put the DataSet in dsEdit mode. The AppendRecord and InsertRecord methods are used to add non-blank rows to a DataSet using a supplied set of field values.

The Delete method deletes the row at the current cursor position. The Edit method allows modification of rows in the DataSet, placing the DataSet in dsEdit mode. The Post method saves these changes to the database, whereas Cancel discards them. This is also true of the Append and Insert methods—you can Post or Cancel them as well.

> **NOTE**
>
> When using Delphi's DataSet components to communicate with the Sybase platform, I've received intermittent failures while attempting database operations of almost any kind. The message received is Connection is in use by another statement. This message occurs due to Sybase's infamous Attempt to initiate query with results pending error message. It's caused by attempting to fire off another query (over a given database connection) while results are still waiting to be retrieved for the previous one. All interactions with the server count as queries, so tables and stored procedures are queries, too, in that sense. A way around this is to call the FetchAll method of the relevant DataSet. FetchAll retrieves all pending rows from the back-end, thereby freeing the connection for a new query, while still allowing you to keep the DataSet open. Here's an example of the use of FetchAll:
>
> ```
> procedure TForm1.btApplyUpdatesClick(Sender: TObject);
> begin
>   With taCALLS do begin
>     FetchAll;
>     ApplyUpdates;
>   end;
> end;
> ```

Local Filters

The Filter, Filtered, and FilterOptions properties facilitate setting up local filters on the DataSet. Local filtering enables you to filter a DataSet from within the application. This can be advantageous with DataSets that have a small number of rows because the entirety of the DataSet will typically be cached by the BDE, anyway, so filtering it locally saves interaction with the database server or network.

Filter enables you to specify a filter expression for restricting the rows visible in the DataSet. The syntax supported in the expression is similar to that of an SQL WHERE clause. Fields can be compared to each other and to static values. The operators shown here can be used to build your filter expressions:

Operator	Use
<	Less than
>	Greater than
>=	Greater than or equal to
<=	Less than or equal to
=	Equal to
<>	Not equal to
()	Encloses individual elements of a compound expression
[]	Encloses field names with spaces
AND, OR, NOT	Joins individual elements of compound expressions

You can also filter records using the `OnFilterRecord` event. An `OnFilterEvent` looks like this:

```
procedure TfmRPROCGD0.taPROPERTYFilterRecord(DataSet: TDataSet; var Accept:
➥Boolean);
{Filters PROPERTY records so that only those properties with gas heat
 are visible}
begin
  Accept:=taPROPERTYGasHeat.Value;
end;
```

The `OnFilterRecord` event handler sets the value of the `Accept` var parameter to indicate whether a row meets the filter criteria. Note that the DataSet to which the filter corresponds is also passed in as a parameter. In the previous example, only those properties with gas heat are visible when the filter is active. Note the use of the `Value` variant property to set the `Accept` parameter.

You can also use the `FindFirst`, `FindNext`, `FindPrior`, and `FindLast` methods to search an unfiltered DataSet using a filter expression. `FindFirst` locates the first row matching the filter expression. `FindNext` locates the next one that does. `FindPrior` locates the previous row matching the filter expression and FindLast locates the last one that does.

`FilterOptions` is a set variable that can include two possible elements:

Element	Meaning
foCaseInsensitive	The filter ignores the case of the DataSet's data
foNoPartialCompare	Partial field matches aren't allowed

You can set them using Delphi's Object Inspector, or by using set addition, like so:

```
With taPROPERTY do FilterOptions:=FilterOptions+[foNoPartialCompare];
```

Ranges

The `SetRangeStart`, `SetRangeEnd`, `EditRangeStart`, `EditRangeEnd`, `ApplyRange`, and `SetRange` methods also allow you to limit the set of rows visible to your application. Unlike Delphi's more flexible Local Filters, the rows within the set must correspond to a consecutive set of keys within the current index. The CancelRange method makes all rows again visible to your application. Ranges are usually faster than filters, because the index tells us exactly what records need to be looked at. Filters may have to download every row in the table; ranges don't.

Locate/Lookup

The Locate and Lookup methods allow you to search for rows in a table. They're much more flexible than the FindKey/SetKey family of functions because they do not require the use of an index and can therefore be used with Query and StoredProc components in addition to Table components. You decide the data you want and the BDE finds the best way to access it.

Locate

The Locate method takes three parameters: a string that identifies the field(s) you want to search, a variant that lists the values to search for, and a TLocateOptions set variable that specifies options for the search. Here's the syntax for the Locate function:

```
function Locate(const SearchColumns: string; const SearchValues: Variant;
➥SearchOptions: TLocateOptions): Boolean;
```

Separate multiple field names with semicolons in Locate's SearchColumns parameter and pass their values as a variant array in its SearchValues parameter. Locate's SearchOptions parameter is of type TLocateOptions and enables you to specify options that control the search. The parameter is a set variable and can have two possible values, loCaseInsensitive and loPartialKey. The first option, loCaseInsensitive, tells Locate to perform a case-insensitive search. The second one, loPartialKey, allows for partial key searches. You case pass either one or both of these using a set constructor like so:

```
[loCaseInsensitive]
```

or,

```
[loCaseInsensitive, loPartialKey].
```

Here's an example of a call to the Locate function:

```
var
  Found : Boolean;
begin
  Found:=taPROPERTY.Locate('Address','2 Chickasha',[loPartialKey]);
end;
```

Locate uses the fastest available means of satisfying your search criteria. If an index exists that can satisfy the search request, Locate uses it. If an index does not exist that can service the search, a BDE filter is constructed. Either way, the fastest possible path to your data is taken.

Locate returns True if it's able to locate the data you request; False if it isn't.

> **NOTE**
>
> Because of a bug in `Locate`, you'll have to be careful to only pass a variant array as its `SearchValues` parameter when you actually have multiple values to search for. That is, don't supply a single element variant array, supply a plain variant, instead. Why is this an issue? If you're writing a generic search routine that makes use of `Locate`, the logical thing to do would be to construct a variant array and fill it with the values to search, regardless of whether there were five values to search for or just one. However, this approach won't work. `Locate` assumes that single values will be passed in as plain variants, not variant arrays, and an exception will be raised if you attempt otherwise. Listing 15.1 shows a function that you can pass to `Locate` to translate single-element variant arrays to plain variants on-the-fly.

Listing 15.1. A function to turn a single-item variant array into a plain variant.

```
function VarArrayToSingle(VarArray : Variant) : Variant;
  {Hoop-jumping code due to a bug in DB.Pas}
  var
    ActualElements, Counter : Integer;
begin
  If VarIsArray(VarArray) then begin
    ActualElements:=0;
    For Counter:=VarArrayLowBound(VarArray,1) to
        VarArrayHighBound(VarArray,1) do
          If (VarArray[Counter]<>'') then Inc(ActualElements);
    If (ActualElements=1) then
      Result:=VarArray[VarArrayLowBound(VarArray,1)]
    else
      Result:=VarArray;
  end Else Result:=VarArray;
end;
```

Lookup

Similarly to the `Locate` function, the `Lookup` function takes three parameters: a string parameter specifying a semicolon-delimited list of columns to search for, a variant or variant array specifying the column values to search for, and a string parameter listing the names of columns to return in the function's result. Here's the syntax for the `Lookup` function:

```
function Lookup(const SearchColumns: string; const SearchValues: Variant;
➡ const ResultColumns: string): Variant;
```

In addition to performing a DataSet search, `Lookup` returns values from the operation as well. If a matching row cannot be found, `Lookup` returns a null variant. If a matching row is found, `Lookup` first processes any lookup fields you've defined for its associated DataSet, then returns the values of the fields you've specified in `ResultColumns`. If `ResultColumns` lists multiple fields, the result is a variant array; otherwise, it's just a simple variant. Here's a sample call to the Lookup function:

```
var
  Results : Variant;
begin
  Results:=dmRentalMan.taTENANT.Lookup('Employer; EmpCity',
    VarArrayOf(['Bricktown Brewery','OKC']), 'TenantNo; Name');
end;
```

Notice the use of the VarArrayOf function to dynamically create the variant array that Lookup requires.

Cached Updates

Delphi's cached updates mechanism enables you to delay applying updates to your database back-end. You can decide when to apply updates, and then apply them all at once. Updates are cached locally until you apply them, so using cached updates can have a dramatic impact on performance.

A side-benefit of using cached updates is the ability to update read-only DataSets. Since you can control the SQL that's generated to update a DataSet, you can set up code to modify result sets that would otherwise be read-only.

There are four method procedures that relate to cached updates: ApplyUpdates, CancelUpdates, CommitUpdates, and RevertRecord. They have the following functions:

Method	Function
ApplyUpdates	Saves cached updates to the database
CancelUpdates	Discards cached updates
CommitUpdate	Notifies the cache that updates have been applied
RevertRecord	Returns a row to its state prior to cached updates to it

There are also a couple of properties that relate directly to cached updates:

Property	Description
CachedUpdates	Toggles cached updates for a DataSet
UpdateRecordTypes	Controls the visible rows in a cached update set

The process of making use of cached updates in an application is as follows:

■ Set the CachedUpdates property of the DataSet whose updates you want to cache to True.

■ Set the UpdateRecordTypes property to control what rows should be visible in the cached set. UpdateRecordTypes is a set property that can have the following values: rtModified, rtInserted, rtDeleted, and rtUnmodified. Each of these control the type of rows that are visible in a DataSet whose updates are being cached.

- Set up an OnUpdateError event handler to handle any errors during a call to ApplyUpdates
- Make changes to the DataSet's data.
- Call the ApplyUpdates method to save your changes, CancelUpdates to discard them.

A good application of cached updates is in data-entry forms. As discussed in Chapter 7, "Application Design 101," there are three basic types of database forms: decision support forms, transaction processing forms, and data-entry forms. Since users of data-entry forms will typically add several rows in succession, it would make sense to cache these additions locally, then save them in one pass. This will reduce table locking on your database and speed up the application.

Updating read-only DataSets is covered in the discussion of the UpdateSQL component later in this chapter.

On...Error

The OnEditError, OnDeleteError, and OnPostError events allow you to react to errors that occur while modifying the data in a DataSet. These events all send the same three parameters to handlers you define for them: the DataSet in which the error occurred, the exception class raised by the error, and a var parameter than lets you specify what action to take once the handler finishes. Here's a sample of the method procedure that Delphi generates for the On...Error events:

```
procedure Form.DataSetPostError(DataSet: TDataSet; E: EDatabaseError;
var Action: TDataAction);
begin
end;
```

You can set Action to one of three values: daFail, daAbort, or daRetry.

TQuery

Unit: DBTables   Class ancestor: TDBDataSet

Like TTable, TQuery is a direct descendent of the DBDataSet class and an indirect descendant of the DataSet class. You use TQuery to send explicit SQL statements to the database engine. This SQL either operates on local tables or is passed directly to your database server. You execute a query that returns a result set using TQuery's Open method or by setting its Active property to True. Provided that the query adheres to Delphi's restrictions on "live" queries, you can then treat the result set as if it were a table, similarly to the way an SQL VIEW works on many database servers. You can update, add to, and delete the rows in this live result set, just as you can when using a TTable component.

Table 15.10 lists the key properties, Table 15.11 lists the key methods, and Table 15.12 lists the key events for the TQuery component.

Table 15.10. TQuery key properties.

Property	Description
Active	Toggles whether the DataSet is open
AutoCalcFields	Determines how calculated fields are calculated
BOF	Reflects whether the DataSet is at its beginning
CachedUpdates	Toggles whether updates are cached
Constrained	Controls allowable updates to live result sets
Database	Identifies the TDatabase in use by the DataSet
DatabaseName	Names the alias used to connect to the database
DataSource	Specifies a TDataSource to retrieve query parameters from
DBHandle	Returns the low-level BDE connection handle
EOF	Reflects whether the DataSet is at its end
FieldCount	Returns the number of fields in the DataSet
FieldDefs	Lists important information about fields in the DataSet
Fields	(Indexed) returns a specific field from the DataSet
Filter	Specifies an expression to filter records by
Filtered	Toggles whether the filtering specified by Filter or OnFilterRecord is active
FilterOptions	Controls the behavior of filters
Handle	Returns the low-level BDE cursor handle
Modified	Reflects whether the current record has been changed in a live result set
ParamCount	Reflects the number of parameters for the SQL query
Params	Specifies the parameters to use with the SQL query
Prepared	Reflects whether the query has been prepared
RecordCount	Returns the number of rows in the DataSet
RequestLive	Specifies whether you want the query result to be updatable
SessionName	Specifies the TSession component to use to connect to the database
SQL	Specifies the SQL statements to execute on the server
State	Returns the state of the DataSet (such as dsEdit or dsBrowse)
StmtHandle	Returns the low-level BDE handle for the last query result
UniDirectional	Specifies that the cursor moves in only one direction

Property	Description
UpdateMode	Determines the type of SQL used to perform data changes
UpdateObject	Specifies the UpdateSQL component to use in conjunction with cached updates

Table 15.11. TQuery key methods.

Method	Function
Append	Appends a blank row to the DataSet
AppendRecord	Appends a row to the DataSet using specified values
ApplyUpdates	Saves cached updates to the database
Cancel	Discards pending modifications to the current row
CancelUpdates	Discards cached updates that are pending
ClearFields	Sets the current row's fields to their default values
Close	Closes the DataSet
Delete	Deletes the current record
Edit	Puts the DataSet in edit mode
ExecSQL	Executes the SQL without returning a cursor
FetchAll	Reads all pending rows from a database server connection
FieldByName	Returns a TField using its database field name
FindKey	Performs an exact search on the DataSet
GetFieldNames	Returns a list of the fields in the DataSet
Insert	Inserts a blank row and allows it to be edited
InsertRecord	Inserts a row using supplied column values
Locate	Finds a record in a DataSet
Lookup	Finds a record in a DataSet and returns values from it
MoveBy	Moves the DataSet cursor by a given number of rows
Open	Opens the DataSet
ParamByName	Returns a query parameter using its name
Post	Saves pending modifications to the current row
RevertRecord	Discards changes to the current record when using cached updates

Table 15.12. TQuery key events.

Event	Catalyst
AfterCancel	Occurs following a Cancel
AfterClose	Occurs following the close of the DataSet
AfterDelete	Occurs following a Delete
AfterEdit	Occurs following an Edit
AfterInsert	Occurs following an Insert or Append
AfterOpen	Occurs after a DataSet is opened
AfterPost	Occurs following a Post
BeforeCancel	Occurs prior to a Cancel
BeforeClose	Occurs before the close of the DataSet
BeforeDelete	Occurs prior to a Delete
BeforeEdit	Occurs prior to an Edit
BeforeInsert	Occurs prior to an Insert or Append
BeforeOpen	Occurs before a DataSet is opened
BeforePost	Occurs prior to a Post
OnCalcFields	Occurs when calculated fields need values
OnDeleteError	Occurs when there is a problem deleting a record
OnEditError	Occurs when there is a problem editing a record
OnFilterRecord	Occurs when filtering is active and the DataSet needs a row
OnNewRecord	Occurs when a new record is added to the DataSet
OnPostError	Occurs when there is a problem posting a record
OnUpdateError	Occurs when there is a problem while applying cached updates
OnUpdateRecord	Occurs for each row saved by a call to ApplyUpdates

Key Elements

SQL statements can also be executed that do not return a result set. This would include calls to the SQL INSERT, UPDATE, and DELETE commands, for example. Use the ExecSQL method for these types of queries.

The DatabaseName property specifies the database you want to query. The SQL property specifies the single SQL statement that you want to use in the query. When you query local tables, use Local SQL. When querying server tables, you can use any SQL syntax that your database server supports, unless you intend for the result set to be updatable. If you want an updatable result set, you must use Local SQL syntax so that the database engine can determine what database tables to actually update.

The SQL statement can be a static SQL statement or one that includes parameters that are dynamically replaced with real values. A query that uses replaceable parameters (known as a dynamic SQL query) uses a colon to delineate those parameters, like so:

```
SELECT * FROM ORDERS
WHERE CustomerNumber=:CustNo
```

In this example, CustNo is the name of the replaceable parameter. You supply these named parameters using TQuery's Params property.

> **TIP**
>
> When editing TQuery's SQL property, you can edit your SQL using Delphi's full-blown code editor. You do this by clicking the Code Editor button from within the SQL property editor. You'll find Delphi's code editor to be much more versatile than the TMemo component that's used to edit the SQL property by default.

The Constrained property enables you to control what updates may be made to a live result set. If you set Constrained to True, updates that would cause a row to be excluded from the result set are not permitted. That is, if you set up a Query component to return only those customers whose last names begin with A, an attempt to change the LastName column in a row to start with B will fail. This works much the same as the WITH CHECK option on SQL VIEWs.

Tasks

To establish a live, or updatable, result set, two things must happen. First, you must set TQuery's RequestLive property to True. Second, the SQL you use to define the query must conform to certain rules. These rules are different based on whether you are querying local tables or server tables. For local tables, the SQL must:

- Use Local SQL syntax only.
- Involve only one table.
- Not have an ORDER BY clause.
- Not contain aggregate functions.
- Not contain calculated fields.
- Use a WHERE clause involving comparisons of column names to scalar constants only. Operators supported include LIKE, >, <, >=, and <=. Individual elements of the clause may be joined by ANDs and ORs as well.

For server tables, the SQL must:

■ Use Local SQL syntax only

■ Involve only one table

■ Not contain aggregate functions

> **NOTE**
>
> The TLiveQuery component detailed in Chapter 26, "Building Your Own Database Components," provides an alternate method of acquiring updatable result sets from database servers. Basically, it creates and opens a temporary view on your server that you may then update as though it were a table. The updates you can make to this "live" result set are limited only by the restrictions your server places on updatable views.

The First method moves to the top of the DataSet, the Last to the bottom. The Prior and Next methods move to the previous and next rows, respectively. Use the MoveBy method to move a number of rows forward or backward from the current row.

Use the BOF property to determine whether the DataSet cursor is at its beginning. Use the EOF property to determine whether the cursor has reached the DataSet's end. These two properties can be useful in looping through the rows in a DataSet.

> **CAUTION**
>
> Be careful that you don't make bad assumptions about the BOF and EOF properties. You can't assume that BOF will be True just because you're on the first row of a query result set. Nor can you assume that EOF will be True when you're on the last row of a result set. Typically, an additional Prior or Next is required to set BOF or EOF to True. For example, the sequence First, Next, Prior won't reset BOF to True, but First, Next, Prior, Prior will. Note that BOF is True immediately after opening a query or calling the First method and EOF is True immediately after calling the Last method.

The Append and Insert methods are used to add blank rows to a DataSet. Append adds a record to the end of the DataSet, whereas Insert adds it at the current cursor position. Along these same lines, the AppendRecord and InsertRecord methods are used to add non-blank rows to a DataSet using a supplied set of field values.

The Delete method deletes the row at the current cursor position. The Edit method allows modification of rows in the DataSet, placing the DataSet in dsEdit mode. The Post method saves these changes to the database, whereas Cancel discards them.

See the previous discussion on the Table component for information on other DataSet-based properties, methods, and events.

TStoredProc

Unit: DBTables   Class ancestor: TDBDataSet

Like TTable and TQuery, TStoredProc is a direct descendent of the DBDataSet class and an indirect descendant of the DataSet class. This means that, in addition to the methods, properties, and events defined by the class itself, TStoredProc inherits several class elements from the DBDataSet class. This establishes a lot of common ground between the three DataSet-based components, TTable, TQuery, and TStoredProc.

You use the TStoredProc component to execute stored procedures from within your Delphi applications. A stored procedure is a compiled set of SQL statements executed as a single program. TStoredProc enables you to interact with the result sets returned by these stored procedures.

Table 15.13 lists the key properties, Table 15.14 lists the key methods, and Table 15.15 lists the key events for the TStoredProc component.

Table 15.13. TStoredProc key properties.

Property	Description
Active	Toggles whether the DataSet is open
AutoCalcFields	Determines how calculated fields are calculated
BOF	Reflects whether the DataSet is at its beginning
CachedUpdates	Toggles whether updates are cached
Database	Identifies the TDatabase in use by the DataSet
DatabaseName	Names the alias used to connect to the database
EOF	Reflects whether the DataSet is at its end
FieldCount	Returns the number of fields in the DataSet
FieldDefs	Lists important information about fields in the DataSet
Fields	(Indexed) returns a specific field from the DataSet
Filter	Specifies an expression to filter records by
Filtered	Toggles whether the filtering specified by Filter or OnFilterRecord is active
FilterOptions	Controls the behavior of filters

continues

Table 15.13. continued

Property	Description
Modified	Reflects whether the current record has been changed in updatable result sets
Overload	Specifies the overload procedure to use on the Oracle platform
ParamBindMode	Determines how Params will be bound to proc parameters
ParamCount	Reflects the number of parameters for the SQL query
Params	Specifies the parameters to use with the SQL query
Prepared	Reflects whether the query has been prepared
RecordCount	Returns the number of rows in the result set
SessionName	Specifies the TSession component to use to connect to the database
State	Returns the state of the DataSet (such as dsEdit or dsBrowse)
StmtHandle	Returns the low-level BDE handle for the last result set
StoredProcName	Specifies the name of the procedure to execute
UpdateObject	Specifies the UpdateSQL component to use in conjunction with cached updates

Table 15.14. TStoredProc key methods.

Method	Function
Append	Appends a blank row to the DataSet
AppendRecord	Appends a row to the DataSet using specified values
ApplyUpdates	Saves cached updates to the database
Cancel	Discards pending modifications to the current row
CancelUpdates	Discards cached updates that are pending
Close	Closes the DataSet
Delete	Deletes the current record
Edit	Puts the DataSet in edit mode
ExecProc	Executes the stored procedure
FetchAll	Reads all pending rows from a database server connection
FieldByName	Returns a TField using its database field name
FindKey	Performs an exact search on the DataSet
GetFieldNames	Returns a list of the fields in the DataSet

Method	Function
GetResults	Returns Sybase stored procedure output parameters
Insert	Inserts a blank row and allows it to be edited
InsertRecord	Inserts a row using supplied column values
Locate	Finds a record in the result set
Lookup	Finds a record in the result set and returns values from it
MoveBy	Moves the DataSet cursor by a given number of rows
Open	Opens a stored procedure that returns a result set
ParamByName	Returns a query parameter using its name
Post	Saves pending modifications to the current row

Table 15.15. TStoredProc key events.

Event	Catalyst
AfterCancel	Occurs following a Cancel
AfterClose	Occurs following the close of the DataSet
AfterDelete	Occurs following a Delete
AfterEdit	Occurs following an Edit
AfterInsert	Occurs following an Insert or Append
AfterOpen	Occurs after a DataSet is opened
AfterPost	Occurs following a Post
BeforeCancel	Occurs prior to a Cancel
BeforeClose	Occurs before the close of the DataSet
BeforeDelete	Occurs prior to a Delete
BeforeEdit	Occurs prior to an Edit
BeforeInsert	Occurs prior to an Insert or Append
BeforeOpen	Occurs before a DataSet is opened
BeforePost	Occurs prior to a Post
OnCalcFields	Occurs when calculated fields need values
OnDeleteError	Occurs when there is a problem deleting a record
OnEditError	Occurs when there is a problem editing a record
OnFilterRecord	Occurs when filtering is active and the DataSet needs a row
OnNewRecord	Occurs when a new record is added to the DataSet

continues

Table 15.15. continued

Event	Catalyst
OnPostError	Occurs when there is a problem posting a record
OnUpdateError	Occurs when there is a problem while applying cached updates
OnUpdateRecord	Occurs for each row saved by a call to ApplyUpdates

Key Elements

Use the DatabaseName property to specify the database you want to access. It points to either a local application-specific alias or one that you've defined using the Database Explorer or BDE Configuration utility.

The StoredProcName property points to the stored procedure on the server that you want to execute.

The Params property enables you to specify parameters for the stored procedure. You can edit this information at design time using the Delphi Object Inspector. If the information is available from the server, the Object Inspector will list the parameters that the stored procedure expects.

You can set these at runtime by assigning values to the Params property. For example, you could use the following code to assign the parameter named CustomerNumber for the stored procedure associated with the TStoredProc:

```
StoredProc1.ParamByName('CustomerNumber').AsString := '123';
```

Note that stored procedure return values are accessed using the Params property, as well. That is, if you've defined an output parameter named Balance in the Params property, you can reference it's return value using ParamByName('Balance').AsFloat following the execution of the procedure.

> **NOTE**
>
> If you intend to return output parameters from a Sybase stored procedure that also returns a result set, you'll need to call TStoredProc's GetResults method in order to retrieve them. Normally, the StoredProc component handles this automatically, but Sybase SQL Server does not return stored procedure output values until all results are read, so you'll need to call GetResults yourself.

Tasks

If a stored procedure returns only one row, or no rows, execute it with the ExecProc method. If it returns multiple rows, use the Open method instead.

Note that you'll need to prepare a stored procedure before executing it. At runtime, you do this using the Prepare method. At design time, you do so by editing the Params property.

The First method moves to the top of the result set, the Last to the bottom. The Next and Prior methods move to the previous and next rows, respectively. Use the MoveBy method to move a number of rows forward or backward from the current row.

The Append and Insert methods are used to add blank rows to the result set of a TStoredProc. AppendRecord and InsertRecord add non-blank rows to the result set, using a supplied set of field values.

The Delete method deletes the row at the current cursor position. The Edit method allows modification of the row at the current cursor position, placing the result set in dsEdit mode. The Post method saves these changes to the database, whereas Cancel discards them.

Cached Updates

As mentioned previously, you can only update stored procedure result sets by using cached updates and a TUpdateSQL component. Basically, you set up the InsertSQL, DeleteSQL, and ModifySQL properties of a TUpdateSQL component to handle the DataSet modifications for you. When you then call the ApplyUpdates method of your TStoredProc, the relevant SQL is executed. Since you can control the SQL that's generated to update a DataSet, you can set up code to modify result sets that would otherwise be read-only.

You do this using an UpdateSQL component that defines SQL statements for handling inserting, modifying and deleting rows. These SQL statements can be complex SQL queries that update multiple tables or even other stored procedure calls, so you should be able to update a stored procedure's underlying tables. You reference UpdateSQL objects using TStoredProc's UpdateObject property.

TStoredProc has two method procedures that relate directly to cached updates: ApplyUpdates and CancelUpdates. ApplyUpdates saves changes you've made to the database. In the case of the StoredProc component, this means that the relevant insert, update, or delete SQL statements are executed in the linked UpdateSQL component. Note that you can set up the OnUpdateError event to handle errors that occur during a call to ApplyUpdates.

There are also a couple of properties that relate directly to the use of cached updates with stored procedures: CachedUpdates and UpdateRecordTypes. CachedUpdates toggles cached update support for the StoredProc component. Unless CachedUpdates is enabled and you've linked and set up an UpdateSQL component properly, you won't be able to update stored procedure result sets. UpdateRecordTypes determines which types of updates remain visible in a DataSet with CachedUpdates set to True.

Updating read-only DataSets is discussed further in the coverage of the UpdateSQL component later in this chapter.

NOTE

I've received spurious error messages when updating stored procedure result sets on the Sybase platform. These errors indicate that the updates and inserts I've attempted have failed, when in fact they have succeeded. There are a couple of ways to handle this. The way that I chose to deal with it was to setup an OnUpdateError handler to quash the bogus messages. Here's an example of such a handler:

```
procedure TForm1.StoredProc1UpdateError(DataSet: TDataSet;
  E: EDatabaseError; UpdateKind: TUpdateKind;
  var UpdateAction: TUpdateAction);
begin
  case (MessageDlg('Error applying updates',mtError,mbAbortRetryIgnore,0)) of
    mrAbort : UpdateAction:=uaAbort;
    mrRetry : UpdateAction:=uaRetry;
    mrIgnore : UpdateAction:=uaApplied;
  end;
end;
```

If the user selects Ignore in the dialog box that's displayed, the routine assumes that the update succeeded in spite of the error message that was received. Alternately, you could code mrIgnore to set UpdateAction to uaFail to cause the update that generated the message to fail. I selected uaApplied here because I knew the error messages to be phony.

TBatchMove

Unit: DBTables   Class ancestor: TComponent

The TBatchMove component enables you to work with sets of records in operations between two tables. These sets can range from a few records to all the records in a DataSet. When working with TBatchMove, you specify both a source and a destination table. You can append, update, and delete rows in the target table. You can even replace the target table completely, if you wish. The actual operation carried out when you call the component's Execute method depends on the setting of the Mode property.

Table 15.16 lists the key properties, Table 15.17 lists the key method, and Table 15.18 lists the key event of the TBatchMove component.

Table 15.16. `TBatchMove` key properties.

Property	Description
Destination	Specifies the destination of the batch move operation
Mapping	Specifies column-to-column mappings between Source and Dest. If your source and destination tables are not identical, you'll need to provide field mappings so that the BDE can figure out where to put your data. If you neglect to do this with tables that aren't identical, the batch move will fail.
Mode	Specifies the type of move (such as `batAppendUpdate` or `batCopy`)
Source	Specifies the source of the batch move operation

Table 15.17. `TBatchMove` key method.

Method	Function
Execute	Initiates the batch move operation

Table 15.18. `TBatchMove` key event.

Event	Catalyst
None	

Key Elements

Set the `Source` property to the DataSet from which you want to copy. Set the `Destination` property to the target DataSet. Set `Mode` to one of the following values depending on what you want to do:

- ■ `batAppend`—Appends rows to a pre-existing target DataSet.

- ■ `batUpdate`—Updates rows in a pre-existing target DataSet with their counterparts in the source table. The mode requires an index in order to locate the rows to update.

- ■ `batAppendUpdate`—Appends new rows to a pre-existing target DataSet and updates existing rows. This mode requires an index in order to locate the rows to update.

- ■ `batCopy`—Copies rows in the source DataSet to the target DataSet. It creates the target table when executed, so an existing target table will be overwritten. Be aware that, since existing tables are deleted and replaced, any dependent objects such as indexes and triggers are deleted as well. *Note that these secondary objects are not recreated.*

- batDelete—Deletes records from the target table that match the source table. This mode requires an index in order to locate the rows to delete.

Tasks

Once Mode is set appropriately, call the Execute method to perform the copy. If there are problems, TBatchMove will behave differently based on the settings of various properties:

- If AbortOnProblem has been set to True, the copy will abort the moment any errors occur.
- If AbortOnKeyViol is set to True, the operation will abort when any key violation errors occur.
- If the ProblemTableName property has been set, any rows causing errors will be placed into it. Obviously, if AbortOnProblem is also set to True, this table will contain no more than one record.
- If the KeyViolTableName property is set, any rows causing key violation errors will be placed into it.
- If the ChangedTableName property is set, rather than discarding updated or changed rows from the target table, TBatchMove will move them to it, instead.

TDataSource

Unit: DBTables   Class ancestor: TComponent

The TDataSource component is the link between data-aware controls and the DataSet components (TTable, TQuery, and TStoredProc). It's what allows data-aware components to interact with physical database objects.

Data-aware controls reference a common TDataSource through their DataSource properties. It, in turn, references the DataSet that supplies them with data. The DataSet supplies data to the TDataSource, which is then passed to the data-aware controls. When data is modified in a data-aware control, the change is passed to the TDataSource, which then passes it to the DataSet.

By abstracting the data control level from the DataSet level, Delphi allows the interaction between the DataSet and data-aware controls to be more easily coordinated. It enables you, for example, to change the DataSet for a number of components without changing them individually. That is, if you want to change the DataSet to which a form's data-aware controls refer, you don't have to change the controls themselves. Instead, you change the DataSet property of the TDataSource to which they refer. This three-tiered approach allows the access of a group of controls to a given DataSet to be more easily controlled.

Table 15.19 lists the key properties, Table 15.20 lists the key method, and Table 15.21 lists the key events for TDataSource.

Table 15.19. TDataSource key properties.

Property	Description
Autoedit	Determines whether modifying the contents of a data-aware control automatically starts Edit mode
DataSet	References the DataSet that provides data to this TDataSource
Enabled	Specifies whether the display of associated data controls is updated
State	Returns the state of the linked DataSet component

Table 15.20. TDataSource key method.

Method	Function
Edit	Switches the associated DataSet into Edit mode

Table 15.21. TDataSource key events.

Event	Catalyst
OnDataChange	Occurs when data is changed or the record pointer moves
OnStateChange	Occurs when the State property changes
OnUpdateData	Occurs when Post or UpdateRecord is called

Key Elements

The DataSet property identifies the TTable, TQuery, or TStoredProc that supplies the component with data. The AutoEdit property determines whether modifying the contents of a data-aware control will automatically switch the DataSet into Edit mode, allowing changes to be made to the underlying data.

Tasks

You can monitor changes to a DataSet and its associated data-aware controls by assigning an event handler to the OnDataChange event.

The OnStateChange event occurs when the State of the DataSet changes. For example, if you switch the DataSet's State from dsBrowse to dsEdit by calling the Edit routine, this event will be triggered. Because OnStateChange can occur for nil DataSets, be sure to check for a nil DataSet before attempting to reference it.

If you want to change the data in the current row before it is posted, set up an OnUpdateData event. It's triggered when Post or UpdateRecord is called.

TUpdateSQL

Unit: DBTables   Class ancestor: TDataSetUpdateObject

The TUpdateSQL component enables you to control the way that DataSets are updated. Since you have complete control over the update process, you can even update read-only DataSets. You do this via TUpdateSQL's InsertSQL, DeleteSQL and ModifySQL properties. They allow you to specify the SQL to execute for row insertions, deletions and updates.

Table 15.22 lists the key properties, Table 15.23 lists the key methods, and Table 15.24 lists the key event for the TUpdateSQL component.

Table 15.22. TUpdateSQL key properties.

Property	Description
DeleteSQL	Specifies the SQL to execute when a row is deleted
InsertSQL	Specifies the SQL to execute when a row is added
ModifySQL	Specifies the SQL to execute when a row is updated

Table 15.23. TUpdateSQL key methods.

Method	Function
Apply	Replaces parameters and calls the SQL you specify (DeleteSQL, InsertSQL, or ModifySQL). Calls both SetParams and ExecSQL
ExecSQL	Executes DeleteSQL, InsertSQL, or ModifySQL, as you specify
SetParams	Replaces the parameters in DeleteSQL, InsertSQL, or ModifySQL, as you specify

Table 15.24. TUpdateSQL key event.

Event	Catalyst
None	

Key Elements

The InsertSQL, ModifySQL, and DeleteSQL properties provide the means of controlling updates to DataSets. These DataSets can be TTables, TQuery result sets, or TStoredProc result sets. The SQL you specify can be a simple SQL INSERT, UPDATE, or DELETE statement, it can be a complex SQL query, it can even be a call to a stored procedure. This flexibility gives you the control you need to update almost any type of result set.

Tasks

To make use of a TUpdateSQL component, follow these steps:

■ Drop a TUpdateSQL component onto a form and set its InsertSQL, DeleteSQL, and ModifySQL statements to update the database object(s) referenced by your DataSet

■ Set the DataSet's UpdateObject property to point to your TUpdateSQL component

■ Set the DataSet's CachedUpdates property to True

■ Call the ApplyUpdates method from within your application when you want to invoke the SQL specified in the TUpdateSQL component

Updates that you make via the DeleteSQL and ModifySQL statements will of course need to be qualified by an SQL WHERE clause. Both of these properties support a special extension to SQL that enables you to refer to a field's original value by prefixing its name with Old_. This is similar to InterBase's Old. context variable. For example, the ModifySQL statement you set up for the CUSTOMER table might look like this:

```
UPDATE CUSTOMER SET Name=:Name
WHERE CustomerNo=:Old_CustomerNo
```

Though this query doesn't actually change CustomerNo, it's a good idea to get into the habit of using the Old_ prefix anyway, since there are updates that aren't possible without it.

> **TIP**
>
> When editing the SQL associated with the TUpdateSQL component, you can edit your SQL using Delphi's full-blown code editor. You do this by clicking the Code Editor button from within the InsertSQL, DeleteSQL, or ModifySQL property editors. You'll find Delphi's code editor to be much more powerful than the TMemo component that's used to edit the three properties by default.

Use your DataSet's OnUpdateRecord event when you want to perform additional processing before sending rows to TUpdateSQL. Once you've completed this additional processing, you can call

TUpdateSQL's Apply method to replace the parameters embedded in your SQL and execute the SQL against your database. Here's a sample OnUpdateRecord handler:

```
procedure TForm1.StoredProc1UpdateRecord(DataSet: TDataSet;
  UpdateKind: TUpdateKind; var UpdateAction: TUpdateAction);
const
  DefaultRate = 5.00;
begin
  if (UpdateKind=ukInsert) then
    StoredProc1.FieldByName('Rate').Value:=DefaultRate;
  UpdateSQL1.Apply(UpdateKind);
  UpdateAction:=uaApplied;
end;
```

Notice that the routine sets the UpdateAction var parameter to tell the cached updates ApplyUpdates routine that no further action is necessary.

TField

Unit: DBTables   Class ancestor: TComponent

The TField component is used to access the columns in a DataSet's rows. Everything that Delphi enables you to configure at the field level is done with the TField component. You can toggle a database field's visibility in a grid, determine what its valid values are, and control whether or not it can be changed—all using the TField component.

Table 15.25 lists the key properties, Table 15.26 lists the key methods, and Table 15.27 lists the key events for TField.

Table 15.25. TField key properties.

Property	Description
Calculated	Reflects whether a field is a calculated field
DataSet	Returns the DataSet to which this TField belongs
EditMask	Specifies an input mask limiting text typed into the control
FieldName	Specifies the associated database field name
Lookup	Reflects whether a field is a lookup field
Value	Return the TField's underlying data value as a variant
Visible	Determines whether the TField is visible (by default) in DBGrid controls

Table 15.26. `TField` key methods.

Method	Function
Assign	Copies the value in one field to another
AssignValue	Assigns a literal value to a `TField`
Clear	Empties a `TField`
GetData	Returns the data from a field in raw format
SetData	Assigns raw data to a field

Table 15.27. `TField` key events.

Event	Catalyst
OnChange	Occurs when any modification is made to a `TField`
OnValidate	Occurs when field's value is changed

Key Elements

If you do not specifically create a set of `TFields` using the Fields Editor in Delphi, field objects are automatically created for you each time a DataSet is opened. This generated list reflects the columns as they appear in the DataSet.

By creating your own list of `TFields` using the Fields Editor, you ensure that your application is indeed accessing the `DataSet` columns it intends to access. Without such a list, changing the underlying table automatically changes the columns your application works with. Using `TField` components makes your application immune to column reordering and causes an exception to be raised if a column's name or data type changes. The only time you shouldn't make use of `TField` components is when building a generic table browser. On all other occasions, you'll want to be sure and establish `TField` components to service your DataSets.

When you establish your own `TField` list, referencing a field that's been renamed or removed from the underlying table raises an exception. This is preferable to allowing the application to possibly work with the wrong data.

A `TField` component itself is never actually created in Delphi applications—it's an abstract class and, therefore, parts of it must be overridden before it can be instantiated. You must create a descendant of `TField` and fill in some of its abstract gaps in order to create a `TField` instance. In OOP parlance, you do this via *inheritance*. The `TField` class type can also be used to typecast and manipulate its descendants. This technical term for this OOP concept is *polymorphism*.

For example, thanks to polymorphism, you're able to use `TField(MyTField-Descendant).AsString` to retrieve the string value of a `TField` descendant, no matter what type the `TField` descendant actually represents. `TField`'s descendant classes are detailed in Table 15.28.

Table 15.28. `TField` descendants.

`TField` *descendant*	*Purpose*
`TStringField`	Fixed-length text data up to 255 characters
`TIntegerField`	Whole numbers from -2,147,483,648 to 2,147,483,647
`TSmallintField`	Whole numbers from -32,768 to 32,767
`TWordField`	Whole numbers from 0 to 65,535
`TFloatField`	Real numbers from $5.0*10^{-324}$ to $1.7*10^{308}$
`TCurrencyField`	Currency values accurate 15 to 16 digits; represented as a binary value with a range of (+/-) $5.0*10^{-324}$ to $1.7*10^{308}$
`TBCDField`	Binary Coded Decimal values with accuracy to 18 digits
`TBooleanField`	Boolean values
`TDateTimeField`	Date and time values
`TDateField`	Date values
`TTimeField`	Time values
`TBlobField`	Variable-length field with no size limit
`TBytesField`	Variable-length field with no size limit
`TVarBytesField`	Variable-length field up to 65,535 characters
`TMemoField`	Variable-length text field with no size limit
`TGraphicField`	Variable-length graphic field with no size limit

You never specifically drop a `TField` descendant onto a form. As I've mentioned, these are created for you, either via the Fields Editor or automatically when a DataSet is opened.

Tasks

`TFields` support a number of column-based settings that you can use to customize your applications. You specify these settings using the Fields Editor of a DataSet. The Fields Editor is accessed by right-clicking a `DataSet` component and selecting Fields Editor from the menu.

For example, to prevent modifications to a field, right-click its DataSet, select Fields Editor, then set its `ReadOnly` property to `True` in the Object Inspector. To make it invisible in a `DBGrid`, set its `Visible` property to `False`. If you want to control the types of characters allowed into the field, set its `EditMask` property. To change the database field to which the `TField` is linked, change its `FieldName` property.

`TFields` also support implicit data conversions. That is, you don't have to know what type of data a `TField` actually stores in order to convert it to another data type. This is facilitated by `TField`'s `Value` property. `Value` is a variant type that is implicitly converted when it is assigned or receives a value. For example, you can assign a string to a Boolean field using its `Value` variant, like so:

```
MyBoolean : TBooleanField;
....
MyBoolean.Value:='T';
```

You can also assign a numeric field to a string control using its `Value` property:

```
MyMoney : TCurrencyField;
....
Edit1.Text:=MyMoney.Value;
```

`TField`'s amazing ability to implicitly convert between different data types makes it chameleon-like in its capacity to adapt to varying data requirements. This simplifies your applications and makes for less work when an application's underlying data structure changes.

What's Ahead

In Chapter 16, I'll discuss the suite of data-aware component classes, their key methods and properties, and the ways in which they're used in applications. Unlike the components just discussed, most of the data-aware controls descend from standard Windows controls, so they will probably be more familiar to you.

Summary

As you can see, the Delphi database class hierarchy is complex, yet easy to use. Great attention has been given to making the hierarchy not only extensive, but also coherent. The VCL database classes strike a good balance between functionality and ease of use.

16

Database Component Reference Part II

The purpose of this chapter and the one preceding it is to enhance the database component information available in the Delphi documentation. The idea is to put as much key information as possible into one place, thereby saving you the trouble of wading through the manuals and on-line help for critical facts. Think of Chapter 15, "Database Component Reference Part I," and this chapter as database component "cheat sheets." They coalesce as much vital information as possible into a limited space.

As I've mentioned, the approach taken in these two chapters is to cover database access components separately from data-aware controls. This chapter focuses on Delphi's data-aware controls. You can find them on the Data Controls page of the Delphi component palette.

Each component narrative consists of three sections:

■ A description of the component and its unit, tables of its key properties, and tables of its key methods and key events (if any)

■ A key elements section

■ A tasks section

The key properties, methods, and events tables are by no means exhaustive—see the Delphi documentation, or, better yet, the VCL source code, for complete lists of these. The idea is to equip you with what you need without overburdening you.

To continue where we left off in Chapter 15, let's begin with the TDBGrid component.

TDBGrid

Unit: DBGrids

The TDBGrid component allows data from a DataSet to be displayed and edited in a spreadsheet-like format. It divides the rows and columns of the DataSet into a grid, hence its name. It works similarly to the StringGrid and DataGrid components, but works directly with the data in a DataSet; thus, it's a data-aware control, just like the other components reviewed in this chapter.

Table 16.1 gives the key properties for TDBGrid, and Table 16.2 gives the key event. There are no key methods for TDBGrid.

Table 16.1. TDBGrid key properties.

Property	Description
Columns	Defines the attributes of the columns displayed by the grid
DataSource	Lists the TDataSource that supplies data to the control
DefaultDrawing	Toggles whether the control is drawn automatically
EditorMode	Toggles whether field editing can be done just by typing

Property	Description
FieldCount	Returns the number of fields referenced by the DBGrid
Fields	(Array property) returns the list of TFields referenced by the DBGrid
Options	Controls the appearance and behavior of the grid
ReadOnly	Determines whether the grid can be edited
SelectedField	Returns the field currently selected in the grid
SelectedIndex	Returns the zero-based index of the current field

Table 16.2. TDBGrid key event.

Event	Catalyst
OnDrawColumnCell	Occurs when the grid needs to draw a cell

Key Elements

A common way of allowing the user to navigate through a DataSet using a TDBGrid is to include a TDBNavigator component that's attached to the same TDataSource as the grid. This way, the user can easily jump a row at a time through the data or jump quickly to its beginning or end. He can also explicitly post and cancel changes made in the grid by using the buttons on the TDBNavigator. There are, in fact, some third-party Delphi component libraries that combine these controls into one.

The Fields property lists the fields in the DataSet associated with the grid. The SelectedField property indicates the grid's currently selected field. The FieldCount property reflects the number of TFields associated with the grid.

Tasks

Since most of DBGrid's behavior is event-driven, performing tasks involves customizing the control's default behavior. You do that via its many properties and its OnDrawColumnCell event.

Customizing the Grid's Behavior

The Options property changes the appearance and behavior of a TDBGrid. You can control whether the grid displays lines between columns, whether it includes column headings, and whether the Tab key moves between columns, among many other things, using the Options property.

Table 16.3 lists the individual elements of the Options property and how they affect the grid.

Table 16.3. The TDBGrid component's Options property.

Option	Determines
dgEditing	Whether editing of the rows in the grid is allowed
dgAlwaysShowEditor	Whether field selection switches to edit mode
dgTitles	Whether column headings are displayed
dgIndicator	Whether a row indicator is displayed at the left
dgColumnResize	Whether columns can be resized
dgColLines	Whether vertical lines should appear between columns
dgRowLines	Whether horizontal lines should appear between rows
dgTabs	Whether the Tab key moves between columns or controls
dgRowSelect	Whether selections are field-oriented or row-oriented
dgAlwaysShowSelection	Whether the selected cell or row remains highlighted when the grid loses focus
dgConfirmDelete	Whether row deletions are confirmed with a prompt box
dgCancelOnExit	Whether unmodified row inserts are canceled when focus moves to another row of the grid

You can also customize many of the aspects of the grid's behavior via its Columns property. To change column attributes via the Columns property, you first need to build a list of columns from the underlying DataSet's field list. To do this, double-click the Columns property in the Object Inspector, then click Add All Fields in its property editor dialog box. Here are some examples of items you can configure with the Columns property:

■ To change the order of a column in the grid, drag it to a new position in the Columns property editor.

■ To prevent a column from being displayed in a TDBGrid, delete it from the list of columns in the Columns editor.

■ To change a column's display color, set its Color property in the Columns editor.

■ To protect the field against modification, set its ReadOnly property to True in the Columns editor.

If you want an entire DataSet to be read-only, set the DataSet's ReadOnly property to True. If you only want to prevent modification of the DataSet through a TDBGrid, set the TDBGrid's ReadOnly property to True.

Editing

Rows can be modified or inserted into a grid, provided the following conditions are met:

- The CanModify property of the associated DataSet is set to True. (CanModify is a runtime and read-only property only. It looks at the value of the ReadOnly property and whether the DataSet is actually editable to determine whether it can be modified.)
- The ReadOnly property of the TDBGrid is set to False.

Posting

Data isn't actually inserted or edited with a TDBGrid until the changes are posted to the database. This can occur automatically, by moving to a different row in the grid, or it can be done explicitly by either using a TDBNavigator or calling the Post method yourself. A place on which you might "hook" your own Post method call would be on the OnColExit event of the grid itself. This would ensure that changes were posted with each column change, rather than waiting until the current row changed.

> **CAUTION**
>
> Because automatically posting changes by the grid requires that you move to a different row, if you merely change the input focus of the form to another data-aware control, *the changes won't be posted*, because you haven't changed the current row.

If you want to cancel the changes you made to a row before they're posted, simply press the Esc key before moving to a new record.

TDBNavigator

Unit: DBCtrls

The TDBNavigator component is a database navigation component. This means that it's used to move through a DataSet and to perform modification of its data. Quite often, it's used in concert with the TDBGrid component, as well as other data-aware controls, in providing a complete data maintenance form.

Table 16.4 gives the key properties, and Table 16.5 lists the key method for TDBNavigator. There are no key events for TDBNavigator.

Table 16.4. `TDBNavigator` key properties.

Property	Description
ConfirmDelete	Determines whether row deletions are confirmed
DataSource	Lists the TDataSource that supplies data to the control
Hint	Specifies the pop-up hint to be displayed
VisibleButtons	Determines which navigator buttons are included

Table 16.5. `TDBNavigator` key method.

Method	Function
BtnClick	Fakes a navigator-button click

Key Elements

Clicking one of `TDBNavigator`'s buttons causes the appropriate action to be carried out on the associated DataSet. Table 16.6 details `TDBNavigator`'s buttons and their respective functions.

Table 16.6. The `TDBNavigator` component's buttons and their functions.

Button	Function
First	Moves to the first record of the DataSet; disables First button
Prior	Moves to the DataSet's previous record
Next	Moves to the DataSet's next record
Last	Move to the DataSet's last record; disables Last button
Insert	Inserts a new record; switches DataSet into edit mode
Delete	Deletes the current row, making the next row the current row
Edit	Switches the DataSet to edit mode
Post	Posts any changes to the current row (disabled if there are none)
Cancel	Cancels any pending record changes (disabled if there are none)
Refresh	Rereads all rows from the DataSet

You use the `VisibleButtons` property to determine which of these buttons are actually included in the control at runtime.

Because the TDBNavigator control consists of several TSpeedButton controls side-by-side, you use its Hints property to specify fly-over hints for the individual buttons. Each line in the Hints property corresponds positionally to a button on the navigator. For those buttons for which you do not specify a hint, Delphi provides a default. Of course, fly-over hints must be enabled in the form itself in order for hints to be displayed.

Tasks

Because the VisibleButtons property controls what buttons appear on the control at runtime, you can use it to limit what functions the user can perform on a DataSet. By default, all buttons are included. If you make a button invisible by changing the Visible property, you make it impossible for the user to perform the button's associated function using the navigator. For example, if you wanted to prevent the user from deleting rows from the table, you could set the nbDelete portion of VisibleButtons to False, thereby removing the button from control. The user would then be unable to delete rows using the TDBNavigator.

There are times when overriding the default OnClick behavior of the navigator is desirable. An example of this is when you want to check referential integrity relationships between the current DataSet and other DataSets before allowing a delete. Of course, the best place to do this sort of checking would be in the DataSet's BeforeDelete event, but, depending on your needs, it may be necessary to do this checking with your navigator component. If so, you can use the navigator's OnClick event to do it.

The TDBNavigator component's OnClick event is a little different than most other visual controls. This is because, in addition to supplying the Sender of the event to its handler, as most controls do, TDBNavigator also supplies the button that was clicked. You can use this information in a case statement to determine what action to take. Here's an example of an OnClick event for a TDBNavigator:

```
procedure TfmDANIEDT0.naANIMALSClick(Sender: TObject; Button: TNavigateBtn);
begin
  Case Button of
  nbDelete : CheckReferentialDelete;
  nbPost : CheckReferentialChange;
  end;
end;
```

There are also times when you may want to duplicate the functions on the TDBNavigator with other buttons on the form. An example of this would be if you were needing to include the navigator for simple DataSet perusal, and larger, textual buttons for significant actions like editing or posting records. The way you do this is through the use of the control's BtnClick method. Basically, this method fakes the clicking of one of the navigator control's buttons. So, if you wanted to drop a TButton onto a form and have it perform the same function as the navigator's Delete button, you'd set the TButton's OnClick event to call the navigator's BtnClick method. For example, the following code would accomplish the same thing as clicking the navigator's Delete button:

```
naANIMALSClick.BtnClick(nbDelete);
```

Note that this is preferable to having the TButton simply call the DataSet's Delete method itself. The reason for this is that you might have defined special handling for the delete function, as mentioned previously, in your navigator control. If so, using BtnClick will ensure that this special handling occurs.

TDBText

Unit: DBCtrls

TDBText is a read-only data-aware control for displaying a column from a DataSet. Because it's a read-only control, TDBText is great for displaying columns from a DataSet that you do not want to enable the user to change. Because it has a different screen appearance than the TDBEdit control, it helps alleviate the confusion sometimes associated with read-only edit controls.

Table 16.7 gives the key properties for TDBText. There are no key methods or key events.

Table 16.7. TDBText key properties.

Property	Description
Alignment	Controls whether text is left-, center-, or right-justified
AutoSize	Determines whether the control is sized by its contents
DataField	References the associated column in the linked DataSet
DataSource	Lists the TDataSource that supplies data to the control
Transparent	Determines whether the control is transparent
WordWrap	Controls whether text wraps at the right to the next line

Key Elements

The TDBText control is similar to the standard TLabel component. It displays text from a DataSet rather than using a Caption property, as the TLabel control does. Also, unlike TLabel, it doesn't have a FocusControl property because it's not used for labeling other fields. It's used instead for displaying read-only data from a DataSet.

Tasks

You specify whether a TDBText control is aligned left-, center-, or right-justified using its Alignment property. Toggle whether it wraps text to the next line using the WordWrap property. Make sure that the control is either sized large enough to handle the largest value its underlying field might present, or that AutoSize is set to True. Neglecting to do this can result in the field being truncated while displayed. Note that the AutoSize and WordWrap settings are mutually-exclusive. Obviously, if a control auto-sizes to fit its data, it will never wordwrap.

If the control needs to appear on top of other controls without obscuring them, set its Transparent property to True.

TDBEdit

Unit: DBCtrls

Very similar to a standard TEdit control, a TDBEdit is a data-aware control for working with single lines of text. If you need to handle a database field that allows multiple lines of text, use the TDBMemo component instead.

Table 16.8 gives the key properties for TDBEdit. Table 16.9 gives the key methods, and Table 16.10 shows the key event.

Table 16.8. TDBEdit key properties.

Property	Description
CharChase	Causes input text to match a particular case
DataField	References the associated column in the linked DataSet
DataSource	Lists the TDataSource that supplies data to the control
EditText	References the control's text, including any mask characters
IsMasked	Indicates whether the associated TField has an edit mask
MaxLength	Determines the maximum number of characters
Modified	Returns whether the text has been modified
PasswordChar	Specifies the character to display for password fields
ReadOnly	Determines whether the field can be edited
SelLength	Indicates the number of characters of text that are highlighted
SelStart	Indicates the character offset of the first character in the high-lighted text block
SelText	Returns the text that has been highlighted
Text	References the control's text, minus any mask characters

Table 16.9. TDBEdit **key methods.**

Method	Function
Clear	Empties the contents of the control
ClearSelection	Deletes the currently selected text in the control
CopyToClipboard	Copies the currently selected text to the clipboard
CutToClipboard	Cuts the currently selected text to the clipboard
GetSelTextBuf	Copies the currently selected text to a buffer
PasteFromClipboard	Pastes the contents of the clipboard into the control
SelectAll	Selects the entirety of the control's contents
SetSelTextBuf	Replaces the selected text with text from a buffer
ValidateEdit	Checks for missing required characters in the field

Table 16.10. TDBEdit **key event.**

Event	Catalyst
OnChange	Occurs when the control's contents are modified (for instance, with each key that's typed into it)

Key Elements

Though you can use TDBEdit's ReadOnly property to prevent the editing of a field, the TDBText control is a better choice if you want to display text in a read-only fashion. If the control needs to be editable at times and read-only at others, TDBEdit is the better choice.

The TDBEdit component surfaces a number of useful properties. The Modified property reflects whether the control's contents have been edited. Modified is reset anytime anything is assigned to the control. For example, if you assign a value to a DBEdit's underlying field, you'll reset its Modified property to value. The PasswordChar property conceals the characters that are typed into it. The MaxLength property determines the maximum number of characters that can be typed into the control. The CharCase property causes the control to convert the characters typed into it to a particular case (upper, lower, or mixed). The AutoSize property determines whether the control resizes itself to accommodate font size changes.

The AutoSelect property causes the text in the TDBEdit to be automatically selected whenever it receives the form's input focus. You can programmatically select all the text in the control using the SelectAll method. To select only part of the text, use the SelStart and SelLength properties. Use the SelText property to determine what text in the control is selected. If you want to clear the selected text, use the ClearSelection method.

Selected text can be copied to the clipboard using the CopyToClipboard method. Cut it to the clipboard using the CutToClipboard method. You can paste from the clipboard using the PasteFromClipboard method. Of course, the normal Windows keys for cutting, copying, and pasting from the clipboard work with the control, as well.

A TDBEdit is editable if the CanModify property of the associated DataSet is set to True. (CanModify is a runtime and read-only property only. It looks at the value of the ReadOnly property and whether the DataSet is actually editable to determine whether it can be modified.)

TDBMemo

Unit: DBCtrls

Very similar to a standard TMemo control, a TDBMemo is a data-aware control for working with multiple lines of text. It's normally used for variable-length text fields like memo or BLOB fields. If you need to handle a database field that allows only a single line of text, use the TDBEdit component instead. Note that the DBEdit control doesn't support centering or right-justification of text, but DBMemo does. This enables you to use a DBMemo that's sized to a single line to emulate a DBEdit that supports these features. Note that TDBMemo is much more sensitive to control-Height/Font-size issues that DBEdit is. If you size a DBEdit control so that it's too short to display the text it contains, it will attempt to display clipped text. Not so with DBMemo—it only displays complete lines of text. This means that if you size a single-line DBMemo so that it's too small to display the text it contains, it won't display anything—the control will be blank.

Table 16.11 gives the key properties for TDBMemo. Table 16.12 shows its key methods, and Table 16.13 lists the key event.

Table 16.11. TDBMemo key properties.

Property	Description
Alignment	Controls whether text is left-, center-, or right-justified
AutoDisplay	Controls whether the underlying field is automatically displayed when the DataSet cursor moves
DataField	References the associated column in the linked DataSet
DataSource	Lists the TDataSource that supplies data to the control
Lines	Returns a TString list of the individual lines that make up the control's text
MaxLength	Specifies the maximum length of the control's text
Modified	Reflects whether the control's contents have been edited by the user
ReadOnly	Determines whether the control's contents can be modified

continues

Table 16.11. continued

Property	Description
ScrollBars	Determines what scrollbars, if any, the control sports
SelLength	Returns the length of the currently selected text
SelStart	Returns the start of the currently selected text
SelText	Returns the selected section of the control's text
Text	Refers to the entirety of the control's text
WantTabs	Determines whether tabs are processed by the control or allowed to change the input focus to another control
WordWrap	Controls whether text wraps at the right to the next line (WordWrap and horizontal scrollbars are mutually exclusive)

Table 16.12. TDBMemo key methods.

Method	Function
Clear	Clears the control's contents
GetSelTextBuf	Copies the currently selected text to a buffer
SelectAll	Selects the entirety of the control's contents
SetSelectTextBuf	Replaces the selected text with text from a buffer

Table 16.13. TDBMemo key event.

Event	Catalyst
OnChange	Occurs when the control's contents are changed (for instance, when text is typed, pasted, or when the current row changes)

Key Elements

The TDBMemo component surfaces a number of useful properties. The Lines property refers to the lines of text that make up the control's contents. To work with the control's lines as a continuous text stream, use the Text property. If you need individual line access, use the Lines property instead.

Establish scrollbars in the control using the ScrollBars property. If you want to break unformatted text into lines, set the WordWrap property to True. Note that WordWrap and horizontal scrollbars are mutually exclusive. If you have a horizontal scrollbar, you have not right margin, hence, no wordwrap.

If you want to allow tabs in the text, set the WantTabs property to True. WantTabs' default setting, False, allows Tab to change the input focus to the next control in the form's tab order.

You can control when the BLOB text appears in the memo with the AutoDisplay property. If AutoDisplay is True, the contents of a memo field are displayed when the row cursor moves in the underlying DataSet. Setting AutoDisplay to False will speed up your application since it won't have to deal with displaying your BLOB text.

The Modified property reflects whether the control's contents have been edited by the user. Note that Modified gets reset each time the current row changes. The MaxLength property determines the maximum number of characters that may be typed into the control. The Alignment property determines whether the control's text is left-, center-, or right-justified.

A TDBMemo is editable if the following conditions are met:

■ The DataSet is in dsEdit mode.

■ The CanModify property of the associated DataSet is set to True. (CanModify is a runtime and read-only property only. It looks at the value of the ReadOnly property and whether the DataSet is actually editable to determine whether it can be modified.)

Tasks

You can programmatically select all the text in the control using the SelectAll method. To select only part of the text, use the SelStart and SelLength properties. Use the SelText property to determine what text in the control is selected. If you want to clear the selected text, use the ClearSelection method.

Selected text can be copied to the clipboard using the CopyToClipboard method. Cut it to the clipboard using the CutToClipboard method. You can paste from the clipboard using the PasteFromClipboard method. Of course, the normal Windows keys for cutting, copying, and pasting from the clipboard work with the control, as well.

Because the Lines property is a TStrings object, you can use TString's Add, Insert, Delete, and Move methods to manipulate the lines in the control. You can also use TString's LoadFromFile and SaveToFile methods to load and save the control's contents.

TDBImage

Unit: DBCtrls

Similar to a TImage component, the TDBImage component is used to edit and display graphic images from a database column.

Table 16.14 gives the key properties for TDBImage. Table 16.15 lists the key methods. There are no key events for TDBImage.

Table 16.14. TDBImage key properties.

Property	Description
AutoDisplay	Controls whether the underlying field is automatically displayed when the current record changes
Center	Determines whether the image is aligned top-left or centered
DataField	References the associated column in the linked DataSet
DataSource	Lists the TDataSource that supplies data to the control
ReadOnly	Determines whether the control can be edited
Stretch	Controls whether the image size matches the control's size

Table 16.15. TDBImage key methods.

Method	Function
CopyToClipboard	Copies the control's contents to the clipboard
CutToClipboard	Cuts the control's contents to the clipboard
LoadPicture	Loads the control's image from its underlying table
PasteFromClipboard	Pastes the contents of the clipboard into the control

Key Elements

As with TDBMemo, use the AutoDisplay property to control when the component's image is displayed. If AutoDisplay is True, the component automatically displays the contents of the underlying BLOB field each time the record focus changes. If it's False, you'll have to call LoadPicture to load the image. Setting AutoDisplay to False can speed navigation through a DataSet since the control doesn't have to stop and display a potentially huge bitmap with every record focus change.

Tasks

Set the Stretch property to True if you want the control's image to always match the size of the control.

If you turn AutoDisplay off, use the LoadPicture method to load the image from the database at runtime.

Like other controls, you can copy an image to the clipboard using the CopyToClipboard method. Cut it using the CutToClipboard method. You can paste the clipboard's contents using the PasteFromClipboard method. Of course, the standard Windows keys for cutting, copying, and pasting (Shift+Del, Ctrl+Insert, and Shift+Insert) work as well.

TDBListBox

Unit: DBCtrls

Like the standard TListBox control, the TDBListBox component is a data-aware control for selecting from a list of items. The value of a column in the current row of a DataSet can be changed by selecting from a list. The item selected becomes the column's new value.

Table 16.16 gives the key properties for TDBListBox. There are no key methods or key events.

Table 16.16. TDBListBox key properties.

Property	Description
DataField	References the associated column in the linked DataSet
DataSource	Lists the TDataSource that supplies data to the control
ItemIndex	Returns the zero-based index of the current item
Items	Returns a list of the items in the control
ReadOnly	Determines whether the control can be modified
SelCount	Reflects the number of selected items
Selected	(Indexed) reflects whether a given item is selected
Sorted	Determines whether the control's items are sorted
Style	Controls the type of listbox control used
TopIndex	Returns the index of the top item in the listbox

Key Elements

The items that the user can select from are specified using the Items property. Likewise, the value displayed in the listbox is the value from the Items list that matches with the table's value. You can add, insert, and delete the listbox's items with the Add, Insert, and Delete methods of the Items object. The currently selected item in the Items property is indicated by its ItemIndex property. Note that, even though DBListBox is a data-aware control, you must manually add items to it—they are not automatically retrieved from the database, even when the associated DataField is a Lookup field.

To prevent the user from changing the underlying field by selecting an item in the listbox, set TDBListBox's ReadOnly property to True.

TDBComboBox

Unit: DBCtrls

Like the standard TComboBox control, the TDBComboBox component is a data-aware combobox control for selecting from a list of items. Like the standard control, the TDBComboBox is basically a combination of the TEdit and TListBox controls. The value of a column in the current row of a DataSet can be changed by selecting from a list or typing in the edit box. The item keyed or selected becomes the column's new value.

Table 16.17 gives the key properties for TDBComboBox, and Table 16.18 lists the key methods. There are no key events.

Table 16.17. TDBComboBox key properties.

Property	Description
DataField	References the associated column in the linked DataSet
DataSource	Lists the TDataSource that supplies data to the control
DropDownCount	Determines the length of the listbox part of the control
ItemIndex	Returns the zero-based index of the current item
Items	Returns a list of the items in the control
ReadOnly	Determines whether the control can be modified
SelCount	Reflects the number of selected items
Selected	(Indexed) reflects whether a given item is selected
Sorted	Determines whether the control's items are sorted
Style	Controls the type of combobox control used

Table 16.18. TDBComboBox key methods.

Method	Function
Clear	Empties the contents of the control
CopyToClipboard	Copies the currently selected text to the clipboard
CutToClipboard	Cuts the currently selected text to the clipboard
PasteFromClipboard	Pastes the contents of the clipboard into the control
SelectAll	Selects the entirety of the control's contents

Key Elements

The items that the user can select from are specified using the Items property. A value that is not in the list may also be typed into the edit box part of the control. You can add, insert, and delete the listbox's items with the Add, Insert, and Delete methods of the Items object. The currently selected item in the Items property is indicated by its ItemIndex property. Note that, despite the fact that DBComboBox is a data-aware control, you must manually add its items—they are not retrieved from the database, even when the associated DataField is a Lookup field.

The Style property controls the runtime appearance of the TDBComboBox component. This property can have the following values:

- csDropDown (default)—A drop-down list of items with an edit box at the top is displayed. Items are strings and all have the same height.

- csSimple—A list of items with an edit box at the top is displayed at all times, rather than as a drop-down list. Items are strings and all have the same height.

- csDropDownList—A drop-down list of items with an edit box at the top is displayed. Items keyed into the edit box must exist in the list. Items are strings and all have the same height.

- csOwnerDrawFixed—Allows items other than strings to be displayed (for example, bitmaps). The height of each item in the list is set according to the ItemHeight property.

- csOwnerDrawVariable—Allows items other than strings to be displayed (for example, bitmaps). Items in the list can also have varying heights.

The maximum number of items displayed at one time in the control's drop-down listbox is determined by the DropDownCount property. When the number of items in the drop-down box exceeds DropDownCount, the list is scrollable. When the number is less than the number specified by DropDownCount, the listbox shrinks to match the list.

Set the Sorted property to True to sort the items in the TDBComboBox alphabetically.

TDBCheckBox

Unit: DBCtrls

Similar to the standard TCheckBox control, the data-aware TDBCheckBox control allows a True/False-type column value to be specified by simply checking or unchecking a checkbox on a form. Likewise, the database field's current value is reflected in the checked state of the TDBCheckBox control.

If the value of a column in the current row of the associated DataSet equals the value of the ValueChecked property, the TDBCheckBox is checked. If the contents match the value of the ValueUnchecked property, the TDBCheckBox is unchecked.

Along these same lines, when the checkbox is checked by a user, the value in the ValueChecked property gets stored in the associated DataSet column. Likewise, when the control is unchecked, the value in the ValueUnchecked property gets stored there. By default, ValueChecked and ValueUnchecked are set to True and False, but you can specify any alphanumeric value for them. You can also specify a semicolon-delimited list of items for each property. For example, you might specify Yes;True;Y for ValueChecked or No;False;F for ValueUnchecked. Comparison with these values is case-insensitive. If you specify more than one value for either property, the first value in the list is the one stored to the database.

Table 16.19 gives the key properties for TDBCheckBox. There are no key methods. Table 16.20 lists the key event.

Table 16.19. TDBCheckBox **key properties.**

Property	Description
Alignment	Controls the alignment of the control's caption
AllowGrayed	Controls whether the control has two or three possible states (checked, unchecked, and indeterminate)
Checked	Returns whether the checkbox is checked or unchecked
DataField	References the associated column in the linked DataSet
DataSource	Lists the TDataSource that supplies data to the control
State	Returns the state (checked, unchecked, or grayed) of the control
ValueChecked	Specifies checked value to use
ValueUnchecked	Specifies unchecked value to use

Table 16.20. TDBCheckBox **key event.**

Event	Catalyst
OnClick	Occurs when the control is "clicked" with the mouse or keyboard

Key Elements

Set the control's Caption property to display a label for the checkbox. To control the alignment of the checkbox with respect to its Caption, use the Alignment property. To allow the TDBCheckBox to be grayed (thereby allowing three possible states for the control: checked, unchecked, and indeterminate), set the AllowGrayed property to True. When a checkbox is grayed, it is neither checked nor unchecked—it is in a third, indeterminate, state.

TDBRadioGroup

Unit: DBCtrls

The TDBRadioGroup component is used to display a set of mutually exclusive choices. Because the control is a data-aware control, the choice made is stored in a DataSet field. Likewise, the value in the associated DataSet field governs which radio button is selected by default.

Table 16.21 gives the key properties for TDBRadioGroup. There are no key methods. Table 16.22 lists the key events.

Table 16.21. TDBRadioGroup key properties.

Property	Description
DataField	References the associated column in the linked DataSet
DataSource	Lists the TDataSource that supplies data to the control
ItemIndex	Returns the zero-based index of the current item
Items	Returns the list of items
ReadOnly	Determines whether the control can be modified
Value	Reflects the value of the underlying DataSet's associated column
Values	Specifies alternate values (other than Items) to use

Table 16.22. TDBRadioGroup key events.

Event	Catalyst
OnChange	Occurs when the control's contents are changed
OnClick	Occurs when the control is "clicked" with the mouse or keyboard

Key Elements

Add radio buttons to the TDBGroupBox using the Items property. The strings you enter in the Items property become the text for the control's radio buttons if the Values property is empty.

If you want values other than the captions displayed on-screen to be stored in your database, use the Values property to specify a corresponding value for each radio button.

Note that radio buttons can be displayed in multiple columns using the TDBRadioGroup's Columns property.

TDBLookupListBox

Unit: DBCtrls

A TDBLookupListBox component is a data-aware listbox whose list of allowable items comes from a second DataSet. The chief difference between a TDBLookupListBox and a TDBListBox is that the TDBListBox control uses a predefined list of allowable items. You set this list up with its Items property. TDBLookupListBox, on the other hand, gets its list from a second table.

Table 16.23 gives the key properties for TDBLookupListBox. There are no key methods or key events.

Table 16.23. TDBLookupListBox key properties.

Property	Description
DataField	References the associated column in the linked DataSet
DataSource	Lists the TDataSource that supplies data to the control
ListField	Specifies the field to display in the listbox
ListSource	Lists the TDataSource that supplies data for the lookup
KeyField	Specifies the column that's used to perform the lookup in ListSource's DataSet
ReadOnly	Controls whether the component's contents can be changed

Key Elements

Set the TDataSource from which to get the list's items using the ListSource property. Set the field to look up using the KeyField property. Specify the column to display from the lookup DataSet using the ListField property. Note that none of this applies if your DataField is already defined as a Lookup field. That is, you won't need to set any of these properties if the DataField you specify refers to a Lookup field in its associated DataSource. A Lookup field defines these properties for you. If you attempt to set them anyway, Delphi will complain that they're already defined in the DataField.

TDBLookupComboBox

Unit: DBCtrls

A TDBLookupComboBox component is a data-aware combobox whose list of allowable items comes from a second DataSet. The chief difference between a TDBLookupComboBox and a TDBComboBox is that the TDBComboBox component uses a predefined list of items. You can add or delete items in this via its Items property. TDBLookupComboBox, on the other hand, gets its list from a second table.

Table 16.24 gives the key properties for TDBLookupComboBox. Table 16.25 lists the key methods, and Table 16.26 shows the key event.

Table 16.24. TDBLookupComboBox key properties.

Property	Description
DataField	References the associated column in the linked DataSet
DataSource	Lists the TDataSource that supplies data to the control
DropDownAlign	Determines whether the text in the drop-down list will be left-aligned, centered, or right-justified
DrowDownRows	Specifies how long the drop-down box is
DropDownWidth	Specifies the width of the drop-down list (default is 0 which means that it matches the control's width)
ListField	Specifies the field to display in the listbox
ListSource	Lists the TDataSource that supplies data for the lookup
KeyField	Specifies the column that's used to perform the lookup in ListSource's DataSet
ReadOnly	Controls whether the component's contents can be changed

Table 16.25. TDBLookupComboBox key methods.

Method	Function
CloseUp	Causes an open drop-down list to close
DropDown	Causes the listbox portion of the control to drop down

Table 16.26. TDBLookupComboBox key event.

Event	Catalyst
OnDropDown	Occurs when the listbox portion of the control is displayed

Key Elements

The ListSource property specifies the TDataSource that the list's items are to come from. The KeyField property specifies the field to look up in the second DataSet. The ListField property sets the column to display from the lookup DataSet. If you leave ListField blank, KeyField is listed instead. Note that you won't need to set any of these properties if the DataField you specify refers to a Lookup field in its associated DataSource. Lookup fields already define all of this information.

TDBCtrlGrid

Unit: DBCGrids

The TDBCtrlGrid component is a database grid control that allows multiple rows from a table to be displayed simultaneously. Each individual table row can occupy multiple screen rows. This is in contrast to the DBGrid control, which limits records to one screen row each. TDBCtrlGrid provides a panel surface that you can drop controls onto. This panel is then replicated at runtime for each row displayed. The TDBCtrlGrid component is comparable to Paradox's Multi-Record Object and PowerBuilder's DataWindow. For you System/38 and AS/400 programmers out there, TDBCtrlGrid has capabilities similar to a subfile.

Not all controls can be placed onto a TDBCtrlGrid. Some controls, such as DBMemo and DBImage, exact enough of a performance penalty that you would normally want to avoid using them in a grid-type control. By definition, a component's ControlStyle property must include the csReplicatable style in order to be eligible for placement on a TDBCtrlGrid. The csReplicatable style indicates that a component can be replicated for each row displayed by a TDBCtrlGrid. The csReplicatable requirement automatically precludes the use of any control except a data-aware control. Within the data-aware controls, some components are replicatable and some aren't. Table 16.27 lists Delphi's data-aware components and whether they're replicatable on a TDBCtrlGrid.

Table 16.27. Data-aware controls and their replicatable status.

Control	Replicatable
DBGrid	No
DBNavigator	No
DBText	Yes
DBEdit	Yes
DBMemo	No
DBImage	No
DBListBox	No

Control	Replicatable
DBComboBox	Yes
DBCheckBox	Yes
DBRadioGroup	No
DBLookupListBox	No
DBLookupComboBox	Yes
DBCtrlGrid	No

Note that even though a data control is initially non-replicatable, you can override this default by subclassing the control in a new component and adding csReplicatable to its ControlStyle.

To make a control replicatable usually requires additional work in the paint routine of the control, too. TDBMemo and TDBImage happen to already contain all the code needed for replication, but have replication turned off for performance reasons.

Table 16.28 lists the key properties and Table 16.29 lists the key method for the TDBCtrlGrid component. There are no key events.

Table 16.28. TDBCtrlGrid key properties.

Property	Description
AllowDelete	Controls whether a user can delete a table row by pressing Ctrl+Delete
AllowInsert	Controls whether a user can append or insert a new table row by pressing Ctrl+Insert or Insert, respectively
ColCount	Determines the number of columns the control uses to display panels
DataSource	Lists the TDataSource that supplies data to the control
RowCount	Determines the number of rows the control uses to display panels
Orientation	Specifies whether the component arranges its panels vertically or horizontally
PanelHeight	Configures the height of the replication panel
PanelWidth	Configures the width of the replication panel

Table 16.29. TDBCtrlGrid key method.

Method	Function
DoKey	Simulates the pressing of a specified key within the control

Key Elements

You'll typically use the RowCount and PanelHeight properties to get your TDBCtrlGrid components set up properly. Unlike the height of the control itself, you can't resize TDBCtrlGrid's replication panel using the keyboard or mouse—you'll have to do it via properties.

Though a TDBCtrlGrid is oriented vertically by default, you can change that if you wish. To switch a TDBCtrlGrid to horizontal orientation, set its Orientation property to goHorizontal. Once a TDBCtrlGrid is horizontally oriented, you use its ColCount and PanelWidth properties to control how rows are displayed by the component.

Tasks

You can call the DoKey method to simulate a keypress within the TDBCtrlGrid control. DoKey takes a single parameter of type TDBCtrlGridKey. Table 16.30 summarizes the values it may have:

Table 16.30. Possible DoKey parameter values and their meanings.

Key	Action	Equivalent key
gkNull	Nothing	
gkEditMode	Toggles EditMode	F2
gkPriorTab	Switches focus to the previous control	Shift+Tab
gkNextTab	Switches focus to the next control	Tab
gkLeft	Moves a column to the left	Left arrow
gkRight	Moves a column to the right	Right arrow
gkUp	Moves up to the previous row	Up arrow
gkDown	Moves down to the next row	Down arrow
gkScrollUp	Makes the previous record the current row	(none)
gkScrollDown	Makes the next record the current row	(none)
gkPageUp	Pages up in the grid	PgUp
gkPageDown	Pages down in the grid	PgDn
gkHome	Moves to the first record	Ctrl+Home
gkEnd	Moves to the last record	Ctrl+End
gkInsert	Inserts a new row (AllowInsert = True)	Insert
gkAppend	Appends a new row (AllowInsert = True)	Ctrl+Insert
gkDelete	Deletes the current row (AllowDelete = True)	Ctrl+Delete
gkCancel	Cancels any pending row modifications	Esc

What's Ahead

Chapter 17, "InterBase," takes you on a guided tour of Borland's client/server DBMS. You'll learn to create databases, build tables and add data to them, and create complex objects like stored procedures and triggers. If you plan to develop database applications for the InterBase platform, you will find this chapter informative.

Summary

As you can see, the data-aware components supplied with Delphi are rich and varied. They provide interface elements and features right out of the box that would have taken months to write just a few years ago.

The interaction between the data components is logical and well-thought out, and the controls themselves are easy to use. Using Delphi's data controls, you can build polished database applications with a fraction of the effort required by other tools.

Hopefully, Chapters 15 and 16 have provided you with essential reference information for building full-featured database applications. And, if you someday find yourself trying to remember some obscure database component detail, you know where to look first.

17

InterBase

The purpose of this chapter is to give you a guided tour through the major parts of Borland's InterBase Client/Server DBMS. The Local InterBase (LIB) Server, a single-user local version of the InterBase DBMS, is included with the client/server edition of Delphi. This chapter uses the included Windows Interactive SQL (WISQL) utility to take you through the major features of InterBase using the LIB Server.

Because the LIBS is used extensively throughout the rest of this book, you may find this chapter a bit redundant. In particular, if you've read Chapter 5, "A No-Nonsense Approach to SQL," and Chapter 22, "Advanced SQL," you can probably safely skip this chapter. The idea here is to bring together in one place all the relevant pieces throughout the book regarding InterBase. If you've already covered those component pieces, this chapter may be old hat for you.

What I've set out to do here is to take you from A to Z, through all the issues of working with InterBase. Everything from building databases to writing stored procedures is covered in this chapter. I've expressly avoided any discussion on database administration topics (such as backing up and restoring databases) in this chapter for a couple of reasons: The focus of this book is on database application development, and information regarding database administration is readily available in your InterBase documentation.

Now that the tour guidelines are nailed down, it's time to begin.

Creating a Database

You may already have a database in which you can create some temporary tables for the purpose of working through the examples in this chapter. If you don't, creating one is easy enough. In SQL, you create databases by using the SQL CREATE DATABASE command. The exact syntax varies from vendor to vendor, but here's the InterBase syntax:

```
CREATE DATABASE 'C:\DATA\IB\ORDENT' USER USERNAME  PASSWORD password
```

Because InterBase's WISQL utility can't prepare the CREATE DATABASE command for execution, you use the Create Database option from its File menu instead. Following are the steps for doing that:

1. Start the Interactive SQL tool (WISQL) from either your Delphi group or from the Task menu of the InterBase Server Manager.

2. Select the Create Database option from the File menu.

3. Type C:\DATA\IB\ORDENT into the Database field of the Create Database dialog, replacing C:\DATA\IB with a valid path. Of course, you may wish to create a special directory in advance in which to store your databases.

4. Click the OK button. InterBase should create the database and connect you to it. In the future, you'll use the Connect to Database option from the File menu to connect to the database without creating it first.

Extending a Database

As your data capacity needs change, you'll probably want to expand databases created in the past. Use the ALTER DATABASE command to increase the allocated size of an existing database. Here's the InterBase syntax:

```
ALTER DATABASE
ADD  FILE 'C:\DATA\IB\ORDENT2.GDB'
```

The *CONNECT* Command

On most server platforms, the CONNECT command is used to change the database context—to connect to and use a specific database. The InterBase syntax is

```
CONNECT "C:\DATA\IB\ORDENT.GDB" USER "SYSDBA" PASSWORD "masterkey";
```

Use the DISCONNECT command to reverse a CONNECT command, as in the following:

```
DISCONNECT  ALL;
```

You can replace ALL with the word DEFAULT to accomplish the same thing. In WISQL, you use the Connect to Database and Disconnect from Database File menu options to connect to and disconnect from databases.

Transaction Isolation Levels

Transaction Isolation Levels (TILs) affect your ability to see changes made by other users to data you're working with and their ability to see changes you've made to it. Use just one TIL througout an entire application.

InterBase supports three Transaction Isolation Levels (TIL). The three supported TILs are SNAPSHOT, SNAPSHOT TABLE STABILITY, and READ COMMITTED. You set the TIL you wish to use via the SET TRANSACTION command. Here's a summary of what each TIL setting means:

■ SNAPSHOT—For the duration of the transaction, the database appears just as it did when the transaction started. Changes made by other transactions aren't visible while the transaction is active.

■ SNAPSHOT TABLE STABILITY—Allows other transactions read-only access to the tables that the transaction is accesses.

■ READ COMMITTED—The most recently committed version of a record is located during updates and deletions; the transaction can make changes if there are no update conflicts with other transactions.

Creating Tables

After a database has been established, you're ready to begin building database objects. Virtually any relational database concept can be demonstrated with a maximum of three tables. For the purpose of working through this chapter, begin by creating the following three tables. Tables are created by using the SQL CREATE TABLE statement. Enter the following syntax in WISQL:

```
CREATE TABLE CUSTOMER
(
CustomerNumber            int                 NOT NULL,
LastName                  char(30)
FirstName                 char(30)
StreetAddress             char(30)
City                      char(20)
State                     char(2)
Zip                       char(10)
)
```

This builds the CUSTOMER table. Next, build the ORDERS table by using a similar syntax:

```
CREATE TABLE ORDERS
(
OrderNumber               int                 NOT NULL,
OrderDate                 date
CustomerNumber            int                 NOT NULL,
ItemNumber                int                 NOT NULL,
Amount                    float
)
```

Now that the ORDERS table is built, only one table remains. Create the ITEMS table by using the following syntax:

```
CREATE TABLE ITEMS
(
ItemNumber                int                 NOT NULL,
Description               char(30)
Price                     float
)
```

Adding and Dropping Table Columns

You use the SQL ALTER TABLE command to add and drop columns from an existing table. Not all servers support dropping columns after the fact (Sybase SQL Server doesn't, for example), but InterBase does. Use the following syntax to add a column:

```
ALTER TABLE CUSTOMER
ADD PhoneNumber char(10)
```

Use the following syntax to drop it:

```
ALTER TABLE CUSTOMER
DROP PhoneNumber
```

Note that you can't add a NOT NULL column to a table that already has rows because it would necessarily have to allow NULLs immediately after being added to the table.

Constraints

A *constraint* is the mechanism by which you limit, or constrain, the type of data a column may store. A constraint can also be used to define a default value for a column. Constraints can be defined when a table is first created by using the CREATE TABLE command, or afterward by using the ALTER TABLE command. Here's an example of a primary key constraint:

```
ALTER TABLE CUSTOMER
ADD CONSTRAINT PRIMARY KEY (CustomerNumber)
```

This syntax adds a primary key constraint to the CUSTOMER table, defining its CustomerNumber field as the table's primary key. This causes a unique index to be created over the table using the CustomerNumber column as the key. Note that you cannot define a column that accepts NULL values as a table's primary key.

A foreign key constraint defines a column in one table whose values must exist in a second, or foreign, table. A foreign key doesn't identify its host table's records uniquely as does a primary key. On the contrary, it exists as a primary or unique key in the second, or referenced, table. Adding a foreign key constraint causes InterBase to automatically build a secondary index over its key columns. The following is an example of the syntax:

```
ALTER TABLE ORDERS
ADD FOREIGN KEY (CustomerNumber) REFERENCES CUSTOMER
```

This constraint defines the CustomerNumber field in the ORDERS table as a foreign key that references the same column in the CUSTOMER table. This means that customer numbers entered into the ORDERS table must first exist in the CUSTOMER table. It also means that customer numbers that are being used in the ORDERS table cannot be deleted from the CUSTOMER table. This capability to enforce the relationship between the two tables simply by defining it is called *declarative referential integrity.* The term simply means that the integrity of the relationship between the tables is ensured by simply defining (or declaring) it, not by the program code you write.

A third type of constraint is one that checks a column against a list of predefined values. Here's an example of such a constraint:

```
ALTER TABLE CUSTOMER
ADD CONSTRAINT INVALID_STATE CHECK (State in ('OK','AR','MO'))
```

Note the negative naming convention used for the constraint. This is done so that front-end tools that report the constraint name will give a somewhat meaningful message to the user. If the message were to read VALID_STATE, the user might wonder what the problem is. By using a simple message as the name of the constraint, you allow for the possibility that the message might actually give the user a hint as to what the problem is. This might save you the effort of having to replace the Delphi exception generated due to the constraint with your own.

Testing Constraints

You should test every constraint that you place on a database. You do this by attempting to add values to the database that the constraint is supposed to disallow. For example, to test the preceding INVALID_STATE constraint, enter this command in WISQL:

```
INSERT INTO CUSTOMER (CustomerNumber, State)
VALUES (123,'CA')
```

Because the constraint limits States entered to 'OK', 'AR', and 'MO', it should reject your attempted row insertion with a –297 error: Operation violates CHECK constraint INVALID_STATE on view or table CUSTOMER.

If a constraint you've defined fails to function as expected, check it to ensure that you successfully added it in the first place and that it's checking the data in the way you intended.

Creating Indexes

You create indexes in SQL by using the CREATE INDEX command. Following is the basic syntax:

```
CREATE INDEX ORDERS02 ON ORDERS (CustomerNumber)
```

where ORDERS02 is the name of the new index, ORDERS is the name of the table on which to build the index, and CustomerNumber is the index key. Note that in InterBase, index names must be unique across the database in which they reside.

You can create an index that prohibits duplicates by using the CREATE UNIQUE INDEX variation of the command, as in the following:

```
CREATE UNIQUE INDEX ORDERS01 ON ORDERS (OrderNumber)
```

Index keys, by default, are arranged in ascending order. InterBase also supports the capability to create descending indexes by using the DESCENDING keyword. For example,

```
CREATE DESCENDING INDEX ORDERS03 ON ORDERS (Amount)
```

helps queries like

```
SELECT * FROM ORDERS
ORDER BY Amount DESCENDING
```

execute more quickly. This is similar to the usage of the DESC() function found in many Xbase dialects.

Activating and Deactivating an Index

InterBase supports a useful mechanism for deactivating an index, then reactivating and rebuilding it later. This capability allows for quick addition of a large number of rows without incurring the penalty of index maintenance with each new row. Here's the syntax:

```
ALTER INDEX CUSTOMER03 INACTIVE
```

To reactivate it, use the following:

```
ALTER INDEX CUSTOMER03 ACTIVE
```

Deactivating and then reactivating an index causes it to be rebuilt. Note that the deactivation of an index is delayed until it's no longer in use—this includes use by a primary or foreign key constraint.

Inserting Data

The SQL INSERT statement is used to add data to a table. You can add data one row at a time using INSERT's VALUES clause, or you can insert several rows at once by selecting them from another table. Use the following syntax to add data to each of the three tables. First, add three rows to the CUSTOMER table by executing the following syntax in WISQL:

```
INSERT INTO CUSTOMER (CustomerNumber, LastName, FirstName, StreetAddress, City,
State, Zip)
VALUES(1,'Doe','John','123 Sunnylane','Anywhere','OK','73115')

INSERT INTO CUSTOMER (CustomerNumber, LastName, FirstName, StreetAddress, City,
State, Zip)
VALUES(2,'Doe','Jane','123 Sunnylane','Anywhere','OK','73115')

INSERT INTO CUSTOMER (CustomerNumber, LastName, FirstName, StreetAddress, City,
State, Zip)
VALUES(3,'Citizen','John','57 Riverside','Reo','AR','65803')
```

Now, add three rows to the ITEMS table with this syntax:

```
INSERT INTO ITEMS (ItemNumber, Description, Price)
VALUES(1001,'WIDGET A',123.45)

INSERT INTO ITEMS (ItemNumber, Description, Price)
VALUES(1002,'WIDGET B',678.90)

INSERT INTO ITEMS (ItemNumber, Description, Price)
VALUES(1003,'WIDGET C',86753.09)
```

Finally, add four to the ORDERS table by using this syntax:

```
INSERT INTO ORDERS (OrderNumber, OrderDate, CustomerNumber, ItemNumber, Amount)
VALUES(101,'07/07/95',1,1001,123.45)
```

```
INSERT INTO ORDERS (OrderNumber, OrderDate, CustomerNumber, ItemNumber, Amount)
VALUES(102,'07/08/95',2,1002,678.90)

INSERT INTO ORDERS (OrderNumber, OrderDate, CustomerNumber, ItemNumber, Amount)
VALUES(103,'07/09/95',3,1003,86753.09)

INSERT INTO ORDERS (OrderNumber, OrderDate, CustomerNumber, ItemNumber, Amount)
VALUES(104,'07/10/95',1,1002,678.90)
```

Note that you don't have to include all the columns or follow the order in which they appear in the table when you specify a column list, *but the list of values you specify must match the content and order of the column list.* Here's an example:

```
INSERT INTO ITEMS (Price, ItemNumber)
VALUES(123.45, 1001)
```

The *UPDATE* Command

Without a doubt, you'll eventually want to change the data you've loaded into a table. You use the SQL UPDATE command to do this. It works much like the dBASE REPLACE ALL command. Here's the syntax:

```
UPDATE CUSTOMER
SET Zip='90120' WHERE City='Beverly Hills'
```

Though the WHERE clause in the preceding query might cause it to change only a single row, depending on the data, you can update all the rows in the table by omitting the WHERE clause:

```
UPDATE CUSTOMER
SET State='CA'
```

You can also update a column using other columns in its host table. You can even use the column itself, as in:

```
UPDATE ORDERS
SET Amount=Amount+(Amount*.07)
```

The *DELETE* Command

You use the DELETE command to delete rows from tables. To delete all the rows in a table, use this syntax:

```
DELETE FROM CUSTOMER
```

The DELETE command can also include a WHERE clause to limit the rows deleted. Here's an example:

```
DELETE FROM CUSTOMER
WHERE LastName<>'Doe'
```

COMMIT and ROLLBACK

A group of changes to a database is formally known as a *transaction*. The SQL COMMIT command makes these transactions permanent; think of it as a database save command. ROLLBACK, on the other hand, throws away the changes a transaction might make to the database; it functions like a database undo command. Both of these commands affect only the changes made since the last COMMIT; you cannot ROLLBACK changes you've just committed.

InterBase's WISQL utility begins a transaction automatically (by issuing the equivalent of the InterBase SET TRANSACTION command) when it first loads. When you exit the utility, it asks whether you'd like to commit your work. You can commit or rollback your work at any time by using the Commit Work and Rollback Work options on WISQL's File menu.

NOTE

Note that, in addition to normal data modifications, transactions control Data Definition Language (DDL) statements, too. DDL statements define and create database objects such as tables and indexes. If you create a database object from within a transaction, then roll the transaction back, the object is removed. The change is immediately visible across the database and supersedes any TIL you may have in place.

The SELECT Command

You can quickly check the contents of each table by using the SQL SELECT command. Issue a SELECT * FROM *tablename*, replacing *tablename* with the name of the table you wish to check (such as CUSTOMER, ORDERS, or ITEMS). At this point, each table should have three rows in it. Figures 17.1, 17.2, and 17.3 show what the tables should look like at this point.

FIGURE 17.1.

The CUSTOMER table as it appears when SELECT * is issued in the WISQL utility.

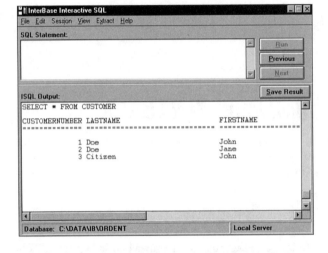

FIGURE 17.2.

The ORDERS table as it appears when SELECT * is issued in the WISQL utility.

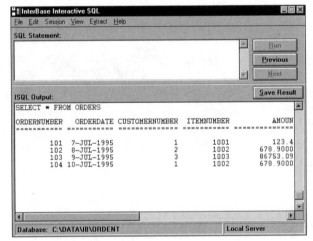

FIGURE 17.3.

*The ITEMS table as it appears when SELECT * is issued in the WISQL utility.*

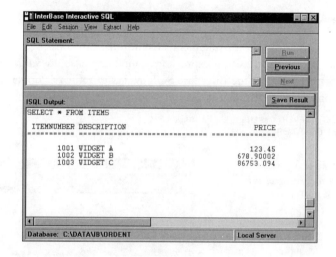

The SELECT * syntax causes all the columns of all the rows in the table to be returned. You could change it to use a comma-delimited field list, instead, as in

```
SELECT CustomerNumber, LastName, State FROM CUSTOMER
```

to qualify what fields you'd like to see. Figure 17.4 lists the output from this query.

FIGURE 17.4.

A SELECT that uses a field list.

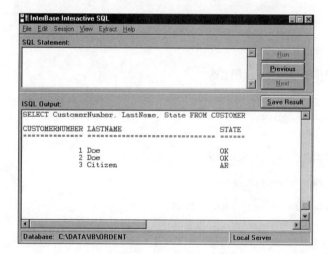

Expression Columns

A column in the SELECT statement's column list can consist of more than just a column in a table. It can also consist of expressions containing absolute values and functions. (See Figure 17.5.) Following is the InterBase SQL syntax to return as uppercased the last name of each customer in the customer table:

```
SELECT UPPER(LastName), FirstName
FROM CUSTOMER
```

FIGURE 17.5.

Using the UPPER function in a SELECT statement.

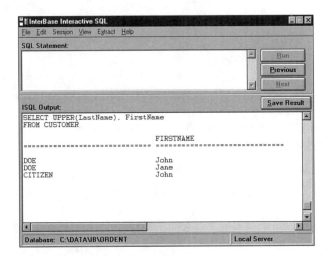

Aggregate Columns

Aggregate columns are actually functions that perform some calculation on a set of data. Examples of aggregates are the COUNT, SUM, AVG, MIN, and MAX functions. Here are some examples of their use:

```
SELECT COUNT(*) FROM CUSTOMER
```

tells how many customers are on file.

```
SELECT MAX(Amount) FROM ORDERS
```

reports the dollar amount of the largest order on file.

```
SELECT SUM(Amount) FROM ORDERS
```

returns the total dollar amount of all orders on file.

The *WHERE* Clause

The SQL WHERE clause is used to qualify the data returned by a SELECT statement. Here are some examples:

```
SELECT * FROM CUSTOMER
WHERE State='OK'
```

returns only those customers that reside in Oklahoma. (See Figure 17.6.)

FIGURE 17.6.

Using a WHERE clause in a
SELECT statement.

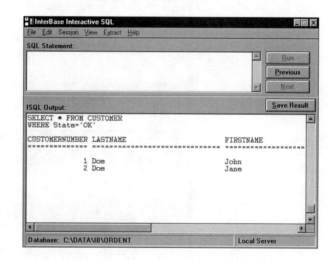

```
SELECT * FROM CUSTOMER
WHERE StreetAddress LIKE '%Sunny%'
```

returns only those customers whose street address contains the word Sunny anywhere in the field. Note that the comparison is case-sensitive. If you want a case-insensitive search, use the UPPER function to uppercase the column and the value you're searching for. Figure 17.7 shows the use of the WHERE clause.

```
SELECT * FROM ORDERS
WHERE Amount > 500
```

returns only the orders exceeding $500, as Figure 17.8 illustrates.

```
SELECT * FROM ORDERS
WHERE OrderDate BETWEEN '07/08/95' AND '07/09/95'
```

returns only those orders occurring between July 8 and July 9, 1995, inclusively. Figure 17.9 shows another use of a WHERE clause with BETWEEN.

FIGURE 17.7.

Using a WHERE clause with LIKE in a SELECT statement.

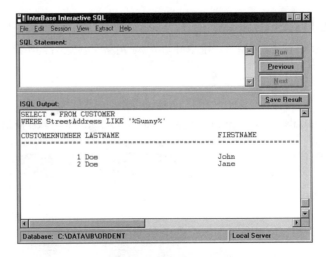

FIGURE 17.8.

Orders exceeding $500.

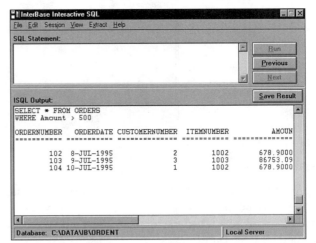

Joins

The WHERE clause is also used in joining one table with another to create a combined result set. Joining one table with another by using the WHERE clause consists of two changes to the basic SELECT statement syntax: You specify additional tables in the SELECT's FROM clause, and you link related fields in the tables using equality conditions in the WHERE clause. (See Figure 17.10.) Here's an example:

```
SELECT CUSTOMER.CustomerNumber, ORDERS.Amount
FROM CUSTOMER, ORDERS
WHERE CUSTOMER.CustomerNumber=ORDERS.CustomerNumber
```

FIGURE 17.9.

Using the WHERE clause with BETWEEN.

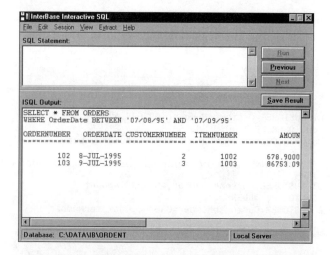

FIGURE 17.10.

The CUSTOMER table joined with the ORDERS table.

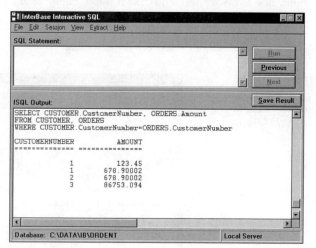

Notice the inclusion of the ORDERS table in the FROM clause. Also notice the use of the equal sign to join the CUSTOMER and ORDERS tables using their CustomerNumber fields. The table on the left of the equal sign is said to be the *outer* table; the table on the right is the *inner* table. They're also commonly referred to as the *left* and *right* tables, respectively, indicating their positions in a *left-to-right* or *left* join—the most popular type of join used in relational database management systems.

Inner Joins Versus Outer Joins

The type of *left* join mentioned in the preceding section is formally known as an *inner* join. An inner join returns only rows if the join condition is met. This is in contrast to an outer join, which returns rows regardless of whether the join condition is met. When the join condition is not met for a given row in an outer join, fields from the inner table are returned as NULL.

ANSI Join Syntax

The ANSI syntax for a left *inner* join looks like this:

```
SELECT CUSTOMER.CustomerNumber, ORDERS.Amount
FROM CUSTOMER LEFT JOIN ORDERS
ON CUSTOMER.CustomerNumber=ORDERS.CustomerNumber
```

Note that the INNER keyword is implicit. InterBase also supports the syntax

```
SELECT CUSTOMER.CustomerNumber, ORDERS.Amount
FROM CUSTOMER, ORDERS
WHERE CUSTOMER.CustomerNumber=ORDERS.CustomerNumber
```

to define left inner joins.

The syntax for a left *outer* join looks like this (see Figure 17.11):

```
SELECT CUSTOMER.CustomerNumber, ORDERS.Amount
FROM CUSTOMER LEFT OUTER JOIN ORDERS
ON CUSTOMER.CustomerNumber=ORDERS.CustomerNumber
```

FIGURE 17.11.

The CUSTOMER and ORDERS tables joined by using an ANSI-SQL outer join.

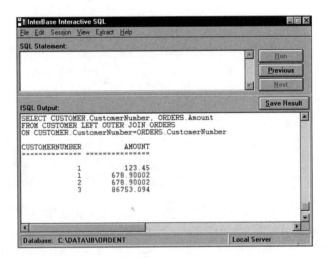

For right outer joins, you simply replace LEFT with RIGHT. Note that a right inner join and left inner join are actually the same thing and do not differ syntactically.

Multi-Tier Joins

A *multi-tier* join is a join that involves more than two tables. Table A is joined with Table B, which is, in turn, joined with Table C. Consider the following query:

```
SELECT C.LastName, C.FirstName, I.Description, O.Amount
FROM CUSTOMER C,
         ORDERS O,
         ITEMS I
WHERE C.CustomerNumber=O.CustomerNumber
and O.ItemNumber=I.ItemNumber
```

In this query, the CUSTOMER and ORDERS tables are joined on their common key, the CustomerNumber field. Then, the ORDERS and ITEMS tables are joined on their common key, the ItemNumber column. The effect is that all three tables are linked together in one result set. Figure 17.12 illustrates the result set returned by this query.

FIGURE 17.12.

The results of the multi-tiered query.

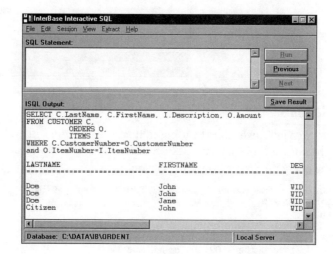

Self-Joins

Aside from joining to other tables, a table can be joined with itself. This type of join is known as a *reflexive* or *self-join*. Consider the following query:

```
SELECT O.CustomerNumber, O.Amount, (O.Amount / SUM(O2.Amount))*100 Percentage
FROM    ORDERS O,
        ORDERS O2
WHERE O.CustomerNumber=O2.CustomerNumber
GROUP  BY O.CustomerNumber, O.Amount
```

This purpose of this query is to list each order a customer has made, comparing the amount of each order to the total orders made by the customer. The only way to perform this type of query in a single SELECT statement is through a self-join. The individual statistics for each customer are gathered and grouped as one would expect, then the ORDERS table is joined back to itself to retrieve the total orders for each customer. The amount of the current order is then divided by this total and converted to a percentage for placement in the result set. The result set is shown in Figure 17.13.

FIGURE 17.13.
The results of the self-join.

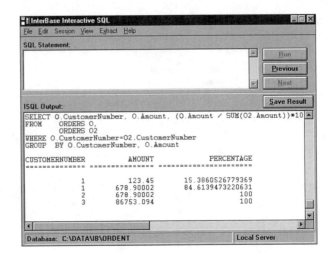

Theta Joins

A *theta* join joins two tables by using comparison operators other than equality operators, usually the not-equal (<>) operator. The following is an example of a theta join; it's a different spin on the query used to demonstrate self-joins:

```
SELECT C.CustomerNumber, O.Amount, Sum(O2.Amount) OTHERS
FROM CUSTOMER C,
ORDERS O,
ORDERS O2
WHERE C.CustomerNumber=O.CustomerNumber
AND C.CustomerNumber<>O2.CustomerNumber
GROUP BY C.CustomerNumber, O.Amount
```

Actually, this query contains two joins. First, it joins the CUSTOMER and ORDERS tables in order to retrieve the orders made by each customer. Second, it uses a theta join to retrieve a total of all the orders *not* made by each customer. Because it's using two different types of joins to link the same table, the query uses two separate table aliases for the ORDERS table. Figure 17.14 shows the results of the query.

Cartesian Products

A *Cartesian product* is the product of all the rows in one table multiplied by the rows in another. Such a result set is usually an accident, the result of missing or improper joins between tables. Here's an example:

```
SELECT ORDERS.OrderNumber, ITEMS.ItemNumber
FROM ORDERS, ITEMS
ORDER BY OrderNumber, ItemNumber
```

Figure 17.15 shows the results of the query.

FIGURE 17.14.

The results of the theta join.

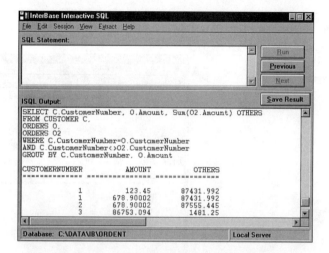

FIGURE 17.15.

The Cartesian product of the ORDERS and ITEMS tables.

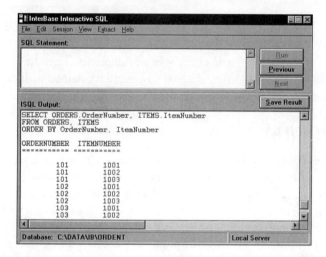

On large tables, a Cartesian product may tie up the server for a long time. So long, in fact, that you may want to kill the server to stop the query. On some platforms (for example, LIBS) you may have to take the machine on which the server is running down. On others (such as NetWare), you may be able to get away with unloading the server NLM. In any event, Cartesian products are probably something you'll want to avoid, especially when dealing with large tables.

Subqueries

A *subquery* is a SELECT statement within the WHERE clause of another SELECT. (See Figure 17.16.) Generally, you use a subquery to return a list of values that you then test the query against. Here's an example:

```
SELECT * FROM CUSTOMER
WHERE CustomerNumber IN (SELECT CustomerNumber FROM ORDERS)
```

FIGURE 17.16.

A subquery within the WHERE clause of another query.

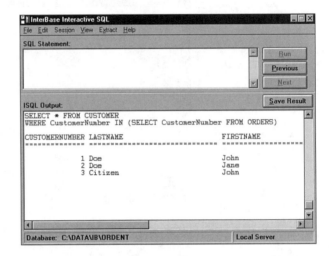

Certain operators operate exclusively on subqueries. They are the ANY, ALL, SOME, EXISTS, and SINGULAR operators. Although the ALL keyword is also used with the SELECT command, it is only used as an operator with subqueries.

GROUP BY

Because SQL is a set-oriented query language rather than a record-oriented query language, statements that group data are integral to the language and, in concert with aggregate functions, are the means by which the real work of data retrieval is done. dBASE programmers find this approach unusual in that they are accustomed to working with data on a record-by-record basis. Looping through a table in order to generate summary information is the way things are normally done in PC database products—not so with SQL. A single SQL statement can do what 10 or even 50 lines of Xbase code can. This magic is performed by using the SELECT statement's GROUP BY clause in conjunction with SQL's aggregate functions. Here's an example of the use of GROUP BY:

```
SELECT CUSTOMER.CustomerNumber, sum(ORDERS.Amount) TotalOrders
FROM CUSTOMER, ORDERS
WHERE CUSTOMER.CustomerNumber=ORDERS.CustomerNumber
GROUP BY CUSTOMER.CustomerNumber
```

This query returns a list of all customers along with the total amount of each customer's orders. (See Figure 17.17.)

FIGURE 17.17.

A query that uses the
GROUP BY clause.

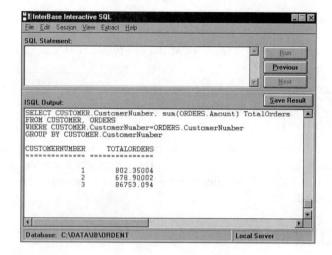

How do you know which fields to include in the GROUP BY clause? With InterBase, you must
GROUP BY all the nonaggregate columns in the column list of the SELECT statement. A GROUP BY
clause implies the use of at least one aggregate column in the SELECT's column list; you cannot
include a GROUP BY clause without one.

HAVING

The HAVING clause is used to limit the rows returned by a GROUP BY clause. (See Figure 17.18.)
Its relationship to the GROUP BY clause is similar to the relationship between the WHERE clause
and the SELECT statement itself. The HAVING clause works like a WHERE clause on the rows in the
result set rather than on the rows in the query's tables.

FIGURE 17.18.

Using HAVING to qualify
GROUP BY.

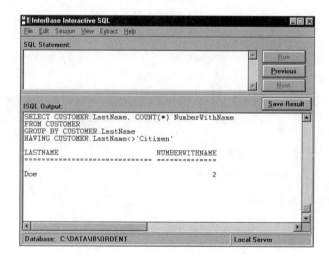

There is usually a better way of qualifying a query than by using a HAVING clause. In general, HAVING is less efficient than the WHERE clause because it qualifies the result set *after* it has been organized into groups, while WHERE does so *before*. Here's an example of the use of the HAVING clause:

```
SELECT CUSTOMER.LastName, COUNT(*) NumberWithName
FROM CUSTOMER
GROUP BY CUSTOMER.LastName
HAVING COUNT(*) > 2
```

About the only valid use of HAVING is to restrict rows returned from the query based on the results of an aggregate calculation. In this case, WHERE is unable to handle the task because the information doesn't exist until after the query has executed and its aggregate columns have been computed.

ORDER BY

You use the ORDER BY clause to order the rows in the result set. (See Figure 17.19.) Here's an example:

```
SELECT * FROM CUSTOMER
ORDER BY State
```

FIGURE 17.19.

Using the ORDER BY clause.

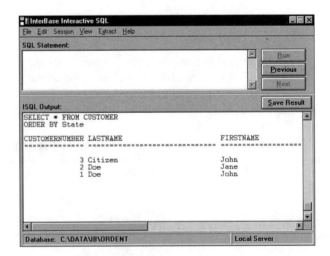

Here's another example:

```
SELECT FirstName, LastName
FROM CUSTOMER
ORDER BY LastName
```

Column Aliases

You may have noticed that I use logical column names for aggregate functions like COUNT()
and SUM(). Labels such as these are known as *column aliases* and serve to make the query and its
result set more readable. In InterBase SQL, you place a column alias immediately to the right
of its corresponding column in the SELECT statement's field list. For example, in the query

```
SELECT CUSTOMER.LastName, COUNT(*) NumberWithName
FROM CUSTOMER
GROUP BY CUSTOMER.LastName
HAVING COUNT(*) > 2
```

the column alias of the COUNT() aggregate is the NumberWithName label. You can use column aliases
for any item in a result set, not just aggregate functions. For example,

```
SELECT CUSTOMER.LastName LName, COUNT(*) NumberWithName
FROM CUSTOMER
GROUP BY CUSTOMER.LastName
```

substitutes the column alias LName for the LastName column in the result set. Note, however,
that you cannot use aliases in other parts of the query, like the WHERE or GROUP BY clauses. You
must use the actual column name or value in those parts of the SELECT statement.

Table Aliases

Rather than always having to specify the full name of a table each time you reference it in a
SELECT command, you can define a shorthand moniker for it to use instead. You do this by
specifying a *table alias* for the table in the FROM clause of the SELECT statement. Place the alias to
the right of the actual table name, as illustrated here:

```
SELECT C.LastName, COUNT(*) NumberWithName
FROM CUSTOMER C
GROUP BY C.LastName
```

Notice that the alias can be used in the field list of the SELECT list before it is even syntactically
defined. This is possible because references to database objects in a query are resolved before
the query is executed.

Views

An SQL table view consists of a SELECT statement that you can treat as a table and, in turn,
issue SELECT statements against it. The view itself does not actually store any data; it's a logical
construct only. Think of a view as a small SQL program that runs each time you query it. It's
similar to a select procedure, which is discussed in the following section, "Stored Procedures."

When you SELECT from a view, the query optimizer takes the SELECT used to create the view, blends in the one you are executing against it, and optimizes the two as a single query against the server.

SQL table views are created by using the CREATE VIEW command. Here's an example:

```
CREATE VIEW OKCUSTOMERS AS
SELECT *
FROM CUSTOMER
WHERE State='OK'
```

After the view is created, it can be queried just like a table, as in

```
SELECT * FROM OKCUSTOMERS
```

Figure 17.20 displays the results from this query. Notice that, even though the SELECT against the view didn't include a WHERE clause, the result set appears as if it did due to the WHERE clause built into the view.

FIGURE 17.20.

The result set is returned when the view is queried.

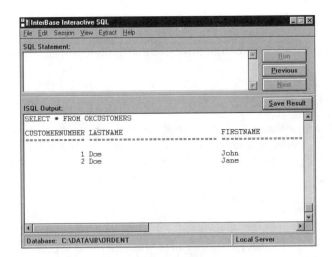

The SELECT statement that makes up a view can do almost anything a normal SELECT statement can do. One thing it can't do is include an ORDER BY clause. This limitation exists on both the InterBase and Sybase platforms.

Additional limitations are imposed if you want to be able to create a view that's updatable. In order for an InterBase view to be updatable, the following conditions must be met:

■ The view's SELECT statement either must be over a single table or reference another updatable view

- Columns from the underlying table that are excluded from the view must allow NULL values in order for the view to support the INSERT command

- The view's SELECT statement must not contain subqueries, a DISTINCT predicate, a HAVING clause, aggregate functions, joined tables, user-defined functions, or stored procedures

When you create an updatable view, you can tell the server to ensure that rows that are updated or added by means of the view meet the selection criteria imposed by the view. That is, you can ensure that an updated or added record doesn't "go out of scope"—doesn't vanish from the view once it's changed or added. You do this by using the WITH CHECK OPTION clause of the CREATE VIEW command. Here's the syntax:

```
CREATE VIEW OKCUSTOMERS AS
SELECT *
FROM CUSTOMER
WHERE State='OK'
WITH CHECK OPTION
```

Now, any record updates or inserts having a State column with anything but 'OK' in them will fail.

Stored Procedures

A *stored procedure* is a compiled SQL program, often consisting of many SQL statements, that is stored in a database with other database objects. Stored procedures come in two basic flavors: *select procedures* and *executable procedures*. Select procedures are used in place of a table or view in a SELECT statement; therefore, they must define one or more values to return. Executable procedures, on the other hand, may or may not return data.

Stored procedures are created by using the CREATE PROCEDURE command. Here's an example of the InterBase syntax:

```
CREATE PROCEDURE listcustomers
AS
BEGIN
  SELECT LastName FROM CUSTOMERS
END
```

If the procedure receives parameters from the caller, the syntax changes slightly. Here's the InterBase syntax:

```
CREATE PROCEDURE listcustomers (State char(2), LastNameMask char(30))
AS
BEGIN
  SELECT LastName FROM CUSTOMERS
  WHERE State=:State AND LastName LIKE :LastNameMask
END
```

Select Procedures

Select procedures define data to return to the caller by using the RETURNS keyword, as in the following:

```
CREATE PROCEDURE listcustomers (State CHAR(2))
RETURNS(LastName CHAR(30))
AS
BEGIN
    FOR SELECT LastName
    FROM CUSTOMER
    WHERE State=:State
    INTO :LastName
    DO
      SUSPEND;
END
```

Note the use of the FOR SELECT...DO syntax to return the result rows to the caller. The SUSPEND command pauses the execution of the procedure until another row is requested from the caller. Values that have been assigned to output parameters are returned before execution is paused.

Executable Procedures

An *executable procedure* differs little from a select procedure except that it is not required to include a RETURNS statement. Here's another example of an executable procedure in InterBase SQL:

```
CREATE PROCEDURE insertcapital (Capital CHAR(30), State CHAR(2))
AS
BEGIN
    UPDATE CAPITALS
    SET Capital=Capital
    WHERE State=:State
END
```

Scripts

It's a good idea to construct Data Definition Language SQL statements, including stored procedures, using SQL script files. You can create these scripts by using a text editor; most good SQL editors support saving their contents to disk. Remember that these scripts must include any necessary CONNECT and SET TERM statements. These can then be executed by using WISQL's Run an ISQL Script option. Listing 17.1 shows an example of such a file.

Listing 17.1. A stored procedure residing in an SQL script file.

```
CONNECT "C:\DATA\IB\ORDENT";

SET TERM ^;
CREATE PROCEDURE GET_CUSTOMER (State CHAR(2))
RETURNS (LastName CHAR(30))
```

```
AS
BEGIN
    FOR SELECT LastName
    FROM CUSTOMER
    WHERE State = :State
    INTO :LastName
    DO
        SUSPEND;
END ^
SET TERM ; ^
EXIT;
```

Notice that the CONNECT statement at the top of the file establishes the connection to the database. Next is the SET TERM command, which changes the SQL statement termination character to a caret (^) rather than the default semicolon (;). This keeps commands embedded in the stored procedure from executing when the CREATE PROCEDURE statement itself is executed. Finally, the SET TERM command is again executed in order to restore the command terminator to its default.

Exceptions

Exceptions are mechanisms for reporting user-defined error conditions in stored procedures and triggers. In InterBase, you use CREATE EXCEPTION to define a new exception and the EXCEPTION command to "raise" or "throw" it. Listing 17.2 is an example of an InterBase exception and a stored procedure that raises it.

Listing 17.2. InterBase exception and stored procedure.

```
CREATE EXCEPTION ORDER_TOO_LOW
"The order is too low. Only orders of $5 or more are allowed."

CONNECT "C:\DATA\IB\ORDENT";

SET TERM ^;
CREATE PROCEDURE insertorder (OrderNumber int, OrderDate date, CustomerNumber int,
ItemNumber int, Amount float)
AS
BEGIN
    IF (:Amount < 5) THEN
        EXCEPTION ORDER_TOO_LOW;
    ELSE
        INSERT INTO ORDERS
        VALUES (:OrderNumber, :OrderDate, :CustomerNumber,
        :ItemNumber, :Amount);
END ^
SET TERM ; ^
EXIT;
```

This procedure limits orders to those of $5 or more. Note the use of the IF...THEN syntax to detect whether the Amount column in the row about to be inserted is less than $5. The EXCEPTION command is used to raise the ORDER_TOO_LOW exception when the Amount is less than $5.

Triggers

Not unlike stored procedures, triggers are SQL routines that are activated when data in a given table is inserted, updated, or deleted. You associate a trigger with a specific operation on a table: an insertion, an update, or a deletion. Here's an example using InterBase SQL:

```
CREATE TRIGGER ORDERSDelete FOR CUSTOMER
BEFORE DELETE
AS
BEGIN
    DELETE FROM ORDERS
    WHERE CustomerNumber=OLD.CustomerNumber;
END
```

This trigger deletes a customer's orders from the ORDERS table when the customer's record is deleted from the CUSTOMER table. This sort of delete is known as a *cascading delete:* A delete made in one table cascades through others using a common key.

Note the use of the OLD context variable. An OLD context variable indicates the current value of a column prior to an UPDATE or DELETE operation. A NEW context variable refers to the new value of a column in an INSERT or UPDATE operation.

Note also the use of the BEFORE keyword. A trigger can be activated before or after an INSERT, UPDATE, or DELETE.

In InterBase, virtually any number of triggers (up to 32,768 of them, to be precise) can be bound to a given table event. You can specify a firing order for multiple triggers bound to the same table event by using the POSITION keyword. Here's an example:

```
CREATE TRIGGER ORDERSDelete FOR CUSTOMER
BEFORE DELETE
POSITION 0
AS
BEGIN
    DELETE FROM ORDERS
    WHERE CustomerNumber=OLD.CustomerNumber;
END
```

POSITIONs begin at 0 and go through 32,767; lower numbers execute first. Multiple triggers with the same POSITION execute in a random order.

Cursors

Cursors are set-oriented SQL's answer to record-oriented databases. Cursors enable you to work with tables one row at a time. Since the BDE automatically creates and maintains cursors for you, you won't generally create your own cursors using SQL. However, you may find them handy in stored procedures.

There are four basic operations you can perform on cursors: You can declare them, open them, fetch from them, and close them. You can also use a cursor to UPDATE and DELETE rows in its base table.

A cursor declaration consists of a SELECT statement and, for updatable cursors, a list of updatable columns. Here's the syntax:

```
DECLARE c_CUSTOMER CURSOR
FOR SELECT * FROM CUSTOMER
```

Before you can retrieve rows using the cursor, it must be opened. You use the OPEN command to initiate the query that makes up the cursor declaration:

```
OPEN c_CUSTOMER
```

OPEN doesn't actually retrieve any rows back to the client application. You must use FETCH for that. Here's the syntax:

```
FETCH c_CUSTOMER
```

This retrieves a single row from the cursor result set. Each subsequent call to FETCH retrieves the next row in the set. Both InterBase and Sybase support one-way cursors only; you cannot FETCH backward. If you wish to move back up in a set, you must CLOSE and re-OPEN the cursor.

> **NOTE**
>
> The fact that the server you happen to be using doesn't support bidirectional cursors doesn't prevent your Delphi applications from using them. This is because the Borland Database Engine emulates bidirectional cursoring at the client level regardless of whether your server back-end supports it.

The table rows returned by updatable cursors can be updated by using special versions of the UPDATE and DELETE commands. A cursor must be declared by using the FOR UPDATE OF clause in order to be updatable. Here's an example:

```
DECLARE c_CUSTOMER CURSOR
FOR SELECT * FROM CUSTOMER
FOR UPDATE OF LastName
```

> **NOTE**
>
> Be sure to list only those columns in the FOR UPDATE OF clause that you actually intend to update. Declaring more updatable fields than you need wastes server resources.

In order to UPDATE or DELETE the current row of an updatable cursor, you use the WHERE CURRENT OF cursorname syntax to qualify the command, as in

```
UPDATE CUSTOMER
SET LastName="Cane"
WHERE CURRENT OF c_CUSTOMER
```

or

```
DELETE FROM CUSTOMER
WHERE CURRENT OF c_CUSTOMER
```

When you finish with a cursor, you use the CLOSE command to close it. Closing a cursor also releases any system resources in use by it. Here's the syntax:

```
CLOSE c_CUSTOMER
```

What's Ahead

Chapter 18, "ReportSmith," discusses Delphi's report writer of choice, ReportSmith. The chapter discusses how to generate all four of ReportSmith's major report types. Techniques on standardizing report layouts, on using DLLs in conjunction with reports and on retrieving data to drive reports are all discussed. If you use or plan to use ReportSmith to create database reports for your Delphi applications, this chapter should prove useful to you.

Summary

You've covered a lot of territory in a relatively short amount of space. This tour began with creating databases and ended with closing cursors. Hopefully, you now feel sufficiently exposed to InterBase. This knowledge, coupled with a thorough knowledge of Delphi, should put you well on your way to developing sophisticated client/server database applications.

18

ReportSmith

You'll find that Delphi's QuickReport components are adequate for most of your reporting needs, but some types of reports are produced more easily by using a reporting tool such as ReportSmith. Complex financial reports or reports that involve a large number of columns are often easier to construct with a report writer. ReportSmith handles the mundane task of inserting, aligning, and formatting report columns, enabling you to concentrate on the more important aspects of report design.

One advantage of building reports with a report writer is that they can be modified by your users or used by them as a basis for new reports. This means, of course, that your users will have to purchase the report writer you used to build the reports. Most vendors enable you to include only a runtime version with your software. They'll also have to be trained in the use of your chosen tool. As easy as they are, report writers still require a certain amount of skill to use them effectively.

Since user modification of your application's reports could cause you support problems, it's probably a good idea to prevent your reports from being modified. Rather than modify your reports, enable the user to base *new* reports on your existing ones.

In this chapter, you'll use Borland's ReportSmith to build several different types of reports. I think the best way to learn ReportSmith is to thoroughly explore its capabilities. Rather than attempting to amaze you with lots of interesting facts regarding ReportSmith, I'd rather show you how to use it to accomplish real work. After all, you have the ReportSmith manual if you feel the sudden urge to read up on ReportSmith's technical specifications. While inundating you with information might or might not equip you properly for developing in ReportSmith, there's no doubt that using it to develop a variety of reports will.

ReportSmith Background Information

ReportSmith is a full-featured graphical report writer. You can buy it with Delphi or separately. Because Delphi and ReportSmith are both Borland products, you can expect ReportSmith to integrate better with Delphi than any other stand-alone report writer. For example, the latest version of ReportSmith, version 3.0, can share database connections with Delphi applications, alleviating the need to separately log in to database servers.

You can produce the following four types of reports with ReportSmith:

- Columnar reports—Reports that list data horizontally in a series of columns
- Crosstab reports—Reports that present data in a tabular format—similar to a spreadsheet
- Form reports—Reports that print a single row per page, usually in a form-like manner, such as an invoice
- Label reports—Reports that print mailing labels (ReportSmith supports both Avery labels and user-defined labels)

You'll build one of each type of report in this chapter. Though you may find some of the alternative methods of report creation listed in Chapter 12, "Reports," preferable to using ReportSmith, building each of these will no doubt sharpen your skills as a report designer.

> **NOTE**
>
> If you've completed Part II, "Tutorial," of this book, you're probably already familiar with report creation using ReportSmith. Chapter 12 covers this subject in depth, and most of the material found here is found there, as well. If you're already comfortable with creating reports in ReportSmith, you might want to skip to Chapter 19, "Business Rules Part I."

Connecting to a Data Source

The first order of business when you build database reports is obtaining the data that will drive the report. ReportSmith supports four basic methods of retrieving report data:

- Native access—ReportSmith provides native support for many popular DBMS formats
- ODBC access—A number of database formats, including Access "databases" and Excel spreadsheets, can be accessed via 32-bit Open Database Connectivity (ODBC) data sources
- BDE (IDAPI)—ReportSmith can use the Borland Database Engine aliases and drivers that you set up for your Delphi applications
- Delphi-based access—ReportSmith can share a database connection with a Delphi application, though there are some limitations with this

Personally, I prefer using BDE connections with ReportSmith. This enables me to utilize the same drivers and aliases that I use within my Delphi applications and doesn't restrict the things I can do when building reports.

Though sharing a database connection between ReportSmith and an application would seem to be preferable to using a separate connection for each of them, doing so severely limits your ability to link tables. If you share a database connection with a Delphi application, you can't join the DataSet provided by Delphi with another table; you must do this from within Delphi. There's really no logical reason for this restriction, so I recommend that you use BDE/IDAPI connections instead.

Before you get started, you'll need to create a suite of Paradox tables on which to build your reports. You'll also want to populate them with data. The reports in this chapter use the tables from the Tutorial section of this book. Their structures are briefly summarized in Tables 18.1

through 18.7. If you haven't already done so, create each of them using the following data dictionary information before you proceed. Begin by creating a BDE alias named RENTMAN that points to a given disk directory, for example, C:\DATA\DELPHI\RENTMAN. This will enable you to keep all the tables together, as though they were in a database of their own, which will make creating reports over them easier. If you need help creating the BDE alias or creating or populating the tables, see Chapter 8, "Your First Real Database Application."

Note that the primary key of each table is boldfaced.

Table 18.1. The WORKTYPE table design.

Column	Type	Size
WorkTypeCode	Short	
Description	Alpha	30
TaskDuration	Number	

Table 18.2. The TENANT table design.

Column	Type	Size
TenantNo	AutoIncrement	
Name	Alpha	30
Employer	Alpha	30
EmpAddress	Alpha	30
EmpCity	Alpha	20
EmpState	Alpha	2
EmpZip	Alpha	10
HomePhone	Alpha	15
WorkPhone	Alpha	15
ICEPhone	Alpha	15
LeaseBeginDate	Date	
LeaseEndDate	Date	
MovedInDate	Date	
MovedOutDate	Date	
RentDueDay	Short	
PetDeposit	Money	
LawnService	Logical	
Comments	Alpha	100

Table 18.3. The EMPLOYEE table design.

Column	Type	Size
EmployeeNo	AutoIncrement	
Name	Alpha	30

Table 18.4. THE PROPERTY table design.

Column	Type	Size
PropertyNo	AutoIncrement	
TenantNo	AutoIncrement	
Address	Alpha	30
City	Alpha	20
State	Alpha	2
Zip	Alpha	10
Addition	Alpha	30
BedRooms	Short	
LivingAreas	Short	
BathRooms	Short	
GarageType	Short	
SchoolDistrict	Alpha	15
Deposit	Money	
Rent	Money	
Range	Logical	
Refrigerator	Logical	
DishWasher	Logical	
CentralHeat	Logical	
CentralAir	Logical	
GasHeat	Logical	
PrivacyFence	Logical	
LastSprayDate	Date	
LastLawnDate	Date	
Comments	Alpha	100

Table 18.5. The WORDERS table design.

Column	Type	Size
WorkOrderNo	AutoIncrement	
PropertyNo	Long	
EmployeeNo	Long	
StartDate	Date	
EndDate	Date	
Comments	Alpha	100

Table 18.6. The WDETAIL table design.

Column	Type	Size
WorkOrderNo	Long	
LineNo	Long	
WorkTypeCode	Short	
Comments	Alpha	100

Table 18.7. The CALLS table design.

Column	Type	Size
CallNo	AutoIncrement	
CallDateTime	Timestamp	
PropertyNo	Long	
Description	Alpha	30
Priority	Alpha	1
WorkOrderNo	Long	
Comments	Alpha	100

> **NOTE**
>
> You can also find these tables on the CD-ROM that accompanies this book. You can use the RENTALMAN application, which is also included on the CD-ROM, to enter additional data into the tables if necessary.

After the tables are created, you'll need to populate them with data if you're to have any hope of testing the reports you base on them. There are a variety of methods for doing this. Because these are Paradox tables, you can use Paradox itself if you have it. You can use the RENTALMAN application that's defined in the Tutorial section of this book, or you can use something like Borland's Database Desktop to insert rows into the tables. Whatever your method, keep in mind that you'll need a good number of rows in each table to test such things as page breaks and grouping levels.

Before You Get Started

If you haven't already constructed the RENTALMAN application outlined in the Tutorial section of this book, you'll need to build a small test application from which you can try out your ReportSmith reports. Obviously, you could design and test your reports all from within ReportSmith. However, you'd then miss out on their use as it relates specifically to Delphi applications, so I'll take you through constructing a small test application.

Start Delphi and create a new application. Drop a MainMenu component onto its main form. Set the Caption property of its main form to Rental Maintenance Management System and save the application as RENTMAN.DPR.

Next, create a new data module form named dmRentalMan and save it as rentdata.pas. Add the rentdata unit to the Uses statement of RENTALMAN's main form. Drop a Table component onto this form for each of the tables you created earlier. In keeping with the naming conventions laid out in Chapter 4, "Conventions," name each component after the physical table it represents, prefixing each name with the letters "ta" (for example, the PROPERTY table's component would be named taPROPERTY). Set the DatabaseName of each component to the RENTMAN alias you created earlier and set each Table's TableName property to the table on disk to which it corresponds. Next, select all seven Table components and open them by toggling the Active property to True in the Object Inspector.

Now that the shell application has been constructed and its data module has been set up, you're ready to begin developing reports.

Columnar Reports

Drop a Report component (located on the Data Access component palette page) onto the dmRentalMan form and name it reRPROLST0. Set its ReportName to rprolst0 and its ReportDirectory to C:\DATA\DELPHI\RENTMAN (or to whatever path you're using). Right-click the component and select Edit Report from the menu. You should see ReportSmith load.

Next, select Columnar Report in the Create a New Report dialog. Once the Tables dialog is displayed, click its Add Table button. When the Select Table dialog appears, select Delphi as the table Type and click the Server Connect button. You should then see listed all the DataSet components in your application that share a form with a Report component. In this case, the DataSets you placed on the dmRentalMan data module should be displayed. (See Figure 18.1.)

FIGURE 18.1.

ReportSmith's Select Table dialog.

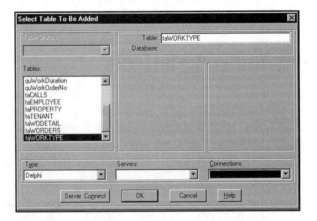

Select the taPROPERTY table, and return to the Tables dialog. Next, click the Done button to return to ReportSmith's main edit screen. You should then see the the PROPERTY table's columns arranged in a sample report that you can modify. Figure 18.2 shows the first rendition of the property list report.

After you've finished this report, it will serve as a model for other reports. Before it can be used as a model, though, the report needs several changes. The page header, detail, and summary sections need to be cleaned up a bit. The fonts and layout you use in each section need to be standardized.

TIP

ReportSmith includes all the columns in a table by default. To change its default behavior to exclude all columns, add the line

```
ExcludeFields = 1
```

to the [Options] section of the RPTSMITH.INI file (you may have to add the section).

FIGURE 18.2.

ReportSmith's main screen shows a default report layout for the PROPERTY table.

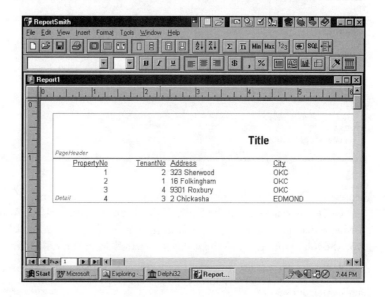

Derived Fields

Before you set up the page header, you'll need to define a couple of *derived fields*: one to return a formatted report name, the other to return the current user name from Windows. You'll use the REPUTILS Dynamic Link Library (DLL) to return the current user name. See Chapter 12 if you need help creating this DLL. Its source code is shown in Listing 18.1.

Listing 18.1. The source text to the Report Utilities Dynamic Link Library (REPUTILS.DLL).

```
library Reputils;

{ Important note about DLL memory management: ShareMem must be
the first unit in your interface section's uses clause if your DLL
exports any procedures or functions that pass string parameters or
function results. This applies to all strings passed to and from
your DLL—even those that are nested in records and classes. ShareMem
is the interface unit to the DELPHIMM.DLL, which must be deployed
along with your DLL. To avoid using DELPHIMM.DLL, pass string
information using PChar or ShortString parameters. }

uses
  SysUtils,
```

continues

Listing 18.1. continued

```
  Classes,
  Windows;

function GetWindowsUserName(UserName : PChar) : PChar; stdcall; export;
var
  Name : Array[0..30] of Char;
  NameLen : Integer;
begin
  NameLen := sizeof(Name);
  If GetUserName(Name, NameLen) then StrCopy(UserName,Name)
  else StrCopy(UserName,'UNKNOWN');
  Result := UserName;
end;

exports
  GetWindowsUserName;
end.
```

Select the Derived Fields option on ReportSmith's Tools menu. Type `ReportName` in the `Derived Field Name` field of the Derived Fields dialog, and click the Add button. In the Choose A Macro dialog, type `GetReportName` in the `Macro Name` field and click the New button. Next, type the following text into the `Macro Formula` field of the Edit Macro dialog:

```
' A function to return the name of the current report without a path or extension.
' NOTE: this function depends on the report name being originally in 8.3 format.
Sub GetReportName()
  SlashPos=0    'Variable to store position of backslash
  PeriodPos=0   'Variable to store position of period
ThisReport$=Right$(ActiveTitle(),12)
' Loop removing all directories from the name
SlashPos=InStr(ThisReport$,"\")
Do While SlashPos<>0
ThisReport$=Mid$(ThisReport$,SlashPos+1,Len(ThisReport$)-SlashPos)
SlashPos=InStr(ThisReport$,"\")
Loop
' Now remove the extension, if there is one
PeriodPos=InStr(ThisReport$,".")
If PeriodPos<>0 then ThisReport$=Left$(ThisReport$,PeriodPos-1)
' Return the end result
DerivedField UCase$(ThisReport$)
End Sub
```

> **NOTE**
>
> ReportSmith's `ActiveTitle()` function already returns the name of the current report, so you may be wondering why you're constructing a derived field to do so. A complete discussion of ReportSmith's macro language is beyond the scope of this book, but the reason for this is simple. `ActiveTitle()` returns the full path—including the filename and its extension—of the currently loaded report. If the path is very long, this name could be meaningless because you have a limited amount of space in which to print it.

Furthermore, the extension of all your reports will likely be the same; there's no point in printing the extension on every report. A better solution is to strip both the path and the extension from the name of the report before it's printed. The preceding derived function does just that. Keep in mind that the preceding code assumes the use of the 8.3 file naming convention, as recommended in Chapter 4. This code doesn't support Windows 95/NT long filenames.

Return to the Choose A Macro dialog by clicking OK, then click OK again to return to the Derived Fields dialog. You'll next define a derived field to retrieve the current Windows user name. Before doing this, make sure that ReportSmith can access the REPUTILS.DLL file you created earlier. The best way to do this is to place it in a directory that's on the system PATH. You can do this by adding the RENTALMAN project's home directory (probably C:\DATA\DELPHI\RENTMAN) to the path, or you can copy REPUTILS.DLL to a directory, such as C:\WINDOWS, that's already on the PATH.

Once REPUTILS.DLL is accessible, you're ready to create the UserName derived field. Type UserName into the Derived Field Name box of the Derived Fields dialog, then click the Add button. Next, type GetUserName into the Macro Name box of the ensuing dialog, then click the New button. Type the following macro code into the Macro Formula box of the Edit Macro dialog:

```
Declare Sub GetWindowsUserName Lib "REPUTILS" (ByVal usrnam as String)
Sub GetUserName()
UName$=string$(30," ")
GetWindowsUserName(ByVal UName$)
DerivedField UName$
End Sub
```

This function calls the GetWindowsUserName function in your REPUTILS DLL. Notice that the Declare Sub code imports the DLL function by name. You can import DLL functions by ordinal index, as well. Though not as intuitive and flexible, importing DLL functions by ordinal index is faster than referencing them by name.

NOTE

Be sure you match the character case used in names of functions imported by name exactly. That is, be sure the case you use in ReportSmith precisely matches the case used in the DLL's source code. If you use a different case when importing the function by name than was used in its DLL, ReportSmith won't be able to locate the function in the host DLL. You can avoid this pitfall completely by importing functions by ordinal index.

Click OK to save your macro, then click OK again to exit the Choose a Macro dialog. Click Done in the Derived Fields dialog to return to ReportSmith's main screen.

Start by removing all the columns on the report except the PropertyNo, Address, City, State, Zip, and Addition columns. You can delete columns simply by clicking them and pressing the Delete key. You can select a number of contiguous columns at once by dragging a rectangle around them (which selects them) and pressing the Delete key. To select non-contiguous columns, click the first one, then hold down the Ctrl key while you click the rest. Notice that when you delete a column, its column heading vanishes with it. This is because ReportSmith is by default in column edit mode. You can toggle between column and field edit mode by clicking the appropriate button on ReportSmith's toolbar.

Before proceeding, set the PropertyNo column heading to No. Change the font of the column headings to Times New Roman, 10 pts., Underlined. Change the font of the columns themselves to Courier New, 10 pts. Resize the columns so that they all fit on screen at the same time. There's no reason to spread them out horizontally, and scrunching them onto a single screen will make report design easier. Figure 18.3 shows what the report should look like thus far.

FIGURE 18.3.

An early version of the Property List report.

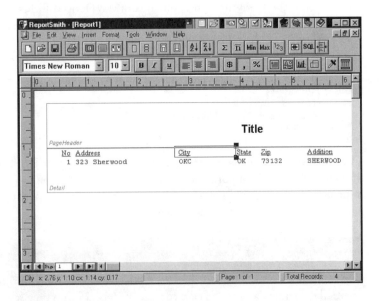

Next, click the Title field in the page heading section and change it to Property Listing. Set the title's font to Times New Roman, 14 pts., Bold. Next, drop a text field just above the Property Listing field. Set its text to Rental Maintenance Management System and its font to Times New Roman, 14 pts., Bold. Center both fields horizontally on the page. (See Figure 18.4.)

FIGURE 18.4.

The page header section of the new report as it should initially appear.

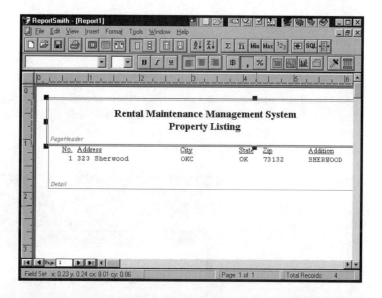

NOTE

You may have noticed that the two title lines in the page header section of the report use the same font. You can easily copy the formatting information from one field to another by following these steps:

1. Click the field whose formatting style you want to copy.
2. Click the Extract Style button on the ReportSmith toolbar (it looks like an eye-dropper).
3. Click the field or fields that you want to format with the extracted style.
4. Click the Extract Style button a second time to end your formatting changes.

You're now ready to begin dropping the remainder of the page heading fields onto it, including the two derived fields you constructed earlier. Drop a text field onto the upper-left corner of the page heading and set its text to `Report:`. Change its font to Times New Roman, 10 pts., Bold.

Next, drop your `ReportName` derived field to the immediate right of this label. To drop the `ReportName` field, select Field from ReportSmith's Insert menu, then select Derived Fields in the drop-down list of the Insert Field dialog. Uncheck the Include field name checkbox, then drag `ReportName` from the list of derived fields to the appropriate place in the page header section. Set its font to Courier New, 10 pts.

After the `ReportName` component is in place, you're ready to drop the `Print Date` system field. It will be positioned just below the `ReportName` field on the left side of the page heading section. Drop a text field onto the left side of the page heading and set its text to `Print date:`. Set its font to Times New Roman, 10 pts., Bold.

Next, click Field on the Insert menu again, then select System Fields in the drop-down list. Drag Print Date to the immediate right of the text field you just placed on the report. As with the `ReportName` field, set its font to Courier New, 10 pts. Figure 18.5 illustrates the proper placement of the `ReportName` and `Print Date` fields.

FIGURE 18.5.

The proper placement of the ReportName *and* Print Date *fields on the new report.*

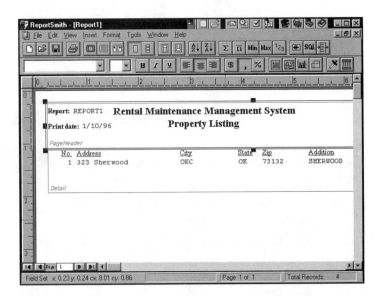

Now that the `ReportName` and `Print Date` fields are in place, you're ready to insert the `UserName` derived field. Drop a text field onto the left of the page heading section, beneath the `Print Date` field. Set its text to `User name:` and its font to Times New Roman, 10 pts., Bold. Follow this by dropping the `UserName` derived field (without a field name) to its immediate right. Copy the formatting style of the `ReportName` field to the `UserName` field using the steps listed previously.

Once you've finished the left side of the page heading, you're ready to move on to the right side. There are only two fields that go on the right side of the page heading. They are the `Page Number` and `Print Time` system fields.

Place the `Page Number` and `Print Time` fields on the right side of the page header. Set up text labels for both of them and format each to match the fields on the left of the section. After you've finished the page header, save your new report as RPROLST0. Figure 18.6 illustrates the new report's completed page heading.

FIGURE 18.6.

The completed page header for the new Property Listing report.

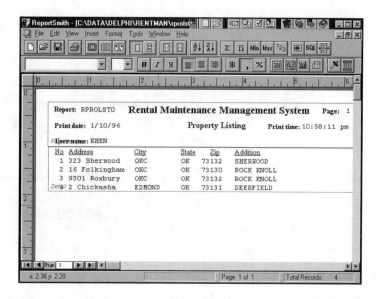

Lookup Fields

Lookup fields that have been defined for a DataSet are not included in the list of fields that ReportSmith receives from Delphi. Unfortunately, this is one of the drawbacks of sharing a database connection with Delphi. To make matters worse, you can't perform the lookups yourself from within ReportSmith by linking tables together. ReportSmith's ability to link one table with another is disabled when ReportSmith and Delphi share a database connection.

To remedy this, you have two options. First, you can set up a query component in Delphi that performs the join for you and returns the composite rows. You can then use this DataSet in ReportSmith when building reports. Second, you can change the report so that it doesn't share a database connection with Delphi. ReportSmith can interact directly with the Borland Database Engine—it doesn't need Delphi for this. You can replace the table connection that references Delphi with one that works directly with the BDE. This is a good way to handle situations where your data needs are more complex than the DataSets defined by your Delphi application.

To switch a report that was originally designed to share a database connection to communicate directly with the BDE, click the Replace table button in ReportSmith's Tables dialog. In the ensuing dialog, change the connection type to the BDE alias you want to use (RENTMAN, in this case). Then double-click the name of the table you want in the Files list. (See Figure 18.7.)

Once back in the Tables dialog, click the Done button to activate your change. ReportSmith will then switch the report's data source without altering the report itself. You won't lose the fields that you've already placed on the report.

FIGURE 18.7.

Changing a report that shares a database connection to communicate directly with the BDE.

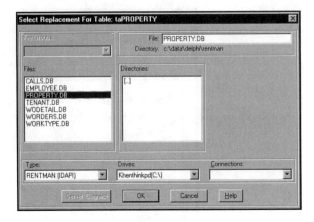

Now that the report interacts directly with the BDE, you can construct the necessary link with the TENANT table to retrieve tenant names. To do this, click the Add table button in the Tables dialog, then double-click the TENANT table in the list. Next, click the Add New Link button. In the Create New Table Link dialog, notice that ReportSmith has already set up a link between the two tables based on a column name they share, the TenantNo column. (See Figure 18.8.)

FIGURE 18.8.

The Create New Table Link dialog.

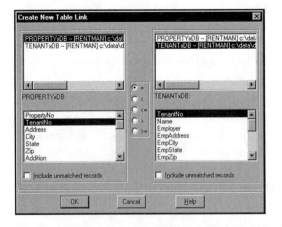

Save your new link by clicking OK, then click Done to exit the Tables dialog. You'll notice that all the fields in the TENANT table now appear to the right of those from the PROPERTY table. Delete all the TENANT fields except the Name column from the report. Figure 18.9 shows the revised report.

The Property Listing report is now essentially complete. The only things that remain to be done are to add a text field placeholder for the report's selection criteria and to add a summary field that counts the total number of properties.

FIGURE 18.9.

The revised Property Listing report links the PROPERTY and TENANT tables.

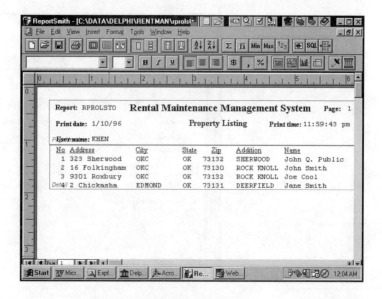

Center a new text field in the report's page header just below the Property Listing field. Its text should be "Report criteria" and its font should be Courier New, 10 pts.

Next, click the Insert/Header/Footer menu option. Leave Entire Report_Group selected and click the Footer checkbox in the Header/Footer dialog, then click OK. This adds a footer to the bottom of the report. Next, click the PropertyNo column, then click the Count button on ReportSmith's toolbar (it's the one with the 123 label). This will place a summary field in the report's footer that counts the total number of properties. (See Figure 18.10.)

FIGURE 18.10.

You insert headers and footers using the Header/Footer dialog box.

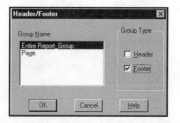

Click the label that ReportSmith automatically supplied for your summary field and set its text to "Total number of properties:" and its font to Times New Roman, 10 pts., Bold. Next, click the summary field that ReportSmith inserted into the Summary section and set its Font to Courier New, 10 pts. Finish up by saving the report. Figure 18.11 shows what it should now look like.

FIGURE 18.11.

The Property Listing report as it appears in ReportSmith.

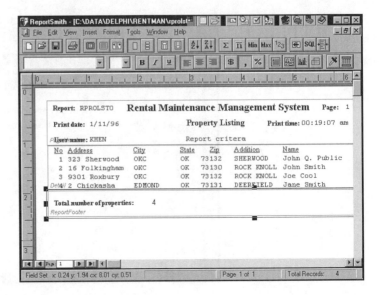

Styles and Templates

Now that you've completed the report, you can use it as the basis for other reports. There are two ways of doing this. The report can be saved as a formatting *style* that you may then apply to other reports, or it can be saved in its entirety, then loaded and modified when building a new report. The second method is preferable because it includes the fields from the original report—report styles don't include fields.

Select the Report Style option on ReportSmith's Format menu. Next, click the New button and type AllReports in the ensuing dialog, then click OK to exit it. Next, click the Done button to return to ReportSmith's main screen. This defines a new report style named AllReports using the formatting information of the current report.

To see the effects of applying the style to a report, select the New option on ReportSmith's File menu. Create a Columnar report, then add the TENANT table to the report in the Tables dialog. Figure 18.12 shows the initial appearance of the report.

Now click the Report Style option on the Format menu a second time, select the AllReports style, and click the Apply button.

You'll notice several changes on the new report. For example, the detail and header fonts will be altered to match those on the Property Listing report. Figure 18.13 shows the changed report.

The fields from the original report aren't included when you create a report style. They're therefore missing when you define a new report that uses the style—you must add them yourself. This points out the principal advantage of saving and reusing actual reports. When you create a new report by loading a copy of another report, you automatically get all the fields in the original report, including those in its page header. The original report becomes a template from which you can construct additional reports.

FIGURE 18.12.

The Tenant Listing report before the AllReports style has been applied to it.

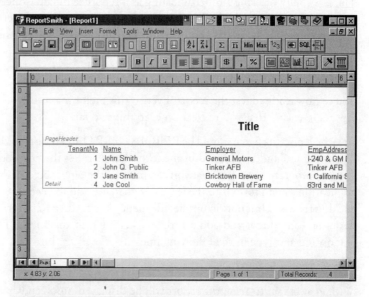

FIGURE 18.13.

The Tenant Listing report after the AllReports style has been applied to it.

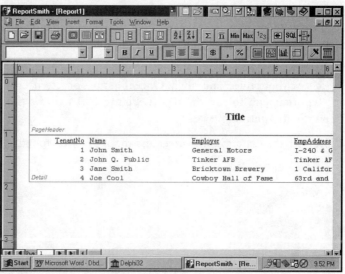

If you don't want the detail columns from the first report, they're easy enough to delete. You probably *will* want the page heading fields and their attributes. They'll all be present along with any report macros you created. This saves time when creating new reports and provides the same basic benefits as using report styles.

To save the Property Listing report as a report template, save the report using a generic name like AllReprt (I've omitted the *o* to keep the name to eight characters). After you've saved the report with this generic name, new reports can be built by simply loading and modifying it. The possibility of using Property Listing as a report template is the reason I had you add the Report criteria text field. The Property Listing report doesn't actually have any governing criteria, but reports you base on it might. For this report, you can simply remove the field.

Testing the Report

You're now ready to test the report. Even at this preliminary stage, it's a good idea to test your reports to ensure that you're clear on everything so far.

Save the report (its name should be RPROLST0.RPT) and return to Delphi. The dmRentalMan data module should be loaded in the form designer. Set the reRPROLST0 Report component's Preview property to True so that you can preview the report before it's printed. Next, load your application's main form into the form designer and add the rentdata unit to its Uses clause by clicking the Use Unit option on the File menu. Next, add a Reports menu to your main form's MainMenu component and add a Property List item to this menu. Double-click the Property List option and type in the following line:

```
dmRentalMan.reRPROLST0.Run;
```

With Preview set to True, the report will be displayed onscreen when the Property List menu option is selected. A variety of functions can then be performed, including both printing the report and saving it to disk. Saving a report to disk enables you to store the report's output in a number of formats. These include the Excel, Lotus 1-2-3, and Quattro Pro spreadsheet formats as well as several text formats.

Next, save your project and run it. Once the app is onscreen, click the Property List option on its Reports menu to run the report. Figure 18.14 shows the report as it appears in the ReportSmith runtime viewer.

Close both the ReportSmith viewer and the application to return to Delphi.

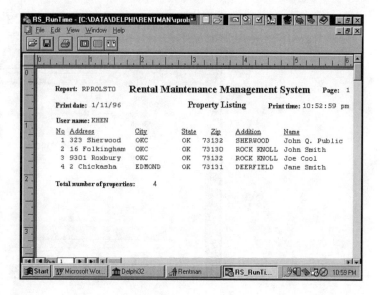

Mailing Labels

The next ReportSmith report you construct will print mailing labels using the TENANT table. Drop a new Report component onto the dmRentalMan data module and name it reRTENLBL0. Set its ReportName property to rtenlbl0. Next, edit the new report in ReportSmith by right-clicking the component and selecting Edit Report. Select Label Report from ReportSmith's list of report types and add the TENANT table to the report.

You're next placed into the Insert Field dialog. You can then drag report field from the TENANT table onto the label report. Drag the TENANT table's Name field onto the upper corner of the label Report, then click the dialog's Done button.

Next, you'll add the PROPERTY table to the report so that you can print the tenant's address on your mailing lables. Click the Table option on the Tools menu, then add the PROPERTY table to the report. Add a link between the TENANT and PROPERTY tables by clicking the Add new link button in the Tables dialog. ReportSmith correctly assumes that you want to link the two tables using the TenantNo column. Click the Done button to return to ReportSmith's main screen.

After you've linked the tables, bring up the Insert Field dialog and drag the Address, City, State, and Zip fields onto the label report. (See Figure 18.15.)

FIGURE 18.15.
The Tenant Mail Labels report as it initially appears.

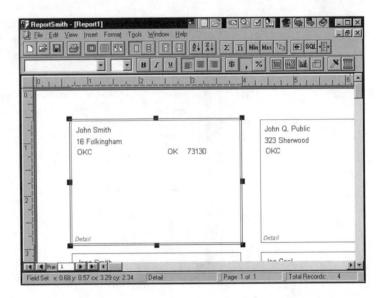

Because they're merely positioned adjacent to one another, the City and State fields are not formatted very well. There is a noticeable gap between them due to space at the end of the City field.

To get rid of this extraneous space, you create a derived field that combines City, State, and Zip into a single field that you can then place on the report. Create a new derived field named CityStateZip by selecting Derived Field on the Tools menu. Define the field using a ReportBasic macro named GetCityStateZip. Type this code into the macro:

```
DerivedField Trim$(Field("City"))+", "+ Trim$(Field("State"))+ " "+
➡Trim$(Field("Zip"))
```

This macro combines the City, State, and Zip fields into a single string and removes unnecessary spaces from each field. It also places the customary comma between the City and State fields. The fields are changed from being formatted like

```
CITY    STATE  Zip
```

to instead look like

```
CITY, STATE Zip
```

which is what we're after.

Save your CityStateZip field and drag it onto the label report. Remove the City, State, and Zip fields from the label, then place the CityStateZip field so that it occupies the position on the label formerly occupied by the three fields. (See Figure 18.16.)

FIGURE 18.16.

The Tenant Labels report with its City, State, *and* Zip *fields reformatted.*

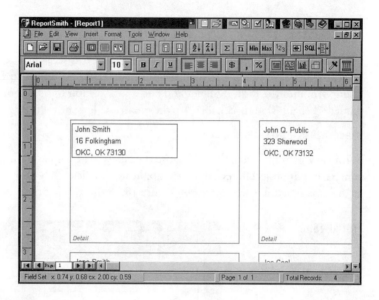

Selecting a Label Type

Before you print the labels, you'll need to select the type of labels you want to use. ReportSmith supports the Avery label family and also enables you to define and use custom labels. Select Page Setup from ReportSmith's File menu and click the Labels radio button. Select the Avery 5162 Address label from the Label type list, then click OK. Figure 18.17 shows the new label selection.

FIGURE 18.17.

The Tenant mailing label report using Avery 5160 address labels.

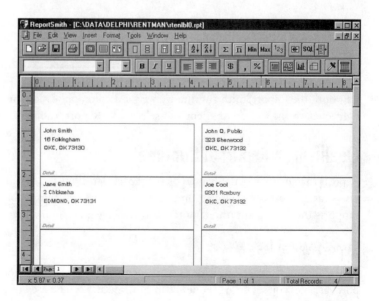

Running the New Report

Once you've configured the type of label you want to use, you're ready to test your mailing labels report. Save the report (name it RTENLBL0) and return to Delphi. Next, load your main form into the form designer and add a new option to its Reports menu. Add an option named "Tenant Mailing &Labels" to the menu and key the following code into its Click event:

```
dmRentalMan.reRTENLBL0.Run;
```

With Preview set to True, this will cause the labels to be displayed onscreen when the report is run. Save your project now and run the application. Click the New option on the Reports menu to make sure that it works correctly. Figure 18.18 shows what the new report should look like.

FIGURE 18.18.

The Tenant Mailing Labels report as it appears at runtime.

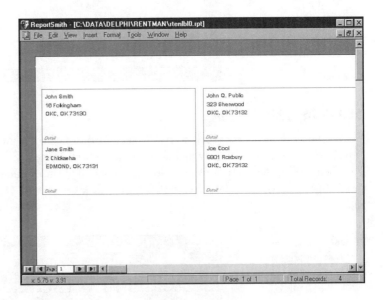

Exit both the ReportSmith runtime viewer and your application and return to Delphi. Next, right-click the Report component and select Edit Report from its context menu.

Qualifying a Report at Runtime

Reports that are to be actually used by people have to allow the data they return to be qualified. Users rarely want entire tables dumped. One of the nicest things about ReportSmith is that it supports this basic reporting requirement in a very graceful manner.

Report Variables

Report variables are special fields that enable the user to specify report criteria at runtime. Report variables you set up are requested at runtime and can be used to qualify data on the report.

You can also print report variables in a report's header. Report variables can be simple text entry fields, Boolean fields, and list- and table-based entries. You can display one column from a table while using another, or you can set up your own list of values. The prompt and dialog title you specify for a report variable are displayed at runtime when the user is prompted to supply a value.

Click the Tools/Report Variables menu option and define a new report variable named `SelectedTenantName`. Set the new field's data type to `String`, its dialog title to `Select Tenant Name`, and its prompt to `Please enter a tenant name or wildcard mask to use when printing labels`. Set its property to `Type-in` and its `Maximum` property to `30`, and then click New. Click Done to exit the dialog. Figure 18.19 shows the completed dialog.

FIGURE 18.19.

Report variables prompt for report criteria at runtime.

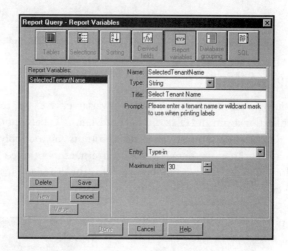

In order to limit the data returned by the report using this new variable, you must modify the row Selections utilized by the report's query. To do this, click Selections on the Tools menu. Next, click the button next to the `Include records in the report…` line in the upper-left of the dialog box and select Add selection criteria from the pop-up menu. Click the TENANTxDB.TenantNo element in the criteria and change it to TENANTxDB.Name instead. Change `is equal to` to `is patterned like` and change the `text` element to `report variable`. Because you have only one report variable, ReportSmith will automatically select it and place it in your selection criteria. Click Done to apply your criteria. Figure 18.20 shows the completed Selections criteria.

When ReportSmith prompts you to supply the `SelectedTenantName` report variable, type in a percent sign (`%`). SQL uses the percent sign as a wildcard character, so ReportSmith will then display all the rows in the TENANT table.

FIGURE 18.20.
*The Report Query
Selections dialog box.*

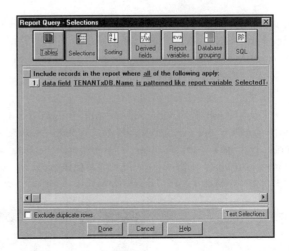

Testing the Report

Once you've finished defining your report variable, save your report and return to Delphi. Run your application again and click the Tenant Mailing Labels option on the Reports menu. Notice that the ReportSmith runtime viewer now prompts you to supply a value for SelectedTenantName. You can supply an entire name or just a pattern, as mentioned previously. Figure 18.21 shows the dialog. Notice that I've supplied John% as the criteria. This will limit the labels printed to the two customers whose first names begin with John.

FIGURE 18.21.
*Prompting for parameters
for the Tenant Mailing
Label report.*

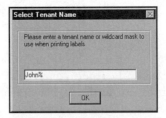

The mailing label report is now finished. The next report you do will be a crosstab report. A crosstab report groups and summarizes data in a spreadsheet-like manner. The crosstab report will be more involved than the mailing label report. It uses several tables and summarizes their data in a table-like fashion.

Crosstab Reports

The crosstab report you'll next build groups and summarizes the maintenance done at each rental property by the type of work actually performed. Each report row is to list a rental property followed by the amount of time spent on each type of maintenance on the property. The report will enable the user to easily tell whether a given type of maintenance, say the monthly lawn care service, has been performed at a property and how much time was spent completing it. Also, the report will allow the total maintenance time on each property to be easily ascertained by providing a total for each property row. Lastly, the report will allow the total time spent performing a given type of maintenance to be easily deduced by providing maintenance type column totals.

Close the report and exit the application. Drop a new `Report` component onto dmRentalMan and name it reRMANWKT0. Set its `ReportName` property to RMANWKT0 and set its `Preview` property to `True`.

Next, right-click the reRMANWKT0 `Report` component and select Edit Report from its context menu. Click the Cancel button in ReportSmith's Create a New Report dialog. Next, open the AllReports generic report template that you created earlier and resave the AllReports template using the name RMANWKT0, using the File/Save As menu option. This ensures that you don't inadvertently modify the template.

Next, click the Tools/Tables menu option and remove the PROPERTY and TENANT tables from the report. The links between the two tables also disappear. After you've done this, you need to add four tables to the report. Add the WODETAIL, WORDERS, PROPERTY, and WORKTYPE tables using the Add report button. Link the WODETAIL and WORDERS tables on the `WorkOrderNo` column. Link the WORDERS and PROPERTY tables on the `PropertyNo` column. Finally, link the WODETAIL table and the WORKTYPE table on the `WorkTypeCode` column. Once you've established these links, click the Done button to exit the Tables dialog.

Next, change the report's title line to read "Property Maintenance Grouped and Summarized by Work Type." Once you've changed the report title, delete all the columns that ReportSmith has automatically inserted in the detail area. Once the columns are removed, select the Detail section itself and delete it. Crosstabs cannot be inserted into the Detail section of a report; they must be inserted into a header or footer section, instead.

Next, resize the Page Footer section so that it occupies all of the remaining screen area. You'll place the crosstab in this section and you need all the room you can get. Next, delete the summary field (and its label) from the report footer. These fields corresponded to the PROPERTY table from which the AnyReport style was built and no longer apply.

You're now ready to insert a crosstab into the report. Click the crosstab button on ReportSmith's toolbar to create a crosstab object for insertion into the report. Once the Crosstab Report dialog is displayed, add the `Address` column from the PROPERTY table to the Rows list, add the WORKTYPE table's `Description` field to the Columns list and its `TaskDuration` column to the Values list. Once this is done, click the crosstab's Options button (it's the leftmost Options button, not the ones under each of the lists) and deselect the Fix Cell Size and Labels options. Set the `Null Value String` to N/A and click OK. Next, click OK to finish defining the crosstab.

ReportSmith then pauses briefly to generate the crosstab. Once it's done, the mouse pointer becomes a crosstab bitmap. You can then click the Page Footer section to insert it. Figure 18.22 shows what it should look like.

FIGURE 18.22.

The crosstab shows the work done on rental properties.

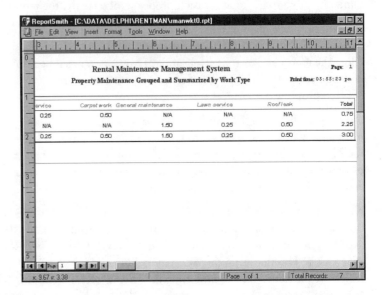

Because the crosstab could conceivably return a large number of columns, you should switch the paper size and orientation of the report. Click the File/Page Setup menu option and switch the report to landscape orientation on legal paper. Now a much larger number of columns will fit on the report. Since you've changed the width of the printed page, you'll need to adjust the fields in the report's page header.

An alternative to changing the paper size and/or the report's print orientation would be to reduce the size of the fonts in use on the report. You might find this preferable to using larger paper because changing paper types may force your users to manually load different types of paper when they print your reports.

The final thing you need to do to finish up the report is to add report variables to control what records are selected for printing. Unlike the other reports you've designed, this crosstab report is the type of report that requires some sort of selection criteria because it's unlikely that the user would want to see all maintenance on all properties from the time of system origination to the present. The amount of maintenance on a property is relevant within the context of the amount of time over which that maintenance was performed.

Add two report variables to the report: one to specify a beginning date for the report, the other an ending date. To do this, click the `Report Variables` option on the Tools menu. Set the new variable's `Name` to `FromDate`, its `Type` to `Date`, its `Title` to `From Date`, and its `Prompt` to `Enter the report's beginning date`, and then click the Add button. Next, click the New button and set up a second Date variable named ToDate. Set its Title to To Date and its Prompt to Enter the report's ending date. When you're finished, click the Done button.

Now that the report variables have been created, you're ready to add them into the report's governing criteria. Click the Selections option on the Tools menu to bring up the Report Query-Selections dialog. Click the 1 on the dialog and select Add Selection Criteria from the menu. Change the data field to the EndDate column in the WORDERS table. Change the expression operator from is equal to to is between and set up the FromDate and ToDate report variables as the operands of expression. Click Done to complete your selection.

With the report variables now in place and controlling what rows are displayed on the report, you need to add them to the report's page heading so that this will be obvious to the user. Click the Report criteria text field in the report heading. This field serves as a placeholder to remind you to include any criteria controlling the rows printed on the report in its heading. You'll replace this field with the actual criteria governing the report.

Delete the Report criteria field from the PageHeader section. Next, create a derived field named ReportCriteria. Set it up to be macro-based and name the macro GetReportCriteria. Set the macro's code to the following:

```
Dim ReturnVar as String
Dim FromDate as String
Dim ToDate as String
FromDate$=GetRepVar("FromDate")
ToDate$=GetRepVar("ToDate")
ReturnVar$=FromDate$+" through "+ToDate$
DerivedField ReturnVar$
```

Place this new field in the position formerly occupied by the Report criteria placeholder. Center it under the report's title line. This will cause the value of the two report variables to be displayed in the report heading when you print the report. Figure 18.23 shows the completed report.

Now that you've completed the report, you're ready to wire it into your application. Save the report and return to Delphi. Load your main form into the visual designer and double-click its MainMenu component. Insert a new menu item on the Reports menu just before the Tenant Mailing Labels item and set its Caption to &Maintenance by Work Type. Double-click it and type in a call to the new Report component's Run method, as in the following:

```
dmRentalMan.reRMANWKT0.Run;
```

This will cause the report to be displayed in preview mode when you select the new menu item. Now save your project and run the application. Select the new menu item, and you'll see the report previewed in the ReportSmith runtime viewer.

The ReportSmith report you just designed is a fairly sophisticated report. Because of the wealth of tools available in ReportSmith, crosstabs among them, complex reports can often be constructed with very little coding.

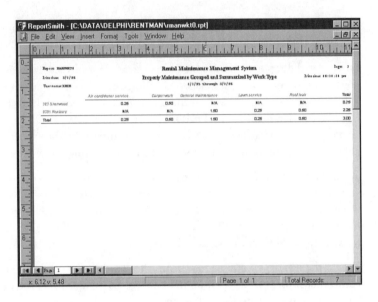

Form Reports

Form reports are used for printing a single row per page in a fixed format, such as an invoice or a work order. Typically, a separate page is generated for each row in the report's main table. You'll build a form report that lists out the TENANT table. The TENANT table is a particularly appropriate subject for a form report because of its numerous fields. Besides printing a table using a fixed-form layout, another good use of a form report is in printing tables with many columns. By listing the TENANT table using a form report, you create a report that is easier to read and more informative than a similar columnar report.

Exit your test application and return to Delphi. Drop a new Report component onto the dmRentalMan form and name it reRTENLST0. Set its Preview property to True and its ReportName property to RTENLST0. Right-click the component and select Edit Report from the menu.

When ReportSmith starts, select Form Report from the Create a New Report dialog. The dialog you see will be the Tables dialog. Click the Add table button and double-click the TENANT table from the list of tables. Click the Done button to exit the Tables dialog. You should then see ReportSmith's main screen with the fields from the TENANT table placed into a default form report layout. (See Figure 18.24.)

FIGURE 18.24.

The form report that ReportSmith generates for the TENANT table.

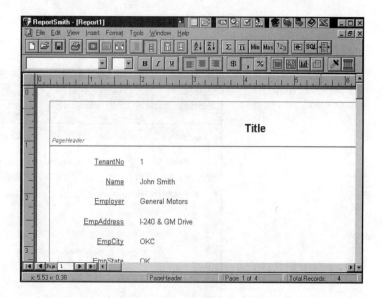

This report needs a few changes before it's ready for prime time. First, you need to add the same fields to its header that you added to all the others. Given that you haven't yet defined a report template for form reports, the easiest way to do this is to load the Property List report (RPROLST0) and copy the fields in its header to the clipboard, then paste them into your new report. To do this, follow these steps:

1. Open RPROLST0 in ReportSmith.
2. Select each of the fields in the report's page heading. You can do this by clicking the first field in the header, then holding down the Shift key while you click the rest of them. After they're all selected, press Ctrl+C to copy them to the clipboard. *Be very careful NOT to select the page heading section itself—only its fields.*
3. Close RPROLST0.
4. Reselect the window containing your new report (you can do this via the Window menu), then click the page heading section, and press Ctrl+V.

NOTE

You'll need to redefine and re-insert the UserName and ReportName derived fields from the Property Listing report. This is due to the unfortunate fact that the copy/paste operation detailed previously converts these two fields to text when they're pasted onto the target report. Instructions for defining and placing these fields are contained in the section, "Columnar Reports."

Change the report's title from Property Listing to Tenant Listing and save the report as RTENLST0. Figure 18.25 shows the completed Tenant Listing report.

FIGURE 18.25.

The completed Tenant Listing report.

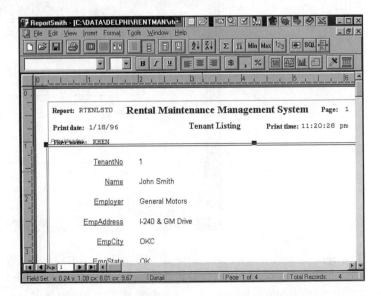

Now that you've completed the report, it's time to wire it into your test application. Exit ReportSmith and return to Delphi. Select the RENTALMAN application's main form and add a Tenant List item to its Reports menu. Set up the new item's OnClick event handler to execute the following line of code:

```
dmRentalMan.reRTENLST0.Run;
```

Then save your application and run it. Figure 18.26 shows what the new report should look like at runtime.

FIGURE 18.26.
The Tenant Listing report at runtime.

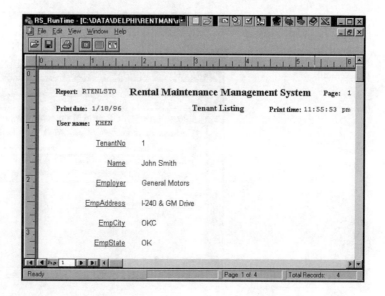

Master/Detail Reports

Master/detail reports show a one-to-many relationship between two tables. The master table is serviced by one query, while the detail query is serviced by another. The rows in the detail portion of a report page correspond to the master row with which they share the page.

Exit the application and return to Delphi. Drop a new Report component onto the dmRentalMan form and set its name to reRWORLST0. Change its ReportName to RWORLST0 and its ReportDirectory to C:\DATA\DELPHI\RENTMAN (or whatever you're using). Toggle Preview to True, then right-click the component and select Edit Report.

Click the Cancel button in the Create a New Report dialog, then click the Open option on ReportSmith's toolbar. Open the AllReports report template that you created earlier. Immediately resave the report template using your new report name, RWORLST0, so that you don't accidentally modify your template.

Select the Tables option from the Tools menu and delete both tables from the report. Next, add the WORDERS table back into the report, and then click Done. You should then be returned to ReportSmith's main screen and should see the fields from the WORDERS table inserted into the report. Change the report's title from Property Listing to Work Order Listing and delete the fields in its ReportFooter section. Figure 18.27 shows the preliminary version of the report.

FIGURE 18.27.

The preliminary version of the Work Order Listing report.

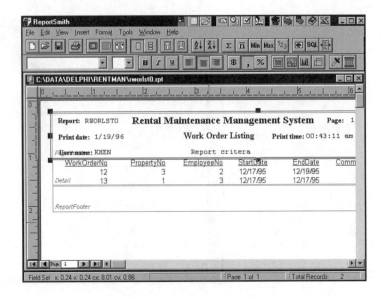

Now click the Detail Report option on the Insert menu. You'll then see the Tables dialog. Click Add table and select the WODETAIL table. Click the Done button, and you'll be placed in the Link Master/Detail Reports dialog. The list on the left side of the dialog should reflect the fields in the WORDERS table; the one on the right should list the fields in the WODETAIL table. Click the Add field to key button under each list to add the WorkOrderNo field to the Key Fields list, then click OK. (See Figure 18.28.)

FIGURE 18.28.

Use the Link Master/Detail Report to link master and detail reports together.

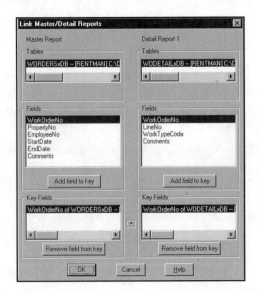

Next, click the `WorkOrderNo` column in the report's detail section and delete it. Because within a group of detail records the `WorkOrderNo` column will never change, there's no point in printing it repetitively. After you've done this, click the Report criteria text field in the report's header and delete it. Click the Detail Report 1 Detail section, then click the Section menu item on the Format menu. Check the New Page After box, and then click OK. This will cause a page break to be generated after each set of detail data. Because a new set of detail data will print for each record in the WORDERS table, this will have the effect of placing each work order on a separate page, which is what you're after. Figure 18.29 shows the completed Master/Detail report.

FIGURE 18.29.

The completed Work Order Listing Master/Detail report.

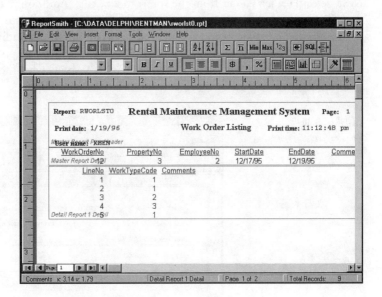

There are many other things you could do to further enhance this report (such as translate the `PropertyNo`, `EmployeeNo`, and `WorkTypeCode` columns), but I've purposely kept it simple so that you could see just how easy it is to build Master/Detail reports using ReportSmith.

Save your report and return to Delphi. After you're back in Delphi, reload your RENTALMAN application's main form into the visual form designer and add a menu item that invokes your new report when clicked. To reiterate, you add a report to your menu system by first adding a new menu item for the report, and then associating a call to the `Report` component's `Run` method with the menu item's `OnClick` event. Refer to the reports that you added to the menu system previously in case you need any help.

Summary-Only Reports

This next report will be only a test. You won't worry about linking into the RENTALMAN application. Start ReportSmith and load the RPROLST0 report you created earlier. In this section, you'll modify the Property List report so that it returns summary information only. *Summary-only reports* are useful when you want to see the "big picture" and aren't concerned with the details behind totals, averages, and other computations on a report.

Select the Report Grouping item on the Tools menu and select the Addition column as the column by which you wish to group the report. Doing this will organize the report so that all the properties of a given addition are listed sequentially, and each addition is distinguished from the others.

Next, select Header/Footer from the Insert menu, click Addition_Group, click Header, and then click OK. You should see a group header section inserted into the report. Next, select Field from the Insert menu and add the Addition column to the Addition_Group header section. Change the font of the field's label to Times New Roman, 10 pts., Bold, and set the font of the field itself to Courier New, 10 pts. Figure 18.30 shows what the report should look like thus far.

FIGURE 18.30.

The Property List report with its Addition_Group section intact.

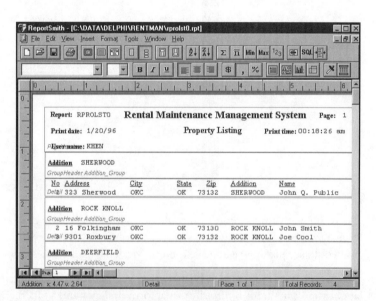

NOTE

You can also insert fields into a header or footer section on a report by dragging them there from elsewhere. You do this by first switching ReportSmith into form mode (also known as field, not column, editing mode), then dragging the field from the detail section to the header or footer.

Now, insert a footer into the report for the Addition_Group report grouping. Select Header/ Footer from the Insert menu, click the Addition_Group selection, click Footer, then click OK. You should see a new group footer inserted into the report for the Addition_Group report grouping. Next, click the `PropertyNo` column and click the Count button on the ReportSmith toolbar. This will insert a summary field into both of the footers (the new Addition_Group footer as well as the original report footer) in your report. You can go ahead and delete the one added to the report footer.

Change the label text of the new field to `Number of properties` and set its font to Times New Roman, 10 pts., Bold. Set the font of the field itself to Courier New, 10 pts. Figure 18.31 shows the report with the new footer in place.

FIGURE 18.31.

The Property List report as it appears with its new Addition_Group footer in place.

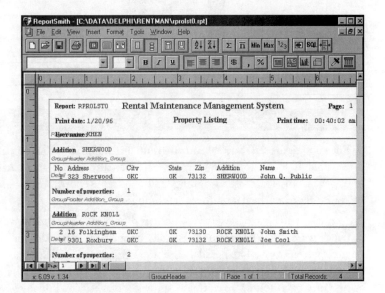

The only thing you have to do now to change the report to a summary-only report is delete its Detail section. Click the Detail section now and press the Delete key. You'll see the Detail rows disappear, but the group header and footer that you established earlier will remain intact. Save the report now as RPROLST1.RPT (be sure to increment the sequence number at the end of the filename so that you don't overwrite the original Property List report). Figure 18.32 shows the report in summary-only form.

FIGURE 18.32.

The Property List report as it looks after it has been converted to a summary-only report.

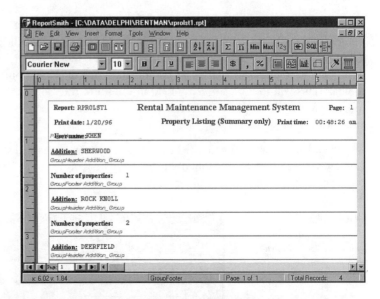

NOTE

For large result sets, you'll want to group and summarize data on a database server, if possible. If you're working with data that actually resides on a database server, you can use the Tools/Database Grouping facility to tell ReportSmith to allow your database server to group the data rather than doing so itself.

Allowing your database server to do this type of work has many advantages. First, you cut down on network traffic drastically because the only data traveling over it are the summarized rows. The detail data doesn't need to traverse the network if you aren't going to print it. Second, the whole purpose of database servers is to group and organize data, so they're normally quite good at it. You'll likely get better performance when you allow your server to do its job. Lastly, some types of queries—especially those that involve huge numbers of rows—simply aren't possible unless they're run on a database server. The time needed to download the detail data to the server might take days, and that might not be practical in your situation.

Conditional Formatting

Something that you'll run into surprisingly often is the need to conditionally format the text in a report. You might want to underline a field value if it falls outside of a certain range, or perhaps display it in red, or maybe not print it at all, depending on your needs. ReportSmith enables you to do all this—and do it more simply—by linking a macro and a field on the report together.

To begin, reload the Tenant Listing report (RTENLST0) you created earlier and select Macros from the Tools menu. Type `PossiblyMove` as the new macro's name and click the New button. Set up the macro to look like the following:

```
Sub PossibleMove()
 Red=RGB( 255,0,0 )
  If (DateValue(Field$("LeaseEndDate"))-30) <= Date Then FieldFont "",0,-1,Red,-1
End Sub
```

Notice the use of the `RGB` function to derive a value for the color `Red`. The `If` statement checks to see if the value of the `LeaseEndDate` field minus thirty days is less than or equal to today's date. If so, the tenant is planning to move within the next thirty days, so the company needs to immediately start running newspaper ads for the property. By linking this macro to the `LeaseEndDate` field on the report, you cause it to be displayed in red if the rental company needs to take action immediately.

Click OK to get back to the Macro Commands dialog, then click the Links button to associate the new macro with a data field on the report. After the Macro Links dialog is displayed, drop down the Object Type list and select DataField. Next, scroll the list of data fields and select LeaseEndDate from the list, and then click OK. After you're back in the Macro Commands dialog, click OK to return to ReportSmith's main screen.

If you now flip through the records in the TENANT table, you should see any `LeaseEndDate` fields that are within 30 days of the current date displayed in red. (See Figure 18.33.)

FIGURE 18.33.

The Tenant Listing report modified to show tenants who are about to move.

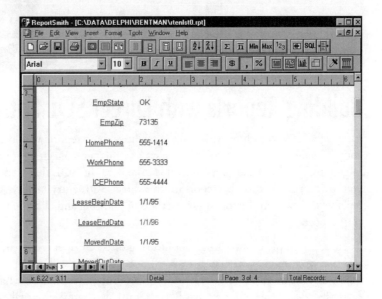

Graphics in Reports

Adding graphics to a report can make it look more professional and friendlier to your clients. ReportSmith supports a couple of different ways of inserting graphics objects into your reports. First, you can plant graphics images in your reports by clicking the Insert Picture button on the ReportSmith toolbar (or by clicking Picture on the Insert menu) and selecting a bitmap. Second, you can use ReportSmith's drawing toolbox to add simple graphics elements to your reports. Figure 18.34 illustrates both of these facilities.

FIGURE 18.34.

Graphics from simple drawing objects to complex bitmap images can be inserted into ReportSmith reports.

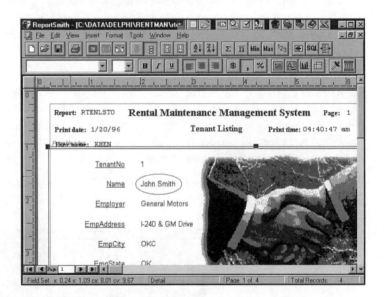

Building Reports with Direct SQL Entry

Although ReportSmith provides all the facilities most reports would ever need, you may find yourself wanting more control over the way that data is collected for your reports. A good way to gain this additional level of control is to replace the SQL that ReportSmith generates with your own. You do this via ReportSmith's direct SQL entry facility. Using direct SQL entry replaces the standard ReportSmith method of pointing and clicking to construct a data set for your report.

There are a couple of ways to go about using direct SQL entry. First, you can create a report that uses your own SQL to begin with. For reports that will be driven by SQL stored procedures, this makes the most sense. Second, you can convert an existing report to a direct SQL report by editing the SQL text that ReportSmith generates. This makes more sense if you're an SQL novice or if you want to save yourself typing in a large number of column names. The following paragraphs will explore both methods.

Click the New report icon on the ReportSmith toolbar and select Columnar Report. Once in the Tables dialog, click the SQL button on the far right. Once in the SQL dialog, key the following simple SQL query, substituting whatever directory you've stored the WORKTYPE table in for C:\DATA\DELPHI\RENTMAN:

```
SELECT * FROM 'C:\DATA\DELPHI\RENTMAN\WORKTYPE.DB'
```

Click the Done button, and you should see ReportSmith build a simple columnar report using the columns from the WORKTYPE table.

Now try a little more complex example. Open the RMANWKT0 report and select SQL Text from the Tools menu. You should see something like the following SQL query:

```
SELECT

'WODETAILxDB'.'WorkOrderNo', 'WODETAILxDB'.'LineNo',
'WODETAILxDB'.'WorkTypeCode', 'WODETAILxDB'.'Comments',
'WORDERSxDB'.'WorkOrderNo', 'WORDERSxDB'.'PropertyNo',
'WORDERSxDB'.'EmployeeNo', 'WORDERSxDB'.'StartDate',
'WORDERSxDB'.'EndDate', 'WORDERSxDB'.'Comments',
'PROPERTYxDB'.'PropertyNo', 'PROPERTYxDB'.'TenantNo',
'PROPERTYxDB'.'Address', 'PROPERTYxDB'.'City',
'PROPERTYxDB'.'State', 'PROPERTYxDB'.'Zip',
'PROPERTYxDB'.'Addition', 'PROPERTYxDB'.'BedRooms',
'PROPERTYxDB'.'LivingAreas', 'PROPERTYxDB'.'BathRooms',
'PROPERTYxDB'.'GarageType', 'PROPERTYxDB'.'SchoolDistrict',
'PROPERTYxDB'.'Deposit', 'PROPERTYxDB'.'Rent',
'PROPERTYxDB'.'Range', 'PROPERTYxDB'.'Refrigerator',
'PROPERTYxDB'.'DishWasher', 'PROPERTYxDB'.'CentralHeat',
'PROPERTYxDB'.'CentralAir', 'PROPERTYxDB'.'GasHeat',
'PROPERTYxDB'.'PrivacyFence', 'PROPERTYxDB'.'LastSprayDate',
'PROPERTYxDB'.'LastLawnDate', 'PROPERTYxDB'.'Comments',
'WORKTYPExDB'.'WorkTypeCode', 'WORKTYPExDB'.'Description',
'WORKTYPExDB'.'TaskDuration'
FROM
'C:\DATA\DELPHI\RENTMAN\WORDERS.DB' WORDERSxDB
RIGHT JOIN 'C:\DATA\DELPHI\RENTMAN\PROPERTY.DB' PROPERTYxDB
ON ('WORDERSxDB'.'PropertyNo' = 'PROPERTYxDB'.'PropertyNo' ),
➥'C:\DATA\DELPHI\RENTMAN\WODETAIL.DB' WODETAILxDB,
'C:\DATA\DELPHI\RENTMAN\WORKTYPE.DB' WORKTYPExDB
WHERE
('WODETAILxDB'.'WorkOrderNo'= 'WORDERSxDB'.'WorkOrderNo' )
AND ('WODETAILxDB'.'WorkTypeCode'= 'WORKTYPExDB'.'WorkTypeCode' )
```

You can now click the Edit SQL button to make your own changes to the SQL that ReportSmith has generated. This is no trivial process, and you should carefully consider whether it's what you really want to do before doing it. After you convert a report to a direct SQL entry report, you can't go back to ReportSmith's visual query tools.

Another way of keying in your own SQL statements is through the use of SQL-based derived fields. The derived fields you've seen in this chapter have all been macro-based, but you can also build them using SQL. In the Report Query - Derived Fields dialog, you simply select Defined by SQL rather than Defined by ReportBasic macro to define a derived field using SQL.

One final way of executing your own SQL from under ReportSmith is through the use of the ExecSQL macro command. ExecSQL enables you to execute stored procedures and other types of SQL that do not return a result set.

What's Ahead

The next chapter begins the first of a two-part series on proper business rules implementation. Chapter 19 gives you the basics needed for developing a sound business rules philosophy in your Delphi applications. You'll want to be sure and read it before building business rules into your Delphi applications.

Summary

You've now completed your quick tour of ReportSmith's many handy facilities. You've learned how to build all four of ReportSmith's basic report types—columnar, crosstab, label, and form—and you've learned to create custom variations of these, as well. You've learned how to set up report groupings, report variables, and derived fields. You've also learned how to set up a Delphi application to properly interact with ReportSmith. You should be well on your way to developing complex database reports using ReportSmith's many extraordinary features.

IV

Advanced Topics

19

Business Rules Part I

This chapter discusses the server side of implementing business rules in database applications. There are those who discuss business rule implementations as a theoretical concept separate from the database constraints and program objects necessary to implement them. While I agree that one must understand an organization's business rule needs completely before implementing them, I think separating them from their practical application is a mistake. This is especially true because they must eventually be reduced to real database or program objects anyway.

There are also those who, from a conceptual standpoint, separate business rules from relational integrity constraints. This seems a bit ill-advised because one of the most basic business rules of any organization is that its database integrity must be assured. No business wants a database riddled with orphaned rows, invalid column values, and gaping security holes. On the contrary, the basic integrity and reliability of the database is a foundation the organization expects to be able to rely on. Thus, the two subjects—business rules and relational integrity—should be discussed together.

There are basically three schools of thought regarding the proper place for business rules: server implementations, client implementations, and middle-ware implementations. This chapter discusses the strengths and weaknesses of each approach and then delves into the server-based approach.

Business Rules Defined

Before discussing the proper location of a business rules implementation, what's required of an effective business rules strategy needs to be defined. An effective business rules implementation guarantees that data residing in a database complies with the rules and policies of an organization. One means of accomplishing this is to set up each column in each table in a database so that it protects against values that violate the organization's policies. In database terms, this means applying constraints to the data to ensure that it contains valid values. This is what usually comes to mind when one hears the term *business rules*.

But this isn't enough. Business rules actually have three separate functions: to keep unwanted data out of the database, to define relationships between columns and tables, and to describe the way that data originates in the database. I'll discuss each of these separately.

Constraints keep invalid data out of a database. They also define default values for columns if no values are supplied. An example of a constraint, in English terms, is, "The `CustomerNumber` column in the INVOICE table must have a corresponding record in the CUSTOMER table." This limits, or *constrains*, the values in the INVOICE table. Another example of a constraint would be, "The `PaymentType` column in all tables must be in the following list: 'C', 'H', 'R'." A constraint that defines a default for a column could be expressed in English as, "If a `PaymentType` is not specified, it defaults to `Cash`."

Business rule definitions can also define relationships between tables (for example, "For every invoice, there must be at least one item ordered") and intra-table relationships between columns (such as, "The `Commission` column in the SALES table equals the `AmountOfSale` column in the SALES table multiplied by the commission percentage stored in the REP table"). I usually like to avoid intra-table relationships between columns, preferring instead to perform calculations like these on the fly, but there are situations where this isn't possible. In this example, the `Commission` column is dependent upon the `AmountOfSale` column, so it could be argued that such dependencies prevent the database from being fully normalized. In any event, there are times when intra-table relationships are necessary, and, when they are, business rules define them.

Business rules can also be used to describe a data element's origin. Describing the origination of a data element describes where it comes from. Where did the database element originate? Is it a summation of column X in table Y? A simple example would be, "The general ledger accounts payable balance is updated by posting new AP transactions to it." This defines the origin or source of the general ledger accounts payable balance.

I should mention here that I think it's a good idea to avoid basing one data element on another when possible. I don't mean to say that this should never be done, just that you should carefully consider all the ramifications of doing so. The reason for this is that deriving one data element from another creates an inter-table dependency. This may be unavoidable, but it may also cause you headaches. If the source data changes, the dependent data will need to change, as well. Typically, you protect against this by implementing data "posting" mechanisms. Data that's been posted updates its dependent elements (as in the example of the GL accounts payable balance), thereby rendering itself uneditable—no further modifications are permitted once the dependent elements have been updated. Systems that avoid dependencies of this type are known as *bucketless* systems because they do not derive data elements for storage elsewhere in the database (in "buckets").

Now that you understand a little more about what business rules are, what's the best way to implement them? As I've mentioned, there are three schools of thought regarding the proper place for business rules. Determining the proper location for business rules largely determines the way in which they will be implemented. Obviously, if you implement business rules on the server, you'll do it via constraints and the like. If you put your business rule implementation on the client, you'll do it via program code. If you implement business rules in some middle-ware product, you'll do it by using the facilities provided by the middle-ware product.

Server-Based Business Rule Implementations

I guess it's the DBA in me, but I am an unabashed proponent of server-based business rules. This means that I adhere to the "fat server" approach to business rules implementation. My basic philosophy is this:

> Because middle-ware business rule tiers are not yet pervasive enough to use with the majority of available tools, business rules should be placed on the server when at all possible, and augmented, when necessary, on the client.

I think the reasons for this philosophy will become more evident as the pros and cons of the three models are discussed.

Server Implementation Strengths

One of the benefits of placing business rules on the database server is that the data itself is protected against tampering and accidental invalidation. Because the controls themselves are intrinsically linked to the data, server-based constraints ensure that data stored in the database will always contain valid values and will be protected against invalid deletions.

Another benefit to implementing business rules on the server is that all client applications that communicate with the database automatically have access to the rules. One of the big problems with the approach of locating business rules in client software is that client development tools are often platform or operating system dependent. Not so with server-based implementations. All of the major client/server DBMS vendors support client connections from a number of different operating systems and hardware platforms. No matter what the client's host operating environment actually is, it is both restricted by and has access to the business rules information on the database server.

Another advantage of implementing business rules on the server is that of speed. Because organizations typically view a database server as an infrastructure investment, they are more willing to purchase the hardware and software needed to ensure that the server performs optimally. If placing business rule constraints on a server severely impedes performance, a corporation is usually more willing to buy the extra resources needed to remedy this than it would be to put high-powered machines on every desktop, *even if the cost of the former exceeds that of the latter.*

Another point to consider is that database servers are usually, by design, scalable. This means that if your needs exceed the maximum performance a particular hardware platform is capable of, you can move your server and its data bank to a more powerful hardware platform without switching DBMS vendors or redesigning your database. This same sort of scalability would have to be present in middle-ware and client-based solutions in order for them to be viable alternatives. At present, this just isn't so. If your clients are Windows clients, you're pretty much locked into the Intel platform. True, Windows NT is also available on a handful of other platforms, but it doesn't begin to be as portable as, say, Sybase SQL Server, which is available on nearly every major hardware platform and operating system.

Server Implementation Weaknesses

One of the weaknesses of going the server-based route is that, obviously, additional constraints on database objects will slow down access to them. This could be so severe that it makes the server unusable.

The answer to this, though, is not to switch to either client or middle-ware-based business rules. It lies, rather, in the same approach one would take if a sudden increase in data volume slowed the server to the point of being unusable: Invest in the additional hardware and software resources to bring the server's performance up to par. In the example of a sudden increase in data volume, tossing the server out in favor of a client-based solution is usually not an option. The same should be true of business rule implementations: Treat the business rule implementation on a server as an integral part of the database and an essential element to have on the server. With that mentality, making the necessary investment to support server-based business rule implementations is less difficult.

Another weakness that's often pointed out by opponents of server-based business rules is that server implementations tend to be either database- or server-centric. This means that conveying business rule constraints between databases or across servers is either difficult or impossible. A table in one database could, presumably, not reference a table in another for the purpose of validating a column entry. Nor could a table on one server acquire a default value from a table on another. Because organizations have a tendency to organize servers by department, this presents a problem.

The answer to these concerns, though, lies in pushing DBMS vendors to improve cross-database and cross-server interoperability. Sybase, for example, already supports cross-database queries and has for years. Furthermore, technology such as Sybase's Replication Server answers the cross-server problem by allowing key tables to be automatically replicated from one server to another. The answer is not in jumping ship to yet another immature technology but in influencing existing vendors to grow their cross-database and cross-server facilities to the point that they're usable.

Another problem with server-based business rule implementations is that there is often a lack of integration between the client software and the server. One result of this is that server messages related to business rules are often improperly handled by the client or ignored altogether. For example, errors raised from within stored procedures or triggers by Sybase's RAISERROR facility are ignored by Delphi applications. Constraint violations are also sometimes mishandled by Delphi applications.

The solution here, though, is not in switching away from a server-based implementation. It lies instead in pushing client software tool vendors (such as Borland) to fully integrate with their supported back ends. That is, if Delphi provides support for Sybase SQL Server, that support should be complete and should support all the client-related facilities that SQL Server provides, including business rule violation detection.

Client Implementation Strengths

One of the strengths of implementing business rules on the client is the level of customization and control one has in dealing with reporting and responding to business rules. Field-by-field control is usually quite easy in front-end tools. Preventing the user from, for example, exiting a form until its entries are valid is normally a simple task.

Another advantage of client-side implementation is the richness of application programming languages when compared with SQL. Object Pascal is magnitudes richer as a language than SQL. Even BASIC is a more full-featured language than SQL.

A final advantage of implementing business rules on the client is that they can be encompassed in components that can then be reused in all applications developed with the tool. Adding business rules to an application then becomes as simple as dropping a component onto a form. The next chapter discusses this approach.

Client Implementation Weaknesses

The chief fallacy in placing business rules exclusively on the client is that doing so requires increasingly more powerful client machines on the desktop. Client machines end up requiring the type of resources that would have made a machine a potential server just a few years ago. You end up putting the latest, greatest hardware you can on the desktop because the client continually complains about performance. Client applications that include business rules have a larger memory footprint and run slower than those that do not. This is especially true with applications that must run server-based queries to support their client-based implementations.

With the constant upgrading of the client hardware comes all the headaches associated with constantly changing hardware and software configurations. Historically, the constant tuning and tweaking of hardware has been relegated to server machines, but this isn't the case in the world of the "fat client." You virtually end up with a server on each desktop, requiring additional personnel and expertise to support.

This approach also violates one of the main tenants of the client/server philosophy—that of the reduced need for client resources. The natural outgrowth of client/server DBMS usage, so the thinking goes, is that because the real work of the DBMS happens on the server, client machines can afford to be less-capable. The idea is that if resource needs increase, they will do so on the server, not the client. The "fat client" model runs directly counter to this thinking.

Another problem with building business rule implementations into client applications is that such implementations are rarely cross-tool, let alone cross-vendor in nature. This means that you'll have to "reinvent the wheel" if you need to, say, develop an application that updates a given table in Delphi one week and one that updates it in Borland C++ the next. Because the Borland C++ application can't access the business rules you built into your Delphi application, you'll have to redo them in the C++ application. The situation is even worse when the prospect of working with tools from multiple vendors is considered. Even if the Borland Database Engine were enhanced to support cross-tool business rules, you would still be hard-pressed to use this capability in applications built with, say, Visual Basic.

Building business rules into applications, rather than on a server, also removes the capability to view the entirety of a database or data bank's business rules from a single vantage point. Because the rules are all encapsulated in program code or objects, you cannot easily tell what constraints are in place on what data, unlike the server-based approach.

A final point to be made regarding the fallacy of client-based solutions is that even though a given application or tool may insulate the database from invalid data, the database itself remains unprotected. This creates an inordinate dependency on client software development tools that is not easily alleviated. It stipulates that all further development of client software must occur with the tool in question. Otherwise, the business rules will either be neglected or duplicated in another tool. Though tool vendors would certainly have no problem with this, it's not a good business strategy. It's far better to have the rules on the server where they can be enforced regardless of the client tool and accessed and shared by all applications, as they were intended to be.

Middle-Ware Strengths

Middle-ware refers to a layer of software between the client and the server. Specifically, middle-ware abstracts clients from servers and servers from clients—they communicate with each other through the middle-ware layer. Middle-ware can consist of anything between the client application itself and the database server. It might be a database connectivity API, such as the BDE, or it might be a business rules server that runs on the same computer as the database server. Middle-ware can have a number of different incarnations. Conceptually, the middle-ware approach may be the best of the available options. In a perfect world, business rules would be defined in operating system objects that would then reference database server objects. Certain operating systems—for example, Steve Job's NeXTSTEP—have made bold strides in this direction.

A middle-ware approach avoids the current difficulties with cross-server and cross-database business rule implementation, because the rules do not reside in a given database or on a given database server.

The middle-ware approach also avoids both the fat client and fat server problems. Presumably, neither the server nor the client will be encumbered by the presence of business rules. You won't have to invest in powerhouse PCs for the desktop, and your server-based resources should be free from the burden of a business rules implementation.

Middle-Ware Weaknesses

The only problem with the middle-ware approach, though, is that sufficient middle-ware tools are not yet available. Though there are a variety of proprietary solutions (PowerBuilder implements such a scheme, for example), these are rarely, if ever, cross-tool, let alone cross-vendor or cross-platform. This means that the business rules you define in PowerBuilder will likely not be usable in other tools. Thus, using PowerBuilder's middle-ware approach to business rules carries with it the same limitations as using the client-based approach.

A logical place for establishing portable business rule definitions would seem to be in either an ODBC or IDAPI database driver. The problem with this approach is that ODBC and IDAPI are inherently Windows-centric. If you need to develop a UNIX-based database application, you're out of luck. You won't be able to use business rules defined at the database driver level in Windows.

What you really need here is a business rules server, which brings back the subject of the server-based approach. The funny thing about this is that some of the very same people who have criticized server-based business rule implementations have called for a business rules server of some type. What is apparently not evident to them is that such a server already exists—it's the database server itself.

There's no reason that the database server and the business server need to be two different physical machines. They must address many of the same issues: connectivity, integrity, and multi-platform support. Thus, as I've said before, given the choice, I would opt for implementing business rules on the database server every time.

Implementing Server-Based Business Rules

Now that I've offered my views on what I think the proper business rules strategy is, what's the best way to implement it? Determining the proper location for business rules largely determines the way in which they will be implemented. If you go the server route, obviously you'll build database objects to support your implementation. The following section discusses those database objects and their respective roles in the business rules equation.

Getting Started

The first thing to do in developing a business rules scheme is to get with the users of the application or database and exhaustively develop every rule and every policy that can be applied to the relevant data. The best way to do this is to use simple sentences written in plain English. A good time to do this is just after you've decomposed your field repository into the database or application's tables. Some examples of English-like business rules are

- Each invoice number must be unique in the INVOICE table.
- Every customer number in the INVOICE table must have a corresponding row in the CUSTOMER table.
- The credit cards accepted are Visa, MasterCard, and American Express.

- Each line item on an invoice is totaled by multiplying the cost of the item by the quantity ordered.

- An invoice total is derived by summing all extended line item totals, adding 7 percent sales tax and $5 shipping and handling.

- An invoice header record may not be deleted as long as there are invoice detail records that correspond with it.

- If not otherwise specified, the default method of shipping is Federal Express.

Every column in every table should be reviewed. Every effort should be made to ensure that each column allows only valid data. Every effort should be made to ensure that relationships between tables are established and protected. Every computation and every data origination should be worked out in advance. You might even consider having your client sign off on the list—especially if you're a consultant. Later, when you develop the constraints to place into the database design, you can check off each business rule on the list, one by one. Being thorough now will save you time (and heartache) later.

Primary Key Constraints

In SQL terms, constraints are the vehicle most often used in implementing server-based business rules. While it's true that triggers can do all that constraints can do and more, my philosophy regarding the trigger versus constraint debate is as follows:

> Constraints always have preference over triggers. Address as much of your business rules implementation as you can by using constraints. Address the remainder with views, triggers, or stored procedures, in that order. Give views preference over triggers and triggers preference over stored procedures.

The first type of constraint to apply is the *primary key constraint*. It denotes which columns in a table uniquely identify each row. A primary key is the default method of accessing a table. Examples of primary keys are the `InvoiceNumber` field in an INVOICE table and the `CustomerNumber` field in a CUSTOMER table. By adding a primary key constraint, you cause the database server to ensure that the values inserted into the primary key column or columns are unique within the table. Although you would normally define a primary key constraint when you create a table, you might also want to define it after the fact. Following is some SQL syntax to add a primary key constraint after a table has been created:

```
ALTER TABLE CUSTOMER ADD PRIMARY KEY (CustomerNumber)
```

Foreign Key Constraints

Foreign key constraints are popular for defining relationships between tables. They force a value in a column in one table to exist in another table. Likewise, they prevent the deletion of data from the second table referenced in the first. You use a foreign key constraint, for example, to ensure that all the customer numbers listed in the `CustomerNumber` field of the INVOICE table exist in the CUSTOMER table. You would normally create a foreign key reference when you construct a table, but you might need to do so afterward. Here's the SQL syntax to add a foreign key constraint after the fact:

```
ALTER TABLE ORDERS ADD FOREIGN KEY (CustomerNumber) REFERENCES CUSTOMER
```

Check Constraints

Another type of constraint is the *check constraint*. A check constraint ensures that a value inserted into a column exists in a given set of fixed values. Suppose that a given retail organization accepts only certain credit cards, for example, Visa, MasterCard, and American Express. Because this is a fixed set of values, it's a good candidate for a check constraint. You could code it as a check constraint by using the following SQL syntax:

```
ALTER TABLE ORDERS ADD CONSTRAINT INVALID_CREDIT_CARD
CHECK (CreditCardType in ('V','M','A'))
```

Defaults

Default values for fields are important in that they determine the value a column gets during an INSERT operation if one is not supplied. There is a tendency among developers to establish column defaults by using program code. For example, you could do this by using Delphi's `OnNewRecord` event. However, this is a bad practice. It makes spelunking through program code necessary in order to find the default values for a given table's columns. It's a far better practice to store those defaults on the server where they can be easily viewed or altered.

Though some vendors provide platform-specific means of establishing column defaults, I'll stick with the ANSI syntax. The ANSI syntax for establishing a column default is as follows:

```
ALTER TABLE ORDERS
ADD CreditCardType char(1)
DEFAULT 'V'
```

Views

There are times when implementing a particular business rule is best done via an SQL table *view*. Simply put, a view is an SQL SELECT statement that you may compile and query as though it were a table itself. The uses of SQL views are many and varied, though one key use of views in implementing business rules is that of performing computations involving columns in a table. For example, here's a view to calculate invoice line item totals:

```
CREATE VIEW INVOICEDETAIL
AS
SELECT InvoiceNumber, LineNumber, PriceEach * UnitsOrdered ExtendedTotal
```

This view implements a business rule that says, "Each line item on an invoice is totaled by multiplying the cost of the item by the quantity ordered."

Triggers

When all else fails, a *trigger* can usually get the job done. Many platforms include special extensions to SQL that give triggers and procedures special capabilities. You should always use a constraint, if possible, rather than a trigger. If you can't do what you need to do using a constraint, chances are a trigger will do the job. Here's an example of a trigger that goes beyond the simple capabilities of a column constraint:

```
CREATE TRIGGER ORDERSInsert FOR ORDERS BEFORE INSERT AS
BEGIN
  IF (New.CreditCardType='V' AND New.Amount<50.00) THEN
  EXCEPTION BELOW_MINIMUM_VISA;
END
```

This trigger ensures that orders made by using a Visa credit card are $50 or more. Because of the conditional nature of the rule, it can't be implemented by using a traditional column constraint. Thus, the use of a trigger is appropriate in this situation.

Stored Procedures

There is a trend in some SQL circles to use *stored procedures* for implementing business rules. The thinking is that one should use stored procedures for all data maintenance, building a separate INSERT, UPDATE, and DELETE stored procedure for each table. This procedure would then ensure that the proper integrity constraints and business rules were observed with each operation.

The problem with this approach is that it prevents the viewing of your database security and business rule implementation from a single vantage point. It also nullifies the use of tools like Delphi, because you basically deprive such tools of their inherent data-aware functions—which is the main reason for using them in the first place.

I don't recommend this approach and advise you to avoid it. Instead, use stored procedures only in situations where neither a traditional constraint nor a trigger can do the job.

An example of such a situation is that of the infamous posting routine. For example, if you want to accumulate the values in a column or columns for posting in a separate table, you'd probably do so via a stored procedure.

Consider the general ledger example mentioned earlier. If you were to write a stored procedure to handle the posting of accounts payable transactions to the general ledger, you would do something like this:

```
CREATE PROCEDURE POSTAP (APACCCOUNT)
AS
DECLARE VARIABLE APTOTAL FLOAT
BEGIN
  SELECT SUM(AmountOfTransaction) TranAmount
  INTO :APTOTAL
  FROM APTRANS;
```

```
   UPDATE GLBAL SET APMonthEndBalance=APMonthEndBalance+:APTOTAL
   WHERE AccountNumber=:APACCOUNT;
END
```

This procedure defines the `APMonthEndBalance` column as originating from the `AmountOfTransaction` column in the APTRANS table. It implements the business rule that says exactly how the general ledger accounts payable account balance is derived each month.

Stored procedures are good for situations like this one because they can perform as many SELECTs as necessary to perform the data operation you need to do. They're particularly well suited for batch-oriented operations like posting routines.

What's Ahead

Chapter 20, "Business Rules Part II," will discuss client-side business rules. At present, it's inevitable that you'll have to fill in the gaps in a server-based implementation with client-side business rules. Chapter 20 explores the many facets of application-based business rules.

Summary

If you take each concept outlined here, break it down, and apply it to your specific circumstances, you should find that implementing server-based business rules is intuitive and rather straightforward. I envision the database objects I've mentioned here as increasingly complex tools for doing a particular job—in this case, the job of implementing business rules. With each business rule, you use the simplest tool capable of meeting your needs. If a given tool can't do what you need, move up to the next one. For example, if a simple column constraint doesn't do the trick, you might need to move up to a view or trigger. Whatever the case, hopefully the examples given in this chapter will get you well on your way to successful business rule implementations.

20

Business Rules Part II

This chapter discusses the application side of successful business rules implementation. As I stated in the previous chapter, I believe that business rules should be implemented on the server side of an application whenever possible. However, it's inevitable that you'll need to augment server-side business rules with client-side rules. It's my hope that someday enough synergy will exist between database servers and software development tools that this will be a nonissue—that the developer won't have to be concerned with *where* business rules are implemented but can instead concentrate on *how* they're implemented.

There is a propensity among longtime software developers to place a significant amount of an application's business rule logic in the application itself. The development tool world is more familiar territory to them, and DBMS platforms have historically lacked the sophisticated business rule facilities that polished applications demand.

Propensities notwithstanding, as I stated in the previous chapter, moving an application's business rules wholesale to the application itself is not the answer. Developers must coerce DBMS vendors into providing the sophisticated business rule interfaces that professional applications require. The answer isn't to simply give up and produce a hackneyed solution that relies on inferior technology. It is, instead, to force DBMS vendors to meet the needs of their customers—to provide business rule support that real applications can use. Until this is done, client/server systems will continue to be little more immune to business rule infractions than their flat-file counterparts of yesteryear.

To their credit, DBMS vendors are making great strides in shoring up their business rule strategies. In the past, most business rule implementations were fairly air tight—they were safe—but they weren't "application-friendly." Developers had difficulty getting database objects and application objects to work together seamlessly. For example, if a Sybase trigger were used to supply default values for a table's rows, how would the application know this and display the default column values on-screen when a user added a row to the table? The developer was left to choose the lesser of two evils: Either ignore the server-based business rule and duplicate it in the developed applications, or blow off the need to synchronize the appearance of the application on-screen with its database counterparts. Neither option was particularly attractive, and, as Jerry Garcia once observed: "Choosing the lesser of two evils is still choosing evil."

Today, DBMS vendors are becoming increasingly more "application aware." Sound business rule design is easier now than ever before. At the same time, database development tools like Delphi are becoming more aware of and more intelligent about their database "pen pals" on the server side of the data link. The result is that development tools and DBMS platforms are converging in their attempts to satisfy the needs of their clients. The winners in all this are you and I. Implementing a sound business rule strategy is becoming increasingly easier as DBMS platforms and development tools learn to work together.

Despite where things are going, you, as a database developer, have to deal with where they are right now. The situation at present is that you will probably have to implement part of an application's business rules in the application itself. As I said in the previous chapter, the approach I take is this: I design all of the business rule strategy that I can on the DBMS platform itself, then I supplement this on the client as needed. It makes no difference whether you're dealing with Paradox tables or a full-blown client/server implementation. What I can't implement on the server, I implement at the client. I fill in the gaps of the server-based implementation with application objects and code.

This chapter addresses the application side of proper business rules implementation. It takes you through the various means of constructing an effective business rule strategy in your applications. You'll learn that there are four major levels of application-based business rule design in Delphi: the data type level, the component level, the TField level, and the TDataSet level. Hopefully, you'll use what you learn here to extend a comprehensive server-based business rule scheme.

Types of Business Rules

Business rules come in two distinct types: *elementary* business rules and *advanced* business rules. Elementary rules provide for simple data validation. They ensure, for example, that numeric data goes into numeric fields, that date columns contain valid dates, and so on. Elementary rules apply no matter what the application is or what the database is being used for.

Advanced rules cover things like the referential integrity between two tables or the value a given column in a given table receives. They tend to be database specific; some are even table specific.

In this book, I use the term *business rules* in its broadest meaning. That is, I include both elementary and advanced rules in the same discussion. Everything from simple data validation to complex relational integrity is included under the business rules umbrella. Though I could, for example, separate data validation techniques from the general business rules discussion, there's nothing to be gained by doing so. The same methods are used to implement elementary business rules as are used to forge complex ones. It's therefore my policy here to discuss effective business rule design in general. It makes no difference whether they're simple rules or advanced ones; they both need careful attention.

Delphi provides a number of ways of constructing elementary business rules with no coding whatsoever and provides a nice suite of tools for constructing advanced rules using a minimal amount of code. This chapter explores both types of rules from the perspective of the application.

Two Rules about Business Rules

There are two fundamental rules regarding successful business rule construction that you'll want to follow in your Delphi applications. You'll solve a number of the typical problems that developers face before they even occur if you follow these two very basic rules.

Rule Number One

The first rule when setting up client-side business rules is to begin by using the appropriate data types in your database. Delphi's VCL enforces a number of built-in, elementary restrictions based on the type of data a column represents. For example, data-aware components won't permit invalid dates in date-type columns, alphabetic characters in numeric fields, nor invalid boolean values in boolean fields. You don't have to do any coding to enforce these constraints; Delphi enforces them automatically. The key thing is that you use the appropriate data types to begin with.

There is sometimes a tendency among veteran developers to make too much use of string types when building databases. I've seen tables, for example, containing date columns that were defined by using string data types. I've also seen numeric data stored in string fields. If a column is to contain dates and dates alone, define it by using a date data type, if your DBMS supports date types. If a field can contain only numbers, define it by using a numeric data type. There's no reason to store numeric values in alphabetic columns.

Another situation where using the right data type is crucial to proper business rule design is in dealing with columns that contain sequential values. While you could certainly effect a sequential numbering system through code or even through database triggers, it's far more preferable to use data types that are inherently sequential in the first place. Sybase calls them *identity columns*; in Paradox, they're known as *auto-increment fields*. By using the right data type in this situation, you relieve yourself of the hassle of maintaining the sequential numbers yourself, and you ensure that the basic business rule you're after—*the numbers in column Y of table X must be sequential*—is enforced with no real work on your part.

Rule Number Two

The second major rule when implementing application-based business rules is to use Delphi components that match up well with their underlying data types. The most common error that developers make in this regard is by using plain text entry components too extensively. These text entry components (such as DBEdit, TEdit, and TMaskEdit) frequently allow data to be keyed into a field that is invalid for the component's underlying data type. This can usually be avoided by using the right component for the job. For example, you shouldn't use a DBEdit for a boolean field. The field can have only two values: True and False. Use a checkbox, radio buttons, or a drop-down list instead. Don't use a DBEdit for a field that is always read-only; use a DBText component instead. This conserves system resources and saves you the trouble of having to set the component's ReadOnly property. Furthermore, you shouldn't use a DBEdit for a numeric column that can have only a handful of valid values. Use a DBRadioGroup instead. Table 20.1 summarizes which components you should use with which basic data types.

Table 20.1. Column data types and their appropriate VCL components.

Data type	Components
Boolean	DBCheckBox, DBRadioGroup, DBComboBox, DBListBox
Date	DBEdit, Calendar, SpinEdit
Numeric (allows a large number of values)	DBEdit, SpinEdit
Numeric (allows only a handful of values)	DBRadioGroup
String (allows a large number of values)	DBEdit
String (allows only a handful of values)	DBComboBox, DBListBox

TIP

You can configure the type of control that's used for a particular field by editing the TControlClass property in the Database Explorer. Once you've set this property, dragging a TField from the Fields Editor onto a form will cause the component you specified to be created.

These are just general guidelines. The rule of thumb here is to use the component that ensures the validity of the data entered into it as much as possible without preventing valid entries.

Custom Components

Because of Delphi's component-based architecture, a number of quality tools and libraries have been released that enable you to bind business rules into components. They usually do this by descending new components from Delphi's DataSet component class and building the desired business rule logic into these descendant components.

These tools typically enable you to specify everything from individual field input masks to complex relationships between tables. Especially with Delphi 1.0, this is a very practical approach to constructing sound business rule implementations.

The downside to this approach, however, is that because developers aren't forced to use the components, Delphi applications can be constructed that do not respect the business rules in place. Furthermore, because the component approach is a Delphi-only solution, applications built in other tools cannot make use of the business rule logic embedded in the DataSet descendants.

My word of advice on these types of tools is this: If you elect to use one of them, be sure to implement all you can of your business rule strategy on your DBMS platform and use these custom components only as a means of enhancing that implementation.

TField Properties and Business Rules

Business rules normally refer to more complex entities than mere field masks and display labels. Still, many properties of the TField component class are relevant in some way to proper business rule implementation. Properties like TField's edit mask attribute are relevant in that they force the data that a given column receives to conform to a specific format. This is an elementary business rules concern, as mentioned earlier. Upon the foundation of these elementary business rules, you build the structure of the more advanced rules, like those that ensure referential integrity between two tables or those that supply a given column with a default value. Successful business rule implementation requires that attention be given to the minutiae of the design strategy as well as to its major elements.

There are two ways of implementing elementary business rules through TField component property settings. The first method is to use Delphi's Data Dictionary and set relevant TField properties using Attribute Sets. The second method is to set those TField properties in your application's DataSet components themselves. Though they both amount to the same thing—TField Attribute Settings you make end up becoming a part of your application's TField components—your first choice should be to use the Data Dictionary to define your TField settings. Establishing TField properties by using the Data Dictionary is more flexible and of more general use than doing so via the Fields Editor of DataSet components. What you cannot define via the dictionary or what makes no sense to define in the dictionary can be set up in the DataSet components themselves. This chapter will explore both methods so that you can see the relative benefits of each approach.

Delphi's Data Dictionary

Beyond choosing the appropriate component class to represent a given data type, the next level of application-based business rule definition is that of *columnar attributes.* Columnar attributes are established by setting the properties of the TField component class. They include such field characteristics as input and display masks, the minimum and maximum allowable values for a column, flags indicating whether a column must have a value and whether it can be modified, and so forth. Beginning with Delphi 2.0, the best way to define such things is through the use of the Data Dictionary. You can access Delphi's Data Dictionary via the Explore option on Delphi's Database menu. The Data Dictionary enables you to define Attribute Sets that you may then apply to table columns in your database. When you then reference these columns in a Delphi application, you'll see the property settings that you specified earlier reflected in Delphi's Fields Editor and in the application itself.

This capability is best illustrated by example. Let's create a small Paradox table and define business rules over it using Delphi's Data Dictionary. Table 20.2 is the table definition for the TENANT table as it was laid out in Part II, "Tutorial," of this book.

> **NOTE**
>
> If you've already created the TENANT table, you can skip this section. The table presented here is exactly the same as the one presented in Part II of this book.

Table 20.2. The TENANT table design.

Column	Type	Size	Req	Allowable values	Default
TenantNo	Auto-Increment		Y		
Name	Alpha	30	Y		
Employer	Alpha	30	Y		
EmpAddress	Alpha	30	Y		
EmpCity	Alpha	20	Y		
EmpState	Alpha	2	Y		
EmpZip	Alpha	10	Y		
HomePhone	Alpha	15	Y		
WorkPhone	Alpha	15	Y		
ICEPhone	Alpha	15	Y		
LeaseBeginDate	Date		Y		
LeaseEndDate	Date		Y		
MovedInDate	Date		Y		
MovedOutDate	Date		N		
RentDueDay	Short		Y	1,15	
PetDeposit	Money		Y		$0
LawnService	Logical		Y		T
Comments	Alpha	100	N		

Note that both the PetDeposit and LawnService columns have default values established for them. Also note that some of the fields are required, while others aren't. You'll learn how to set up these types of columns using Delphi's Data Dictionary.

Before you create the table, create a Borland Database Engine (BDE) alias that points to the directory where the table will reside if you haven't already done so. In Part II of this book, this alias is named RENTMAN and points to the C:\DATA\DELPHI\RENTMAN directory, though you can put the table anywhere you want.

You can use Delphi's Database Explorer to create the alias if you like. To do so, right-click the Databases entry on the Explorer's Databases page and select New from the menu to define a new BDE database alias. Name the alias RENTMAN, set its Type to STANDARD, and set its PATH to the directory on your hard disk where you want the TENANT table to reside.

Next, create the TENANT table using the tool of your choice. You can use Paradox itself, Delphi's Database Desktop, or some other tool. After the table is created, select the Explore option on Delphi's Database menu. Figure 20.1 shows the Database Explorer.

FIGURE 20.1.

Delphi's Database Explorer.

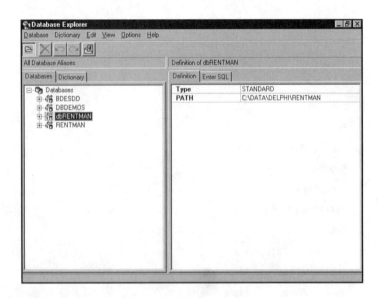

The opening screen of the Database Explorer displays two tabs: a Databases tab and a Dictionary tab. The Databases page lists the BDE database aliases that have been defined so far. Note the special icon next to the dbRENTMAN database in Figure 20.1. Its icon differs from the others listed because it's an application-specific database alias. It was defined earlier for use with the RENTALMAN application that was built in the Tutorial section of this book. Because the RENTALMAN application was the active project in Delphi when I started the Explorer, it shows up as one of the aliases in the list. Because it's an application-specific alias, it would disappear from the list if I returned to Delphi, unloaded the RENTALMAN project, and restarted the Database Explorer.

The Dictionary page is where you define the Attribute Sets of which I spoke earlier. You'll define an Attribute Set for several of the columns in the TENANT table, then associate them with their respective columns from within Delphi. Click the Dictionary tab, then expand the

Databases branch. You should see the demo database, DBDEMOS, in the Databases list. Next, click the Import Database option on the Explorer's Dictionary menu. When the Import Database dialog is displayed, select the RENTMAN BDE alias you defined earlier and click OK.

Importing the RENTMAN database into Delphi's Data Dictionary enables you to define TField attributes for specific columns in the database. As opposed to defining an Attribute Set in the Data Dictionary, then associating it with a number of columns from within Delphi, you can easily define one that is directly associated with a given column from within the Data Dictionary itself. You do this by right-clicking the Attribute Sets node under a given column, then selecting New from the menu. When you add an Attribute Set this way, it's also added to the "master" list of Attribute Sets so that you may use it with other columns in the database.

Besides creating Attribute Sets that are initially associated with a particular table column, you can also create ones that are for a more general use and can be utilized within any number of tables. You do this by right-clicking the root Attribute Sets branch on the Dictionary page and selecting New from the menu. You then key in a name for the new Attribute Set and establish the TField properties you want it to specify. Then, after you're back in Delphi, you can right-click a DataSet and associate the Attribute Set with one of its columns. The TField attributes that you defined in the Attribute Set will then be reflected in forms that use the DataSet.

You'll define Attribute Sets using both methods so that you can get a good feel for how they work. In the Data Dictionary, expand the Tables\TENANT table branch of the RENTMAN database. Click the Fields branch to expand it and expand the HomePhone column. You should see an Attribute Sets node under the HomePhone column. (See Figure 20.2.)

FIGURE 20.2.

The HomePhone column as it appears on the Database Explorer's Data Dictionary page.

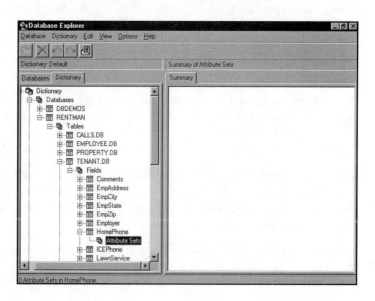

Right-click the Attribute Sets node and select New from the menu. Name the new Attribute Set PhoneNo and click the Apply button on the Explorer toolbar. Next, select the Edit Mask property in the list of `TField` attributes on the right of the screen and key in `!\(999\)000-0000;1;` then press Enter. This sets up a mask for the PhoneNo Attribute Set that will cause phone numbers to be edited using the customary United States format. Click the Apply button to save your change. (See Figure 20.3.)

FIGURE 20.3.

You can set up `TField` *attributes using Delphi's Attribute Sets.*

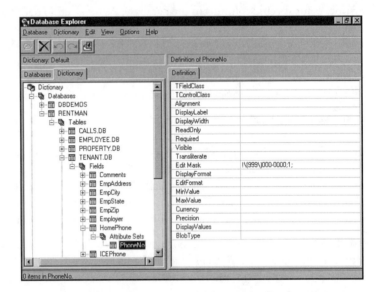

Now, exit the Database Explorer and return to Delphi. Start a new project and drop a `Table` and a `DataSource` component onto its main form. Change the `Table` component's name to taTENANT, set its `DatabaseName` property to point to the RENTMAN database and its `TableName` property to TENANT.DB. Change the `DataSource` component's name to dsTENANT and set its `DataSet` property to taTENANT.

Next, right-click the `taTENANT` component and select Fields Editor from the menu. After the Fields Editor is on the screen, right-click it and select Add fields from the pop-up menu. Add all the fields in the TENANT table to the list, including the `HomePhone` column. Now, exit the Fields Editor and double-click taTENANT's `Active` property to open it.

Next, drop a `DBEdit` component onto the form and set its `DataSource` property to point to dsTENANT and its `DataField` property to refer to the `HomePhone` column in the TENANT table. You should then see the `Edit Mask` you established in the Database Explorer reflected in your `DBEdit` component. (See Figure 20.4.)

Now that you've established a column-specific Attribute Set, it's time to define one for general use. Return to the Database Explorer and select its Dictionary page. Right-click the Attribute Sets branch and select New. Name the new Attribute Set Date and click the Apply button to

save your addition. Next, click the Edit Mask property on the right of the display and set it to
!99/99/00;1;_. Click the Apply button again to save your work, then exit the Explorer and
return to Delphi.

FIGURE 20.4.

TField attributes that you establish in Delphi's Data Dictionary are reflected in your applications.

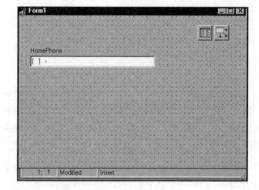

Next, right-click the taTENANT component and select Fields Editor. Right-click the
LeaseBeginDate in the list and select Associate attributes from the pop-up menu. You should
then see the Attribute Sets that are currently defined displayed in a list from which you may
select. Double-click the Date Attribute Set you just created to associate it with the LeaseBeginDate
column. After you've done this, close the Fields Editor and change the
DataField property of your DBEdit to reference the LeaseBeginDate column. You've now linked
the Attribute Set you created in Delphi's Data Dictionary with the LeaseBeginDate column in
the TENANT table. Figure 20.5 shows the effect of the Attribute Setting at runtime.

FIGURE 20.5.

The Date Attribute Setting sets up a special Edit Mask for the LeaseBeginDate column.

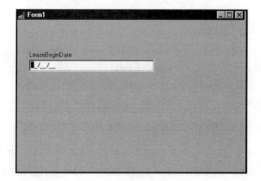

There are numerous other TField attributes that you could establish using Attribute Sets. The
point of all this is that Delphi's Data Dictionary provides a nice facility for defining elementary business rules through TField properties. The advantage to defining business rules in the

Data Dictionary as opposed to doing so in the DataSets themselves is that the business rules you set up in the Data Dictionary can be used by any Delphi application that references the tables in question. This provides a similar benefit to the approach taken by some tool vendors of bundling business rules into custom components, yet it suffers from none of the drawbacks of using third-party components.

Defining Business Rules Using *TFields*

In addition to using Delphi's Data Dictionary to define TField attributes, you can also define them using TFields themselves. Delphi adds TField components to a form's class when you select Add fields from a DataSet's Fields Editor menu. When you do this, the attributes you defined for these TFields in the Data Dictionary are reflected in Delphi's Object Inspector.

As an example, right-click the taTENANT component and select Fields Editor. You should see listed the TField components you added earlier. Click the LeaseBeginDate field and notice its EditMask property in the Delphi Object Inspector—it's set to the same EditMask you specified in the Data Dictionary. At this point, you could change the setting or set other properties—columnar attributes you receive from the Data Dictionary are only a starting point.

Required

You could, for example, toggle whether a field is required to have a value. Click the Name field, then double-click its Required property in the Object Inspector. This forces the user to supply a value for the Name field whenever a TENANT record is added. Here, one of the most elementary business rules of all is established: For every TenantNo entry you must also have a Name entry.

Calculated Fields

Calculated fields are useful for everything from deriving simple field values to performing complex computations involving the fields in a table. You can perform mathematical operations, table lookups, data validation, and so on, using Delphi's calculated fields mechanism. Calculated fields are especially handy for data that you want to display but have no need to store.

To set up a calculated field, you must do two things:

■ Define the field in the appropriate DataSet's Fields Editor
■ Assign the field a value in its DataSet's OnCalcFields event

To try this out, right-click the taTENANT component and select Fields Editor from the list. When the Fields list appears, right-click it and select New field from the menu. In the New Field dialog, key PropertyCount for the new field's Name, set its data Type to Integer, and click the Calculated radio button in the Field type radio button group. Click OK to finish your definition. (See Figure 20.6.)

FIGURE 20.6.

You use the New Field dialog to define calculated fields.

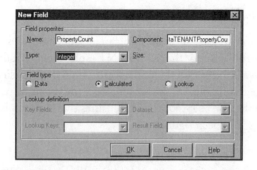

When you return to the Fields Editor, you should see the new field's properties listed in Delphi's Object Inspector. Notice that the `Calculated` property is set to `True`.

Now that the field is defined, you can set up `taTENANT`'s `OnCalcFields` event to do something like the following:

```
With quPropertyCount do begin
    ParamByName('TenantNo').AsInteger:=taTENANTTenantNo.AsInteger;
    Open;
    taTENANTPropertyCount.Value:=quPropertyCountPropertyCount.Value;
    Close;
  end;
```

This code won't actually compile, so don't bother trying. It relies on a `Query` component, `quPropertyCount`, that you haven't yet created. Nevertheless, you can study the code to learn how calculated fields work. The line

```
ParamByName('TenantNo').AsInteger:=taTENANTTenantNo.AsInteger;
```

supplies the `Query` component with its only parameter, `TenantNo`. This is followed by the call to the `Query` component's `Open` method, which executes its SQL query. After the query executes, the line

```
taTENANTPropertyCount.Value:=quPropertyCountPropertyCount.Value;
```

assigns the `Query` component's `PropertyCount` field to the calculated field's `Value` property. Setting a field's `Value` property does exactly what you'd think—it specifies the calculated field's value.

Calculated fields are particularly useful for performing fixed computations involving a table's columns. You could, for example, use a calculated field to encode the amount of money your organization pays per mile when an employee takes his or her personal vehicle on company business. Or, you might build the amount of sales commission your firm typically pays its salespeople into an `OnCalcFields` event. The possibilities are endless. An important thing to remember is to keep these calculations as nimble as possible so that you don't overburden your applications.

OnValidate

Now it's time to look at establishing an advanced business rule using TField properties. Bring up the Fields Editor for the taTENANT table, then click the MovedInDate field. Next, click the Events page in Delphi's Object Inspector, then double-click its OnValidate event. Here, you'll write a small code snippet that ensures that the MovedInDate for a given tenant is always later in time than the LeaseBeginDate. This ensures that a person isn't allowed to move into a property until a lease has been signed.

Key the following code into the code editor:

```
If (taTENANTMovedInDate.Value < taTENANTLeaseBeginDate.Value) then
    raise EDatabaseError.Create('A tenant must sign a lease before moving in');
```

This code checks to see if MovedInDate column is earlier in time than the LeaseBeginDate column. If so, it displays an error message and exits the routine. First of all, notice the name that Delphi automatically generates for TFields you add via the Fields Editor. The name consists of the table in which the field exists, followed by its name. It's important to note that the TField component that Delphi generates via the Fields Editor is owned by the TForm component, just like the Table component that you used to create it. That is, even though you used the Fields Editor of the taTENANT table to create the TField definitions, they exist as children of the TForm on which taTENANT resides—they're form components in every sense of the word. This is the reason the If statement in the preceding code doesn't have to refer directly to the taTENANT component; it only refers to the TField components themselves.

Note the use of the TField's Value property to retrieve the current value of its underlying field. Value is a variant data type that you can use to access a field's underlying data, regardless of its type. You can also use the AsString, AsDateTime, AsFloat, AsInteger, and AsBoolean TField properties to translate Value to a particular type of data. For example,

```
If (taTENANTMovedInDate.AsDateTime < taTENANTLeaseBeginDate.AsDateTime) then
    raise EDatabaseError.Create('A tenant must sign a lease before moving in');
```

performs exactly the same function as the code you typed earlier (note the use of AsDateTime).

> **NOTE**
>
> Variants are new in Delphi 2.0. The AsXXXX family of properties are a carryover from Delphi 1.0. As a rule, you should use the Value property when referencing a TField's underlying data. This is more flexible and more immune to changes in the associated table.

Finally, notice how Delphi's exception mechanism is used to flag the entry as invalid. No valid variable or switch is explicitly set. However, by raising the EDatabaseError exception from within the OnValidate event, you automatically invalidate it. When the field receives an invalid value, the message that is passed into EDatabaseError's Create constructor is displayed on-screen, and the entry is refused.

OnExit

Another common place to implement business rules in Delphi applications is in the OnExit event of data-aware components such as DBEdit.

Click the DBEdit that you dropped earlier, then click the Events page in the Object Inspector. Double-click its OnExit event and key in the following code:

```
DecodeDate(taTENANTLeaseBeginDate.Value, Year, Month, Day);
taTENANTLeaseEndDate.Value:=EncodeDate(Succ(Year), Month, Day);
```

Be sure to include a var section in the event method's header, like so:

```
var
  Year, Month, Day : Word;
```

This code causes the LeaseEndDate column to default to one year later than the LeaseBeginDate column. It uses Delphi's DecodeDate and EncodeDate to break down, then reconstruct, the LeaseBeginDate so that its year element may be incremented by one.

You can try this now by dropping a second DBEdit onto your form and setting its DataSource to dsTENANT and its DataField to LeaseEndDate. Now run your test application and key a date into first DBEdit. Press Tab to exit it and jump to the second one. You should see the date you originally entered into the first DBEdit appear in the second one, incremented by a year. (See Figure 20.7.)

FIGURE 20.7.

Exiting the first DBEdit supplies the second with a value because of the OnExit event.

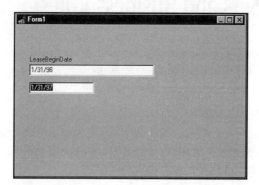

This example uses the OnExit event to supply a default value for another field, but you can also use it to validate the value of the current field. For example, you can use the following code to validate the TENANT table's EmpState field:

```
If (not taSTATES.FindKey([taTENANTEmpState.AsString])) then begin
    ActiveControl:=deEmpState;
    raise EDatabaseError.Create('Invalid state');
  end;
```

Of course, this code assumes the existence of a STATES table, which it uses to check your EmpState column. Note the use of the FindKey method of the Table component to look up an indexed value in a table. You may find this brute force method of establishing a relationship between two tables preferable to the more civilized means of doing so.

Another common use of the OnExit event is to execute a query that looks up information in other tables for display in a form. For example, you might use a query to quickly calculate a customer's current balance for display on an order entry form. You could attach a lookup of this type to the OnExit event of a DBEdit that is linked to, for example, the CustomerNo field. Here's a code sample to illustrate:

```
procedure TForm1.deCustomerNoExit(Sender: TObject);
begin
  With quCalcBalance do begin
    ParamByName('CustNo').AsString:=taCUSTOMERCustNo.AsString;
    Open;
    laBalance.Caption:=quCalcBalanceCurrentBalance.AsString;
    Close;
  end;
end;
```

In the code sample, the Caption property of the label laBalance is changed to reflect the customer's current balance. Another way of doing this would be to link a DBText field to the Query's CurrentBalance field. By using a plain label control, though, you remain in control of (and become responsible for) when the control's text gets updated.

DataSets and Business Rules

The next level of application business rule design is the DataSet level. There are three events of the DataSet component class (from which the Table, Query, and StoredProc components all descend) that merit special consideration: OnNewRecord, BeforeDelete, and BeforePost.

OnNewRecord

The OnNewRecord event occurs any time a new record is added to a Table. You can use it to supply values for a table's columns. Here's a code sample that supplies a default value for the PetDeposit and LawnService columns:

```
procedure TForm1.taTENANTNewRecord(DataSet: TDataSet);
begin
  taTENANTPetDeposit.AsInteger:=0;
  taTENANTLawnService.AsBoolean:=True;
end;
```

BeforeDelete

BeforeDelete occurs just prior to a row deletion, as its name suggests. You can use it to verify that a deletion the user is attempting is a valid one. For example, you can use it to prevent the deletion of a row in one table while rows in other tables depend on it. You would be effecting a code-based referential integrity scheme in doing this. By raising an exception within this event, you thwart the pending deletion. For example, here's a code snippet that uses the TENANT table and the PROPERTY table from Part II of this book to affect a simple RI scheme:

```
taPROPERTY.IndexName:='TenantNo';
If taPROPERTY.FindKey([taTENANTTenantNo.AsInteger]) then
  raise EDatabaseError.Create('TenantNo is in use - delete failed');
```

BeforePost

The BeforePost event, as its name suggests, occurs just prior to a row being saved to its table. You can use the BeforePost event to validate the values in a new row or the changes to an existing one. If you raise an exception from within this event, you stop the post. Here's a code sample that ensures that the LeaseEndDate always falls chronologically after the LeaseBeginDate:

```
procedure TForm1.taTENANTBeforePost(DataSet: TDataSet);
begin
  If (taTENANTLeaseBeginDate.AsDateTime > taTENANTLeaseEndDate.AsDateTime) then
    raise EDatabaseError.Create('Lease ending date must come after its beginning
➥date');
end;
```

There are a number of other special DataSet events that you may want to use to implement application-based business rules. Table 20.3 includes a list of events supported by the DataSet component class that are relevant to business rule design.

Table 20.3. DataSet methods that you may find useful in implementing application-based business rules.

Event	Catalyst
AfterCancel	Occurs following a Cancel
AfterClose	Occurs following the close of the DataSet
AfterDelete	Occurs following a Delete
AfterEdit	Occurs following an Edit
AfterInsert	Occurs following an Insert or Append
AfterOpen	Occurs after a DataSet is opened
AfterPost	Occurs following a Post
BeforeCancel	Occurs prior to a Cancel
BeforeClose	Occurs before the close of the DataSet
BeforeEdit	Occurs prior to an Edit
BeforeInsert	Occurs prior to an Insert or Append
BeforeOpen	Occurs before a DataSet is opened

continues

Table 20.3. continued

Event	Catalyst
OnCalcFields	Occurs when calculated fields need values
OnDeleteError	Occurs when there is a problem deleting a record
OnEditError	Occurs when there is a problem editing a record
OnFilterRecord	Occurs when filtering is active and the DataSet needs a row

What's Ahead

In the next chapter, you'll be introduced to concurrency control and the many facets of adequately controlling multi-user access to your applications. In particular, pessimistic and optimistic locking schemes are discussed, as well as transaction isolation levels and controlling transactions via SQL.

Summary

In this chapter, you've learned about the four major levels of application-based business rule design in Delphi: the data type level, the component level, the TField level, and the TDataSet level. Each of these simplifies the levels that follow it. That is, if you've picked the correct data type for a field, picking the best user-interface component with which to service it becomes much easier. Likewise, if you set TField's properties appropriately, the work you must do at the DataSet level becomes much simpler. I tend to think of constructing business rules this way as similar to building a pyramid: As you get the lower, more fundamental levels built correctly, the higher ones become easier and smaller. Likewise, if you botch the lower levels, the higher ones are more difficult to build and less stable. It's important to pay careful attention to the fine points of application-based business rules. Even the smallest of details can make a big difference in the robustness of your implementations.

21

Concurrency Control

The term *concurrency control* refers to sharing resources among multiple users simultaneously. This broad subject can be broken into two major sections: transaction-isolation and concurrency-control systems. Transaction-isolation levels control the degree of access a transaction has to database changes made by concurrent transactions. Closely related to transaction isolation, concurrency-control systems affect not only the ability of one transaction to access another transaction's updates, but also the way in which database updates are performed.

Transaction Isolation

Transaction isolation refers to the mechanism used by database management systems to insulate one transaction from the effects of another. Transaction isolation in Delphi is organized into three distinct levels, each with its own characteristics. These *Transaction-Isolation Levels* (TILs) affect the accessibility of one transaction to database changes made by other concurrent transactions.

Normally, Delphi handles transaction-related issues for you by establishing a default transaction-isolation level and by automatically starting and committing transactions when your application updates a database. If you need more control than this, you can control transaction processing yourself through the TDatabase component or via Passthrough SQL. Controlling transactions via the TDatabase component is the preferred method since it ensures that Delphi "sees" the transaction processing you do.

Choosing an Appropriate Transaction-Isolation Level

Most database servers, including InterBase, support three separate TILs. Speaking strictly from a management point of view, it's advantageous to use a single TIL across an entire application. Using a single TIL for *all* database applications is even more airtight. This strategy protects the integrity of the database and ensures that changes you attempt to make occur as they are supposed to.

Nevertheless, depending on the requirements of a particular application, you may not be able to use this simplistic approach. Taking a one-size-fits-all approach to transaction isolation usually results in overkill or questionable database integrity. You may end up needlessly locking tables or preventing harmless database updates. *The trick to a successful TI implementation is to first ensure the integrity of the database, then address performance concerns by optimizing your TI scheme as much as possible.*

Classic Transaction-Isolation Problems

The types of problems that transaction-isolation schemes encounter can be divided into five basic groups:

■ *Dirty reads*—These occur when the uncommitted changes made by one transaction are read by another. Because the uncommitted changes can be rolled back, they can cause the transaction that read them beforehand to possess dirty reads.

■ *Nonrepeatable reads*—These occur when one transaction is allowed to change rows that another transaction is continually reading. Because the iterative reads by the second transaction are not reproducible due to the changes by the first transaction, they are said to be nonrepeatable. By their very design, READ COMMITTED transactions permit nonrepeatable reads because they can read changes made by other transactions as they are committed.

■ *Phantom rows*—These occur when a transaction is allowed to select an incomplete set of the new rows written by a second transaction. Phantom rows are not prevented by the READ COMMITTED TIL.

■ *Lost updates*—These occur when one transaction inadvertently overwrites a change made by another simultaneous transaction.

■ *Update side-effects*—These can occur when the values in one row depend upon the values in another and these dependencies are not protected by the proper integrity constraints. When two or more simultaneous transactions read and update the same data, undesirable side-effects can occur if a transaction copies a value in one row to a second that the other transaction subsequently changes in the first row. These types of orphaned transactions are known as *interleaved* transactions.

The way that the TIL you select with the TransIsolation property addresses these problems depends upon the RDBMS platform you're working with and on the server TIL that TransIsolation is translated to. Both of these subjects are discussed in the following sections.

Transaction Management with *TDatabase*

You manage transactions via the TDatabase component using the TransIsolation property and the StartTransaction, Commit, and Rollback methods.

Transaction Isolation

The TransIsolation property controls the transaction-isolation level on the database server for your particular connection. As mentioned, the TIL on the server controls the accessibility of transactions concurrent with yours to changes you've made and your transaction's ability to see changes they've made.

TransIsolation has three possible values, tiDirtyRead, tiReadCommitted, and tiRepeatableRead. It defaults to tiReadCommited. The three possible values of TransIsolation have the following significance:

■ tiDirtyRead—Uncommitted changes by other transactions are visible.

■ tiReadCommitted—Only committed changes by other transactions are visible.

■ `tiRepeatableRead`—Changes by other transactions to previously read data are not visible, which means that every time a transaction reads a given record it always gets the *exact same* record.

Transaction Control

The `TDatabase` component's `StartTransaction` method marks the beginning of a transaction—a group of database changes that you want treated as a unit. They will either all be applied to the database or none of them will be.

`Commit` makes permanent the database changes that have occurred since the transaction was started. Think of it as a database `save` command.

`Rollback` discards the database changes that have been made since the transaction began. Think of it as a database `undo` command.

TransIsolation and DBMS TILs

The isolation levels supported by `TDatabase`'s `TransIsolation` property may be different or not supported at all on your database server. When a `TransIsolation` level you request is not supported by your server, it's promoted to the next highest isolation level.

Table 21.1 cross-references the TILs supported by the `TransIsolation` setting with their implementations on the various DBMS platforms.

Table 21.1. `TransIsolation` **and DBMS TILs.**

TransIsolation Setting	*InterBase*	*Oracle*	*Sybase & Microsoft*
`tiDirtyRead`	Read committed	Read committed committed	Read
`tiReadCommitted`	Read committed	Read committed	Read committed
`tiRepeatableRead`	Repeatable Read	Repeatable read (READ ONLY)	Error (unsupported)

Controlling Transactions with SQL

You can also control transaction processing on your server using Passthrough SQL. To do this, you issue SQL commands that change the transaction processing on your server. The following examples use InterBase's SQL syntax.

> **CAUTION**
>
> Be aware that setting the transaction-isolation level with SQLPASSTHRUMODE set to SHARED AUTOCOMMIT or SHARED NOAUTOCOMMIT could cause your new TIL setting to inadvertently affect other transactions initiated by your application.

Transaction Isolation

To set the TIL you wish to use via SQL, you use the SET TRANSACTION command. The three TILs supported by InterBase, for example, are SNAPSHOT, SNAPSHOT TABLE STABILITY, and READ COMMITTED. To install one of these as the new TIL, use the SET TRANSACTION ISOLATION LEVEL SQL command.

Here's a summary of what each setting means:

- SNAPSHOT—Restricts the view of the database to a snapshot of the way it appeared when the transaction started. Changes made by other active transactions aren't visible using this TIL.

- SNAPSHOT TABLE STABILITY—Places a table lock on tables this transaction is reading and writing, allowing other transactions read-only access to the tables.

- READ COMMITTED—Shows the most recently committed version of a row during updates and deletions, and allows the transaction to make changes provided there are no update conflicts with other transactions. READ COMMITTED supports the following two optional parameters:

    - NO RECORD_VERSION (default)—Shows only the most recent version of a row. If SET TRANSACTION's WAIT parameter has been specified, the transaction waits until the most recent version of a record is committed or rolled back, then retries the read.

    - RECORD_VERSION—Reads the most recent *committed* version of a row, even if a newer uncommitted version is present in the database.

Server Transaction Isolation and the Classic TI Problems

As a rule, each DBMS vendor has its own way of dealing with the classic transaction-isolation problems previously mentioned. Each TIL supported by the server is designed to address the problems mentioned previously in some fashion. Table 21.2 is a summary of how each InterBase TIL deals with them:

Table 21.2. InterBase transaction-isolation levels and the five classic transaction-management problems.

TIL	Problem	Solution
SNAPSHOT	Lost updates	Other transactions can't update rows updated by this transaction
	Dirty reads	Doesn't read changes made by other transactions; other transactions see a previous version of a row updated by this transaction
	Nonrepeatable reads	Can read only the version of a row committed when the transaction began
	Phantom rows	Can read only the version of a row committed when the transaction began
	Update side-effects	Doesn't read changes made by other transactions; other transactions see a previous version of a row updated by this transaction
READ COMMITTED	Lost updates	Other transactions can't update rows updated by this transaction
	Dirty reads	Other transactions see a previous or committed version of a row updated by this transaction
	Nonrepeatable reads	Are allowed by design
	Phantom rows	May be encountered because this TIL sees committed changes by other transactions
	Update side-effects	Other transactions see a previous or committed version of a row updated by this transaction

TIL	Problem	Solution
SNAPSHOT TABLE STABILITY	Lost updates	Prevents updates by other transactions on tables it controls
	Dirty reads	Prevents access by other transactions to its updated tables
	Nonrepeatable reads	Can read only the version of a row committed when the transaction began; prevents access by other transactions to its updated tables
	Phantom rows	Prevents access by other transactions to tables it controls
	Update side-effects	Prevents updates by other transactions to tables it controls

Selecting the Right Transaction-Isolation Level

As you can see, with few exceptions each transaction-isolation issue is adequately covered by all three InterBase TILs. The one you should choose depends largely on your application's needs.

The default TIL is SNAPSHOT. For most applications, either SNAPSHOT or READ COMMITTED should be chosen. SNAPSHOT TABLE STABILITY can lock other users out of tables indefinitely that they may need access to. It should therefore be avoided unless you actually need its specialized features.

The choice between SNAPSHOT and READ COMMITTED should be based on whether you need to see committed updates by other transactions during your transaction. If not, use SNAPSHOT. If so, READ COMMITTED is your best choice. Generally speaking, the READ COMMITTED TIL will produce a lower amount of lock contention.

Transaction Control

You control InterBase transactions using the SET TRANSACTION, COMMIT, and ROLLBACK SQL commands. SET TRANSACTION has a variety of uses, including setting the transaction-isolation level, as mentioned previously. COMMIT works just like TDatabase's Commit method—it acts as a database save command. ROLLBACK functions just like the TDatabase Rollback method—it discards changes made to a database since the last COMMIT.

SET TRANSACTION

You use the SET TRANSACTION command to begin a transaction, like so:

```
SET TRANSACTION
```

If you want the transaction to be a READ ONLY transaction, you can also include the optional READ ONLY keyword:

```
SET TRANSACTION READ ONLY
```

Many RDBMS platforms also support named transactions, as well. This enables you, for instance, to nest transactions within one another. In InterBase SQL, data-modification commands (including INSERT, UPDATE, and DELETE) can also make direct use of a named transaction. Here's the InterBase syntax for starting a named transaction:

```
SET TRANSACTION :UpdateCustomers
```

Note that :UpdateCustomers must be a previously declared and initialized host language variable.

Here's the Sybase Transact-SQL syntax for doing the same thing:

```
BEGIN TRANSACTION UpdateCustomers
```

COMMIT and ROLLBACK

The SQL COMMIT command makes the changes that occurred during a given transaction permanent. Think of it as a database save command. ROLLBACK, on the other hand, throws away the changes a transaction might make to the database—it functions like a database undo command. Both of these commands affect the changes made only since the last COMMIT—you cannot ROLLBACK changes you've just committed.

> **NOTE**
>
> You should attempt to include only statements that actually modify data between a SET TRANSACTION and its corresponding COMMIT or ROLLBACK. Perform all lookups or other data gathering before you initiate the SET TRANSACTION. This helps ensure that you lock other users out of database resources as little as possible.

InterBase's WISQL utility begins a transaction automatically (by issuing the equivalent of the InterBase SET TRANSACTION command) when it first loads. When you exit the utility, it asks whether you'd like to commit your work. You can commit or rollback your work at any time using the Commit Work and Rollback Work options on WISQL's File menu.

Concurrency-Control Systems

The concepts behind concurrency-control systems are relatively simple if you reduce them to everyday terms. For example, you might compare a concurrency-control system to the system that manages trains on a railroad system. If there were just one train, there'd be no concurrency problem. Add several trains to the system, though, and you have to quickly devise a way of keeping the trains from colliding while still picking up and delivering their cargoes in a timely fashion. The same types of problems you encounter in this scenario apply equally well to databases. You have to find a way of keeping the updates users make to the database from "colliding"—from overwriting one another—while still providing the functionality users expect.

Obviously, if you only query a database, you have no concurrency problems. Concurrency problems rear their ugly heads when two or more users attempt to change the same data at the same time. When a user's changes to the database are lost or prevented because of changes made by another user, a `lost update` or `update conflict` occurs. Effective concurrency-control systems address these problems without reducing the usability or functionality of the database.

Concurrency-control systems come in two basic flavors: pessimistic control systems and optimistic control systems. They are distinguished by their different assumptions regarding whether concurrent transactions are likely to attempt to change the same data at the same time. A pessimistic concurrency-control system assumes that this is a likely occurrence, whereas an optimistic system regards such contention as abnormal and treats it as an exception. An optimistic concurrency-control system assumes that most queries are read-only and that updates to a given data element rarely occur at the same time.

Pessimistic Concurrency Control

Because a pessimistic control system assumes `update conflicts` are likely, it locks the resources a given transaction uses in order to remove the possibility of a conflict. Other transactions needing the resources locked by the transaction will have to wait until it completes before proceeding.

Though a pessimistic control system can utilize both read-inhibit and write-inhibit locks, you never see a read-inhibit lock in the real world. Instead, you normally see locks that permit only the reading of data, or permit both reading and writing. This locking is usually maintained at a given level—ranging from multiple table locks all the way down to single columns.

Table, row, and page (Sybase) locks are the most common, sometimes occurring in sequence. That is, you will often see several row locks followed by the locking of the entire table in which they reside. This is called *lock escalation* and occurs when your database server believes that enough row or page locks exist to justify replacing them with a complete table lock. Sybase, for example, promotes a transaction's page locks to a table lock after the transaction accumulates more than 200 page locks on a given table.

In practice, you never see locks on individual columns; they're too resource-intensive and serve no real purpose. Preventing a change to a column in a row that is not being updated by another transaction is rarely useful.

Typically, as the locking used within a database becomes more granular, it permits more users to access more database resources simultaneously. As this usage increases, the number of locks also increases. Obviously, if you lock just one table, you have just one lock. But if you lock multiple rows in multiple tables, you have many locks. As the number of locks increases, the server resources needed to manage them also increases, as does the time required to establish and remove them. Like many things, increased functionality brings with it increased resource requirements.

Because of their propensity to lock entire tables, pessimistic control systems are susceptible to deadlock situations. A deadlock occurs when transaction 1 locks tables needed by transaction 2, and vice versa. Because neither transaction is able to unlock the tables it needs to complete, the two are locked in a deadly embrace—resulting in neither of them ever completing without outside intervention.

Database servers, as a rule, implement pessimistic control schemes. This is a throwback to the days when the resources did not exist at the workstation level to implement optimistic control mechanisms. Because Delphi itself implements a type of optimistic control scheme, you may be faced with the challenges of both approaches in the database applications you develop.

Most database servers lock the appropriate elements for you automatically as you make changes to a database. For example, most servers will lock a row while you update it to prevent other users from updating it simultaneously. If you delete a large number of rows, the server may lock the entire table, depending on the platform.

Sybase SQL Server provides both table and page locking, but doesn't lock individual rows. When you attempt to change a given row, the page on which it resides is locked during the update. The thinking is that updates usually occur in batches to rows that are concentrated in a given area of the database. By locking these rows by the page, one lock typically suffices for several rows. This conserves server resources, but it can prevent access to rows unrelated to the update. Updates to single rows are particularly a problem with this approach. Despite the trade-offs, Sybase's approach works about as well in practice as those taken by other DBMS vendors.

Optimistic Concurrency Control

Optimistic concurrency-control systems assume that most updates are nonconflicting and that most users read, but do not update, the database. The best way to visualize the workings of an optimistic control system is by way of an example. Imagine a book editor who supervises the editing of book manuscripts to be published by a publishing house. As manuscripts are received, he duplicates and distributes them to other editors to be edited. These editors mark up the duplicates and send them back to the supervising editor, who must consolidate the changes and apply them to the original manuscript. After the changes are applied, editors who receive the manuscript will get the changed version, so that they don't repeat editing work that's already been done.

This is a good example of optimistic concurrency control for a couple of reasons. First, notice that the original manuscript never leaves the supervising editor. In optimistic concurrency-control systems, a *copy* of the data is initially changed, not the data itself. When a change is applied to the server, it is done in such a way as to prevent it from overwriting changes made by other users.

Also notice that changes made by the editors are naturally partitioned. One editor might review the manuscript's grammar; another might check it for technical accuracy. As a rule, two editors would never edit the same manuscript in the same manner simultaneously. This is a basic premise of optimistic concurrency control systems. Database updates are normally partitioned by department, management level or some other criteria. This works out well for optimistic systems because database resources are not locked to begin with.

Optimistic Concurrency Control in Delphi Applications

Delphi implements its version of optimistic concurrency control using the `UpdateMode` property of the `TTable` and `TQuery` `DataSet` components. As with all optimistic concurrency systems, Delphi retrieves a copy of a row from the server, enables you to change it, then sends your changes to the server. Changes are sent to the server using the SQL `UPDATE` command. This `UPDATE` command contains a `WHERE` clause that locates the row that is to be changed. `UpdateMode` controls which columns from the table are listed in the `WHERE` clause.

`UpdateMode` can have three possible values:

- ■ `upWhereAll` (default)—The `WHERE` clause includes every column in the table.
- ■ `upWhereChanged`—The `WHERE` clause includes the `DataSet`'s key columns and columns that have changed.
- ■ `upWhereKeyOnly`—The `WHERE` clause includes only the `DataSet`'s key columns (use this only if you have exclusive use of the database table).

Both the `TTable` and `TQuery` components publish an `UpdateMode` property. It defaults to `upWhereAll`, which means that updating a row in a table causes a `WHERE` clause to be generated that lists every column in the table. This can be quite cumbersome, especially with large tables. An alternative, and faster, approach is the use of the `upWhereChanged` setting. It generates a `WHERE` clause that includes the table's key fields and the fields that were changed. This is best demonstrated by means of an example.

Let's say your Delphi application had just modified the `LastName` field of the CUSTOMER table. With `upWhereAll`, here's the type of SQL that would be generated—notice the lengthy `WHERE` clause:

```
UPDATE CUSTOMER
SET LastName='newlastname'
WHERE CustomerNumber=1
AND LastName='Doe'
AND FirstName='John'
AND StreetAddress='123 SunnyLane'
AND City='Anywhere'
AND State='OK'
AND Zip='73115'
```

By contrast, here's the statement generated by upWhereChanged:

```
UPDATE CUSTOMER
SET LastName='newlastname'
WHERE CustomerNumber=1
AND LastName='Doe'
```

Notice how much shorter it is. Notice also that it avoids the possibility of overwriting another user's changes to the LastName field by including its original value in the WHERE clause. If another user changes the LastName field in between the time the row is read and when it is updated by the current user, the UPDATE generated by upWhereChanged will fail, which is what you'd want. Obviously, this isn't as bullet proof as the upWhereAll method. Another user could delete the row after your application has read it, then add a new record to the table that happens to have the same key and LastName value as the original record. When your record applied its UPDATE, it would be updating the wrong record. But this scenario is usually a remote possibility at best.

UpdateMode's other setting, upWhereKeyOnly, is even less bulletproof, but it does have its use. Because it checks only the key value of the row you're changing, it doesn't allow for the possibility that another user has changed the field you're updating in the time since you originally read the record. This may be a safe assumption, and, then again, it may not be. *In most multiuser applications, it would be unsafe to assume that another user has not changed a record you've previously read into a client application.* This is, therefore, the kind of optimization that you do only on a rare occasion and out of necessity. Because the WHERE clause generated by the upWhereKeyOnly setting would naturally be shorter, it would tend to be faster than one that included other columns as well. Nevertheless, you should check with your Database Administrator before using this option; it could lead to data loss if used improperly.

In practice, you should stick with upWhereAll unless you have a specific reason for deviating from it. upWhereChanged is a good alternative if the table you're working with has a large number of columns and upWhereAll is just too slow. UpWhereKeyOnly is safe to use only when you have exclusive use of the table—don't use it otherwise. One practical application of upWhereKeyOnly would be in the collection of data from a machine of some type. If you need to update values in a database table using this data as it's collected, you'll probably be the only user updating the table, and quick execution of the SQL UPDATE may be critical. If so, perhaps upWhereKeyOnly is what you need, but I recommend that you check with your Database Administrator before using it.

Transaction Log Management

Ever wonder how database servers keep from permanently saving changes to a database that is interrupted by a power outage or machine crash? Does the server keep some kind of undo list? How does it know what transactions to rollback when the database is recovered?

The answer to all these questions is that changes you make to a database are normally made to the database's transaction log *first*, then later committed to the database itself after the transaction completes successfully. This means that, despite its name, the transaction log is more than a mere log—it's where all the action is! If the power fails on the server machine before a change you've made has been committed to the database, there's no change to reverse off the database—the change never occurred. Because the uncommitted changes you were making were applied strictly to the transaction log, the server software can easily roll back incomplete transactions without affecting the database.

One subject that doesn't usually come to mind when developers think of database application development is transaction log management. Usually relegated to the area of database administration, transaction log management tends to be neglected by database application developers—much to the chagrin of DBAs.

There are, however, a couple of areas of transaction log management that the competent database developer will be familiar with and design his applications to take into consideration. The first area to be concerned with is in keeping transaction log information to a minimum. The second is in breaking large transactions into smaller ones to avoid filling the transaction log. I'll discuss each of these separately.

Keeping Transaction Logs to a Minimum

A common mistake made by client/server developers coming from flat-file databases like dBASE and Paradox is using programming constructs, rather than SQL, to perform batch data updates. This is best illustrated using an example. Let's say that you needed to convert all the last name fields in the CUSTOMER table to uppercase. If you're a former dBASE developer, you might code the following Object Pascal to perform your updates:

```
With taCUSTOMER do begin
    First;
    While not EOF do begin
        FieldByName('LastName').AsString :=
➥UpperCase(FieldByName('LastName').AsString);
        Next;
    end;
end;
```

This approach would not only be slow, it would have the undesirable effect of beginning and committing a transaction for every row in the table. Furthermore, if a problem occurred while your loop was executing, part of the rows would be updated, and part would not be—some last names would be uppercased, some would remain unchanged. You could remedy the partial update problem by calling your TDatabase component's StartTransaction method prior to the loop, but you'd still have the problem of very inefficient updates. For every iteration of your loop, a separate SQL UPDATE statement would be generated, complete with its own WHERE clause to locate the very next row in the table. With an extremely large CUSTOMER table, the process would probably crawl along very slowly.

A far better approach, and one that uses the transaction log as it was intended, is to use a TQuery or TStoredProc component to carry out your update. The same update written in SQL would look like this:

```
UPDATE CUSTOMER

SET LastName=UPPER(LastName)
```

Because the statement will itself be treated as a single transaction, either all the updates will occur, or none of them will. Furthermore, the transaction log will escape being thrashed by the constant initiation and committal of one transaction after another.

Another means of limiting the log information generated by a transaction is to avoid unqualified SQL DELETE commands. Each row deleted with the DELETE command is copied to the transaction log first so that the transaction may be rolled back should the need arise. With a large table, it's easy to quickly run out of transaction log space. If you need to delete all the rows in a table, use your server's table-truncation command rather than the DELETE command. Many servers support a command similar to the dBASE ZAP command that quickly empties a table of its contents. Sybase, for example, provides the TRUNCATE TABLE command for this purpose. Not only is it always faster than the DELETE command, it isn't saved to the transaction log, so there's no log activity associated with it. If your server doesn't support any type of table-truncation command, you may find that simply dropping and recreating the table in question is an option, depending on the way it's used elsewhere in the database and by other applications.

Yet another way of avoiding log activity is the use of SELECT INTO rather than INSERT SELECT when copying rows from one table to another. Rows inserted using INSERT SELECT are stored in the transaction log, so large inserts are to be avoided. SELECT INTO, as implemented by Sybase and others, is a nonlogged operation—it adds no entries to the transaction log. Not all DBMS platforms support this syntax (InterBase doesn't, for instance), so you may not be able to use this technique.

The Sybase Transact-SQL syntax for using SELECT INTO in this manner is as follows:

```
SELECT LastName, FirstName
INTO NEWCUSTOMER
FROM CUSTOMER
```

This creates a table called NEWCUSTOMER and inserts into it the LastName and FirstName columns from the CUSTOMER table. It's functionally equivalent to this syntax:

```
CREATE TABLE NEWCUSTOMER
(LastName CHAR(30),
 FirstName CHAR(30))
```

```
INSERT INTO NEWCUSTOMER (LastName, FirstName)
SELECT LastName, FirstName
FROM CUSTOMER
```

You can use SELECT INTO to avoid creating transaction log entries in the following scenario:

- You need to create a table, then copy rows from a second table into it.
- All of the columns in the new table need to receive values from the second table.
- You aren't interested in being able to roll back the row inserts.

Breaking Up Large Transactions

There are times that you must perform a mass data modification of some kind that unavoidably creates large numbers of transaction log entries. Unchecked, these types of updates can cause your transaction log to fill and create serious problems on your server. They can also generate locks that prevent access to entire tables by other users. Because of this, it's a good idea to break these types of large transactions into smaller ones. There are a couple of ways of doing this; which one you use depends upon your DBMS platform and the specific needs of your application.

One way of breaking a large update into smaller ones is to breakdown a single UPDATE or DELETE into several UPDATEs or DELETEs that each use a more restrictive WHERE clause. Using the previous example, if we have a CUSTOMER table of a million records and were needing to uppercase each last name in each record, we might do the following:

```
SET TRANSACTION;
UPDATE CUSTOMER
SET LastName=UPPER(LastName)
WHERE CustomerNumber between 1 and 100000;
COMMIT;

SET TRANSACTION;
UPDATE CUSTOMER
SET LastName=UPPER(LastName)
WHERE CustomerNumber between 100001 and 200000;
COMMIT;

SET TRANSACTION;
UPDATE CUSTOMER
SET LastName=UPPER(LastName)
WHERE CustomerNumber between 200001 and 300000;
COMMIT;
```

This is a simple technique that can make the difference between an update being feasible and it not being feasible.

Another technique for limiting the rows affected by an UPDATE or DELETE statement is to limit the number of rows the command has access to. Not all DBMS platforms support this (Sybase does, for example, but InterBase does not), so you may not be able to use it.

Basically, you use a command specific to the server that limits the rows processed by your UPDATE or DELETE. You then repeat your UPDATE or DELETE as many times as necessary to process all rows. Here's an example using Sybase's Transact-SQL:

```
SET ROWCOUNT 50000 /* Limits the UPDATE to 50000 rows at a time */
WHILE (EXISTS (SELECT * FROM ORDERS WHERE Amount<>0))
BEGIN
    UPDATE ORDERS SET Amount=0
    WHERE Amount<>0 /* Keeps the UPDATE from looping infinitely */
END
```

Because the rows we're updating are still in the table with each iteration of the loop, we have to have a way of excluding them as they're processed. One way to do this is to test in the UPDATE's WHERE clause for a value that's exclusive of the one we're setting with the UPDATE. In other words, we test the Amount column using <>0 because we are assigning Amount to 0 with the UPDATE. This allows the UPDATE to essentially flag each row as processed by updating it. This flagging keeps a row from being updated twice.

Here's an example using the DELETE command:

```
SET ROWCOUNT 50000 /* Limits the DELETE to 50000 rows at a time */
WHILE (EXISTS (SELECT * FROM ORDERS WHERE Amount=0))
BEGIN
    DELETE FROM ORDERS
    WHERE Amount=0
END
```

What's Ahead

In the next chapter, we'll return to a discussion of SQL, specifically advanced SQL. You'll further the SQL skills you've garnered thus far by exploring stored procedure creation, database triggers and the like. Between Chapter 22, "Advanced SQL," and Chapter 5, "A No-Nonsense Approach to SQL," you should be able to glean all you need of the SQL database query language.

Summary

As you can see, there are a number of issues to consider regarding transaction isolation and concurrency control. Elements such as the TransIsolation and UpdateMode properties need to be fully appreciated in order to properly design Delphi database applications. Although tools like Delphi greatly insulate the developer from having to worry about low-level details such as transaction isolation, you'll still need to tweak these things occasionally. With this chapter, you now have the basic skills you need to do so.

22

Advanced SQL

This chapter doesn't attempt to pick up exactly where Chapter 5, "A No-Nonsense Approach to SQL," left off. There is a wide gap between entry-level SQL and advanced SQL. There is therefore a gap between this chapter and the introductory SQL chapter. This chapter is targeted for the person with advanced SQL skills; the introductory chapter is targeted for the beginner.

I assume that you're already familiar with how to connect to a database and execute SQL commands against it using your favorite SQL editor. The examples in this chapter make use of the Windows Interactive SQL (WISQL) editor. Feel free to use whatever suits you.

This chapter makes extensive use of the database and tables first created in Chapter 5. To work through the following examples, you'll need to reuse the objects you created in that chapter or create them now. See Chapter 5 for more information.

Some of the tables used in this chapter were defined in the Tutorial section of this book. Though they're not essential to understanding the concepts presented, you can refer to Chapter 8, "Your First Real Database Application," for information on creating them.

In this chapter, the two main families of SQL syntax—the ANSI and Sybase families—are compared. InterBase is highly ANSI-compliant, so examples using InterBase syntax will work on most other ANSI-compliant platforms (such as Oracle). Sybase SQL Server, on the other hand, deviates from ANSI in many important ways, as does its licensed cousin, Microsoft SQL Server.

I've expressly tried to avoid replicating what you can already easily find in your SQL platform's documentation. The goal of this chapter is to touch on a variety of advanced SQL topics—some are "advanced" because they are not beginner topics, some are "advanced" because they are indeed complicated and difficult to grasp. Advanced SQL is a huge subject capable of filling several books all by itself; this chapter covers enough topics that there will be something for everyone.

You'll notice that I go to great lengths to "speak" in SQL. Rather than beat around the bush and attempt to explain SQL with English, I explain SQL with SQL. I liken this to a French teacher teaching in French and forcing all students to converse in French. If SQL is the language in which you're supposed to be fluent, let's talk SQL!

Extending a Database

As your data capacity needs change over time, you'll probably want to expand databases that you created in the past. Use the ALTER DATABASE command to increase the allocated size of an existing database. Here's the InterBase syntax:

```
ALTER DATABASE
ADD 'C:\DATA\IB\ORDENT2'
```

The preceding command adds a second operating system file to the database.

Sybase supports a similar syntax. Here's an example:

```
ALTER DATABASE ORDENT
ON ORDENT2=100
```

Segments

A popular way of improving performance on a large database is to spread it over several different disk drives. Sybase calls these pieces of the database *segments*. With Sybase System 10, you can use segments to allocate specific database objects on specific disk drives. Dramatic performance improvement can be seen by placing a table on one disk drive and its indexes on another, especially if the disks have separate disk controllers. Using segments involves four basic steps:

1. Create a new link to a physical drive (a *device*, in Sybase terminology) using the Sybase DISK INIT command:

   ```
   DISK INIT
   name = "INDDEV",
   physname = "SYS:DATA\INDDEV.DAT",
   vdevno = 25,
   size = 51200
   ```

2. Expand the database on to the drive using the ALTER DATABASE command:

   ```
   ALTER DATABASE ORDENT
   ON INDDEV=100
   ```

3. Create a new segment that resides on the newly allocated device using the sp_addsegment command

   ```
   sp_addsegment 'indexeseg','ORDENT','INDDEV'
   ```

   where 'indexeseg' is the name of the new segment, 'ORDENT' is the database name and 'INDDEV' is the name of the newly added device.

4. Create a database object on the newly created segment. For example, you could create an index on the new segment using the following syntax:

   ```
   CREATE INDEX INVOICES02 ON INVOICES (CustomerNumber) ON indexeseg
   ```

The INVOICES table and the INVOICES02 index now reside on different segments and, it's hoped, on different disk drives, thereby eliminating head contention when the table is accessed by using the INVOICES02 index.

Proper database design on the Sybase platform mandates the consideration of segmentation *before* objects are built within a database, because they cannot be easily moved afterward. There are two rules to follow when deciding how to segment a database:

■ Attempt to split tables from their corresponding non-clustered indexes. The most basic way of doing this is to place all the tables in a database on one disk drive and all the indexes on another. Note that you cannot place a table's clustered index on a different device than the table itself. If you attempt to, the table will "follow" its clustered index and eventually migrate to the segment you've specified for the clustered index. (Clustered indexes are discussed later in the chapter.)

■ Attempt to further separate major tables, especially those that are likely to be accessed simultaneously, from each other onto separate drives. If your database has three major tables and scads of other less-significant tables, the ideal disk drive configuration includes at least eight separate disks: one each for the three major tables, one for the less-significant tables, and a corresponding index disk for each table disk.

Note that none of this applies to InterBase—it doesn't support segmentation as defined by Sybase.

Creating Indexes

You create indexes in SQL using—you guessed it—the CREATE INDEX command. Here's the basic syntax

```
CREATE INDEX INVOICES02  ON INVOICES  (CustomerNumber)
```

where *INVOICES02* is the name of the new index, *INVOICES* is the name of the table on which to build the index, and *CustomerNumber* is the index key.

In InterBase, index names must be unique across the database in which they reside. In Sybase, they need be unique only across each table.

Unique indexes are created using the CREATE UNIQUE INDEX variation of the command, as in the following:

```
CREATE UNIQUE INDEX INVOICES01 ON INVOICES (InvoiceNo)
```

Index keys are, by default, arranged in ascending order. Note that you can create descending indexes in InterBase using the DESCENDING keyword. Here's an example:

```
CREATE DESCENDING INDEX INVOICES03 ON INVOICES (Amount)
```

helps queries such as the following execute faster:

```
SELECT * FROM INVOICES

ORDER BY Amount DESCENDING
```

Clustered Versus Nonclustered Indexes

Sybase supports an extension to the basic CREATE INDEX syntax that enables the creation of clustered indexes. *Nonclustered indexes* are indexes in the traditional sense—at the lowest level, they store a key value that must then be cross-referenced with the physical table in order to retrieve data from the table. *Clustered indexes* store the actual record data at the lowest level of the index tree. That is, rather than merely storing a key value at the lowest level of a clustered-index tree, SQL Server stores the entire row there. By definition, then, there can be only one clustered index per table.

In a clustered index, the data itself is basically sorted by the specified key, providing much better performance than traditional indexes. There is no need to return to the physical table to look up a key located in the index. The clustered index and the table are basically the same thing—there is no separate table in which to look up anything.

The Sybase syntax for creating a clustered index is as follows:

```
CREATE CLUSTERED INDEX INVOICES01 ON INVOICES (OrderNumber)
```

Unfortunately, there is no equivalent facility in InterBase.

Covered Indexes

Though not a separate index type, covered indexes offer a performance boon similar to that of clustered indexes. A *covered index* is a nonclustered index that happens to include, as part of its key, all the columns a given query might access. That is, in addition to real key values, the index key of a covered index contains other columns needed to satisfy a particular query. Thus, the index "covers" the query.

Here's an example of the use of a covered index:

```
CREATE INDEX INVOICES04 ON INVOICES (InvoiceDate, Amount)
```

Now the query

```
SELECT InvoiceDate, SUM(Amount) TotalAmount
FROM INVOICES
GROUP BY InvoiceDate
```

can be optimized by the database server to read only from the index, without having to look up the Amount column in the table itself.

Activating and Deactivating an Index

In InterBase, you can temporarily disable an index, then reactivate and rebuild it later. While an index is deactivated, you can add a large number of rows to its table without incurring the penalty of index maintenance with each new row. Here's the syntax:

```
ALTER INDEX INVOICES03 INACTIVE
```

Just replace INACTIVE with ACTIVE to reactivate it, like so:

```
ALTER INDEX INVOICES03 ACTIVE
```

Deactivating and reactivating an index causes it to be rebuilt. You'll want to wait until an index is not in use before attempting this because index deactivations are delayed until they're no longer in use.

Server Query Optimization

All leading database servers optimize the SQL queries passed to them by clients. They look at the SQL you pass them and attempt to determine the most effective way of executing them. Most servers refer to the strategy they come up with to optimally execute SQL as a query execution *plan*. Factors such as available indexes, the amount of disk that must be traversed, statistical information regarding index key distribution, and so forth are taken into account when this plan is developed. More often than not, the server comes up with the best plan for resolving your query; however, it may need some assistance from you.

Helping the Optimizer

One way you can help the query optimizer is to update the statistics it stores regarding index selectivity. *Index selectivity* refers to the distribution of key values within an index. By keeping this information up-to-date, you ensure that the query optimizer bases the decisions it makes on the most accurate information possible.

The syntax for updating index selectivity in InterBase is

```
SET STATISTICS INDEX INVOICES03
```

where *INVOICES03* is the name of the index to recompute.

This is the Sybase syntax

```
UPDATE STATISTICS INVOICES.INVOICES03
```

where *INVOICES* is the name of the table on which the index is built and *INVOICES03* is the name of the index itself. Because Sybase indexes are unique only within the table on which they're built, the name of the table is required with this command. The advantage to this approach, though, is that all the indexes for a given table can be created at once by omitting the name of a specific index:

```
UPDATE STATISTICS INVOICES
```

Displaying the Query Optimizer's Plan

With most SQL servers, you can display the server's execution plan when you execute a query. You can do this with InterBase from within WISQL. To view the plans InterBase generates to service your queries, set the Display Query Plan option to True in the Basic Settings dialog box on WISQL's Session menu (see Figure 22.1).

FIGURE 22.1.

The Basic ISQL Set Options dialog box.

This is equivalent to the SET PLAN ON command.

You also can display statistical information about each query after it executes by using the SET STATS ON command. This command is not to be confused with the SET STATISTICS command (which updates index information) mentioned previously.

On Sybase, you use the SET SHOWPLAN ON command to display the optimizer's plan. In conjunction with the SET NOEXEC option, you can review the server's query execution plan without executing the query.

You can also review statistical information related to query execution via the Sybase SET STATISTICS command. SET STATISTICS IO ON causes SQL Server to display statistical I/O information for each query it executes. SET STATISTICS TIME ON causes SQL Server to display timing information for each query executed.

Reviewing the plan generated by your query optimizer helps you better understand why queries behave the way they do and possibly assists you in fine-tuning them. For example, if you run the preceding covered index query without a covered index in place and display the generated query plan, you get the output shown in Figure 22.2.

FIGURE 22.2.

The query plan without the covered index.

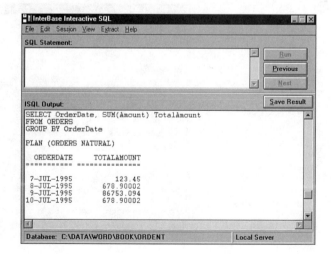

Let's add an index that includes only the OrderDate column and then rerun the query. Figure 22.3 illustrates that the query optimizer uses the new index.

FIGURE 22.3.

The query plan uses the OrderDate index.

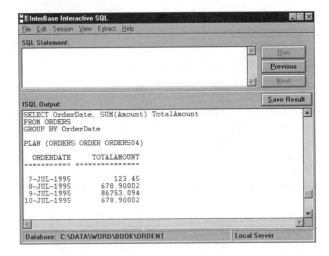

Now, let's add the covered index back in. Re-create it using this syntax:

```
CREATE INDEX INVOICES04 ON INVOICES (OrderDate, Amount)
```

Rerun the query. Note that the query optimizer uses the covered index rather than the one built only on the OrderDate column. (See Figure 22.4.)

FIGURE 22.4.

The query plan uses the covered index.

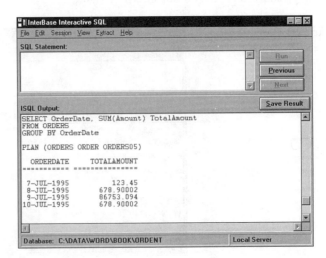

This example shows the real value of being able to see the plan that the server develops for executing a query. By carefully reviewing the plan, you are able to come up with ways of optimizing the query.

Forcing the Use of a Plan

InterBase supports an extension to the SELECT statement that enables you to tell the optimizer to use a specific query execution plan rather than develop its own. Here's the syntax:

```
SELECT LastName, FirstName
FROM CUSTOMER
PLAN (CUSTOMER ORDER CUSTOMER03)
ORDER BY LastName
```

Notice the PLAN clause. The first argument tells the optimizer which of the query's tables the plan is for, and second argument tells the optimizer what it is you're doing—in this case, you're ordering the table. The last argument tells the optimizer what it is you want to use to carry out your plan—in this case, the CUSTOMER03 index. Figure 22.5 illustrates the results of the forced plan.

FIGURE 22.5.

The plan specified in the SELECT statement forces the use of the CUS-TOMER03 index.

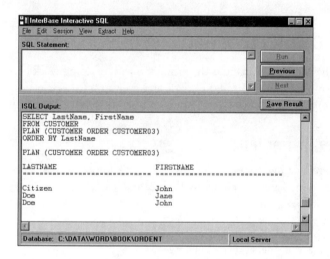

This facility can be useful in situations where you don't think that the optimizer is taking the best approach to optimizing a query.

Sybase SQL Server has a similar, but undocumented, capability. As with any undocumented feature, keep in mind that it could be removed from the product at any time.

There is a way in SQL Server–based queries to force the Sybase query optimizer to use a particular index. The syntax to do this looks like this:

```
SELECT LastName, FirstName
FROM CUSTOMER (3)
ORDER BY LastName
```

Notice the 3 surrounded by parentheses after the table name. This tells the optimizer to use the third index created over the CUSTOMER table. (This is the reason that I name indexes using the table as a base, followed by a number. Remembering the order of the index is a snap.)

Adding and Dropping Table Columns

Columns are added and dropped from tables using the SQL ALTER TABLE command. Some server platforms, such as Sybase, don't support dropping columns after the fact. InterBase, on the other hand, does. Here's the syntax to add a column to a table

```
ALTER TABLE CUSTOMER
ADD PhoneNumber char(10)
```

and here's the syntax to drop it:

```
ALTER TABLE CUSTOMER
DROP PhoneNumber
```

Note that you can't add a NOT NULL column to a table that already has rows, because it would necessarily have to allow NULLs immediately after being added to the table.

Advanced *SELECT* Syntax

The SELECT command is the primary means of doing work in SQL. You can use SELECT commands to join tables, return data, and even to serve as selection criteria for other SELECT statements. The following paragraphs enumerate some of the many uses of the SELECT command.

Multi-Tier Joins

Joins that involve more than two tables are known as *multi-tier joins.* For example, in a multi-tier join, Table1 is joined to Table2, and Table2 is joined to Table3. Here's an example of a multi-tier join:

```
SELECT w.WorkOrderNo, p.Address, t.Name
FROM WORDERS w, PROPERTY p, TENANT t
WHERE w.PropertyNo=p.PropertyNo
and p.TenantNo=t.TenantNo
```

In this query, the WORDERS and PROPERTY table are joined using their PropertyNo columns, and the PROPERTY and TENANT table are joined using their TenantNo columns. The effect is that all three tables are linked together in one result set. (See Figure 22.6.) Listing 22.1 illustrates the result set returned by this query.

Self-Joins

In addition to joining with other tables, a table joins with itself. This type of join is known as a *reflexive-* or *self-join.* Here's a self-join query:

```
SELECT I.CustomerNumber, I.Amount, (I.Amount / SUM(I2.Amount))*100 Percentage
FROM    INVOICES I,
        INVOICES I2
WHERE I.CustomerNumber=I2.CustomerNumber
GROUP  BY I.CustomerNumber, I.Amount
```

FIGURE 22.6.

The results of the multi-tiered query.

This query lists the invoices on file for each customer and the percentage of all invoices for the customer that a given invoice's total represents. A self-join is the only way to retrieve this type of information in one pass. Each customer's data is gathered and grouped as would be expected, then the INVOICES table is joined back to itself to retrieve the total of the invoices for each customer. The amount of each invoice is then divided by this total and converted to a percentage for placement in the result set.

Theta Joins

Theta joins link two tables using non-equality comparison operators (such as <>). Here's an example of a theta join:

```
SELECT C.CustomerNumber, O.Amount, Sum(O2.Amount) OTHERS
FROM CUSTOMER C,
INVOICES O,
INVOICES O2
WHERE C.CustomerNumber=O.CustomerNumber
AND C.CustomerNumber<>O2.CustomerNumber
GROUP BY C.CustomerNumber, O.Amount
```

This query is composed of two joins. The first join consists of linking the CUSTOMER and INVOICES tables to retrieve each customer's invoices. The second join is a theta join that retrieves the total of all the invoices that do *not* belong to each customer. Since it's joining with the INVOICES table using two different join types, two separate table aliases are used for the INVOICES 4table.

Cartesian Joins

A *Cartesian join* is used to build a result set containing all the rows from two different tables. Here's an example:

```
SELECT t.Name, w.Description
FROM TENANT t, WORKTYPE w
```

Cartesian products usually happen by accident. They're normally the result of an errant join clause. Nevertheless, Cartesian joins can be useful for obtaining a composite view of the data in two separate tables. For example, the previous query could be used to construct a work table that lists the work done for each tenant. Figure 22.7 shows the results of the query.

FIGURE 22.7.

The results of the Cartesian join.

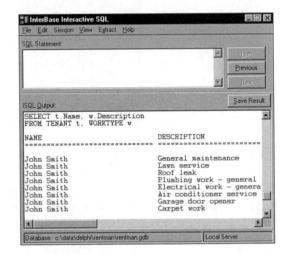

Views

Views consist of compiled SELECT statements that you can query as though they were tables. Views do not actually store any data—they consist of compiled SQL only. Views are similar to stored procedures, especially select procedures. When a view is queried, the server combines the SELECT used to create the view with the one used to query it, and executes the combined query against the view's underlying tables.

Use the CREATE VIEW command to construct views. Here's an example:

```
CREATE VIEW NEWTENANTS AS
SELECT *
FROM TENANT
WHERE MovedInDate >"12/01/95"
```

Once the view is created, it can be queried just like a table, as in the following:

```
SELECT * FROM NEWTENANTS
```

Figure 22.8 displays the results from this query. Notice that, even though the SELECT against the view didn't include a WHERE clause, the result set appears as though it did due to the WHERE clause being built into the view.

FIGURE 22.8.

The result set returned when the view is queried.

The SELECT statement that makes up a view can do almost anything a normal SELECT can do except include an ORDER BY clause. This is true of both the InterBase and Sybase platforms.

Updatable views impose additional restrictions. For a view to be updatable on the InterBase platform, it must meet the following conditions:

■ The SELECT statement must reference either a single table or another updatable view.

■ In order for the view to support the INSERT command, columns in the underlying table that are excluded from the view must allow NULL values.

■ Subqueries, the DISTINCT predicate, the HAVING clause, aggregate functions, joined tables, user-defined functions, and SELECTs from stored procedures are not supported.

To create an updatable view that ensures that rows inserted or updated through it meet the selection criteria imposed by the view, use the WITH CHECK OPTION clause of the CREATE VIEW command. The WITH CHECK OPTION clause causes the view to refuse updates or inserts that would create a row that its selection criteria would exclude. Here's the syntax:

```
CREATE VIEW OKPROPERTY AS
SELECT *
FROM PROPERTY
WHERE State="OK"
WITH CHECK OPTION
```

Now, any record updates or inserts whose State column is not equal to "OK" will fail.

Sybase views are a little more flexible than InterBase views in that they can span multiple tables and remain updatable. Still, there are many limitations. Here's a summary of the limitations that exist with Sybase views:

■ The ORDER BY and COMPUTE clauses, the keyword INTO, and the UNION operator are not allowed in the SELECT statement that makes up a view.

■ Views cannot be created over temporary tables.

■ Triggers and indexes cannot be built over views.

■ Readtext and writetext cannot be used on text or image columns in views.

There are additional limitations with updatable views:

■ Views over multiple tables do not support the DELETE command.

■ Columns from the underlying table that are excluded from the view must allow NULL values in order for the view to support the INSERT command.

■ Views that contain calculated columns do not support the INSERT command.

■ Views over multiple tables that were created using the DISTINCT or WITH CHECK OPTION switches do not support the INSERT command.

■ Views created with the DISTINCT switch do not support the INSERT or UPDATE commands.

■ When updating a view over multiple tables, all affected columns must belong to the same table.

■ Columns in a view that consist of a calculation are not updatable.

■ Views that contain aggregate columns are not updatable.

Dynamic Views

A view is a compiled SELECT statement that emulates a table and can be queried like a table. When a view is queried, the SQL that comprises it is retrieved and executed by the server. Though the data returned by the query may vary dramatically, the SELECT statement executed on the server rarely does.

A *dynamic view* is a view that renders a different SELECT statement based on conditions at the time it is accessed. The preceding example limited the property records shown to just those residing in Oklahoma. The criteria the view used never changes, even though the rows it returns might; it is therefore a *static view*. A dynamic view, on the other hand, changes the criteria it passes to the server based on conditions external to it when it is accessed. Here's an example, written in Sybase's Transact-SQL dialect

```
CREATE VIEW CONTACTLISTV
SELECT * FROM CONTACTLIST
WHERE EnteredBy=suser_name()
```

where EnteredBy is a column in the CONTACTLIST table that records the name of the user entering a new record. It is automatically set by using a DEFAULT constraint each time a record is added. Each time a user of the application adds a record, his suser_name() is stored in this field. Because of this, you're able to restrict the view a user sees of the entire CONTACTLIST to just those records he entered. The search criteria used by the server varies based on who the current user of the application is—that is, it's dynamic.

Views and Access Rights

A user need not have rights to a view's underlying tables in order to access the view. Access permissions on views are separate from those on their underlying tables. The one exception to this is that users who create views must have the proper access rights to the underlying tables.

If users have access rights to perform a given operation on a view, *even if they lack those same rights on its underlying tables,* they can access the underlying tables through the view. In fact, no less than Sybase itself recommends using views in this way as security mechanisms.

This is not a good practice for several reasons. By placing part of your access permissions in views, you make it impossible to manage your system security from a single central point—you cannot see all access rights from any one perspective. You must instead look in at least two different places—the traditional placement of rights via GRANT and REVOKE, as well as your system's table views—to have a complete system access picture. Furthermore, most administrative tools aren't advanced enough to point out to you that a user does not have rights to a table that he is accessing via a view. If you want to give a user limited rights to a table, I recommend you do so via tables, not views.

Stored Procedures

Stored procedures are compiled SQL programs. They are often made up of numerous SQL statements and are stored in a database with other database objects. There are two types of stored procedures: select procedures and executable procedures. Select procedures can be used in place of a table in a SELECT statement. Executable procedures, by contrast, are executed—they may or may not return data.

You create stored procedures using the CREATE PROCEDURE command. Here's an example of the InterBase syntax:

```
CREATE PROCEDURE CLEARCALLS
AS
BEGIN
   DELETE FROM CALLS WHERE CallDateTime < '01/01/96';
END
```

Here's the same procedure coded in Sybase's Transact-SQL:

```
CREATE PROCEDURE CLEARCALLS
AS
  DELETE FROM CALLS WHERE CallDateTime < '01/01/96'
```

If the procedure receives parameters from the caller, the syntax changes slightly. Here's the InterBase syntax:

```
CREATE PROCEDURE CLEARCALLS (BeginningDate DATE)
AS
BEGIN
    DELETE FROM CALLS WHERE CallDateTime < :BeginningDate;
END
```

Here's the Sybase syntax for the same procedure:

```
CREATE PROCEDURE CLEARCALLS (@BeginningDate datetime)
AS
  DELETE FROM CALLS WHERE CallDateTime < @BeginningDate
```

Select Procedures

Select procedures define data to return to the caller by using the RETURNS keyword, like so:

```
CREATE PROCEDURE LISTPROP (State char(2))
RETURNS (PROPERTYNO INTEGER,
ADDRESS VARCHAR(30))
AS
BEGIN
        FOR SELECT PropertyNo, Address
        FROM PROPERTY
        WHERE State = :State
        INTO :PropertyNo, :Address
        DO
           SUSPEND;
END
```

You use the FOR SELECT...DO syntax to return results to the caller. SUSPEND pauses execution of the procedure until the caller requests another row. Output parameters are returned before execution is paused.

It's a good practice to store the source code to stored procedures in SQL script files. These scripts can be created and maintained using nearly any text editor. Remember to include any necessary CONNECT and SET TERM statements. These can then be executed using WISQL's Run an ISQL Script option. Listing 22.1 is an example of such a file.

Listing 22.1. A stored procedure residing in a SQL script file.

```
CONNECT "C:\DATA\DELPHI\RENTMAN\RENTMAN.GDB" USER SYSDBA PASSWORD masterkey;

SET TERM ^ ;

/* Stored procedures */
CREATE PROCEDURE LISTPROP
RETURNS (PROPERTYNO INTEGER, ADDRESS VARCHAR(30))
AS

BEGIN
        FOR SELECT PropertyNo, Address
        FROM PROPERTY
```

```
        INTO :PropertyNo, :Address
        DO
          SUSPEND;
END
  ^
SET TERM ; ^
```

The CONNECT statement at the top of the file establishes a connection to the database. The SET TERM command temporarily changes the SQL statement termination character to a caret (^) from the default semicolon (;). This keeps commands within the stored procedure definition from executing when the CREATE PROCEDURE command is executed. After CREATE PROCEDURE executes, SET TERM is again called to restore the SQL command terminator. This business of temporarily changing the termination character is a peculiarity of SQL scripts—you don't have to worry about this in WISQL itself.

Executable Procedures

Executable stored procedures differ little from select procedures in that they're not required to include a RETURNS statement. Here's an example of an InterBase executable procedure:

```
CREATE PROCEDURE insertWORKTYPE (WorkTypeCode smallint, Description char(30),
TaskDuration float)
AS
BEGIN
    INSERT INTO WORKTYPE VALUES  (:WorkTypeCode, :Description, :TaskDuration);
END
```

That same procedure written in Sybase's Transact-SQL would look like this:

```
CREATE PROCEDURE insertWORKTYPE (@WorkTypeCode smallint, @Description char(30),
@TaskDuration float)
AS
  INSERT INTO WORKTYPE VALUES  (@WorkTypeCode, @Description, @TaskDuration)
```

Exceptions

Exceptions are supported by both InterBase and Sybase. In InterBase, you use CREATE EXCEPTION to define a new exception and the EXCEPTION command to raise or throw it. Sybase doesn't define a separate exception object, though you can still raise one on-the-fly using the RAISERROR command. You also can build user-defined messages in advance that can then be used with the RAISERROR command. Here's an example of an InterBase exception and a stored procedure that raises it:

```
/* The exception */
CREATE EXCEPTION CREDIT_TOO_HIGH
"The requested credit is too high. All Casino advances must be less then $5000";

/*The SQL script for a procedure that uses the exception */
CONNECT "C:\DATA\IB\CASINO";
```

```
SET TERM ^;
CREATE PROCEDURE insertCREDIT (VoucherNumber smallint, VoucherDate date,
CustomerNumber int, Amount float)
AS
BEGIN
    IF (:Amount > 5000) THEN
        EXCEPTION CREDIT_TOO_HIGH;
    ELSE
        INSERT INTO CREDIT
        VALUES (:VoucherNumber, :VoucherDate, :CustomerNumber, :Amount);
END ^
SET TERM ; ^
EXIT;
```

This procedure limits casino credit requests to $5,000 or less. Note the use of the IF...THEN syntax to detect whether the Amount column in the row about to be inserted is greater than $5,000. The EXCEPTION command is used to raise the CREDIT_TOO_HIGH exception when the Amount is greater than $5,000.

Here's the Sybase SQL Server syntax to do the same thing (I've coded it as though it were stored in a separate script file, as recommended earlier):

```
sp_addmessage 20001,
  "The requested credit is too high. All Casino advances must be less then $5000."
GO
use CASINO
GO
CREATE PROCEDURE insertCREDIT (@VoucherNumber smallint, @VoucherDate date,
@CustomerNumber int, @Amount float)
AS
    IF @Amount > 5000
        RAISERROR 20001
    ELSE
        INSERT INTO CREDIT
        VALUES (@VoucherNumber, @VoucherDate, @CustomerNumber, @Amount)
GO
```

Note that Sybase also supports the inclusion of placeholders within the message text, similar to the Delphi Format function and the C printf() function. So, the message and previous procedure could have been constructed this way:

```
sp_addmessage 20001,
"The requested credit of %1 is too high. All Casino advances must be less then
$5000."
GO
use ORDENT
GO

CREATE PROCEDURE insertCREDIT (@VoucherNumber smallint, @VoucherDate date,
@CustomerNumber int, @Amount float)
AS
    IF @Amount > 5000
        RAISERROR 20001, @Amount
    ELSE
        INSERT INTO CREDIT
        VALUES (@VoucherNumber, @VoucherDate, @CustomerNumber, @Amount)
GO
```

Notice the use of the %1! placeholder. The Sybase syntax supports up to 20 numbered message parameters. Note also the modified call to RAISERROR. The @Amount variable is passed in as the command's second parameter. Even though an optional message string is normally the second parameter to RAISERROR, it detects that a user-defined message number has been passed to it and, therefore, uses the remaining arguments as message parameters. A user-defined message is distinguished by the fact that its message number is greater than 20000.

Sybase also supports the ability to bind a user-defined message to a system event, such as a constraint violation. Here's an example:

```
ALTER TABLE INVOICES
ADD CONSTRAINT INVALID_CUSTOMER
FOREIGN KEY (CustomerNumber)
REFERENCES CUSTOMER(CustomerNumber)
GO
exec sp_addmessage 20005, "The customer number you've specified is not on file.
Please specify a valid customer number."
GO
exec sp_bindmsg INVALID_CUSTOMER,20005
GO
```

Note the use of the constraint name in the call to sp_bindmsg. This is what establishes the relationship between the constraint created by the ALTER TABLE command and the message created by the call to sp_addmessage.

Triggers

Triggers are SQL routines that are activated when certain table events occur. They're very similar to stored procedures, so much so in fact that InterBase defines special extensions to SQL that apply to both stored procedures and triggers. Triggers are associated with specific table events—INSERTS, UPDATES, or DELETES. Here's an example of an InterBase trigger:

```
CREATE TRIGGER DELETE_DETAIL FOR WORDERS
ACTIVE BEFORE DELETE
AS BEGIN    DELETE FROM WODETAIL    WHERE WODETAIL.WorkOrderNo=Old.WorkOrderNo;
END
```

This trigger deletes the detail rows associated with a work order whenever their master record is deleted. This type of delete is known as a *cascading delete*—a delete made in one table cascades through to another using a common key.

Note the use of the OLD context variable. You can use the OLD context variable to reference the value of a column prior to an UPDATE or DELETE operation. The NEW context variable refers to the new value of a column in an INSERT or UPDATE operation.

Notice the use of the BEFORE keyword. Triggers can be activated before or after an INSERT, UPDATE, or DELETE.

In InterBase, up to 32,768 triggers can be bound to a given table event. The POSITION keyword specifies their firing order. Triggers with the same POSITION designation execute in a random order. Here's an example:

```
CREATE TRIGGER GENERATE_WORKTYPECODE FOR WORKTYPE
ACTIVE BEFORE INSERT
POSITION 0
AS BEGIN
  NEW.WorkTypeCode = GEN_ID(WorkTypeCodeGEN, 1);
 END
```

Sybase SQL Server supports a slightly different trigger syntax:

```
CREATE TRIGGER INVOICES delete ON CUSTOMER
FOR DELETE AS
DELETE FROM INVOICES WHERE INVOICES.CustomerNumber=(SELECT CustomerNumber FROM
deleted)
```

Notice the use of the logical deleted table. This table is conceptual in nature only—it is used to reference the row about to be deleted from the trigger table. SQL Server also defines an updated table that serves the same purpose in update and insert operations.

SQL Server provides a useful mechanism for determining what columns are being updated in update queries. You use the IF UPDATE(*columnname*) syntax, replacing *columnname* with the name of a column in the table. You can then limit the trigger's actions based on what columns have or have not been changed.

Cursors

Cursors enable you to access the rows in a table one at a time. There are four basic commands that relate to cursors: DECLARE, OPEN, FETCH, and CLOSE. You also can use the UPDATE and DELETE commands with updatable cursors.

Cursors are defined using SELECT statements. If a cursor is to be updatable, it must also include a list of updatable columns. Here's the syntax:

```
DECLARE c_PROPERTY CURSOR

FOR SELECT * FROM PROPERTY
```

You must open a cursor before you can retrieve rows from it. The OPEN command initiates the query that makes up the cursor declaration. Here's an example:

```
OPEN c_PROPERTY
```

Note that OPEN doesn't retrieve rows from the cursor. The FETCH command is used for that. Here's the syntax:

```
FETCH c_PROPERTY
```

FETCH retrieves one row at a time from the cursor's underlying table. With each call to FETCH, a new row is retrieved. InterBase and Sybase support forward cursors only—you cannot FETCH backward. To move backward in a cursor result set, close the cursor and re-open it.

> **NOTE**
>
> Even though Sybase and InterBase don't support bi-directional cursors, this doesn't mean you can't use them in your Delphi applications. The BDE provides a bi-directional cursoring mechanism to Delphi applications regardless of whether the underlying platform supports them.

You can update the rows returned by updatable cursors using special versions of the UPDATE and DELETE commands. A cursor must be declared using the FOR UPDATE OF clause in order to be updatable. Here's an example:

```
DECLARE c_PROPERTY CURSOR
FOR SELECT * FROM PROPERTY
FOR UPDATE OF Address
```

List just those columns in the FOR UPDATE OF clause that you might actually update. Declaring unneeded updatable fields wastes server resources.

Use the WHERE CURRENT OF cursorname syntax to UPDATE or DELETE the current row of an updatable cursor. Here's the syntax:

```
UPDATE PROPERTY
SET Address="357 Riverside Avenue"
WHERE CURRENT OF c_PROPERTY
```

To delete a row, use:

```
DELETE FROM PROPERTY
WHERE CURRENT OF c_PROPERTY
```

Use the CLOSE command to close cursors you're finished with. Here's the syntax:

```
CLOSE c_PROPERTY
```

On the InterBase platform, CLOSE also releases any system resources related to the cursor. On Sybase, you use the DEALLOCATE CURSOR command. Here's the syntax:

```
DEALLOCATE CURSOR c_PROPERTY
```

What's Ahead

In the next chapter, you'll learn about optimizing Delphi client/server applications. You'll learn a number of techniques for making your applications run faster and more reliably on client/server platforms. Performance optimizations as well as optimal SQL coding techniques are discussed in detail. If you want the lowdown on client/server optimization, you'll want to take a hard look at Chapter 23, "Optimizing Delphi Client/Server Applications."

Summary

This chapter covered a wide range of advanced SQL topics. Advanced SQL is a large topic, capable of filling several books by itself. The review here should prove useful in your Delphi database application work.

23

Optimizing Delphi Client/Server Applications

This chapter introduces several means of optimizing Delphi client/server applications. It's divided into two sections: Delphi-application optimization and server-based optimization. Server optimization is further divided into optimal SQL-coding techniques and performance considerations. Note that the examples contained herein are in no way exhaustive. I cover a number of optimization techniques in a relatively small space. The idea is to whet your appetite for the many benefits of proper client/server optimization. There's no substitute for getting intimately familiar with your chosen DBMS platform and learning its own peculiarities and nuances.

Keep Server Connections to a Minimum

Opening unneeded connections to a server that has limited connection resources to begin with is something you'll want to avoid. This wastes resources on the server, slows the client application down, and is in general problematic.

Use a *TDatabase*

One way to protect against opening unneeded server connections is to use a single TDatabase component for an entire application. Here are the steps for doing this:

1. Drop a TDatabase component onto your application's main form.
2. Set the AliasName property of the TDatabase to point to the BDE alias you want the application to use.
3. Set its DatabaseName property to the name you want published elsewhere as an application-specific alias.
4. When you use a TDataSet (TTable, TQuery, or TStoredProc), choose the DatabaseName you chose for the TDatabase, instead of a regular BDE alias, for the TDataSet's DatabaseName property.

When a TDataSet that has been set up this way is opened, it will use the connection provided by the TDatabase component, rather than creating its own.

There is one caveat you should be aware of when using a TDatabase rather than a separate BDE alias to provide connections to your server. If you open a TDataSet that refers to the application-specific alias while in the Delphi form designer,

■ The form that contains the TDatabase component must be open in the form designer, as well.

■ Opening a TDataSet (by setting its Active property to True in the Object Inspector) that refers to a TDatabase causes the TDatabase to automatically connect to the server. Because TDatabase's KeepConnection property is set to True by default, subsequently closing the TDataSet *will not close the connection to the server.* Instead, when you later save your project and exit Delphi, the TDatabase's connection status is saved with the project. When the project is later reloaded, you'll be immediately prompted for a password because the TDatabase is trying to reestablish its previous connection to the server.

You can remedy this by setting the TDatabase's KeepConnection property to False; however, this brings with it the undesirable side effect of having to log back into the server each time you close the last active DataSet and then try to open another. You can override having to log back in, but, again, this is the default behavior.

SQLPASSTHRU MODE

Another way you can limit the number of connections your application makes to your back-end server is through the use of the SQLPASSTHRU MODE setting in the BDE Configuration program. SQLPASSTHRU can be set for either an entire driver family or for individual aliases. Setting it for a driver family only affects new aliases defined from that point forward—it does not affect existing aliases. It has one of three possible values: NOT SHARED, SHARED AUTOCOMMIT, and SHARED NOAUTOCOMMIT. Setting this to either of the SHARED settings helps minimize connections to the server because it allows the BDE to share connections made by your application to the server for its own use.

Use Stored Procedures

Compiled code is generally faster and more efficient than interpreted code, no matter what programming language you're dealing with. The same is true of SQL. Rather than using TQuery components and Delphi's dynamic SQL, use stored procedures when possible and pass them parameters instead. This is faster than sending dynamic SQL statements because the server compiles and optimizes stored procedures in advance. Interpreted code must go through this same process every time it needs to be executed, so the more of the process you can accomplish in advance, the better.

There is one area where I feel it's inappropriate to use stored procedures pervasively. This is in the area of commonplace data modification—the kind normally done with INSERT, UPDATE, or DELETE statements. A trend has arisen in the last few years to move data modification away from data-aware controls and toward doing it via stored procedures. The reasons given for this range from improved security and speed to greater control over the database.

These are all valid reasons, but the one thing not mentioned is that doing this basically emasculates client/server-aware development tools like Delphi. In Delphi apps, the only automatic way to use stored procedures for normal data modifications is through the TUpdateSQL component. Though TUpdateSQL handles this task quite well, it still requires you to build hard-coded SQL to update your tables. Your stored procedure calls will no doubt require a list of field values for insertion, deletion, or modification of table rows. As the table structure changes, your SQL will have to change with it. This is problematic in nature and should be avoided.

This isn't to say that there aren't occasions where using TUpdateSQL isn't appropriate. But you should first attempt to use Delphi's built-in mechanism for updating tables, resorting to performing data modifications through TUpdateSQL only when absolutely necessary.

If you perform stored procedure-based updates without using TUpdateSQL, you lose the ease of Delphi's data-aware controls altogether. You must then manually set up normal controls to simulate data-aware controls by limiting the types of data they accept, retrieving values for them when a form is first displayed, and sending changed values to the server via stored procedures when the form is closed. This is all very tedious and highly error prone. It removes one of the biggest reasons for using a tool like Delphi—its ability to retrieve and act on meta-data from the server. You might as well be using a tool that has no inherent ability to communicate with the server and make direct database API calls, instead.

Another disadvantage to this approach is the fact that you circumvent the security mechanisms provided by the server. Most administrative tools aren't going to show whether stored procedure XYZ has the DELETE privilege on table XYZ. You lose the ability to view the system-security configuration—rights that have been granted or revoked for users or groups on individual database objects—from a single place. You must look not only at the rights you've granted using GRANT or REVOKE, but also at the contents of the stored procedures in your database.

NOTE

Unlike Sybase, InterBase allows rights to database objects to be granted and revoked from triggers as though they were users. This security information is stored as part of the server's meta-data and could be queried by a database administration tool in order to provide a comprehensive view of the server's security. I still believe, however, that it's a bad idea to implement database security in this manner.

There was a time when the tools available for client/server development were primitive enough that doing simple data modification via stored procedures was a necessary evil. However, with the advent of tools like Delphi, those days are long gone, so I recommend you take full advantage of Delphi's built-in data modification mechanisms. Use stored procedures for complex queries and for tasks other than simple data manipulation.

Use Prepare

Call the Prepare method of TQuery components before opening them. Prepare sends an SQL query to the database engine for parsing and optimization. If Prepare is explicitly called for a dynamic SQL query that will be executed more than once, Delphi sends only the query's parameters—not the entire query text—with each successive execution. If Prepare is not explicitly called in advance, the query is automatically prepared each time it's opened. By preparing it first, you remove the need for the database engine to do so, allowing the query to be opened/closed several times in succession without being re-prepared. This is bound to make query-intensive operations run faster.

UpdateMode

Both the `TTable` and `TQuery` components publish an `UpdateMode` property. This property determines the type of SQL `WHERE` clause that's used to perform data modifications made using data-aware controls. It defaults to `UpWhereAll`, which means that the BDE generates a SQL `WHERE` clause that lists every column in a table. With large tables especially, this can be quite cumbersome. An alternative, faster approach is the use of the `UpWhereChanged` setting. It generates a `WHERE` clause that mentions only the table's key fields along with the fields that were changed. This is best demonstrated by means of an example.

Let's say your Delphi application had just modified the `LastName` field of the CUSTOMER table. With `UpWhereAll`, here's the type of SQL that would be generated—notice the lengthy `WHERE` clause:

```
UPDATE CUSTOMER
SET LastName='newlastname'
WHERE CustomerNumber=1
AND LastName='Doe'
AND FirstName='John'
AND StreetAddress='123 SunnyLane'
AND City='Anywhere'
AND State='OK'
AND Zip='73115'
```

By contrast, here's the statement generated by `UpWhereChanged`:

```
UPDATE CUSTOMER
SET LastName='newlastname'
WHERE CustomerNumber=1
AND LastName='Doe'
```

Notice how much shorter it is. Notice also that it avoids the possibility of overwriting another user's changes to the `LastName` field by including its original value in the `WHERE` clause. If another user changes the `LastName` field in between the time the row is read and when it is updated by the current user, the `UPDATE` generated by `UpWhereChanged` will fail, which is what you'd want. Obviously, this isn't as bulletproof as the `UpWhereAll` method. Another user could delete the row after your application has read it, then add a new record to the table that happens to have the same key and `LastName` value as the original record. When your record applied its `UPDATE`, it would be updating the wrong record. But this scenario is only a remote possibility, at best.

`UpdateMode`'s other setting, `UpWhereKeyOnly`, is even less bulletproof, but it does have its uses. Because it checks only the key value of the row you're changing, it doesn't allow for the possibility that another user has changed the field you're updating in the time since you originally read the record. This may be a safe assumption, and, then again, it may not be. *In most multiuser applications, it would not be safe to assume that another user has not changed a record you've previously read into a client application.* This is, therefore, the kind of optimization that you do only on a rare occasion and out of necessity. Because the WHERE clause generated by the UpWhereKeyOnly setting would naturally be shorter, it would tend to be faster than one that included other columns as well. Nevertheless, you should check with your Database Administrator before using this option; it could lead to disastrous results if used improperly.

Updatable *TQuerys*

As a rule, avoid updatable TQuerys. Use views on your server instead. I say this for a couple of reasons. First, updating a TQuery puts the burden of dissecting a SQL query and updating its underlying table(s) on the client application (specifically on the Borland Database Engine), not on the server. In client/server systems, the server is the proper place for this SQL reverse-engineering. It's the place that resources have been dedicated to do complex database work. The server will also tend to understand its own SQL dialect better than a client application. This leads to more flexible updatable queries and faster updates.

Dynamic Forms

Another method of optimizing Delphi applications—including Delphi database applications—is to delay allocating resources for forms until they're actually needed. By default, all the forms in an application are created when the application starts, even though only a handful are ever used simultaneously. Be especially cautious about wasting database resources. Every open connection into the server burns a certain amount of database resources and slows down other connections. Far better to explicitly create and destroy nonessential forms than to have them needlessly wasting system resources.

You'll have to use program code to create and destroy forms that you do not permit to be created automatically. This can be quite simple—especially for modal forms. Here's a method of dynamically creating and destroying forms:

1. Bring up the Project Options dialog from within Delphi.

2. Move all but the most essential forms out of the Auto-create forms list and into the Available forms list.

3. On each form that you wish to create and destroy dynamically, set up its OnClose event to set Action := caFree.

4. Use the Application.CreateForm(*TForm1*, *Form1*) syntax to create a form when you need to show it, replacing *TForm1* with the form's class type and *Form1* with the form's instance variable.

5. Show the form using its ShowModal method.

6. Destroy the form by closing it.

Cached Updates

You can use Delphi's cached updates mechanism to minimize the database locks caused by your application. Cached updates are stored locally until you explicitly apply them to the database. They're then sent to the server en masse. This reduces server locks and can speed up your application dramatically. To enable cached updates in a Delphi application, follow these steps:

1. Set the CachedUpdates property to True for the DataSet whose updates you want to cache.

2. Set the DataSet's UpdateRecordTypes property to control the visible rows in the cached set. UpdateRecordTypes can have the following values: rtModified, rtInserted, rtDeleted, and rtUnmodified.

3. Establish an OnUpdateError event handler to handle any errors during a call to ApplyUpdates.

4. Make changes to the DataSet's data within the app.

5. Call the ApplyUpdates method to save your changes, CancelUpdates to discard them.

Use SQL Monitor

Delphi 2.0's SQL Monitor tool is handy for watching the SQL that's generated by your applications. Use it to inspect the SQL generated by operations that seem inordinately slow. Depending on the situation, you may find that you need to switch the SQL to a view or stored procedure on the server. You may also discover that the way you're searching for or updating data is inefficient—perhaps the application can be streamlined to remedy this. Whatever the case, be sure to take advantage of the behind-the-scenes information that SQL Monitor provides. You can find the SQL Monitor tool on Delphi's Database menu.

Schema Caching

The Borland Database Engine now supports schema caching—storing structural information about database objects locally. Enabling schema caching can speed up your applications significantly because the BDE is not forced to constantly re-retrieve data-definition information from the server.

You can enable schema caching in the BDE Configuration utility. There are four settings that are related to schema caching. Table 23.1 lists them.

Table 23.1. BDE Configuration settings that affect schema caching.

Setting	Action
ENABLE SCHEMA CACHE	Enables/disables schema caching (this is a driver-level setting)
SCHEMA CACHE SIZE	Specifies the number of tables for which to cache schema data
SCHEMA CACHE TIME	Specifies the number of seconds to cache schema information
SCHEMA CACHE DIR	Specifies a directory in which to store schema information (this is a driver-level setting)

Both the ENABLE SCHEMA CACHE and SCHEMA CACHE DIR settings are driver-level settings only—you can't set them for individual database aliases. Note that SCHEMA CACHE TIME defaults to -1 which means that schema information is retained in the cache until the database is closed. Valid values for SCHEMA CACHE TIME range from 1 to 2,147,483,647 seconds.

Especially over WAN connections, enabling schema caching can make a remarkable difference in how your applications perform. Note that the BDE's schema cache facility naturally expects your database schema not to change. This means that some databases aren't good candidates for schema caching. In particular, you shouldn't use schema caching for databases

- Where table columns are often added or dropped
- Where table indexes are frequently added or dropped
- Where column NULL/NOT NULL designations are frequently changed

If you attempt to use schema caching with databases that aren't appropriate for it, you can expect the following Unknown SQL Errors:

- Unknown Column
- Invalid Bind Type
- Invalid Type
- Invalid Type Conversion
- Column Not a Blob

Local Filters

Use Delphi's local filtering facility to qualify small result sets on the client side of your client/server applications. For small DataSets, local filters can be faster than re-querying the database because they do not involve interaction with the server or network. Small DataSets will often be cached on the client machine in their entirety, anyway, so it makes sense to filter them locally when possible. To enable Delphi's local filters in an application, follow these steps:

1. Set the `Filter` property of a DataSet you want to qualify locally to an expression that includes the desired rows. (See Chapter 15, "Database Component Reference Part I," for more information on filter expressions.)

2. Alternately, you can set the `OnFilterRecord` event to include/exclude rows using its `Accept` parameter.

3. Set the DataSet's `Filtered` property to `True`.

4. When you access the DataSet from within the application, it will appear as though it only contains rows that match the filter criteria.

Threads

One of the more powerful aspects of 32-bit Windows is the ability to create multi-threaded applications. Delphi enables you to create threads easily and safely using its `TThread` object. Multi-threading can also be used in database applications. A useful application of threading in database apps is in background query execution. If you have a query that executes for an extended period of time, you can execute it on its own thread and allow your application to continue running. Threads can also be used to speed access to the database. For example, if you're reading records from a set of operating system files and inserting them into tables on your SQL server, you might allocate a separate thread for each file so that insertions from one file don't wait on those from another. There are a number of good uses of multi-threading in database applications. Listings 23.1 through 23.5 show a simple database program that uses multi-threading to execute a user-entered query in the background.

Listing 23.1. Project source code for the multi-threaded example program, "thrdex."

```
program thrdex;

uses
  Forms,
  thrdex00 in 'thrdex00.pas' {fmQuery},
  thrdex01 in 'thrdex01.pas' {fmBackground};

{$R *.RES}

begin
  Application.Initialize;
  Application.CreateForm(TfmQuery, fmQuery);
  Application.Run;
end.
```

Listing 23.2. Unit source code for thrdex00.pas, the first of the two units in the multi-threaded example program.

```
unit thrdex00;

interface

uses
  Windows, Messages, SysUtils, Classes,
  Graphics, Controls, Forms, Dialogs,
  StdCtrls, ExtCtrls, DB, DBTables;

type
  TfmQuery = class(TForm)
    Panel1: TPanel;
    btExecute: TButton;
    edUserName: TEdit;
    edPassword: TEdit;
    meQuery: TMemo;
    cbAliases: TComboBox;
    Label1: TLabel;
    Label2: TLabel;
    Label3: TLabel;
    procedure btExecuteClick(Sender: TObject);
    procedure FormCreate(Sender: TObject);
  private
    { Private declarations }
  public
    { Public declarations }
  end;

var
  fmQuery: TfmQuery;

implementation

uses thrdex01;

{$R *.DFM}

procedure TfmQuery.btExecuteClick(Sender: TObject);
begin
  ExecuteQuery(meQuery.Text,
               cbAliases.Items[cbAliases.ItemIndex],
               edUserName.Text, edPassword.Text);
end;

procedure TfmQuery.FormCreate(Sender: TObject);
begin
  Session.GetAliasNames(cbAliases.Items);
  cbAliases.Sorted:=True;
end;

end.
```

Listing 23.3. Form .DFM file for thrdex00.pas, the first of the two units used by the multi-threaded example program thrdex.

```
object fmQuery: TfmQuery
  Left = 72
  Top = 107
  Width = 521
  Height = 300
  Caption = 'fmQuery'
  Font.Color = clWindowText
  Font.Height = -11
  Font.Name = 'MS Sans Serif'
  Font.Style = []
  OnCreate = FormCreate
  PixelsPerInch = 96
  TextHeight = 13
  object Panel1: TPanel
    Left = 0
    Top = 232
    Width = 513
    Height = 41
    Align = alBottom
    TabOrder = 0
    object Label1: TLabel
      Left = 96
      Top = 1
      Width = 75
      Height = 13
      Caption = 'Choose an alias'
    end
    object Label2: TLabel
      Left = 256
      Top = 1
      Width = 100
      Height = 13
      Caption = 'Enter your user name'
    end
    object Label3: TLabel
      Left = 392
      Top = 1
      Width = 96
      Height = 13
      Caption = 'Enter your password'
    end
    object btExecute: TButton
      Left = 8
      Top = 8
      Width = 75
      Height = 25
      Caption = '&Execute'
      TabOrder = 0
      OnClick = btExecuteClick
    end
    object edUserName: TEdit
      Left = 253
```

continues

Listing 23.3. continued

```
      Top = 16
      Width = 121
      Height = 21
      TabOrder = 2
    end
    object edPassword: TEdit
      Left = 387
      Top = 16
      Width = 121
      Height = 21
      PasswordChar = '*'
      TabOrder = 3
    end
    object cbAliases: TComboBox
      Left = 96
      Top = 16
      Width = 145
      Height = 21
      ItemHeight = 13
      TabOrder = 1
    end
  end
  object meQuery: TMemo
    Left = 0
    Top = 0
    Width = 513
    Height = 232
    Align = alClient
    TabOrder = 1
  end
end
```

Listing 23.4. Unit source code for thrdex01.pas, the second of the two units used by the multi-threaded example program thrdex.

```
unit thrdex01;

interface

uses
  Windows, Messages, SysUtils,
  Classes, Graphics, Controls, Forms, Dialogs,
  ExtCtrls, DB, DBTables, Grids,
  DBGrids, StdCtrls, ComCtrls;

type
  TfmBackground = class(TForm)
    quBackGround: TQuery;
    stBackground: TStatusBar;
    dgBackground: TDBGrid;
    dsBackground: TDataSource;
    seBackground: TSession;
    dbBackground: TDatabase;
```

```
  private
    { Private declarations }
  public
    { Public declarations }
  end;

procedure ExecuteQuery(SQLToExecute,
                       AliasToUse,
                       Username, Password: string);

implementation

{$R *.DFM}

{ TQueryThread }

type
  TQueryThread = class(TThread)
  private
    fmBackground: TfmBackground;
    StatusMessage: string;
    procedure UpdateDisplay;
    procedure UpdateStatusBar;
  protected
    procedure Execute; override;
  public
    constructor Create(AfmBackground: TfmBackground);
  end;

constructor TQueryThread.Create(AfmBackground: TfmBackground);
begin
  fmBackground := AfmBackground;
  FreeOnTerminate := True;
  inherited Create(False);
end;

procedure TQueryThread.Execute;
begin
  try
    with fmBackground do begin
      seBackground.SessionName :=
          Format('%s%x', [Session.Name,GetCurrentThreadID]);
      dbBackground.SessionName := seBackground.SessionName;

      dbBackground.DatabaseName :=
          Format('%s%x', [dbBackground.Name, GetCurrentThreadID]);
      quBackground.SessionName := dbBackground.SessionName;
      quBackground.DatabaseName := dbBackground.DatabaseName;

      quBackground.Open;

      Synchronize(UpdateDisplay);

      StatusMessage := 'Executed query';
      Synchronize(UpdateStatusBar);
    end;
```

continues

Listing 24.3. continued

```
except
  on E: Exception do
  begin
    StatusMessage := Format('%s: %s.', [E.ClassName, E.Message]);
    Synchronize(UpdateStatusBar);
  end;
end;
end;

procedure TQueryThread.UpdateDisplay;
begin
  with fmBackground do dsBackground.Dataset := quBackground;
end;

procedure TQueryThread.UpdateStatusBar;
begin
  with fmBackground do stBackground.Panels.Items[0].Text := StatusMessage;
end;

procedure ExecuteQuery(SQLToExecute, AliasToUse, Username, Password: string);
var
  fmBackground: TfmBackground;
begin
  fmBackground := TfmBackground.Create(Application);
  with fmBackground do begin
    Show;
    quBackground.SQL.Text:=SQLToExecute;
    dbBackground.AliasName := AliasToUse;
    dbBackground.Params.Values['USER'] := Username;
    dbBackground.Params.Values['PASSWORD'] := Password;
  end;

  TQueryThread.Create(fmBackground);
end;


end.
```

Listing 23.5. Form .DFM file for thrdex01.pas, the second of the two units used by the multi-threaded example program thrdex.

```
object fmBackground: TfmBackground
  Left = 159
  Top = 83
  Width = 443
  Height = 332
  Caption = 'fmBackground'
  Font.Color = clWindowText
  Font.Height = -11
  Font.Name = 'MS Sans Serif'
  Font.Style = []
  Position = poDefault
  PixelsPerInch = 96
  TextHeight = 13
```

```
object stBackground: TStatusBar
  Left = 0
  Top = 286
  Width = 435
  Height = 19
  Panels = <
    item
      Width = 200
    end>
  SimplePanel = False
end
object dgBackground: TDBGrid
  Left = 0
  Top = 0
  Width = 435
  Height = 286
  Align = alClient
  DataSource = dsBackground
  TabOrder = 1
  TitleFont.Color = clWindowText
  TitleFont.Height = -11
  TitleFont.Name = 'MS Sans Serif'
  TitleFont.Style = []
end
object quBackGround: TQuery
  Left = 8
  Top = 11
end
object dsBackground: TDataSource
  Left = 8
  Top = 106
end
object seBackground: TSession
  Left = 8
  Top = 74
end
object dbBackground: TDatabase
  LoginPrompt = False
  SessionName = 'Default'
  Left = 8
  Top = 43
end
end
```

This tiny application includes a form whose whole purpose in life is to execute queries in the background. When the application's ExecuteQuery procedure is called, it instantiates the background query form and its associated query thread. The thread then executes the specified query in the background, freeing your application to run in the foreground. No matter what the query does, your app is free to continue doing other things. If you key in this source code (or load it from the accompanying CD-ROM) you'll notice that the background and foreground threads don't interfere with one another. They each execute independently. You can use this to your advantage in Delphi client/server applications by off-loading lengthy tasks onto their own threads. Study these source code listings for the details on how to do this.

Use *TFields*

Define and use TField components when at all possible. Don't use FieldByName or the Fields property unless you have to. Persistent TFields are more efficient because they store basic information about the field with the application, saving it from having to be retrieved from the server. They're also safer because they automatically raise an exception if a column's underlying data type has changed. The FieldByName function and the Fields property, on the other hand, must scan the table's schema information to derive a column's basic information. They're slower and less reliable. Use TFields instead—they're easier, safer, and more immune to changes in the underlying database objects.

Use the Data Dictionary

In my opinion, you should always attempt to first locate your application's business rules on the server if at all possible. This subject is discussed in detail in Chapter 19, "Business Rules Part I." However, there will be times when you'll have to define business rules at the application level. In situations where you have to do this, use Delphi's Data Dictionary and its Attribute Sets to define as many of your client-based business rules as possible. When you've defined all you can of your client-side business rules in the Data Dictionary, then resort to defining the remainder of the business rules strategy using DataSet components and TField attributes. By defining client-side business rules using the Data Dictionary rather than within a specific application, you make the rules more readily accessible by other applications.

DBText and Read-Only Fields

If a field is to be read-only, don't use a DBEdit component for it; use a DBText component instead. DBText fields are leaner and provide the same function. You also might want to consider using static Label components for column data that cannot change once a form is onscreen. You need a DBText if the data might change, otherwise, you can assign a TLabel component's Caption property in the form's OnShow event and save yourself the resources needed by data-aware controls, even lean ones like DBText. Using the leanest possible data controls in your applications will not only help your applications have a smaller resource footprint, it will also help them run faster since there will be less interaction with the database.

Server-Based Optimization

Server-based optimization consists of tweaking your SQL, network settings, database configuration, and so forth. Making server-based optimizations generally helps any app that uses the server, not just Delphi apps.

SQL Code Optimization

SQL code optimization consists not only of writing SQL that runs faster, but also of using optimal coding techniques—techniques that are easy to follow and maintain. Some of these techniques don't make your code run any faster, but they save you time by helping you avoid common pitfalls and by making your code easier to read.

Use ANSI Syntax

When possible, use ANSI SQL syntax. The only exception I make to this is in the case of joins. The Sybase syntax for joins is more compact and easier to read than is the ANSI syntax. At least be aware of the differences between the SQL you use and the ANSI syntax.

This will potentially help others who look at your work, because you will be using syntax that a number of DBMS vendors have agreed upon. It will also broaden the field of books and training materials that you may find useful; there should be more that cover ANSI SQL than that cover a given vendor's dialect. Finally, it will better equip you for cross-platform and cross-vendor projects.

Column Qualification

Whenever you code SQL that involves more than one table, always fully qualify the columns you list. Do not rely on the fact that only one of the tables in the query contains a given column name and, hence, enables you to omit the column's table identifier. Always label each column with the table in which it's located. If you later add a table that happens to share column names with some of the tables already in the query, you won't have to revise the query to remove ambiguous column references. This can be a real time-saver with extremely large queries.

Table Aliases

Use table aliases to make your SQL easier to read. Don't type the full name of the table before each column in your select list; use a table alias instead. This cuts down on typing, shortens the textual size of the query, and makes it easier to read.

Column Names on *INSERT* Statements

The introductory SQL chapter pointed out that column names on INSERT statements are optional if you are inserting values for all the columns in the table. It's still a good idea, though, to list the columns anyway. This enables you to be doubly sure that what you're inserting is what you want to insert. It forces you to match up each of the insert values with their corresponding column names. Again, this isn't mandatory, but it's a good idea.

GROUP BY

Always GROUP BY all nonaggregate columns in queries that contain aggregates. Failing to do so, as mentioned in the chapter on advanced SQL, renders generally useless query results and can make long queries run indefinitely. Note that InterBase will refuse to execute a query that doesn't GROUP BY all nonaggregate columns.

WHERE

The following techniques list coding optimizations you can make to the SQL WHERE clause. The WHERE clause is used to qualify the all-powerful SELECT command, so clear and concise WHERE clause construction is crucial to readable queries.

Avoid Cartesian Products

For each table in a multi-table SELECT, you must have a valid join to at least one other table, and each join should be connected with the other joins in the statement using the AND keyword. Failing to do this, as pointed out in the previous chapter on advanced SQL, renders some part of the Cartesian product of the tables involved. A Cartesian product consists of all the rows in one table multiplied by those in another. If the tables involved are very large, the query may run indefinitely. Cartesian products have a very limited usefulness; they generally occur by accident.

Use Parenthesis

Use parenthesis to break up complex WHERE clauses composed of ANDs and ORs. This establishes precedence among the elements in the clause and makes it easier to read.

Stored Procedures

The following tips relate to optimal stored procedure coding techniques. Because much of the real work of large client/server systems is done via stored procedures, it's important to use consistent coding practices when building them.

Comments

Nested-comment support varies from platform to platform and should be avoided. Also, commenting SQL excessively should be avoided. There is a school of thought that says that all program code, be it a traditional programming language or SQL, should be commented extensively. I don't happen to subscribe to this way of thinking. The reason I think extensive comments are unneeded in SQL (and, in fact, get in the way of good SQL coding) is that SQL is supposed to be English-like in and of itself. That is, the language as originally designed by IBM was to be a Structured English Query Language—that's where the SQL acronym comes from. SQL that is written properly will often be virtually self-documenting.

Excessive footnotes detract from the readability of a book; they cause the reader to constantly leave the book's text to find some tiny message at the bottom of the page. The same is true of embedding too many comments in SQL code. They can make wading through a complex SQL script tedious.

Placing too many comments in your code also doubles your work—when you change the code, you have to change the comments, too. If your code is too obscure to understand just by reading through it along with a few well-placed comments, it probably needs to be redesigned.

This is not a general prohibition against commenting your SQL code—not at all. A moderate amount of source-code commenting is essential, even in English-like languages. It's important to realize, though, that times have changed and the query language being used is, to a large extent, self-documenting. If the queries constructed with it are designed properly, extensive commenting should be unnecessary.

BEGIN...END

Use the BEGIN...END bracketing syntax even in situations where you do not have to. For example, in Sybase's Transact-SQL, you can omit the BEGIN...END after an IF statement if only one SQL statement depends on the IF. Use BEGIN...END in all IF and looping constructs, even where it's not required. This will make your code more readable and will allow one-line conditionals to be easily expanded to multi-line conditionals should the need arise.

Performance

The following optimizations related specifically to performance improvements. Making use of these techniques can speed up your database access dramatically.

Clustered Indexes

On platforms that support it, use a clustered index rather than a nonclustered index for a table's primary key. Dramatic performance gains can be seen with some types of queries simply by using clustered indexes rather than nonclustered ones. With a clustered index, the physical data is located at the lowest level of the index tree; the table and the index are one and the same.

Normally, the lowest level of an index tree stores a key value and the location in the associated table where its row can be found. This location reference might be a page number, a segment address, or even a record number. When a row is looked up using the index, this location reference is used to locate the row in its table.

With clustered indexes, the entire row is stored with the index key. In fact, there is no separate table. Thus, retrieving the index key's associated row requires one less step with clustered indexes than with non-clustered ones.

Covered Indexes

Although not a separate index type per se, covered indexes offer a performance boon similar to that of the clustered index. A covered index is a nonclustered index that happens to include, as part of its key, all the data a given query might need to access. That is, in addition to key values, the index key of a covered index contains other data elements needed to satisfy a particular type of query. Thus, the index "covers" the query—hence the name.

Here's an example of the use of a covered index:

```
CREATE INDEX ORDERS04 ON ORDERS (OrderDate, Amount)
```

Now the query

```
SELECT OrderDate, SUM(Amount) TotalAmount
FROM ORDERS
GROUP BY OrderDate
```

can be optimized by the database server to read only from the index, without having to look up the Amount column in the table itself.

Use of *EXISTS*

When you need to qualify a query based on the existence of data in a table, don't use

```
IF (SELECT COUNT(*) FROM TABLENAME WHERE condition) > 0
```

This counts all the records in the table that match the WHERE condition before returning to the IF to be evaluated. On large tables, this could take forever. Instead, use

```
IF EXISTS (SELECT * FROM TABLENAME WHERE condition)
```

Most servers optimize this query to return the moment a single row is located that meets the specified criteria.

SELECT DISTINCT

The use of SELECT DISTINCT is almost always unnecessary. To understand why this is, we must first understand what it is that DISTINCT does. The DISTINCT keyword eliminates duplicates from the result set returned by a SELECT command. The question must be asked, "Why did the result set contain duplicates in the first place? Was it the result of an inefficient query?" If so, the query is the place to fix this. More often than not, SELECT DISTINCT is used to mask a Cartesian product of which the coder cannot figure out how to rid himself. Use of SELECT DISTINCT should be limited to those times when it is the *only* way to get the desired result, not the *easiest* way.

WHERE

The WHERE clause is probably the single most-likely candidate for SQL optimizations that dramatically improve performance. The SELECT command is so multi-faceted and complex, whole books could be written on how to optimize it and its component pieces, such as the WHERE clause. The following techniques give you a few pointers on how to make your WHERE clauses more efficient.

Limit the DataSet

The first job of a WHERE clause is to reduce the set of rows that the query must work with. Organize your WHERE clauses so that they first limit the number of rows being manipulated. If at all possible, this should be accomplished via indexes. If you are constantly limiting a DataSet by means of a WHERE clause that has no corresponding index, perhaps it's time to add another index.

Key Fields in Functions and Expressions

Avoid modifying index key fields with function calls or expressions when you use them in a WHERE clause. Doing so can prevent the server's query optimizer from using an index. For example, here's an InterBase query that prevents the InterBase query optimizer from using an index:

```
SELECT * FROM ORDERS
WHERE CAST (OrderDate AS CHAR(8)) >= '07/01/95'
```

The preceding example is a poor usage of CAST() for two reasons. First, it's unnecessary because InterBase handles the comparison between a date and a character variable implicitly. Second, it confuses the InterBase query optimizer into not using the index that exists over the OrderDate column.

Use of *LIKE*

When you use the LIKE keyword, be careful that you don't prevent the use of an index. For example, the following query prevents the use of an index:

```
SELECT * FROM CUSTOMER
WHERE LastName LIKE "%Joh%on"
```

The fact that the wildcard character is on the left of the LIKE expression prevents an indexed look-up. By contrast, this is perfectly acceptable

```
SELECT * FROM CUSTOMER
WHERE LastName LIKE "Joh%on"
```

because the query optimizer can look up the first matching entry using only Joh as a key. The rows that are qualified via Joh can then be further limited to those that end with on using a conventional sequential scan. The moral of the story is that the potential set of matching records is locatable using an index due to the type of LIKE expression used. It simplifies the job of limiting the records retrieved from the table to just those with the specified last-name mask.

Subqueries

Subqueries are to be avoided and replaced, where feasible, with hard-coded lists of values. For example, let's say you are writing a query that must summarize a table of millions of credit-card receipts. In the summarization, you want to see only receipts that match types corresponding to individual, not corporate, customers. You have a table that lists the types of customers you have (let's say there are 10 different types) and flags each of them as either corporate or individual in nature. You could write a query like this

```
SELECT UseDate, SUM(Amount) AmountSpent
FROM RECEIPTS
WHERE CardType in (SELECT CardType FROM CARDTYPE WHERE Type='I')
GROUP BY UseDate
```

but this isn't the most efficient way of doing things. First, you could hard code the list of individual types if it rarely changes. This leaves open the possibility that a user might add a record to the CARDTYPE table and that your report would fail to include it. You'll have to be the judge of whether this is an approach you could consider.

Another (and, I think, superior) approach is to create the query dynamically in Delphi. Here are the steps you'd follow to construct the query dynamically:

1. Open a TQuery whose SQL queries the server for the card types associated with individuals.

2. Loop through the result set returned by the TQuery and build a string containing a comma-delimited list of all the returned card types. The string would look something like this:

   ```
   '1,2,4,12,13,20'
   ```

3. Pass the string to a dynamic SQL query to be used in the query's IN clause. Here's an example of what the query should look like:

   ```
   SELECT UseDate, SUM(Amount) AmountSpent
   FROM RECEIPTS
   WHERE CardType in (:CardTypeList)
   GROUP BY UseDate
   ```

4. Prepare and open the dynamic SQL query.

This method keeps the query as flexible as possible, allowing for future additions to the CARDTYPE table. At the same time, it avoids the use of the subquery in the summarization process.

ORDER BY

The ORDER BY clause should be avoided. It's an inefficient mechanism that can cause a server to needlessly sort a large result set. Unless you actually need the ordering provided by the clause, don't use it. Note that clustered indexes implicitly order result rows on many platforms. Also note that the GROUP BY clause orders data on some platforms. Though SQL as a language guarantees no natural row order, some platforms do provide for implicit row ordering by one means or another. Check your server documentation for more information.

HAVING

There is almost always a better way of qualifying a query than by using a HAVING clause. In general, HAVING is less efficient than the WHERE clause because it qualifies the result set *after* it has been organized into groups, whereas WHERE does so *beforehand*. Here's an example of an unnecessary use of the HAVING clause:

```
SELECT CUSTOMER.LastName, COUNT(*) NumberWithName
FROM CUSTOMER
GROUP BY CUSTOMER.LastName
HAVING CUSTOMER.LastName<>'Citizen'
```

Now, here's the same query properly rewritten using the WHERE clause:

```
SELECT CUSTOMER.LastName, COUNT(*) NumberWithName
FROM CUSTOMER
WHERE CUSTOMER.LastName<>'Citizen'
GROUP BY CUSTOMER.LastName
```

This is a better approach because it does not include data in the grouping phase that we know we do not want. In the case of the HAVING clause, most servers would group the data first, then filter it by the criteria specified in the HAVING clause. This is less efficient than simply ignoring the unwanted data to begin with.

The only valid use of HAVING is to qualify the result set by aggregate columns—columns that are the result of computations over the result set. Since these aggregates aren't known until after the server has created the result set, you can't use them in the WHERE clause. Instead, if you want to qualify a result set using an aggregate, you must do so via the HAVING clause. Here's an example:

```
SELECT CUSTOMER.LastName, COUNT(*) NumberWithName
FROM CUSTOMER
WHERE CUSTOMER.LastName<>'Citizen'
GROUP BY CUSTOMER.LastName
HAVING COUNT(*) > 2
```

Since NumberWithName isn't known until after the result set is built, you use HAVING to qualify it.

COMPUTE

Sybase's Transact-SQL supports a way of totaling columns returned by a SELECT statement without actually using aggregates in the SELECT itself. This is done via the COMPUTE clause. It follows the other clauses that make up the SELECT statement and simply totals a returned column using a normal aggregate function such as SUM(). Here's an example:

```
SELECT CustomerNumber, Amount
FROM ORDERS
COMPUTE SUM(Amount)
```

There are several good reasons not to use this facility. First, most front-end tools don't know how to properly process it as part of a result set. Second, COMPUTEs have the nonsensical limitation of not being able to total aggregate columns in the SELECT. So, if the preceding query were written

```
SELECT CustomerNumber, SUM(Amount) TotalOrders
FROM ORDERS
GROUP BY CustomerNumber
```

you wouldn't be able to use a COMPUTE clause to return a grand total for TotalOrders. Third, and most importantly, the query can be designed to return the desired total without need of a COMPUTE clause, as in:

```
SELECT O.CustomerNumber, O.Amount, SUM(O2.Amount) TotalOrders
FROM    ORDERS O,
        ORDERS O2
GROUP  BY O.CustomerNumber, O.Amount
```

This keeps the data in a format that most front-ends can deal with. An even better and more efficient approach would be to make two separate passes over the data: one to retrieve a subset of the data into a temporary table, and a second to total it up. In any event, there are a number of ways of deriving the desired figures without resorting to the clumsy COMPUTE clause.

GROUP BY

Group columns according to index keys, if possible. For example, given the two queries:

```
SELECT OrderDate, CustomerNumber, SUM(Amount) TotalOrders
FROM ORDERS
GROUP BY OrderDate, CustomerNumber
```

and

```
SELECT OrderDate, CustomerNumber, SUM(Amount) TotalOrders
FROM ORDERS
GROUP BY CustomerNumber, OrderDate
```

only the second approach will use an index over the ORDERS table that was created like so:

```
CREATE INDEX ORDERS03 ON ORDERS (CustomerNumber, OrderDate)
```

If no index exists that was created using OrderDate as the high-order key, the query optimizer will be precluded from using an index in resolving the query.

Stored Procedures

The following techniques relate to stored procedure performance optimization. Sometimes just switching to stored procedures interpretive SQL can greatly improve an application's performance. Additionally, there are several things you can do to further improve performance by optimizing the stored procedures themselves.

Go Easy on the Parameters

The parameters you pass to a stored procedure should be as small and as few as possible. As with traditional programming languages, parameters passed on the stack should be kept to a minimum. This is even more true of stored-procedure parameters because they must be sent over the network to your database server, possibly causing network bottlenecks. Pass small integers where possible and expressly avoid passing large character strings.

Sybase's *SET NOCOUNT ON*

By default, Sybase SQL Servers pass a count of the rows processed by each statement in a stored procedure back to the client that executed the stored procedure. Normally, the client throws these counts away. You can improve the performance of Sybase stored procedures by using the SET NOCOUNT ON syntax. The only side effect of using SET NOCOUNT is that the READTEXT command, when used in conjunction with the dbreadtext() DB-Library function, may not operate properly. Since this circumstance is extremely rare, SET NOCOUNT ON should be regarded as safe to use and should be included in stored-procedure definitions by default.

Local-Variable Assignments

Stored procedures that use SELECT statements to set local variables should do so in a single SELECT, if possible. On some platforms, there is overhead associated with the first variable assignment of each SELECT statement. Grouping the variables into a single SELECT is more efficient. Here's an example in InterBase SQL:

```
SELECT City, State, Zip
INTO :City, :State, :Zip
FROM CUSTOMER
```

and one in Sybase's dialect:

```
SELECT @City=City, @State=State, @Zip=Zip
FROM CUSTOMER
```

Looking Up Ancillary Information

Look up ancillary information last in stored procedures. List small, secondary tables last in multitable joins. This is again in keeping with limiting the DataSet first, then looking up auxiliary information second.

For example, if you are summarizing a credit-card table that contains several million rows, don't look up each card's customer name during the summarization; look it up after you've reduced the result set as much as possible and are ready to return the rows to your client application. The most effective way of doing this is to execute the query in multiple passes, storing the reduced result set in temporary tables with each successive pass. After the data has been fully qualified, join it with the CUSTOMER table to return the supplemental customer information to the client application.

Though it might seem counter-intuitive to make multiple passes over a large result set, keep in mind that the server itself makes multiple passes when necessary. All you do by making them yourself is effectively become your own query optimizer. The single biggest thing you can do to optimize SQL queries is limit your result set as quickly as possible. This sometimes requires multiple passes and the use of temporary tables.

Cross-Tab Queries

There are times when the standard method of grouping data via a SELECT statement is not enough. In particular, cross-tab queries can be difficult to implement in SQL. A cross-tab query organizes data into rows and columns, much like a spreadsheet. If your data is organized linearly, as most data is, it may be challenging to represent it in a cross-tab fashion.

This is best explained by way of an example. Let's say you are writing a query that returns sales information for the Big Three American auto makers: Ford, General Motors, and Chrysler. The client wants the type of automobile (subcompact, compact, sports car, truck, and so on) to be listed on the left of a report, with columns for the sales figures for each of the auto makers to the right. Normally, the SQL to derive the needed information would look something like

```
SELECT CarType, Maker, Sales TotalSales
FROM BIGTHREESALES
```

However, due to your report writer's inability to generate cross-tabs on its own, the data can't be formatted in the way the client wants without jumping through some hoops. Specifically, you'll have to create a work table that mimics the output format the client is after, then fill it with the appropriate data. Here's an example:

```
CREATE TABLE CARCROSS
(CarType            CHAR(10)
 FordSales          FLOAT
 GMSales            FLOAT
 ChryslerSales      FLOAT)
```

Typically you'd make multiple passes over this table, filling it with the appropriate data, before finally returning the completed data set to your report writer. Here's an example:

```
INSERT INTO CARCROSS (CarType, FordSales)
Select CarType, Sales FordSales
FROM BIGTHREESALES
WHERE Maker='Ford'
```

Then you'd either use a cursor and update the appropriate columns for the other two manufacturers, or you'd use UPDATE statements within loops to update their respective columns en masse, like so:

```
SELECT Sales
INTO :GMSales
FROM BIGTHREESALES
WHERE Maker='GM'
AND CarType='SC'

UPDATE CARCROSS
SET GMSales=:GMSales
WHERE CarType='SC'
```

Or, alternately, you might use the following Sybase syntax:

```
UPDATE CARCROSS
SET GMSales=Sales
FROM SALES S, CARCROSS C
WHERE Maker='GM'
AND S.CarType=C.CarType
```

There is, however, a better way. It leverages one of SQL's greatest strengths—its ability to easily group and summarize data—to give you data in a cross-tab format with a minimal amount of effort. It does this by means of query *folding* or *flattening*. Here's an example of the previous query using the flattening technique:

First, collect and place the Ford information in the appropriate column:

```
INSERT INTO CARCROSS (CarType, FordSales)
Select CarType, Sales FordSales
FROM BIGTHREESALES
WHERE Maker='Ford'
```

Now, do the same for GM:

```
INSERT INTO CARCROSS (CarType, GMSales)
Select CarType, Sales GMSales
FROM BIGTHREESALES
WHERE Maker='GM'
```

And, now, for Chrysler:

```
INSERT INTO CARCROSS (CarType, ChryslerSales)
Select CarType, Sales ChryslerSales
FROM BIGTHREESALES
WHERE Maker='Chrysler'
```

At this point, the rows in CARCROSS look something like that shown in Figure 23.1.

You flatten the CARCROSS table using this query:

```
SELECT CarType, SUM(FordSales) FordSales, SUM(GMSales) GMSales, SUM(ChryslerSales)
➥ChryslerSales
FROM CARCROSS
GROUP BY CarType
```

FIGURE 23.1.

*The CARCROSS table
before being flattened.*

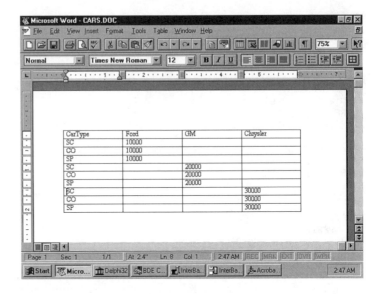

The result set returned by the query is shown in Figure 23.2.

FIGURE 23.2.

*The result set following the
flattening operation.*

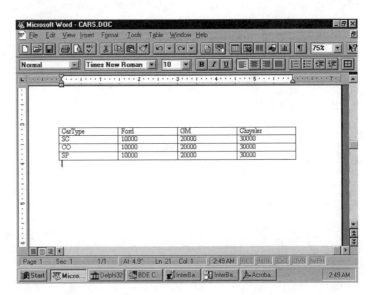

As you can see, you now have the format the report required without any of the kludgy, needlessly
complicated techniques mentioned previously.

In-Line Summarization

One of the classic problems facing database designers and query authors is the proper handling of detail versus summary data. Over time, an organization will normally summarize large amounts of detail data. Usually, in addition to being able to query this data while in detail form, users also want to access it after it's been summarized. This presents a suite of interesting problems for the database professional. The first problem is finding an appropriate place to store the summarized data. If it's stored in the same database as the system's detail data, should it reside in special summary tables? Perhaps it should reside in a special summary database? How then will it be accessed? Will this double my administrative work? And what of the stored procedures and reports that were developed for the detail data—should they be redeveloped to work with summary data, as well?

There is an answer to this conundrum that trades slightly higher storage requirements for solutions to the preceding problems. It lies in what I call *in-line summarization*. It basically consists of organizing detail tables in such a way that summarized rows can reside in the same table with detail rows and be queried by the same queries that query detail rows. This eliminates the need for summary tables or databases and makes separate, summary-oriented stored procedures or reports unnecessary.

The best way to explain this is by way of example. Let's say you have a credit-card database that stores millions of credit-card transactions. Each month, you want to summarize the transactions by day, credit-card number, and transaction location. You want to summarize both the total number of transactions and their total amount. That is, if John Doe had three purchases at Foley's on January 1st, you want to see only one record. It would list John Doe's credit-card number, the date, the location number for the Foley's store, the number of transactions, and the total amount of the purchases.

Rather than store the summary information in a separate table, you can store it back in the original table with only a few minor changes to the design of the table. For example, let's say the original layout of the table looked like this:

```
CREATE TABLE CARDTRANS
(CardNumber          char(20)        NOT NULL,
 TransactionDate     date            NOT NULL,
 Location            int             NOT NULL,
 Amount              float           NOT NULL)
```

And let's say you'd query the data either for reporting or permanent summarization using a SELECT statement like this one:

```
SELECT CardNumber, TransactionDate, Location, COUNT(*) NumberTrans, SUM(Amount)
➥Amount
FROM CARDTRANS
WHERE TransactionDate between '01/01/95' AND '02/01/95'
GROUP BY CardNumber, TransactionDate, Location
```

You can accommodate summary data in this table and its related query by making only minor changes. Here's a revised table layout that supports in-line summarization:

```
CREATE TABLE CARDTRANS
(CardNumber                char(20)        NOT NULL,
 TransactionDate           date            NOT NULL,
 Location                  int             NOT NULL,
 NumberTrans               int             NOT NULL,
 Amount                    float           NOT NULL)
```

Notice the inclusion of the NumberTrans column. What does it store in a detail row? It stores the same thing a summary row does—a transaction count for a given row in the table. For detail rows, NumberTrans will always be set to 1; in fact, you could define a DEFAULT constraint that would ensure this. For summarized rows, NumberTrans would contain the number of transactions represented by the row's key fields. In the case of our John Doe example, the value would be 3, but it could be any number, up to the maximum supported by the int data type. Now, here's the query mentioned previously, revised to handle either detail or summary rows:

```
SELECT CardNumber, TransactionDate, Location, SUM(NumberTrans) NumberTrans,
➥SUM(Amount) Amount
FROM CARDTRANS
WHERE TransactionDate between '01/01/95' AND '02/01/95'
GROUP BY CardNumber, TransactionDate, Location
```

Note that the only change was to go from using COUNT(*) to determine the number of transactions to using SUM(NumberTrans). This approach works for both summary and detail rows because of our inclusion of the NumberTrans column in detail rows.

Typically, the summarization process would summarize a month's data into a temporary table using a query similar to the previous one. Then, the original detail data would be deleted from the CARDTRANS table. Finally, the summarized data would be inserted back into the table. This would all be executed as a single transaction on the server to prevent accidental deletion of the data in the event of an unforeseen problem.

It should be noted that the example summarization process here would be responsible for stripping the time information from the TransactionDate column during summarization. In detail rows, TransactionDate would include a valid transaction time along with the transaction date. This is necessary to ensure a unique key for the table. In summarized rows, the time field would be zeroed because the summarization requirements specified grouping the data by day.

Note also that you may have to increase the size of fields such as the Amount field to allow them to hold summary data. For example, if you'd defined Amount as a smallmoney Sybase data type, you'd probably want to redefine it using the larger money data type.

This is a viable method for avoiding the common pitfalls of summarizing detail data into separate summary tables or databases. It trades a small amount of storage per record for the convenience of being able to treat detail and summary data identically.

What's Ahead

The next chapter, Chapter 24, "Delphi's Database Drivers Demystified," helps you set up and troubleshoot database connections. Specific information is given for connecting to the Sybase, InterBase, Oracle, and Microsoft platforms. The chapter also takes you through setting up ODBC data sources and using them to interact with Access tables and Excel spreadsheets. If you want to know more about the nuts-and-bolts of setting up and troubleshooting database connections, you'll want to be sure and read this chapter.

Summary

Optimizing Delphi client/server applications can be broken into two areas of optimization: client-application optimization and server optimization. Server optimization can further be divided into two types of optimization: optimal SQL-coding techniques and performance considerations. The optimizations listed in this chapter are by no means exhaustive. They should, however, give you a good idea as to the many methods of optimizing Delphi client/server applications. The best optimizations come from years of experience with a given platform. Regarding client/server optimization, there's no substitute for simple trial and error.

24

Delphi's Database Drivers Demystified

The purpose of this chapter is to help you through the virtually endless maze between database applications and database servers. What I'm referring to, of course, is properly configuring database clients and the many layers between them and their servers. Beyond the development of the application itself, one of the biggest challenges of building client/server applications is tweaking the many links in the chain between the application and the server.

What makes the process so tough is that so many pieces are involved. To have even a fighting chance as a commando in the client/server jungle, you've got to have considerable skill at a number of technological disciplines. You must be adept at LAN protocol configuration, LAN client setup, LAN server management, advanced Windows concepts, database engine nuances, and database server setup and management.

Because the possible combinations of the pieces in the client/server puzzle are nearly infinite, it seems that no one book gives you all the answers. A good book on network protocols may offer nothing on database driver configuration. A good one on database drivers may be lacking in database servers. No one book can solve all the problems you might encounter. This one is no exception—it only touches on a few key areas which you may have to consider. Because many of the technologies involved are so new and are changing so quickly, only years of experience can actually prepare you for the hand-to-hand combat that is client/server deployment.

This chapter doesn't cover every configuration element, or even every database driver, exhaustively. It points out some potential pitfalls and caveats of which you should be aware. Sometimes a word of caution from someone who knows the bridge is out ahead is more valuable than a detailed road atlas.

The chapter is divided into two major sections. The first one deals with the native database drivers that ship with Delphi, the second deals with setting up ODBC connections using the Borland Database Engine's ODBC socket. Additionally, you'll explore a few issues that are specific to running client/server applications over WANs and running them against UNIX-based database servers.

Delphi Client/Server ships with high-performance native database drivers for four DBMS platforms: Sybase SQL Server, Oracle, InterBase, and Microsoft SQL Server. You'll look at each of these separately.

Sybase SQL Server

To connect from Windows 95 or Windows NT client machines to a Sybase server, you need to install Sybase's Net Library software. There are two versions of this software for the Windows 95/NT family, and they are *not* the same. The version for Windows NT (it comes as part of Sybase's Open Client for Windows NT package) installs *only* for NT—it will not install or work under Windows 95. Attempting to install it under Windows 95 will generate an error 422 message.

The second version installs under both Windows 95 and Windows NT. You know you have the dual-purpose version of the software by the fact that its splash screen says that it works for either OS. This version of the software is the later of the two and is the preferred one to use because it works with both Windows 95 and Windows NT.

Net Library/Open Client Error 422 Under NT

The Windows NT-only version also has the dubious distinction of sometimes not installing correctly under NT. As of early 1996, Sybase's installation program often generated an error 422 message the first time through the installation process—even under Windows NT. Turns out that the solution is simple. Despite the fact that the Sybase Release Bulletin accompanying the software instructs you to empty your Windows TEMP directory before installing, you need to do just the opposite. If the software crashes with error 422 the first time you run it, it leaves a handful of temporary files in your TEMP directory. Don't delete them. Run the installation again and all will go well.

Configuring the Client

Whichever version of the software you end up using, you'll use Sybase's SQLEDIT program to edit your connection information. Here's a quick rundown of how to set up a server connection by using SQLEDIT:

1. Start SQLEDIT and type the name you want to use for your database server into the Input Server Name box.
2. Click on the Add button to add it to the Server Entry list.
3. Click on the Service Type drop-down list and select Query from the list.
4. In the Platform list, select Windows 95 or NT, depending on which one you're running.
5. Select the appropriate Net-Library driver from the Net-Library Driver drop-down list. Most likely this is either the NLWNSCK (TCP/IP Winsock) or NLNWLINK (IPX) driver.
6. Type your database server's network address and port number (separated by commas) into the Connection Information/Network Address box. This is a TCP/IP address if you are using the TCP/IP protocol and an IPX network address if you're using IPX. Here's a sample connection string:

   `100.10.15.12,3000`

   In this example, `100.10.15.12` is the TCP/IP address, and `3000` is the port number. Consult with your network or system administrator if you're unsure of your database server's address or port number.

> **NOTE**
>
> You can also use HOSTS file entries in place of actual TCP/IP addresses in your server connection strings. For example, assuming you had a HOSTS entry of this:
>
> ```
> 100.10.15.12   marketing
> ```
>
> you can use the following
>
> ```
>  marketing,3000
> ```
>
> for your connection string.

7. Once you set up the connection information, click on the Add Service button to add the service to the Connection Service Entry list.

8. Once the service is added, you're ready to test it. Click on the Ping button in the lower right of the screen. Ping attempts to open, then close, a connection with the server you specify. If you properly configure your client, it should succeed.

9. Now press Ctrl+S to save your connection information, then exit SQLEDIT.

> **NOTE**
>
> These same instructions apply whether you configure a server connection when you install the software or by running SQLEDIT separately.

SYBPING

You can also use Sybase's SYBPING utility to test your server connections. It should be located in your SYBASE program folder. Simply click on the name of your server in the list presented by SYBPING, then click on the Ping button. If your machine can "see" the server in question, all is well.

Win 3.x Drivers

If you still have 16-bit clients (Win 3.x) that you must support, here are a few tips that may save you some grief:

■ All releases of Sybase SQL Server prior to System 10 use Sybase's DB-Library to establish client/server connections. System 10 and later use CT-Library. Although you can connect from Win 3.x clients to System 10 servers using DB-Library, you likely won't have access to System 10-specific features. Delphi 1.0 connects using DB-Library, Delphi 2.0 connects using CT-Lib. Be sure you know which library is in use on a client before you attempt to configure it.

■ All versions of DB-Library are not created equal. Some work better than others. I've had the best luck with the one dated 3-1-94, although you may find that a different one works best for you. One sure sign that you need to check your DB-Library version is data-type conversion problems. For example, I once experienced a problem with date fields when using Delphi 1.0 and Sybase's June 1994 DB-Library. That particular DB-Library appended the time portion of a datetime value twice when converting from a string data type. If you have odd conversion-related problems when running Windows 3.*x* applications against your Sybase server(s), you might try a different DB-Library version.

■ Versions of SQL Server prior to System 10 used a different method of canceling queries. These versions relied on Out-Of-Bound Data (OOBD) support in order to cancel a query and properly discard its unretrieved results. OOBD support is built into the IPX protocol, but you need to ensure its presence in your particular TCP/IP connectivity package. For example, only later versions of Novell's LAN WorkPlace TCP/IP software support OOBD out of the box; earlier ones require a patch.

■ In order to make use of OOBD to cancel queries on Sybase Win 3.*x* clients, you use the URGENT connection string parameter. Basically, you just tack URGENT onto the end of the connection string:

```
100.10.15.12,3000,URGENT
```

This ensures that queries that are aborted using DB-Library's `dbcancel()` function return control as quickly as possible to the application.

■ Win 3.*x* versions of DB-Library all require 386 Enhanced mode, although they do not reveal this when you attempt to use them. If you attempt to connect to a Sybase SQL Server using DB-Library under Windows 3.*x* in Standard mode, your connection will simply fail; DB-Library won't bother to tell you that you need to switch modes.

Setting Up a BDE Alias

Once you're able to ping your database server, you're ready to build a BDE alias so that your Delphi applications can access it. This subject is covered elsewhere in this book, but is reviewed here for your convenience and to establish the relationship between configuring your database driver software and setting up a BDE alias.

You can create BDE aliases by using either the BDE Configuration utility or Delphi's Database Explorer. The following instructions use the BDE Configuration program.

Start the BDE Configuration program, select the Aliases page, and click on the New Alias button. When the Add Aliases dialog box comes up, type the name of your new alias, then select SYBASE in the Alias type drop-down list. (See Figure 24.1.)

FIGURE 24.1.

The Add New Alias dialog box.

Once the new alias is added, you need to configure it. You do this via the Parameters panel on the Aliases page. Click on your new alias, if it isn't already selected, and then click on the DATABASE NAME entry in the Parameters grid. Set it to the name of the database on your Sybase server that you want to access with the new alias. Keep in mind that you can still access objects in other databases using this alias by fully qualifying their names (for example, database.owner.table).

Set the SERVER NAME parameter to the name of the server you created using Sybase's SQLEDIT utility. Optionally, you can also set the USER NAME parameter to the name of the database server user you want to use by default. The user name you specify is displayed as the default whenever Delphi's built-in login dialog box is shown. Figure 24.2 illustrates the Parameters list.

FIGURE 24.2.

The alias Parameters list in the BDE Configuration program.

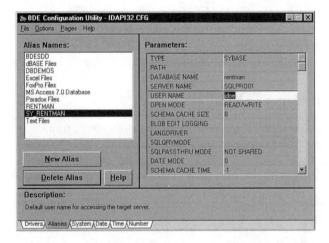

As you can see, there are a number of other parameters you can set via this screen. The rest of them are optional, though, and you can leave them set to their defaults for now.

Finish up by saving the configuration file and exiting the BDE Configuration utility.

Miscellaneous Sybase SQL Server Issues

The following are miscellaneous issues that you may encounter when interacting with Sybase SQL Server from your Delphi applications.

Numeric and Decimal Data Types

System 10 introduces the new Numeric and Decimal data types. The BDE supports these by translating them to its floating-point type, fldFloat. Note, however, that both types are retrieved from the server in their native formats (xltNONE), so no data is lost in the translation.

Identity Columns

System 10's new auto-incrementing "identity" fields are translated by the BDE to its fldINT32 subtype, fldstAUTOINC. This means that, unlike Delphi 1.0, you can use these field types in your Delphi applications.

Cross-Database/Server Tables

You can access Sybase objects in other databases by fully qualifying them. For example, you can open ACCOUNTING.DEMO.CUSTOMER, a table that lives in the ACCOUNTING database and is owned by user DEMO, just by fully specifying its name.

Troubleshooting Sybase Connection Problems

If you have problems connecting to a Sybase SQL Server, try the following:

1. Use Sybase's SYBPING utility to ping your server. If the server pings fine, you probably have a problem with your BDE alias configuration. Return to the BDE Configuration program and examine the parameters you specified (particularly the server name) to ensure that they're correct.

2. If SYBPING fails, you probably have a protocol problem. If you're using TCP/IP to connect to the server, use the PING utility that comes with Windows 95 and Windows NT to attempt to PING the host computer. Try both the machine's name, as it appears in the HOSTS file, and its IP address.

3. If the machine pings appropriately with the IP address, but not with its host name, you may have a problem with your HOSTS file. You can fix the problem temporarily by changing your connection string (with SYBEDIT) to use the IP address rather than the host name, to connect. You should resolve the HOSTS file problem as soon as possible because this is a more flexible way of connecting to remote machines.

4. If you're using IPX to connect with your server, be sure that the Novell server's IPX network number matches the one you're specifying with SYBEDIT. If this is the case and you still can't connect, or, if you're using some other protocol to connect, consult with your network administrator for further assistance.

5. If you're using TCP/IP and you have no success when trying to PING the host machine using either its host name or its IP address, you probably have a network problem. Be sure to check obvious things such as whether the IP address you have for the server is correct. Try pinging the TCP/IP loopback address, 127.0.0.1, to see whether your TCP/IP stack is working properly. This address loops back to your machine, enabling you to PING yourself. If it fails, you have a serious problem with your protocol configuration. You may need to consult your network administrator for help with your network connection.

6. If SYBPING fails, but PING works fine, check to see that the port number you specified in your connection string is the one on which the database server is listening. You can consult with your database administrator to determine what port(s) your host machine is listening on for connections. Listener ports are configured under System 10 using the Sybase SYBINIT utility.

7. If everything seems to be configured properly, you might try switching protocols, if that's an option for you. For example, I have personally seen a version of System 10 for Novell Netware that will not work reliably using Novell's own home-grown protocol, IPX—yet it works fine with TCP/IP. Because the server can be configured to listen on both protocols simultaneously, this isn't an either/or situation; you can configure the server to listen on a protocol that works until you resolve problems with other ones.

Microsoft SQL Server 6.0

Many of the tips in the previous section on Sybase SQL Server apply equally well to Microsoft SQL Server 6.0. Until recently, Microsoft licensed Sybase's SQL Server code and simply re-packaged a port of it. Beginning with version 6.0, the two product lines have diverged, and the two companies have parted ways as well.

Because SQL Server 6.0 is inexpensive and runs under Windows NT, you may find yourself developing applications where the client and the server are the same machine. SQL Server's low price has had the effect of positioning it as an entry-level solution, and many small companies have adopted it for single-machine applications. If this is your situation, be very careful to make your application as bulletproof as possible. If you manage to crash NT, something that's not easily done, you're not only taking down the client, you're also taking down the server, possibly corrupting its data in the process. This admonition holds true no matter what platform or what SQL server you're using. If your client and server are on the same machine, be *very* careful.

Despite being dangerous, running your Delphi applications on the same machine as your SQL Server has the benefit of making database connections easier to configure. For example, rather than having to know or use the machine's actual TCP/IP address, you can use the TCP loopback address, 127.0.0.1, instead.

Numeric and Decimal Data Types

Here's another miscellaneous tip: SQL Server 6.0 introduces the new Numeric and Decimal data types. The BDE supports these by translating them to its floating-point type, `fldFloat`. Note, however, that both types are retrieved from the server in their native formats (`xltNONE`), so no data is lost in the translation.

Troubleshooting Microsoft SQL Server Connection Problems

If you have problems connecting to a Microsoft SQL Server, try the following:

1. Use Microsoft's ISQL/w utility to connect to your server. If you're able to connect with ISQL/w, but not from your Delphi applications, you probably have a problem with your BDE alias configuration. Return to the BDE Configuration program and examine the parameters you specified (particularly the server name) to ensure that they're correct.

2. If ISQL/w fails to connect, you probably have a protocol problem. If you're using TCP/IP to connect to the server, attempt to PING the host computer using the PING utility that accompanies both Windows 95 and Windows NT. Try both the machine's name, as it appears in the HOSTS file, and its IP address.

    If you're using named `pipes` to connect to the server, try the `net view` `\\`*servername* command, where *servername* is the name of the NT server on which the SQL server is running. If net view succeeds, try `netuse` `\\`*servername*`\IPC$`, replacing *servername* with the name of your server. If both of these commands succeed, try the `makepipe/` `readpipe` facility. Run `makepipe` on the server, then run `readpipe /S`*servername* `/ D`*teststring* from a client machine. The `makepipe/readpipe` facility tests the integrity of the named `pipes` services. Press Ctrl+C or Ctrl+Break to terminate `makepipe`. If any of these tests fail, get with your NT system administrator. You may have problems with the named `pipes` services on the server.

3. If the machine pings appropriately with the IP address, but not with its host name, you may have a problem with your HOSTS file. You can fix the problem temporarily by changing your connection string to use the IP address, rather than the host name, to connect. You should resolve the HOSTS file problem as soon as possible because this is a more flexible way to connect to remote machines.

4. If you're using named `pipes` to connect to the server, try the `net view` `\\`*servername* command, where *servername* is the name of the NT server on which the SQL server is running. If `net view` succeeds, try `netuse` `\\`*servername*`\IPC$`, replacing *servername* with the name of your server. If both of these commands succeed, try the `makepipe/` `readpipe` facility. Run `makepipe` on the server, then run `readpipe /S`*servername* `/ D`*teststring* from a client machine. The `makepipe/readpipe` facility tests the integrity of the named `pipes` services. Press Ctrl+C or Ctrl+Break to terminate `makepipe`. If any of these tests fail, get with your NT system administrator. You may have problems with the named `pipes` services on the server.

5. If you're using IPX to connect with your server, check to see if the server is visible to your client machine. You can do this by running isql /L from the OS prompt. Isql /L calls dbserverenum, which lists all available servers from the Bindery. If your server is not in the list, you've probably got a network problem. Consult with your network administrator for further assistance.

6. If you're using TCP/IP and you have no success when trying to PING the host machine using either its host name or its IP address, you probably have a network problem. Be sure to check obvious things such as whether the IP address you have for the server is correct. Try pinging the TCP/IP loopback address, 127.0.0.1, to see whether your TCP/IP stack is working properly. This address loops back to your machine, enabling you to PING yourself. If it fails, you have a serious problem with your protocol configuration. You may need to consult your network administrator for help with your network connection.

7. If ISQL/w fails to connect, but PING works fine, check to see that the port number you specified in your connection string is the one on which the database server is listening. You can consult with your database administrator to determine what port(s) your host machine is listening on for connections.

8. If everything seems to be configured properly, you might try switching protocols, if that's an option for you. Because the server can be configured to listen on multiple protocols simultaneously, you can configure it to listen on a protocol that works until you resolve problems with ones that don't.

Oracle

To connect to an Oracle database server, you need to install and configure Oracle's SQL Net connection software. To install the software, you simply run Oracle's ORAINST general-purpose installation program. To configure the software, you define Database Aliases—a collection of settings containing all the information necessary to connect to a database server. These are not unlike Delphi's own database aliases; it's just that they work at the level of the Oracle driver rather than that of all database drivers.

To configure an Oracle database alias using the SQL Net configuration program, start the SQL Net configuration program, select Add Database Alias, and then click on OK.

The next dialog box asks you to choose a database alias. Because you're adding one, type in the new name you'd like to use and click on OK.

The next dialog box asks you to select a network protocol. Select the one that you want to use to connect to your server (such as TCP/IP).

The next dialog box requests additional information about your server. If you selected TCP/IP as your network protocol, you are asked to enter the server's host name as it appears in your HOSTS file. You can also enter its IP address. If you're connecting to a Personal Oracle server on the same machine, you can enter the TCP/IP loopback address, 127.0.0.1, as your server's IP address. If you selected SPX as your connection means, you are prompted for an SPX service name instead. Enter the requested information and click on OK.

The final dialog box displays the connection information for the database alias you're about to create. Click on OK to add the database alias. (See Figure 24.3.)

FIGURE 24.3.

The Confirm Adding Database Alias dialog box.

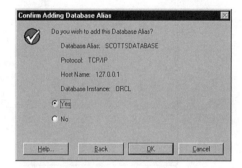

When you return to the SQL Net configuration program's main menu, select Exit, and then click on OK to close the application.

Once the database alias is configured, you should test it by using it to connect to your database server. To do this, start Oracle's SQL Plus utility and enter the following command at its command line

CONNECT *USERNAME / PASSWORD@ALIASNAME*

where *USERNAME* and *PASSWORD* are the user name and password you want to use, and *ALIASNAME* is the name of the database alias you just created. (See Figure 24.4.)

Note that you can also use Oracle's TNSPING program to test a server connection. It uses the same syntax as the familiar UNIX PING command. It's a character-mode application, so you may prefer the SQL Plus method over it.

NOTE

When connecting to a Personal Oracle server running on the same machine, I've found the TCP/IP protocol to be the least problematic. Using TCP/IP enables you to use the TCP/IP loopback address, 127.0.0.1, as the server's IP address. TCP/IP is included with both Windows 95 and Windows NT; you need only to install it to have everything you need to connect to Oracle.

FIGURE 24.4.

Connecting to an Oracle server using SQL Plus.

Setting Up a BDE Alias

Once you're able to connect to your database server, you're ready to build a BDE alias so that your Delphi applications can access it. This subject is covered elsewhere in this book, but let's review it here for your convenience and to establish the relationship between configuring your database driver software and setting up a BDE alias.

You can create BDE aliases by using either the BDE Configuration utility or Delphi's Database Explorer. The following instructions use the BDE Configuration program.

Start the BDE Configuration program, select the Aliases page, and click on the New Alias button. When the Add Aliases dialog box comes up, type the name of your new alias, and then select ORACLE in the Alias type drop-down list. You don't have to use the same name you used in the SQL Net configuration program, but it's probably a good idea. (See Figure 24.5.)

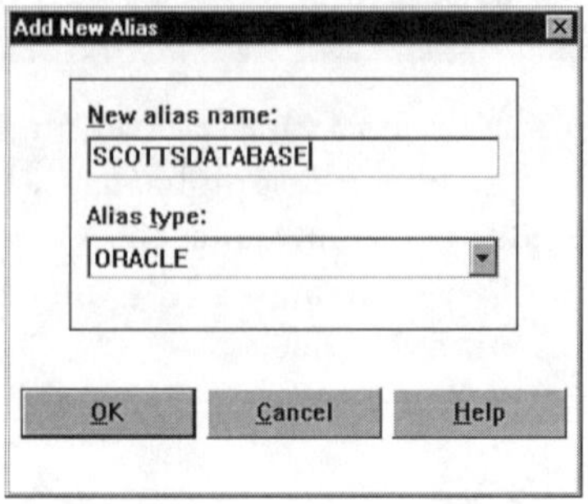

FIGURE 24.5.

The BDE Configuration program's Add New Alias dialog box.

Once the new alias is added, you need to configure it. You do this via the Parameters panel on the Aliases page. Click on your new alias, if it isn't already selected, then click on the SERVER NAME entry in the Parameters grid. Set it to the name of the database alias you created in the SQL Net configuration program.

Next, click on the NET PROTOCOL entry and set it to the network protocol you chose in the SQL Net configuration program.

> **NOTE**
>
> If you're connecting to Personal Oracle and using the TCP/IP protocol, don't select TCP/IP here. As of early February 1996, a problem existed wherein selecting TCP/IP here would create a BDE alias that was unusable—attempting to use it to connect to the server would result in an error. Instead, you must use Oracle's TNS (Transparent Network Substrate) protocol. Configuring the Oracle database alias to use TCP/IP and the BDE alias to use TNS seems to work fine.

Optionally, you can also set the USER NAME parameter to the name of the database server user you want to use by default. The user name you specify is displayed as the default whenever Delphi's built-in login dialog box is shown. Figure 24.6 shows the Parameters list.

FIGURE 24.6.

The BDE Configuration program's alias Parameters list.

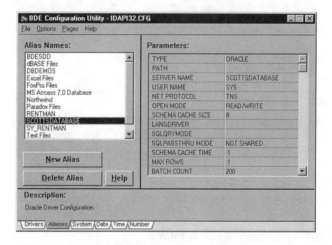

As you can see, there are a number of other parameters you can set via this screen. The rest of them are optional, though, and you can leave them set to their defaults for now.

Finish up by saving the configuration file and exiting the BDE Configuration utility.

Miscellaneous Oracle Issues

The following are miscellaneous issues that you may encounter when interacting with Oracle from within Delphi applications.

Synonyms

Oracle enables you to set up alternate object names known as *synonyms*. You can use a special database driver setting, LIST SYNONYMS, to specify how you want Oracle synonyms handled. You specify this special setting using the Params property of the Database component. Table 24.1 lists the setting's possible values.

Table 24.1. Possible values for LIST SYNONYMS.

Value	*Translation*
NONE	No synonyms are included.
PRIVATE	Only private synonyms are included.
ALL	Include all (public and private) synonyms.

To specify one of these values, double-click on the Database component's Params property and type the name of the setting followed by its value, like so:

```
LIST SYNONYMS=ALL
```

Public Synonyms

When you set LIST SYNONYMS to ALL, Oracle's PUBLIC synonyms show up in the table list. However, to open a PUBLIC synonym, you must have SELECT privileges on the synonym's underlying base object. If you (or the user running your application) lack the necessary access rights, the synonym will appear not to exist when you attempt to open it.

Included in Oracle's public synonyms are a set of dynamic performance tables. Only the DBA user SYS, by default, can access them. These synonym names are in the format V$*NAME*, where *NAME* is the remainder of the synonym name (such as LOCK, OPEN_CURSOR, and so on).

Cross-Database/Server Tables

You can access Oracle objects in other databases or on other servers by fully qualifying them. For example, you can open DEMO.CUSTOMER@ACCOUNTING, a table that lives on the ACCOUNTING server, by fully specifying its name.

Troubleshooting Oracle Connection Problems

If you have problems connecting to Oracle, try the following:

1. Use Oracle SQL Plus utility to connect to your server. If you're able to connect with SQL Plus, but not from your Delphi applications, you probably have a problem with your BDE alias configuration. Return to the BDE Configuration program and examine the parameters you specified (particularly the server name) to ensure that they're correct.

2. If SQL Plus fails to connect, you probably have a protocol problem. If you're using TCP/IP to connect to the server, attempt to PING the host computer using the PING utility that accompanies both Windows 95 and Windows NT. Try both the machine's name, as it appears in the HOSTS file, and its IP address.

3. If the machine pings appropriately with the IP address, but not with its host name, you may have a problem with your HOSTS file. You can fix the problem temporarily by changing your connection string in the SQL Net configuration program to use the IP address rather than the host name. You should resolve the HOSTS file problem as soon as possible because this is a more flexible way to connect to remote machines.

4. If you're using SPX to connect with your server, be sure that the server's SPX service number matches the one you're specifying in the SQL Net configuration program. If this is the case and you still can't connect, or, if you're using some other protocol to connect, consult with your network administrator for further assistance.

5. If you're using TCP/IP and you have no success when trying to PING the host machine using either its host name or its IP address, you probably have a network problem. Be sure to check obvious things such as whether the IP address you have for the server is correct. Try pinging the TCP/IP loopback address, 127.0.0.1, to see whether your TCP/IP stack is working properly. This address loops back to your machine, enabling you to PING yourself. If it fails, you have a serious problem with your protocol configuration. You may need to consult your network administrator for help with your network connection.

6. If SQL Plus fails to connect, but PING works fine, check to see that the Oracle home directory is on your PATH. If your PATH is correct, make sure that (ORACLE HOME DIRECTORY)\NETWORK\ADMIN\TNSNAMES.ORA file is set up properly. It's a text file, so you can look at using the TYPE command or an editor, but don't edit it directly—use the SQL Net configuration program to edit it instead. Here's an excerpt that shows what the file should look like:

```
SCOTTSDATABASE.world =
  (DESCRIPTION =
    (ADDRESS_LIST =
      (ADDRESS =
        (COMMUNITY = tcp.world)
        (PROTOCOL = TCP)
        (Host = 127.0.0.1)
        (Port = 1521)
```

```
              )
              (ADDRESS =
                (COMMUNITY = tcp.world)
                (PROTOCOL = TCP)
                (Host = 127.0.0.1)
                (Port = 1526)
              )
          )
          (CONNECT_DATA = (SID = ORCL)
          )
      )
```

7. If everything seems to be configured properly, you might try switching protocols, if that's an option for you. Because the server can be configured to listen on multiple protocols simultaneously, you can configure it to listen on a protocol that works until you resolve problems with ones that don't.

InterBase

Unlike the servers mentioned thus far, InterBase doesn't have a separate database connection element that you must define in order to access InterBase servers. The only requirement to access an InterBase server is that the server must have an entry in your TCP/IP HOSTS file, like so:

```
100.10.15.12  marketing
```

A line must also be added to your TCP SERVICES file that identifies the InterBase access protocol:

```
gds_db  3050/tcp
```

This is done automatically when you install InterBase, or you can add the line yourself. Once your TCP/IP access is configured, you're ready to create a BDE alias.

Setting Up a BDE Alias

Once you're able to connect to your database server, you're ready to build a BDE alias so that your Delphi applications can access it. This subject is covered elsewhere in this book, but let's review it here for your convenience and to establish the relationship between configuring your database driver software and setting up a BDE alias.

You can create BDE aliases by using either the BDE Configuration utility or Delphi's Database Explorer. The following instructions use the BDE Configuration program.

Start the BDE Configuration program, select the Aliases page, and click on the New Alias button. When the Add Aliases dialog box comes up, type the name of your new alias, then select INTRBASE in the Alias type drop-down list. (See Figure 24.7.)

FIGURE 24.7.

The Borland Database Engine Configuration utility's Add New Alias dialog box.

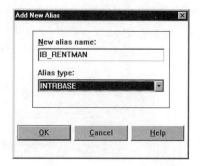

Once the new alias is added, you need to configure it. You do this via the Parameters panel on the Aliases page. Click on your new alias, if it isn't already selected, then click on the SERVER NAME entry in the Parameters grid. Set it to the name of the server as you entered it in your HOSTS file, followed by the full path to the database file itself. Usually this file will have a GDB extension. Your entry should look something like this

```
MIS:/data/interbase/accounting.gdb
```

where MIS is the name of your server and /data/interbase/accounting.gdb is the full path to the file containing its database.

> **TIP**
>
> If you're connecting to the Local InterBase Server, you don't need to include a server name in the SERVER NAME field. Instead, just specify the full path to your database file, like so:
> ```
> C:\DATA\INTERBASE\ACCOUNT.GDB
> ```

Optionally, you can also set the USER NAME parameter to the name of the database server user you want to use by default. The user name you specify is displayed as the default whenever Delphi's built-in login dialog box is shown. See Figure 24.8, which shows the parameters list.

As you can see, there are a number of other parameters you can set via this screen. The rest of them are optional, though, and you can leave them set to their defaults for now.

Finish up by saving the configuration file and exiting the BDE Configuration utility.

FIGURE 24.8.

The BDE Configuration utility's alias Parameters list.

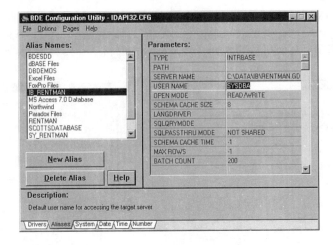

Troubleshooting InterBase Connection Problems

If you have problems connecting to an InterBase server from within your Delphi applications, try the following:

1. Use the InterBase WISQL utility to connect to your server. If you're able to connect to the server, but still have problems doing so within your Delphi applications, you probably have a problem with your BDE alias configuration. Return to the BDE Configuration program and examine the parameters you specified (particularly the server name) to ensure that they're correct.

2. If WISQL fails, you probably have a protocol problem. Use the PING utility included with Windows 95 or Windows NT to attempt to PING the host computer. Try both the machine's name, as it appears in the HOSTS file, and its IP address.

3. If the machine pings appropriately with the IP address, but not with its host name, you may have a problem with your HOSTS file. You have to resolve the HOSTS file problem in order to connect to the server, because InterBase uses it to find your server. You should have an entry in your HOSTS file for each server you want to access that looks like this:

   ```
   100.10.15.12  marketing
   ```

4. If you're using TCP/IP and you have no success when trying to PING the host machine, using either its host name or its IP address, you probably have a network problem. Be sure to check obvious things such as whether the IP address you have for the server is correct. Try pinging the TCP/IP loopback address, 127.0.0.1, to see whether your TCP/IP stack is working properly. This address loops back to your machine, enabling you to PING yourself. If it fails, you have a serious problem with your protocol configuration. You may need to consult your network administrator for help with your network connection.

5. If WISQL fails, but PING works fine, attempt to telnet into the server machine using the TELNET utility that accompanies both Windows 95 and Windows NT. The syntax for TELNET is the following:

```
TELNET 100.100.100.100
```

where `100.100.100.100` is the TCP/IP address of the host computer. If TELNET fails, you may have a problem with the inet daemon on the server machine.

6. If TELNET succeeds, but WISQL still fails, make sure, first of all, that the InterBase server software is installed correctly and currently running on the host computer. Second, check to see that required entry in the TCP SERVICES file is present. It should look like this:

```
gds_db    3050/tcp
```

7. If these steps fail to resolve your problem, you should consult with your network administrator and/or your database administrator for further assistance.

ODBC

In this section, you go through the process of using ODBC database drivers with your Delphi applications. The first exercise is setting up ODBC access to a Microsoft Access database.

Access

The first thing you need to do when accessing ODBC database drivers is to define an ODBC Data Source using the ODBC configuration program. To create a new ODBC Data Source, start the ODBC configuration program from the Windows Control Panel, then click on the Add button.

The first dialog box you're presented with asks you to select an ODBC driver set on which to base the new Data Source. If you installed the Professional version of Microsoft Office, or installed Access separately, you should see the Access ODBC driver in the list. (See Figure 24.9.) Double-click on the Access driver to select it.

FIGURE 24.9.

The Data Sources dialog box.

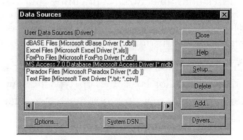

You're next presented with the Setup dialog box for the Access ODBC driver. Type Northwind in the Data Source Name box and ODBC DSN for the Northwind Traders database for the Description.

Next, click on the Database button and select an Access database to open. The Northwind Traders database is located in the C:\MSOFFICE\ACCESS\SAMPLES directory by default.

Once you specify a database, you're finished with the Data Source definition. Click on OK to save your new Data Source. Figure 24.10 shows the completed definition.

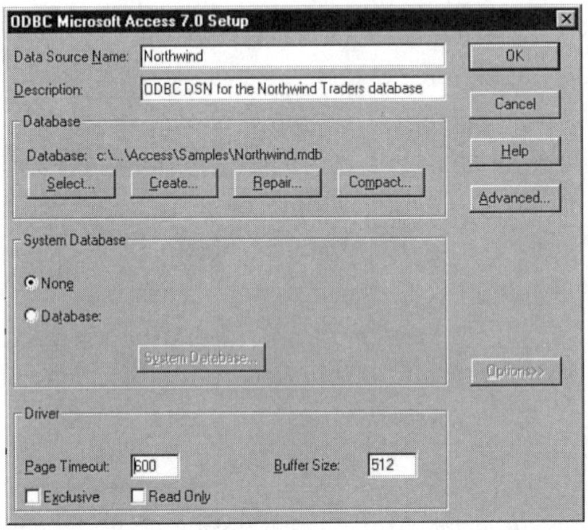

FIGURE 24.10.

The ODBC Microsoft
Access 7.0 Setup window.

Now that your ODBC Data Source is defined, you're ready to build a BDE alias.

Setting Up a BDE Alias

After you define a Data Source to interface the Access ODBC driver, you're ready to build a BDE alias so that Delphi applications can use the Access database referenced by the Data Source. This subject is covered elsewhere in this book, but let's review it here for your convenience and to establish the relationship between configuring your Data Source and setting up a BDE alias.

You can create BDE aliases by using either the BDE Configuration utility or Delphi's Database Explorer. These instructions use the BDE Configuration program.

Start the BDE Configuration program, select the Aliases page, and click on the New Alias button. When the Add Aliases dialog box comes up, type the name of your new alias, then select Access Data (*.mdb) in the Alias type drop-down list. (See Figure 24.11.)

FIGURE 24.11.

The Add New Alias dialog box.

Once the new alias is added, you need to configure it. You do this via the Parameters panel on the Aliases page. Click on your new alias, if it isn't already selected, then click on the ODBC DSN entry in the Parameters grid. Set it to the name of the Data Source that you created in the ODBC Administrator program.

Optionally, you can also set the USER NAME parameter to the name of the user you want to use by default. The user name you specify is displayed as the default whenever Delphi's built-in login dialog box is shown. Figure 24.12 shows the Parameters list.

FIGURE 24.12.

The alias Parameters list.

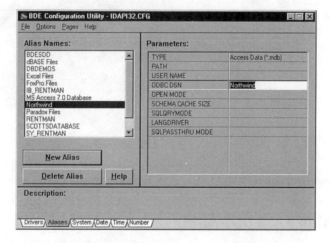

As you can see, there are a number of other parameters you can set via this screen. The rest of them are optional, though, and you can leave them set to their defaults for now.

Finish up by saving the configuration file and exiting the BDE Configuration utility.

The next exercise is setting up the Excel ODBC driver.

Excel

Start the ODBC Administration program from the Windows Control Panel, then click on the Add button.

Next, double-click on the Microsoft Excel driver to select it from the list of available ODBC drivers. You're next presented with the Setup dialog box for the Excel ODBC driver. Type XL_RENTMAN in the Data Source Name box and Excel ODBC DSN for RENTMAN System for the Description.

Next, click on the Select Workbook button and select an Excel workbook to open. Note that you need to name the ranges (in Excel) within the workbook that you intend to access. These ranges will appear in table lists (for instance, for the TableName property) in Delphi. Delphi lists the named ranges on all the pages in a workbook, and you can have multiple named ranges per page.

After you specify a workbook, you're finished with the Data Source definition. Click on OK to save your new Data Source. Figure 24.13 shows the completed definition.

FIGURE 24.13.

ODBC Microsoft Excel Setup window.

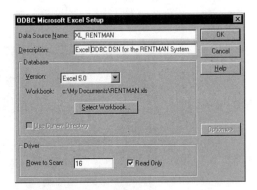

Now that your ODBC Data Source is defined, you're ready to build a BDE alias.

Setting Up a BDE Alias

Once you define a Data Source to interface the Excel ODBC driver, you're ready to build a BDE alias so that Delphi applications can use the Excel workbook referenced by the Data Source. This subject is covered elsewhere in this book, but we'll cover it here for your convenience and to establish the relationship between configuring your Data Source and setting up a BDE alias.

You can create BDE aliases using either the BDE Configuration utility or Delphi's Database Explorer. The instructions in the following paragraphs use the BDE Configuration program.

Start the BDE Configuration program, select the Aliases page, and click on the New Alias button. When the Add Aliases dialog box comes up, type the name of your new alias, then select Excel Files (*.xls) in the Alias type drop-down list, as shown in Figure 24.14.

FIGURE 24.14.

The Add New Alias dialog box.

Once the new alias is added, you need to configure it. You do this via the Parameters panel on the Aliases page. Click on your new alias, if it isn't already selected, then click on the ODBC DSN entry in the Parameters grid. Set it to the name of the Data Source that you created in the ODBC Administrator program. (See Figure 24.15.)

FIGURE 24.15.

The alias Parameters list in the BDE Configuration program.

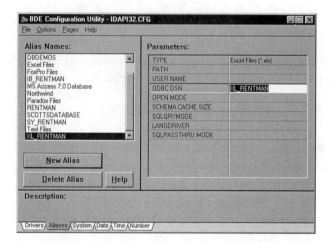

As you can see, there are a number of other parameters you can set via this screen. The rest of them are optional, though, and you can leave them set to their defaults for now.

Finish up by saving the configuration file and exiting the BDE Configuration utility.

TIP

You can set the AUTO ODBC flag to True in the BDE Configuration program to cause the utility to create an alias automatically for every ODBC Data Source defined in the ODBC.INI file. This can save you time initially setting up ODBC-related aliases.

WAN Considerations

The term WAN, as used here, refers to a Wide Area Network that typically runs over 56KB or T-1 (1.544 megabit) digital lines. Because even a speedy T-1 line is only about one-seventh as fast as a 10MB/second Ethernet network, you have to be a lot more conscientious about bandwidth utilization in apps you target for WANs. Here are a few tips related to optimally configuring database connections over WANs:

■ If your network connection protocol supports oversized packets (such as Novell's Large Internet Packet support), you might give it a try. The fewer packets you pass over relatively slow WAN connections, the better.

■ Consider creating nonessential forms dynamically rather than automatically. Every database connection you establish uses up network bandwidth. Over relatively speedy local network connections, this is barely perceptible. The difference it makes can be very substantial over WAN connections, however. You have to weigh the slowness of creating and destroying forms as you need them against the reduced overall bandwidth requirements to see whether this is worth doing, but it's something you should consider.

■ When building applications that will communicate over a WAN, grid controls, such as DBGrid and DBCtrlGrid, should be viewed with a skeptical eye. Though certainly appropriate in local network applications, grids retrieve much more data than is actually needed by the application. They cause bandwidth to be wasted and your applications to run more slowly.

■ Keep master/detail relationships to a minimum.

■ Consider using Label components and static Lookup/Locate operations rather than DBText components for read-only data from secondary tables. Though it's certainly easier to set up data-aware DBText components, every data-aware control you use can eat up bandwidth on the WAN. Eat up enough of the bandwidth and you suddenly find yourself with an application that is unusable.

■ Consider setting TDatabase's KeepConnection property to false. Though this slows down your application each time it reconnects to your server, it has the advantage of leaving as much bandwidth as possible free to other users at a remote site. This is crucial when deploying applications that run across WANs. Another benefit of this approach is the conservation of user connections on your database server. If you have a limited number of concurrent connections on your database server, dropping inactive connections (KeepConnections:=False) can conceivably allow more users access to your system.

■ Use stored procedures and queries to consolidate large amounts of information on your server before sending it across the WAN to your application. That is, don't do row-by-row processing in your application if you can avoid it—use server-based stored procedures instead.

■ Use Cached Updates to group your updates together so that they can be applied as a batch rather than one at a time.

■ Enable the BDE's schema caching to cache database schema information on the local machine. You do this by setting ENABLE SCHEMA CACHE to True in the BDE Configuration utility.

■ Use Delphi's local filters to qualify small result sets at the local machine level. This saves having to re-access them over the relatively slow WAN connection.

■ Use Delphi's BatchMove facilities to move large numbers of rows between tables; don't do *anything* one row at a time.

UNIX Issues

The following are tips specific to UNIX:

■ By default, the TCP/IP protocol waits until a packet is full before sending it. This can cause performance degradation when the data that needs to be sent exceeds the size of the packet being used. You can turn off this delay on most servers with a simple configuration change. You'll have to check with your UNIX system administrator to get the specifics, but this is usually a configuration option on either the host computer as a whole or the database server program itself. Sybase SQL Server, for example, implements the TCP_NODELAY setting via a trace flag (1610) on the command line to its dataserver program. You pass the command line option -T1610 to implement it on Sybase UNIX-based servers.

■ Depending on your UNIX vendor, you may be able to tweak various settings of the TCP/IP protocol that could potentially help your applications run more efficiently. Here's a list of some that I've come across:

```
ndd -set /dev/tcp tcp_rexmit_interval_max value
ndd -set /dev/tcp tcp_conn_req_max value
ndd -set /dev/tcp tcp_close_wait_interval value
ndd -set /dev/tcp tcp_keep_alive_interval value
```

Exact syntax and phrasing vary from platform to platform, but most high-end UNIX servers enable you to adjust the behavior of the TCP/IP protocol extensively. If your client applications use TCP/IP to communicate with your database server, streamlining its operation might very well improve the usability of your systems.

What's Ahead

Chapter 25, "The Borland Database Engine," introduces you to the engine that's behind your Delphi database applications. You'll get to look "under the hood" of Delphi's database access and discover how Delphi pulls off many of its database tricks. If you want to get down to the nitty-gritty of database access under Delphi, you'll definitely want to check out the next chapter.

Summary

As you can see, properly configuring client/server applications is a black art indeed. It's a painstaking process that you must approach with an ample supply of both patience and tenacity. Trial and error is often the best way to work your way through the maze that is client/server configuration. This guide should help you avoid a few pitfalls along the way.

25

The Borland
Database Engine

The Borland Database Engine is the set of Dynamic Link Libraries through which all Delphi's database access occurs. Not only is the BDE used by Delphi, it's also used by several other Borland products (such as Paradox, dBASE for Windows, Borland C++, and so forth). You may have seen it in other Borland products under its old name, IDAPI (Independent Database Application Programming Interface). Borland originally released IDAPI as an open database connectivity product, but Microsoft's ODBC has eclipsed it in that regard.

Delphi encapsulates nearly all the functionality of the BDE in its database components. You rarely, if ever, need to interact directly with the BDE. Delphi's method of doing things is infinitely easier and more bulletproof than making direct BDE calls. Contrary to what you might think, you don't give up a lot in terms of performance by using these components, either.

Why then do you need a chapter on the BDE? This chapter explains the internals of the engine so that you can better understand why Delphi does things the way it does and addresses those few times that you might need BDE capabilities not found in Delphi's database components.

There are a couple of things you should keep in mind when making direct BDE calls. First, you don't have the exception safety-net that Delphi's VCL provides when accessing databases. You need to check return codes from BDE functions closely and react to them accordingly. Second, because Delphi's database components won't be aware of your low-level access, you may need to re-synchronize them with your database. In some situations, this may entail only calling the Refresh method; in others, you may have to close and reopen a DataSet—it depends on what you're doing.

This chapter discusses the BDE in terms of how you can use it to extend the database access provided by Delphi's VCL, not as an alternative to it. You'll explore the key BDE structures with which you should be familiar, BDE functions that you may have a need to use, and ways you can use Delphi components and BDE API calls together.

BDE Versus ODBC

In terms of a direct comparison between the BDE and ODBC, you'll find BDE drivers to be faster and more feature-rich than corresponding ODBC drivers. ODBC's jack-of-all-trades approach has made it a master of none. When dealing with ODBC drivers, it often feels as though you're working with the least common denominator in terms of database features. Even when a particular ODBC driver includes vendor-specific enhancements, you often cannot access them without making direct ODBC API calls—they aren't supported by the herd of tools out there that purport ODBC compliance.

This isn't the case with the BDE. As a rule, its SQL Link drivers support their respective database platforms rather completely, and that functionality flows through into Delphi's components. For example, SQL database servers provide transaction control mechanisms that enable you to group a batch of database changes together so that they either occur or do not occur in their entirety. The SQL syntax needed to initiate a transaction group varies from server to server. Local tables, on the other hand, do not support transactions. Despite the variance among vendors regarding transaction SQL syntax, and despite the lack of transaction support in local tables, the BDE provides a single API call for starting a transaction on any platform it supports: DbiBeginTran. This facility even works for local tables—the BDE provides its own transaction control mechanism for them. Delphi envelops this BDE API call in the BeginTransaction method of its TDatabase component, so you can initiate transactions on your server platform without being concerned with the actual SQL syntax it may require, and you can use transactions with local tables despite the fact that the tables know nothing of it. This is a good example of unique BDE features showing themselves in the Delphi VCL.

The Architecture

The BDE uses a driver-based architecture. This means that you need a separate driver for each DBMS you access. Sometimes a single driver supports multiple versions of a DBMS platform (for instance, there's just one driver for the dBASE platform, regardless of whether you're dealing with dBASE III, IV or V, or FoxPro or Clipper).

To help you better understand the BDE architecture, consider this: when you access a database object from under Delphi, the sequence of events goes something like this:

1. You make a call to a Delphi database component.
2. The component calls the BDE.
3. The BDE calls its local database or SQL Links driver.
4. If you're using a local driver, the driver accesses your database tables,

   or

   if you're using an SQL Links driver, the driver calls your DBMS vendor's client driver.

The BDE is object-oriented. This means that it's easy to use and easy to extend. If you need to access a DBMS platform for which the BDE does not provide out-of-the-box support, simply install the BDE or ODBC driver for that platform. It's extremely unlikely that the BDE itself would have to be reworked to support your new platform.

The BDE is client/server ready. This means that it supports all the advanced features users have come to expect from a client/server DBMS. These include transaction processing, updatable cursors, stored procedure support, and more. Because the drivers and API are separate in the BDE, moving from platform to platform has never been easier. Scaling from local tables to client/server platforms can be as easy as changing the database alias an application uses to point to the new platform.

Shared Services

One of the strengths of the BDE design is that it provides a number of services that database drivers may share. These services alleviate the need for each driver to create or establish the service itself. This leads to overall better performance and consistency among the drivers.

OS Services

Because the BDE provides a full battery of OS services to its drivers, isolating them from interacting directly with the OS and network, it is highly portable.

Buffer Manager

The first OS service is the shared buffer manager. This is a priority-based manager that enables all BDE drivers to share the same buffer pool. Though the use of the pool isn't required, drivers that use the common pool help conserve system resources.

Memory Manager

To make smaller memory allocations more efficient, the BDE provides its own memory suballocation mechanism. This enables drivers to avoid going to the OS every time they need a small amount of memory. BDE allocates larger chunks of RAM, then hands it out to clients making memory requests.

BLOB Cache

To expedite access to Binary Large OBjects (BLOBs), the BDE provides a BLOB cache. This frees developers from having to worry about setting up their own and enables, among other things, random access to BLOB information so that BDE users don't have to concern themselves with writing the contents of a BLOB to an external file. This random access is supported even on platforms that provide no random BLOB access.

Sort Engine

The BDE provides a speedy sort engine that is used by the query engine, the dBASE drivers, and the Paradox drivers. Borland holds two different patents on this engine's architecture.

Query Engine

BDE's query engine is a robust, full-featured query processor that produces complex result sets quickly. It supports both the Query By Example (QBE) and direct SQL methods of querying databases against any of the drivers it supports. For example, you can use SQL to query dBASE tables, even though they have no inherent support for SQL.

SQL Generator

As mentioned previously, the BDE enables you to query databases by using the QBE method made famous by Paradox or by using traditional SQL statements. When a QBE query is sent to a SQL server, the BDE translates it to SQL before sending it.

Restructure

The Restructure shared service enables you to make modifications to the structures of dBASE and Paradox tables without having to be concerned with the fine details of the process. For example, the service handles creating any temporary tables or saving and reloading data for you automatically.

Data Translation Service

The BDE provides a service for translating data between different formats. This enables BDE functions and services to do cross-database operations. When the need to convert between similar formats arises, the data conversion service determines the best method of conversion and performs it.

Batch Table Functions

The BDE provides a powerful mechanism for moving data from one format to another and for handling the merging of similar tables. This service is the basis of the Delphi TBatchMove component and the Data Pump tool that accompanies Delphi.

In-Memory Tables

As is the case with many client/server DBMS platforms, the BDE supports temporary tables that exist only in memory. This speeds up access to data, enables sorts to happen much faster, and provides the necessary foundation for cached updates.

Linked Cursors

The BDE supports linked cursors at the engine level, alleviating the need for Delphi's VCL to handle it manually and also freeing the developer from having to be concerned with it. Linking one cursor with another causes it to move anytime the other cursor does. A common use of linked cursors is in establishing master/detail relationships between tables.

SQL Drivers Services

A suite of mini-services is provided for SQL-based drivers. Among these are translation of navigational commands to SQL so that access to local tables and SQL tables is seamless, data dictionary and object directory services, and cached BLOB manipulation.

System Manager

The system manager is the BDE's traffic cop. It loads drivers when necessary and frees resources when they are no longer needed.

Configuration Manager

The BDE's configuration manager service enables clients to read and write driver configuration information. Aliases can be created, driver parameters can be queried, and so forth.

Language Drivers

The BDE's language drivers provide support for the international market. Because the approach taken to supporting foreign languages is driver-based, developers need not concern themselves with porting the BDE between languages.

The BDE API

The BDE API is a cursor-based API that provides a single, unified set of API calls for both local ISAM-based data sources and remote, SQL-based ones. Each type of database has influenced the API in favor of the other. For example, even though navigating bi-directionally through SQL server database objects has traditionally not been supported very well by DBMS vendors, Delphi provides the ability to navigate both forward *and* backward in remote result sets, something you normally expect from local tables, not remote ones. Likewise, even though dBASE and Paradox, as local file formats rather than database servers, have no inherent support for transactions, the BDE provides a transaction control mechanism for them that uses the same API calls as those platforms that do their own transaction management.

The BDE API avoids being a jack-of-all-trades-and-a-master-of-none by supporting the individual nuances of each DBMS platform. For example, Clipper indexes are now supported by the BDE dBASE driver. Primary indexes are supported by the Paradox driver. Stored procedures are supported on the SQL platforms that have them, and so on.

Minimum Functionality

For the platforms on which a native BDE driver or ODBC driver is available, the following five functions are always supported:

- ■ Opening/closing of databases
- ■ Retrieving/establishing property values for BDE system objects
- ■ Reading/writing data in database objects

■ Creating database objects such as tables and indexes

■ Executing cross-database operations such as copying data from one database to another

Key BDE Structures

In order to develop applications that interface with the BDE, it's helpful to know the key data structures used by the engine. Table 25.1 lists the structures used by the BDE.

Table 25.1. Key BDE data structures.

Structure	Description
BATTblDesc	Batch table descriptor
CANHdr	Filter node class header
CBPROGRESSDesc	Callback routine for progress indicator
RESTcbDesc	Callback routine for table restructure
CFGDesc	Configuration descriptor
CLIENTInfo	Client application info
CRTblDesc	Table attributes descriptor
CURProps	Cursor property descriptor
DBDesc	Database descriptor
DBIEnumFld	Enumerated field
DBIEnv	BDE environment descriptor
DBIErrInfo	Error info descriptor
DBIQryProgress	Query status indicator
DRVType	Driver info descriptor
FILEDesc	File descriptor
FILTERInfo	Filter info descriptor
FLDDesc	Field descriptor
FLDType	Field type descriptor
FMLDesc	Language driver descriptor
FMTBcd	Binary-coded decimal format
FMTDate	Date format
FMTNumber	Number format
FMTTime	Time format

continues

Table 25.1. continued

Structure	Description
DbiFUNCArgDesc	Remote datasource function argument descriptor
DbiFUNCDesc	Remote datasource function descriptor
IDXDesc	Index descriptor
IDXType	Index type descriptor
LDDesc	Language driver descriptor
LOCKDesc	Lock descriptor
RECProps	Record properties descriptor
RINTDesc	Referential integrity descriptor
SECDesc	Security descriptor
SESInfo	Session info descriptor
SPDesc	Standard procedure descriptor
SPParamDesc	Standard procedure parameters descriptor
SYSConfig	System configuration info descriptor
SYSInfo	BDE system status descriptor
SYSVersion	BDE system version info descriptor
TBLBaseDesc	Basic table information descriptor
TblExtDesc	Additional table information descriptor
TBLFullDesc	Complete table information descriptor
TBLType	Table capability descriptor
USERDesc	User descriptor
VCHKDesc	Validity check descriptor
XInfo	Transaction descriptor

In addition to these structures, the BDE defines the objects listed in Table 25.2.

Table 25.2. Object defined by the BDE.

Object	Type	Description
hDBICur	hDBIObj	Handle to cursor
hDBIDb	hDBIObj	Handle to database
hDBIObj	UINT32	Handle to nonspecific object
hDBIQry	hDBIObj	Handle to query

Object	Type	Description
hDBISes	hDBIObj	Handle to session
hDBIStmt	hDBIObj	Handle to new query statement
hDBIXact	UINT32	Handle to transaction
hDBIXlt	hDBIObj	Handle to translation
phDBICfg	^hDBICfg	Pointer to configuration handle
phDBICur	^hDBICur	Pointer to cursor handle
phDBIDb	^hDBIDb	Pointer to database handle
phDBIObj	^hDBIObj	Pointer to nonspecific object handle
phDBIQry	^hDBIQry	Pointer to query handle
phDBISes	^hDBISes	Pointer to session handle
Phdbistmt	^hdbistmt	Pointer to statement handle
phDBIXact	^hDBIXact	Pointer to transaction handle
phDBIXlt	^hDBIXlt	Pointer to translation handle

You'll find the hDBIDb and hDBICur variables to be the ones most often used in your applications. An hDBIDb is returned when you open a database, and an hDBICur is returned when you open a table. These correspond to the DBHandle and Handle properties of TDataSet, respectively.

Building a Native BDE Application

As mentioned previously, you'll probably never need to write an entire application using BDE calls rather than Delphi's database components. Nevertheless, it's still helpful to understand what such an application requires, because that will no doubt help you understand the process Delphi goes through to provide you with database access. To build an application using only BDE API calls, you must follow 12 basic steps:

1. Initialize the engine.
2. Set up the debug layer.
3. Open a database.
4. Set the work directory.
5. Set the temporary directory.
6. Create a cursor by opening a table.
7. Retrieve the table's properties.
8. Allocate a record buffer area.

9. Move the cursor to the record you want.

10. Retrieve the record from the cursor.

11. Retrieve the field you want from the record.

12. Free all allocations.

Listing 25.1 shows a unit that illustrates these 12 steps. Basically, I've taken the BDE Help template application and converted it from C to Object Pascal, then inserted it into the OnClick event of a button component.

Listing 25.1. The BDE Help template application rewritten in Object Pascal and converted to a button OnClick handler.

```
{*********************************************************}
{                                                         }
{                  BDE Template Program                   }
{                                                         }
{         Copyright (c) 1996 Borland International         }
{                                                         }
{*********************************************************}
{

Conversion to Object Pascal by Ken Henderson.

}
unit BDETemp;

interface

uses
  Windows, Messages, SysUtils, Classes, Graphics, Controls, Forms, Dialogs,
  StdCtrls, BDE;

type
  TForm1 = class(TForm)
    Button1: TButton;
    procedure Button1Click(Sender: TObject);
  private
    { Private declarations }
  public
    { Public declarations }
  end;

var
  Form1: TForm1;

implementation

{$R *.DFM}

procedure TForm1.Button1Click(Sender: TObject);
var
    hDb : hDBIDb;           // Handle to the Database
    hCur : hDBICur;         // Handle to the cursor (table)
```

```
      szTblName : String;
      szTblType : String;
      CursorProps : CURProps;  // Properties of the cursor
      pRecBuf : pBYTE;         // Pointer to the record buffer
      TenantNo : Integer;
      isBlank : BOOL;


function Chk(ErrorValue : DBIResult) : DBIResult;
var
   dbi_status : string;
   dbi_string : string;
   ErrInfo : DBIErrInfo;
   count : integer;
begin
   dbi_status:='';
   dbi_string:='';
   if (ErrorValue <> DBIERR_NONE) then begin
      DbiGetErrorInfo(TRUE, ErrInfo);

      if (ErrInfo.iError = ErrorValue) then begin
      dbi_status:='  ERROR '+ ErrInfo.szErrCode;

      With ErrInfo do
        for count:=low(szContext) to high(szContext) do
           if (strcomp(ErrInfo.szContext[count], '')<>0) then
               dbi_status := dbi_status+'    '+ ErrInfo.szContext[count];
      end else begin
         SetLength(dbi_string, DBIMAXMSGLEN);
         DbiGetErrorString(ErrorValue, PChar(dbi_string));
         dbi_status := '  ERROR '+dbi_string;
      end;
      MessageBox(0, PChar(dbi_status), 'BDE Error', MB_OK or MB_ICONEXCLAMATION);
   end;
   result:=ErrorValue;
end;

begin
   hDb := nil;
   hCur := nil;

   ShowMessage('Initialize engine');
   Chk(DbiInit(nil));         // Step 2

   ShowMessage('Set debug layer options');
   DbiDebugLayerOptions(DEBUGON or OUTPUTTOFILE or FLUSHEVERYOP, 'TRACE.TXT');//
➥Step 3

   ShowMessage('Open database');
   Chk(DbiOpenDatabase(                 // Step 4
      nil,               // Database name - nil for standard database
      nil,                  // Database type - nil for standard database
      dbiREADWRITE,              // Open mode - Read/Write or Read only
      dbiOPENSHARED,             // Share mode - Shared or Exclusive
      nil,                  // Password - not needed for the STANDARD
➥database
```

continues

Listing 25.1. continued

```
    0,                          // Number of optional parameters
    nil,                        // Field Desc for optional parameters
    nil,                        // Values for the optional parameters
    hDb));                      // Handle to the database

ShowMessage('Set table directory');

Chk(DbiSetDirectory(           // Step 5
    hDb,                       // Handle to the database which is being
➡modified
    'c:\data\delphi\rentman'));    // The new working directory

ShowMessage('Set private directory');
Chk(DbiSetPrivateDir(          // Step 6
    'c:\temp'));               // Select a directory on a local drive not used
                               // by other applications.

szTblName:='TENANT';
szTblType:=szPARADOX;
ShowMessage('Open table');
Chk(DbiOpenTable(              // Step 7
    hDb,                       // Handle to the standard database
    PChar(szTblName),          // Name of the table
    PChar(szTblType),          // Type of the table - only used for local tables
    nil,                       // Index Name - Optional
    nil,                       // IndexTagName - Optional. Only used by dBASE
    0,                         // IndexId - 0 = Primary.
    dbiREADWRITE,              // Open Mode - Read/Write or Read Only
    dbiOPENSHARED,             // Shared mode - SHARED or EXCL
    xltFIELD,                  // Translate mode - Almost always xltFIELD
    FALSE,                     // Unidirectional cursor movement.
    nil,                       // Optional Parameters.
    hCur));                    // Handle to the cursor

ShowMessage('Get cursor properties');
Chk(DbiGetCursorProps(         // Step 8
    hCur,                      // Handle to the cursor
    CursorProps));             // Properties of the cursor (table)

ShowMessage('Allocate a record buffer');
GetMem(pRecBuf,CursorProps.iRecBufSize * sizeof(BYTE));       // Step 9
if (pRecBuf = nil) then
    ShowMessage('Error allocating buffer')
else begin
    ShowMessage('Set cursor to the crack before the first record');
    Chk(DbiSetToBegin(hCur)); // Step 10
                              // Position the specified cursor to the crack
                              // before the first record

    ShowMessage('Get the next record');
    Chk(DbiGetNextRecord(                    // Step 11
        hCur,      // Cursor from which to get the record.
        dbiNOLOCK,                           // Lock Type
        pRecBuf,                             // Buffer to store the record
        nil));                               // Record properties - don't need in
```

```
➥this case

      ShowMessage('Get a field out of the record buffer');
      Chk(DbiGetField(
         hCur,              // Cursor which contains the record
         1,                 // Field Number of the "TenantNo" field.
         pRecBuf,           // Buffer containing the record
         @TenantNo,         // Variable for the Customer Number
         isBlank));         // Is the field blank?

      ShowMessage('The retrieved field value is '+ IntToStr(TenantNo));
   end;

   ShowMessage('Clean-up');

   if (pRecBuf <> nil) then
      freemem(pRecBuf);       // Free the record buffer

   if (hCur <> nil) then
      Chk(DbiCloseCursor(hCur));
                              // Close the cursor

   if (hDb <> nil) then
      Chk(DbiCloseDatabase(hDb));
                              // Close the database

   DbiExit;                   // Close the BDE.

end;

end.
```

As you can see, this code is attached to the OnClick event of a button on a Delphi form. You can key this code into your own OnClick event to see how it works. Note that it opens the TENANT table in the RENTMAN database (C:\DATA\DELPHI\RENTMAN, by default), so the table should exist in advance if it's to be opened.

Note the use of the BDE unit in the unit's Uses clause. The BDE unit contains all the procedure and data type information for the database engine. Add it to your Uses clause any time you want to interact directly with the BDE.

Although most Delphi developers never construct an application whose database access is made entirely of BDE API calls, the preceding code provides a nice template from which to work should the need arise.

Accessing the BDE from Delphi Applications

A far more likely scenario is one in which you do almost all your database access by using Delphi's built-in components, but perform a few specialized functions by using direct BDE calls. The LiveQuery component, detailed in Chapter 26, "Building Your Own Database Components," illustrates this type of arrangement. It uses the `DBiQExecDirect` BDE function to execute a query in the `BeforeOpen` event of a `TTable` descendent. Listing 25.2 shows its source code.

Listing 25.2. The `LiveQuery` component uses the `DBiQExecDirect` BDE function.

```
{
LiveQuery Delphi Component

Supports editing of SQL server result sets through
the use of temporary views.  This allows any result
set to be updated that would be editable had the
user created it as a view on the back-end.  Any updates
that would be supported by the back-end against views
are therefore supported.

Written by Ken Henderson.

Copyright (c) 1995 by Ken Henderson.

A couple of caveats:

1)  This magic is performed through the use of temporary views, so

    a)  Since some platforms, like Sybase, don't support temporary' views,
            I have to construct a temp name and both create and drop the view.  I use
            the date and time to create a name, so name collisions with other users
            are remotely possible.  See the source code.  You can handle the exception
            that is raised, if this happens, and simply re-issue the Open -- it's up
            to you.

    b)  Your users will need permission to create views, obviously

    c)  Because it create views, the component is only usable on servers that
            support views, i.e. remote servers -- you can't use it with dBASE and
            Paradox tables.

On the positive side, you can:

1)  Use any syntax your server supports for updatable views, including:

    a)  as many tables as you want via joins

    b)  where and having clauses

This puts all the burden on the server, where, in my opinion, it belongs.
It also may mean that the SQL you execute will be compiled ahead of time,
which should make it execute more efficiently.  If your server doesn't
like an update you try to perform, obviously an exception will be raised.

}

unit Liveqry;

interface
```

```
uses
  SysUtils, WinTypes, WinProcs, Messages, Classes, Graphics, Controls,
  Forms, Dialogs, DB, DBTables, BDE;

const
  DEFAULTCREATEVIEWSQL = 'CREATE VIEW %s AS ';
  DEFAULTDROPVIEWSQL = 'DROP VIEW %s';
  DEFAULTTABLENAMEFORMAT = 'TV%s';

type
  TLiveQuery = class(TTable)
  private
    { Private declarations }
    FCreateViewSQL : String;
    FDropViewSQL : String;
    FTableNameFormat : TFileName;
    FSQL : TStrings;
    procedure SetQuery(Value: TStrings);
  protected
    { Protected declarations }
    procedure CreateTemporaryView;
    procedure DropTemporaryView;
    procedure DoBeforeOpen; override;
    procedure DoAfterClose; override;
  public
    { Public declarations }
    constructor Create(AOwner: TComponent); override;
    destructor Destroy; override;
  published
    { Published declarations }
    property CreateViewSQL : String read FCreateViewSQL write FCreateViewSQL;
    property DropViewSQL : String read FDropViewSQL write FDropViewSQL;
    property SQL : TStrings read FSQL write SetQuery;
    property TableNameFormat :
              TFileName read FTableNameFormat write FTableNameFormat;
  end;

procedure Register;

implementation

constructor TLiveQuery.Create(AOwner: TComponent);
begin
  inherited Create(AOwner);
  FSQL := TStringList.Create;
  FCreateViewSQL := DEFAULTCREATEVIEWSQL;
  FDropViewSQL := DEFAULTDROPVIEWSQL;
  FTableNameFormat := DefaultTableNameFormat;
end;

destructor TLiveQuery.Destroy;
begin
  If Active then begin
    Close;
    DropTemporaryView;
  end;
```

continues

Listing 25.2. continued

```
  SQL.Free;
  inherited Destroy;
end;

procedure TLiveQuery.SetQuery(Value: TStrings);
begin
  CheckInActive;
  SQL.Assign(Value);
end;

procedure TLiveQuery.CreateTemporaryView;
var
  TemporaryDB : TDatabase;
  WorkSQL : TStrings;
begin
  WorkSQL := TStringList.Create;
  WorkSQL.AddStrings(SQL);
  TableName:=Format(TableNameFormat,[FormatDateTime('yymmddhhnnss',Now)]);
  WorkSQL.Insert(0,Format(CreateViewSQL,[TableName]));
  TemporaryDB:=Session.OpenDatabase(DatabaseName);
  If (TemporaryDB<>nil) then
    try
      If (TemporaryDB.IsSQLBased) then begin
        If (DbiQExecDirect(TemporaryDB.Handle,qrylangSQL,
                           PChar(WorkSQL.Text),nil)<>DBIERR_NONE) then
          raise EDatabaseError.Create('Error creating temporary view');
      end else
        raise EDatabaseError.Create('Cannot use this component with local tables')
    finally
      Session.CloseDatabase(TemporaryDB);
      WorkSQL.Free;
    end;
end;

procedure TLiveQuery.DoBeforeOpen;
begin
  inherited DoBeforeOpen;
  CreateTemporaryView;
end;

procedure TLiveQuery.DropTemporaryView;
var
  TemporaryDB : TDatabase;
  WorkSQL : TStrings;
begin
  WorkSQL:=TStringList.Create;
  WorkSQL.Add(Format(DropViewSQL,[TableName]));
  TemporaryDB:=Session.OpenDatabase(DatabaseName);
  If (TemporaryDB<>nil) then begin
    try
      If (TemporaryDB.IsSQLBased) then begin
        If (DbiQExecDirect(TemporaryDB.Handle,qrylangSQL,
            PChar(WorkSQL.Text),nil)<>DBIERR_NONE) then
          raise EDatabaseError.Create('Error dropping temporary view');
      end else
```

```
        raise EDatabaseError.Create('Cannot use this component with local tables')

    finally
      Session.CloseDatabase(TemporaryDB);
      WorkSQL.Free;
    end;
  end;
end;

procedure TLiveQuery.DoAfterClose;
begin
  DropTemporaryView;
  inherited DoAfterClose;
end;

procedure Register;
begin
  RegisterComponents('Data Access', [TLiveQuery]);
end;

end.
```

Note the use of the DBiQExecDirect function. Once the routine has built the WorkSQL SQL statement, the next order of business is to execute it. Because you're using a Table component descendent, there is no immediate way of executing your own SQL. Were LiveQuery a descendent of the Query component, you'd have access to the ExecSQL routine, but this isn't the case. This is where DBiQExecDirect comes into play. A temporary hDBIDb is created and passed into the DbiQExecDirect function along with the contents of WorkSQL to execute the SQL query.

> **NOTE**
>
> If compatibility with Sybase were not a concern, LiveQuery's own DBHandle property could have been used in place of the temporary database connection that's created by the component. Sybase SQL Server prohibits the initiation of a new query while query results are pending, so using LiveQuery.Database.Handle with DBiQExecDirect is unwise in a Sybase environment.

Notice that the third parameter of the DbiQExecDirect function requires a PChar data type. Recall that PChar strings are Pascal's version of the char * string in C and C++. Beginning with Delphi 2.0, translating a Pascal-style string to a C/C++ one is as simple as typecasting it. Pascal strings are now terminated with a null character, so you don't have to be concerned with that, either. Additionally, Pascal strings also contain a length field. This saves you from having to scan the string for a null character to determine its length, as you must with C.

Making Native Calls to Your DBMS

The BDE also gives you access to the native connection handle for your particular DBMS. This enables you to make calls to functions in your DBMS vendor's client libraries, completely bypassing Delphi's database components and the BDE. You may find that, in certain circumstances, this improves performance dramatically, or that it affords you functionality missing from the BDE.

You use the DbiGetProp function to retrieve your DBMS vendor's native connection handle. Table 25.3 summarizes the type of information that is available for each platform.

Table 25.3. DBMS platform information returned by DbiGetProp.

Platform	Handle Type	Length
InterBase	gds_db_handle	4
Sybase	DBPROCESS NEAR *	2
Oracle	LDA	64
ODBC Socket	HDBC	4

The following code snippet contains some sample syntax you can use with the Sybase platform to retrieve the name of the current database:

```
type
  DBPROCESS = Pointer;

var
  Form1:  TForm1;
  DBProc: DBPROCESS;
  SizeDBProc: Word;

function dbname(DBProc: DBPROCESS) : PChar; external 'LIBSYBDB';

implementation

{$R *.DFM}

procedure TForm1.Button1Click(Sender: TObject);
begin
  DbiGetProp(hDBiObj(Table1.DBHandle),dbNATIVEHNDL,
            DBProc, SizeOf(DBProc), SizeDBProc);
  Edit1.Text:=dbname(DBProc);
end;
```

In this example, the DB-Library function dbname is referenced externally in the LIBSYBDB Dynamic Link Library. It requires a single parameter, the DBPROCESS handle of the current connection. This handle is retrieved by calling DbiGetProp and passing it the dbNATIVEHNDL parameter.

Retrieving Platform-Specific Info Using the BDE

If you intend to enable the user to build queries at runtime, you'll want to be able to list not only the tables and columns on the selected DBMS platform, but also the functions that the platform supports for querying data. You'll need to be able to display things like the platform's supported aggregates, the string, date and numeric functions it supports, and so on. The BDE provides a function that facilitates this called DbiOpenFunctionList. DbiOpenFunctionList opens a cursor into the list of functions supported by the associated DBMS platform. You can then call DBiGetNextRecord to retrieve each supported function name, one by one. Listings 25.3 through 25.5 show a simple Delphi program that uses DbiOpenFunctionList to list the table objects present on the current DBMS platform as well as the functions supported by the platform. The program presents a drop-down list of BDE alias that you can select and query for table and function information.

Listing 25.3. The project source file for the BDE DbiOpenFunctionList example program, FuncEx.

```
program FuncEx;

uses
  Forms,
  FuncEx00 in 'FuncEx00.pas' {Form1};

{$R *.RES}

begin
  Application.CreateForm(TForm1, Form1);
  Application.Run;
end.
```

Listing 25.4. The unit source file for FuncEx00.PAS, the only unit in the BDE DbiOpenFunctionList example program, FuncEx.

```
unit FuncEx00;

interface

uses
  Windows, Messages, SysUtils, Classes, Graphics, Controls, Forms, Dialogs,
  BDE, StdCtrls, DB, DBTables;

type
  TForm1 = class(TForm)
    Database1: TDatabase;
    ListBox1: TListBox;
    ComboBox1: TComboBox;
    ListBox2: TListBox;
    Label1: TLabel;
    Label2: TLabel;
```

continues

Listing 25.4. continued

```
    Label3: TLabel;
    procedure Button1Click(Sender: TObject);
    procedure FormCreate(Sender: TObject);
    procedure ComboBox1Change(Sender: TObject);
  private
    { Private declarations }
  public
    { Public declarations }
  end;

var
  Form1: TForm1;

implementation

{$R *.DFM}

procedure TForm1.Button1Click(Sender: TObject);

function Chk(ErrorValue : DBIResult) : DBIResult;
var
   dbi_status : string;
   dbi_string : string;
   ErrInfo : DBIErrInfo;
   count : integer;
begin
   dbi_status:='';
   dbi_string:='';
   if (ErrorValue <> DBIERR_NONE) then begin
      DbiGetErrorInfo(TRUE, ErrInfo);

      if (ErrInfo.iError = ErrorValue) then begin
      dbi_status:='  ERROR '+ ErrInfo.szErrCode;

      With ErrInfo do
        for count:=low(szContext) to high(szContext) do
           if (strcomp(ErrInfo.szContext[count], '')<>0) then
              dbi_status := dbi_status+'    '+ ErrInfo.szContext[count];
      end else begin
         SetLength(dbi_string, DBIMAXMSGLEN);
         DbiGetErrorString(ErrorValue, PChar(dbi_string));
         dbi_status := '  ERROR '+dbi_string;
      end;
      MessageBox(0, PChar(dbi_status), 'BDE Error', MB_OK or MB_ICONEXCLAMATION);
   end;
   result:=ErrorValue;
end;

var
  hCur : hDBiCur;
  FuncInfo : DBiFUNCDESC;
  counter : integer;
  Res : Word;
```

```
begin
  counter:=0;
  Chk(DbiOpenFunctionList(Database1.Handle, fnListINCL_USER_DEF, @hcur));
  if (hCur<>nil) then begin
    while (DBiGetNextRecord(hCur,dbinolock,@FuncInfo,nil)<>DBIERR_EOF)
    and (counter <50) do  begin
      ListBox1.Items.Add(FuncInfo.szName);
      inc(counter);
    end;
    DbiCloseCursor(hCur);
  end else  ShowMessage('Error opening cursor');
end;

procedure TForm1.FormCreate(Sender: TObject);
begin
  Session.GetDatabaseNames(ComboBox1.Items);
  ComboBox1.ItemIndex:=0;
end;

procedure TForm1.ComboBox1Change(Sender: TObject);
function Chk(ErrorValue : DBIResult) : DBIResult;
var
   dbi_status : string;
   dbi_string : string;
   ErrInfo : DBIErrInfo;
   count : integer;
begin
   dbi_status:='';
   dbi_string:='';
   if (ErrorValue <> DBIERR_NONE) then begin
      DbiGetErrorInfo(TRUE, ErrInfo);

      if (ErrInfo.iError = ErrorValue) then begin
      dbi_status:='  ERROR '+ ErrInfo.szErrCode;

      With ErrInfo do
        for count:=low(szContext) to high(szContext) do
           if (strcomp(ErrInfo.szContext[count], '')<>0) then
               dbi_status := dbi_status+'   '+ ErrInfo.szContext[count];
      end else begin
         SetLength(dbi_string, DBIMAXMSGLEN);
         DbiGetErrorString(ErrorValue, PChar(dbi_string));
         dbi_status := '  ERROR '+dbi_string;
      end;
      MessageBox(0, PChar(dbi_status), 'BDE Error', MB_OK or MB_ICONEXCLAMATION);
   end;
   result:=ErrorValue;
end;

var
  hCur : hDBiCur;
  FuncInfo : DBiFUNCDESC;
  Counter : integer;
```

continues

Listing 25.4. continued

```
begin
  With Database1 do begin
    Connected:=False;
    ListBox2.Items.Clear;
    AliasName:=ComboBox1.Items[ComboBox1.ItemIndex];
    Open;
   Session.GetTableNames(AliasName,'',False, False,ListBox1.Items);
  end;
  counter:=0;
  If (Chk(DbiOpenFunctionList(Database1.Handle, fnListINCL_USER_DEF, @hcur)) =
➥DBIERR_NONE) then begin
    if (hCur<>nil) then begin
      while (DBiGetNextRecord(hCur,dbinolock,@FuncInfo,nil)<>DBIERR_EOF)
      and (counter <50) do  begin
        ListBox2.Items.Add(FuncInfo.szName);
        inc(counter);
      end;
      DbiCloseCursor(hCur);
      ListBox2.Sorted:=True;
    end else  ShowMessage('Error opening cursor');
  end;
end;

end.
```

Listing 25.5. The form (.DFM) file for FuncEx00.PAS, the lone unit in the BDE DbiOpenFunctionList example program, FuncEx.

```
object Form1: TForm1
  Left = 200
  Top = 108
  Width = 435
  Height = 300
  Caption = 'Form1'
  Font.Color = clWindowText
  Font.Height = -11
  Font.Name = 'MS Sans Serif'
  Font.Style = []
  OnCreate = FormCreate
  PixelsPerInch = 96
  TextHeight = 13
  object Label1: TLabel
    Left = 33
    Top = 0
    Width = 36
    Height = 13
    Caption = 'Aliases:'
```

```
    end
    object Label2: TLabel
      Left = 32
      Top = 40
      Width = 35
      Height = 13
      Caption = 'Tables:'
    end
    object Label3: TLabel
      Left = 216
      Top = 40
      Width = 98
      Height = 13
      Caption = 'Supported functions:'
    end
    object ListBox1: TListBox
      Left = 32
      Top = 56
      Width = 177
      Height = 209
      ItemHeight = 13
      TabOrder = 0
    end
    object ComboBox1: TComboBox
      Left = 32
      Top = 14
      Width = 177
      Height = 21
      Style = csDropDownList
      ItemHeight = 13
      TabOrder = 1
      OnChange = ComboBox1Change
    end
    object ListBox2: TListBox
      Left = 216
      Top = 56
      Width = 177
      Height = 209
      ItemHeight = 13
      TabOrder = 2
    end
    object Database1: TDatabase
      AliasName = 'RENTMAN'
      DatabaseName = 'Database1'
      Params.Strings = (
        'USER NAME=testuser')
      SessionName = 'Default'
    end
end
```

Figure 25.1 shows the FuncEx application at runtime.

FIGURE 25.1.

The FuncEx application shows the available tables and functions on a DBMS platform.

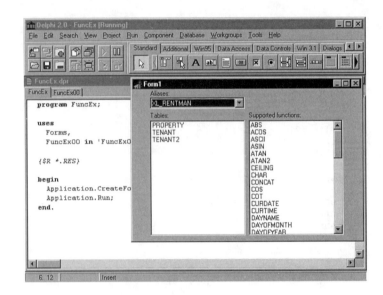

Expression Indexes

One of the neat things about the fact that the BDE supports dBASE's expression indexes is that you can make use of the expression evaluator used to process expression index keys in your own apps. This means that you can build an expression evaluator with the richness of dBASE indexes into your Delphi applications. Expressions evaluated by the mechanism would support all the operators and functions of dBASE's indexes. You might use an expression evaluator as a simple calculator or in some other capacity where you need complex expression evaluation.

The way you access the BDE expression evaluator is by creating an expression index over a dummy dBASE DBF table. To do this, create a dBASE table with a single row in it (structure doesn't matter), then set up an app to allow an expression to be entered. This expression doesn't have to have a thing to do with the table—we'll only use the table to create an index in order to evaluate the expression. When an expression is entered into your app, create an expression index over the table using the entered expression as its key. Next, switch the new index to be the table's current index and use the BDE DbiExtractKey function to return the raw (or evaluated) key value. You'll then have your evaluated expression. Here's a code fragment from an app that uses this technique:

```
procedure TForm1.Button1Click(Sender: TObject);
var
  IndexDesc : IDXDesc;
  KeyString : String;
```

```
begin
  With Table1 do begin
    If not Active then Open;
    AddIndex('EVAL2',Edit1.Text,[ixExpression]);
    Close;
    IndexName:='EVAL2';
    Open;
    DbiGetIndexDesc(Table1.Handle,0,IndexDesc);
    SetLength(KeyString,IndexDesc.iKeyLen);
    DbiExtractKey(Table1.Handle, nil, PChar(KeyString));
    Edit2.Text:=KeyString;
    Close;
    DeleteIndex('EVAL2');
    IndexName:='DUMMY';
  end;
end;
```

The key to all this is the DbiExtractKey routine; it returns the translated or evaluated key value from the index. This nifty facility enables you to add an interpreter-like expression evaluation facility to your compiled Delphi applications. Figure 25.2 illustrates an app that uses DbiExtract key to evaluate complex expressions.

FIGURE 25.2.

An app that includes an expression evaluation mechanism courtesy of the BDE DbiExtractKey function.

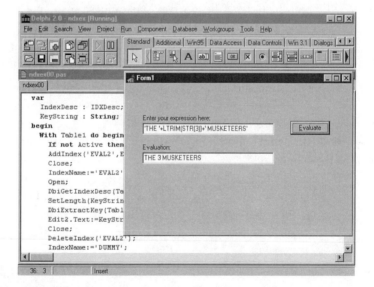

Optimizing the BDE

Optimizing the BDE can be a tricky process, but here are some general guidelines. There seems to be no "silver bullet," here—you may find that the engine is fast enough that you don't want or need to tune it:

■ Updates to data are slowed down by numerous secondary indexes. Limit them to just the ones you must have. You may find that it's actually faster to drop your indexes, insert your data, then rebuild the indexes.

- Opening a table exclusively speeds access to it because other users don't have to be taken into consideration.

- Avoid manipulating rows one at a time when possible. Use the BDE's batch operations instead.

- Try to work with multiples of the physical block size when working with the `DbiWriteBlock` function.

- You can use `DbiAcqPersistTableLock` on a dummy table to force the creation of the .LCK file so that it's not repetitively deleted and re-created as you open and close tables.

- Use in-memory tables for work tables rather than disk tables. Keep in mind that you can't index, batch copy, or save an in-memory table permanently.

Optimizing BDE for SQL Access

Optimzing SQL is covered more completely in Chapter 22, "Advanced SQL," and Chapter 23, "Optimizing Delphi Client/Server Applications," of this book. Here are some general tips on optimizing the BDE's SQL access:

- When making a series of updates to an SQL server, use explicit transactions so that an implicit one isn't started and committed with each modification.

- Set up complex queries and stored procedures to use PassThrough SQL. This causes the BDE to get your SQL to the server as quickly as possible and also enables you to use whatever SQL your back-end supports.

- Make native calls to your DBMS using the information provided by `DbiGetProps`, as mentioned previously.

- Make the first goal of a query to reduce its result set. Perform any grouping or joins after you've reduced the result set as much as possible. Perform as much of this work as possible on the server.

- In some cases, you may find that copying the results of a query to a local table is advantageous.

- `DbiAddFilter`, `DbiSetRange`, and `DbiSetFieldMap` help reduce the amount of data actually accessed. Anytime you can reduce the amount of raw data being processed, you're bound to speed up things. Note that all three of these facilities are supported directly by Delphi's DataSet controls.

- Creating a descending index on a table in which you frequently scroll backward can save the server a lot of time.

- You should avoid `DbiSetToEnd` and `DbiSetToKey` when you're in the middle of a large table or the table includes a composite index. Calling either of these at the wrong time can result in your application traversing sequentially through a huge number of rows in large tables.

What's Ahead

Chapter 26 takes you through the process of constructing database components to enhance Delphi and Delphi applications. You'll learn to build components ranging from the simple to the complex and you'll learn how they can be used in the applications you build with Delphi.

Summary

This chapter covers the BDE in sufficient detail so that you should have a greater appreciation for what goes on behind the scenes in Delphi's database components. You now have a new set of tools that you can put to good use when you need capabilities beyond the VCL.

26

Building Your Own Database Components

In this chapter, you'll learn the secrets of building your own Delphi database components. You'll learn the general approach to building components of any type, and you'll learn the specific nuances of constructing database components.

This book is not about authoring Delphi components. That subject could fill many volumes all by itself. The technical editor of this book Danny Thorpe, has written a book entitled *Delphi Component Design* that covers component development in-depth. I highly recommend it.

Despite the fact that this book isn't about component development, it's probably a safe bet that you'll eventually need to write a component or two. Real applications often demand them. Because most "real" Delphi applications will no doubt be database applications, I think a quick initiation into the black art of component authorship is appropriate here.

You'll build four separate database components in this chapter:

TArrayTable	A TTable descendent that treats its rows and columns as an array
TLiveQuery	A TTable descendent that provides better "live" query support than TQuery through server-based views
TDBNavSearch	A replacement for the DBNavigator component that features a search button
TZoomDlg	A dialog box that enables the allowable values for a field to be chosen from a second table

Each of these has its own characteristics and unique heritage. TArrayTable is a simple TTable descendent. TLiveQuery is a more-complex TTable descendent. TDBNavSearch is created by cloning, then modifying the DBNavigator source code. TZoomDlg is a nonvisual component that displays a form. They all have their own nuances, and each brings something different to the table as far as learning about component development is concerned.

The Four Basics of Component Construction

The four things you must do in order to construct a new Delphi component are:

1. Descend a new component from a member of Delphi's Visual Component Library (VCL) using the New Component option on the File menu.
2. Add new (or override inherited) methods and properties in the new component.
3. Code a Register procedure to register your component with Delphi's component palette.
4. Add the component to the component palette.

You can create new components manually or by using Delphi's Component Expert. Choosing the New Component option on Delphi's File menu invokes the expert. I recommend you use the Component Expert whenever possible. Unless you need to combine a number of components into a single unit, there's little reason not to use the expert to at least get you started.

TArrayTable

The TArrayTable component provides an array-like interface to a database table. This means that it enables you to address the records and fields in a table as though they were rows and columns in a two-dimensional array. This type of functionality is handy for building spreadsheet-like displays. For example, you could use TArrayTable in conjunction with Delphi's built-in TStringGrid component to roll your own DBGrid control. Rather than having to manually position yourself to the appropriate row in the DataSet, TArrayTable gives you the ability to refer to a table's records as though they were the first dimension of a two-dimensional array. Likewise, you can refer to the table's fields using a pseudo-array syntax that equates them to the array's second dimension.

To begin creating the TArrayTable component, choose New from the File menu and double-click the Component option. Key TArrayTable for the new component's Class Name, select TTable as its ancestor class, and set its Palette Page to Data Access. (See Figure 26.1.)

FIGURE 26.1.

The Component Expert's initial dialog box.

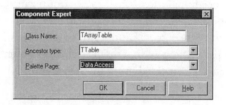

Click the OK button to exit the dialog. You'll notice that the Component Expert generates a unit for you containing the code definition of the new component. Go ahead and save the unit now as ArrTab.PAS. Listing 26.1 shows the unit as it originally appears.

Listing 26.1. Delphi's Component Expert generates a skeleton unit for you when you build a new component.

```
unit ArrTab;

interface

uses
  Windows, Messages, SysUtils, Classes, Graphics, Controls, Forms, Dialogs,
  DB, DBTables;

type
  TArrayTable = class(TTable)
  private
    { Private declarations }
  protected
    { Protected declarations }
  public
    { Public declarations }
```

continues

Listing 26.1. continued

```
published
  { Published declarations }
end;

procedure Register;

implementation

procedure Register;
begin
  RegisterComponents('Data Access', [TArrayTable]);
end;

end.
```

Notice the Register procedure. It lists the new component and names the page it will reside on. In order for a component to be installed on to Delphi's component palette, it must include a Register procedure. Note that this does not mean that the Register procedure must reside in the same source code unit as the component itself does. It's a common practice to gather the registration procedures for a number of components into a single "registration unit" that is used in their place when adding them to the component palette. For example, Delphi's built-in components are registered using the registration units located in the Lib directory.

You'll add just one new property, the Records property, to this new component. The Records property is a read only, runtime only property and provides access to the first dimension of the two-dimensional record/field array feigned by the component.

When a property is added to a component, a read and write method is also normally supplied for it. These methods enable you to store and retrieve the property's value from a more primitive class variable, but they also enable you to execute extra code when a property's value is queried or changed. Modify TArrayTable's class definition to match the following:

```
TArrayTable = class(TTable)
  private
    { Private declarations }
    function GetRecord(RecNum : Longint) : TDataSet;
  protected
    { Protected declarations }
  public
    { Public declarations }
    property Records[RecNum : Longint] : TDataSet read GetRecord;
  published
    { Published declarations }
  end;
```

As you can see, not much has been done to the class definition. The fact is that the changes necessary to provide the array interface you're after aren't very substantial. First, notice the addition of the GetRecord function to the class's private section. It's a standard practice to name the Read function for a property Get... followed by the name of the property. Likewise, the Write procedure for a property is normally named Set... followed by the property's name.

Next, notice the property definition itself. It's an indexed property. This means that when you access it, you specify an index value, much like you would with an array. Notice the way in which the link between the Records property and the GetRecord function is established. Simply put, you set up Read functions using the read keyword and Write functions using the write keyword. The index you specify when referencing the Records property is passed directly to its Read function, GetRecord, which then uses it to access the record you're after.

Notice the data type of the Records property; it's a TDataSet. You may be wondering why this is. It would seem logical that this should be some sort of TRecord class. Bear with me, and you'll see the reasoning behind this in a moment.

Now that you've modified the class definition, you're ready to construct the GetRecord function. This function will be called whenever you reference the Records property at runtime. Key the following definition for the GetRecord function:

```
function TArrayTable.GetRecord(RecNum : Longint) : TDataSet;
begin
  First;
  MoveBy(RecNum);
  Result:=Self;
end;
```

Note GetRecord's return type. Just like the Records property that it services, it, too, returns a result of type TDataSet. Why? Because Delphi's TField components don't reside within record classes of any sort. That is, Delphi's DataSets aren't composed of TRecord classes that must be interrogated to access field level information. On the contrary, Delphi's TField components can be accessed directly from the DataSet itself via its Fields property. The Fields property itself is an indexed property. This, in conjunction with the Records property, provides the basis for the pseudo-array interface to the DataSet provided by the component.

Notice the code that gets executed every time you query the Records property. The property sends the record number you've requested into the GetRecord function, which then does the following:

1. Positions to the first of the DataSet.

2. Moves a fixed number of rows from the top of the DataSet based on the record number you requested.

3. Returns a pointer to the TArrayTable itself as the function's result.

By first moving the record cursor, then returning a pointer to the DataSet itself, TArrayTable provides for the following syntax:

```
X:=ArrayTable1.Records[4].Fields[2].AsInteger;
```

See the array similarities? In a manner not unlike retrieving an array value, by using TArrayTable you're able to access any column in any row in the table.

Believe it or not, that's basically all there is to the TArrayTable component. Listing 26.2 shows the complete source for the new component.

Listing 26.2. The complete source for the TArrayTable component.

```
unit ArrTab;

interface

uses
  SysUtils, WinTypes, WinProcs, Messages, Classes, Graphics, Controls,
  Forms, Dialogs, DB, DBTables;

type
  TArrayTable = class(TTable)
  private
    { Private declarations }
    function GetRecord(RecNum : Longint) : TDataSet;
  protected
    { Protected declarations }
  public
    { Public declarations }
    property Records[RecNum : Longint] : TDataSet read GetRecord;
  published
    { Published declarations }
  end;

procedure Register;

implementation

function TArrayTable.GetRecord(RecNum : Longint) : TDataSet;
begin
  First;
  MoveBy(RecNum);
  Result:=Self;
end;

procedure Register;
begin
  RegisterComponents('Data Access', [TArrayTable]);
end;

end.
```

Now that you've finished the component, you're ready to install it on to Delphi's component palette. Save your work, then select Install from the Component menu. Figure 26.2 shows the Install Components dialog box.

FIGURE 26.2.

You use the Install Components dialog to add components to Delphi's component palette.

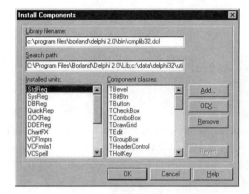

Click the Add button, then type in the full path to the ArrTab.PAS unit you created earlier and click OK. After you return to the Install Components dialog, click OK again to recompile Delphi's component library.

Using the Component in an Application

After the component is present on Delphi's component palette, you're ready to use it in an application. Click New Application on Delphi's File menu. Next, click the Data Access page in the component palette and select the `ArrayTable` component. It should be on the far right of the page and should have the same icon as the `Table` component. Drop the `ArrayTable` component on to the form. Notice it lists the same properties in the Delphi Object Inspector as the `Table` component. This is because it's a descendent of the Table component class and defines no new published properties of its own (only published properties show up in the Object Inspector). Next, drop a Button and a `StringGrid` onto the form. Double-click the button and change its event handler to look like the following:

```
procedure TForm1.Button1Click(Sender: TObject);
var
  RCount, FCount : Integer;
begin
  With ArrayTable1, StringGrid1 do begin
    ColCount:=Succ(FieldCount);
    RowCount:=Succ(RecordCount);

    Cells[0,0]:=TableName;

    For FCount:=0 to Pred(FieldCount) do
      Cells[Succ(Fcount),0]:=Fields[FCount].FieldName;

    for RCount:=1 to RecordCount do
      for FCount:=0 to Pred(FieldCount) do
        Cells[Succ(FCount),RCount]:=Records[RCount].Fields[FCount].AsString;
  end;
end;
```

As I mentioned earlier, by using the `ArrayTable` component in conjunction with a `StringGrid`, you can simulate a read-only `DBGrid` control fairly well.

Regarding the preceding code, first note the two assignment statements that begin the routine:

```
ColCount:=Succ(FieldCount);
RowCount:=Succ(RecordCount);
```

`ColCount` and `RowCount` are properties of the `StringGrid` component. By setting them respectively to the `FieldCount` and `RecordCount` properties of the `ArrayTable` component, you size the grid so that it can display all the table's rows and columns. Note the use of `Succ(FieldCount)` and `Succ(RecordCount)` here because you don't want to place any data in the grid's first column or first row.

The assignment

```
Cells[0,0]:=TableName;
```

places the `ArrayTable`'s `TableName` in the upper-left corner of the grid.

The first loop

```
For FCount:=0 to Pred(FieldCount) do
  Cells[Succ(Fcount),0]:=Fields[FCount].FieldName;
```

initializes the first row of the `StringGrid` with the names of the fields it will display. Notice that the name of each field is retrieved using its `FieldName` property.

The second loop

```
for RCount:=1 to RecordCount do
  for FCount:=0 to Pred(FieldCount) do
  Cells[Succ(FCount),RCount]:=Records[RCount].Fields[FCount].AsString;
```

uses the novelty of `TArrayTable`'s pseudo-array to reference the values in the table in numeric sequence.

Now that you've written the code for the `Button` component's `OnClick` event, you'll need to set the `ArrayTable` component's key properties. Click the `ArrayTable` component in the visual designer and set its `DatabaseName` and `TableName` properties so that they point to a valid database and table combination. In my code, I used the RENTMAN database and the WODETAIL table from Part II, "Tutorial." Next, double-click `ArrayTable`'s `Active` property to open it. Lastly, save your work and run the application. Figure 26.3 shows the test application at runtime.

When you click the button, `StringGrid` is populated with data and looks much the same as a `DBGrid` control whose `ReadOnly` property has been set.

FIGURE 26.3.

The `ArrayTable` *component can be used with the* `StringGrid` *to simulate a* `DBGrid` *component.*

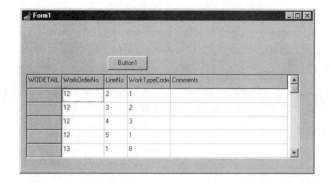

TLiveQuery

The `TLiveQuery` component class supplements the functionality provided by Delphi's *live* query facility. Live, or updatable, queries are normally created in Delphi by setting the `RequestLive` property of a `Query` component to `True`. The SQL that the component uses must comply with Delphi's restrictions on updatable queries. `LiveQuery` gets around these restrictions by turning the SQL you specify into a server-based view that it then opens like any other table. If your server allows updates to views, you should then be able to update the result set returned by `LiveQuery`.

Because `LiveQuery` creates its view by using the SQL `CREATE VIEW` syntax, your DBMS platform must support the `CREATE VIEW` statement in order for you to use the component. This means that you can't use `TLiveQuery` with local tables like dBASE and Paradox tables. On the positive side, every type of table view update that your database server supported is also supported against `TLiveQuery`'s because they are, in fact, views themselves.

`LiveQuery` takes the responsibility of decomposing complex queries away from the application and places it back on the server, where, in my opinion, it belongs. DBMS vendors are the best experts on their own SQL dialects, so it makes sense to allow them to dissect their own queries. In order for the result set associated with a query to be updated, its columns must be traced back to their roots. Each result set column must be reduced to the actual table and column name from where it came. The criteria used to select the result set rows must also be carefully inspected. Not only must the correct table columns be updated, but the right records must be extrapolated, as well. This can be rather difficult with elaborate queries involving calculated columns, multilevel joins, and complex `WHERE` and `HAVING` clauses. That's why I say it's better to leave this divination to the host database server. It knows its own SQL dialect and its own database objects best.

Begin by creating a new component named `TLiveQuery` that descends from the `TTable` class. Place it on the Data Access page as you did the `ArrayTable` component. After Delphi's Component Expert generates the source code to support your new component, save it as LiveQry.PAS.

You'll need to make several minor changes to the generated source code. You'll add four additional published properties plus their support code and class variables. Listing 26.3 shows the changes you need to make to the component's class definition.

Listing 26.3. The class definition for the `LiveQuery` component.

```
TLiveQuery = class(TTable)
  private
    { Private declarations }
    FCreateViewSQL : String;
    FDropViewSQL : String;
    FTableNameFormat : TFileName;
    FSQL : TStrings;
    procedure SetQuery(Value: TStrings);
  protected
    { Protected declarations }
    procedure CreateTemporaryView;
    procedure DropTemporaryView;
    procedure DoBeforeOpen; override;
    procedure DoAfterClose; override;
  public
    { Public declarations }
    constructor Create(AOwner: TComponent); override;
    destructor Destroy; override;
  published
    { Published declarations }
    property CreateViewSQL : String read FCreateViewSQL write FCreateViewSQL;
    property DropViewSQL : String read FDropViewSQL write FDropViewSQL;
    property SQL : TStrings read FSQL write SetQuery;
    property TableNameFormat :
             TFileName read FTableNameFormat write FTableNameFormat;
  end;
```

Note that you'll need to preface the class definition with a set of constant definitions that the component relies on. These are

```
const
  DEFAULTCREATEVIEWSQL = 'CREATE VIEW %s AS ';
  DEFAULTDROPVIEWSQL = 'DROP VIEW %s';
  DEFAULTTABLENAMEFORMAT = 'TV%s';
```

Note that you can't actually use these in the header of `TLiveQuery`'s class definition because Delphi supports only integer and set constants when defining default values for properties. That is, even though you would expect to be able to define the default value of the `TableNameFormat` property like this

```
property TableNameFormat : TFileName read FTableNameFormat
    write FTableNameFormat default DEFAULTTABLENAMEFORMAT;
```

you can't because Delphi doesn't support the use of string constants when defining default values for properties. Note that this default mechanism is used only by Delphi itself to determine whether you've set a property to other than its default value so that it can be written to disk if necessary. The actual assignment of default values to properties happens elsewhere, usually in a component's `Create` constructor.

CreateViewSQL

You use the `CreateViewSQL` property to specify the SQL `CREATE VIEW` syntax supported by your particular DBMS platform. The component defaults to using ANSI compatible syntax. Note the `%s` in the preceding `DEFAULTCREATEVIEWSQL` constant. The `%s` is a placeholder that Delphi's `Format` function replaces with the name of the temporary view generated by the component. This works much the same as the `sprintf()` function in C and C++.

DropViewSQL

The `DropViewSQL` property is the destructive counterpart of the `CreateViewSQL` property. It enables you to specify the `DROP VIEW` syntax supported by your database server's SQL dialect. Again, the `%s` in the `DEFAULTDROPVIEWSQL` constant is a placeholder that Delphi's `Format` function replaces with the name of the temporary view that is created by the component.

TableNameFormat

`TableNameFormat` enables you to specify any special formatting of the table view's name as required by your DBMS platform. Some DBMS platforms require that the name of an object's owner precede any reference to it. If you're working with a database server that has such requirements, you can use `TableNameFormat` to specify the required formatting.

After the class's header information is specified, you next need to supply its body. Listing 26.4 lists the implementation of the `LiveQuery` component.

Listing 26.4. The body of the `LiveQuery` component.

```
constructor TLiveQuery.Create(AOwner: TComponent);
begin
  inherited Create(AOwner);
  FSQL := TStringList.Create;
  FCreateViewSQL := DEFAULTCREATEVIEWSQL;
  FDropViewSQL := DEFAULTDROPVIEWSQL;
  FTableNameFormat := DefaultTableNameFormat;
end;

destructor TLiveQuery.Destroy;
begin
  If Active then begin
    Close;
```

continues

Listing 26.4. continued

```
    DropTemporaryView;
  end;
  SQL.Free;
  inherited Destroy;
end;

procedure TLiveQuery.SetQuery(Value: TStrings);
begin
  CheckInActive;
  SQL.Assign(Value);
end;

procedure TLiveQuery.CreateTemporaryView;
var
  TemporaryDB : TDatabase;
  WorkSQL : TStrings;
begin
  WorkSQL := TStringList.Create;
  WorkSQL.AddStrings(SQL);
  TableName:=Format(TableNameFormat,[FormatDateTime('yymmddhhnnss',Now)]);
  WorkSQL.Insert(0,Format(CreateViewSQL,[TableName]));
  TemporaryDB:=Session.OpenDatabase(DatabaseName);
  If (TemporaryDB<>nil) then
    try
      If (TemporaryDB.IsSQLBased) then begin
        If (DbiQExecDirect(TemporaryDB.Handle,qrylangSQL,
                            PChar(WorkSQL.Text),nil)<>DBIERR_NONE) then
          raise EDatabaseError.Create('Error creating temporary view');
      end else
        raise EDatabaseError.Create('Cannot use this component with local tables')
    finally
      Session.CloseDatabase(TemporaryDB);
      WorkSQL.Free;
    end;
end;

procedure TLiveQuery.DoBeforeOpen;
begin
  inherited DoBeforeOpen;
  CreateTemporaryView;
end;

procedure TLiveQuery.DropTemporaryView;
var
  TemporaryDB : TDatabase;
  WorkSQL : TStrings;
begin
  WorkSQL:=TStringList.Create;
  WorkSQL.Add(Format(DropViewSQL,[TableName]));
  TemporaryDB:=Session.OpenDatabase(DatabaseName);
  If (TemporaryDB<>nil) then begin
    try
      If (TemporaryDB.IsSQLBased) then begin
        If (DbiQExecDirect(TemporaryDB.Handle,qrylangSQL,
            PChar(WorkSQL.Text),nil)<>DBIERR_NONE) then
          raise EDatabaseError.Create('Error dropping temporary view');
      end else
```

```
        raise EDatabaseError.Create('Cannot use this component with local tables')
    finally
      Session.CloseDatabase(TemporaryDB);
      WorkSQL.Free;
    end;
  end;
end;

procedure TLiveQuery.DoAfterClose;
begin
  DropTemporaryView;
  inherited DoAfterClose;
end;

procedure Register;
begin
  RegisterComponents('Data Access', [TLiveQuery]);
end;
```

The Constructor

This section will discuss each element of the implementation individually. First, look at the component's constructor:

```
constructor TLiveQuery.Create(AOwner: TComponent);
begin
  inherited Create(AOwner);
  FSQL := TStringList.Create;
  FCreateViewSQL := DefaultCreateViewSQL;
  FDropViewSQL := DefaultDropViewSQL;
  FTableNameFormat := DefaultTableNameFormat;
end;
```

The first thing it does is call the Create constructor of its ancestor, TTable. It does this by using the inherited keyword. The line

```
inherited Create(AOwner);
```

calls TTable's Create constructor and passes it the AOwner component parameter that was originally passed to TLiveQuery.

Next, the constructor instantiates a TStringList object and assigns it to the FSQL private class variable. This private class variable will store the value of the SQL property that you use to specify your live query's SQL statement.

The next three statements take the string constants that you defined earlier and assign them to the private class variables that correspond to properties the component publishes. A component's Create constructor is the best place to assign default values for its properties. Don't be fooled by the Default syntax support in the class's type definition. This only establishes a means for Delphi's component streaming mechanism to determine whether you've changed a property's default value so that it can store it to disk if necessary. The actual assignment of a property's default value happens in its component's `Create` constructor.

The Destructor

The next procedure in `LiveQuery`'s implementation is its destructor. It looks like this:

```
destructor TLiveQuery.Destroy;
begin
  If Active then begin
    Close;
    DropTemporaryView;
  end;
  SQL.Free;
  inherited Destroy;
end;
```

The destructor is called whenever the component needs to be destroyed. First, the destructor closes the component's database cursor, if it's still open, and drops the temporary view. Then it finishes up by freeing the `TStrings` object created for the SQL property and calling the destructor of its ancestor, `Ttable`.

SetQuery

The next routine is the `Set...` procedure for the SQL property, `SetQuery`. It looks like this:

```
procedure TLiveQuery.SetQuery(Value: TStrings);
begin
  CheckInActive;
  SQL.Assign(Value);
end;
```

The first thing `SetQuery` does is call its inherited `CheckInActive` routine. `CheckInActive` is used to ensure that a DataSet is inactive before making a change to it that affects its data link. If the component isn't inactive, an exception is raised, causing the operation to abort.

The last thing the routine does is call the SQL property's `Assign` method. The `Assign` method of the `TStrings` class copies the contents of one `TStrings` object to another. In this case, it copies the value you type in Delphi's Object Inspector to the SQL property.

CreateTemporaryView

The `CreateTemporaryView` method is next in the body of the `LiveQuery` component. The routine does exactly what its name suggests: It creates the table view on your database server that becomes the `LiveQuery` component's DataSet. The view is temporary in that it will be deleted when the component is closed or destroyed. There are several interesting elements of the `CreateTemporaryView` method procedure. Take a look at its source code:

```
procedure TLiveQuery.CreateTemporaryView;
var
  TemporaryDB : TDatabase;
  WorkSQL : TStrings;
begin
  WorkSQL := TStringList.Create;
  WorkSQL.AddStrings(SQL);
  TableName:=Format(TableNameFormat,[FormatDateTime('yymmddhhnnss',Now)]);
  WorkSQL.Insert(0,Format(CreateViewSQL,[TableName]));
  TemporaryDB:=Session.OpenDatabase(DatabaseName);
  If (TemporaryDB<>nil) then
    try
      try
        If (TemporaryDB.IsSQLBased) then begin
          If (DbiQExecDirect(TemporaryDB.Handle,qrylangSQL,
                             PChar(WorkSQL.Text),nil)<>DBIERR_NONE) then
            raise EDatabaseError.Create('Error creating temporary view');
        end else
          raise EDatabaseError.Create('Cannot use this component with local tables')
      finally
        Session.CloseDatabase(TemporaryDB);
      end;
    finally
      WorkSQL.Free;
    end;
end;
```

The first thing to note about `CreateTemporaryView` is that it creates a scratch area, `WorkSQL`, where it manipulates the query contained in the SQL property. It creates this area when the procedure begins, and it uses a `Try...Finally` block to ensure that it gets destroyed when it's no longer needed.

Next, it assigns the inherited `TableName` property using Delphi's `Format` function, the `TableNameFormat` property specified in the component, and the current date and time. Unfortunately, `TableName` is still a published property in the `LiveQuery` component; however, unlike the `Table` component, there is no purpose in enabling the user to specify it, and doing so does nothing. The reason `TableName` remains a published property in the `LiveQuery` component is that Delphi doesn't enable you to "unpublish" component properties. You can promote a public property to a published one, but you cannot demote a published property to a public one.

After a `TableName` is derived, the routine again uses the `Format` function to paste a `CREATE VIEW` statement onto the top of your SQL query using the `CreateViewSQL` property. This is where `LiveQuery`'s magic is performed; it simply turns any SQL query you give it into a `CREATE VIEW` statement that your server must then decide how to handle. That is, first and foremost, the syntax must be supported by your server; you must be allowed to use the type of query you supply in the SQL property from within views. Second, if you intend to update the view, your server must support updatable views (most do), and it must allow views using the SQL syntax you've specified to be updated. The burden of dissecting the query and updating the property columns and rows is placed squarely on the server, not the application or BDE.

After the WorkSQL SQL statement is built, the next order of business is to execute it. Because you're using a Table component descendent, there is no immediate way of executing your own SQL. If LiveQuery were a descendent of the Query component, you would have access to the ExecSQL routine, but this isn't the case. LiveQuery addresses this by creating its own pipe into the database server and by using the BDE function DbiQExecDirect to execute the SQL query (contained in WorkSQL) that creates the temporary view.

Notice the third parameter of the DbiQExecDirect function. Since it requires a PChar variable to be passed into it, you can simply typecast the Text property of the WorkSQL object as a PChar. Delphi's compiler handles the conversion.

Note the use of the IsSQLBased property of the temporary Database component. As I said earlier, this component can't be used with local DBMSs that don't support views like dBASE and Paradox, so it's imperative that the component checks for this and raises an exception, if necessary.

The routine finishes up by closing the temporary database connection and freeing the scratch area from memory. Note that it does both of these inside the finally section of a try...finally block. By placing code inside the finally section, you ensure that it gets executed even if an exception is raised by the code that follows the try keyword.

DoBeforeOpen

The DoBeforeOpen method performs a very simple function: It overrides the default DeBeforeOpen routine and sets up the creation of the temporary view when the component's Open method is called. Because CreateTemporaryView also assigns the component's TableName property, this has the effect of creating and assigning the view just prior to opening it like any other table. Note that DoBeforeOpen calls its ancestor's DoBeforeOpen routine before it does anything. This has the effect of executing any code the user has tied to the BeforeOpen event in the component prior to creating the temporary view.

DropTemporaryView

The next method in LiveQuery's implementation is the DropTemporaryView routine. As the name suggests, it drops the view created by the CreateTemporaryView method. As with its counterpart, DropTemporaryView uses a temporary database connection and a call to the DbiQExecDirect routine to execute an SQL query that drops the view.

DoAfterClose

DoAfterClose executes after the component is closed and is responsible for calling DropTemporaryView to delete the view created earlier. Note that DoAfterClose calls the inherited DoAfterClose method, which has the effect of executing any code that the user has attached to the component's AfterClose event.

Other than the registration procedure, that about wraps it up for the LiveQuery component. Listing 26.5 shows the complete source code.

Listing 26.5. The LiveQuery source code.

```
{
LiveQuery Delphi Component

Supports editing of SQL server result sets through
the use of temporary views.  This allows any result
set to be updated that would be editable had the
user created it as a view on the back-end.  Any updates
that would be supported by the back-end against views
are therefore supported.

Written by Ken Henderson.

Copyright (c) 1995 by Ken Henderson.

A couple of caveats:

1)  This magic is performed through the use of temporary views, so

  a)  Since some platforms, like Sybase, don't support temporary' views,
        I have to construct a temp name and both create and drop the view.  I use
        the date and time to create a name, so name collisions with other users
        are remotely possible.  See the source code.  You can handle the exception
        that is raised, if this happens, and simply re-issue the Open -- it's up
        to you.

  b)  Your users will need permission to create views, obviously

  c)  Because it create views, the component is only usable on servers that
        support views, i.e. remote servers — you can't use it with dBase and
        Paradox tables.

On the positive side, you can:

1)  Use any syntax your server supports for updatable views, including:

  a)  as many tables as you want via joins

  b)  where and having clauses

This puts all the burden on the server, where, in my opinion, it belongs.
It also may mean that the SQL you execute will be compiled ahead of time,
which should make it execute more efficiently.  If your server doesn't
like an update you try to perform, obviously an exception will be raised.

}

unit Liveqry;

interface
```

continues

Listing 26.5. continued

```
uses
  SysUtils, WinTypes, WinProcs, Messages, Classes, Graphics, Controls,
  Forms, Dialogs, DB, DBTables, BDE;

const
  DEFAULTCREATEVIEWSQL = 'CREATE VIEW %s AS ';
  DEFAULTDROPVIEWSQL = 'DROP VIEW %s';
  DEFAULTTABLENAMEFORMAT = 'TV%s';

type
  TLiveQuery = class(TTable)
  private
    { Private declarations }
    FCreateViewSQL : String;
    FDropViewSQL : String;
    FTableNameFormat : TFileName;
    FSQL : TStrings;
    procedure SetQuery(Value: TStrings);
  protected
    { Protected declarations }
    procedure CreateTemporaryView;
    procedure DropTemporaryView;
    procedure DoBeforeOpen; override;
    procedure DoAfterClose; override;
  public
    { Public declarations }
    constructor Create(AOwner: TComponent); override;
    destructor Destroy; override;
  published
    { Published declarations }
    property CreateViewSQL : String read FCreateViewSQL write FCreateViewSQL;
    property DropViewSQL : String read FDropViewSQL write FDropViewSQL;
    property SQL : TStrings read FSQL write SetQuery;
    property TableNameFormat :
             TFileName read FTableNameFormat write FTableNameFormat;
  end;

procedure Register;

implementation

constructor TLiveQuery.Create(AOwner: TComponent);
begin
  inherited Create(AOwner);
  FSQL := TStringList.Create;
  FCreateViewSQL := DEFAULTCREATEVIEWSQL;
  FDropViewSQL := DEFAULTDROPVIEWSQL;
  FTableNameFormat := DefaultTableNameFormat;
end;

destructor TLiveQuery.Destroy;
begin
  If Active then begin
    Close;
    DropTemporaryView;
  end;
```

```
  SQL.Free;
  inherited Destroy;
end;

procedure TLiveQuery.SetQuery(Value: TStrings);
begin
  CheckInActive;
  SQL.Assign(Value);
end;

procedure TLiveQuery.CreateTemporaryView;
var
  TemporaryDB : TDatabase;
  WorkSQL : TStrings;
begin
  WorkSQL := TStringList.Create;
  WorkSQL.AddStrings(SQL);
  TableName:=Format(TableNameFormat,[FormatDateTime('yymmddhhnnss',Now)]);
  WorkSQL.Insert(0,Format(CreateViewSQL,[TableName]));
  TemporaryDB:=Session.OpenDatabase(DatabaseName);
  If (TemporaryDB<>nil) then
    try
      If (TemporaryDB.IsSQLBased) then begin
        If (DbiQExecDirect(TemporaryDB.Handle,qrylangSQL,
                          PChar(WorkSQL.Text),nil)<>DBIERR_NONE) then
            raise EDatabaseError.Create('Error creating temporary view');
      end else
        raise EDatabaseError.Create('Cannot use this component with local tables')
    finally
      Session.CloseDatabase(TemporaryDB);
      WorkSQL.Free;
    end;
end;

procedure TLiveQuery.DoBeforeOpen;
begin
  inherited DoBeforeOpen;
  CreateTemporaryView;
end;

procedure TLiveQuery.DropTemporaryView;
var
  TemporaryDB : TDatabase;
  WorkSQL : TStrings;
begin
  WorkSQL:=TStringList.Create;
  WorkSQL.Add(Format(DropViewSQL,[TableName]));
  TemporaryDB:=Session.OpenDatabase(DatabaseName);
  If (TemporaryDB<>nil) then begin
    try
      If (TemporaryDB.IsSQLBased) then begin
        If (DbiQExecDirect(TemporaryDB.Handle,qrylangSQL,
            PChar(WorkSQL.Text),nil)<>DBIERR_NONE) then
          raise EDatabaseError.Create('Error dropping temporary view');
      end else
        raise EDatabaseError.Create('Cannot use this component with local tables')
```

continues

Listing 26.5. continued

```
    finally
      Session.CloseDatabase(TemporaryDB);
      WorkSQL.Free;
    end;
  end;
end;

procedure TLiveQuery.DoAfterClose;
begin
  DropTemporaryView;
  inherited DoAfterClose;
end;

procedure Register;
begin
  RegisterComponents('Data Access', [TLiveQuery]);
end;

end.
```

TDBNavSearch

The DBNavSearch component is a clone of the DBNavigator component that incorporates a search button into the speed button set presented by DBNavigator. Because of the way that Borland has implemented DBNavigator, it's not possible to simply inherit from it and create a new component that includes a search button. On the contrary, the source code to DBNavigator must be duplicated and modified to allow for the new button. If you have the Delphi VCL source code, you should find the source to DBNavigator in the DBCtrls.PAS file in the Source\VCL subdirectory under your Delphi directory. The changes to the original DBNavigator source are too numerous to list individually, so I'll first list the entirety of the modified source and then discuss the necessary changes in general terms. Listing 26.6 shows the source to DBNavSearch.

Listing 26.6. The complete source code to DBNavSearch.

```
{*********************************************************}
{                                                        }
{        Delphi Visual Component Library                 }
{                                                        }
{        Copyright (c) 1995 Borland International        }
{                                                        }
{*********************************************************}
{
DBNavSearch Delphi Component

Enhances the standard DBNavigator component by adding a search button to
it.  This button allows a table to be scanned using the key fields of its
current index.  A second unit, DBSearch, contains the search form that
DBNavSearch instantiates when the button is clicked.
```

```
Written by Ken Henderson.
Original code written and copyrighted by Borland International, Inc.
Modifications by Ken Henderson.
Copyright (c) 1995 by Ken Henderson.
}

unit DBNavSch;

interface

uses SysUtils, Windows, Messages, Classes, Controls, Forms,
  Graphics, Menus, StdCtrls, ExtCtrls, DB, DBTables, Mask, Buttons, DBCtrls,
  DBSearch;

type
  TNavButton = class;
  TNavDataLink = class;

  TNavGlyph = (ngEnabled, ngDisabled);
  TNavigateBtn = (nbFirst, nbPrior, nbNext, nbLast,
                    nbInsert, nbDelete, nbEdit, nbPost, nbCancel, nbRefresh,
                    nbSearch);
  TButtonSet = set of TNavigateBtn;
  TNavButtonStyle = set of (nsAllowTimer, nsFocusRect);

  ENavClick = procedure (Sender: TObject; Button: TNavigateBtn) of object;

{ TDBNavSearch }

  TDBNavSearch = class (TCustomPanel)
  private
    FDataLink: TNavDataLink;
    FVisibleButtons: TButtonSet;
    FHints: TStrings;
    ButtonWidth: Integer;
    MinBtnSize: TPoint;
    FOnNavClick: ENavClick;
    FocusedButton: TNavigateBtn;
    FConfirmDelete: Boolean;
    function GetDataSource: TDataSource;
    procedure SetDataSource(Value: TDataSource);
    procedure InitButtons;
    procedure InitHints;
    procedure Click(Sender: TObject);
    procedure BtnMouseDown (Sender: TObject; Button: TMouseButton;
      Shift: TShiftState; X, Y: Integer);
    procedure SetVisible(Value: TButtonSet);
    procedure AdjustSize (var W: Integer; var H: Integer);
    procedure SetHints(Value: TStrings);
    procedure WMSize(var Message: TWMSize);   message WM_SIZE;
    procedure WMSetFocus(var Message: TWMSetFocus); message WM_SETFOCUS;
    procedure WMKillFocus(var Message: TWMKillFocus); message WM_KILLFOCUS;
    procedure WMGetDlgCode(var Message: TWMGetDlgCode); message WM_GETDLGCODE;
    procedure CMEnabledChanged(var Message: TMessage); message CM_ENABLEDCHANGED;
```

continues

Listing 26.6. continued

```
protected
  Buttons: array[TNavigateBtn] of TNavButton;
  procedure DataChanged;
  procedure EditingChanged;
  procedure ActiveChanged;
  procedure Loaded; override;
  procedure KeyDown(var Key: Word; Shift: TShiftState); override;
  procedure Notification(AComponent: TComponent;
    Operation: TOperation); override;
  procedure GetChildren(Proc: TGetChildProc); override;
public
  constructor Create(AOwner: TComponent); override;
  destructor Destroy; override;
  procedure SetBounds(ALeft, ATop, AWidth, AHeight: Integer); override;
  procedure BtnClick(Index: TNavigateBtn);
published
  property DataSource: TDataSource read GetDataSource write SetDataSource;
  property VisibleButtons: TButtonSet read FVisibleButtons write SetVisible
    default [nbFirst, nbPrior, nbNext, nbLast, nbInsert, nbDelete,
      nbEdit, nbPost, nbCancel, nbRefresh, nbSearch];
  property Align;
  property DragCursor;
  property DragMode;
  property Enabled;
  property Ctl3D;
  property Hints: TStrings read FHints write SetHints;
  property ParentCtl3D;
  property ParentShowHint;
  property PopupMenu;
  property ConfirmDelete: Boolean read FConfirmDelete write FConfirmDelete
➥default True;
  property ShowHint;
  property TabOrder;
  property TabStop;
  property Visible;
  property OnClick: ENavClick read FOnNavClick write FOnNavClick;
  property OnDblClick;
  property OnDragDrop;
  property OnDragOver;
  property OnEndDrag;
  property OnEnter;
  property OnExit;
  property OnResize;
  property OnStartDrag;
end;

{ TNavButton }

  TNavButton = class(TSpeedButton)
  private
    FIndex: TNavigateBtn;
    FNavStyle: TNavButtonStyle;
    FRepeatTimer: TTimer;
    procedure TimerExpired(Sender: TObject);
```

```
  protected
    procedure Paint; override;
    procedure MouseDown(Button: TMouseButton; Shift: TShiftState;
      X, Y: Integer); override;
    procedure MouseUp(Button: TMouseButton; Shift: TShiftState;
      X, Y: Integer); override;
  public
    destructor Destroy; override;
    property NavStyle: TNavButtonStyle read FNavStyle write FNavStyle;
    property Index : TNavigateBtn read FIndex write FIndex;
  end;

{ TNavDataLink }

  TNavDataLink = class(TDataLink)
  private
    FNavigator: TDBNavSearch;
  protected
    procedure EditingChanged; override;
    procedure DataSetChanged; override;
    procedure ActiveChanged; override;
  public
    constructor Create(ANav: TDBNavSearch);
    destructor Destroy; override;
  end;

procedure Register;

implementation

uses BDE, Clipbrd, DBConsts, Dialogs;

{$R DBNAV}

{ TDBNavSearch }

const
  SSearchRecord = 65535;
  BtnStateName: array[TNavGlyph] of PChar = ('EN', 'DI');
  BtnTypeName: array[TNavigateBtn] of PChar = ('FIRST', 'PRIOR', 'NEXT',
    'LAST', 'INSERT', 'DELETE', 'EDIT', 'POST', 'CANCEL', 'REFRESH', 'SEARCH');
  BtnHintId: array[TNavigateBtn] of Word = (SFirstRecord, SPriorRecord,
    SNextRecord, SLastRecord, SInsertRecord, SDeleteRecord, SEditRecord,
    SPostEdit, SCancelEdit, SRefreshRecord, SSearchRecord);

constructor TDBNavSearch.Create(AOwner: TComponent);
begin
  inherited Create(AOwner);
  ControlStyle := ControlStyle - [csAcceptsControls, csSetCaption] + [csOpaque];
  if not NewStyleControls then ControlStyle := ControlStyle + [csFramed];
  FDataLink := TNavDataLink.Create(Self);
  FVisibleButtons := [nbFirst, nbPrior, nbNext, nbLast, nbInsert,
    nbDelete, nbEdit, nbPost, nbCancel, nbRefresh, nbSearch];
  FHints := TStringList.Create;
  InitButtons;
  BevelOuter := bvNone;
```

continues

Listing 26.6. continued

```
  BevelInner := bvNone;
  Width := 241;
  Height := 25;
  ButtonWidth := 0;
  FocusedButton := nbFirst;
  FConfirmDelete := True;
end;

destructor TDBNavSearch.Destroy;
begin
  FDataLink.Free;
  FDataLink := nil;
  inherited Destroy;
end;

procedure TDBNavSearch.InitButtons;
var
  I: TNavigateBtn;
  Btn: TNavButton;
  X: Integer;
  ResName: string;
begin
  MinBtnSize := Point(20, 18);
  X := 0;
  for I := Low(Buttons) to High(Buttons) do
  begin
    Btn := TNavButton.Create (Self);
    Btn.Index := I;
    Btn.Visible := I in FVisibleButtons;
    Btn.Enabled := True;
    Btn.SetBounds (X, 0, MinBtnSize.X, MinBtnSize.Y);
    FmtStr(ResName, 'dbn_%s', [BtnTypeName[I]]);
    Btn.Glyph.Handle := LoadBitmap(HInstance, PChar(ResName));
    Btn.NumGlyphs := 2;
    Btn.Enabled := False;   {!!! Force creation of speedbutton images !!!}
    Btn.Enabled := True;
    Btn.OnClick := Click;
    Btn.OnMouseDown := BtnMouseDown;
    Btn.Parent := Self;
    Buttons[I] := Btn;
    X := X + MinBtnSize.X;
  end;
  InitHints;
  Buttons[nbPrior].NavStyle := Buttons[nbPrior].NavStyle + [nsAllowTimer];
  Buttons[nbNext].NavStyle  := Buttons[nbNext].NavStyle + [nsAllowTimer];
end;

procedure TDBNavSearch.InitHints;
var
  I: Integer;
  J: TNavigateBtn;
begin
  for J := Low(Buttons) to High(Buttons) do
    Buttons[J].Hint := LoadStr (BtnHintId[J]);
  J := Low(Buttons);
  for I := 0 to (FHints.Count - 1) do
```

```
  begin
    if FHints.Strings[I] <> '' then Buttons[J].Hint := FHints.Strings[I];
    if J = High(Buttons) then Exit;
    Inc(J);
  end;
end;

procedure TDBNavSearch.SetHints(Value: TStrings);
begin
  FHints.Assign(Value);
  InitHints;
end;

procedure TDBNavSearch.GetChildren(Proc: TGetChildProc);
begin
end;

procedure TDBNavSearch.Notification(AComponent: TComponent;
  Operation: TOperation);
begin
  inherited Notification(AComponent, Operation);
  if (Operation = opRemove) and (FDataLink <> nil) and
    (AComponent = DataSource) then DataSource := nil;
end;

procedure TDBNavSearch.SetVisible(Value: TButtonSet);
var
  I: TNavigateBtn;
  W, H: Integer;
begin
  W := Width;
  H := Height;
  FVisibleButtons := Value;
  for I := Low(Buttons) to High(Buttons) do
    Buttons[I].Visible := I in FVisibleButtons;
  AdjustSize (W, H);
  if (W <> Width) or (H <> Height) then
    inherited SetBounds (Left, Top, W, H);
  Invalidate;
end;

procedure TDBNavSearch.AdjustSize (var W: Integer; var H: Integer);
var
  Count: Integer;
  MinW: Integer;
  I: TNavigateBtn;
  Space, Temp, Remain: Integer;
  X: Integer;
begin
  if (csLoading in ComponentState) then Exit;
  if Buttons[nbFirst] = nil then Exit;

  Count := 0;
  for I := Low(Buttons) to High(Buttons) do
  begin
    if Buttons[I].Visible then
```

continues

Listing 26.6. continued

```
    begin
      Inc(Count);
    end;
  end;
  if Count = 0 then Inc(Count);

  MinW := Count * MinBtnSize.X;
  if W < MinW then W := MinW;
  if H < MinBtnSize.Y then H := MinBtnSize.Y;

  ButtonWidth := W div Count;
  Temp := Count * ButtonWidth;
  if Align = alNone then W := Temp;

  X := 0;
  Remain := W - Temp;
  Temp := Count div 2;
  for I := Low(Buttons) to High(Buttons) do
  begin
    if Buttons[I].Visible then
    begin
      Space := 0;
      if Remain <> 0 then
      begin
        Dec(Temp, Remain);
        if Temp < 0 then
        begin
          Inc(Temp, Count);
          Space := 1;
        end;
      end;
      Buttons[I].SetBounds(X, 0, ButtonWidth + Space, Height);
      Inc(X, ButtonWidth + Space);
    end
    else
      Buttons[I].SetBounds (Width + 1, 0, ButtonWidth, Height);
  end;
end;

procedure TDBNavSearch.SetBounds(ALeft, ATop, AWidth, AHeight: Integer);
var
  W, H: Integer;
begin
  W := AWidth;
  H := AHeight;
  AdjustSize (W, H);
  inherited SetBounds (ALeft, ATop, W, H);
end;

procedure TDBNavSearch.WMSize(var Message: TWMSize);
var
  W, H: Integer;
begin
  inherited;

  { check for minimum size }
```

```
    W := Width;
    H := Height;
    AdjustSize (W, H);
    if (W <> Width) or (H <> Height) then
      inherited SetBounds(Left, Top, W, H);
    Message.Result := 0;
end;

procedure TDBNavSearch.Click(Sender: TObject);
begin
  BtnClick (TNavButton (Sender).Index);
end;

procedure TDBNavSearch.BtnMouseDown(Sender: TObject; Button: TMouseButton;
  Shift: TShiftState; X, Y: Integer);
var
  OldFocus: TNavigateBtn;
begin
  OldFocus := FocusedButton;
  FocusedButton := TNavButton (Sender).Index;
  if TabStop and (GetFocus <> Handle) and CanFocus then
  begin
    SetFocus;
    if (GetFocus <> Handle) then
      Exit;
  end
  else if TabStop and (GetFocus = Handle) and (OldFocus <> FocusedButton) then
  begin
    Buttons[OldFocus].Invalidate;
    Buttons[FocusedButton].Invalidate;
  end;
end;

procedure TDBNavSearch.BtnClick(Index: TNavigateBtn);
const
  MaxKey = 15;
  FldHeight = 30;
var
  c : Byte;
  Labels : Array[0..MaxKey] of TLabel;
  DBEdits : Array[0..MaxKey] of TDBEdit;
  Ruler : String;
  WidestLabelWidth, FieldWidth : Byte;
begin
  if (DataSource <> nil) and (DataSource.State <> dsInactive) then
  begin
    with DataSource.DataSet do
    begin
      case Index of
        nbPrior: Prior;
        nbNext: Next;
        nbFirst: First;
        nbLast: Last;
        nbInsert: Insert;
        nbEdit: Edit;
        nbCancel: Cancel;
```

continues

Listing 26.6. continued

```
        nbPost: Post;
        nbRefresh: Refresh;
        nbDelete:
          if not FConfirmDelete or
            (MessageDlg(LoadStr(SDeleteRecordQuestion), mtConfirmation,
            mbOKCancel, 0) <> idCancel) then Delete;
        nbSearch: begin
          WidestLabelWidth:=0;
          SearchForm:=TSearchForm.Create(Self);
          try
            With FDataLink.DataSet as TTable do begin
              for c:=0 to IndexFieldCount-1 do begin
                Labels[c]:=TLabel.Create(SearchForm.ScrollBox1);
                Labels[c].Parent:=SearchForm.ScrollBox1;
                Labels[c].AutoSize:=True;
                Labels[c].Caption:=IndexFields[c].FieldName;
                If (c<>0) then Labels[c].Top:=Labels[Pred(c)].Top+FldHeight
                else Labels[c].Top:=2;
                Labels[c].Left:=2;
                If (Labels[c].Width>WidestLabelWidth) then
                  WidestLabelWidth:=Labels[c].Width;
              end;

              {Use two separate loops so that the widest label can be
               detected and allowed for.}
              for c:=0 to IndexFieldCount-1 do begin
                DBEdits[c]:=TDBEdit.Create(SearchForm.ScrollBox1);
                DBEdits[c].Parent:=SearchForm.ScrollBox1;
                DBEdits[c].DataSource:=Self.DataSource;
                DBEdits[c].DataField:=IndexFields[c].FieldName;

                FieldWidth:=IndexFields[c].DisplayWidth+2;
                SetLength(Ruler,FieldWidth);
                FillChar(Ruler[1],FieldWidth,'M');
                DBEdits[c].Width:=Canvas.TextWidth(Ruler);

                If (c<>0) then DBEdits[c].Top:=DBEdits[Pred(c)].Top+FldHeight
                else DBEdits[c].Top:=2;
                DBEdits[c].Left:=WidestLabelWidth+5;
              end;
              SetKey;
              If (SearchForm.ShowModal=mrOK) then begin
                {I don't test the return value of GotoKey because
                 GotoNearest is a procedure, preventing consistent
                 behavior for exact and inexact searches.}
                If SearchForm.LocateExact.Checked then GotoKey
                else GotoNearest;
              end else Cancel;
            end;
          finally
            SearchForm.Free;
          end;
        end;
      end;
    end;
  end;
end;
```

```
    if not (csDesigning in ComponentState) and Assigned(FOnNavClick) then
      FOnNavClick(Self, Index);
end;

procedure TDBNavSearch.WMSetFocus(var Message: TWMSetFocus);
begin
  Buttons[FocusedButton].Invalidate;
end;

procedure TDBNavSearch.WMKillFocus(var Message: TWMKillFocus);
begin
  Buttons[FocusedButton].Invalidate;
end;

procedure TDBNavSearch.KeyDown(var Key: Word; Shift: TShiftState);
var
  NewFocus: TNavigateBtn;
  OldFocus: TNavigateBtn;
begin
  OldFocus := FocusedButton;
  case Key of
    VK_RIGHT:
      begin
        NewFocus := FocusedButton;
        repeat
          if NewFocus < High(Buttons) then
            NewFocus := Succ(NewFocus);
        until (NewFocus = High(Buttons)) or (Buttons[NewFocus].Visible);
        if NewFocus <> FocusedButton then
        begin
          FocusedButton := NewFocus;
          Buttons[OldFocus].Invalidate;
          Buttons[FocusedButton].Invalidate;
        end;
      end;
    VK_LEFT:
      begin
        NewFocus := FocusedButton;
        repeat
          if NewFocus > Low(Buttons) then
            NewFocus := Pred(NewFocus);
        until (NewFocus = Low(Buttons)) or (Buttons[NewFocus].Visible);
        if NewFocus <> FocusedButton then
        begin
          FocusedButton := NewFocus;
          Buttons[OldFocus].Invalidate;
          Buttons[FocusedButton].Invalidate;
        end;
      end;
    VK_SPACE:
      begin
        if Buttons[FocusedButton].Enabled then
          Buttons[FocusedButton].Click;
      end;
  end;
end;
```

continues

Listing 26.6. continued

```
procedure TDBNavSearch.WMGetDlgCode(var Message: TWMGetDlgCode);
begin
  Message.Result := DLGC_WANTARROWS;
end;

procedure TDBNavSearch.DataChanged;
var
  UpEnable, DnEnable: Boolean;
begin
  UpEnable := Enabled and FDataLink.Active and not FDataLink.DataSet.BOF;
  DnEnable := Enabled and FDataLink.Active and not FDataLink.DataSet.EOF;
  Buttons[nbFirst].Enabled := UpEnable;
  Buttons[nbPrior].Enabled := UpEnable;
  Buttons[nbNext].Enabled := DnEnable;
  Buttons[nbLast].Enabled := DnEnable;
  Buttons[nbDelete].Enabled := Enabled and FDataLink.Active and
    FDataLink.DataSet.CanModify and
    not (FDataLink.DataSet.BOF and FDataLink.DataSet.EOF);
end;

procedure TDBNavSearch.EditingChanged;
var
  CanModify: Boolean;
begin
  CanModify := Enabled and FDataLink.Active and FDataLink.DataSet.CanModify;
  Buttons[nbInsert].Enabled := CanModify;
  Buttons[nbEdit].Enabled := CanModify and not FDataLink.Editing;
  Buttons[nbPost].Enabled := CanModify and FDataLink.Editing;
  Buttons[nbCancel].Enabled := CanModify and FDataLink.Editing;
  Buttons[nbRefresh].Enabled := not (FDataLink.DataSet is TQuery);
  Buttons[nbSearch].Enabled := (FDataLink.DataSet is TTable) and
                               (TTable(FDataLink.DataSet).IndexFieldCount<>0);
end;

procedure TDBNavSearch.ActiveChanged;
var
  I: TNavigateBtn;
begin
  if not (Enabled and FDataLink.Active) then
    for I := Low(Buttons) to High(Buttons) do
      Buttons[I].Enabled := False
  else
  begin
    DataChanged;
    EditingChanged;
  end;
end;

procedure TDBNavSearch.CMEnabledChanged(var Message: TMessage);
begin
  inherited;
  if not (csLoading in ComponentState) then
    ActiveChanged;
end;

procedure TDBNavSearch.SetDataSource(Value: TDataSource);
```

```
begin
  FDataLink.DataSource := Value;
  if not (csLoading in ComponentState) then
    ActiveChanged;
  if Value <> nil then Value.FreeNotification(Self);
end;

function TDBNavSearch.GetDataSource: TDataSource;
begin
  Result := FDataLink.DataSource;
end;

procedure TDBNavSearch.Loaded;
var
  W, H: Integer;
begin
  inherited Loaded;
  W := Width;
  H := Height;
  AdjustSize (W, H);
  if (W <> Width) or (H <> Height) then
    inherited SetBounds (Left, Top, W, H);
  InitHints;
  ActiveChanged;
end;

{TNavButton}

destructor TNavButton.Destroy;
begin
  if FRepeatTimer <> nil then
    FRepeatTimer.Free;
  inherited Destroy;
end;

procedure TNavButton.MouseDown(Button: TMouseButton; Shift: TShiftState;
  X, Y: Integer);
begin
  inherited MouseDown (Button, Shift, X, Y);
  if nsAllowTimer in FNavStyle then
  begin
    if FRepeatTimer = nil then
      FRepeatTimer := TTimer.Create(Self);

    FRepeatTimer.OnTimer := TimerExpired;
    FRepeatTimer.Interval := InitRepeatPause;
    FRepeatTimer.Enabled := True;
  end;
end;

procedure TNavButton.MouseUp(Button: TMouseButton; Shift: TShiftState;
                             X, Y: Integer);
begin
  inherited MouseUp (Button, Shift, X, Y);
  if FRepeatTimer <> nil then
    FRepeatTimer.Enabled := False;
end;
```

continues

Listing 26.6. continued

```pascal
procedure TNavButton.TimerExpired(Sender: TObject);
begin
  FRepeatTimer.Interval := RepeatPause;
  if (FState = bsDown) and MouseCapture then
  begin
    try
      Click;
    except
      FRepeatTimer.Enabled := False;
      raise;
    end;
  end;
end;

procedure TNavButton.Paint;
var
  R: TRect;
begin
  inherited Paint;
  if (GetFocus = Parent.Handle) and
     (FIndex = TDBNavSearch (Parent).FocusedButton) then
  begin
    R := Bounds(0, 0, Width, Height);
    InflateRect(R, -3, -3);
    if FState = bsDown then
      OffsetRect(R, 1, 1);
    DrawFocusRect(Canvas.Handle, R);
  end;
end;

{ TNavDataLink }

constructor TNavDataLink.Create(ANav: TDBNavSearch);
begin
  inherited Create;
  FNavigator := ANav;
end;

destructor TNavDataLink.Destroy;
begin
  FNavigator := nil;
  inherited Destroy;
end;

procedure TNavDataLink.EditingChanged;
begin
  if FNavigator <> nil then FNavigator.EditingChanged;
end;

procedure TNavDataLink.DataSetChanged;
begin
  if FNavigator <> nil then FNavigator.DataChanged;
end;
```

```
procedure TNavDataLink.ActiveChanged;
begin
  if FNavigator <> nil then FNavigator.ActiveChanged;
end;

procedure Register;
begin
  RegisterComponents('Data Controls',[TDBNavSearch]);
end;

end.
```

CAUTION

Borland does not recommend that you make any modifications to the VCL source code. Technically speaking, DBNavSearch isn't so much a modification to the VCL as it is a new component class. You're not replacing DBNavigator or modifying its source code; you're creating a new component. Still, you should tread lightly when modifying complex source code that you did not write—no matter who its author is.

NOTE

The parts of the DBNavSearch component source code that were originally authored by Borland are used here with Borland's permission.

The *DBSearch* Form

DBNavSearch makes use of second unit, DBSearch, that contains the form it creates when the search button is clicked. There are two key aspects of DBSearch's implementation. First, a fixed pitch font, Courier New, is used by the form to ensure that accurate calculations can be made regarding the width of the DBEdits placed on the form. Second, a ScrollBox component is used to ensure that any number of index key fields can be used as search criteria. If the number of fields (and, hence, the number of DBEdits generated by DBNavSearch) exceeds the form's capability to display them vertically, the ScrollBox component on which they reside will allow them to be scrolled on to the screen and accessed. Figure 26.4 shows the DBSearch form.

FIGURE 26.4.

The DBSearch *form as it appears in Delphi's form designer.*

Resources

DBNavSearch also makes use of a resource file, DBNAV.RES, that it incorporates via the $R directive. DBNAV contains two resources: One defines the appearance of the new search button on the navigator's toolbar, and the other defines the hint string that appears when the mouse pointer rests over the search button. Listing 26.7 shows the textual source of DBNAV.RES.

Listing 26.7. The source of DBNAV.RES.

```
/*******************************************************************************



dbnav.rc

produced by Borland Resource Workshop



*******************************************************************************/


DBN_SEARCH BITMAP LOADONCALL MOVEABLE DISCARDABLE
{
 '42 4D 46 01 00 00 00 00 00 00 76 00 00 00 28 00'
 '00 00 1C 00 00 00 0D 00 00 00 01 00 04 00 00 00'
 '00 00 D0 00 00 00 00 00 00 00 00 00 00 00 00 00'
 '00 00 10 00 00 00 00 00 00 00 00 00 80 00 00 80'
 '00 00 00 80 80 00 80 00 00 00 80 00 80 00 80 80'
 '00 00 80 80 80 00 C0 C0 C0 00 00 00 FF 00 00 FF'
 '00 00 00 FF FF 00 FF 00 00 00 FF 00 FF 00 FF FF'
 '00 00 FF FF FF 00 80 08 88 88 88 88 88 87 78 88'
 '88 88 88 88 73 33 00 00 88 88 88 88 88 77 77 88'
 '88 88 88 88 11 00 0F 00 08 88 88 88 88 7F 77 78'
 '88 88 88 88 CE CC 80 F0 00 88 88 88 88 87 F7 77'
 '88 88 88 88 73 33 88 0F 00 00 00 78 88 88 7F 77'
 '77 77 78 88 18 00 88 80 F0 07 88 70 88 88 87 F7'
 '77 88 77 88 CC CC 88 88 00 78 8F 87 08 88 88 77'
 '78 8F 87 78 73 33 88 88 07 88 88 F8 77 88 88 77'
 '88 88 F8 77 19 00 88 88 07 88 88 8F 80 88 88 77'
 '88 88 8F 87 CE CC 88 88 07 8F F8 88 80 88 88 77'
 '8F F8 88 87 73 33 88 88 77 7F F8 88 77 88 88 77'
```

```
'7F F8 88 77 10 00 88 88 80 77 88 87 08 88 88 87'
'77 88 87 78 CC CC 88 88 88 07 77 70 88 88 88 88'
'77 77 77 88 77 33'
}


STRINGTABLE
{
 65535, "Search for a record"
}
```

Of course, you won't want to type all this in manually. The STRINGTABLE resource presents no challenge, but typing in the "source" to a bitmap is no fun. Rather than typing it in, you can make use of the DBNAV.RES that's on the CD-ROM accompanying this book. You can also draw the bitmap yourself using a resource editor like Delphi's Image Editor or Borland's Resource Workshop. Figure 26.5 shows the bitmap as it appears in the Resource Workshop.

FIGURE 26.5.

*The DBN_SEARCH
bitmap as it appears in
Borland's Resource
Workshop.*

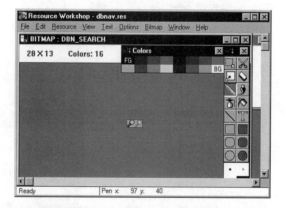

> **NOTE**
>
> Although Resource Workshop isn't included with Delphi 2.0, you can acquire it separately from Borland or as part of the Borland C++ package. Be sure to get the 32-bit version of the product because Delphi supports only 32-bit resources. I prefer Resource Workshop to the Image Editor because it can edit more types of resources and is generally more capable than Image Editor.

The *key* Routine

DBNavSearch's key routine is the nbSearch section of the BtnClick method. Basically, the routine looks at the component's underlying DataSet and adds a DBEdit to the DBSearch form for each key field in the DataSet's current index. After this is done, it pops the DataSet into SetKey mode, then displays the form. This blanks the DBEdits on DBSearch and allows search values to be keyed into them. When the user has keyed these values, DBNavSearch calls GotoKey or GotoNearest to position the DataSet appropriately. Listing 26.8 is a code fragment listing the nbSearch section of the BtnClick method.

Listing 26.8. The nbSearch section of BtnClick.

```
nbSearch: begin
          WidestLabelWidth:=0;
          SearchForm:=TSearchForm.Create(Self);
          try
            With FDataLink.DataSet as TTable do begin
              for c:=0 to IndexFieldCount-1 do begin
                Labels[c]:=TLabel.Create(SearchForm.ScrollBox1);
                Labels[c].Parent:=SearchForm.ScrollBox1;
                Labels[c].AutoSize:=True;
                Labels[c].Caption:=IndexFields[c].FieldName;
                If (c<>0) then Labels[c].Top:=Labels[Pred(c)].Top+FldHeight
                else Labels[c].Top:=2;
                Labels[c].Left:=2;
                If (Labels[c].Width>WidestLabelWidth) then
                  WidestLabelWidth:=Labels[c].Width;
              end;

              {Use two separate loops so that the widest label can be
               detected and allowed for.}
              for c:=0 to IndexFieldCount-1 do begin
                DBEdits[c]:=TDBEdit.Create(SearchForm.ScrollBox1);
                DBEdits[c].Parent:=SearchForm.ScrollBox1;
                DBEdits[c].DataSource:=Self.DataSource;
                DBEdits[c].DataField:=IndexFields[c].FieldName;

                FieldWidth:=IndexFields[c].DisplayWidth+2;
                SetLength(Ruler,FieldWidth);
                FillChar(Ruler[1],FieldWidth,'M');
                DBEdits[c].Width:=Canvas.TextWidth(Ruler);

                If (c<>0) then DBEdits[c].Top:=DBEdits[Pred(c)].Top+FldHeight
                else DBEdits[c].Top:=2;
                DBEdits[c].Left:=WidestLabelWidth+5;
              end;
              SetKey;
              If (SearchForm.ShowModal=mrOK) then begin
                {I don't test the return value of GotoKey because
                 GotoNearest is a procedure, preventing consistent
                 behavior for exact and inexact searches.}
                If SearchForm.LocateExact.Checked then GotoKey
                else GotoNearest;
              end else Cancel;
            end;
          finally
            SearchForm.Free;
          end;
        end;
```

Component Icons

You may be wondering by now how it is you go about specifying icons for the components you create. After all, you've done nothing to specify icons for the ones you've created so far. Neglecting to specify an icon for a new component means that Delphi decides what icon to use when you drop it onto a form. For a component descending from a component that includes its own icon, this means that the ancestor's icon will be used. For components that descend from those that don't define icons, Delphi provides a default.

Obviously, a component looks more professional and is easier to distinguish from other components when you give it its own icon. The procedure for doing this is very simple. You simply define a bitmap resource that you store in a file named the same as the component's source code unit, using the extension .DCR. For example, the component icon for the DBNavSearch component is stored in DBNavSch.DCR because DBNavSch.PAS is the component's source code unit. Figure 26.6 shows the component icon for the DBNavSearch component as it looks in the component palette.

FIGURE 26.6.

The DBNavSearch *component icon as it appears in the component palette.*

DBNavigator Component icon

Testing the New Component

If you haven't done so already, create the DBNavSearch component as it is previously listed and install it onto the component palette. After you've done this, you're ready to create a simple application for testing it.

Drop a Table component, a DataSource, a DBGrid, and a DBNavSearch component onto a form. Set the Table's DatabaseName and TableName properties to point to a table that includes at least one index (I used the WODETAIL table from the Tutorial section of this book). Set the Table's IndexName property to point to one of its indexes, then double-click its Active property to open it.

Set the DataSet property of the DataSource component to point to the Table you placed on the form. Next, set the DataSource property of the DBGrid and DBNavSearch components to point to the DataSource you dropped. After you've completed these steps, you're ready to run the application to test it; press F9 to run the application. After the application is up on-screen, click the Search button (magnifying glass) on the DBNavSearch component. You should see the DBSearch form populated with a DBEdit for every key field in your table's current index. (See Figure 26.7.)

FIGURE 26.7.
The DBSearch *form at runtime.*

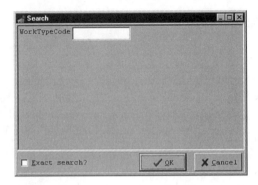

The *ZoomDlg* Component

The ZoomDlg component provides an easy way for you to select the allowable values for a table column from a second table. With the advent of Delphi's Lookup fields, the need for this capability has diminished somewhat, but there is still much to be learned from constructing it.

ZoomDlg defines a single published method, Execute, that is intended to be linked with the OnDblClick event of a data-aware control such as a DBEdit. That is, typically you would invoke ZoomDlg's Execute method when a given DBEdit is double-clicked. Like other dialog components, the Execute method displays the form that is associated with the component. This form is stored in the ZoomForm unit. It enables the user to "drill-down" into a column and to select a value for it from a second table. In my applications, I make a habit of coloring controls that support this mechanism differently so that their innate capabilities are obvious to the user.

As with the DBNavSearch component, the source code to ZoomDlg is too extensive to cover in detail here. I, therefore, will list it and then discuss it in general terms. Listing 26.9 includes the complete source code for the ZoomDlg component (this includes the source found in ZoomDlg.PAS and ZoomForm.PAS).

Listing 26.9. The ZoomDlg component.

```
{ ZoomDlg.PAS

ZoomDlg Delphi Component

Supports drilling down into a table column to select a value for it
from a second table. This is a non-visual component that is invoked
using its Execute method, as with other dialog components. When
Execute is called, ZoomForm is instantiated and displays the second
table. Once a selection from the second table is made, the appropriate
column value is assigned to the column in the first table.

Written by Ken Henderson.

Copyright (c) 1995 by Ken Henderson.

}
```

```
unit Zoomdlg;

interface

uses
  SysUtils, WinTypes, WinProcs, Messages, Classes, Graphics, Controls,
  Forms, Dialogs, ZoomForm, DBTables, DsgnIntf, TypInfo;

type
  TZoomDialog = class(TComponent)
  private
    { Private declarations }
    FCaption : string;
    FSourceTable : TTable;
    FSourceField : string;
  protected
    { Protected declarations }
  public
    { Public declarations }
  published
    { Published declarations }
    procedure Execute(Sender : TObject);
  published
    { Public declarations }
    property Caption : string read FCaption write FCaption;
    property SourceTable : TTable read FSourceTable write FSourceTable;
    property SourceField : string read FSourceField write FSourceField;
  end;

procedure Register;

implementation

procedure TZoomDialog.Execute(Sender : TObject);
begin
  fmZoom:=TfmZoom.Create(Self);
  try
    fmZoom.ShowForm(Sender,Caption,SourceTable,SourceField);
  finally
    fmZoom.Free;
  end;
end;

{ TSourceFieldProperty }

type
  TSourceFieldProperty = class(TStringProperty)
  public
    function GetAttributes: TPropertyAttributes; override;
    procedure GetValueList(List: TStrings);
    procedure GetValues(Proc: TGetStrProc); override;
    function GetTablePropName: string; virtual;
  end;

function TSourceFieldProperty.GetAttributes: TPropertyAttributes;
begin
```

continues

Listing 26.9. continued

```
  Result := [paValueList, paSortList, paMultiSelect];
end;

function TSourceFieldProperty.GetTablePropName: string;
begin
  Result := 'SourceTable';
end;

procedure TSourceFieldProperty.GetValues(Proc: TGetStrProc);
var
  I: Integer;
  Values: TStringList;
begin
  Values := TStringList.Create;
  try
    GetValueList(Values);
    for I := 0 to Values.Count - 1 do Proc(Values[I]);
  finally
    Values.Free;
  end;
end;

procedure TSourceFieldProperty.GetValueList(List: TStrings);
var
  Instance: TComponent;
  PropInfo: PPropInfo;
  SourceTable : TTable;
begin
  Instance := GetComponent(0);
  PropInfo := TypInfo.GetPropInfo(Instance.ClassInfo, GetTablePropName);
  if (PropInfo <> nil) and (PropInfo^.PropType^.Kind = tkClass) then
  begin
    SourceTable := TObject(GetOrdProp(Instance, PropInfo)) as TTable;
    if (SourceTable <> nil) then
      SourceTable.GetFieldNames(List);
  end;
end;

procedure Register;
begin
  RegisterComponents('Dialogs', [TZoomDialog]);
  RegisterPropertyEditor(TypeInfo(string), TZoomDialog, 'SourceField',
➥TSourceFieldProperty);
end;

end.

{ZoomForm.PAS

Zoom form for the
ZoomDlg Delphi Component

Supports drilling down into a table column to select a value for it
from a second table.  This is a non-visual component that is invoked
using its Execute method, as with other dialog components.  When
```

Execute is called, ZoomForm is instantiated and displays the second
table. Once a selection from the second table is made, the appropriate
column value is assigned to the column in the first table.

Written by Ken Henderson.

Copyright (c) 1995 by Ken Henderson.

```
}
unit ZoomForm;

interface

uses
  SysUtils, WinTypes, WinProcs, Messages, Classes, Graphics, Controls,
  Forms, Dialogs, ExtCtrls, DBCtrls, StdCtrls, Buttons, DB, DBTables,
  Grids, DBGrids, DBNavSch, Tabs;

type
  TfmZoom = class(TForm)
    dsZoom: TDataSource;
    Panel1: TPanel;
    nsZoom: TDBNavSearch;
    Panel2: TPanel;
    dgZoom: TDBGrid;
    Panel3: TPanel;
    bbOK: TBitBtn;
    bbCancel: TBitBtn;
    procedure bbOKClick(Sender: TObject);
    procedure FormClose(Sender: TObject; var Action: TCloseAction);
    procedure FormShow(Sender: TObject);
  private
    { Private declarations }
    FSourceTable : TTable;
    FSourceField : string;
  public
    { Public declarations }
    Caller : TObject;
    procedure ShowForm(Sender : TObject; Cap : String; SourceTab : TTable;
➥SourceFld: String);
    property SourceTable : TTable read FSourceTable write FSourceTable;
    property SourceField : string read FSourceField write FSourceField;
  end;

var
  fmZoom: TfmZoom;

implementation

{$R *.DFM}

procedure TfmZoom.ShowForm(Sender : TObject; Cap : String; SourceTab : TTable;
SourceFld: String);
begin
  Caption:=Cap;
```

continues

Listing 26.9. continued

```
  Caller:=Sender;
  SourceTable:=SourceTab;
  SourceField:=SourceFld;
  dsZoom.DataSet:=SourceTable;
  ShowModal;
end;

procedure TfmZoom.bbOKClick(Sender: TObject);
begin
  If Caller is TDBEdit then begin
      With Caller as TDBEdit do begin
        If (not (DataSource.DataSet.State in [dsInsert, dsEdit])) then
          DataSource.DataSet.Edit;
        DataSource.DataSet.FieldByName(DataField).AsString:=
          dsZoom.DataSet.FieldByName(SourceField).AsString;
      end;
  end else If Caller is TCustomEdit then begin
    With Caller as TCustomEdit do begin
      Clear;
      Text:=dsZoom.DataSet.FieldByName(SourceField).AsString;
    end;
  end else If Caller is TComboBox then begin
    With Caller as TComboBox do begin
      Clear;
      Text:=dsZoom.DataSet.FieldByName(SourceField).AsString;
    end;
  end else If Caller is TDBComboBox then begin
    With Caller as TDBComboBox do begin
      If (not (DataSource.DataSet.State in [dsInsert, dsEdit])) then
        DataSource.DataSet.Edit;
      DataSource.DataSet.FieldByName(DataField).AsString:=
        dsZoom.DataSet.FieldByName(SourceField).AsString;
    end;
  end;
  ModalResult := mrOK;
end;

procedure TfmZoom.FormClose(Sender: TObject; var Action: TCloseAction);
begin
  with SourceTable do if Active then Close;
end;

procedure TfmZoom.FormShow(Sender: TObject);
begin
  With SourceTable do
    If not Active then Open;
end;

end.
```

ZoomDlg is unusual for a couple of reasons. First, it not only includes a Register procedure to register itself on the Delphi component palette, but it also registers a special property editor for its SourceField property. This enables you to select from a DataSet's available fields when you specify a value for `SourceField`, just as you can with other field-type properties in Delphi's VCL (such as the `DataField` property). The code involved in creating and registering the property editor is shown in Listing 26.10.

Listing 26.10. The property editor code.

```
{ TSourceFieldProperty }

type
  TSourceFieldProperty = class(TStringProperty)
  public
    function GetAttributes: TPropertyAttributes; override;
    procedure GetValueList(List: TStrings);
    procedure GetValues(Proc: TGetStrProc); override;
    function GetTablePropName: string; virtual;
  end;

function TSourceFieldProperty.GetAttributes: TPropertyAttributes;
begin
  Result := [paValueList, paSortList, paMultiSelect];
end;

function TSourceFieldProperty.GetTablePropName: string;
begin
  Result := 'SourceTable';
end;

procedure TSourceFieldProperty.GetValues(Proc: TGetStrProc);
var
  I: Integer;
  Values: TStringList;
begin
  Values := TStringList.Create;
  try
    GetValueList(Values);
    for I := 0 to Values.Count - 1 do Proc(Values[I]);
  finally
    Values.Free;
  end;
end;

procedure TSourceFieldProperty.GetValueList(List: TStrings);
var
  Instance: TComponent;
  PropInfo: PPropInfo;
  SourceTable : TTable;
begin
  Instance := GetComponent(0);
  PropInfo := TypInfo.GetPropInfo(Instance.ClassInfo, GetTablePropName);
  if (PropInfo <> nil) and (PropInfo^.PropType^.Kind = tkClass) then
  begin
    SourceTable := TObject(GetOrdProp(Instance, PropInfo)) as TTable;
    if (SourceTable <> nil) then
      SourceTable.GetFieldNames(List);
  end;
```

continues

Listing 26.10. continued

```
end;

...

RegisterPropertyEditor(TypeInfo(string), TZoomDialog, 'SourceField',
➥TSourceFieldProperty);

...
```

Rolling Your Own Property Editor

Careful study of the code in Listing 26.10 will show you how to construct custom property editors. You must follow these four basic steps in order to create your own property editor:

1. Derive a new property editor type from one of those defined in the DsgnIntf unit.
2. Set up routines to allow the property to be both edited and displayed as text. If your property isn't a string type, your property editor will have to provide the necessary conversion mechanism.
3. Publish the specific attributes of your property editor so that the Object Inspector can properly determine how to handle it.
4. Register your property editor by using the RegisterPropertyEditor procedure.

In Listing 26.10, the SourceFieldProperty editor is derived from DsgnIntf's TStringProperty class. The only difference between the SourceField property and any other string property is that it needs to be able to display a drop-down list of available fields from which to select.

Because the property is a string property to begin with, there's no need to define new routines to get and set the property using string values. The routines inherited from the StringProperty class will work just fine.

SourceFieldProperty advises the Object Inspector of its specific attributes by overriding the GetAttributes function of the TStringProperty class. The function itself contains just one line:

```
Result := [paValueList, paSortList, paMultiSelect];
```

This single line of code specifies three aspects of the SourceFieldProperty editor. The first thing it signifies is that the property is to be a list-type property—that it will allow selection from a list of possible values. The second attribute, paSortList, instructs the Object Inspector to sort the list returned by the GetValues routine. Though I personally dislike the way that field names are sorted alphabetically by the Object Inspector, I've copied that behavior here for consistency's sake. The last attribute, paMultiSelect, indicates that the SourceField property is the type of property that can be displayed/changed when more than one component is selected. Some types of properties (such as the Name property) don't lend themselves to multiselection.

Finally, the property editor is registered via a call to `RegisterPropertyEditor`, as in the following:

```
RegisterPropertyEditor(TypeInfo(string), TZoomDialog,
                       'SourceField', TSourceFieldProperty);
```

When you call `RegisterPropertyEditor`, you specify four parameters:

- The property data type to which the editor is to apply. This is always done via a call to the built-in `TypeInfo` function.

- The type of component to which the editor is to be linked. You can specify `nil` for this parameter, and the editor will be used with all components containing the specified property type.

- The property name the editor is to edit. This has meaning only if you named a component type in the second parameter.

- The property editor class to register for the specified property type.

In this case, `RegisterPropertyEditor` is called with parameters indicating that the property is a string data type and that the editor is to apply only to the `SourceField` property of `ZoomDialog` component.

Other *ZoomDlg* High Points

The central routine to the `ZoomDlg` component is the code attached to the `Click` event of `ZoomForm`'s OK button. To reiterate, this code is

```
procedure TfmZoom.bbOKClick(Sender: TObject);
begin
  If Caller is TDBEdit then begin
    With Caller as TDBEdit do begin
      If (not (DataSource.DataSet.State in [dsInsert, dsEdit])) then
        DataSource.DataSet.Edit;
      DataSource.DataSet.FieldByName(DataField).AsString:=
        dsZoom.DataSet.FieldByName(SourceField).AsString;
    end;
  end else If Caller is TCustomEdit then begin
    With Caller as TCustomEdit do begin
      Clear;
      Text:=dsZoom.DataSet.FieldByName(SourceField).AsString;
    end;
  end else If Caller is TComboBox then begin
    With Caller as TComboBox do begin
      Clear;
      Text:=dsZoom.DataSet.FieldByName(SourceField).AsString;
    end;
  end else If Caller is TDBComboBox then begin
    With Caller as TDBComboBox do begin
      If (not (DataSource.DataSet.State in [dsInsert, dsEdit])) then
        DataSource.DataSet.Edit;
      DataSource.DataSet.FieldByName(DataField).AsString:=
        dsZoom.DataSet.FieldByName(SourceField).AsString;
    end;
```

```
  end;
  ModalResult := mrOK;
end;
```

The most notable aspect of this code block is its extensive use of Runtime Type Information (RTTI). Typically, natively compiled languages don't support RTTI. However, as you've probably figured out by now, Delphi's is not typical: It provides lots of features missing in other tools. Here, the ZoomForm uses RTTI to determine the type of component that invoked it so that it can properly assign the component's value using the selection made from its list of possible values.

Note the use of the With...as syntax to typecast the Caller variable. This is known as a "safe" typecast in that an exception is raised if the typecast is invalid. Normally in languages that support casting one data type as another, if you miscast a variable, you can count on an access violation of some sort. You can protect against this possibility by using the With...as syntax to safely typecast your class variables. You can then handle the exceptions raised due to miscasts in an orderly fashion.

What's Ahead

Chapter 27, "Deploying Your Applications," is the final chapter of this book. In this chapter, which discusses database application deployment in-depth, you'll learn to use the InstallShield Express software that ships with Delphi to create professional-looking, reliable installation programs for deploying your database applications. You'll also learn about the many issues you must address before venturing out into the world with your applications.

Summary

You've learned how to create a variety of different types of components in this chapter. Not only are these components educational, they're also useful. You can use them in your own programs if you like. While it's doubtful that you'll need to create reams of new components in order to build professional database applications, I have a sneaking suspicion that you may still need to build custom components every now and then. If so, going through the examples in this chapter should get you up to speed for building the components you need.

27

Deploying Your Applications

Delphi includes a slick tool called InstallShield to help you deploy your applications. Specifically, InstallShield assists in the development of installation programs. You specify a few parameters regarding the type of installation program you want, and InstallShield does the rest—right down to copying your installation images to diskette or CD-ROM. Although InstallShield is comprehensive, you need to do several things before you begin to develop your setup procedure.

Get Organized

The first thing you should do, when you think your application development is done and you're ready to face the world with your software, is to get organized. Determine what files make up your application and arrange them logically. Divide your files into essential and non-essential elements. Consider the support files that your application needs that your users likely won't have. Planning ahead will assist you greatly when it comes time to build distribution disks.

Ascertain Client Network Requirements

After you've organized your application's required files, you'll need to ascertain the networking requirements of your application. Does it require TCP/IP? Is TCP/IP installed on your client's machine? Does it require access to a shared network directory? Does the client have sufficient access rights to the directory? These questions and others are the kinds of things you must address before deploying your application.

Ascertain Client Database Driver Requirements

Beyond whether the proper network pieces are in place, does your application require a vendor-specific database driver? For example, if your application relies on tables that reside on a Sybase server, your client will need Sybase's Open Client software. If your application requires an ODBC driver, is the driver installed on the client machine? This is a concern only with client/server and ODBC-based applications, but it's a crucial issue that must be resolved before you can deploy database applications that you develop.

Ascertain Client Database Server Requirements

If your application is designed to work with a database server, you need to ensure that your client has the proper access to the server. First, is the server an existing one or are you expected to set it up? Second, is the server a remote or a local one? Third, does your client have a login and the proper access rights on the database server? You'll have to address these items before deployment, or the deployment could become a nightmare.

Ascertain Database Preparation Requirements

You'll need to determine in advance what's involved with setting up the database so that your client can access it. First, for remote systems, do you need to contact your DBA to create the database objects your application requires, or do you need to create those objects yourself? Second, if you are to create those database objects, what will you use to create them? Will you use Database Desktop, SQL scripts, or some other tool? If you're going to use SQL scripts, you'll need to write them in advance, of course.

If you're dealing with local tables, you'll need to prepare clean copies of your tables for inclusion with the installation program. You'll want to make a separate copy of the tables and delete any test data from them.

These issues and others represent the types of things that must be addressed before you begin to generate those master disks. The main thing you must do is plan, plan, and plan some more. Deploying database applications, particularly client/server apps, is like being dropped into a jungle with only your parachute and your commando gear to help you survive. It's important to prepare as much as possible beforehand.

After you're ready to begin building installation disks, you'll need to fire up Delphi's InstallShield Express tool. This tool will enable you to create setup programs that range in complexity from the simple to the moderately complicated. In this chapter, I'll take you through the development of both a basic installation program and an advanced one. In the basic program, you'll specify only the options necessary to build a setup program using InstallShield. In the advanced setup, you'll build a moderately complex installation program that uses a number of InstallShield's optional features.

Basic Setup

When you first start InstallShield Express, you're asked whether you'd like to open an existing setup project or create a new one. Click Create a new Setup Project to start a new project.

You're next presented with the New Project dialog box. Here, you'll specify the Project Name, Type, Directory, and whether or not to create a Custom setup option. A Custom setup option enables the user to tailor the installation process to his or her own needs. The user can install selected components without having to install all of them.

This first exercise will stick with the basics, so key in a name for your project in the Project Name box. After you've keyed in a name, click the Create button to initialize the project. (See Figure 27.1.)

FIGURE 27.1.

You specify new project parameters in the New Project dialog box.

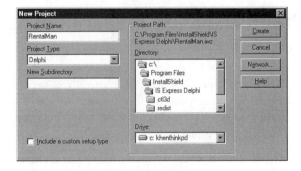

The next screen you see is the InstallShield main screen. It lists the nine major tasks necessary to create a new setup program. Each of these tasks is broken down into a handful of smaller steps that you can complete sequentially to construct your setup program. InstallShield helps you keep track of what to do next by displaying a pointer to the left of the next logical step. When you create a new project, this will be the Application Information step of the Set the Visual Design task. Figure 27.2 shows InstallShield's main screen.

FIGURE 27.2.

The InstallShield main screen.

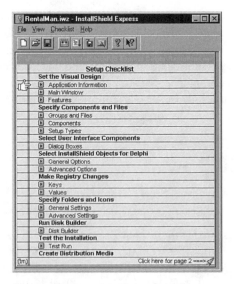

Set the Visual Design

The first of the nine major tasks prompts for basic application information and a variety of settings that affect the visual appearance of your setup program. Click the Application Information button to begin specifying application-specific information such as the name of your primary executable, its current version, and so on.

Application Information

The App Info section enables you to specify your application's name, primary executable, and version number. You can also specify your company name if it's different from the one you specified when InstallShield was first installed.

The Application Name entry defaults to the project name you specified previously in the New Project dialog. Keep in mind that the default destination path is set to match whatever you specify here. Even though you can use up to 80 characters to name your application, you probably won't want to.

Application Executable specifies your application's primary executable file. Whatever you enter here is automatically added to the Program Files group in the Groups and Files dialog (provided no entries have yet been made to Groups and Files). An icon is also created in the General Icon Settings dialog (provided no entries have been made there yet). Click the ellipsis button next to the Application Executable entry to browse for your executable.

You probably won't need to change the Version or Company settings at this point, so your application information should be complete. Figure 27.3 illustrates the App Info page.

FIGURE 27.3.

The App Info page enables you to specify application information.

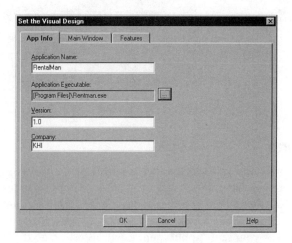

Notice that the Main Window and Features items from InstallShield's main screen are available via tabs in this dialog. You don't have to return to the main screen to select them. This is true with all nine of the major tasks; you can access their composite steps from a single dialog.

Main Window

Click the Main Window tab to select it. On the Main Window page, you can specify the title for your setup application's main window, you can specify your logo bitmap, and you can set the background color used by the installer. The Main Title setting defaults to the Application

Name you specified on the App Info page, but you can change it. You can change it to something more descriptive than just your setup project's name. You can also change it to be a bitmap rather than text. Be careful not to get too liberal with the text you specify because the title is displayed in a rather large font in a fixed amount of horizontal space.

If you elect to have the setup program display a logo bitmap, you'll specify the bitmap to use on this page. Remember that you can click the browse button (ellipsis) to search for it.

The Background Color defaults to Dithered Blue, though you can change it to something that better suits your tastes. For now, you don't need to change anything on the page. Just take the defaults and move to the next page. Figure 27.4 illustrates the Main Window page.

FIGURE 27.4.
InstallShield's Main
Window page.

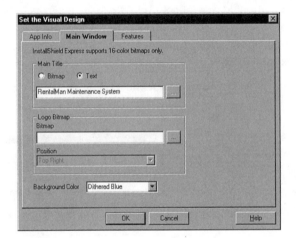

Features

Click the Features tab to select it. The only item on the Features page is a checkbox that toggles whether the setup program creates an automatic uninstall program. One of the requirements of the Windows 95 logo is that applications include an uninstall facility, so it's best to leave this option enabled. When you run the uninstaller, it removes all the files that were initially installed by your setup application. It will also clean up the Windows Registry, removing any entries that were created by default by InstallShield. Note, however, that it won't remove registry entries that you specify in addition to the default entries. You'll have to add uninstall keys for any entries that you've added. Figure 27.5 shows the Features page.

Click OK to save your Visual Design settings.

FIGURE 27.5.

The Features page enables you to specify whether an automatic uninstall program should be generated.

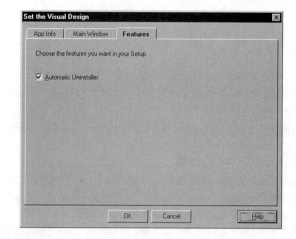

Specify Components and Files

You use this section to define the components that make up your application. Using components to define your application gives you a flexible method of allowing different types of setups. Because a component usually contains a family of related files, you could enable the user the omit certain optional components via a Custom setup. For now, you'll just define the basics need to generate the install program.

Groups and Files

Groups contain sets of related files—files that will exist in the same directory on the target machine. There's only one group by default, the Program Files group. Click the Groups and Files button to open its dialog, then click the expand button (the plus sign to its left) next to the Program Files group. Notice that the executable you specified earlier is the only file in the group.

Add to this group the other files that the application needs in order to run. Don't worry about stock Delphi items such as the Borland Database Engine or the ReportSmith runtime; those are covered later in the chapter. Potential candidates for this group would be elements that are usually local to the application, like the report files it uses (such as ReportSmith RPT files), data tables (and their supporting files) that it references, DLLs that only the application itself needs, and so forth. DLLs and OCXs that might be used by more than one application should be placed in a directory that can be shared by all applications. A good directory to use is the Common Files subdirectory under Program Files.

Click the Launch Explorer button to start the Windows Explorer so that you can drag files into the group. Locate a file that needs to be in the Program Files group, then drag it from the Explorer into the group.

Keep in mind that you can create additional groups in order to place files in different directories. To add a group, type the name of your new group into the Group Name box, then change the Destination Directory to point to the directory the group's files should be copied to on the target machine. Click the Add Group button to actually create the group.

Special Directory Identifiers

You can use any of InstallShield's special directory identifiers in the Destination Directory box. These identifiers enable you to specify paths on the target machine without knowing the exact directories that will be created in advance. Examples of these directories include the Windows SYSTEM directory on the target, the Program Files directory, and many others. Table 27.1 lists the InstallShield special directory identifiers and what each of them signifies.

Table 27.1. InstallShield directory identifiers.

Identifier	Replaced with
<INSTALLDIR>	The target directory as specified by the user
<WINDIR>	The directory in which Windows resides
<WINSYSDIR>	The Windows SYSTEM directory (SYSTEM32 for Windows NT)
<WINSYS16DIR>	Specifies the 16-bit SYSTEM directory under Windows NT
<WINDISK>	The driver letter of the disk containing Windows
<WINSYSDISK>	The driver letter of the disk containing the Windows SYSTEM directory
<ProgramFilesDir>	The Program Files directory
<CommonFilesDir>	The Common Files directory
[group name]	The group's Destination Directory

Keep in mind that you can specify a subdirectory in conjunction with any of the preceding identifiers. That is, you can append a literal subdirectory specification to the end of any of those shown here. For example, <ProgramFilesDir>\Borland will render the Borland subdirectory under C:\Program Files, by default.

After you've finished dragging files and defining groups, you're ready to move on to Components. Figure 27.6 shows the Groups dialog page.

FIGURE 27.6.

*The Groups dialog page
enables you to define files
groups and their contents.*

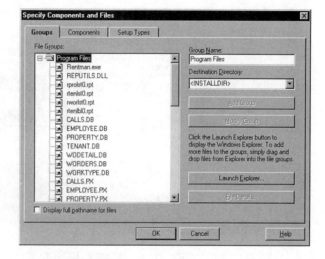

Components

Unless you're defining a Custom setup, you don't need to use the Components dialog page. Components are used to break your application into pieces that can be optionally installed or omitted. Skip this page for now; you'll come back to it in the "Advanced Setup" section.

Setup Types

Unless you're defining a Custom Setup, you don't need to access the Setup Types dialog page. Obviously, if you have only one setup type (Typical), there's nothing to specify here. You'll return to this page when you build the advanced setup project in the "Advanced Setup" section.

Click OK to save your component and file settings.

Select User Interface Components

There's only one step needed to complete this task: the Dialog Boxes step. You use this step to specify which dialogs your setup project displays.

Dialog Boxes

Click the Dialog Boxes button. Figure 27.7 shows the dialog.

You can click the dialogs that you want displayed sequentially in your setup project. There are several to choose from, and Table 27.2 summarizes them.

FIGURE 27.7.

The Dialog Boxes dialog enables you to specify what dialogs to include in your setup application.

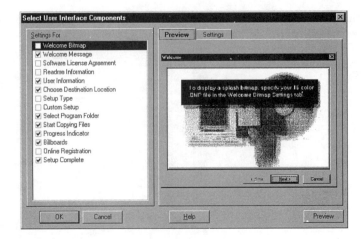

Table 27.2. Dialog boxes you can include in your setup application.

Dialog	Purpose
Welcome Bitmap	Specifies a bitmap to display when your setup starts
Welcome Message	Specifies an introductory message to display
Software License Agreement	Shows a license agreement that you specify
Readme Information	Displays a "readme" file that you provide
User Information	Enables the user to key user-specific information
Choose Destination Location	Enables the user to specify the installation target directory
Setup Type	Enables the user to specify a Custom, Compact, or Typical setup
Custom Setup	Enables the user to specify what to include in a custom setup
Select Program Folder	Enables the user to specify in which folder to place new icons
Start Copying Files	Enables the user to initiate the file copy process
Progress Indicator	Shows the current progress of the file copy process
Billboards	Displays a bitmap during the copy process
Online Registration	Enables the user to register online
Setup Complete	Shows a completion message after the install finishes

Simply place a check mark next to the dialogs that you want to include. Several of them have additional settings that you may want to specify if you select them. Click the Settings tab that corresponds to a given item to specify these special parameters.

Readme and Software License Agreement

You can include your application's Readme and Software License Agreement as text files for display in your installation program. Keep in mind that the text you specify is not auto-formatted to fit the multiline edit in which it's displayed. You'll have to embed hard returns in your text if you want it to be formatted properly. Also note that the text displayed in the preview is "canned," not updated to reflect changes you make on the Settings tab.

Custom Setup

The Custom Setup dialog displays only if the user selects Custom setup in the Setup Type dialog. This means, of course, that it won't be displayed if you don't enable the Setup Type dialog. The Custom Setup dialog allows selection of the components the user wishes to install.

Bitmaps

Note that InstallShield Express supports only 16-color bitmaps. Keep this in mind when selecting bitmaps for the Welcome Bitmap and Billboards dialogs. Also note that the Welcome Bitmap sample won't change to reflect any bitmap you specify.

Billboards

In order to use a bitmap with the Billboards dialog, you'll need to name your bitmap file SETUP1.BMP or SETUP1.WMF. You can specify the bitmap's home directory on the Settings tab.

Online Registration

If you want to use the online registration wizard, you'll need to contact Pipeline Communications (1-800-WIN95REG or `WIN95REG@pcpipeline.com`) in order to obtain the necessary login ID and phone number. You'll then need to enter this information on the Online Registration Settings tab.

For now, just take the defaults on this screen and click the OK button to proceed. These items are covered in more detail in the "Advanced Setup" section.

Select InstallShield Options for Delphi

The next task involves selecting which Delphi-specific options your application requires. If your application is a database application, it will no doubt require the Borland Database Engine. If it accesses remote servers using Borland's SQL Links drivers, you'll need them, too. Finally, if you run ReportSmith reports from within your application, you'll need the ReportSmith runtime, as well.

General Options

Click the General Options button to specify which Borland components your application requires. Keep in mind that selecting either SQL Links or ReportSmith runtime requires that you also include the Borland Database Engine. Figure 27.8 displays the General Options dialog page.

FIGURE 27.8.

The General Options dialog enables you to specify which Borland components to include.

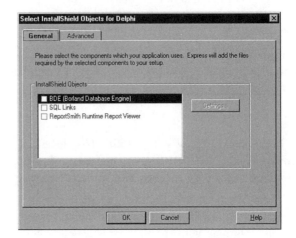

Including the BDE

Click the BDE checkbox to select it. Immediately, InstallShield displays a second dialog asking whether you want to include a full BDE installation or only a partial one. Choose the default, Full, for now and click the Next button.

Defining BDE Aliases to Include

The next four dialogs enable you to configure BDE aliases to be created when your installation program runs. You'll want to be sure to include any aliases that your application requires so that it will run correctly after it's installed. Click the New button and type the name of the new alias when prompted. (See Figure 27.9.)

Click the Next button to proceed.

After you've named your alias, you're asked whether the alias should be installed for both the 16-bit and 32-bit versions of the Borland Database Engine. As a rule, you probably won't need to do this, so you can leave this box unchecked and click the Next button.

FIGURE 27.9.

InstallShield enables you to define BDE aliases to create when your application is installed.

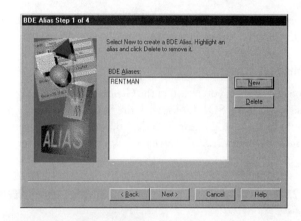

The third step enables you to define the specifics of the aliases you want to be created on the target machine. The Alias Name you specified is carried forward from the previous screen; you specify a Type for the new alias on this screen.

If you're defining a local table-based alias (such as Paradox or dBASE), you'll need to specify a path in which to locate your data files. Keep in mind that you can use InstallShield's special directory identifiers when specifying this path. For example, when building simple setup projects, you'll probably just use the <INSTALLDIR> directory identifier.

You can also specify other alias parameters in the multiline edit at the bottom of the screen. If you're connecting to a remote database server, for example, you might specify the server name or user name in this area. To specify these parameters, just type the parameter name followed by an equal sign and its value, as in the following:

```
SERVER=SYBSQL01
```

Figure 27.10 illustrates this dialog.

FIGURE 27.10.

Use this dialog to define the specifics for your new alias.

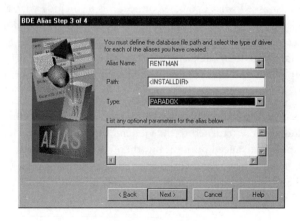

The fourth of the four dialogs involved with defining BDE aliases simply tells you that you're finished. Click the Finish button to complete your alias definition.

Including SQL Links

After you click Finish, you return to the General Options dialog. If you're connecting to a remote database server using SQL Links, click the SQL Links option. You are then asked to select the SQL Links drivers you'd like to include. You can include drivers for Sybase SQL Server, Oracle, InterBase, or Microsoft SQL Server. Click the ones you want, then click the Finish button. (See Figure 27.11.)

FIGURE 27.11.

Use this dialog to select the SQL Links drivers you want to install on the target machine.

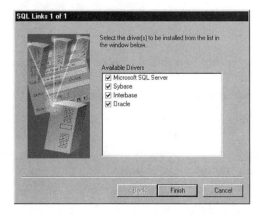

Including the ReportSmith Runtime

If your application includes ReportSmith reports, you'll need to include the ReportSmith runtime in order for your users to be able to view or print them. Click the ReportSmith Runtime Report Viewer selection to include the runtime with your application.

You're next asked what database connections to include with the runtime. After you've made your selection, click the Next button to proceed. The next dialog enables you to configure each of the connections that you selected on the previous screen. Specify the necessary configuration parameters, then click the Next button. The final ReportSmith configuration dialog you see simply tells you that you're finished. Click the Finish button to complete the inclusion of the ReportSmith runtime.

After you've finished defining which of the three basic Delphi-specific components you want to include, you're returned to the General Options dialog. Here, you can click the Advanced tab to specify advanced options, but there's little reason to do this. The Advanced tab, for example, enables you to modify the files that are included as part of a particular Borland component. This is something you should probably not do; InstallShield already has it covered. Click the OK button to finish selecting InstallShield objects for Delphi.

Make Registry Changes

The next major task is to specify the Registry entries that your application requires. For most applications, you'll find that you don't need to make any changes to the Registry. Therefore, skip it for now and proceed with specifying icons for your application.

Specify Folders and Icons

In this task, you configure the folders and icons created by your installation program. The General Settings dialog enables you to specify the icons you want to place in your application's folder. This folder will be placed on the Start Programs menu. General Settings also enables you to define command line parameters for your application.

The Advanced Settings dialog enables you to place an individual icon on the Start Programs menu for your application. Using the Advanced Settings dialog, you can also select an alternate working directory, load an icon from an external resource, and specify an application shortcut key.

For this basic setup, you won't need to do any of this. As mentioned earlier, an icon has already been added to the General Settings dialog page that corresponds with your application's primary executable. For most installations, this is sufficient. There's little reason to configure most of the other available settings in basic setups. You'll return to this task in the "Advanced Setup" section later in the chapter.

Run Disk Builder

The last of the major tasks that you should perform on your own machine is the Run Disk Builder task. Run Disk Builder creates the disk images that comprise your application and its installation program. You can specify the target media for these images so that they will be correctly sized. I advise you to save your current setup project before proceeding.

Next, click the Disk Builder button. In the lower left of the ensuing dialog, you can select the size of the target media—the default is 1.44MB. This can also be set to CD-ROM and a variety of other floppy sizes. When you're ready to actually build the images, click the dialog's Build button. Figure 27.12 illustrates this dialog box.

Provided there are no problems, your disk images should be built, and you should see a set of icons representing them on the left of the screen (if your target media is CD-ROM, you'll see just one diskette icon). After you're finished generating these image files, click the Close button.

FIGURE 27.12.

The Disk Builder dialog box enables you to create disk images containing your application and its setup program.

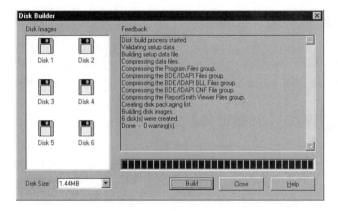

Test Run

You're now ready to do a test run, but before you do, there are a couple of things you should know. First, I strongly recommend that you perform your test installs on a separate machine. Don't use your development machine to test your installation program; use a separate machine that's configured as closely as possible to the target machine(s). This will make your test more true to life and can alert you to potential problems before you attempt installation on a client's machine.

Second, if you make the mistake of installing a project on your machine that includes any of the stock Borland components, be aware that you can't safely uninstall them. This is because the uninstall program will remove key elements that you'll later need in order to build Delphi applications. Particularly susceptible to this is the ReportSmith runtime. Because Delphi itself does not use the runtime (it uses ReportSmith instead), Windows may think that the runtime is unused and allow the uninstall program to remove it. Because your installation program installs these files to exactly the same directories as the Delphi installation program, uninstalling them has the net effect of removing your copy of the ReportSmith runtime engine.

To make matters worse, after these files are removed, you won't even be able to run your Disk Builder task again because it requires the files in order to build your disk images. You'll have to re-install your missing files from the Delphi CD-ROM or distribution diskettes in order to undo the damage done by the uninstall routine.

The moral of the story is this: Don't test InstallShield-based setup programs on anything but test machines unless you want configuration problems or have no intention of ever uninstalling the application. It's also a good idea to backup your test machine (especially the Windows directory and system registry) before installing an application. Later, you can restore your backup prior to making additional install runs.

Create Distribution Media

The last of the nine major tasks is to create your distribution media. Building your distribution media entails copying the disk images that you built earlier to physical media for distribution. This will usually either be in the form of floppies or a writeable CD-ROM drive. There's nothing to this step: Click the Copy to Floppy button, then click the Copy All Disk Images button on the resulting dialog. InstallShield will then copy your disk images to successive diskettes. (See Figure 27.13.)

FIGURE 27.13.

The Copy To Floppy dialog enables you to copy your disk images to physical media for distribution.

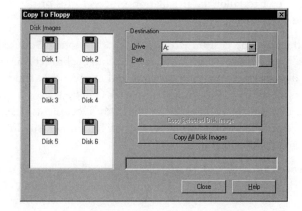

You've now got all you need to go to a client's machine and install your application. Before you install the application on any client machines, though, you should install from your distribution media onto a test machine. This gives you yet another test run of the installation routine and ensures that your installation master diskettes are in good shape.

After you're satisfied with your setup project, save it so that you can build new distribution media in the future.

Advanced Setup

This section goes through a more advanced exercise. You'll learn to set up an installation project that includes a Custom setup. A Custom setup enables the user to select what files to include in an installation. This is the preferred method of operation for many advanced users, and you should allow optional parts of your application to be excluded, if possible. Including a Custom setup option helps keep your application's disk footprint to a minimum and gives the application a more polished appearance.

Getting Started

When you start InstallShield Express, you're asked whether you'd like to open an existing setup project or create a new one. You can open a project you created previously, or you can create a completely new project. To get the full benefit of this exercise, click Create a new Setup Project to start a new project.

You're next presented with the New Project dialog. Here, you'll specify the Project Name, Type, Directory, and whether or not to create a Custom setup option. A Custom setup option enables the user to tailor the installation process to his or her own needs. The user can install selected components without having to install all of them.

Click the Include a custom setup type checkbox so that your users can customize their installations. Next, key in a name for your project into the Project Name box. Also, change the project's home directory to C:\My Documents and create a new subdirectory for the project named Installs (substitute the appropriate drive for C: if My Documents is on a different drive). To create the new directory, first change to C:\My Documents, then type Installs into the New Subdirectory box. When you create the project, the new subdirectory will be created, and your new project will be placed into it.

After you've finished with the details, click the Create button to initialize the project. (See Figure 27.14.)

FIGURE 27.14.

You specify new project parameters in the New Project dialog box.

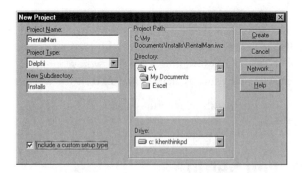

The next screen you see is the InstallShield main screen. It lists the nine major tasks necessary to create a new setup program. Each of these tasks is broken down into a handful of smaller steps that you can complete sequentially in order to construct your setup program. InstallShield helps you keep track of what to do next by displaying a pointer to the left of the next logical step. Table 27.3 lists these major tasks.

Table 27.3. The nine major tasks you must complete in order to build an InstallShield installation program.

Task	*Purpose*
Set the Visual Design	Specifies parameters affecting the installer's visual appearance
Specify Components and Files	Enables you to group files and create flexible setups
Select the User Interface Components	Specifies which canned dialogs to include
Select InstallShield Objects for Delphi	Specifies the Borland components to include
Make Registry Changes	Enables automation of necessary registry modifications
Specify Folders and Icons	Enables you to define what folders and icons to create
Run Disk Builder	Creates the disk images necessary to distribute your application
Test the Installation	Enables you to test your installation on your current machine
Create Distribution Media	Copies your disk images to physical media

When you create a new project, InstallShield's pointer will initially point to the Application Information step of the Set the Visual Design task.

Set the Visual Design

The first of the nine major tasks prompts for basic application information and a variety of settings that affect the visual appearance of your setup program. Click the Application Information button to begin specifying application-specific information such as the name of your primary executable, its current version, and so on.

Application Information

The App Info section enables you to specify your application's name, primary executable, and version number. You can also specify your company name if it's different from the one you specified when InstallShield was first installed.

The Application Name entry defaults to the project name you specified previously in the New Project dialog. Type in a descriptive name here for your project; you don't have to keep it to one word. Keep in mind that the default destination path is set to match whatever you specify here. Even though you can use up to 80 characters to name your application, you probably won't want to.

The entry you make in the `Application Name` field is used in many ways:

- It's used in the text area of the Welcome Message and Choose Destination Location dialogs.
- It becomes the default path in the Choose Destination Location dialog. The default destination directory is C:\Program Files\Your Company\Application Name.

> **NOTE**
>
> Modifications to the Application Name box automatically overwrite the setting in the Choose Destination Location box. Any changes you've made to the default destination will be lost.

The entries on this dialog also server as the keyname in the paths of three different automatic registry entries: the Uninstall key, the App Paths key, and the user information key. The first key, the uninstall key, looks like this:

```
HKEY_LOCAL_MACHINE\SOFTWARE\Microsoft\Windows\CurrentVersion\Uninstall\
➥Application Name
```

Two entries are made under this key: the DisplayName (displayed in Control Panel's Add/ Remove Programs list) and UninstallString (used to run UNINST.EXE, InstallShield's uninstaller).

The second key, the App Paths key, looks like this:

```
HKEY_LOCAL_MACHINE\SOFTWARE\Microsoft\Windows\CurrentVersion\
➥App Paths\YOUREXE.EXE
```

The third key, the user information key, looks like this:

```
HKEY_LOCAL_MACHINE\SOFTWARE\Company\Application Name\Version
```

This key stores the user's name, company, and, optionally, serial number so that you may access this information from your application.

Application Executable specifies your application's primary executable file. Whatever you enter here is automatically added to the Program Files group in the Groups and Files dialog (provided no entries have yet been made to Groups and Files). An icon is also created in the General Icon Settings dialog (provided no entries have been made there yet). Click the ellipsis button next to the Application Executable entry to browse for your executable.

The Version entry enables you to specify your application's current version. This can be handy in distinguishing two different versions of your software from one another on the same machine. InstallShield scans your executable for a Windows VERSIONINFO resource and, if it finds one, defaults the Version entry to it.

TIP

See Chapter 13, "Finishing Touches," for information on creating Windows VERSIONINFO resources. Included in Part II, "Tutorial," Chapter 13 shows, among other things, how to create and utilize a Windows VERSIONINFO resource in Delphi applications.

Company defaults to the company you specified when you first installed InstallShield. You can change this if you like; as mentioned before, it will be used in the automatic registry entries made by the installation program.

After you've specified your Version and Company settings, your application information should be complete. Figure 27.15 shows the App Info page of the dialog box.

FIGURE 27.15.

The App Info page enables you to specify application information.

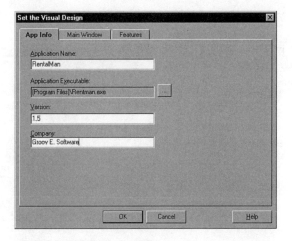

Notice that the Main Window and Features items from InstallShield's main screen are available via tabs in this dialog. You don't have to return to the main screen to select them. This is true with all nine of the major tasks; you can access their composite steps from a single dialog.

Main Window

Click the Main Window tab to select it. On the Main Window page, you can specify the title for your setup application's main window, you can specify your logo bitmap, and you can set the background color used by the installer. The Main Title setting defaults to the Application

Name you specified on the App Info page, but you can change it if you wish. You can change it to something more descriptive than just your setup project's name. You can also change it to be a bitmap rather than text. Be careful not to get too liberal with the text you specify because the title is displayed in a rather large font in a fixed amount of horizontal space.

If you elect to have the setup program display a logo bitmap, you'll specify the bitmap to use on this page. Remember that you can click the browse button (ellipsis) to search for it.

The Background Color defaults to Dithered Blue, though you can change it to something that better suits your tastes.

Type a descriptive name into the Main Title box. Remember that you have a fixed amount of space, so don't specify an extremely long title.

Next, click the browse button next to the Logo Bitmap box and specify a bitmap to display for your product's logo. There are several canned bitmaps in the Images\Splash subdirectory under your Delphi directory.

After you specify a bitmap, you'll need to position it. The default position is the top-right corner of the screen. This is a good choice, so there's no need to change it.

The default Background Color is also a good choice, so leave it in place, as well.

Figure 27.16 illustrates the Main Window page.

FIGURE 27.16.

InstallShield's Main Window page.

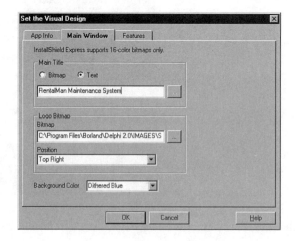

Features

Click the Features tab to select it. The only item on the Features page is a checkbox that toggles whether the setup program creates an automatic uninstall program. One of the requirements of the Windows 95 logo is that applications include an uninstall facility, so it's best to leave this option enabled. When the uninstaller is run, it removes all the files that were initially installed by your setup application. It will also clean up the Windows Registry, removing any entries that were created by default by InstallShield. Note, however, that it won't remove Registry entries that you specify in addition to the default entries. You'll have to add uninstall keys for any entries that you've added.

Click OK to save your Visual Design settings.

Specify Components and Files

You use this section to define the components that make up your application. Using components to define your application gives you a flexible method of allowing different types of setups. Because a component usually contains a family of related files, you could enable the user to omit certain optional components via a Custom setup. You'll create groups that will place the application's data in a separate directory and enable the user to omit installing report support if the user desires.

Groups and Files

Groups contain sets of related files—files that will exist in the same directory on the target machine. If you don't allow for a Custom setup type, there's only one group by default, the Program Files group. If you add a Custom setup type, there are three groups by default: the Program Files group, the Help Files group, and the Sample Files group.

Click the Groups and Files button to open its dialog, then click the expand button (the plus sign to its left) next to the Program Files group. You'll notice that the executable you specified earlier is the only file in the group.

Add to this group the other files that the application needs in order to run. Don't worry about stock Delphi items such as the Borland Database Engine or the ReportSmith runtime; those will be taken care of later in the chapter. Also, for now don't concern yourself with the application's data files or report files (such as ReportSmith RPT files); you'll create separate groups for them in a moment. Potential candidates for this group would be elements that are usually local to the application, such as DLLs that only it needs, auxiliary configuration executables, or information files, and so on. DLLs and OCXs that might be used by more than one application should be placed in a directory that can be shared by all applications. A good directory to use is the Common Files subdirectory under Program Files.

Click the Launch Explorer button to start the Windows Explorer so that you can drag files into the group. Locate the files that need to be in the Program Files group, then drag them from the Explorer into the group.

After the Program Files group is completed, you're ready to drag your application's help files to the Help Files group. Certainly, during a Custom setup, installation of Help files should be optional. They often go unused and can be quite large. Use the Windows Explorer to drag the help files your application uses into the Help Files group.

After you're done with the Help Files group, delete the Sample Files group if your application does not include any type of example or sample files. Most custom applications don't include sample files, so it simplifies things to remove the group.

Next, create a group for your application's report files. In the case of ReportSmith, these report files have the extension .RPT and are opened by the runtime engine when an application runs a report. To create a new group, type the new name in the Group Name box and click the Add New Group button. Name the new group Report Files and leave the Destination Directory unchanged.

Next, fire up the Windows Explorer and drag the report files to the Report Files group. By setting these up separately, you enable the user to omit them if he or she does not need to print reports.

Now create a group for your application's data files. To create the new group, type the name `Data Files` into the Group Name box and change the Destination Directory to <INSTALLDIR>\Data. Then click the Add New Group button.

After the group is created, drag your application's data files from the Windows Explorer into the Data Files group. By setting these up separately, you keep your application's program files and data separate—a practice that can be helpful when backing up the data.

After you've finished dragging files and defining groups, you're ready to move on to Components. Figure 27.17 shows the Groups dialog page.

FIGURE 27.17.

The Groups dialog page enables you to define file groups and their contents.

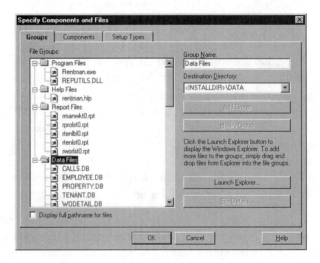

Components

Components are used to break your application into pieces that can be optionally installed or omitted. You'll use this page to associate the groups you created on the Groups page with installation components than can be either installed or omitted by the user. As a rule, there will be a one-to-one correspondence between the groups you set up earlier and the components you set up on this page.

As with the Groups page, by default there are three items on the Components page: the Application Files component, the Help and Tutorial Files component, and the Sample Files component. If you deleted the Sample Files group on the Groups page, there's no reason to keep its component around; go ahead and delete it if it's not needed.

Using this screen, you can add components that it does not have by default, and modify the names and descriptions of the existing components to suit your needs.

Because the application requires its data files in order to function correctly, you don't need to create a separate component for the Data Files group; you'll associate it with the Application Files component. On the other hand, the Report Files group that you added earlier does need its own component so that it may be optionally omitted.

In order to add the Report Files component, simply type the name of the component, `Report Files`, into the Component Name box and type its description into the Description box, then click the Add Component button.

Next, change the name of the Help and Tutorial Files component to be more concise. If your application is like many apps, it doesn't include a tutorial. If not, change the name of the Help and Tutorial Files component to just `Help Files`. Do this by clicking the component and typing the new name into the Component Name box. Change the component's Description to "Help files needed for online help." Click the Modify Component button to save your changes.

Now that all the components are defined, it's time to establish what groups belong in what components. To add a group to a component, click the target component in the Application Components list, then click the group in the File Groups list and click the Add to Application Component button below the File Groups list. If a group is already associated with a component, the Add button will be disabled.

Because of the default associations that InstallShield makes for you, there are only two groups that you need to assign to a component. Associate the Data Files group with the Application Files component, and associate the Report Files group with the Report Files component. Figure 27.18 illustrates the component definition process.

FIGURE 27.18.

Use components to break your application into pieces that can be installed or omitted.

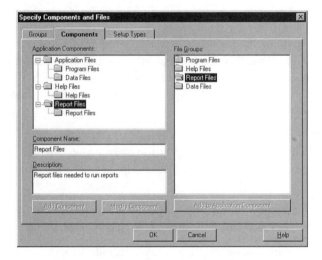

After you've defined your application's components, you're ready to move on to setup types.

NOTE

After you've completed the Select InstallShield Objects for the following Delphi section, you'll need to return to this section to associate those objects with components so that the user can optionally install or omit them.

Setup Types

Click the Setup Types tab to select it. On this page, you associate the components you created on the previous page with one of the three built-in setup types: Compact, Custom, or Typical. InstallShield supports only these three; you can't add new ones or make changes to the existing setup types.

Associating a component with a setup type is easy. You just click the component in the Application Components list, click the setup type in the Setup Types list, then click the Add to Setup Type button.

Be default, all defined components are associated with the Custom setup type. This is because all of them need to be present so that the user can decide whether to include or omit them.

As a rule, you'll probably also want to associate all your application components with the Typical setup type, as well. Chances are, if an option was important enough to include in one of the components, it needs to be part of a Typical install. Of course, there are exceptions to this, but failing to include all your application components as part of a Typical setup forces the user to select a Custom setup in order to "get all the goods." Because of this, I recommend that you associate all application components with the Typical setup type.

The Compact setup type enables you to specify the bare minimum that's required for the application to be functional. You could, for example, omit the Report Files and Help Files components in the Compact setup type. Users who select this type usually want to minimize the disk space occupied by an application, so you should see to it that the Compact setup type has as small a disk footprint as possible.

Because the Custom setup type is already configured properly, you only need to configure the Typical and Compact types. Click the Typical setup type, then add all your application components to it.

Next, click the Compact setup type and add just the Application Files component to it. Assume that your application will run correctly without its reports or help files.

Click OK to save your groups, components, and setup types. Figure 27.19 shows the Setup Types dialog page.

FIGURE 27.19.

The Setup Types dialog page enables you to associate application components with setup types.

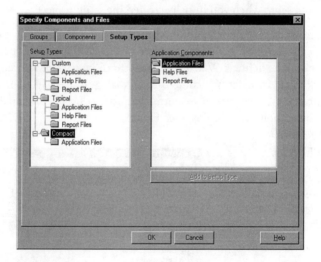

Select User Interface Components

There's only one step needed to complete this task: the Dialog Boxes step. You use this step to specify which dialogs your setup project displays.

Dialog Boxes

Click the Dialog Boxes button. Figure 27.20 shows the dialog box.

FIGURE 27.20.

Specify the dialogs you want in your setup application.

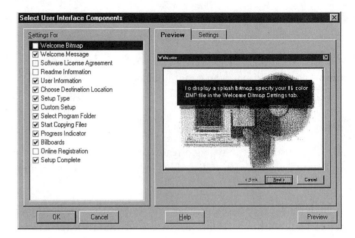

Simply place a checkmark next to the dialogs that you want to include. Notice that the Setup Type and Custom Setup options are already checked. This is because you elected to include a Custom setup when you initially created the setup project.

Several of the dialogs have additional settings that you may want to specify if you select them. You click the Settings tab that corresponds to a given item to specify these special parameters. For example, define a Welcome Bitmap to display when the setup program starts. Click the checkbox next to the Welcome Bitmap dialog to select it, then click its Settings tab. On its Settings page, click the browse button (ellipsis) to locate a bitmap that you want displayed when the setup application begins. (See Figure 27.21.)

FIGURE 27.21.

Use the Settings tab to specify special parameters for dialogs on the Select User Interface Components screen.

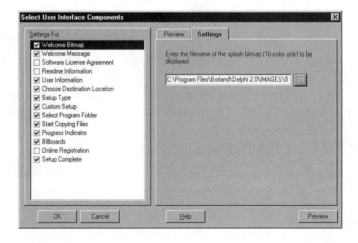

Keep in mind that clicking the Preview button while this dialog is selected won't show your new bitmap. The bitmap that's displayed is an example only; you'll have to run the installation program to see how your bitmap looks at runtime. Note that InstallShield Express supports only 16-color bitmaps. Keep this in mind when selecting bitmaps for the Welcome Bitmap and Billboards dialogs.

Readme and Software License Agreement

You can include your application's Readme and Software License Agreement as text files for display in your installation program. Keep in mind that the text you specify is not auto-formatted to fit the multiline edit in which it's displayed. You'll have to embed hard returns in your text if you want it to be formatted properly. Also note that the text displayed in the preview is "canned," not updated to reflect changes you make on the Settings tab.

Billboards

In order to use a bitmap with the Billboards dialog, you'll need to name your bitmap file SETUP1.BMP or SETUP1.WMF. You can specify the bitmap's home directory on the Settings tab.

Online Registration

InstallShield enables you to build setup programs that register your programs on-line, provided the user running the program has a modem. Contact Pipeline Communications (1-800-WIN95REG or WIN95REG@pcpipeline.com) if you want your setup program to use the on-line registration wizard. Pipeline will issue the login ID and phone number your setup program will need in order to register on-line. You'll enter this information on the Online Registration Settings tab.

Click the OK button to save your changes and proceed.

Select InstallShield Options for Delphi

The next task involves selecting which Delphi-specific options your application requires. If your application is a database application, it will no doubt require the Borland Database Engine. If it accesses remote servers using Borland's SQL Links drivers, you'll need them, too. Finally, if you run ReportSmith reports from within your application, you'll need the ReportSmith runtime, as well.

General Options

Click the General Options button to specify which Borland components your application requires. Keep in mind that selecting either SQL Links or ReportSmith runtime requires that you also include the Borland Database Engine.

Including the BDE

Click the BDE checkbox to select it. Immediately, InstallShield displays a second dialog asking whether you want to include a full BDE installation or only a partial one. Choose the default, Full, for now and click the Next button.

Defining BDE Aliases to Include

The next set of dialogs enables you to configure BDE aliases to be created by your installation program. Include any aliases that your application requires so that it will run correctly after it's installed. Click the New button and key the name of the new alias when prompted. Figure 27.22 illustrates this dialog.

FIGURE 27.22.

InstallShield enables you to define BDE aliases for your setup program to create.

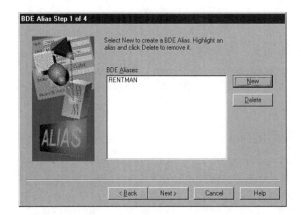

Click the Next button to move on.

After you've named your alias, you're asked whether the alias should be installed for both the 16-bit and 32-bit versions of the Borland Database Engine. As a rule, you probably won't need to do this, so you can leave this box unchecked and click the Next button.

The third step enables you to define the specifics of the aliases you want created on the target machine. The Alias Name you specified is carried forward from the previous screen; you specify a Type for the new alias on this screen.

If you're defining a local table-based alias (such as Paradox or dBASE), you'll need to specify a path in which to locate your data files. Because you located your data files in the <INSTALLDIR>\Data directory, you'll need to be consistent with that here. Rather than retyping the target directory of your Data Files group, though, you can simply specify the name of the group itself, in brackets, to specify its target directory as the alias Path. That is, rather than retyping <INSTALLDIR>\Data, you can instead type [Data Files] in the Path entry box. InstallShield will replace the group name with its target directory when your installation program runs.

You can also specify other alias parameters in the multi-line edit at the bottom of the screen. If you're connecting to a remote database server, for example, you might specify the server name or user name in this area. To specify these parameters, just type the parameter name followed by an equal sign and its value, as in the following:

```
SERVER NAME=SYBSQL01
```

Figure 27.23 illustrates this dialog box.

FIGURE 27.23.
Use this dialog box to define the specifics for your new alias.

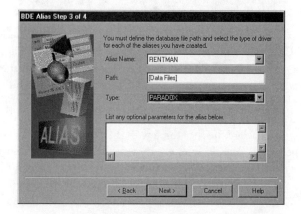

The fourth of the four dialogs involved with defining BDE aliases simply tells you that you're finished. Click the Finish button to complete your alias definition.

Including SQL Links

Once you click Finish, you're placed back in the General Options dialog. If you're using SQL Links to connect to remote database servers, click the SQL Links option. If you click the SQL Links option, you're asked to select the SQL Links drivers you'd like to include. You can include drivers for Sybase SQL Server, Oracle, InterBase, or Microsoft SQL Server. Click the ones you want, then click the Finish button.

Including the ReportSmith Runtime

If your application includes ReportSmith reports, you'll need to include the ReportSmith runtime in order for your users to be able to view or print them. Click the ReportSmith Runtime Report Viewer selection to include the runtime with your application.

You're next asked what database connections to include with the runtime. After you've made your selection, click the Next button to proceed. The next dialog enables you to configure each of the connections that you selected on the previous screen. Specify the necessary configuration parameters, then click the Next button. The final ReportSmith configuration dialog you see simply tells you that you're finished. Click the Finish button to complete the inclusion of the ReportSmith runtime.

After you've finished defining which of the three basic Delphi-specific components that you want to include, you're returned to the General Options dialog. Here, you can click the Advanced tab to specify advanced options, but there's little reason to do this. The Advanced tab, for example, enables you to modify the files that are included as part of a particular Borland component. This is something you should probably not do; InstallShield already covers it. Click the OK button to finish selecting InstallShield objects for Delphi.

> **NOTE**
>
> After you've decided which Delphi-specific pieces to include, you'll need to return to the Components page of the Specify Components and Files dialog and associate these items with your currently defined components. If you install the BDE, the SQL Links Drivers, and the ReportSmith runtime viewer, you should have four additional groups that need association with a component: the BDE/IDAPI Files group, the BDE/IDAPI BLL Files group, the BDE/IDAPI CNF File group, and the ReportSmith Viewer Files group. Associate the first three with the Application Files component. Associate the ReportSmith Viewer Files group with the Report Files component. This way, if your user elects not to install reporting support, he or she won't have a dormant copy of the ReportSmith runtime engine installed on his or her system.

Make Registry Changes

The next major task is to specify the custom Registry entries that your application requires. For most applications, you'll find that you don't need to make any changes to the Registry. InstallShield already establishes several default Registry entries for your application. If you do create any additional Registry keys, remember that you'll also need to define uninstall keys so that they'll be removed when your application is uninstalled. The Windows Setup Guidelines require that your application clean up after itself when it's uninstalled.

> **CAUTION**
>
> Be very careful when removing keys from the Windows Registry. Removing the wrong key could disable other applications. Centrally locating all the configuration information on a machine has it advantages and disadvantages. One of the disadvantages is that it's all too easy to foul up another program by inadvertently modifying or deleting its Registry entries. When changing the Windows Registry, remember the admonition of the Old World maps: "Here Be Dragons."

Specify Folders and Icons

In this Task, you configure the folders and icons created by your installation program. The General Settings dialog enables you to specify the icons you want to place in your application's folder. This folder will be placed on the Start Programs menu. General Settings also enables you to define command line parameters for your application.

The Advanced Settings dialog enables you to place an individual icon on the Start Programs menu for your application. By using the Advanced Settings dialog, you can also select an alternate working directory, load an icon from an external resource, and specify an application shortcut key.

Click the General Settings button to display its dialog. As mentioned earlier, an icon has already been added to the General Settings dialog that corresponds with your application's primary executable. Change the icon's Description to be a bit more informative, though. Click the Description box on the dialog and change it from the project name to a two- or three-word description of the application. Keep in mind that this text will be displayed beneath the icon in your program folders, so don't get too carried away. Click the Modify Icon button to save your change.

Save your changes and return to InstallShield's main screen by clicking the OK button.

Run Disk Builder

The last of the major tasks that you should perform on your own machine is the Run Disk Builder task. Run Disk Builder creates the disk images that comprise your application and its installation program. You can specify the target media for these images so that they will be correctly sized. I advise that you save your current setup project before proceeding.

Next, click the Disk Builder button. In the lower left of the resulting dialog, you can select the size of the target media; the default is 1.44MB. This can also be set to CD-ROM and a variety of other floppy sizes. When you're ready to actually build the images, click the dialog's Build button. Figure 27.24 illustrates this dialog.

Provided there are no problems, your disk images should be built, and you should see a set of icons representing them on the left of the screen (if your target media is CD-ROM, you'll see just one diskette icon). After you're finished generating these image files, click the Close button.

FIGURE 27.24.

The Disk Builder dialog enables you to create disk images containing your application and its setup program.

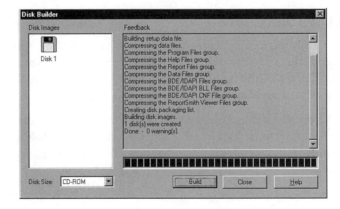

Test Run

You're now ready to do a test run. Be sure to perform this test run on a test machine. Don't do it on a production machine. As previously mentioned, after Delphi companion items such as the ReportSmith runtime engine are installed during a test run, you can't safely uninstall them without impairing your ability to run reports in the future or build new installation disks.

You can feel free to go through a test run on a production machine up to the point where the installation program is ready to begin copying files; however, don't allow it to begin copying files, or you could cause yourself a myriad of problems.

Create Distribution Media

The last of the nine major tasks is to create your distribution media. Building your distribution media entails copying the disk images that you built earlier to physical media for distribution. This will usually either be in the form of floppy disks or a writeable CD-ROM drive. There's nothing to this step: Click the Copy to Floppy button, then click the Copy All Disk Images button on the ensuing dialog. InstallShield will then copy your disk images to the target you specify.

You've now got all you need to go to a client's machine and install your application. Before you install the application on any client machines, though, you should install from your distribution media onto a test machine. This gives you yet another test run of the installation routine and ensures that your installation master diskettes are in good shape.

After you're satisfied with your setup project, save it so that you can build new distribution media in the future.

Installing the Application on a Client Machine

This section details running the installation program on a client machine from start to finish. Screen shots are provided to give you a feel for what the installation program is doing.

To install your application on client's machine, insert the first disk from those created by the Copy to Floppy option and run its Setup program. Figure 27.25 shows an example of the Setup program's Welcome Bitmap.

FIGURE 27.25.

The Setup program's opening screen displays its Welcome Bitmap if you've specified one.

After the user clicks the Next button, Setup displays its Welcome Message dialog, as Figure 27.26 illustrates.

FIGURE 27.26.

The Setup program's Welcome Message dialog.

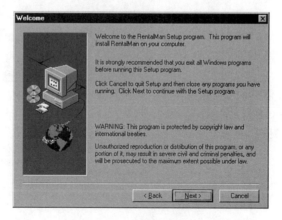

The next screen prompts for user information. (See Figure 27.27.)

FIGURE 27.27.

Setup requests personal information via its user information dialog.

After the user clicks Next, Setup prompts for a destination directory. This defaults to C:\Program Files*Company Name**Application Name*, where *Company Name* and *Application Name* correspond to the entries you made in the Application Information dialog. (See Figure 27.28.)

FIGURE 27.28.

Your Setup program enables the user to choose a target directory for the installation.

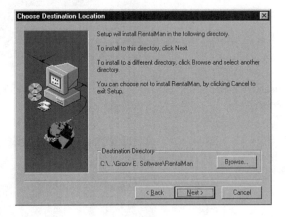

After the user has selected a destination directory for the installation, he or she is asked to select a setup type. (See Figure 27.29.)

FIGURE 27.29.

Once a destination directory is selected, the user selects a setup type.

If the user selects the Custom setup type, the next dialog asks which components should be installed. A running tally of the amount of required disk space is displayed, as well as the program groups that make up each component. (See Figure 27.30.)

FIGURE 27.30.

Selecting the Custom setup type enables the user to select which components to install.

The next dialog that's displayed requests the folder to which the application's icons should be added. By default, a new folder, named after the application, is added. (See Figure 27.31.)

FIGURE 27.31.

The user can tell the Setup program which folder is to be home to the new application's icons.

Just prior to copying the files to disk, your setup program displays a confirmation dialog that details the installation that's about to occur and asks the user to click the Next button to begin copying files. (See Figure 27.32.)

FIGURE 27.32.

Before actually copying the files, Setup displays a confirmation dialog.

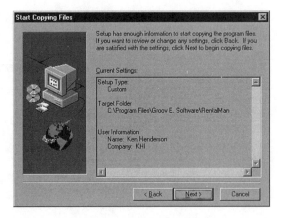

After the user clicks Next, Setup begins copying files. As the files are copied, a meter indicates the estimated progress into the installation process. (See Figure 27.33.)

After the installation is complete, the Setup program displays a completion dialog as illustrated in Figure 27.34.

FIGURE 27.33.

Your Setup program displays a status bar to apprise the user of the progress into the installation process.

FIGURE 27.34.

The installation program displays a completion dialog when it has completed.

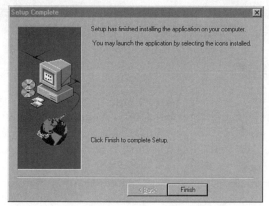

After you exit the installation program and return to the Windows desktop, you'll notice the new program folder that that Setup program created. It will include the application icon you specified in InstallShield. (See Figure 27.35.)

FIGURE 27.35.

The new program folder as it was created by the installation program.

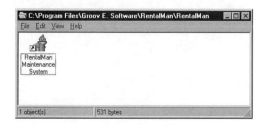

After you complete these steps, you've successfully installed the application on the client machine. If you now want to uninstall the application, you can do so via Control Panel's Add/ Remove Programs facility, as illustrated in Figure 27.36.

FIGURE 27.36.

You can remove the new application by using Control Panel's Add/ Remove Programs facility.

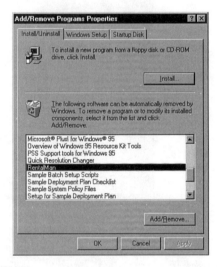

Summary

In this chapter, you learned to create both a basic and an advanced setup program. You learned the many subtleties of using InstallShield to turn your application into something you can deploy on client machines. You also learned that there is a wealth of preparation that must occur before any diskettes are copied. Deploying applications is like baking a cake: if you get the ingredients wrong or put the icing on the cake before you bake it, no one will want it. It's important to get organized and plan ahead before venturing into the uncertain world of client computing.

Epilogue

Never one to pass up the opportunity to speak to a captive audience, I thought I'd offer a few thoughts before we part company. The following are just my opinions—I offer them as nothing more. They reflect my concern for the computing industry as a whole, where I think we are and where I think we're going.

I wrote my first computer program back in the late 1970s. It was a simple little thing, really—just a few lines of BASIC that printed the words "I'M ALIVE!" over and over. That version of BASIC required line numbers (remember them?) and supported only two string variables, so I was rather proud of myself when it filled the screen with its endless proclamation.

Since then, making software has been my primary method of expressing myself creatively. Because I was developing software (back then we called it programming) before there even was an IBM PC, I've had the privilege of watching the PC revolution from its infancy. I've witnessed numerous trends, observed a number of fads, and seen computer companies come and go.

To be sure, it's been thrilling to see technology improve the way that it has. When dBASE II was the PC DBMS standard, few could have predicted the giant leaps and bounds that computing would make in the next decade. Before Microsoft Windows even existed and back when a 20MB hard drive was considered huge, no one could have imagined the near-vertical flight that the personal computer industry would take in the years to come.

Why have things changed so much so rapidly? Mainly, I think, because people have been empowered to change their worlds for their own betterment. That is, in terms of computing, people using personal computers have what they need to continually improve their environments. Personal computers are affordable and require no interaction with system administrators or large host machines. The interaction with the computer can be a one-on-one experience—the CPU of the human brain matched with that of the PC in front of it.

The upshot of this empowerment is a natural evolution in available technology. The cycle works like this: people select a piece of hardware or software, use it, and find out what they'd like changed about it. Vendors come out with products that have the improvements the user is looking for at affordable prices. The user selects a new product (or a new release of an old one) and the cycle starts over. The end result is an ever-escalating, ever-improving technology base that grows well with users' needs.

Nevertheless, a disturbing trend has been on the rise lately. I didn't notice it myself, at first. I think, more than anything, the recent hype regarding the Internet has brought it to the forefront of my thinking. The "it" I refer to is hype-based product selection. This amounts to a shift from selecting hardware and software because it's better, to instead selecting it because it's the "flavor of the month"—it's what everyone else is using, or, at least what we *think* everyone else is using.

Part of the reason for this is what I call "brand-name-itis." People are putting more stock today in brand names than ever before. For example, a product with "Microsoft" in its title has a better chance of selling than one that includes almost any other vendor's name. This is unfortunate since most industry experts would agree that Microsoft's products are not, as a whole, markedly better than anyone else's. In many people's estimation, Borland products have consistently out-performed Microsoft's for years, yet Microsoft has had the greater success. Why? Is marketing the whole story?

No, I think the problem goes much deeper than that. Only a handful of companies, Microsoft among them, have discovered that technical people—potential purchasers of computing products—are consumers, too. They need to be wooed and won over just like consumers of other types of products.

Whatever the reason, people are buying computing products for reasons other than technical superiority now more than ever. Hype and marketing play a bigger role in purchasing decisions than they ever have before. I attribute this in part to the maturation of the industry—it's not as though computing is alone in this—most industries suffer from this same problem and have for a long time. Still, it can't *all* be attributed to the industry's coming of age.

The danger with selecting computing products because they are popular rather than better is that in doing so, you stymie technological evolution. You thwart the very process by which computing technology has grown and improved as quickly as it has. The fittest no longer survive—the most popular do. And as long as popularity is the chief means by which computing products survive, marketing, not innovation, will be the primary focus of companies that survive. The end result is that hardware and software will be of an inherently lower quality.

The worst thing about all this is that taking the bandwagon approach to buying computing products creates a sort of vicious cycle. By buying a product simply because it's more popular than another, you encourage companies that specialize in marketing rather than innovation to flourish, since they now have more of your money with which to do that. They, in turn, use the money you paid them to undertake other marketing efforts, again stressing salesmanship over ingenuity. The result is a vicious cycle that is difficult to break.

The road is littered with products that were better, but suffered because they weren't produced by the right company or sufficiently hyped-up. WordPerfect for Windows is one example, OS/2 Warp is another. Quattro Pro for Windows is yet another. I don't mean to say that these products are dead—just that they failed to reach their full potential due largely to marketing and hype. None of these products had "Microsoft" in their names and they suffered dearly for it. Many companies select one product over another simply because of who manufacturers it. They suffer from acute "brand-name-itis."

It used to be that people selected computing products according to what worked best for them. When interaction between different products became an issue, people pressured vendors to get their products to cooperate more seamlessly, and they responded. There was no need to buy everything from a single vendor.

This overriding concern for picking the best product led to a steady stream of hardware and software innovations. It was also more conducive to small-time development. A dynamite piece of software developed by an individual or small team of people had just as much chance of succeeding as one produced by the "big boys." In fact, most of the so-called big boys began as meager garage operations, themselves. This was good for the industry and good for the people in it.

Nowadays, though, the trend is toward trends, the fad toward fads. People care less about a computing product's actual merits and more about who markets it and whether their neighbors are using it. Already, this has taken its toll on the industry. Already, we are beset with inferior products. Visual Basic is a fine example of this. PowerPoint is another.

Don't get me wrong. I'm not saying that these products don't have their good points. However, there are a number of better development tools than Visual Basic (Delphi among them) and a number of better presentation packages than PowerPoint. They aren't marketed by Microsoft, but they are, in fact, better.

I realize much of this is subjective on my part; as I've said, these are only my opinions. However, I don't think anyone could reasonably argue that marketing and hype aren't a much bigger part of the computing picture than they've ever been before. Products are being selected because companies know how to market rather than develop, to sell rather than create, and to litigate rather than innovate. If this trend continues, we are all in trouble.

What can you do about this? Can anything be done? Yes, there is one crucial way that you can help turn the tide: buy products because they're better, not because the trade journals you read say everyone else is using them and not because Vendor XYZ manufactures them. Sure, the vendor that produces a product has to be part of your evaluation of the product—you need a vendor that's going to be around and that will be there to support you after the purchase. However, vendor selection can't be the whole decision. It can't be the only thing you consider when buying a product. There is a truism that once applied to the computing industry, and, I'd like to think, still does: if people base their purchasing decisions on which products best meet their needs, vendors that produce good products *will* be around—they *will* survive.

Of course, a company can mismanage itself into non-existence, but that's really pretty rare, especially when it has products that are selling. The trick with running a successful computing company, as with any business, is matching income with what is spent. This may mean that the company can afford four employees, it may mean that it can afford four thousand. Whatever the case, if producing products that meet people's needs is the company's mainstay, and if people buy products because they meet their needs, the company has at least a fighting chance of survival. But this all depends on people making purchases for the right reasons.

So, stepping down from my soapbox, I leave you with this one admonition: please don't take the easy way out and jump on the technological bandwagons that seem to pass by on a daily basis. Do your homework, find out how products compare with each other, then select the one that best meets your needs. Once you've made your selection, fight for what you believe in, hold dear the informed decisions you make—because the survival of the industry as we know it depends on people making the right choices for the right reasons.

I

Index

Symbols

A

If you are a Developer looking for the best way to access Btrieve™ from Borland's Delphi™, look no further than...

TITAN
for Delphi

"In thirty minutes time, (with no prior experience with the product) I was able to build a complete Btrieve file-browser! To reinforce the significance of this, it took me roughly two days of work to duplicate this effort with Visual Basic, calling WBTRCALL directly. I now have a fast, professional looking browser, and I didn't even have to miss my Star Trek re-run!"

Jim Barber,
Btrieve Developer's Journal
Autumn, 1995

FEATURES & BENEFITS:

- ☒ Bypasses ODBC for high speed access to the Btrieve engine.
- ☒ Supports all Delphi data-aware components like DbGrid, DbEdit, etc.
- ☒ Supports "Live" display of Btrieve data at design time.
- ☒ Provides "low-level" access to Btrieve.
- ☒ Supports Delphi Master/Detail relations and Delphi Database experts.
- ☒ Supports Btrieve memo fields with Delphi DbMemo component.
- ☒ Works with 3rd Party components like InfoPower, Orpheus, & QuickReports.
- ☒ No need to distribute BDE runtime.
- ☒ No runtime license fees.

SCALABLE SQL SUPPORT:

- ☒ Supports Delphi TQuery component, allowing SQL statements.
- ☒ Mix & Match Delphi TTable & TQuery information.
- ☒ SQL Stored Procedures & Substitution variables fully supported.

PRICING:

☒	Titan Only:	$295.00
	- with Source:	$495.00
☒	Titan+SQL:	$395.00
	- with source:	$595.00
☒	Titan 32-Bit:	February

"Titan has been instrumental in resolving reliability and performance concerns with Btrieve ODBC alternatives. Using Titan, we have been able to integrate our applications with other Btrieve applications without a single hitch."
- Roy Kingsley, Lynk Soft-

TO ORDER TITAN CONTACT:

AmiSys, Inc.
1390 Willow Pass Rd
Suite 930
Concord, CA 94520

Phone: (510) 671-2103
Fax: (510) 671-2104
Cserve: 70441,3250
Email: amisys@amisysinc.com
Web: www.reggatta.com

© Copyright 1996 - Reggatta Systems.

Titan for Delphi requires Borland's Delphi1.0, Btrieve Version 5.XX or greater, Btrieve Data Definition Files (DDF's) and a tool to create/modify them, and 2 MB of disk space. Titan + SQL requires all of the above and Scalable SQL™ from Btrieve Technologies.

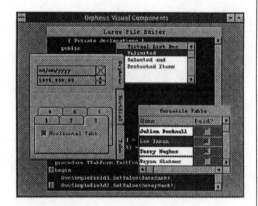

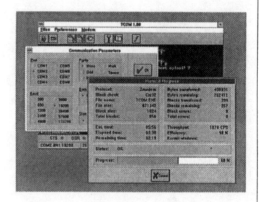

ProtoView DataTable
The Fastest Grid Component Anywhere

DataTable is an industrial grid control. DataTable strength lies in its ability to handle massive amounts of data in an efficient manner. With a compact size, only 90K of memory, virtual memory, and advanced data cache scheme, DataTable is clearly designed for industrial, real-world applications.

Set colors, fonts, and picture formatting for cells. Has built-in column sorting. It's visual and easy. Supports the clipboard, hidden columns, row, and column selection and resizing. Cells may have drop-down combo boxes or check boxes. Full message and property set. MFC classes and message based programming interface. 16- and 32-bit DLL version, VBX and OCX available. Source code is available.

New features include bitmaps in cells, horizontal and vertical splitter window, numeric column totaling, column searching, cell overwriting, improved keyboard handling, auto row insert, region selection, European formatting for date, time, and numbers, and 3D effects. Windows 95-compatible look.

ProtoView Interactive Diagramming Object
The Visual Way to Add Diagramming To Your Application

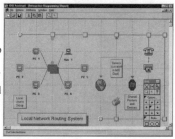

The Interactive Diagramming Object gives you advanced capabilities for creating easy to read diagrams. Choose from a wide assortment of shapes, pictures, lines, and arrows to design pleasing presentation visuals, outlines, process flows, hierarchy charts, floor plans, and much more.

With it you can: load and save diagrams, set colors, fonts and 3D effects, create custom design palettes, and respond to notifications and events for complete program control. It supports diagrams of any size with scrolling, zooming, printing, and the clipboard. Simply drop the IDO on a form and it's ready to go. It's easy to use and easy to program. Whether you want to explain a process or present a plan, the IDO helps you effectively communicate ideas and create applications that are more powerful, yet easier to use. Available as OCX or DLL. Source code is available.

ProtoView Interface Component Set
Polished User Interface Components

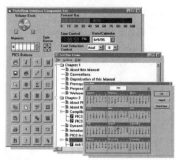

PICS offers sophisticated controls for calendar, date, time, and numeric input using your choice of odometer, LED readout, and normal display. Add to these a slick looking percent/gauge control, multi-directional spin button, a stereo volume control, and fancy icon buttons. You also get a font and point size selection control for your toolbars or dialogs. Also included are 21 PICS button controls with bitmap images.

You also get a powerful hierarchical list box that includes: setting unlimited number of bitmaps per list, lines between bitmaps and names, over 100 functions for complete control of subtrees, selection, display, search and item manipulation.

Complete on-line help, MFC classes, and message based programming interface. 16- and 32-bit DLL, VBX, and OCX available. Source code is available. Windows 95 compatible look. With PICS you can create the sharpest looking applications in no time at all.

ProtoView Visual Help Builder
The Fastest Way To Build Help Systems!

The ProtoView Visual Help Builder is the fastest way to author help systems. Developers can document an application, whether they have that application's "source" programs or not. With a few clicks of the mouse, ProtoView Visual Help Builder captures every dialog box, menu, and control field of an application and creates a full blown help system. Only ProtoView Visual Help Builder brings you these innovative features. Add multimedia support for video, sound, and high-res graphics. It provides the advanced features you need to create help systems, including macros, secondary windows, multiple hotspot graphics, help topics, hypertext links, jumps, browse sequences, and more.

Integrates into version control software. Includes help compiler. Requires Microsoft Word 2.0/6.0/7.0.

PROTOVIEW™
The Visual Development Edge™

Add to Your Sams Library Today with the Best Books for Programming, Operating Systems, and New Technologies

The easiest way to order is to pick up the phone and call

1-800-428-5331

between 9:00 a.m. and 5:00 p.m. EST.
For faster service please have your credit card available.

ISBN	Quantity	Description of Item	Unit Cost	Total Cost
0-672-30704-9		Delphi Developers Guide (book/CD)	$49.99	
0-672-30858-4		Delphi 2 Unleashed, Second Edition (book/CD)	$55.00	
0-672-30913-0		Database Developers Guide with Visual C++ 4, Second Edition (book/CD)	$59.99	
0-672-30474-0		Windows 95 Unleashed (book/CD)	$39.99	
0-672-30602-6		Programming Windows 95 Unleashed (book/CD)	$49.99	
0-672-30745-6		HTML & CGI Unleashed (book/CD)	$49.99	
0-672-30837-1		Visual Basic 4 Unleashed (book/CD)	$45.00	
0-672-30568-2		Teach Yourself OLE Programming in 21 Days (book/CD)	$39.99	
0-672-30855-X		Teach Yourself SQL in 14 Days	$29.99	
0-672-30620-4		Teach Yourself Visual Basic 4 in 21 Days, Third Edition	$35.00	
0-672-30736-7		Teach Yourself C in 21 Days, Premier Edition	$35.00	
0-672-30717-0		Tricks of the DOOM Programming Gurus (book/CD)	$39.99	
		Shipping and Handling: See information below.		
		TOTAL		

❑ 3 ½" Disk

❑ 5 ¼" Disk

Shipping and Handling: $4.00 for the first book, and $1.75 for each additional book. Floppy disk: add $1.75 for shipping and handling. If you need to have it NOW, we can ship product to you in 24 hours for an additional charge of approximately $18.00, and you will receive your item overnight or in two days. Overseas shipping and handling adds $2.00 per book and $8.00 for up to three disks. Prices subject to change. Call for availability and pricing information on latest editions.

201 W. 103rd Street, Indianapolis, Indiana 46290

1-800-428-5331 — Orders   1-800-835-3202 — FAX   1-800-858-7674 — Customer Service

Book ISBN 1-672-30862-2

Installing Your CD-ROM

The companion CD-ROM contains the author's sample databases, plus an assortment of useful third-party tools and product demos. The disc is designed to be explored using a browser program. Using Sams' Guide to the CD-ROM browser, you can view information concerning products and companies, and install programs with a single click of the mouse. To install the browser, here's what to do:

Windows 3.1/NT Installation Instructions:

1. Insert the disc into your CD-ROM drive.
2. From File Manager or Program Manager, choose Run from the File menu.
3. Type `<drive>\setup` and press Enter, where `<drive>` corresponds to the drive letter of your CD-ROM. For example, if your CD-ROM is drive D:, type `D:\SETUP` and press Enter.
4. Installation creates a Program Manager group named DDG with Delphi 2. To browse the CD-ROM, double-click on the Guide to the CD-ROM icon inside this Program Manager group.

Windows 95 Installation Instructions:

1. Insert the disc into your CD-ROM drive. If the AutoPlay feature of your Windows 95 system is enabled, the setup program will start automatically.
2. If the setup program does not start automatically, double-click on the My Computer icon.
3. Double-click on the icon representing your CD-ROM drive.
4. Double-click on the icon titled Setup.exe to run the installation program. Follow the onscreen instructions that appear. When setup ends, double-click on the Guide to the CD-ROM icon to begin browsing the disc.

Following installation, you can restart the Guide to the CD-ROM program by pressing the Start button, selecting Programs, then DDG with Delphi 2 and Guide to the CD-ROM.

NOTE

The Guide to the CD-ROM program requires at least 256 colors. For best results, set your monitor to display between 256 and 64,000 colors. A screen resolution of 640×480 pixels is also recommended. If necessary, adjust your monitor settings before using the CD-ROM.